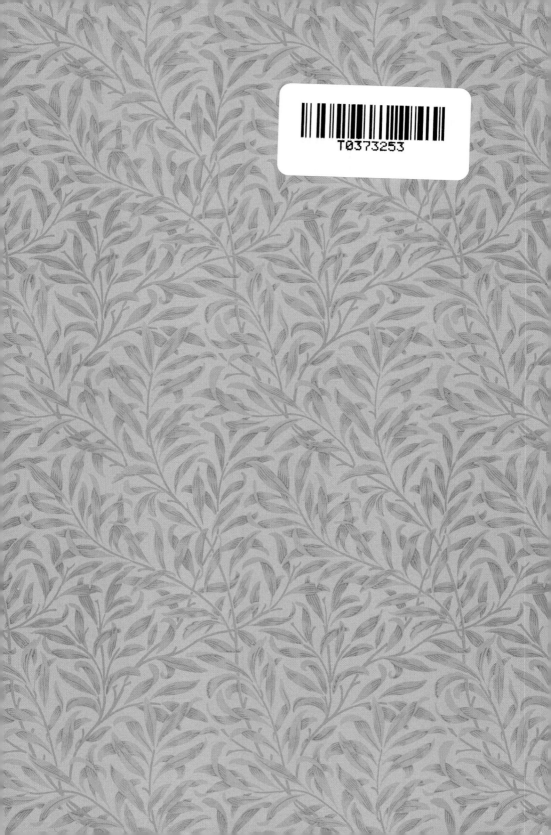

"Doug O'Donnell's expository labors provide preachers and teachers with a sure-footed guide to and through the wonders of Mark's Gospel. His work rests on his having systematically marinated his thought in the carefully wrought literary and theological contours of Mark's account, so that his homiletical divisions are true to Mark's mounting argument and a boon to expositors. O'Donnell's exegesis and homiletical wisdom rest not only on the shoulders of past preachers but also on his having mined the refreshing Marcan exegesis available in today's journals and superb new commentaries—resulting in increased precision and homiletical clarity. In this respect, O'Donnell has long been a notable wordsmith. The shepherding, pastoral tone that permeates this commentary is evident on nearly every page, with astute applications that can come only from a sensitive preacher in touch with life and contemporary culture, as well as with illustrations that actually do serve the sacred text. Confidently recommended."

R. Kent Hughes, Senior Pastor Emeritus, College Church, Wheaton, Illinois

"Sound theological exegesis. Engaging exposition. Helpful subtitles for sermon outlines. Ready-made illustrations ripe for the picking. Personal stories that nudge your own memory. Practical takeaways. Just an all-around enjoyable read. What more does a preacher need when preparing for Sunday? Doug O'Donnell has not replaced your quality time with God in sermon preparation; he has enriched it. Keep his reflections handy. You and God's people will be the better for it."

S. Jonathan Murphy, Department Chair and Professor of Pastoral Ministries, Dallas Theological Seminary

"There is no more reliable guide to teaching or preaching the Gospels effectively than Doug O'Donnell. In these pages, readers will find fresh insights and ideas for communicating the heart of the biblical text in a way that puts the person and work of Christ at the center and connects to the hearts of real people."

Nancy Guthrie, Bible teacher; author

"This learned, profound, utterly practical commentary is a great model for preachers of the Gospel of Mark. It will help them to practice faithful biblical exegesis, goad them to keep their teaching focused on Jesus, and thereby encourage those who listen to their sermons to 'arise and follow the Son.' O'Donnell here reminds you why you answered God's call to be a minister of the Word and supports you in your efforts to unpack this precious book."

Douglas A. Sweeney, Dean and Professor of Divinity, Beeson Divinity School, Samford University

"The most obvious virtue of this commentary is its thoroughness. It is a triumph of scholarship—a one-volume library of the best that has been written on the Gospel of Mark. But it is more than that—a blend of head and heart, with the author's intermittent sharing of his life experiences lending both human interest and a testimony to the reality of the good news."

Leland Ryken, Emeritus Professor of English, Wheaton College

"With seamless synergy between exegesis and the everyday, Doug O'Donnell masterfully dissects and demystifies the Gospel of Mark to aid preachers in feeding their flocks. Having once preached through Mark myself, I wish this resource had been available then. Thankfully, it exists now, and it will be of tremendous benefit to clear preachers and engaged hearers as well as zigzagging preachers and meandering listeners."

    Matthew D. Kim, Professor of Practical Theology and Raborn Chair of Pastoral Leadership, Truett Theological Seminary, Baylor University; author, *A Little Book for New Preachers*

"The church has long been nourished by pastor-theologians who have the intellectual gifts and pastoral sensibilities to understand God's Word and apply it to God's world. Doug O'Donnell is a modern-day representative who serves in this historic office. In his *Expository Reflections on the Gospels: Mark*, O'Donnell conducts a symphony involving a critical (in the good sense!) interpretation of the biblical text in its historical context, a confessional understanding of the theological subject matter of Scripture, and a contextual integration that applies the message of the Gospel of Mark to the lives and realities of the reader. This is a top-tier resource for every pastor and preacher."

    Edward W. Klink III, Senior Pastor, Hope Evangelical Free Church, Roscoe, Illinois; Professor, Trinity Evangelical Divinity School; author, *John* (Zondervan Exegetical Commentary on the New Testament)

"Following some of the best Protestant expository traditions, Doug O'Donnell's lucid expositions of Mark remind us how to read the Gospels as the anchor of the New Testament and the centerpiece of the story of Jesus the Messiah! Lovers of the second Gospel should have this volume before them regularly. Each sermonic chapter faithfully explains the significance of Mark's portrayal of redemption in the promised Son for us. My joy in reading Mark deepened with the turn of every page of this work."

    Eric C. Redmond, Professor of Bible, Moody Bible Institute; Associate Pastor of Preaching and Teaching, Calvary Memorial Church, Oak Park, Illinois

"Doug O'Donnell's commentary on Mark's Gospel is a remarkable piece of work. Grounded in a meticulous study of the text and sensitive to its theological contours, he offers fresh insight that is readily accessible to the preacher and layperson alike. O'Donnell's poetic turns of phrase, engaging wit, and pastoral sensibility make it a resource that every Christian will want to have on the shelf."

    Chris Castaldo, Senior Pastor, New Covenant Church, Naperville, Illinois; author, *The Upside Down Kingdom: Wisdom for Life from the Beatitudes*

"Readers who want an in-depth understanding of the Gospels yet also want to be fed spiritually will often turn to commentaries, only to realize that the gap between critical interpretation and exposition—between historical-theological analysis and everyday life—can be hard to cross. It's difficult to find either a lively exposition of the text that is responsive to cutting-edge scholarship or an erudite commentary that comes alive. Thankfully, in reading the Gospel of Mark alongside us, Doug O'Donnell has provided us with both—in one book."

Nicholas Perrin, President, Trinity International University

"Doug O'Donnell's expository reflections on Mark do for us what the Gospel itself does: they focus us on Jesus, the saving Son of God, and call us to 'arise and follow the Son.' Informed by sound scholarship yet easily accessible, grounded in a close reading of the text yet applied to real life, these reflections lead us again and again to Christ—to his words and his works, his cross and his resurrection, his rule and his return. Read, mark, and learn!"

Murray Smith, Lecturer in Biblical Theology and Exegesis, Christ College, Sydney

"Doug O'Donnell has given us a thorough exposition that is wonderfully refreshing. What particularly struck me is that there is a model here for today's preacher: arresting and accessible teaching for the ignorant new generations, and yet serious nourishment for the mature believer and the Bible student. And that sounds something like an echo of the master teacher in the Gospel records."

Dick Lucas, Former Rector, St. Helen's Bishopsgate, London; Founder, The Proclamation Trust

"With the mind of a scholar and the heart of a pastor, O'Donnell has provided an exegetically rich and practically applicable exposition of this shortest Gospel account. This commentary takes us into the heart of the text and reveals with clarity how to apply the text to our own hearts. Highly recommended!"

Matthew Newkirk, President and Professor of Old Testament, Christ Bible Seminary, Nagoya, Japan

Expository Reflections on the Gospels

Mark

VOLUME 3

Expository Reflections on the Gospels

Mark

Arise and Follow the Son

Douglas Sean O'Donnell

CROSSWAY

WHEATON, ILLINOIS

Expository Reflections on the Gospels, Volume 3: Mark

© 2024 by Douglas Sean O'Donnell

Published by Crossway
1300 Crescent Street
Wheaton, Illinois 60187

Cover design: Jordan Singer

Image credit: The Stapleton Collection / Bridgeman Images

First printing 2024

Printed in China

For other versions cited, please see Appendix.

All emphases in Scripture have been added by the author.

Hardcover ISBN: 978-1-4335-9063-4
ePub ISBN: 978-1-4335-9065-8
PDF ISBN: 978-1-4335-9064-1

Library of Congress Cataloging-in-Publication Data

Names: O'Donnell, Douglas Sean, 1972- author.
Title: Mark : arise and follow the son ESV expository reflections on the Gospels / Douglas Sean O'Donnell.
Description: Wheaton, Illinois : Crossway, 2024. | Series: Expository reflections on the Gospels ; vol. 3 | Includes bibliographical references and index.
Identifiers: LCCN 2023022760 (print) | LCCN 2023022761 (ebook) | ISBN 9781433590634 (hardcover) | ISBN 9781433590641 (pdf) | ISBN 9781433590658 (epub)
Subjects: LCSH: Bible. Mark--Commentaries.
Classification: LCC BS2585.3 .O36 2024 (print) | LCC BS2585.3 (ebook) | DDC 226.3/07--dc23/eng/20230728
LC record available at https://lccn.loc.gov/2023022760
LC ebook record available at https://lccn.loc.gov/2023022761

Crossway is a publishing ministry of Good News Publishers.

RRDS		34	33	32	31	30	29	28	27	26	25	24
13	12	11	10	9	8	7	6	5	4	3	2	1

To my granddaughter Sydney Gene, one of my greatest joys!

Contents

Tables

Preface

Throughout history every major branch of the Christian church—Roman Catholic, Eastern Orthodox, and Protestant—has preached through the Four Gospels more than any other section of Scripture. This is due to (1) liturgical traditions in which the Gospel reading is the final Scripture reading and the preacher's sermon or homily is typically on that reading and (2) the fact that the Gospels have rightly been viewed by pastors as directly evangelistic and essential for discipleship.

A few times throughout church history pastor-theologians have written commentaries on the Four Gospels. The *ESV Expository Reflections on the Gospels* follows in this tradition, especially that of J. C. Ryle's *Expository Thoughts on the Gospels*, with his accessible and applicable exegesis. The writing style is homiletic (in the best sense!), seeking to be carefully structured, exegetically deep, highly applicable, deeply personable and engagingly humorous, and rhetorically excellent.

When I reached out to Dick Lucas, a preacher I greatly admire, to write a commendation, I was delighted that he said yes and was honored that he would write of my work that I have given the church "thorough exposition that is wonderfully refreshing," sermons that echo "the Master Teacher in the Gospel records" and that offer "a model for today's preacher, arresting and accessible teaching." May it be so as you journey, with me as your guide, through the Gospels!

Preface

In God's kind providence my Christian life has centered around the Four Gospels. When I was nineteen, the Lord used the Gospels—particularly the story of the rich young ruler—to open my eyes to the reality of my sin and to draw me to Christ as Savior. Early in my pastoral ministry Pastor Kent Hughes invited me to write a commentary on Matthew for the Preaching the Word series. So the first sermon series I preached at New Covenant Church in Naperville, Illinois, was on the First Gospel. A decade ago, when Queensland Theological College in Brisbane, Australia, invited me to be their senior lecturer in biblical studies and practical theology, they asked me to teach two classes on the Synoptic Gospels and the Gospel of John. What a joy to teach, and learn from, my students down under. Shortly thereafter, under the splendid supervision of professors John Nolland and Nicholas Perrin, I completed my PhD dissertation at the University of Aberdeen on the topic of faith in Matthew's Gospel.[1] Now, in this newest commentary, I am privileged to share with you what was first shared with the congregation of Westminster Presbyterian Church in Elgin, Illinois—expositions on the Gospel of Mark.

Mark, who in Acts is also called John Mark (Acts 12:12, 25; 15:37),[2] was not an apostle, but he was in the apostolic inner circle. He was part of the

---

1   Douglas Sean O'Donnell, *"O Woman, Great Is Your Faith!" Faith in the Gospel of Matthew* (Eugene, OR: Pickwick, 2021).

2   Mark was from Jerusalem and part of a wealthy family (his mother's home was large enough to house a prayer meeting, Acts 12:12; perhaps Mark 14:14) and was connected with other wealthy Christians (Barnabas, Acts 4:36–37). From Acts 12:25 we learn that he joined Barnabas and Paul on their missionary journeys. Mark is also mentioned in Colossians 4:10; 2 Timothy 4:11; Philemon 24; and 1 Peter 5:13. Peter labels Mark his "son" (1 Pet. 5:13). This personal and familial relationship with Peter suggests the possibility that Peter was Mark's source regarding the life of Jesus (so testified by Papias of Hierapolis, Irenaeus, Justin Martyr, Tertullian, and Origen).

group that met in the upper room after Jesus' death. Likely Simon Peter was his source, and likely he wrote this book near the end of Peter's life (AD 64–68) but before the destruction of the temple in Jerusalem (AD 70).[3] We do not know where Mark was when he wrote his Gospel (likely Rome)[4] or to what city or community he first sent his Gospel (a growing number of scholars believe that he intended his Gospel to circulate among as many Christian communities as possible).[5] It is possible that Mark wrote to unbelievers, seeking to persuade them to become believers.[6] But it is more likely that he wrote to believers, with these goals: (1) to remind them of what they were to believe about Jesus, (2) to instruct them in Jesus' teachings, (3) to urge them to share those stories about who Jesus is and what he has done for others, and (4) to encourage them to persevere through persecution.

In 13:14 Mark interjects, "Let the reader understand." This interjection comes in the Olivet Discourse, after Jesus speaks of the "abomination of desolation."[7] Mark's earnest desire is that his Christian readers would understand Jesus' teaching on the destruction of the temple and his second coming. But he also desires his readers to understand far more. He wants us to understand Jesus' identity as the Son of God, the Son of David, and the Son of Man. Moreover, Mark wants us to understand Jesus' mission—that he came to conquer the powers of evil (demons, disease, and death)—through the cross. He wants us to know by heart and embrace with our whole heart the fact that, in Jesus' own words, "even the Son of Man came not to be served but to serve, and to give his life as a ransom for many" (Mark 10:45). Finally, Mark wants us to understand the cost of discipleship—that we should arise and follow the Son by picking up our cross, sacrificing for others, and sharing the good news of the kingdom of heaven with the world.

3   "If one relies on external evidence, it is plausible to assume that Mark wrote in Rome before the death of Peter, whose teaching he wrote down, and that he wrote before the end of Paul's imprisonment. . . . This would mean that Mark wrote his Gospel between AD 60–62." Eckhard J. Schnabel, *Mark: An Introduction and Commentary*, TNTC (Downers Grove, IL: IVP Academic, 2017), 17; cf. Robert H. Gundry, *Mark: A Commentary on His Apology for the Cross* (Grand Rapids, MI: Eerdmans, 1993), 1042–43.
4   From 1 Peter 5:13 we learn that Peter and Mark were in Rome (labeled "Babylon") together. "The city of *Rome* is the most plausible provenance" (Schnabel, *Mark*, 14).
5   That the Gospels were written for a broad audience, see Richard Bauckham, ed., *The Gospel for All Christians: Rethinking the Gospel Audiences* (Edinburgh: T&T Clark, 1998).
6   Gundry (*Mark*, 3–4) argues that Mark's Gospel is "an apology for the cross" in that Mark is showing that through Jesus' crucifixion (theology of suffering) Jesus inaugurates the eschatological salvation (theology of glory) of the kingdom of God. "Mark writes . . . to convert non-Christians despite the shame of the Cross" (1026).
7   See note 6 in chapter 37.

As stated above, these expositions were first preached at Westminster Presbyterian Church. I am grateful for the encouragement I received from both the session and the congregation, and I am thankful for a church community that supported my laboring, through my studies and writings, for the larger church. I am also appreciative to Frederick Dale Bruner for editing the entire second draft, Emily Gerdts for reviewing the third draft, and Elliott Pinegar and Davis Wetherell for their honest pushback, wise suggestions, theological tightening, and careful stylistic and substantive sharpening of sentences.

Abbreviations

1 Macc.	*1 Maccabees*
4 Macc.	*4 Maccabees*
AB	Anchor Bible
ABRL	Anchor Bible Reference Library
ACCS	Ancient Christian Commentary on Scripture
ACW	Ancient Christian Writers
AD	Anno Domini (in the year of our Lord)
Ag. Ap.	*Against Apion* (Josephus)
AMP	Amplified Bible
Ant.	*The Jewish Antiquities* (Josephus)
b. Bat.	Babylonian Talmud, Baba Batra
b. Ber.	Babylonian Talmud, Berakot
b. Mak.	Babylonian Talmud, Makkot
b. Šabb.	Babylonian Talmud, Šabbat
b. Sukk.	Babylonian Talmud, Sukkah
b. Taʿan.	Babylonian Talmud, Taʿanit
BC	Before Christ
BECNT	Baker Exegetical Commentary on the New Testament
BJRL	*Bulletin of the John Rylands University Library of Manchester*
BNTC	Black's New Testament Commentaries
BST	Bible Speaks Today
CBQ	*Catholic Biblical Quarterly*
CCC	Crossway Classic Commentaries
CGTC	Cambridge Greek Testament Commentary
CHSB	*ESV Church History Study Bible: Voices from the Past Wisdom for the Present.* Edited by Stephen J. Nichols, Gerald Bray, and Keith A. Mathison. Wheaton, IL: Crossway, 2022.
CSB	Christian Standard Bible
d.	Died
Did.	*Didache*

DJG	*Dictionary of Jesus and the Gospels*. Edited by Joel B. Green, Jeannie K. Brown, and Nicholas Perrin. 2nd ed. Downers Grove, IL: InterVarsity, 2013.
DNTB	*Dictionary of New Testament Background*. Edited by Craig A. Evans and Stanley E. Porter. Downers Grove, IL: InterVarsity, 2000.
EBC	Expositor's Bible Commentary
EBT	Explorations in Biblical Theology
EGGNT	Exegetical Guide to the Greek New Testament
ESVEC	ESV Expository Commentary
FC	Fathers of the Church
Haer.	*Against Heresies* (Irenaeus)
HCSB	Holman Christian Standard Bible
HTR	*Harvard Theological Review*
ICC	International Critical Commentary
Int	*Interpretation*
Ira	*De Ira* (Seneca)
JBL	*Journal of Biblical Literature*
JSNTSS	Journal for the Study of the New Testament Supplement Series
JSOT	*Journal for the Study of the Old Testament*
JTS	*Journal of Theological Studies*
J.W.	*Jewish War* (Josephus)
KJV	King James Version
LCC	Library of Christian Classics
LXX	Septuagint
m. ʾAbot	Mishnah, ʾAbot
m. B. Qam.	Mishnah, Baba Qamma
m. Ber.	Mishnah, Berakot
m. Giṭ.	Mishnah, Giṭṭin
m. Kel.	Mishnah, Kelim
m. Ketub.	Mishnah, Ketubbot
m. Ned.	Mishnah, Nedarium
m. Pesaḥ.	Mishnah, Pesaḥim
m. Roš Haš	Mishnah, Roš Haššanah
m. Šabb.	Mishnah, Šabbat
m. Sanh.	Mishnah, Sanhedrin
m. Taʿan.	Mishnah, Taʿanit
m. Ṭehar.	Mishnah, Ṭeharot
m. Yebam.	Mishnah, Yebamot
mg.	Margin note (textual footnote)

MSG	The Message
NAC	New American Commentary
NASB	The New American Standard Bible
NCBC	New Cambridge Bible Commentary
Neot	*Neotestamentica*
NET	The NET Bible
NICNT	New International Commentary on the New Testament
NIGTC	New International Greek Testament Commentary
NIV	New International Version
NIVAC	New International Version Application Commentary
NJB	New Jerusalem Bible
NLT	New Living Translation
NRSV	The New Revised Standard Version
NT	New Testament
NTL	New Testament Library
OT	Old Testament
PHILLIPS	J. B. Phillips New Testament
PNTC	Pillar New Testament Commentary
PRS	Perspectives in Religious Studies
Pss. Sol.	*Psalms of Solomon*
PTW	Preaching the Word
REC	Reformed Expository Commentary
SHBC	Smyth & Helwys Bible Commentary
SNTSMS	Society for New Testament Studies Monograph Series
SP	Sacra Pagina
Str-B	Strack, H. L. and P. Billerbeck. *Kommenntar zum Neuen Testament aus Talmud und Midrasch.* 6 vols. Munich: Beck, 1922–1961.
t. Dan	Tosefta, Dan
t. Iss.	Tosefta, Issachar
TLB	The Living Bible
TNTC	Tyndale New Testament Commentaries
Tob.	*Tobit*
TTCS	Teach the Text Commentary Series
Verr.	*In Verrem* (Cicero)
WBC	Word Biblical Commentary
WLC	Westminster Larger Catechism
WUNT	Wissenschaftliche Untersuchungen zum Neuen Testament
ZECNT	Zondervan Exegetical Commentary on the New Testament

Arise and Follow the Son

MARK 1:1

The beginning of the gospel of Jesus Christ, the Son of God.
Mark 1:1

While attending a Christian college I began an outreach ministry at the local community college. Once a week a group of Christian students would scatter around campus and ask people whether they were interested in taking a religious survey. I do not remember all the questions we asked, but I do remember one question and the most popular answer to it. To the question "Who is Jesus?" the usual reply was "the Son of God." When we followed up that answer with more probing questions, we discovered that Jesus as "the Son of God" can mean a lot of different things to a lot of different people.

The Gospel of Mark was written to give God's inspired answer to the question, Who is Jesus? Put differently, it was penned to answer, explain, and illustrate the identity of the real Jesus. So, we might say, this Gospel was written to answer the question, Who is Jesus the Son of God? It was written also to answer the questions, Why should we follow him? and, if we are compelled to follow him, How should we follow him?

Our text for this introductory chapter is quite simple: "The beginning of the gospel of Jesus Christ, the Son of God" (Mark 1:1). But our task is more complex. Here we set out to discover—or rediscover—Jesus. Who is he? What is the good news about him? And, if drawn to him, how should we respond?

Who Is Jesus?

First, who is Jesus? In Mark **1:1** the Evangelist introduces us to the man Jesus. The name Jesus, which means "Yahweh saves," was one of the most common names in Israel at that time. A number of recent studies indicate that the most popular male names among Palestinian Jews living between 330 BC and AD 200 were (1) Simon, (2) Joseph, (3) Lazarus, (4) Judas, (5) John, and

(6) Jesus.[1] So the Jesus of the Gospels was not the only Jesus in Galilee. He was not even the only Jesus of Nazareth. If someone yelled "Jesus" in Jerusalem, like Mary and Joseph must have done when looking for their son (see Luke 2:41–52), more than a few heads would have turned. It would be like yelling "Patrick" in an Irish bar in Boston or "Tony" at a bocce ball tournament at Arthur Avenue in the Bronx.

So the once trendy Jewish name "Jesus" does not define, or set apart, the Jesus we know and love. But the two titles that follow do so: "Christ" and "the Son of God." The term "Christ" is not a last name but a designation. It means "anointed one," or "Messiah." It speaks of Jesus' being the promised King from the line of David (2 Sam. 7:11–16; Isa. 9:1–7; 11:1–16). Mark uses this title eight times. Besides in this verse (Mark 1:1), which serves not only as the start of his Gospel but also as its summary sentence, the name is used regularly in other important moments as well. For example, at the structural center (see table 1.1) and theological hinge of the Gospel (Mark 8:27–29) Peter answers Jesus' question, "Who do you say that I am?" with "You are the Christ" (8:29). At Jesus' trial the high priest asks Jesus, "Are you the Christ?" (14:61), to which Jesus replies, "I am" (*egō eimi*, 14:62). The final time that this word is used is in 15:32, where Jesus is reviled on the cross, "Let the Christ, the King of Israel, come down now from the cross that we may see and believe." His mockers understand correctly that the Christ is the "King of Israel," but they fail to understand that the mission of the promised King is crucifixion. (More on that in a moment.)

Table 1.1: Outline of the Gospel of Mark

1:1–15	Introduction to the Gospel: John the Baptist and Jesus
1:16–3:6	Jesus in Galilee: Ministry and Controversy
3:7–6:6	Jesus in Galilee: Jesus Teaches and Shows His Power
6:7–8:26	Jesus in Galilee: Jesus' Acts Yield a Confession
8:27–10:52	After a Key Confession, Jesus Heads to Jerusalem and Prepares His Disciples for the Suffering That Is to Come
11:1–16:8	In Jerusalem Jesus Meets Controversy and Rejection, Leading to His Death and Resurrection, as He Also Teaches of Suffering, Judgment, and Vindication[2]

---

1 See Richard Bauckham, *Jesus and the Eyewitnesses: The Gospels as Eyewitness Testimony* (Grand Rapids, MI: Eerdmans; Cambridge: Cambridge University Press, 2006), 85.

2 Darrell Bock, *Mark*, NCBC (Cambridge: Cambridge University Press, 2015), 36, emphasis mine. Whether we divide the Gospel at Mark 8:26 (before Peter's confession) or after it (8:30),

Jesus is the "Christ." He is also "the Son of God." This designation does not mean that God the Father, sometime two thousand years ago, birthed a son who did not previously exist. It does not mean Jesus is a son of God in the same way every member of God's covenant community is a child of God. And it is not merely a synonym for Christ. Rather, in Mark 1:1, and also when the Father at Jesus' baptism and transfiguration says, "This is my beloved Son" (9:7; cf. 1:11),[3] the title "Son of God" means that "Jesus is eternally Son of the Father, sharing his divine nature."[4]

This is obviously an important title, and, like the good silverware and china, Mark brings it out only for special occasions. He uses it three times, and every usage is significant. First, it is employed in Mark's introductory but also summary sentence (1:1). Second, it is found in two key confessions by two unexpected characters. At 3:11 we read, "Whenever the unclean spirits saw him, they fell down before him and cried out, 'You are the Son of God.'" The demons recognized Jesus' identity before the disciples did! Then at 15:39 the historical record states, "When the centurion, who stood facing him [Jesus on the cross], saw that in this way he breathed his last, he said, 'Truly this man was the Son of God!'" This scene and confession is dripping with irony. The Gentile solider responsible for carrying out the orders to crucify Jesus is the first person in history to look to the crucified Christ and confess him as "the Son of God."

So, Jesus is the "Christ" and "the Son of God." You may notice, however, that I have subtitled this commentary *Arise and Follow the Son*. I use the word *Son* because Jesus as the Son of God is an important identity marker. But I subtitle the commentary *Arise and Follow the Son* and not *Arise and Follow the Son of God* because Mark uses two other Son titles that help us better identify this Jesus we seek to discover: Son of David and Son of Man.

"the first half of the gospel presents Jesus as the mighty Messiah and Son of God . . . [and] the second half develops the theme of his suffering role." Mark L. Strauss, *Mark*, ZECNT (Grand Rapids, MI: Zondervan, 2014), 18. Note that "Mark employs a geographical and temporal structure to help the audience join episodes and relate them one to another" and that "temporal vocabulary—such as ἡμέρα (5x), πρωΐ (5x), and ὀψία (6x)—joins episodes"; Elizabeth Evans Shively, "Mark," in *The Greek New Testament, Produced at Tyndale House, Cambridge, Guided Annotating Edition*, ed. Daniel K. Eng (Wheaton, IL: Crossway, 2023), 129. Cf. Shively, "The Eclipse of the Markan Narrative: On the (Re)cognition of a Coherent Story and Implications for Genre," *Early Christianity* 12 (2021): 369–87.

3 Cf. 2 Samuel 7:11–14; Psalms 2:7; 89:26.

4 Hans F. Bayer, *A Theology of Mark: The Dynamic between Christology and Authentic Discipleship*, EBT (Phillipsburg, NJ: P&R, 2012), 51. Jesus is also called the Father's "beloved Son" at Jesus' baptism and transfiguration (Mark 1:11; 9:7). Other references to Jesus as the "Son" include "my son" (12:6) in the parable of the tenants, the demons' declaration ("the Son of the Most High God," 3:11; 5:7), and Jesus' own usage (he calls himself the "Son" in 13:32) and affirmation (his "I am" to the question, "Are you . . . the Son of the Blessed?"; 14:61, 62). For an excellent summary on the textual variant "Son of God" in Mark 1:1 see Strauss, *Mark*, 60–61.

More will be said about those titles when we come to them in the various narratives. For now, I will simply say that Son of David is closely connected to Christ (12:35), and Son of Man to Son of God. Jesus is the Christ (the anointed King) from the lineage of David. He fulfills the Davidic covenant. Moreover, Jesus is the Son of Man.[5] He is the Son of Man in his humble human state (Matt. 8:20) and in his humiliation — his rejection and sufferings (Mark 8:31; 10:45; 14:21, 36). But also, alluding to the Son of Man in Daniel 7:13–14, Jesus is the exalted figure who is worshiped alongside the Ancient of Days. In Mark, Jesus as the Son of Man acts like God: he forgives sins (Mark 2:10), rules over the Sabbath (2:28), and will judge the world (8:38; 13:26). The Christ is the Son of David; the Son of God is the Son of Man. Jesus Christ is the Son of David, the Son of God, and the Son of Man.

Three times in Mark questions are raised about Jesus' identity. After hearing his wise words and witnessing his mighty works, Jesus' hometown asks, "Is not this the carpenter, the son of Mary and brother of James and Joses and Judas and Simon?" (6:3). Then, after the calming of the storm the disciples ask, "Who then is this, that even the wind and the sea obey him?" (4:41). Finally, Jesus asks, "Who do people say that I am?" (8:27). If we survey the whole of the Gospel, what follows are Mark's answers to those questions. Some call him teacher, rabbi, and Jesus of Nazareth.[6] Some believe he is a prophet (see 6:15; 8:28). But Jesus is more than a prophet and teacher from Nazareth. Mark makes sure we know that Jesus is the King of the Jews (15:2; cf. King of Israel, 15:32), the Lord (1:3), the Holy One of God (1:24), the Son of David (10:47), the Son of Man (2:10), the Son of the Most High God (5:7), the stone that the builders rejected (12:10), the bridegroom (2:19), the Christ (1:1), and the Son of God (1:1; cf. God's beloved son, 1:11; 9:7; the Son, 12:6; 13:32; the Son of the Blessed, 14:61). Jesus' *identity* is important to Mark!

Before we turn our attention to the phrase "the gospel of Jesus" (1:1), we should take away three important ideas from the phrase "Jesus Christ, the Son of God." First, we must read this Gospel with Jesus in focus. Oftentimes we read, or are tempted to read, the Bible existentially. What does the Bible say to me directly? For example, we read about the healing of the paralytic and think, "Jesus can heal my bad back," or we read about his teaching on fasting and think, "Jesus can help me keep my diet." Maybe our interpretations and applications are not that off base. But I hope you understand my point. We tend to think about ourselves first and then, if ever, about the

---

5 This title is used fourteen times in Mark, and every reference comes from Jesus and is about Jesus.
6 "Teacher" (Mark 4:38; 5:35; 9:17, 38; 10:17, 35; 12:14, 19, 32; 13:1; 14:14), "rabbi" (9:5; 10:51; 11:21; 14:45), "the Nazarene" (14:67; cf. 1:24; 16:6).

original message to the original audience. In his opening verse Mark makes sure that our focus is Godward. He opens his Gospel with a statement not about us but about God's Son. He does this because he wants to know how much Jesus matters. He wants to introduce us to a character—the hero in his great drama.

The second takeaway is that understanding who Jesus is really matters. Jesus' identity matters to Mark, and should matter to us, *because* our salvation depends on it. Jesus' atonement is directly connected to his incarnation. The Son of God became fully and completely human in order to die for our sins. So, when people say, "It does not matter what church you go to as long as it believes in Jesus," we need to reply, "But what 'Jesus' does that church believe in and teach about? Does it confess and profess that Jesus is the Christ, the Son of God?" Moreover, when we encounter a religious group that denies the deity of Jesus, we need to recognize that our conversation is a matter of life and death. We are saved from our sin not by the man Jesus but by the God-man, the one who atoned for all our sins and turned away God's judgment upon that sin because he is fully God and fully man.

The third takeaway from the line "Jesus Christ, the Son of God" involves how we should read each and every section of Mark's Gospel. Mark has given us the lens with which to see Jesus properly. So when we read of Jesus' claiming to be the Lord of the Sabbath (2:27–28), sleeping through a storm (4:38); loving a hungry crowd (8:2); blessing the little children (10:14–16); cursing a fig tree and condemning the temple thieves (11:15–25); teaching the greatest commandment (12:28–34); predicting his sufferings, death, and resurrection (8:31; 9:12, 31; 10:33, 45; 14:23–24), along with his second coming (13:24–27); and then actually dying and rising (15:21–39; 16:1–8), for each and every action and saying we should think, "This is the Christ, the Son of God!"

What Is the Gospel about Jesus?

What is the importance of getting Jesus' identity right? Everything! Why does Mark start this way? Because if we get the *person* of Jesus wrong, we will get the *plan* of Jesus wrong. If we do not know that Jesus is the Christ and the Son of God, then the gospel about him ("the beginning of the *gospel* of Jesus Christ, the Son of God," 1:1) makes no sense. So then, moving from answering the question, Who is Jesus? let us next answer the question, What has Jesus done, and why is it good news for us?

Jesus' first recorded speech in the Gospel of Mark is "The time is fulfilled, and the kingdom of God is at hand" (1:15). That announcement follows directly after Mark's statement that "Jesus came into Galilee, proclaiming the

gospel of God" (1:14). Jesus came to announce the good news of the kingdom of God. However, he came to do more than announce the gospel and
kingdom; he came to declare and demonstrate his rule as the King of that
kingdom. And he does so through his authoritative teaching and powerful
miracles.[7] His every *word* and *work* attest to his identity and mission.

His memorable *words* include the following: "I came not to call the righteous, but sinners" (2:17); "What does it profit a man to gain the whole world
and forfeit his soul?" (8:36); "If anyone would be first, he must be last of all
and servant of all" (9:35); "Whoever would be first among you must be slave
of all" (10:44); "Render to Caesar the things that are Caesar's, and to God
the things that are God's" (12:17); "You shall love your neighbor as yourself"
(12:31); "This is my blood of the covenant, which is poured out for many"
(14:24); "My God, my God, why have you forsaken me?" (15:34). Jesus' last
words are his cry upon the cross. How telling is that!

Jesus' every word attests to his identity and mission, as does every work.
Here is a sampling of his *works*: he feeds thousands of people with a few
pieces of bread and fish (6:30–44; 8:1–10); expels demons (1:21–28; 5:1–20;
7:24–30; 9:14–29); heals the leper (1:40–45), the paralytic (2:1–12), and the
deaf and mute (7:31–37); raises the dead (5:21–43); calms a storm (4:35–41);
walks on water (6:45–52). And, of course, Jesus suffers, dies, and rises. And
before he accomplishes those works, he interprets all his actions in one short
clause: "The Son of Man came . . . to give his life as a ransom for many"
(10:45). In 2:10 Jesus claims to have the authority to forgive sins, and in 15:37
("And Jesus . . . breathed his last") that forgiveness is accomplished and finally,
through faith, applied to us. And that is good news! Jesus paid it all. He has
canceled our debt. We who were enslaved to sin, death, and Satan have been
set free. In his rejection and resurrection the Christ conquers all the evils we
face and that have long held us captive. Praise God! What a Savior he has
sent! "The *gospel* of Jesus Christ, the Son of God" (1:1).

Read, Mark, Learn

Whenever I set out to preach on a book of the Bible, I read the book many
times. So when I decided that the Gospel of Mark was what my congregation
needed to hear preached, I read through it devotionally. Then, when it came

7   Elizabeth Struthers Malbon calls Jesus' actions "enacted Christology." "'Reflected Christology':
     An Aspect of Narrative 'Christology' in the Gospel of Mark," *PRS* 26 (1999): 136. Adela Yarbo
     Collins claims, "Jesus is portrayed as Son of God narratively, by recounting his mighty deeds,
     his authoritative teaching, his prophecy, and his death for the benefit of others." "Mark and His
     Readers: The Son of God among Greeks and Romans," *HTR* 93 (2000): 100.

time to study it in greater depth, I printed out the book in its entirety and I started to read Mark and mark Mark up.

The first time I read through Mark, I got a feel for it, noting its unusual literary form (a gospel)[8] and its variety of genres—narratives, discourses, commands, parables, and apocalyptic pronouncement and prophecies. The second time I put a box around every title for Jesus and underlined every time there was a question about Jesus' identity. The third time I noted some of the details. I highlighted the geography, noting that Jesus moves from Galilee to Jerusalem. I noted Mark's use of the OT, writing an *OT* next to all the OT quotations and possible allusions. I highlighted the times Jesus commands people to be quiet. I noticed that Mark has a disputed ending. Does it end at 16:8 or 16:20?[9] I noticed that Mark's storytelling skills remind me of the live report from an on-the-scene journalist.[10] I observed his "dualisms"[11] (i.e., he says one phrase and then says the same thing with minor variations) and interpretive intercalations (an episode within an episode; e.g., 5:21–43).[12] I saw that Mark's Gospel not only is shorter than the other canonical Gospels[13] but has a fast-paced quality to it.[14] Often with the adverb

---

8   As a genre, Mark's Gospel was "a completely new kind of book. . . . No one had ever written [a Gospel] before. In fact, no one would have known what a Gospel was!" Sinclair B. Ferguson, *Let's Study Mark* (Carlisle, PA: Banner of Truth Trust, 2016), xiii. That said, Mark's narrative shares some features of Greco-Roman *bioi* (biographies of important people). Moreover, and more notably, it resembles OT biographical material (e.g., the life of David in 1–2 Samuel) in that it has a didactic purpose.

9   The oldest Greek manuscripts (ℵ, Codex Sinaiticus; B, Codex Vaticanus) do not contain Mark 16:9–20. "In the oldest commentary on Mark's Gospel, by Victor of Antioch, we find a note attached to the longer ending . . . that says, 'In most copies this additional material according to Mark is not found.'" Eckhard J. Schnabel, *Mark: An Introduction and Commentary,* TNTC (Downers Grove, IL: IVP Academic, 2017), 19. Based on external (above) and internal (e.g., nine new words are introduced) evidence, the scholarly consensus since 1881 (Westcott and Hort, *The New Testament in the Original Greek*) is that the longer ending is not original. Cf. James W. Voelz, *Mark 8:27–16:8*; Christopher W. Mitchell. *Mark 8:27–16:20*, Concordia Commentary (St. Louis: Concordia Publishing House, 2019), 1201–1204, esp. "Excursus 19: A Consideration of the 'Longer Ending' of Mark: 16:9–20" (1222–37).

10 "Mark is . . . fond of the *historical present tense* (151 times), a Greek construction that uses present tense verbs in narrative to describe past actions. Though characteristic of a less-refined Greek style, it also gives that narrative a vivid style, like an on-the-spot report" (Strauss, *Mark*, 46).

11 E.g., "that evening at sundown," or more literally, "evening having come," which is the same as saying, "when the sun set" (Mark 1:32; cf. 1:35; 2:20; 4:35; 10:30; 13:29).

12 These are also called "Markan sandwiches." See Tom Shepherd, *Markan Sandwich Stories* (Berrien Springs, MI: Andrews University Press, 1993).

13 In the Greek texts Mark has 11,304 words (with the longer ending), Matthew 18,346, Luke 19,482, and John 15,635. Mark's Gospel especially lends itself to memorization and public recitation. Some scholars believe that this was Mark's original intent, suggesting that the written Gospel could be based on an oral Gospel that was performed.

14 "Compared with Matthew and Luke, who report lengthy sections of Jesus' teaching, and compared with John, who provides more substantial and explicit theological interpretation, Mark

immediately and the conjunction *and* Mark quickly moves his readers from one story to the next.[15] Yet I also noticed that the tempo slows down during the week of Jesus' crucifixion. Mark describes each day of Jesus' final week and nearly each hour of his passion and death. With the slow motion, frame-by-frame depiction Mark is answering this question: What has Jesus accomplished, and why is it good news for us? The fourth time through I underlined what Jesus says and does, and how people respond to him. To those observations we turn to next.

How Should We Respond to the Gospel? Arise and Follow

Mark does not just talk about who Jesus is and what he has done. He also highlights various responses to him. There are wrong responses and right ones. And through the various characters who encounter Jesus, we ourselves enter into the drama. With each character we should ask ourselves, Should we imitate their response to Jesus or not?

For example, we *should not* say about Jesus, as the scribes did, "He is possessed by Beelzebul" (3:22); or join Peter at the transfiguration in making Jesus equal with Moses and Elijah (wanting to build a tent for each, 9:5); or follow the rich man in not following Jesus' call (10:17–22); or betray Jesus like Judas does (14:43–46); or repeatedly deny Jesus like Peter does (14:66–72); or ridicule Jesus as Pilate does (15:9, 26); or mock him like the Roman soldiers (15:16–20), the chief priests, and the scribes do (15:31–32). But we *should* follow Jesus like Simon, Andrew, James, and John (1:16–20); join the leper on our knees before Jesus, saying, "Make me clean" (1:40); and humbly acknowledge, as the father of the demon-possessed boy does, our need for Jesus' help—not only to deliver us from evil but to grow our faith: "[We] believe; help [our] unbelief" (9:24). We should also see with blind Bartimaeus that Jesus, as the Son of David, is able to cure both physical and spiritual blindness: "Son of David, have mercy on me!" (10:47). And we should shout

---

wrote a vivid, action-packed narrative. . . . Mark's paratactical, anecdotal style leaves his hearers and readers with the impression of fast-paced action. The evangelist moves Jesus and the disciples quickly from event to event. . . . Mark presents Jesus' ministry as a series of dramatic events with hardly a pause" (Schnabel, *Mark*, 1, 5).

15 I learned later that καί ("and"), which is used over a thousand times, and εὐθύς ("immediately") forty-seven times are "paired 25 times in Mark's Gospel (and only three other times in the rest of the NT)," and that Mark, imitating "the paratactic style of Hebrew prose narrative," uses often καί and rarely δέ ("but"). Moreover, Mark's uses of doubling (e.g., "that evening at sundown," 1:32) and tripling (e.g., "rise, take up your bed, and walk," 2:9, 11, 12) "evokes a sense of progressive intensity." Thus I agree with scholars throughout the ages, and most recently Shively, whom I quote above and next: "Together these terms convey a sense of urgency and forward movement" ("Mark," 130).

aloud with the crowd, "Hosanna! Blessed is he who comes in the name of the Lord! Blessed is the coming kingdom of our father David! Hosanna in the highest!" (11:9–10). Yes, indeed. Lord, save us! We should, moreover, like the woman who comes with an expensive bottle of perfume, pour out a year's wages upon Jesus (14:3–9) and join in the centurion's cry at the cross, "Truly this man was the Son of God!" (15:39).

In 13:14 Mark exclaims, "Let the reader understand." But Mark wants his readers to understand not only the Olivet Discourse (where we find that interjection). He wants us to understand who Jesus is, what he has done for us, and how we should respond to him. One way in which Mark teaches his readers to respond to Jesus is through key characters; we are to respond like him and her and them. Another way is through key commands. For example, in 8:27–38 Jesus asks his disciples about his identity: "Who do people say that I am?" The disciples cite various wrong answers. Some say that Jesus is John the Baptist; others Elijah or one of the prophets. "But who do you say that I am?" Jesus asks. Peter answers, "You are the Christ." This is the correct answer. Peter understands Jesus' identity. But, as we soon learn, he does not yet understand Jesus' mission. When Jesus next talks about the necessity of his death, Peter takes him aside to rebuke him. It is the worst counseling session in the history of the world.

In Mark, identity (who Jesus is) and mission (why Jesus came and why his coming is good news) go together. As does the call to discipleship. How do we respond to the good news of the death and resurrection of Jesus, the Christ and the Son of God? Jesus tells us in Mark 8:34: "If anyone would come after me, let him deny himself and take up his cross and follow me." What a challenge! The cost of discipleship. No cheap grace from gracious Jesus.

How will we respond to Jesus? I hope that we do so the way Mark wants us to. Will we follow, listen to, obey, and humbly serve Jesus? Will we suffer for Jesus, look to Jesus' death and resurrection as our only hope of salvation, and await Jesus' return? To Mark, those who genuinely believe the good news of Jesus the Christ and the Son of God respond in certain ways. Self-denial. Cross-bearing. Total dependence. Radical allegiance.

Arise and *follow* the Son!

Answering Life's Big Questions

In a strip from the thought-provoking comic *Calvin and Hobbes*, the curious boy Calvin asks Hobbes, his stuffed tiger who comes to life in his imagination, "Why do you suppose we're here?" They are both sitting on the ground, leaning against a large tree. Hobbes replies, "Because we walked here." "No, no," Calvin retorts, "I mean here on earth." Hobbes replies, "Because earth can support life." "No, I mean why are we anywhere? Why do we exist?" Again, Hobbes comments, "Because we were born." Frustrated, Calvin moves around to the other side of the tree, lowers his head and says, "Forget it." Hobbes concludes, "I will, thank you."[16]

The Gospel of Mark does not set out to answer the question, Why do we exist? Instead it answers these questions: Who is Jesus? What is the gospel about him? How do we respond to the gospel of the kingdom about Christ Jesus, the Son of God? But in answering those questions it helps us find the answer to the question of our existence. Why are we here? In this world filled with evil, injustice, and oppression, where we are faced with trials, pains, and sufferings, why do we exist? Mark tells us that we exist to join Jesus in his victory. Arise and follow the Son! Through Jesus' sufferings the power of death has been broken, the reign of God has begun, and salvation has arrived. "In the midst of a world of bad news," we have the good news of Jesus the Christ, the Son of God.[17]

---

16 Bill Watterson, *Weirdos from Another Planet* (Kansas City, MO: Universal Press Syndicate, 1990), 21.
17 For some of the words and ideas for this paragraph see Strauss, *Mark*, 20.

In the Wilderness

MARK 1:2–13

The Spirit immediately drove him out into the wilderness.
Mark 1:12

The Man Who Eats Locusts, the Descending Dove, and the Tempted Son

Recently I learned that the professor who taught me Greek exegesis has Alzheimer's disease. Each morning for many years my professor and his wife would listen to the Bible read aloud. He would listen to the English, with his Greek text open. She would read along with various English translations in order to try to get a feel for what her husband understood and appreciated. Today, each morning, they still read together. He has forgotten Greek. So he reads a comic strip version of the Bible. He looks at pictures and reads captions. And he loves it. His picture Bible is as worn and tattered as his Greek NT is.

As we focused on Mark 1:1 in the last chapter, we answered three questions. In this chapter, as we turn our attention to verses 2–13, we open Mark's version of a picture Bible. In the first frame (1:2–8) we see an old scroll, an unusual man, and mass baptisms in the Jordan River. In the second frame (1:9–11) we find a descending dove, a baptized son, and a Father's voice from heaven. In the third frame (1:12–13) we witness wild animals, ministering angels, slithering Satan, and the tempted Son.

The Testimony of John the Baptist

To start let us focus on the first frame. Each of the four Gospels begins in a different way. Matthew gives us Jesus' genealogy, Luke a dedication to Theophilus in which he provides a rationale for his writing, and John his *logos* Christology. Mark begins, "The beginning of the gospel of Jesus Christ, the Son of God" (1:1). Then, from those two titles for Jesus, he immediately grounds his Gospel in the OT. Only Mark starts with Scripture:

As it is written in Isaiah the prophet:

"Behold, I send my messenger before your face [an idiom for
        "ahead of you"],
    who will prepare your way,
the voice of one crying [or "shouting"] in the wilderness:
    'Prepare the way of the Lord,
    make his paths straight.'" (**1:2–3**)

Here Mark quotes from Isaiah 40:3, in combination with Exodus 23:20 and
Malachi 3:1. He names Isaiah, and not Moses and Malachi, likely because
he wants us to note the connection between the "beginning of the gospel
of Jesus" (Mark 1:1) and Isaiah's vision of a new exodus, a time of restoration and salvation through judgment (e.g., of "reward" and "recompense,"
Isa. 40:10). In Exodus 23:20 God promises to send a messenger ahead of the
Israelites in the wilderness, and in Malachi 3:1 the messenger is the prophet
Elijah (see Mal. 4:5), who is sent to prepare for Yahweh's coming judgment
on wicked Israel. Obviously, Mark is claiming that the Elijah-like messenger
is John and Yahweh the coming judge is Jesus.

Mark grounds the "gospel of Jesus" (Mark 1:1) in the OT Scriptures
(1:2–3)[1] in order to show that Jesus' whole ministry is rooted in the whole
story of Israel. As Scot McKnight notes,

The Story of Jesus Christ . . . isn't a story that came out of nowhere like
the Book of Mormon, and it isn't a timeless set of ideas, as with Plato's
philosophical writings. The story of Jesus Christ is locked into one people, one history, and one Scripture: it makes sense only as it follows and
completes the Story of Israel.[2]

Mark also grounds "the gospel of Jesus" (1:1) in this prophecy from Isaiah
(1:2–3). Similar to the scene in Acts 8, in which Philip explains the prophet
Isaiah to the Ethiopian eunuch ("Philip opened his mouth, and beginning
with this Scripture [Isaiah 53], he told him the good news about Jesus,"
Acts 8:35), Mark wants to take us to the good news about Jesus through the

---

1   While Mark 1:1 functions as a title statement of the whole of the Gospel, it also connects theo-
    logically with 1:2–15, in that it (1) grounds the gospel in the OT, (2) introduces the ministry of
    John as the "beginning" of the gospel story about Jesus, and (3) is bookended by Jesus' "gospel"
    (1:15) proclamation.
2   Scot McKnight, *The King Jesus Gospel: The Original Good News Revisited* (Grand Rapids, MI:
    Zondervan, 2011), 50.

predicted ministry of John the Baptist. Jesus, who "died for our sins *in accordance with the Scriptures* . . . [and] was raised on the third day *in accordance with the Scriptures*" (1 Cor. 15:3–4), first had a messenger (the prophet John) prepare the way *in accordance with the Scriptures* (the prophet Isaiah). Long ago, even before the creation of the world (Rev. 13:8), God had planned the coming of his Son and the prophetic preparation necessary to announce Jesus' arrival. The advent of John and Jesus was no afterthought.

With that foundation laid, I will give an overview and explanation of the important quotation "Behold, I send my messenger before your face" (Mark 1:2). John is God's messenger who is to "prepare the way of the Lord" (1:3). In the OT quotation "the Lord" is Yahweh; here in Mark it is clearly Jesus.[3] This Lord, as John the Baptist preaches, is powerful ("He who is mightier than I"), righteous ("The strap of whose sandals I am not worthy to stoop down and untie," **1:7**), and transformative ("He will baptize . . . with the Holy Spirit," **1:8**). In John 3:30 John says of his relationship to Jesus, "He must increase, but I must decrease." Here in Mark he demonstrates that humility. He views himself as being below the level of a slave, and his water baptism as incomparable to the Spirit baptism to come.[4] And, by labeling Jesus "He who is mightier than I" (Mark 1:7), he apparently acknowledges that Jesus is Yahweh himself, the coming Lord.

John will prepare the way "in the wilderness" (1:3)—the place in OT history of safety, testing, and disobedience—in two ways. First, he dresses for the job ("John was clothed with camel's hair and wore a leather belt around his waist") and consumes the proper ascetic diet ("locusts and wild honey," **1:6**; cf. Isa. 7:15). He is intentionally resembling the prophet Elijah (2 Kings 1:8),[5]

---

3   "By taking OT passages that speak of the coming of Yahweh himself (Isa. 40:3; Mal. 3:1) and applying them to Jesus, the narrator confirms that Jesus represents God's presence on earth and fulfills his purpose. An implicit divine Christology runs throughout Mark's Gospel." Mark L. Strauss, *Mark*, ZECNT (Grand Rapids, MI: Zondervan, 2014), 67. What C. Kavin Rowe said of Luke 3:4–6 is true of Mark 1:3: "Because 3:4–6 is an Old Testament quotation the κύριος in 3:4 is unquestionably the κύριος of the Old Testament; because John the Baptist in Luke's narrative literally does prepare the way for Jesus structurally, sequentially, and as his prophet, the κύριος indubitably refers to Jesus." *Early Narrative Christology: The Lord in the Gospel of Luke* (Grand Rapids, MI: Baker Academic, 2009), 71.

4   John is likely predicting what happens at Pentecost (Acts 2) and throughout Acts (e.g., 2:38), as the ascended Jesus pours out his Spirit on the church. For the OT foundation for this see Isaiah 44:3; Ezekiel 36:26–27; Joel 2:28. If this is the case, then what Jesus offers, which is greater than what John offers, is an internal (not merely water on the body, but change in the heart) baptism that establishes a right relationship with God and transforms people from the inside out. Put simply, this internal baptism is "the regeneration of the Holy Spirit, his cleansing from sin, and his empowering to godliness." R. Kent Hughes, *Mark: Jesus, Servant and Savior*, PTW, 2 vols. (Wheaton, IL: Crossway, 1989), 1:25.

5   "John's message was also similar to Elijah's. The people had broken the covenant with God. They were under his judgment. Only by turning away from their sins and turning back to the

offering a prophetic protest against materialism and demonstrating a life of complete dependence on God's sustenance for survival. Second, he preaches ("crying [out]," Mark 1:3; "proclaiming," **1:4**; "preached," 1:7) "a baptism of repentance for the forgiveness of sins" (1:4) and baptizes all who come to him and confess their sins (**1:5**). Whatever the baptism looks like—a Jewish ceremonial washing or a Gentile proselyte immersion—the water symbolizes a cleansing of the soul by turning from sin to God ("repentance," 1:4). And John's ministry is a success! He has a megachurch in the desert: "All the country of Judea and all Jerusalem were going out to him and were being baptized" (1:5). Mark exaggerates to make a point. The point is not that everyone from Herod the Great to Simon the Sorcerer is there, but that a revival is occurring. John is announcing that in Jesus the exile is over and a new eschatological exodus is at hand. The exile is not from Babylon back to Jerusalem or out of Egypt into the promised land. Rather, as Mark will explain, it is freedom from the bondage of sin (1:4) through God in the flesh, who has come to be baptized into our bondage (1:9) so as to lead all who are baptized in him through faith (1:15) into the presence of God.

From Explanation to Application

From that explanation of Mark 1:2–8, let me offer two applications.

First, the ministry of John the Baptist teaches us about genuine revival. Do not overlook Mark 1:5: "All the country of Judea and all Jerusalem were going out to [John] and were being baptized." How do we get "all" from the 20- to 200-mile radius to come to church? More than that, how do we get them to say, "I need to change. Help me change. Help me turn from sin to God?" Let me suggest that we preach repentance for the forgiveness of sins. Perhaps the church in North America is not flourishing because we are not preaching what the world needs to hear. We are not following the lead of John (1:4), Jesus (1:15; Revelation 2–3), and the apostles.[6] We do not read that all those people were coming to John because he dressed well, spoke well, and was offering a nice stay in a wilderness resort, which included a quick dip in

Lord and his ways would they be ready when the long-promised Messiah came." Sinclair B. Ferguson, *Let's Study Mark* (Carlisle, PA: Banner of Truth Trust, 2016), 3.

6   "There is not a sermon recorded in the Synoptics and Acts that does not assume everyone is a sinner, under the judgment of God, and thus in need of 'repentance toward God and of faith in our Lord Jesus Christ' (Acts 20:21). The consistent proclamation is that 'all people everywhere' should 'repent' (17:30) and 'believe in the gospel' (Mark 1:15)." Douglas Sean O'Donnell, "'If You, Then, Who are Evil': Sin in the Synoptic Gospels and Acts," in *Ruined Sinners to Reclaim: Human Corruption in Historical, Biblical, Theological, and Pastoral Perspective*, ed. David Gibson and Jonathan Gibson (Wheaton, IL: Crossway, forthcoming).

the pool. Rather, they came to a man dressed in camel's hair to be washed in a dirty river in the Middle East because God was at work through his word.

In 1995, from March 19 to March 23, I witnessed a revival on the campus of Wheaton College. For five days and five nights, hundreds of students publicly confessed their sins. These were good kids, with sometimes horrific sins. I felt dirty hearing everyone's confessions. Yet I also felt God's grace upon us all. I especially knew it was a true work of God when my own timid wife said that she did not go forward to the microphone but confessed a specific sin to her parents. Oh for that sort of revival! A revival of repentance. It will not come through preaching that "Jesus offers you your best life now." It will come only through calling people to adhere to Jesus' first sermon, "*Repent and believe in the gospel*" (Mark 1:15).

Second, we should see Jesus through John's eyes. Many people today think it is fine to mold Jesus into their own image; others think it is fine to be indifferent to Jesus. To the question, "Do you know Jesus as your personal Savior?" the response might be, "Oh, I haven't given Jesus much thought." Some people think that deciding for Jesus is like deciding what flavor of ice cream to lick. It is inconsequential. They do not view Jesus as John did. And those who do not view Jesus as John did are not getting into the kingdom of God. The entrance into the kingdom is small. It is only for those who can become like little children, those who can say with John, "[Jesus, you] must become greater and greater, and I must become less and less" (John 3:30 TLB).

With that said, as we come next to Jesus' baptism (Mark 1:9–11), we need to recognize *who* is going down into the waters. He is no weakling. The one in the waters is "he who is mightier than I" (1:7), mightier than the man Jesus calls "more than a prophet" and than whom there is "no greater" human being (Matt. 11:9, 11). Jesus is no sinner. The one in the waters is so holy that the holiest prophet in the history of Israel is not worthy enough to touch his sandals. And he is no mere human. John is preparing "the way of the Lord" (Mark 1:3).

The Baptism of the Beloved Son

With that in mind we come next to 1:9–11, the picture of Jesus' baptism. We flip a page in our Markan "picture Bible" and read,

> In those days Jesus came from Nazareth of Galilee and was baptized by John in the Jordan. And when he came up out of the water, immediately he saw the heavens being torn open and the Spirit descending on him like a dove. And a voice came from heaven, "You are my beloved Son; with you I am well pleased."

Notice four important details. First, the Jesus we were introduced to in
1:1 as "Christ" and "Son of God" has a hometown. He hails from "Nazareth of Galilee" (**1:9**). Nazareth was a small and obscure village in southwest
Galilee. Other than in the NT, Nazareth is not mentioned in any ancient
Jewish writings, which indicates that Jesus is from a town that is not on
the map. Charles Spurgeon, commenting on Jesus' genealogy in Matthew,
writes, "Marvelous condescension that [God] should be a man, and have
a genealogy."[7] Here in Mark we might say, "Marvelous condescension, that
God should be a man and have a humble hometown."

Second, other than naming Jesus' titles and hometown ("Nazareth," 1:9),
Mark gives no other biographical details. We do not learn how Jesus was
conceived, who his mother was, where Jesus was born, what tribe he was
from, or how he was related to John. We also do not learn how old he was at
this time, if he was educated, or what he looked like. Instead Mark focuses
solely on the man and his mission. Jesus reveals his messianic credentials
through entering into the waters of baptism and the wilderness of temptation. The man from the lowly town is lowering himself into our world.

Third, going from low to lower to lowest, Jesus is baptized. We are not
given John's initial protest and a clear explanation from Jesus as to why
he was baptized, as we find in Matthew. So, we wonder, if John's baptism
is "a baptism of repentance for the forgiveness of sins" (1:4), why is Jesus
baptized?

Fourth, the Father's verbal and the Spirit's visual approval of the Son's
baptism answer that question. As soon as Jesus comes out of the water, the
heavens are "torn open" and Jesus sees the Holy Spirit "descending on him
like a dove" (**1:10**). "Mark's forceful language of 'tearing' or 'ripping open'
. . . of the heavens indicates a theophany, or revelation of God [Isa. 64:1],"[8]
and another tearing will occur in Mark 15:38–39 when the curtain of the
temple is torn in two. After the temple curtain is torn the announcement at
the foot of the cross comes: "Truly this man was the Son of God!" (15:39).
A similar confession comes after Jesus' baptism: "You are my beloved Son"
(1:11). More on that important announcement in a page.

Here in 1:10 notice also the detail about the dove. We are not told whether
the Spirit took on the body of a dove and came upon the scene in a swooping
manner like he hovered or fluttered over the waters at creation (Gen. 1:2).
The dove symbolism alludes to Isaiah's prophecy of the Davidic king:

7   C. H. Spurgeon, *The Gospel of the Kingdom* (repr. Pasadena, TX: Pilgrim Publications, 1996), 1.
8   Strauss, *Mark*, 69.

> The Spirit of the LORD shall rest upon him,
>> the Spirit of wisdom and understanding,
>> the Spirit of counsel and might,
>> the Spirit of knowledge and the fear of the LORD. (Isa. 11:2)

Throughout Mark Jesus lives in constant dependence on the Father through the Holy Spirit. As creation was the work of the Trinity, one God in three persons, so too is redemption![9]

In Mark **1:11** we find another heavenly response ("a voice came from heaven"). The Father follows the Spirit's silent affirmation with a vocal one: "You are my beloved Son; with you I am well pleased."[10] Jesus sees the Spirit and hears the Father. And what Jesus hears helps answer the question of why Jesus was baptized. The title "Son" is an echo not just of Mark 1:1 but of Psalm 2, in which God's anointed Son is enthroned to judge the nations. The adjective "beloved" is an allusion to Genesis 22:2, in which Abraham takes his beloved son, Isaac, to be sacrificed. And the phrase "With you I am well pleased" (Mark 1:11) harks back to Isaiah again, in which God's chosen and Spirit-anointed servant ("Behold my servant, whom I uphold, my chosen, in whom my soul delights; I have put my Spirit upon him," Isa. 42:1) was "pierced for our transgressions . . . [and] crushed for our iniquities" (53:5), and through whose "offering" (53:10) of his life ("He poured out his soul to death") he "bore the sin of many" (53:12).

What does all this mean? It means that when all those people from Judea and Jerusalem went down into the waters, the water that covered them symbolized God's cleansing from their sins. When Jesus went down into the same waters, the opposite occurred. All the spiritual dirt from all the elect washed over him—a sign that God's plan of sin substitution began. As Kent Hughes summarizes,

> Because Jesus was sinless, he needed no baptism of repentance. But in his baptism he associated himself with us sinners and placed himself

---

9 "The Trinity appears very clearly: the Father in the voice, the Son in the man, the Spirit in the dove." Augustine, "Tractates on the Gospel of John," no. 6, quoted in *CHSB*, 1472. Moreover, Irenaeus correctly observes that by Mark's starting his gospel with a quote from Isaiah he is highlighting that "the prophets did not announce one and another God, but one and the same" (*Against Heresies*, quoted in *CHSB*, 1472).

10 Notice how the "Lord" (1:3) is described as Father (1:1, 11), Son (1:1, 11) and Spirit (1:8, 11, 12). "This is one of the great 'trinitarian' passages of the New Testament. Here the Spirit and the Father both bear witness to the Son. As in the book of Genesis God created by his word and through the Spirit (Gen. 1:2–3), so it is fitting that, at the very commencement of God's new work of re-creation, there would be the same operation of the whole Godhead." R. Alan Cole, *Mark*, TNTC (Downers Grove, IL: IVP Academic, 1989), 108.

among the guilty—not for his own salvation but for ours—not for his guilt but for ours—not because he feared the wrath to come, but to save us from it. His baptism meant the Cross![11]

How is Jesus going to deal with the sin problem that John is seeking to address? This is the other side of the question of why God the Father is so well pleased with God the Son. In Jesus' baptism we see the first glimpse into the mission of Jesus, namely, that the Son of David (Psalm 2) and suffering servant (Isaiah 42; 53) will lay down his life (Genesis 22) so sinners might experience fully and completely the forgiveness of their sins.

The First Temptation of Christ

Having looked at the first two frames of Mark's picture Bible, we turn to the final frame in this opening section: "The Spirit immediately drove him out into the wilderness. And he was in the wilderness forty days, being tempted by Satan. And he was with the wild animals, and the angels were ministering to him" (Mark 1:12–13).

Whenever I study a section of Scripture, I look for repeated words. I do this because repeated words usually signal key themes. So, in Mark 1:2–13, I noticed "sins" (2x), "voice" (2x), "Spirit" (3x), and "baptism" (5x). I also noticed the phrase "in the wilderness," which appears four times. Just as John was "in the wilderness" at the start of our text (1:3, 4), so Jesus is led "into the wilderness" at the end (1:12). In Luke Jesus' ministry begins in the holy city; in John in the heavenly council chamber of God; but in Mark (and Matthew) Jesus starts in the wilderness—a hot, arid, and overall lifeless place (with the exception of creatures that can kill with a sting or bite). Jesus has quickly moved from opened heavens to a hellish place. Unlike Adam, who was tempted in a protected garden, this second Adam (1 Cor. 15:45, 47) faces Satan in the untamed wilderness.

Wasting no time ("immediately"), the Spirit who came upon him as a gentle dove at his baptism now acts as a strong shove: "The Spirit . . . drove him out into the wilderness" (Mark 1:12). Matthew and Luke soften "drove him" to "was led" (Matt. 4:1; Luke 4:1). Mark's description is more forceful and vivid. Jesus needs to get into the wilderness as soon as possible because

11 Hughes, *Mark*, 1:24. Cf. Ferguson: "Jesus' water baptism inaugurated him into a ministry which reached its fulfillment later in his baptism in blood upon the cross (see Luke 12:50). What we have here is Jesus' public acknowledgement that he had come to stand where sinners should stand, receive what they should deserve, and in return to them his gift of grace and fellowship with God" (*Let's Study Mark*, 6).

the mission of saving his people has begun. There is no time for Jesus to linger at the Jordan River, basking in the glory of his public inauguration.

But why the wilderness, and why forty days? The combination of "wilderness" and "forty" evokes Israel's wilderness wanderings (Num. 14:34–35). As Israel was tested, so now Jesus is tested,[12] and whereas Israel only had to fight against its own flesh, Jesus fights against Satan, the supernatural creature who possesses people (Mark 3:23) and hinders gospel growth (4:15). Matthew (4:1–11) and Luke (4:1–13) record Satan's three temptations and how Jesus answers and resists each. Mark's focus is on the victory alone (where Israel failed, Jesus succeeds), a victory that is not directly stated but *pictured*.

By the end of Mark **1:13** Jesus is surrounded by heavenly ("the angels") and earthly ("wild animals") creatures. The picture here could be an allusion to Eden, where in the garden Adam and Eve would have coexisted and had mastery over the animals (Gen. 1:28). Or it could be a picture of Jesus surrounded by the hostile animals of the desert and yet protected by angels. Envision Jesus sleeping at night while angels fly around him, wielding swords that cut off the scorpion's tail, the leopard's teeth, the jackal's claws, the boar's tusks, and the snake's fangs. If so, the point is that Jesus is up against both physical and spiritual enemies—deadly creatures and demonic forces—but is not alone in his battle. I favor the more peaceful image, that Mark subtly but brilliantly portrays the dawn of the new age, a taste of the fulfillment of Isaiah 11:6–9 (cf. Isa. 35:3–10; Ezek. 34:23–31), a picture of wild animals recognizing their King and Creator before anyone else does, an image of the animals and angels bowing before the Son of God. Yes, here, the one who has been announced as the coming King at his baptism now sits enthroned in the desert, with all the forces of heaven and earth in subjugation to him.

However, both interpretations above make a similar point: Jesus comes out of his temptation in the wilderness against Satan alive and unscathed. Unlike Matthew and Luke, Mark does not offer a clear conclusion to Jesus' battle with Satan. He does not record "Then the devil left him" (Matt. 4:11). But the sense Mark gives is similar to Luke's, who writes, "The devil . . . departed from him until an opportune time" (Luke 4:13). Mark wants us to know that Satan's war against the King of the kingdom of God is not over. So Mark 1:12–13 records not the last temptation of Christ but the first. Jesus will encounter demons as early as 1:23, and he will be repeatedly tempted to take the crown without the cross. Yet here in 1:13 the first round in a cosmic battle is over. Jesus wins.

---

12 Mark presents Jesus "the Son of God" (Mark 1:1) as a "new Israel," or, as James R. Edwards put it, "Israel-reduced-to-one." *The Gospel According to Mark*, PNTC (Grand Rapids, MI: Eerdmans; Leicester, UK, 2002), 40. Jesus is the individual embodiment of all God's covenant people.

What then is the significance of the testing of Jesus for us? Should we live in the Mojave Desert and see whether angels will protect us from rattlesnakes, the midnight cold, and skin cancer? I doubt that is Mark's intention. Should we join Francis in preaching the gospel to all God's creatures? Well, that supposed saint might have preached to the birds, but I doubt he ever preached to the black widows and the brown snakes. What then? What shall we do with this strange section of Scripture?

Mark's intention is harder to decipher than Matthew's because Matthew details what temptations Jesus was up against and how to combat them. Matthew clearly gives followers of Jesus a lesson on discipleship: know and use the Word to fight Satan and resist his attacks. But Mark too has some lessons on discipleship. His portrait of Christ is both a window and a mirror. It is a window we look through to see Jesus. That Jesus would be baptized *and tested* for us is something we must appreciate. What a humble Savior and loving Lord! It is a mirror in that we can hold this inspired text before us. What should be our response to this revelation? How should it change and shape us? What might it teach us? Here are three lessons.

First, we should learn that testing is God-ordained. Our text reads not "Satan drove Jesus out into the wilderness" but rather "The Spirit . . . drove him out" (Mark 1:12). God does not tempt, but God does allow testing. The purpose of such testing is to define and refine. The strongest Christians are those most refined by trials, tests, and temptations.

Second, we should trust that God, as he did for Jesus, will protect and provide for us during temptation. In 1 Corinthians 10:13 Paul writes, "No temptation has overtaken you that is not common to man. God is faithful, and he will not let you be tempted beyond your ability, but with the temptation he will also provide the way of escape, that you may be able to endure it." We could not resist Satan for forty days in the wilderness. Imagine the hunger and loneliness. The idleness. An idle mind, the ancient saying goes, is the devil's playground. We have never been tempted like Jesus. The temptations in our lives are comparably small and certainly resistible. But they are resistible only with God's help. Jesus had help and took help. We have help and need to take help as well. Notice the verbs in Mark 1:13: "And he *was . . . being tempted* by Satan. And he *was* with the wild animals, and the angels *were ministering* to him." We know that Jesus was not passive during his temptation, but here in Mark it is only the angels who are portrayed with an active verb. Also, the ESV correctly translates the imperfect tense of the Greek verb as "were ministering," which gives the sense that they were attending to and assisting Jesus every hour of the forty days. The point then is well stated by Alan Cole: "Son of God though he was, Jesus did not fight alone; all the powers of heaven were on his side, as they are on ours, even if unseen."[13] Do we believe that? Do we believe in God's protective powers? If we believe that we wrestle not "against flesh and blood, but against the rulers, against the authorities, against the cosmic powers over this present darkness" (Eph. 6:12), then we should not doubt that angels wrestle for us here on earth.

We do not have a guardian angel but guardian angels (cf. Matt. 26:53). More than that, we have the King of the angels! Jesus, who was tempted in the wilderness and tempted in every way that we are (see Heb. 4:15; 5:7), is not just an example of how to resist temptation but a constant help in resisting temptation. When I sin, I usually pray, "God, be merciful to me, a sinner" (Luke 18:13). When tempted, I often offer the first and last petitions of the prayer the Lord Jesus taught us to pray: "Our Father in heaven, hallowed be [thy] name. . . . Lead us not into temptation, but deliver us from evil" (Matt. 6:9, 13). We have heaven's help against hell's onslaught.

Third, identify with Jesus. How so? In communing with creation? No. Preaching to it? No. Self-denial? Yes. Picking up your cross? Yes. Following him? Precisely. Here, in the first scene of Jesus' life, the Lord denies himself and picks up his cross. Notice that Jesus is first baptized and then tempted. His baptism, which "pleased" the Father, did not exclude Jesus from the wilderness temptations or the cross of Golgotha. For Jesus baptism was a sign of his immersion into this world of sin and into the horrific destiny of his mission. For us baptism is a sign of our forgiveness of sin in Christ. Yet for both our Lord and us baptism signals a new journey, a difficult journey that embraces the costly commitment of following God's will, whether such a will "produces comfort or not, happiness or not, fulfillment or not,"[14] whether such a will leads to an old rugged cross or to paradise or to both. To be baptized into Christ is to enter into a spiritual wilderness and a spiritual warfare. So we should understand that through Jesus' baptism and his temptation Mark drives home his "central theme of the costliness of commitment of God's way of salvation,"[15] a costliness for Jesus and a costliness for us.

Greek Exegesis beyond the Classroom

For the Greek exegesis class that I took with the professor I mentioned at the start, a group of seven students sat around a table and translated Greek into

13 R. Alan Cole, "Mark," in *New Bible Commentary*, ed. Gordon J. Wenham, J. A. Motyer, D. A. Carson, and R. T. France (Downers Grove, IL: InterVarsity, 1994), 950.

14 Donald English, *The Message of Mark: The Mystery of Faith*, BST (Leicester, UK: Inter-Varsity, 1992), 45–46.

15 English, *The Message of Mark*, 45.

English. I loved the teacher, but I disliked the class. It was hard. We each had to look at the text and translate it on the spot. I was the worst student in the class. No joke. But the professor was always gracious with me. He listened, corrected, and helped. He never belittled me or anyone else.

His memory is now fading, but so too is mine. I do not remember each and every aspect of the Greek of 1 Timothy, the text we translated together that semester, but I do remember bits of that book quite well. I remember 1 Timothy 1:15, which has become a life verse: "The saying is trustworthy and deserving of full acceptance, that Christ Jesus came into the world to save sinners, of whom I am the foremost." I remember the section in chapter 2 about our great God "who desires all people to be saved" and who tells us that "there is one God, and there is one mediator between God and men, the man Christ Jesus, who gave himself as a ransom for all" (2:3–6), and the poem of 3:16, which begins, "He was manifested in the flesh, vindicated by the Spirit, seen by angels," and phrases like "train yourself for godliness" (4:7). I also remember warnings about those who have "strayed after Satan" (5:15) and the simple statements like "We have food and clothing, with these we will be content" (6:8) and the admonition that follows, "But those who desire to be rich fall into temptation, into a snare, into many senseless and harmful desires that plunge people into ruin and destruction" (6:9). Finally, I remember that epistle's opening line (partly because it is easy in the Greek), "Paul, an apostle of Christ Jesus by command of God our Savior and of Christ Jesus our hope."

Jesus is our hope. He is our hope, according to both Paul (1 Tim. 1:1) and Mark (Mark 1:2–13), because he came in lowliness and humility to bathe his body in the river and to test his soul in the heat of the wilderness. What then is left to say? Only a doxology is fitting: "To the King of ages, immortal, invisible, the only God, be honor and glory forever and ever. Amen" (1 Tim. 1:17).

Proclaiming the Gospel of God

MARK 1:14-20

The time is fulfilled, and the kingdom of God is at hand;
repent and believe in the gospel.
Mark 1:15

The first movie I saw in the theater was *Raiders of the Lost Ark*. I went with my mother, who covered my eyes for half the film. The next movie she took me to was *Chariots of Fire*, a very religious, moral, and unhurried movie. It was so slow in the mind of this nine-year-old boy, who had just been juiced up on Indiana Jones! *Raiders of the Lost Ark* starts with Indiana Jones eluding one dangerous trap after another in order grab a golden idol, which then triggers a large boulder that races after him as he barely escapes certain death, only to be captured by a tribe of poison-dart-spitting Amazon warriors. From there the film is one action-packed scene after another.

The Gospel of Mark is not an action-adventure film, but it does have the pace of one. When Jesus enters the drama, he is baptized. Then immediately the sky opens. The Spirit descends. A heavenly voice booms. Then the divine director yells, "Cut." Scene one is done in three verses. Onto the next scene. Jesus' temptation begins: "And immediately" the Spirit drove Jesus into the wilderness. Jesus is there for forty days. But how many verses does Mark use to cover those forty days? Two!

This is Mark's pattern and pace throughout chapter 1. Jesus preaches his first sermon. The sermon, as Mark records it, is less than twenty words and takes less than seven seconds to say. From there, Jesus calls his first disciples, and they "immediately" follow—no dialogue or discussion, just action. Then, as soon as Jesus enters a synagogue in Capernaum, we read, "And immediately there was . . . a man with an unclean spirit" (1:23). How long does it take for Jesus to deal with the demon? Not long at all. With two brief commands, "Be silent [or "be muzzled"]" and "Come out of him!" this spirit is sent packing. Does Jesus then stick around to shake hands? No. "And immediately he left the synagogue" (1:29). Onto the next scene. There are still seventeen verses left in chapter 1, and four or five action-packed scenes left.

While Mark might have a fast pace, the preacher should take it slow, like the opening scene in *Chariots of Fire*, in which the Olympic runner Eric Liddell's fast strides upon the West Sands in St. Andrews, Scotland, are played in slow motion. We should go slow because each and every word of this fast-paced, God-inspired Gospel is important. And if we take the high speed "film" of Mark and run it in slow motion, we will notice two consistent strides of Jesus as he moves forward out of the wilderness and into his ministry: his words and his works. Through both his words and his works Jesus gains quite the following ("His fame spread everywhere," 1:28; cf. 1:32–33, 37, 45). It is not Jesus' popularity that is most important but his authority. Before the exorcism in the synagogue Mark writes, "And they were astonished at his teaching, for he taught them as one who had authority" (1:22). The focus is on Jesus' authoritative words. Then, after the exorcism, the crowd exclaims, "What is this? A new teaching with authority!" (1:27). Even Jesus' authoritative works point to his authoritative words. Throughout Mark, and beginning here in Mark 1, we will see them stride side by side. For this chapter we focus just on the first. We will slow down to see the authoritative *words* of Jesus: his authoritative sermon (1:14–15) and his authoritative calling (1:16–20).

Jesus' First Sermon

We begin with Mark **1:14–15**, Jesus' first sermon: "Now after John was arrested, Jesus came into Galilee, proclaiming the gospel of God, and saying, 'The time is fulfilled, and the kingdom of God is at hand; repent and believe in the gospel.'"

The setting is interesting. The text does not read, "Now after Jesus was tempted in the wilderness, he came into Galilee." Instead it says, "Now after John was arrested" (1:14). We know what happened to John from Mark 6:14–29. He was beheaded by Herod. John went from "all" the people in Judea and Jerusalem coming to him (1:5) to John's head coming to Herod on a platter (6:28). So the phrase "After John was arrested" has an ominous tone. It is the same verb (Gk. *paradothēnai*) used when Judas betrays Jesus (14:10). It foreshadows what will happen to Jesus. He will move from popularity to death, from fame to infamy. Moreover, it is a reminder that those who side with Jesus have a dangerous and sometimes deadly road ahead (3:33–35; 8:34; 10:29–30).

What is also interesting about the setting is the mention of Galilee. "Jesus came into Galilee" (1:14). Why Galilee? Why not Jerusalem, the holy city of the people of God? Why not Rome, the capital city of the Roman Empire? Of course, Jesus was raised in Nazareth of Galilee. But to the ancient world that designation would have meant either nothing (Where is that?) or very little (cf. Nathanael's cry, "Can anything good come out of Nazareth?" John 1:46). Jesus of Nazareth begins his ministry, and spends the great majority of his ministry, in Galilee because his whole ministry is a descent into greatness. Visualize it this way. Jesus, who came from the heavens that opened at his baptism, is walking to the cross, and with each step on the way—into the waters in the Jordan, through the wilderness, around Galilee, up to Jerusalem and Golgotha—he descends. Jesus descends so as to teach us about humility ("Whoever would be great among you must be your servant, and whoever would be first among you must be slave of all," Mark 10:43–44). Jesus also descends to show us his humility, a humility that opens for us the gates to paradise ("The Son of Man came not to be served but to serve, and to give his life as a ransom for many," 10:45).

Thus far we have heard the voice of John the Baptist (1:3) and the voice of God the Father (1:11); now we hear the voice of the Son of God. He is "proclaiming the gospel of God, and saying, 'The time is fulfilled, and the kingdom of God is at hand; repent and believe in the gospel'" (1:14–15).

Let me explain and apply, and at times illustrate, this verse by asking and answering three key questions. First, what does Jesus mean by the phrase "the kingdom of God"? This is an important question because Jesus frequently talks about the kingdom.[1] The word "kingdom" obviously relates to a king and his rule. That this kingdom is called "the kingdom of God" (elsewhere called "the kingdom of heaven") tells us that it is not an earthly kingdom and does not have a purely earthly monarch. God is King—specifically Jesus, the Son of God, is the Christ (1:1, 11). The subjects of Jesus' kingdom will be all those who repent and believe. More on that (1:15) and them (1:16–20) later. The geographical boundaries of this kingdom seem to be both as broad as the cosmos (Ps. 103:19) and as narrow as those who call Jesus "Christ" and act like he is truly the divine "Son of God" (Mark 1:1).

Here in Mark 1, and throughout his Gospel, the emphasis is on how the king of the kingdom starts to spread his sovereignty by eradicating evil. Jesus exorcises demons, heals the sick, and forgives sins. This is good news! The kingdom of the heavens on the earth through Jesus is gospel for cursed-ridden people. This "gospel of God" (1:14), which is both from God and about God, is "the declaration and demonstration that ultimate salvation has dawned

---

1   Jesus uses the phrase to explain the growth of the kingdom (Mark 4:11, 26, 30), that the kingdom is a present reality (1:15) and future fulfillment (9:1; 14:25), something to be hoped for (15:43), and that its entrance relates to sacrifice (9:47), childlike faith (10:14–15), dependence on him (10:23–25), and love of God and neighbor (12:34).

with the coming of Jesus"[2] (note the echo of "the gospel of Jesus Christ, the Son of God," 1:1). The gospel of the kingdom is the wonderful announcement that "human history is not an endless cycle of sin, suffering, and death." With the arrival of Jesus, "the endgame has begun." "God's plan of redemption and restoration" is unfolding.[3] His rule is spreading over all the world.

However, with the arrest of John, obviously the kingdom that Jesus announces has not eradicated evil. So, if the kingdom has arrived, why is there still disease, death, and demons? The answer Mark gives us is that the kingdom is already and not yet. It has been inaugurated with the first coming of Christ, but it will be consummated with his second coming. God's saving rule is working its way out in stages throughout history. With the first coming, Jesus shows that he can deliver us from evils;[4] in the second, he will complete the deliverance with complete deliverance. So as we await Christ's coming and complete reign, we must hold out hope amid a world of awful injustices, incomprehensible cruelties, and inexplicable ambiguities. When Christ returns in power and glory, the world will be made right. "Justice [will] roll down like waters, and righteousness like an ever-flowing stream" (Amos 5:24). So, chin up! We are part of a kingdom that will win, a reign that will eventually eradicate all evils—pain, disease, poverty, death, plagues, demons. With the return of Christ, the restoration of all the cursed creation will be complete.

Second, what does Jesus mean by the clauses "The time is fulfilled" and "The kingdom . . . is at hand" (Mark 1:15)? "Time" refers to the designated moment in history at which God ushered in a new epoch in the story of salvation. As Paul puts it in Galatians 4:4–5, "When the *fullness* of *time* had come, God sent forth his Son, born of woman, born under the law, to redeem those who were under the law, so that we might receive adoption as sons." When Jesus, then, talks about this time being "fulfilled" and "at hand" (Mark 1:15), which are parallel ideas, he is saying that both chronologically and physically what has been prophesied and waited for has now arrived. "Time's up! God's kingdom is here" (MSG).

Third, it is obvious that the call Jesus issues in the gospel is to "repent and believe" (1:15), but what does it mean to repent and believe? To repent does

2 Christopher D. Marshall, *Faith as a Theme in Mark's Narrative*, SNTSMS 64 (Cambridge: Cambridge University Press, 1989), 49.
3 Mark L. Strauss, *Mark*, ZECNT (Grand Rapids, MI: Zondervan, 2014), 85. Cf. Lischer: "[Jesus] spoke of the kingdom as an eruption *in* history rather than outside it or at its end." Richard Lischer, *Reading the Parables*, Int (Louisville: Westminster/John Knox, 2014), 21.
4 "The kingdom is still future because Jesus is launching the plan that will bring about the final restoration of all things. His exorcisms reveal that the power of the Adversary is being neutralized; his healings demonstrate that fallen humanity is being restored (Isa 35:5, 6); his offer of forgiveness confirms that the power of sin is being broken; and his nature miracles show his divine authority to restore a fallen creation" (Strauss, *Mark*, 85).

not mean simply saying, "I'm sorry." It also is not something superficial and temporary, like it was for Huck Finn's father:

> The old drunk cried and cried when Judge Thatcher talked to him about temperance and such things. Said he'd been a fool and was agoing to turn over a new leaf. And everyone hugged him and cried and said it was the holiest time on record. And that night he got drunker than he had ever been before.[5]

Repentance is not a onetime "I'm sorry" or a superficial one-moment stance. Rather, it has a consistence and persistence to it. It is a continuous present tense. We repent and repent and repent and keep on repenting.

There is also movement to repentance. Those baptized by John in the Jordan walked a long way to get there. The same is true if the first four disciples model repentance. They walk away from their nets and follow Jesus. These examples of walking to and away help illustrate part of the nature of true repentance, which involves three steps. First, we walk away from our sins and, for some people, from an entire way of living (1:5; perhaps 1:18, 20; certainly 2:14). Second, we confess our sins (1:5). Third, we walk in a new direction (1:18, 20; 2:14), namely, after Jesus and in the ways of Jesus. Here is where repentance seamlessly blends into faith.[6] We turn away from sin and turn to Jesus.

Recently I had lunch with an elderly man named Gary. He shared a story that perfectly illustrates repentance and faith. When he was fourteen, he was part of a gang. One day these boys came upon a car. One boy turned to the others and said, "We should steal it." Gary said, "No. It is a set up." Well, the gang went ahead with their plan. But this fourteen-year-old turned the other way. Gary was many miles from home, but he began to walk. When he came upon a pay phone, he called his mother and told her not to wait up. He arrived home at four in the morning. Along the way he prayed to God, he talked with God, and he began to walk toward God.

"Repent!"

"Repent and *believe* in the gospel." Notice that the object of faith is not one's own faith but the gospel. To believe in the gospel is to believe in the announcement of the kingdom of God by the king of that kingdom. And it

---

5 David E. Garland, *Mark*, NIVAC (Grand Rapids, MI: Zondervan, 1996), 65. This is Garland's summary of the end of chapter 5 in Mark Twain's *Adventures of Huckleberry Finn*.

6 "In Mark's view repentance and faith are inseparable. Repentance, which Schlatter notes, is at heart the abandonment of trust in one's self (*Selbstvertrauen*), must lead to faith, a new condition of trust in God's ultimate disclosure" (Marshall, *Faith as a Theme*, 52).

is not merely to assent to the fact that Jesus is the Messiah and has come to save and judge. Even the demons ace their theology exam. They call Jesus "the Holy One of God" and know why he has come—to "destroy" them (1:24; cf. James 2:19). Christian faith involves *notitia* (the gospel of the life, death, and resurrection of Jesus as the content of our faith), *assensus* (the conviction that that gospel is true), and *fiducia* (personal trust and reliance on the king and submission to his call and commands). The imperative to believe (Mark 1:15) is in the present continuous tense ("be believing"). Our initial reception of Jesus as king leads to an ongoing relationship, a "continuing state of trusting obedience, a readiness to do whatever the will of God requires."[7]

Jesus' First Followers

Here in our study of Mark's action-packed Gospel we are slowing down. We are slowing down to notice, appreciate, and apply the authoritative words of Jesus. We have looked at his first sermon. Now we turn to the calling of his first disciples. In Mark **1:16–20** we read,

> Passing alongside the Sea of Galilee, he saw Simon and Andrew the brother of Simon casting a net into the sea, for they were fishermen. And Jesus said to them, "Follow me, and I will make you become fishers of men." And immediately they left their nets and followed him. And going on a little farther, he saw James the son of Zebedee and John his brother, who were in their boat mending the nets. And immediately he called them, and they left their father Zebedee in the boat with the hired servants and followed him.

First, notice that Mark uses the phrase "passing alongside" (1:16). How remarkable that Mark sets the scene here of a great act of authority, and an incredible response to it, with a casual introductory statement—as though Jesus just happened to walk by the shore of the Sea of Galilee.

Second, notice the focus on Simon Peter. Peter was not the first pope, but he was the first among equals. He is always named first in the list of the apostles (e.g., 3:16–19). Other than Jesus, he speaks the most in the Four Gospels. Acts features Peter's acts first and then Paul's. And here in Mark the first person that Jesus sees and calls is Peter: "He saw Simon and Andrew *the brother of Simon*" (1:16). Poor Andrew. He barely gets a shout-out.

---

7   Marshall, *Faith as a Theme*, 53.

Third, notice that the four men Jesus calls first are "fishermen." Think about it. If you set out to establish a kingdom that would be more universal and lasting than the Roman Empire, who would you call to join your leadership team? I would call wealthy patrons, academic elites, powerful politicians, religious leaders, strong soldiers, and influential celebrities. Jesus chooses fishermen!

Galilean fishermen in the early first century were not necessarily lower class.[8] Notice that these men had boats (1:19, 20; cf. Luke 5:3) and nets (Mark 1:18, 19); the father of James and John had "hired servants" (1:20). This does not mean these four men were influential, theologically astute, and well esteemed by the religious professionals, though, either. Fishermen—whether poor or wealthy from their trade—worked with their hands. They rowed and sailed boats, caught fish, and mended nets. They were strong (Luke 5:2), sometimes spoke abrasively (Luke 9:54; John 18:10), and worked long and odd hours (Luke 5:5; John 21:3). They were not sitting in school under some rabbi, as most future members of the Sanhedrin were. They were not learning the skills of oration, as the senators in Rome would have been. They lived their days, and sometimes nights, on the sea, catching stinky fish. The point is simply this: God uses ordinary people to do extraordinary things.

My father was born in rural Ireland and raised in a two-room stone house with a dirt floor and no running water. He was the first in his village to graduate from college. My mother was abandoned by her mother and sent by her alcoholic father to Glasgow to be raised by her aunt. I have an elite education, but I have also delivered newspapers, worked retail, laid carpet and tile, washed windows, been a janitor and a security guard (for almost a decade), waited tables, and, in the most blue-collar profession of all, pastored (for nearly two decades).

What is your story? Are you like poor Bartimaeus? Middle-class John? Rich Joseph of Arimathea? Educated Saul of Tarsus? Aristocratic Isaiah? God loves to invest in and utilize all sorts of people from all sorts of backgrounds. But he especially loves to use ordinary people. Are you ordinary, or even less than ordinary? God has a special place for you in the mission of the kingdom of God.

Fourth, notice the phrase "for they were fishermen" (Mark 1:16). The past tense is revealing. Jesus has nothing against fishermen. His first meal after his resurrection is fish from these fishermen (Luke 24:42–43). He is not saying

---

8 See Craig S. Keener, *The Gospel of Matthew: A Socio-Rhetorical Commentary* (Grand Rapids, MI: Eerdmans, 2009), 151.

that all fishermen should abandon their trade to become evangelists. He is saying that these men encounter the Almighty incarnate, and that this encounter changes the trajectory of their lives.

Fifth, notice the swiftness of their change in vocation. The phrase "and immediately" (Mark 1:18, 20)—a phrase found little in Matthew, Luke, and John—leaps off the page. "And immediately" what? "And immediately" they go from fishermen to "fishers of men." They go from venturing out into the deep waters to catch fish to learning from Jesus ("I will make you become," 1:17) how to drive out demons and preach the gospel (3:14–15). In the OT the image of fishing for people is used in Jeremiah 16:16; Ezekiel 29:4–5; Amos 4:2; and Habakkuk 1:14–17. In these passages the fishing and catching is always related to judgment. You do not want God fishing for you! Here in Mark, however, Jesus uses the image positively—not for damnation but for salvation. Jesus is enlisting these four men to reach out to people and bring them into God's kingdom. Or perhaps, if we combine both the positive and the negative connotations, Jesus is telling them that their mission is to rescue people from God's judgment. As J. C. Ryle writes, "They were to labor to draw people out of darkness into light, and from the power of Satan to God. They were to strive to bring people into the net of Christ's church, so that they might be saved and not perish everlastingly."[9]

Sixth, notice that Jesus calls family members. He calls two sets of brothers. It is beautiful when families follow Christ together. Some of us are believers because a sibling followed Christ, then invited us to follow as well. Others are Christians because they grew up in a Christian home (your parents followed Christ, then you followed your parents in together following Christ). That said, the story of salvation is not always a safe-for-the-whole-family story. The statement "they left their father Zebedee in the boat" (Mark 1:20) has a tinge of tragedy to it. What happens to Zebedee? We know that his wife believes in the kingdom (Matt. 20:20) and that she is even at the cross (Matt. 27:56). But what happens to him? Does he keep the business, disown his sons, and divorce his wife? We do not know. What we do know is that it is tragic when family stays behind or, worse, when family opposes the way of God and persecutes the people of God (see Matt. 10:34–38). For some believers, cross bearing involves severed family ties. Jesus asks, "'Who are my mother and my brothers?' And looking about at those who sat around him [his followers], he said, 'Here are my mother and my brothers! For whoever does the will of God, he is my brother and sister and mother'" (Mark 3:33–35).

---

9 J. C. Ryle, *Mark: Expository Thoughts on the Gospels*, CCC (Wheaton, IL: Crossway, 1993), 7.

Seventh, for these four men, all it takes for them to leave their nets and follow Jesus is Jesus' authoritative call ("Follow me," 1:17).[10] To Christ's radical message ("The time is fulfilled, and the kingdom of God is at hand; repent and believe in the gospel," 1:15) and his radical call ("Follow me," 1:17) these four respond with radical obedience ("Immediately they left their nets and followed him," 1:18; cf. 1:20).

Table 3.1: Calling and Response of the Four Disciples

Characters	Calling	First Response	Second Response
Peter and Andrew	Follow me	They left	Followed him
James and John	Follow me (assumed)	They left	Followed him

As was said, or hinted at, it might be that their leaving and following illustrate repentance and faith. Put differently, they embody the right response to the gospel of the kingdom. I say "might be" because there is no indication that they are repenting of some sin. It might be that they have been running a shady fishing operation. It might be that they love work more than God, family more than God, or money more than God. It might be that they are indifferent to God or working on the Sabbath. What is more certain is that the phrase "followed him" is faith-filled. As James Edwards notes, "'Following' is a load-bearing term that describes the proper response of faith . . . , and is indeed *practically synonymous with faith*."[11] In total dependence on Jesus they right then and there leave their formal loyalties—finances and family—to follow Jesus.[12]

What a challenge these verses are! Jesus is not calling any of us to become apostles (see 3:13–19; Eph. 2:20). He is not calling all of us to change professions or move from our current vocation into full-time ministry. But our Lord is certainly calling all of us to follow him first: first above occupation

---

10 "The disciple does not hurry along to Jesus, but rather is chosen and called by Him"; Adolf Schlatter, quoted in Cranfield, *The Gospel according to St Mark*, CGTC (repr., Cambridge: Cambridge University Press, 2000), 71.

11 James R. Edwards, *The Gospel according to Mark*, PNTC (Grand Rapids, MI: Eerdmans, 2002), 81–82, emphasis mine.

12 "Without any psychological preparations (contrast John 1[:35–51]), they are called and claimed by the word of Jesus, which puts an end to the past they knew and opens up a future they cannot comprehend. All they can do is obey Jesus' word and follow." John P. Meier, *The Vision of Matthew: Christ, Church, and Morality in the First Gospel* (New York: Crossroad, 1991; repr., Eugene, OR: Wipf & Stock, 2004), 62. In Luke's version the motive is also enhanced. The sons of Zebedee "left everything and followed him" (Luke 5:11) after they witnessed a net-breaking catch of fish.

(Mark 1:17), first above wealth (1:20; 10:21–24), and first above family (1:19; 3:33–35; 10:29). Jesus is king. He is the king of the kingdom of the then-inaugurated and soon-to-be-consummated kingdom.

The Urgency and Immediacy

For some of you, you may be reading about Jesus, listening to sermons about Jesus, or checking out websites about Jesus and are still uncertain what to make of Jesus. Perhaps you need more time. Or perhaps Jesus' call "follow me" demands an "immediately" in your life. The calls of the kingdom—repent, believe, follow—are urgent, and the response should be immediate. You do not need every question answered: "I will repent and believe and follow once I understand the hypostatic union." You do not need any more excuses: "I will repent and believe and follow once every Christian everywhere stops being a hypocrite."

Have you never felt the weight of sin? Have you never experienced the consequences of sin? Are you not afraid of the wages of sin—death and damnation? And have you not seen enough of the glories of Christ? Have you not seen the compelling paradoxes of his person, his holy majesty and infinite condescension, his highest glory and lowest humility, his absolute majesty and extraordinary meekness, his complete sovereignty over the world and yet his perfect resignation to the will of God—to death even on a cross?[13] Why wait? "There was and is a radical 'nowness' to Jesus' preaching. *Now* is the time to repent, and *now* is the time to believe."[14] *Now* is the time to follow. *Now* is the time to leave behind your old lifestyle, to bow before the King, to come into the kingdom of God, and to walk in God's ways. Today Jesus says *to you*, "Repent, believe, follow me."

---

13 See Jonathan Edwards, "The Excellency of Christ," in *The Works of Jonathan Edwards*, ed. Edward Hickman, 2 vols. (repr., Carlisle, PA: Banner of Truth, 1992), 1:680–82.

14 R. Kent Hughes, *Mark: Jesus, Servant and Savior*, PTW, 2 vols. (Wheaton, IL: Crossway, 1989), 1:36.

A New Teaching with Authority!

MARK 1:21-39

What is this? A new teaching with authority! He commands
even the unclean spirits, and they obey him.
Mark 1:27

In the Gospel of Mark *immediately* is an important word used in an interesting way. It is used thirty-six times, the first time in 1:10 (at Jesus' baptism) and the last time in 14:72 (when the rooster crows after Peter's denial). The word is not used at the end of the Gospel because the action slows down (no need for an *immediately*) when we come to Jesus' trial (15:1–20), crucifixion (15:21–41), burial (15:42–47), and resurrection (16:1–8). For this reason and others many scholars think of Mark's Gospel as a passion narrative with an extended introduction. This is a valid point, for we misunderstand the message of Mark if we miss the importance of Jesus' death. All the action—this "immediately" happens, then that "immediately" happens—is moving us toward that climatic moment. That said, what we find in Mark 1:1–14:72 is not just a long introduction or an apology for the cross, an explanation as to *why* Jesus had to die. Rather, it is an explanation of *who* went to the cross and of *what* the cross of Christ would accomplish. Thus, the first chapter of Mark is especially Important in setting the scene of this awesome drama that is to unfold. With the voice from heaven ("You are my beloved Son," 1:11), the defeat of Satan in the wilderness (1:12–13), the announcement of the arrival of God's rule ("The kingdom of God is at hand," 1:15), and the compelling call of Christ ("Follow me. . . . And immediately they . . . followed him," 1:17–18), Mark tells us that a cosmic change has occurred.

So too do Jesus' first miracles. How does Jesus the "Christ" (1:1) and "beloved Son" (1:11) demonstrate that he is establishing God's dominion? First, he deals with demons. In 1:21–28 Jesus is teaching in the synagogue on the Sabbath when "immediately" an unclean spirit cries out, "What have you to do with us, Jesus of Nazareth?" (1:24).[1] Then Mark repeats the term "unclean spirit" two more times (1:26, 27) so we do not miss the fact that this is an unclean scene and that Jesus is up against otherworldly forces.[2]

And how does our Lord fare? He defeats the demons. Over and over and over again. As the day ends ("that evening at sundown," 1:32) our text ends as it began: those who were "oppressed by demons" were brought to him; Jesus "cast out many demons" (1:34); "And he went throughout all Galilee, preaching in their synagogues and casting out demons" (1:39). The theme here is obvious: Jesus has authority over evil. Or, in the words of the astonished congregation in Capernaum, "What is this? A new teaching with authority! He commands even the unclean spirits, and they obey him" (1:27).

With that overview of these nineteen verses in place, I will tackle this text in a directly applicable way. That is, in what follows, I will provide three lessons. This is not to say that I will not show you how I derive these lessons from the text within its original context. But it is to say, as noted last chapter, that time is short (there is an *immediacy* to preaching Mark) and it is best that we know sooner than later what to do with this section of God's Word.

Demons Exist and Wreak Havoc in This World

Our first lesson is that we must believe that demons exist and wreak havoc in this world. There is no doubt that Mark's original audience believed in demons. To them spiritual warfare, with real physical manifestations, was a given. "They were all amazed" in **1:27**[3] not because a person could be possessed by a demon but because Jesus' sermon was revolutionary ("a new teaching") and supported by supernatural power ("with authority!"). Today, however, it is not normal to say "I believe demons exist and wreak havoc in the world." This is because the devil has duped many people.

Before I wrote this chapter I reread one of my favorite books, *The Screwtape Letters*, C. S. Lewis's brilliant treatment on the reality of demons and how they work in the world. This fictitious book about the facts of unseen spiritual realities consists of a series of letters written by Screwtape, an important official in Satan's "Lowerarchy," to Wormwood, a junior devil. These short

---

1   Obviously "Nazareth" is where Jesus was raised (Mark 1:9). This title, however, might indicate more. "As exorcists sought to gain power over a demon through knowledge of the demon's name, this particular demon may be attempting to counter Jesus' power by claiming to have himself the power of knowledge about Jesus." Eckhard J. Schnabel, *Mark: An Introduction and Commentary*, TNTC (Downers Grove, IL: IVP Academic, 2017), 58.

2   Mark's term "unclean spirit" is synonymous with the title "demon" (cf. Mark 6:7, 13; 7:25–26).

3   The Greek word *thambeō* ("amazed"; 1:27) is a unique word to Mark, used only here and in 10:24, 32.

epistles are instructions on how to corrupt the thoughts and ways of Worm-wood's "patient," a young man who is in danger of becoming (and eventually does become) a Christian. In Screwtape's seventh letter he gives the following instruction on how to avoid detection:

> My Dear Wormwood, I wonder you should ask me whether it is essential to keep the patient in ignorance of your own existence. That question, at least for the present phase of the struggle, has been answered for us by the High Command [the devil]. Our policy, for the moment, is to conceal ourselves. Of course this has not always been so [read Mark 1]. We are really faced with a cruel dilemma. When humans disbelieve in our existence we lose all the pleasing results of direct terrorism and we make no magicians. On the other hand, when they believe in us, we cannot make them materialists and skeptics. At least, not yet.

Screwtape continues,

> I have great hopes that we shall learn in due time how to emotionalize and mythologize their science to such an extent that what is, in effect, a belief in us (though not under that name) will creep in while the human mind remains closed to belief in the Enemy [God]. . . . If once we can produce our perfect work, the Materialist Magician, the man, not using, but veritably worshipping, what he vaguely calls 'forces' while denying the existence of 'spirits'—then the end of the war will be in sight.

Screwtape concludes,

> But in the meantime, we must obey our orders. I do not think you will have much difficulty in keeping the patient in the dark. The fact that 'devils' are predominantly comic figures in the modern imagination will help you. If any faint suspicion of your existence begins to arise in his mind, suggest to him a picture of something in red tights, and persuade him that since he cannot believe in that (it is an old textbook method of confusing them) he therefore cannot believe in you.[4]

For many people today those Wormwoods of this world (who are presented unapologetically to us in Scripture) need an apologetic for their

---

4   C. S. Lewis, *The Screwtape Letters* (New York: MacMillan, 1948), 39–40.

existence. In a culture in which demons and devils are seen as team mascots, the idea of an evil creature possessing a person is so far from our conception of reality. Yet it ought not to be! For, if we are to get into this text and understand and apply it rightly, we need to move from the popular worldview into the biblical one. We need to move from today's "Materialist Magicians"—those who, on the one hand, do not believe in anything unless there is scientific evidence to support it and who yet, on the other hand, believe in almost anything that has the ring of "magic" to it—to the realities the Scriptures present. We need to believe in the existence and the effects of unseen evil spirits.

Jesus Has Come to Destroy the Works of the Devil

Our first lesson is that we must believe that demons exist and wreak havoc in this world. Our second lesson is that we must know that Jesus has come to destroy the works of the devil.

Look next at Mark **1:24.** Jesus goes into Capernaum, a small town on the upper northwest coast of the Sea of Galilee about 3 miles from where the Jordan River runs into the lake, a place that would serve as a base for our Lord's itinerant ministry ("his own city," Matt. 9:1). He enters a synagogue on the Sabbath. He teaches. Perhaps he teaches samples from the Sermon of the Mount ("You have heard that it was said . . . , but I say to you," Matt. 5:27, 28) or what he taught at his hometown synagogue: "Today this Scripture has been fulfilled in your hearing" (Luke 4:21). Perhaps he teaches Mark 1:15, namely, that a new era of world history, one promised by the prophets, has arrived with his arrival ("The time is fulfilled, and the kingdom of God is at hand") and that entrance into this new covenant community is related not to blood ties with Abraham, Sabbath keeping, hand washing, or temple sacrifices but to repenting of sin and believing in him ("Repent and believe in the gospel"). What boldness! What extraordinary authority. People are amazed. Taken aback.

Then in **1:23** Mark adds an "immediately." He writes, "And immediately there was in their synagogue a man with an unclean spirit. And he cried out [on behalf of the demons in the area],[5] 'What have you to do with us, Jesus of Nazareth? Have you come to destroy us?'" We might interject here with an answer to that second sensible question. Yes! Yes, he has. "The Holy One of God"—that is what the demon will call him next ("I know who you are—the

---

5 It is likely that "this particular demon speaks in his initial encounter on behalf of the whole threatened fraternity." R. T. France, *The Gospel of Mark*, NIGTC (Grand Rapids, MI: Eerdmans, 2002), 103.

Holy One of God," 1:24; cf. 3:11; 5:7)—has come to rid the world of the unholy. And at the top of the list of unholy things in the world are impure and
insubordinate angels, otherwise known as demons: "But Jesus rebuked him,
saying, 'Be silent ["Shut up" captures the harsh tone],[6] and come out of him!'"
(**1:25**). Here Jesus issues a short and simple command (no long incantation,
no stage props, no appeal to heaven), but also an incredibly powerful one.
"And the unclean spirit, convulsing him [the victim] and crying out with
a loud voice, came out of him" (**1:26**). The evil spirit puts up a fierce but
fast-lived fight. The convulsing gives the image of the demon's wrestling with
Christ for dominion over this poor man's body and soul. This is no epileptic
fit, but it looks like that, or worse. This is all happening, we have to remember, during the synagogue service! Songs have been sung. Prayers prayed.
The Law and the Prophets read. Jesus has preached. Then this unexpected
commotion. Imagine the scene. Envision, at this point in the drama, as the
synagogue ruler says, "Let us conclude our service with the Eighteen Bene-
dictions," how Jesus makes a move. He comes to the lectern and announces,
"Let us together sing a new song. It is called 'A Mighty Fortress Is Our God.'"
And he sings, "For lo! his doom is sure, one little word shall [did!] fell him."

Notice also that detail about speech. Jesus says, "Be silent" (1:25). Does
this demon obey? Yes and no. Yes, in that "the unclean spirit . . . came out of
him." No, in that the unclean spirit cries out "with a loud voice" (1:26). One
last rebellious cry. The man's body must have been shaking on the floor as the
sound of a hound-like hellish groan reached down into the pit of the inferno
and tried, with all its hideous strength, to reach the deepest level of hell for
help. But to no avail. Evil is ousted almost immediately.

All in a day for Jesus. Or should we say a morning? Look what happens
next: "And immediately he left the synagogue and entered the house of Simon
and Andrew, with James and John" (**1:29**). So he is finally home, or at least in
a home. Peter and Andrew's home. Living with them, presumably, are their
wives and children, along with Peter's mother-in-law, as the matriarch likely
planned to lay out quite the spread when Peter and the other men returned
from synagogue. Perhaps the day before she envisioned a cheese plate with
some bread, olives, honey, and nuts, along with a fruit plate featuring black-
berries, figs, and pomegranates. She might even have envisioned some roast

---

6 "This command is the first example of Jesus giving the order not to reveal who he is (cf. 1:44; 5:43;
   7:36; 8:26 in the context of healings; 8:30 in the context of Peter's confession of Jesus' messianic
   identity). Revelations about his identity spoken by demons could be a 'potential embarrassment'
   and could lead to 'premature and misdirected popular adulation' (France, p. 105)." Schnabel,
   Mark, 58. In the next chapter the so-called messianic secret is discussed in greater depth.

lamb with mint sauce for the special occasion of hosting Peter's new wonder-working boss.

In the first century, women typically served men lunch. But here, as we are about to see, the man Jesus serves her. He serves her not by giving her lunch but by giving her life. The reason for this role reversal is that she is incapacitated by a fever. Without modern medicine, fevers were deadly enemies, as capable as demons to take one to the grave. How then does Jesus serve her? Once again he ousts the evil. Mark **1:31** is the gospel in miniature: "And he came and took her by the hand and lifted her up, and the fever left her, and she began to serve them."

Look back at **1:30**. Look especially at the second half. The first half documents the medical issue. The host of the house has a fever. But it is no ordinary fever. Preachers have preached sermons with high temperatures, athletes played in championship games, singers sung operas, and city workers plowed snow. This woman cannot get out of bed. Her fever must have been hot (a "high fever," Luke 4:38), closing in on the temperature of the underworld. This dear woman is down for the count when—at the last second—Jesus steps in. But he does not throw in the towel. Rather, he puts on the gloves. He will box this beast. He will fight it by removing his gloves, lowering his hand, and touching the dying woman: "And he came and took her by the hand and lifted her up and the fever left her" (Mark 1:31). What tenderness. What resurrection strength! What beautiful compassion; there was no need to touch her—remember the one verbal command exorcism in the synagogue?

What next? Angels come and minister to her? No. "And she began to serve them" (1:31). What is the significance of this small detail? Three aspects are significant.

First, it tells us that she has been completely and instantaneously healed.

Second, this dramatic change from lying to serving is symbolic of what happens to people who have been touched by Jesus. She models Christian greatness as defined by Jesus in Mark 9:35: "If anyone would be first, he [or she!] must be last of all and *servant of all.*" Christian = servant. Great Christian = servant of all. Peter's mother-in-law *serves us* well in showing that servanthood is a necessary and exalted act in Christ's church.

Third, her serving not only is symbolic of the call to servanthood for all Christ-followers but also points to Christ as the Servant of the servant of the servants of God. Perhaps the most important statement that Jesus makes in Mark comes in 10:45. There, after Jesus teaches his disciples that "whoever would be great among you must be your servant, and whoever would be first among you must be slave of all" (10:43–44), he concludes: "For even the Son of Man came not to be served but to serve, and to give his life as a ransom for many." So how does Jesus serve? By expelling the demon in the Capernaum synagogue? Yes. By touching Peter's mother-in-law? Yes. By healing the multitudes who come to the house (see 1:32–34)? Yes. But ultimately he serves us by paying for our sins by dying in our place on the cross.

Here is where we get to the heart of our second lesson: Jesus has come to destroy the works of the devil. He has come to destroy demons. He has come to destroy sickness that leads to death by dying in our place. He has come to "give his life as a ransom" (Mark 10:45). The cross is the ultimate symbol and the substitutionary embodiment of servanthood.

The Gospel of Mark is the earliest Gospel. Matthew, when he wrote his Gospel, had Mark or something like Mark in front of him. What then did Matthew do with Mark? He certainly rearranged material, as well as omitting and adding other material. For example, below is his record of this same scene. Look at what he does. Notice the major difference.

> And when Jesus entered Peter's house, he saw his mother-in-law lying sick with a fever. He touched her hand, and the fever left her, and she rose and began to serve him. That evening they brought to him many who were oppressed by demons, and he cast out the spirits with a word and healed all who were sick. This was to fulfill what was spoken by the prophet Isaiah: "He took our illnesses and bore our diseases." (Matt. 8:14–17)

The major difference is the final verse, which includes a quotation from Isaiah 53. Matthew's addition can be thought of as we might think of a sermon application. How does Matthew apply Mark? Matthew sees this day of healings as pointing to the cross. And we should too. Jesus' healing ministry points to his *healing* ministry. The exorcism, the cooling touch, and the once-afflicted multitudes' skipping home in the dark all point to the salvation accomplished in Jesus' death.

The Priority of Prayer and Preaching

Our first lesson is that we must believe demons exist and wreak havoc in this world. Our second lesson is that we must know that Jesus has come to destroy the works of the devil. Our third lesson is that we must follow Jesus' priorities.

This is a demanding and exhausting day for Jesus, a day in which he demonstrates his spectacular supernatural powers. In the morning he exorcises a demon. Before lunch he cools a fever. Then at night he helps hundreds of sick and demon-possessed people. Look at Mark **1:32–34**, with some running commentary, and just marvel at our Messiah:

> That evening at sundown [the Sabbath ended][7] they [desperate people] brought to him [those who apparently could not bring themselves] all who were sick [those in bed with fevers, paralyzed legs, and the like] or oppressed by demons. And the whole city was gathered together at the door. [What a scene! Everyone in town knew someone who needed help, and now who to go to. And what did Jesus do?] And he healed many ["great numbers," TLB][8] who were sick with various diseases, and cast out many ["great numbers" of] demons. And he would not permit the demons to speak, because they knew him [i.e., his true identity].

If Jesus were a modern-day faith-healer, he would have capitalized on his fame ("His fame spread everywhere throughout all the surrounding region of Galilee," 1:28). He would also have let the underworld tell the world who was in town—"the Holy One of God."[9] Come one, come all to see God in the flesh! At the very least, if he were a TV evangelist, he would have opened shop in Capernaum and started a new campus, one with click-of-the-button ways to take donations. And then the social media and television ads would go out: "One day; one hundred miracles! Come back tomorrow for more amazing displays of power. A bum leg, no problem. Issue with acne, not an issue." But Jesus has different priorities. He heals people. Indeed, he does. And in doing so he demonstrates that the kingdom is at hand, a kingdom that will conquer demons and diseases. His priority, however, is not healing. Rather, as verses 35–39 make clear, it is prayer and preaching.

> And rising very early in the morning, while it was still dark, he departed and went out to a desolate place, and there he prayed. And Simon and those who were with him searched for him, and they found him and said to him, "Everyone is looking for you." And he said to them, "Let us go

7 Note that Jesus did not wait for the end of the Sabbath to exorcise the demon.
8 The word "many" (Gk. *polloi*) is not an exclusive term (some among many) but inclusive (a great number).
9 "The problem was not primarily the inappropriate nature of the witness but the knowledge of the demons that he is 'the Holy One of God' (1:24), 'the Son of God' (3:11), the 'Son of the Most High God' (5:7), indeed 'the Messiah' (Luke 4:41, the parallel passage to Mark 1:34). The time and manner of the revelation of Jesus' identity as Messiah and unique Son of God is Jesus' own prerogative, revealed only to those close to him (8:29–30) and understood only in connection with Jesus' crucifixion" (Schnabel, *Mark*, 60).

on to the next towns, that I may preach there also, for that is why I came out." And he went throughout all Galilee, preaching in their synagogues and casting out demons.

Jesus' ministry priorities are prayer and preaching. Let us first look at prayer. In **1:35** we read, "And rising very early in the morning, while it was still dark, he departed and went out to a desolate place, and there he prayed."

When does Jesus pray? "Rising very early in the morning, while it was still dark." The phrase "rising very early" tells us that his priority is prayer, not sleep. He needs sleep like every human, but he knows, now that he has entered into his public ministry, that prayer, not just sleep, will get him through the days ahead.

Where does Jesus pray? We are told that he goes to a "desolate place" (1:35). So he leaves the house and journeys out into the countryside (Capernaum is a lakeshore city), and there he prays. He models his own teaching on prayer (cf. Matt. 6:5–6). Jesus prays where no one would see him, where no one could possibly praise his early morning piety.

How does Jesus pray? We are not told his posture. Elsewhere, however, Jesus prays standing, kneeling, or with his face flat on the ground.

What does Jesus pray about? Again, we are not told. But perhaps he prays the prayer he will teach his disciples to pray, the Lord's Prayer. Of course, he would not pray for forgiveness, but he certainly would pray "Your kingdom come." That is his mission. His mission is to bring in the reign of God in heaven to earth.

Why does Jesus pray? Think about it. Jesus has just demonstrated superpowers. So why would he need any help from anyone? Moreover, Jesus is the second member of the Trinity, so why would the divine Son of God pray to God the Father? Because in the incarnation, and with the mission of the cross before him (see Phil. 2:5–8), Jesus is totally dependent on the Father and Spirit for his daily sustenance. Jesus is truly God and truly human, but to be truly human is to say, "Our Father in heaven . . . give us this day our daily bread . . . lead us not into temptation." As the author of Hebrews reflects, "In the days of his flesh, Jesus offered up prayers and supplications, with loud cries and tears" (Heb. 5:7). Can you imagine!

Jesus prays. He prays at his baptism (Luke 3:21), at the start of his Galilean ministry (Mark 1:35), before he chooses the twelve (Luke 6:12–13), after he feeds the five thousand (Mark 6:46; Luke 9:18) and cleanses the leper and heals the paralytic (Luke 5:16), before and during his transfiguration (Luke 9:28, 29), and in the garden of Gethsemane (Mark 14:32–39) before courageously carrying the cross. And he repeatedly teaches his disciples to pray

(9:29; 11:24; 13:18; 14:38). But, do we pray? How often? When? Where? How? Do we share Jesus' awareness of the necessity of prayer and sustained communion with God?

Prayer is one of Jesus' top priorities.

So too is preaching,[10] as featured in Mark **1:36–39**. Peter and the brothers awake. Jesus is nowhere to be found. They have just left everything to follow him, but now they have no leader to follow. So they search the area. They finally find him. Peter offers a bit of a rebuke: "Everyone is looking for you" (1:37). He talks to Jesus like a parent who has been searching for his lost child in the supermarket. Then, after the rebuke, Jesus does not respond. Instead he clarifies his mission. "'Let us go on to the next towns, that I may *preach* there also, for that is why I came out ["This is why I have come," HCSB].' And he went throughout all Galilee, *preaching* in their synagogues and casting out demons" (1:38–39). Jesus casts out demons. But his priority is prayer and preaching. His mission is to herald the kingdom, to proclaim "the gospel of God," to announce that "the time is fulfilled, and the kingdom of God is at hand; repent and believe in the gospel" (1:14–15).

This is a lesson that Peter and the eleven will eventually understand. In Acts 6 we read about physical needs arising within the early church; look at what the twelve do:

> The twelve summoned the full number of the disciples and said, "It is not right that we should give up preaching the word of God to serve tables. Therefore, brothers, pick out from among you seven men of good repute, full of the Spirit and of wisdom, whom we will appoint to this duty. But we will devote ourselves to prayer and to the ministry of the word [preaching]." (Acts 6:2–4)

Then, after these men are appointed and the twelve get back to their appointed task, what happens next is that "the word of God continued to increase, and the number of the disciples multiplied greatly in Jerusalem" (Acts 6:7). My equation for church growth comes from Acts. Here is the not-so-secret formula: Prayer + Preaching + Persecution = Growth. That might not be what you find in today's inspiring books on church growth, but it is what you will find in our God-inspired book. So let me ask: How are we doing with the three *P*s? Are our churches prayerful? Do our churches faithfully preach

---

10 Mark consistently portrays Jesus as a "teacher" (4:38; 5:35; 9:17, 38; 10:17, 20, 35; 12:14, 19, 32; 13:1; 14:14) who teaches (1:21–22; 2:13; 4:1–2; 6:2, 6, 34; 8:31; 9:31; 10:1; 11:17; 12:14, 35; 14:49).

the gospel? And are we persecuted for living out and reaching out with the good news of Jesus?

On the Hearing of God's Word

Richard Baxter wrote something for his congregation called "On the Hearing of God's Word." In answer to the question, What ought you to be listening for in a good message? he gave four directives. First, hear with understanding. Second, remember what you hear. Third, be duly affected by it. Fourth, sincerely practice it.

My hope is that these three lessons—that we must believe demons exist and wreak havoc in this world, that Jesus has come to destroy the works of the devil, and that Jesus' priorities of prayer and preaching are to be ours—would touch our heads and hearts and hands; that we would understand, remember (our heads), be duly affected (our hearts), and practice what we have just read (our hands). That we would suppress and scatter the forces of Satan by the power of prayer and the preaching of the power of the cross.

Curing the Unclean

MARK 1:40–45

Moved with pity, he stretched out his hand and touched
him and said to him, "I will; be clean." And immediately the
leprosy left him, and he was made clean.
Mark 1:41

Psalm 33:13 states, "The LORD looks down from heaven; he sees all the children of man," and Hebrews 4:13 that "nothing in all creation is hidden from
God's sight" (NIV). Imagine who and what God sees. He sees the successful
Wall Street investor driving his luxury sports car, the king of England sitting on
his throne, the Bollywood star acting out her first lines for a new film, the Bra-
zilian model walking the catwalk, the Kenyan marathoner breaking the world
record, the Japanese poet laurate sitting under an elm tree pondering his next
metaphor, and the Australian physicist testing a new theory. He sees the rich,
the powerful, the famous, the beautiful, the strong, the clever, and the smart.
He sees Asians, Africans, Europeans, and Americans. He even sees those down
under! He sees people. He sees the tall and short, the fat and skinny, the healthy
and the sick, the newborn and the dying, the kind and the cruel, the dirty and
the clean, the frightened and the secure. He sees people, billions of people.

True enough. So what? What is the point? The point is the awesomeness
of the incarnation. It is awesome not only that the Son of God became man
and dwelled among us but that, of all the people in the world with whom our
Lord could have associated, it was not the rich but the poor, not the powerful
but the powerless, not the establishment but the outsiders, not the healthy but
the sick with whom he associated.

Mark does not tell us of Jesus' lowly birth. He does not say that Jesus
was born of a poor Jewish maiden who was to be wed to a carpenter from
Nazareth, a couple who could not find any room in the inn for the birth of
their boy. He gives no detail about the manger, the swaddling clothes, or the

shepherds' visit. But he does tell us about the people Jesus surrounded himself with and had compassion on. Jesus called four fishermen (1:16–20), then a tax collector (2:13–14), then seven others, all from common backgrounds (3:13–19). His ministry was preceded by John the Baptist, a man who wore the latest fashions from PQ/Prophets Quarterly (sporting "camel's hair" with "a leather belt," 1:6) and a man who experienced the common fate of many prophets (imprisonment and execution by the authorities, 6:14–29).

But besides John and the first four of the twelve, the people who come to Jesus, and those for whom Jesus has come, are people in great need, spiritually and physically: the demon possessed, paralyzed, crippled, dying, bleeding, blind, deaf and mute, and leprous.

In this chapter we will look at Jesus' cleansing of the leper. But before we do so we will pause and look to Jesus, to see how he has been portrayed thus far in Mark's Gospel. Even though he is the "Christ, the Son of God" (1:1)—the one for whom the heavens open, the Spirit descends (1:10), and the voice of approval sounds "You are my beloved Son; with you I am well pleased" (1:11)—in each frame of Mark's fast-action film Jesus is portrayed as the humble servant of sinners and of the sick. He is baptized in the same waters as all the sinners who come to John "confessing their sins" (1:5). He is tempted in ways that all humans are tempted (1:13). He calls sinners like the four fishermen, whose first line in Mark is a rebuke to Jesus ("Everyone is looking for you," 1:37). He stations his mission to save the world in Capernaum, a small and fairly insignificant city in a small and fairly insignificant country within the vast and quite significant Roman Empire. From there he reaches out to people in even smaller and less significant towns and villages (see 1:38–39). That is the set of scenes that Mark has presented to us before we read the lines "And a leper came to him" (1:40). In one sense this is a surprising line; in another sense, it is just the next piece of the puzzle that fits right into place. It is a piece of the portrait Mark has been painting, the portrait of Jesus as the humble servant and Savior of sinners and the sick.

With that perspective in place, we turn now to Act 1, scene 7, otherwise known as Mark 1:40–45, a text that divides into three sections: coming to Christ (1:40), the compassionate Christ (1:41–42), and the command of Christ (1:43–45).

Coming to Christ

We start with a look at this leper. Mark **1:40** tells us *who* came to Jesus, *how*, and *why:* "And a leper came to him, imploring him, and kneeling said to him,

'If you will, you can make me clean.'" As was emphasized in the introduction to this chapter, do not overlook the *who*. A leper.[1]

Recently I broke out with a rash around my mouth. I was embarrassed. I worked at home. I also, and finally, went to the dermatologist. She examined me. She looked concerned. She put on special green gloves. She felt around the sides of my mouth and under my lips and chin, at the redness. She said, "Well, good news. You don't have *Killamaninlessthansevendays*" or something like that. I said, "What? My Latin is a bit rusty." She said, "You don't have anything serious." She took off the gloves. A good sign. She gave me antibiotics and some special cream. The rash disappeared.

Leprosy is not some easily curable skin inflammation. In Jesus' day, especially in his Jewish context, a leper was the most unholy person. Mark moves us from Jesus' encounter with the most unholy creature (a demon) to the most unholy person (a leper). When the Jewish audience of Jesus' day read, heard, or saw, "A leper came to him," they would have been taken aback. They would have recoiled like we do when we hear someone in the airplane say after she has sneezed in our direction, "I just can't get over this flu."

Of course, leprosy is much worse than some temporary sickness. Without a cure (and there was none in those days), this disease was a slow, ugly, and lonely way to die. "It is a radical disease of the whole person. It attacks not merely the skin but the blood, the flesh and to the bones, until the unhappy patient begins to lose his extremities and to rot by inches."[2] Paul Brand, world-famous leprosy researcher and physician, labeled leprosy a "painless hell." He did so because "the disease acts as an anesthetic, bringing numbness to the extremities as well as to the ears, eyes, and nose." So if you have leprosy and thus cannot feel the temperature of water when you bathe, the cut of a blade when you shave, or the nibble of a rat on your toes while you sleep, what happens is that you burn your body, lose fingers and toes, break bones. You might even scratch off your nose. Soon enough you look hideous and smell disgusting. You are like a walking corpse.[3]

Brand's label "painless hell" only captures one aspect of this terrible sickness. It is painless for the body but not for the soul. Not only does it slowly

---

1 Leviticus 13–14 speaks of "all kinds of skin-disease" (NJB), including Hansen's disease, as we would label it. It is likely that this man has that type of "leprosy" because, as stated above, Mark is moving his readers from a narrative on the most unclean creature (a demon) to the most unclean person (a leper).

2 J. C. Ryle, *Mark: Expository Thoughts on the Gospels*, CCC (Wheaton, IL: Crossway, 1993), 15.

3 "Luke the physician, in a parallel account (Luke 5:12), describes him as 'covered with leprosy.' The disease had run its course. . . . His body was *full* of leprosy, mutilated from head to foot, rotten, stinking, repulsive." R. Kent Hughes, *Mark: Jesus, Servant and Savior*, PTW, 2 vols. (Wheaton, IL: Crossway, 1989), 1:54.

destroy the sensory nerves; it quickly destroys all human interaction.[4] How painful! According to OT law (see Num. 5:2) lepers were banished from God's people, including from religious worship in the temple. So as not to spread the disease they were separate from society. If they ever came near people, they had to cover their mouths and cry out "Unclean! Unclean!" (Lev. 13:45–46). Moreover, as Kent Hughes summarizes,

> By Jesus' time, rabbinical teaching, with its absurd strictures, had made matters even worse. If a leper even struck his head inside a house, it was pronounced unclean. It was illegal to even greet a leper. Lepers had to remain at least 100 cubits away if they were upwind, and four cubits if downwind. [A cubit is the distance from the elbow to the fingertip.] Josephus, the famous Jewish historian, summarized by saying that lepers were treated "as if they were, in effect, dead men."[5]

That is the *who*. Next, we turn to the *how*. How does this leper approach Jesus? Verse 40 reads: "And a leper came to him, imploring him, and kneeling said to him, 'If you will, you can make me clean.'" Have you ever diagrammed sentences? Awful but useful exercises. I did not diagram this sentence, but I did notice the seven verbs: came, imploring, kneeling, said, will, can, make clean. Some are main verbs ("he came") and others supporting ones ("imploring"). But each verb matters.

The first verb (the leper "came" to Jesus) is important for two reasons. First, it shows remarkable courage. When you think about the religious stigma and social separateness this man lives with day after day, it is quite the bold and brave move to come out into public. It is also quite remarkable for him to get so close to Jesus. He is crossing all sorts of purity lines, and he knows it. Second, his movement—*coming* to Jesus—demonstrates a trait of faith. This verb (Gk. *erchomai*) is a common verb but is used often in narratives in which someone expresses faith in Jesus, such as blind Bartimaeus's *coming* to Jesus for healing (Mark 10:50; cf. 2:3; 5:22, 27; 7:25; 14:3).

The second and third verbs demonstrate this man's prayerful posture. Like the psalmists who beg God to rescue them, so he *implores* Jesus. And he does so not face to face but face to foot. He *kneels* before him. There are only three

---

4 "This ostracism, together with the fear of contagion and a slow painful death, made leprosy one of the most dreaded diseases in the ancient world." Mark L. Strauss, *Mark*, ZECNT (Grand Rapids, MI: Zondervan, 2014), 111.

5 Hughes, *Mark*, 1:55, summarizing William Barclay, *The Gospel of Matthew*, 2 vols., rev. ed. (Philadelphia: Westminster, 1975), 2:301.

instances in Mark at which people kneel before Jesus: this leper kneels, the rich young ruler kneels (10:17), and the soldiers who torture and mock Jesus before his crucifixion do so ("kneeling down in homage [*proskuneō*] to him," 15:19).[6] This, then, is the only time that the kneeling connotes authentic worship.

The fourth verb ("he said") simply reinforces the first verb. Not only does the man come to Jesus, but he opens his mouth once he gets there. Both actions take courage. Imagine how difficult it must be for this outcast to speak in public. The verb "he said" says a lot about his faith. He is risking his life because he firmly believes that Jesus can save his life *and limbs*.

We come next to the fifth, six, and seventh verbs, which are found in the leper's petition: "If you will, you can make me clean." He does not say, "Lord, *if you can*, make me clean," but "If you will, *you can* make me clean." He expresses absolute trust in Jesus ("You can heal me")[7] and absolute poverty of spirit before him ("only if you will"). He begs Jesus to act both like God and like the coming Messiah (see Isa. 35:5–6; Matt. 11:5).

These final verbs move us from the *who* and *how* to the *why*. The reason why the leper comes to Jesus is simple. He wants to be cleansed of his leprosy. This is no felt need (e.g., "I feel that you need to affirm my worth") but a very real one ("I will die a slow and awful death if you do not help").

The Compassionate Christ

How then does Jesus respond? I have called this next section "The Compassionate Christ" for a reason. Mark **1:41–42** records: "Moved with pity, he stretched out his hand and touched him and said to him, 'I will; be clean.' And immediately the leprosy left him, and he was made clean."

Here Mark records Jesus' inner emotions, tender technique, and incredible authority. First, his inner emotions. Jesus is "moved with pity" (1:41) or, as other translations say, "moved with compassion" (KJV; NASB).[8] In Greek it is one word—*splanchnizomai*—used twelve times in the NT and each time related to

---

6   In both Mark 1:40 and 10:17 Mark uses the Greek word *gonupeteō*, not *proskuneō*. (Note that both men do not heed Christ's specific commands to them.) Mark uses *proskuneō* only once (15:19), obviously ironically.

7   "What is striking is the leper's recognition of the supreme significance of the will of Jesus. . . . The will of Jesus is being set on a par with that of God." John Nolland, *The Gospel of Matthew*, NIGTC (Grand Rapids, MI: Eerdmans, 2005), 349.

8   Some Greek manuscripts have "indignance" instead of "compassion." "Compassion" is in the majority of the manuscripts and our best ones. However, if "indignance" is the original, the sense would be similar to what we find in John 11:33, 38, where "Jesus is angry at the power of sin and death in this world, specifically the physical, emotional, and social anguish that the person has experienced"; Grant R. Osborne, *Mark*, TTCS (Grand Rapids, MI: Baker, 2012), 33. Or, in line with his later command to obey Leviticus (Mark 1:44), it could be that Jesus is indignant because this man has disobeyed OT law by not keeping his distance.

Jesus. The word means "to feel deeply," as into the depths of one's bowels or, as we would put it, "in the pit of the stomach." Here Jesus feels gut-wrenching pity.

This inner feeling leads to action. Jesus decides to heal with a touch (*haptō*),[9] a word that means "to grasp hold of" or "to fasten oneself to." "Moved with pity, he stretched out his hand and touched [grabbed] him [tightly]" (1:41). Perhaps Jesus hugs the leper. Whatever the nature of the touch, imagine the sheer delight surging through the man's long-lost nose down to his shriveled toes. We do not know how long this man has been a leper, or how long it has been since someone has touched him. Two years? Ten years? Can you imagine no one touching you for a month—no hug, no holding your hand, no playful rub of the head, no hand on your shoulder? And Jesus "stretched out his hand and touched him." Frederick Dale Bruner calls this grasp "the gospel"[10] because, on the one hand, it is a demonstration of God's tangible compassion in Christ and, on the other hand, it is Jesus' taking on all our infirmities. It is Isaiah 53:5 (by "his wounds we are healed") and 2 Corinthians 5:21 ("For our sake he [the Father] made him [the Son] to be sin who knew no sin, so that in him we might become the righteousness of God"). Jesus takes on our flesh and all our impurities, and in doing so we take on, through faith, all his purity. According to Leviticus 5:3 Jesus becomes unclean the moment he touches this leper. Yet by means of his healing touch, it is as though he transcends the law without abolishing it.[11] Jesus' touch does not make him unclean; rather, it cleanses the unclean.

Thus far we have seen Jesus' inner emotions ("moved with pity") and his tender technique ("He . . . touched him," 1:41). Finally we come to our Lord's incredible authority: Jesus "said to him, 'I will; be clean.' And immediately the leprosy left him, and he was made clean" (1:41–42). Jesus does not wonder whether he can cure the incurable.[12] There is no hesitation here (he stretches out his hand), and, at first, there are no words. And when Jesus does speak, it is a direct answer to the man's question ("If you will, you can make me clean," 1:40; Jesus says, "I will," 1:41), followed by a short command ("Be clean," 1:41) and a sudden and complete cleansing ("And immediately the leprosy left him, and he was made clean," 1:42).

9 This is the second of nine touches in Mark (1:31, 41; 5:41; 6:5; 7:33; 8:23; 9:27, 36; 10:16).
10 Frederick Dale Bruner, *Matthew: A Commentary, Volume 1: The Christbook, Matthew 1–12*, rev. ed. (Grand Rapids, MI: Eerdmans, 2007), 374.
11 "Under the law the touch of a leper was infectious, but as Christ possesses such purity as to repel all filth and defilement, he does not by touch either pollute himself with leprosy or become a transgressor of the law." John Calvin, *Commentary on a Harmony of the Gospel*, quoted in *CHSB*, 1474.
12 There are no accounts of someone's curing a leper in ancient Jewish and pagan literature; in all the biblical accounts, God always miraculously intervenes (Ex. 4:6–8; Num. 12:9–15; 2 Kings 5:1–27; Luke 17:11–19).

Notice that Jesus moves from a loving touch, like a mother's forcefully plant-ing a cold cloth on the forehead of her feverish child, to an imposing command, like a foreman's yelling out orders to a wrecking crew. Jesus gives the command ("Be clean"), and the walls of sin and sickness and separation are demolished. Scales fall off the man's skin. Bruises and wounds are instantaneously healed. The tips of toes and fingers grow back. His face is now unblemished. His breath is fresh and clean. His voice restored. Something as awesome as Genesis 1 has occurred. Perhaps better. A new creation. A sort of resurrection from the dead.

In an article in *Preaching Today* Dr. Duane Litfin shares this story:

> I remember a student preaching a sermon on the Gospel of Mark, where Jesus is casting out demons. The student preached a sermon basically on how to cast out demons. When he was through, we began probing what he had done with the text. I asked him, "Do you think Mark was trying to tell us here how to cast out demons?"
>
> He said, "Mmm, no, probably not."
>
> "What do you think Mark was doing?"
>
> "Well, Mark was teaching us about Jesus."
>
> "What was he teaching us about Jesus?"
>
> "That he had power over the occult, the forces of evil, and the universe."
>
> I said to him, "Why didn't you preach it that way?"
>
> He said, "I couldn't think how to apply it."
>
> And I said to him, "How about if we apply it this way: 'Let's all get down on our knees and worship Jesus?'"
>
> And he said, "I didn't think of that."[13]

What has Mark been up to with the first few miracle stories? Why these nar-ratives? Simple. Mark wants to show us that Jesus has authority over evil. He has the power to conquer demons, death, and disease. Moreover, Mark wants us to follow the leper's lead. We should all make it a habit to get down on our knees and worship Jesus.

The Command of Christ

But to what extent should we follow the leper's lead? Having looked at the coming to Christ (1:40) and the compassionate Christ (1:41–42), we conclude with the command of Christ (**1:43–45**):

13 Duane Litfin, "Redeeming How to Preach," *Preaching Today*, https://www.preachingtoday.com/books/art-and-craft-of-biblical-preaching/style/felt-needs-preaching.html, accessed April 2, 2021.

And Jesus sternly charged him and sent him away at once, and said to him, "See that you say nothing to anyone, but go, show yourself to the priest and offer for your cleansing what Moses commanded, for a proof to them." But he went out and began to talk freely about it, and to spread the news, so that Jesus could no longer openly enter a town, but was out in desolate places, and people were coming to him from every quarter.

What a seemingly odd ending. Why the command to say nothing? Why the command to obey the law of Moses? And what is with the saved man's disobedience—is it good or bad behavior? Let me tackle each question in turn.

First, why does Jesus say, "See that you say nothing to anyone" (1:44)? Why be silent about something that makes one want to shout? This is the first time Jesus has talked like this, but it will not be the last. Scholars call it the "messianic secret," those efforts Jesus makes to keep his messianic identity and mission under wraps.[14] What do we make of such secrecy? The answer involves the identity of the man and the timing of his mission. Many of the Jews of Jesus' day thought of the coming Messiah as a conquering king, not a suffering servant. But our Lord had no wish to be labeled a revolutionary, let alone an insurrectionist. He did not want an erroneous opinion broadcast that he had come to fight Rome. He did not want to be tagged as a celebrity miracle worker or exorcist. He did not want word about him getting out too soon or in a way that was misinformed about his purposes. He wanted his disciples slowly but surely to understand his identity and mission and then, after the cross and resurrection, to proclaim it on the housetops. He wanted them to announce that the Son of Man, Son of David, and Son of God is the suffering servant and that through his horrific sufferings and glorious resurrection the powers far greater than Rome—the powers of hell—have been destroyed. Death is killed. Satan is crushed under his heel.

Second, why does Jesus command the leper to heed this law? "Go, show yourself to the priest and offer for your cleansing what Moses commanded, for a proof to them" (1:44).[15] Why go to the priest when Jesus is the only priest we need? Why obey the ceremonial law of Moses when a new day

---

14 See Mark 1:25, 34, 44; 3:12; 5:43; 7:36; 8:30; 9:9.

15 "As described in Leviticus 13–14, this involved sacrifice, shaving the entire body, washing one's body and clothes, and a waiting period after which the procedure would be repeated. During the Second Temple period, part of this process took place at the temple complex. In the northwest corner of the court of the women was the chamber of the lepers, where those who had been cured would come to bathe on the eighth day of their purification process and wait for their guilt, sin, and burnt offerings to be sacrificed by the priests" (Osborne, *Mark*, 33).

has dawned, when "the time is fulfilled, and the kingdom of God is at hand" (1:15)? Again, the answer relates to timing. The kingdom has come, but it has not yet been consummated. Moreover, this kingdom is a continuation of God's rule throughout history. "Jesus has not come to reaffirm the law . . . or to abolish it, . . . but to fulfill it (Matt 5:17)—to bring it to its prophesied consummation in the kingdom of God."[16] Jesus plays by the Book! Leviticus 14 says that someone who is part of God's covenant community is to do what Jesus asks this man to do. Jesus is indeed establishing a new kingdom, but one founded upon the old one. After the cross, Mosaic cleansing rituals will be null and void. But at this time in history they actually testify to Jesus. They witness that someone greater than Moses is here, that the kingdom of heaven is breaking into the world, and that the Christ has come: "The blind receive their sight and the lame walk, *lepers are cleansed* and the deaf hear, and the dead are raised up, and the poor have good news preached to them" (Matt. 11:5).

Finally, what are we to make of the man's disobedience? Mark 1:45 concludes, "But he went out and began to talk freely about it, and to spread the news, so that Jesus could no longer openly enter a town, but was out in desolate places, and people were coming to him from every quarter." Some take the leper's behavior as not only inevitable but commendable. Jesus' imperious command is impossible to keep! Who could keep quiet when something so wonderful has happened? Just as the glory of Jesus' "secret epiphanies . . . cannot be hidden," this man's tongue cannot be tied.[17] This man joins in Jesus' mission. He is already fishing for men. Osborne says,

> This is not really disobedience, for anyone touched by God cannot fail to tell others. . . . The man cannot keep quiet. He has experienced the hand of God and been healed. One simply cannot remain silent. That is Mark's point. When Christ has changed your life, you must go public with the incredible joy you feel.[18]

That will preach, but I do not think it is the point Mark wants preachers to preach.

Mark takes the man's disobedience as a disappointment. I say so for four reasons. First, the man clearly disobeys Jesus' word. That is never a good thing, especially when the command is so clear and stern ("See to it that you obey it!" gets the feel of it). Those saved by Christ should follow what his mother, Mary, said to the servants at the wedding in Cana: "Do whatever he tells you" (John 2:5), no matter how ridiculous it might seem (see John 2:7–8). Second, this man clearly disobeys OT law. That is never a good thing either, especially at that era in salvation history. Third, since there is "no indication . . . given that the healed man obeyed Jesus' command to go to the priest," he is risking reintegration into his culture (in order to be properly restored to society, he first needs to show proof to the priest), and he is failing to give testimony to Jesus as Messiah. Fourth, the end results are the opposite of what Jesus had hoped. Jesus did not want to "storm Israel" with messianic claims but instead to "knock quietly at its door, leper by leper, little by little."[19] Jesus did not want to start a popular healing ministry, be crowned an earthly king, or lead an army. And he did not want his fame to spread to the extent that he "could no longer openly enter a town" (1:45). He wanted to enter the towns openly and proclaim the gospel of the kingdom. Look at the start of Mark 2:1–2: "And when he returned to Capernaum after some days, it was reported that he was at home. And many were gathered together, so that *there was no more room*, not even at the door. And *he was preaching* the word to them."

Jesus would work with the effects of his fame. But one gets the sense in 2:1–12 that he wants to ensure that people understand his priorities now that the word is getting out. Sin is the deeper issue. That is why Jesus will say, "Son, your sins are forgiven" (2:5), before he says, "Rise, pick up your bed, and go home" (2:11). With all that said, and if I am right, then one lesson for us is to take Jesus at his word and trust his timing even if it does not make sense to us at the time. And, as in 2:1–12, another lesson might be that salvation from sin (what Jesus is preaching about throughout Galilee) is a greater salvation than salvation from sickness, even from the dreadful disease of leprosy.

A View from Above

In his book *At Home* Bill Bryson begins by recounting the time he and his wife rented a Victorian house in Norfolk, England. He talks about climbing up into the attic to "look for the source of a slow but mysterious drip." Once up there, he found a secret door in an external wall, one "not visible from anywhere outside the house." He opened it and discovered a "tiny rooftop space." He wondered why some architect would "put in a door to a space so lacking in evident need or purpose." But then he recognized the intention and genius of the design. From this secret rooftop space he could see the whole village

19 Bruner, *Christbook*, 377.

and the "quiet, agreeable, timeless English countryside." He could see all that he had seen before, but now from a new, different, perhaps preferred angle.[20]

I hope in our study of Mark 1:40–45 we have found a new view of the familiar narrative of Jesus and the leper. And I hope we have viewed a very great man on a very humble but life-saving mission. It astounds me, as we look afresh from this new view, that God became a man, that he came to the outposts of civilization, that he touched the least of society, and that he resisted the lure of popularity. He pushed it away to be on his way—to the cross. He was no religious performer, like the ones we have today and the ones they had back then, trying to gain a crowd for money, fame, and self-gratification. He resisted the pull to fame and fortune and flattery.

I hope we also see, like Bryson did the beautiful English countryside, in the distance the hill of Calvary. We see that this miracle points to something beyond the cleansing of an unclean leper and someone beyond a good physician. It points to the Great Physician, who has come "not to call the righteous, but sinners" (2:17) and to save them not from a physical disease but from a spiritual one—the damning disease of sin—and from eternal death.

---

20 Bill Bryson, *At Home: A Short History of Private Life* (New York: Doubleday, 2013), 1.

Our Greatest Need

MARK 2:1-12

Which is easier, to say to the paralytic, "Your sins are for-
given," or to say, "Rise, take up your bed and walk"?
Mark 2:9

On January 24, 2018, Larry Nassar, a sports physician for USA Gymnastics
and Michigan State University, was sentenced to 175 years in prison for his
decades-long sexual abuse of female gymnasts. One hundred fifty of his victims testified in court against him. Rachael Denhollander, the last to testify,
made the most profound public statement I have ever heard a Christian athlete make. Toward the end of her courtroom testimony she spoke directly to
her abuser who was seated before her:

> In our early hearings, you brought your Bible into the courtroom, and
> you have spoken of praying for forgiveness. And so it is on that basis
> that I appeal to you. If you have read the Bible you carry, you know the
> definition of sacrificial love portrayed is of God himself loving so sacri-
> ficially that he gave up everything to pay a penalty for the sin he did not
> commit. By his grace, I, too, choose to love this way.
>
> You spoke of praying for forgiveness. But Larry, if you have read the
> Bible you carry, you know forgiveness does not come from doing good
> things, as if good deeds can erase what you have done. It comes from re-
> pentance which requires facing and acknowledging the truth about what
> you have done in all of its utter depravity and horror without mitigation,
> without excuse, without acting as if good deeds can erase what you have
> seen in this courtroom today.
>
> If the Bible you carry says it is better for a stone to be thrown around
> your neck and you thrown into a lake than for you to make even one
> child stumble. And you have damaged hundreds.

The Bible you carry speaks of a final judgment where all of God's wrath and eternal terror is poured out on men like you. Should you ever reach the point of truly facing what you have done, the guilt will be crushing. And that is what makes the gospel of Christ so sweet. Because it extends grace and hope and mercy where none should be found. And it will be there for you.

I pray you experience the soul crushing weight of guilt so you may some-day experience true repentance and true forgiveness from God, which you need far more than forgiveness from me—though I extend that to you as well.[1]

Forgiveness. The forgiveness of sin offered in Jesus Christ is God's supreme accomplishment. It is his accomplishment, if that is the right word (perhaps "greatest grace"?), because forgiveness is our greatest need. It is the greatest need for the greatest sinners (like the man in the dock that day), as well as for the purest saints. We all fall short of God's glory. We all suffer from the sickness of sin, a disease more insidious, grotesque, and deadly than leprosy.

In this chapter we will learn about the faith of a few friends and the reaction of a large crowd. But the central focus will be on the forgiveness of sin, specifically, on the forgiveness of sin offered in Jesus Christ as God's supreme accomplishment—because the forgiveness of our sin is our greatest need.

The Setting

Mark starts this story about forgiveness in this way: "And when [Jesus] returned to Capernaum after some days, it was reported that he was at home. And many were gathered together, so that there was no more room, not even at the door. And he was preaching the word to them" (Mark **2:1–2**). First, notice the shift in geography. Chapter 1 ends with Jesus "in desolate places" (1:45). Now, at the start of chapter 2, he is back in Capernaum. He left Capernaum to preach in other towns (1:38) and because of the leper's disobedience. Because the leper "talked freely" about his cleansing when Jesus told him not to (see 1:44–45), Jesus "could no longer openly enter a town" (1:45). Crowds met him at every city gate and in every synagogue. So "after some days" (2:1) indicates that Jesus is hoping, after a short period of time (perhaps a few weeks), that the spread of his fame has subsided some.

---

1   "Read Rachael Denhollander's Full Victim Impact Statement about Larry Nassar," *CNN*, January 30, 2018, 7:34 a.m. EST, https://www.cnn.com/2018/01/24/us/rachael-denhollander-full-statement/.

He can go "home" (2:1), likely Peter and Andrew's house, which served as our Lord's ministry headquarters.

Second, notice the full house. Someone sees something. "It was reported that he was at home" (2:1). Imagine a nosy neighbor's noticing Jesus and the four fishermen sneaking in the front door before the break of dawn. This neighbor quickly tells Esther, who tells Jonah, who tells Hannah, who tells Saul, who tells Miriam, who tells Judith—and, once word gets to Judith, well, forget about it. The whole town knows the news! "And many were gathered together, so that there was no more room, not even at the door" (2:2). A packed house.

Here is perhaps how it played out. At 6:00 a.m. comes the first knock. Peter opens the door. His friends Samuel and Sarah arrive. "Oh," Peter says, "Come in, come in." Then another knock. And another. "You sit here," Peter says, "and you here." Soon the living room is full. Then the kitchen. The bedrooms. Eventually, the hallway. People are pushed all the way to the door.

Luke's version adds this interesting detail—the "Pharisees and teachers of the law were sitting there, who had come from every village of Galilee and Judea and from Jerusalem" (Luke 5:17). He also adds, "And the power of the Lord was with him to heal." However, Mark focuses once again not on Jesus' miraculous powers but on his preaching. Of the Gospel writers, only Mark records "And he was preaching the word to them" (Mark 2:2). We do not know for certain what the "word" was that he was preaching, but we can safely surmise that he was preaching the theme of his ministry: the arrival of the kingdom—and thus the need for repentance and faith (1:15).[2]

Their Faith

In fact, I like to imagine that, at the moment Jesus gave the call to believe, the first few bits of the ceiling started to fall. At first Jesus looked up, but then he continued. He preached, "Repent and believe." But soon it became apparent, as the roof above him was cut open and a man lowered down, that this would be a good time to pause. I honestly think that he, at first, was upset. He came to preach the gospel, not to open a hospital. But then I imagine his heart softening. It does not take much for the compassionate Christ to move from righteous indignation to tender mercy. We read in **2:3–5**:

> And they came, bringing to him a paralytic carried by four men. And when they could not get near him because of the crowd, they removed

---

2   In Acts the apostles are often (nearly 40x!) depicted as preaching "the word." The content of their message includes the themes of the lordship of Jesus, the forgiveness of sins, and the coming judgment.

the roof above him, and when they had made an opening, they let down the bed on which the paralytic lay. And when Jesus saw their faith, he said to the paralytic, "Son, your sins are forgiven."

In a page we will focus on the heart of our text—the forgiveness of sin. For now we focus on faith. Verse 5 says that "Jesus saw their faith." What does faith look like? Mark wants to teach us that faith has some movement to it. It is not merely cerebral (e.g., "I believe that Jesus is the Son of God"). Rather, it is cerebral ("I hold certain truths about Jesus and his mission"), as well as active. Faith "comes" to Jesus ("and they came," 2:3). And here faith does not move mountains, but it does remove roofs (Gk. "They unroofed the roof," 2:4). The only thing Jesus *saw* was the newly installed sunroof above him. Their unroofing was a sure sign of faith, despite the four months of community service, I am sure, that they had to serve for this act of vandalism.

A typical Jewish house in Capernaum in those days would have had a stone foundation covered with pebbles or tiles and limestone walls with mortar made of clay, shells, and potsherds and coated with a whitewashed stucco-like substance. The roof would have been flat and durable, with just a slight slope for rainwater to drain. This roof would have served as an outdoor second floor, like a balcony. Because it was flat and durable, people could have walked on it, stored their tools, hung their laundry, dried fruit, and gathered in the cool of the evening to talk. Sometimes, in the warm summer months, people would even have slept outside. The roof would have been made of wooden crossbeams going one way and matted branches the other, then filled in with straw and covered with mud and clay and finally thatch. Stairs, at the back of the house, would have led up to the roof.

So the "faith" that Jesus "saw" (in the sense of "grasped what must have happened") was as follows. Four men carried their friend to the house, knocked at the door repeatedly, and received no answer or the answer no. Perhaps Peter said, "Enough is enough. The house is full. Go home!" They persevered in their faith because they loved their friend and believed in Jesus. They saw the stairs and climbed them. All the while, let us remember, they were carrying another man, an extra 100-plus pounds. I like to imagine he was 250 pounds, but I have a flair for the dramatic. But this is a dramatic scene! Whatever the weigh-in, they made it to the roof. What next? They knew why they climbed the stairs. Time for some remodeling. They started peeling off the thatch and pounding through the clay. Finally they got to the dried mud, branches, and straw. They quickly pulled all of it out and peeled it aside. One big push through the ceiling and they were in. They cleared away the opening and lowered their friend through it. Then people grabbed him and laid him before our Lord. Above, four hopeful faces peered through the opening.

As I said, this passage is not primarily about faith. But of course there is much we can learn from their faith, and I think it is right to include the paralytic here as well,[3] for either they said, "Friend, we are taking you to Jesus," or he said, "Friends, please take me to Jesus." I think he first asked them. I say this because Jesus addressed the man, not the friends. Jesus recognized the man wanted to be healed and knew something of the man's own sin issue, perhaps one that caused the paralysis. Job's sufferings were not due to a sin. The blindness of the man in John 9:2–3 was not due to some sin (cf. Luke 13:1–5; 2 Cor. 12:7; Gal. 4:13–14). But in other places in the Bible some sin is the cause of some sickness. Think of the Corinthian church. Some who misused the elements of the Lord's Supper were bedbound; others were in the grave (1 Cor. 11:30; cf. Deut. 28:27; Ps. 107:17–18; John 5:14; Acts 5:1–11; James 5:15).

Obviously, we do not know the cause of his paralysis. However, we do know that his friends refused to give up on him. They still loved him and believed in him, despite all his stupid antics and sinful actions. They brought him to Jesus. They raised the roof for him. Faith does not sit still, even for those immobile from the waist down. Faith acts. Faith is "a trust which is manifest in action."[4] Faith acts. Faith moves. Faith does. Faith risks. Faith presses on. Faith steps forward (or up the stairs and through the roof, as the case may be) no matter the social or material cost.

His Forgiveness

From *their faith* we move to *his forgiveness*. "And when Jesus saw their faith, he said to the paralytic, 'Son, your sins are forgiven'" (2:5). With a tender term ("[my] son") Jesus forgives not one sin (perhaps the cause of the man's paralysis, or what the man thinks is the cause) but all his "sins."

I believe in the forgiveness of sins! Do you?

---

3   Mark does not make clear that the paralytic shared his friends' faith in Jesus' power to heal, but he does emphasize that the man obeys Jesus' command to "Rise, pick up your bed, and go home" (2:11). That "he rose and immediately picked up his bed and went out before them all" (2:12) is an example of active and obedient faith. In the middle of a packed room he heeded Jesus' word. And just as his friends had walked him to Jesus, so he walked away from Jesus, knowing firsthand that Jesus had come to "save his people from their sins" (Matt. 1:21), even those unable to lift a finger.

4   Amy-Jill Levine, *The Social and Ethnic Dimensions in Matthean Salvation History* (Lewiston, NY: Mellen, 1988), 115.

And do the scribes in the house? They do as well. But there is one major problem. This lovely healing story turns into a major conflict. We read in 2:6–7: "Now some of the scribes were sitting there, questioning in their hearts, 'Why does this man speak like that? He is blaspheming! Who can forgive sins but God alone?'"[5] These are reasonable thoughts and good questions. I am sympathetic to both sinners and scribes. I suppose I am sympathetic because I am both. I am a sinner. Come follow me for a week and you will gather enough evidence to convict me of that. But I am also a scribe. I have spent nearly thirty years carefully studying the Bible. And I not only study but I am very reserved about my assessment of biblical texts and what other scholars make of the Bible. This is a sacred text. It is sometimes very difficult to understand. I want to hear what other scholars think. I want to be open to new ideas. I want to be willing to change my mind if someone has presented a better view than mine. That is how these scribes in the room think. But then comes Jesus. He does not play by the rules. He makes a public announcement that only God can make, or, in their context, only a priest in the temple after an animal sacrifice and *on God's behalf* makes.

And, as though this amazing show of authority were not enough, Jesus ups the ante. They sit there. They do not say a word. But Jesus, he will speak. He has said something that sounds like the ravings of a lunatic (2:5); he will say something ever more seemingly insane. Look at **2:8–12**:

> And immediately Jesus, perceiving in his spirit that they thus questioned within themselves, said to them, "Why do you question these things in your hearts? Which is easier, to say to the paralytic, 'Your sins are forgiven,' or to say, 'Rise, take up your bed and walk'? But that you may know that the Son of Man has authority on earth to forgive sins"— he said to the paralytic—"I say to you, rise, pick up your bed, and go home." And he rose and immediately picked up his bed and went out before them all, so that they were all amazed and glorified God, saying, "We never saw anything like this!"

The scribes, and the crowd, have never heard anything like what Jesus has said. But now, after the miracle, they have never *seen* anything like this.

---

5   More literally their question can be rendered: "Who is able to forgive sins if not one, God?" Cf. Joel Williams, "The nominative ὁ θεός ['the God'] stands in apposition to εἷς ['one'] to clarify who is the one, and the only one, who can forgive sins: God alone"; *Mark*, EGGNT (Nashville: B&H Academic, 2020), 47. And the phrase εἷς ὁ θεός is likely an echo of the Shema (κύριος ὁ θεὸς ἡμῶν κύριος εἷς ἐστιν, Deut. 6:4 LXX), as pointed out by Joel Marcus, *Mark*, AB 27, 2 vols. (New York: Doubleday, 2000), 1:222.

The whole scene is spectacular. We do not know whether Jesus is omniscient when he reads their minds or just a good observer of people (reading their body language or into their mutterings). Either way, he gets to the issue he has raised. He perceives (2:8) that they are thinking that what he has just said is blasphemous. Only God can forgive sins. Who does this *man* think he is—God? In verses 9–12 Jesus is going to lay all his cards on the table in front of this packed house.

How so? He plays the role of the philosopher and then the physician. First, the philosopher. Using an a fortiori argument (if something more difficult can be achieved, then this guarantees the validity of the claim of something less difficult), he asks the religious elite: "Which is easier, to say to the paralytic, 'Your sins are forgiven,' or to say, 'Rise, take up your bed and walk'?" (2:9). Their answer would be our answer. It is easier to say, like a Catholic priest in a confessional booth, "I absolve you of your sins," than to make a man laid out on a stretcher get up and walk home. Even the wicked "faith" healers today do not attempt this one. So the odds are two million to one on Jesus' next saying "Rise, take up your bed and walk" and *then* demonstrating that he is not just hot air. Ah, but surprise, surprise, he bets against the odds and beats the odds. "'But that you may know that the Son of Man has authority on earth to forgive sins'—he said to the paralytic—'I say to you, rise, pick up your bed, and go home.' And he rose and immediately picked up his bed and went out before them all" (2:10–12).

I love this miracle, and I love the Miracle Man. This is not a tender miracle, as the last one was: "He stretched out his hand and touched" (1:41) the incredibly unclean leper. This is an audacious show of authority. He calls himself "the Son of Man." He speaks of his authority to forgive sins. He gives the paralytic three direct commands ("I say to you"): "Rise, pick up your bed, and go home." Does he think he is the divine being described in Daniel 7? Yes, he does. Does he think he is God's representative on earth to forgive whoever's sins he wants to forgive? Yes, he does. "Through the Son of Man, God's heavenly forgiveness has now come to earth."[6] Does he think he has resurrection power? (No one in the history of the world has ever seen a paralyzed man stand up and walk away!) Yes, he does. He has resurrection power. He can recreate the heavens and the earth, if he wants to—and one day he will do so.

6   Mark L. Strauss, *Mark*, ZECNT (Grand Rapids, MI: Zondervan, 2014), 124. Cf. Eckhard J. Schnabel, "The phrase *on earth* does not limit the authority that Jesus claims to have, but underlines the boldness of his claim: forgiveness is now not exclusively a heavenly function, the prerogative of God in heaven, but is exercised *on earth* because of the presence of the Son of Man who, according to Daniel 7:13–14, was to receive from God authority over the earth"; *Mark: An Introduction and Commentary*, TNTC (Downers Grove, IL: IVP Academic, 2017), 69.

But this display of authority is not just Jesus' sending out the full fleet of the oceanic creatures to fight for him (Leviathan and the like) or commanding the air forces of angels to swoop down and destroy. It is the ultimate picture of what he has come to do. He has come to forgive sins. And, to God, the forgiveness offered in Jesus is a mighty power. It is a power that says to a paralytic, rise up and walk out.

Their Ironic Astonishment

Look at the final part of the final verse: "And he rose and immediately picked up his bed and went out before them all, so that they were all amazed and glorified God, saying, 'We never saw anything like this!'" (2:12).

Let me say something positive and negative about the crowd and the religious leaders, whom I take to be included in the "all" ("They were all amazed"). What is positive is their show of excitement. Perhaps you can think of a better word to express their astonishment ("They were all amazed"), their worship ("And glorified God"), and their corporate confession ("We never saw anything like this!").

What then is negative about their reaction? Two subtle details, one from the text and one from the context. It is right to glorify God, but it would also be right to praise Jesus, as that is part of the point he has proven. Only God can forgive sins. Jesus demonstrates that he too can forgive sins. Thus, both Father and Son should be glorified. Read Revelation 4, then 5: "Worthy are you, our Lord and God to receive . . . honor" (4:11); "Worthy is the Lamb who was slain to receive . . . honor" (5:12). The other negative has to do with how this first reaction to Jesus by the crowds, but especially by the religious leaders, is ironic. It is ironic because this Gospel ends with the religious leaders' sentencing him to death for blasphemy (the high priest said, "'You have heard his blasphemy. What is your decision?' And they all condemned him as deserving death," 14:64) and the crowd's chanting "Crucify him" (15:14).

Recently I watched the movie *The Gathering Storm*, based on Winston Churchill's book of that same title, which recounts his leadership before the Second World War. In the early 1940s Churchill could see that storm of war on the horizon. Similarly, in Mark, by the time we get to 3:6 ("The Pharisees went out and immediately held counsel with the Herodians against him, how to destroy him") the Evangelist has already signaled to his readers that the dark clouds are moving in on Jesus. In each of the five episodes in 2:1–3:6[7] opposition arises to Jesus' authority: "He is blaspheming! Who can forgive

---

7   Mark 2:1–12, 13–17, 18–22, 23–28; 3:1–6.

sins but God alone" (2:7); "Why does he eat with tax collectors and sinners?" (2:16); "Why do . . . your disciples . . . not fast?" (2:18); "Why are [the disciples] doing what is not lawful on the Sabbath?" (2:24); "The Pharisees went out and immediately held counsel with the Herodians against him, how to destroy him" (3:6). The storm is gathering. Mark knows it. We should know it. Jesus knows it, and he walks right into it. He does so because that is why he came. He is the Lord of the Sabbath (2:28). True. He is the bridegroom (2:19, 20). True as well. *And* just as he is the Son of Man who has authority to forgive sins (2:10), so too is he the great physician who came to call sinners (2:17). So true.

Calling All Sinners

In the next chapter we will explore the calling of an unrighteous rogue, Levi the tax collector. In this chapter, however, I want us to think about Larry Nasser, the sinner sentenced to 175 years in prison for his horrendous crimes. Do you think he is beyond the reach of God? We might hesitate, but the answer is no. Were Levi, Zacchaeus, the thief on the cross, the Roman centurion who crucified Christ, or Saul of Tarsus (who murdered Christians) beyond God's reach? No. God is a holy God, and he will right every wrong. He will punish all evil. God is also a merciful God, a God who sent his own Son to die for all our sins, a God who delights in saving sinners, even the chief of sinners, even still today.

Do you remember Jeffrey Dahmer? What an unforgettable monster! Dahmer was a serial killer. But he was not just a serial killer. He murdered his victims in the most gruesome and grotesque ways imaginable. Most of us know the details of his wicked deeds. But do you know the end of his life story? It is just as disturbing, in a very different way.

While in prison Dahmer was sent books and tracts on the Christian gospel. He read them. Over time, he began to meet with a local pastor. Dahmer himself writes about how he came to grips with how he was a sinner and accountable before a holy God. In a television interview with Stone Philips he said, "I've . . . come to believe that the Lord Jesus Christ is truly God, and I believe that I, as well as everyone else, will be accountable to him." In that same interview he called Jesus his "Lord and Savior." From all accounts—his own, his father's, the pastor's—he came to a saving faith in Christ. He believed and was baptized. The most notorious sinner in my lifetime was baptized in the name of the Father, Son, and Holy Spirit! Then, one day after attending chapel, a fellow inmate attacked him. He lived. Soon after, while working in the prison gym, he was attacked again. This time he died. Then what? Did the appalling Jeffrey Dahmer enter into the presence of a holy God? He tortured and killed people—lots of people. And sure, he professed faith in Christ, but he died so shortly after. He hardly had a chance to prove himself worthy of the kingdom.

Do you believe in the forgiveness of sins? Do you believe that the forgiveness of sin offered in Jesus Christ is God's supreme accomplishment? God's greatest grace! Do you believe that what "makes the gospel of Christ so sweet," in Rachael Denhollander's words, is that "it extends grace and hope and mercy where none should be found"?

Critical Questions Answered While Sipping New Wine with Old Sinners

MARK 2:13-22

I came not to call the righteous, but sinners.
Mark 2:17

"Romeo, Romeo, wherefore art thou Romeo?" "Who is Godot, and when is he coming?" "Mirror, mirror on the wall, who is the fairest one of all?" "Anybody home, McFly?" "What has it got in its nasty little pocketses?" "What's up, Doc?" "Where's the beef?" "Pardon me, do you have any Grey Poupon?" "How do you spell relief?" "Who you gonna call?"

From classic literature to famous books, movies, shows, and advertisements, questions are used to draw our attention, reveal character, invoke laughter, create suspense, provoke conflict, and intensify tension. The Bible, like all good literature, is full of questions. There are over three thousand questions—questions intended to make us ponder the person and powers of God and our relationship with him. "Shall not the Judge of all the earth do what is just?" (Gen. 18:25). "Is there no balm in Gilead?" (Jer. 8:22). "What is man that you are mindful of him?" (Ps. 8:4). "Where were you when I laid the foundation of the earth?" (Job 38:4). "What must I do to be saved?" (Acts 16:30). "If God is for us, who can be against us?" (Rom. 8:31).

The Gospel of Mark features over one hundred questions. Jesus asks questions, such as "Who do you say that I am?" (Mark 8:29) and "My God, my God, why have you forsaken me?" (15:34). The twelve ask questions, such as "Who then is this, that even the wind and the sea obey him?" (4:41) and "How can one feed these people with bread here in this desolate place?" (8:4). The demons ask questions, such as "Have you come to destroy us?" (1:24) and "What have you to do with me, Jesus, Son of the Most High God?" (5:7). And the religious and political powers of the day ask Jesus questions, such as "Is it lawful to pay taxes to Caesar, or not?" (12:14) and "By what authority are you doing these things?" (11:28).

In Mark 2:13–22 Jesus is asked two critical questions. I use the word *critical* in two ways: first, in the sense of negative criticism; second, in a positive sense of obtaining important, or critical, information. The scribes ask the first question, "Why does he eat with tax collectors and sinners?" (2:16); the people ask the second, "Why do John's disciples and the disciples of the Pharisees fast, but your disciples do not fast?" (2:18). Notice that both of these are food-related questions. Why eat with sinners? Why not fast from food? Notice also that what is recorded in verses 15–22 takes place on one day and in and around one place—the dinner table in Levi's house. But before we get to the dinner party and the two questions, Mark first presents quite a provocative prelude.

Prelude to the Party

In Mark **2:13–14** we read of Jesus: "He went out again beside the sea, and all the crowd was coming to him, and he was teaching them. And as he passed by, he saw Levi the son of Alphaeus sitting at the tax booth, and he said to him, 'Follow me.' And he rose and followed him." Once again Mark begins a pericope by featuring Jesus' priorities. Jesus moves from the private miracle in Peter's house back to his public ministry. Jesus wants to tour the towns around the Sea of Galilee so that he might continue to proclaim the kingdom. "He went out again beside the sea, and all the crowd was coming to him, and he was teaching them." His popularity has not shifted his priorities. Let that be a lesson for every Christian church. We should be known for our teaching ministries. "And he was *teaching* them."

Beyond that detail, notice who is coming to Jesus and who is not. "All the crowd was coming to him" (2:13), while Levi was "sitting at the tax booth" (2:14).[1] What a striking juxtaposition! The phrase "all the crowd" obviously does not mean everyone; in light of verse 14 it might mean "everyone but one."[2] There are perhaps two reasons for Levi's uninterest. First, he apparently has no need. Tax collectors are wealthy. And he must be in good health. Second, he has no desire to listen to the message of this holy man. He has

---

1   Jesus is likely on "the great caravan road (Via Maris, or the Great Trunk Road)" which "leads from Damascus down to the harbor" on the Sea of Galilee and where "Herod has set up a tollbooth to charge fees from both the foreign merchants and the people of the area who took their wares into the city," and "the right to charge tolls" would have been "leased out to the highest bidder." Bo Giertz, *The New Testament Devotional Commentary: Volume 1: Matthew, Mark, Luke*, trans. Bror Erickson (Irving, CA: 1517 Publishing, 2021), 152.

2   "Levi took no notice of him, inquired not about him, and had no thought of leaving his employ and going after him." John Gill, *Exposition of the Bible*, quoted in *CHSB*, 1475.

no desire to submit to the reign of Jesus' righteous rule—to repent and believe. Yet, as we know, he underestimated our Lord's love for sinners and the sovereign power of Christ's call. "And as he passed by, he saw Levi the son of Alphaeus sitting at the tax booth, and he said to him, 'Follow me.' And he rose and followed him" (2:14). Luke adds that Levi "left everything behind" (Luke 5:28 NASB).[3]

Mark sets up Levi's life-changing moment with the clause "and as he passed by" (Mark 2:14). Jesus is passing by to perform a miracle as miraculous as his words to the leper ("Be clean," 1:41) or the paralytic ("Rise, pick up your bed, and go home," 2:11). Our Lord, and soon to be Levi's, said to the man sitting, perhaps counting his coins, "Follow me."

Now, before we see whether he follows or not, picture the frame frozen on Levi's startled expression. Jesus' eyes ("he saw," 2:14) meet Levi's. A name like Levi is not only undoubtedly Jewish; it is as religious as it gets. He is likely a member of the tribe of Levi,[4] the priestly class. In the OT and at this time in history, the only men who could mediate between a holy God and sinful people were the Levitical priests. Levi, also called Matthew, is from good religious stock.

But something has happened. He is a child of the covenant, but he is no keeper of the covenant. He has broken God's law through his very occupation. Levi is sitting at the tax booth (basically a toll booth where he collects tariffs) because he is a tax collector. Big deal, you might think. So he works for the IRS. No. The IRS may have its incidents of corruption, and certainly to most of us getting an unexpected notice from the Internal Revenue Service is disconcerting. But Levi does not work for the IRS. He works for Rome. The Roman Empire had its immorality issues. There are plenty of books and movies about that. But worse than the big boss (Caesar in Rome), Levi works for Rome's pawn in Galilee (Herod Antipas). You might remember Herod's father: Herod the Great. You can read about him in Levi's Gospel (Matthew 2). Near the time of Jesus' birth this diabolical despot ordered the slaughter of every baby boy in Bethlehem under the age of two. This not-great man raised a no-good son. And Levi is under Herod Antipas's evil thumb.

But how does someone with the name Levi end up working for Mr. Caesar and Mr. Antipas? The same way a bunch of good Italian Catholics end up

---

3   Luke's aorist participle (Gk. *katalipōn*) followed by the imperfect indicative (*ēkolouthei*), stresses "his decisive break from his old life" and "his continuing life of discipleship." I. Howard Marshall, *The Gospel of Luke: A Commentary on the Greek Text*, NIGTC (Grand Rapids, MI: Eerdmans, 1978), 219.

4   "Most people named Levi in the first century were Levites." Mark L. Strauss, *Mark*, ZECNT (Grand Rapids, MI: Zondervan, 2014), 130.

working for Al Capone. Baby steps toward sin. Levi gives in to this compromise, then that one, and then *that one*. He makes a deal or a hit that indicates to everyone that there is no turning back from this lifestyle. He is not breaking bad; he has broken bad. He is the one man in town that everyone knows and fears. Do not mess with Levi, or you might just find your thumbs served as fish bait or your brother's head buried under the stone floor of that new lakeside development.

Levi is working for the underworld in the above-board world. He has Rome's complete backing to rob people. He is the most immoral person a pious Jew could imagine. He is thought of in this way because he extorts and defrauds his own people, even the poor among them. The tax is low enough. Perhaps Rome wants the cost of a cup of coffee to cross the sea and bring in some goods to sell. But Rome encourages its collectors to take a cut. Charge whatever you want. So Levi charges twenty bucks a boat. What an inordinate surcharge! A handsome living for an ugly business.

Do you remember the story of the conversion of Zacchaeus? That little man was a big sinner. He was a "chief tax collector" (Luke 19:2). However, after he encountered Jesus, he repented, in part, by giving four times the amount back to those he had defrauded (see Luke 19:8). There he admits two facts: first, that he defrauded people and, second, that this rich man made his riches on the backs of his fellow Jews. Tax collectors were rich. They were shady. Worst of all, they were traitors. They worked for the oppressive establishment. They went against everything it meant to be a good Jew. This is why "the Mishnah prohibits even receiving alms from a tax collector at his office since the money was presumed to have been gained illegally (m. B. Qam. 10.1);" this is why, when a tax collector "entered a house, all that was in it became unclean (m. Ṭehar. 7:6)."[5] Moreover, "he was disqualified as a judge or a witness in a court session, was excommunicated from the synagogue, and in the eyes of the community his disgrace extended to his family."[6]

With that background in place on the name "Levi" and the occupation "tax collector," here are two applications we need to read correctly Jesus' command ("Follow me") and Levi's response ("And he rose and followed him").

First, know that conversion to Christ is a resurrection from the dead. Levi "rose." Sure, he rises from the chair at the tax collector's booth. But that little resurrection is caused not by his own self-determination. ("You know, Mrs. Levi, I was thinking just this morning, I ought to get out of this racket. We

5   Strauss, *Mark*, 130.
6   William L. Lane, *The Gospel of Mark*, NICNT (Grand Rapids, MI: Eerdmans, 1974), 101–2.

have enough money, don't we? Let's just retire to Jericho, join a synagogue, tithe our savings, and live the good and righteous life.") No! He is sitting there because he wants the next squeeze, the next dime from some middle-class fisherman like Peter. But then what happens? Life is breathed into dead bones! "Lazarus, come out" (John 11:43). With one call Levi, a man "dead in [his] trespasses and sins" (Eph. 2:1), rises to new life.

If you think you came to Christ because you were cleverer than others, think again. If you think you came to Christ because you were more righteous than others, think again. You came to Christ because Christ called you like he called Levi. He said, "Follow me," and there was something inside you (the breath of God; his efficacious grace) that made you get up.

So, first, conversion to Christ is a resurrection from the dead. Know that!

My second application is that the call of Christ moves us after Christ. We get up and we go after. Jesus said to Levi, "'Follow me.' And he rose and followed him."

In the last two chapters I have spoken of faith as movement. True Christian faith involves movement! For someone to say, "Why, yes, I am a Christian because five years ago I raised my hand to receive Christ," does not cut it. Have you moved since then? Like the paralyzed man, have you moved? Like Peter and Andrew, James and John, have you moved? Like Levi, have you moved? Did you follow? Are you following? The call of Christ moves us after Christ. We get up and we go after. We follow.

Why Eat with Sinners?

Let us *move* on in our text. From that provocative prelude Mark whisks us away to a dinner party at Levi's house. "And as [Jesus] reclined at table in [Levi's] house, many tax collectors and sinners were reclining with Jesus and his disciples, for there were many who followed him" (**2:15**). On this life-changing day Levi's first step is to leave the past, his second is to follow Jesus, and his third is to introduce his bad company to his good Lord. (Those are some good steps for us to follow as well.)

Grasp the scandal of this scene. This is a formal meal. We know that from the fact that the men around the table are reclining. A short table is in the middle. They are lying on sides or stomachs, with their feet stretched behind them. They lean on one elbow as they use their other arm to feast on what is in front of them. Table fellowship in the ancient Near East was the most intimate and personal expression of friendship. Levi is now Jesus' friend, and Jesus is now a friend of this sinner. (What a friend we have in Jesus!) And Levi's purpose for this party is to invite his friends to meet the friend of sinners, if they have not already done so (see the end of 2:15). He knows first-hand that no one—even the most uninterested or undeserved sinner—is but an instant away from experiencing the sovereign call of Christ.

In verses 15–17 the two most repeated words are "tax collectors" (3x) and "sinners" (4x). Jesus reclines at table with "many tax collectors and sinners" (2:15). The word "many" is striking, especially in context. The last time the word was used was in verse 2: "And *many* were gathered together, so that there was no more room, not even at the door." Mark gives the impression that Levi's house is packed. The word "sinners" here does not mean your regular sinful human being ("We are all sinners"). Rather, it implies a criminal class of people. The term "sinners" is usually connected with "tax collectors" or "prostitutes." I do not think prostitutes were at this meal. It was likely all men. But I do think people like prostitutes were there; that is, people who made a lawless living. As Mark Strauss says, "These were the unscrupulous riffraff, the scoundrels of first-century Jewish life."[7]

This background should make sense of the question that comes from the purity police: "And the scribes of the Pharisees, when they saw that he was eating with sinners and tax collectors, said [not directly to Jesus but] to his disciples, 'Why does he eat with tax collectors and sinners?'" (2:16).

The "scribes of the Pharisees" are experts in OT law and rabbinic oral traditions. So they are genuinely shocked by the situation. They wonder why Jesus would recline with the reprehensible, dine with the detestable, communicate with the unclean, and sip wine with such swine. Jesus will tell them why. In 2:17 he provides a proverb with parallel contrasts: "And when Jesus heard it, he said to them, 'Those who are well have no need of a physician, but those who are sick. I came not to call the righteous, but sinners.'" Jesus depicts himself as a doctor. A doctor hangs out with sick people because his job is to cure the sick. This is why Jesus has accepted Levi's invitation to dinner. He is happy to use Levi's dinner table for his operating table, to perform some surgery of the soul.

What Jesus says in verse 17 is so important not only for us to grasp but for us to apply. We can live out verse 17 in three ways.

First, we should not be spiritual snobs. Like the Pharisees, we too can neglect the weightier matters of the law—like justice and mercy (love for others, even the unlovely)—for our own human-made traditions. Do we have an unspoken church dress code that, if someone breaks, we stare at him and whisper among ourselves? Do we care more about the pipe organ than we do the poor? Do we have a class system for sins—the respectable sins (like worry)

7 Strauss, *Mark*, 131.

are permissible and the disrespectable ones (like swearing) are not? We must remember, and constantly remind ourselves, that Jesus was no respecter of persons. That is, he did not choose from the religious class or the upper class when he formed the twelve apostles. And, while it is true that some from the religious and rich have followed and do follow him, his pattern throughout history has been what we see here in our text. God chooses the unlikely, the despised, and the weak so as to shame the smart and strong and successful, and so that no one may boast before him (see 1 Cor. 1:25–31).

Second, following our Lord's lead, let us employ incarnational tactics. That is, let us be intentional about the places we go to minister. Jesus spent the majority of his time in holy places—synagogues, the temple, and the homes of pious Jews. But he also, as he demonstrates here, hung out with the unholy. Missionary C. T. Studd said, "Some want to live within the sound of Church or Chapel bell; I want to run a rescue shop within a yard of hell."[8] Jesus was running a rescue shop that day in Levi's house.

We need to follow that pattern, as best we can. Of course, we need to know ourselves. If you are a man who struggles with alcohol, don't start a new ministry at the local public house. If you are a woman who struggles with same-sex attraction, do not start a ministry to prostitutes outside the casino. If you are a teenager who struggles with a sense of belonging, do not start a ministry to the neighborhood gang. Be wise. Know yourself. Know that you are not Jesus. He resisted all temptations. We cannot and do not always do that.

But, that said, an important mission of the church is beyond the church walls. We gather on Sunday so we might be encouraged to scatter on Monday through Saturday. We gather not to celebrate our separateness from the world but to remind ourselves of our mission to the world. Most church's mercy ministries target some of the best places to meet people—people in need physically and financially, but also so often spiritually. So think about serving at a homeless shelter, visiting those in prison or on parole, or helping on the HIV/AIDS ward at the hospital; in these places and with such people you will find a receptivity level far higher than that of the soccer moms by the field or the business moguls at the country club. Why? Because those who are messed up or have messed up usually know and admit something of the mess, whereas those who have never been convicted of crime, served time, or lost loved ones due to foolish decisions do not see the need for help. Why go to a doctor if one is (seemingly) healthy?

8 Quoted in Odd Arne Westad, *Restless Empire: China and the World Since 1750* (New York: Basic Books, 2012), 190.

Third, and most theologically foundational, let us remember that Jesus alone sovereignly saves. The word "I" in the phrase "I came not to call" (Mark 2:17) looms large. We must go out into the world with the message of salvation, but our only hope of success is that we believe in irresistible grace, that the Lord of the universe, who said "Let light shine out of darkness" at creation, is the same sovereign who shines in the human heart at re-creation "to give the light of the knowledge of the glory of God in the face of Jesus Christ" (2 Cor. 4:6).

Why Not Fast?

In Mark 2:15–22 Jesus is asked two critical questions. We have looked at the first question: Why eat with sinners? Let us turn our attention next to the second, asked in **2:18**: "Now John's disciples and the Pharisees were fasting [on that day]. And people came and said to him, 'Why do John's disciples and the disciples of the Pharisees fast, but your disciples [and *you*] do not fast?'" The first question came from the religious leaders, "the scribes of the Pharisees" (2:16). This second question comes from the laity ("people," 2:18). The people here might be just as confused as the scribes are as to why Jesus is supping with sinners, but they are certainly confused as to why he is eating on a day when he should be fasting. They think Jesus and his disciples should be fasting because, in following a man-made law,[9] this was what pious Jews of Jesus' day did. They fasted on Mondays and Thursdays. Only the tax collectors and sinners celebrated Margarita Mondays and Taco Thursdays.

In **2:19–22** Jesus will clear up their confusion by offering a few everyday analogies to help explain and justify his and his disciples' behavior.

And Jesus said to them [he has a question of his own!], "Can the wedding guests fast while the bridegroom is with them? As long as they have the bridegroom with them, they cannot fast. The days will come when the bridegroom is taken away from them, and then they will fast in that day. No one sews a piece of unshrunk cloth on an old garment. If he does, the patch tears away from it, the new from the old, and a worse tear is made. And no one puts new wine into old wineskins. If he does,

---

9   "The Mosaic law established only one fast, on the Day of Atonement (Lev 16:29, 31; 23:27–32; Num 29:7; cf. Acts 27:9), but Zech 8:19 mentions four fasts during the postexilic period—in the fourth, fifth, seventh, and tenth months of the Jewish year (cf. Zech 7:5). A fifth fast, associated with the festival of Purim, is established in Esth 9:31. Pious Pharisees of Jesus' day were even more scrupulous, fasting twice a week, on Monday and Thursday (Luke 18:12; *Did.* 8.1; b. Ta῾an. 12a; cf. m. Ta῾an. 2.9). [On the day depicted in our passage] the disciples of the Pharisees were probably observing one of these biweekly fasts." Strauss, *Mark*, 138.

the wine will burst the skins—and the wine is destroyed, and so are the skins. But new wine is for fresh wineskins."

The first analogy is that of a wedding and the groom and his guests. Jewish weddings lasted seven days. The food was plentiful and the wine abundant. At that event no one says to the waiter as he brought around the finger foods, "Sorry, no thanks. I'm fasting." It is a wedding. Everyone eats and drinks at a wedding!

What is especially interesting about Jesus' statement is that, in the OT, God is called the bridegroom, and thus both the Pharisees and other Jews "would never have called the Messiah 'the Bridegroom.'"[10] But, quite provokingly, Jesus uses this title for himself. The reason all those who follow Jesus can eat on any day they want, despite the tradition of the elders, is that God in the flesh is in the house. This seemingly simple meal at Levi's is a foretaste of the messianic banquet at the end of history—the marriage supper of the Lamb (Rev. 19:6–10). When Jesus is "taken away" (Mark 2:20; likely referring to Jesus' arrest and crucifixion [cf. Isa. 53:8] or when he returns to the Father after his ascension), then his disciples will fast. They will fast not to follow some man-made rules but to express the hunger they have for the return of Christ. We fast because we desire that eschatological feast. Because we long for the Lamb!

Three Analogies and Two Parables

With all that Jesus says, one has to imagine that some of what our Lord teaches goes right over everyone's heads. "Wait—bridegroom? Who is the bridegroom? Why would he be taken away? What wedding is he talking about? When is this wedding—now or in the future, or both?" Similarly, Jesus' second answer must have been, at points, just as perplexing. In 2:21–22 Jesus offers three analogies in two short parables that make the same point, namely, the irrationality of putting something new into something old.

The first analogy is that of a person trying to patch up an old garment—something like, in our context, a pair of jeans. No one with two wits about him, Jesus teaches, uses a new patch (a not yet shrunk patch) on old jeans, because as soon as the patch shrinks (and it will once it is washed and dried) it will tear away from the old. The jeans will be ruined. You might as well throw them out. Or sell them at the latest designer jeans shop.

The second analogy makes the same point. New wine is not poured into old, dry, and brittle goat skins, because as soon as the fermentation begins

10 Giertz, *New Testament Devotional*, 153.

the wine expands and the skins crack.[11] The wine is wasted and the wineskins rendered inoperable.

Both the "unshrunk cloth" (the new patch) and the "new wine" represent Jesus' new message, namely, that the kingdom of heaven has arrived on earth with his coming, so repent and believe (1:15). Remember what the crowd said in 1:27: "What is this? A new teaching with authority!" That new teaching can only be received by proper vessels. The person and mission and teachings of Jesus, if poured into the traditions of the Pharisees, will crack and spill out onto the ground. But, if they are poured into receptive hearts, perhaps like those of the tax collectors and sinners around that table, they will settle perfectly into their place. They will keep and grow.

Therefore, the point of these twin parables is plain: Jesus is saying that his coming changes everything. The new life he offers in the gospel of the new covenant (Jer. 31:31–34) is absolutely incompatible with the institutions, structures, and obligations of Pharisaical Judaism.

So there you have it. Questions asked and answered. Here in Mark 2:15–22, while supping with sinners, Jesus answers two critical questions. Question 1: Why eat with sinners? Answer: The sick need a doctor. Jesus has come to heal the spiritually unwell. Question 2: Why not fast? Answer: For those around the table, who are willing to repent and believe, fasting is inappropriate. New life has come to Levi and to many in his house. A wedding-like celebration is the only reasonable response.

Growing Up

Each year my family receives a Christmas letter from our friends Karil and Karl. As usual, we get a brief update on their children. Here is what Karil wrote when one of their daughters was four years old:

> Ingrid has followed the lead of Elsa with her love of dance. She flits about the house and yard and loves to make an artistic entrance . . . even at bedtime. Bedtime is incomplete if there isn't sufficient time to put on her "regalia" (a princess dress over her PJ's with various accessories) before reading a bedtime story. She loves to swing in our yard, snuggle at bedtime, read about volcanoes and weather, go on "hiking adventures" in

---

11 "Such wineskins are still used in the Middle East, for example, by water merchants in the streets. They consist of an animal hide that is prepared on the inside and sown up. The throat or one of the legs can be strung and used as a bottleneck. At first, the skin has much elasticity and can expand, but in a year, they become stiff and brittle." Giertz, *New Testament Devotional Commentary*, 153.

the yard with Elsa holding sticks to stave off "predators," and give some of the tightest bear hugs of anyone I know. Ingrid wants to be a ballerina, pipe organist, or volcanologist (as long as she can wear something pretty) when she grows up.

We do not know what Levi, as a boy, wanted to be when he grew up. Perhaps he wanted to be a rabbi, or a priest at the big temple in the big city. I doubt he wanted to be a tax collector. But, through one bad decision after another, he found himself out of fellowship with God and his people—until one day, when Jesus offered him a fresh start, an invitation to join him on the journey of a lifetime. And, by God's grace, he took it. A fresh start. A new life! Salvation from all his sin.

I do not know where you are. You are reading a Bible commentary right now. That is a good sign! However, I do not know what idols you might have in your hearts. You might very well be sitting in your own personal "tax booth" and sitting complacently with your love of money and your involvement with the darker side of this world. If so, let me tell you that Jesus offers you now the same hand of fellowship that he did to this wicked tax collector. "Follow me." He wants you to follow him. And I pray that you, by God's sovereign grace, feel compelled to heed that call. For, I assure you, not only a joyful journey but a great feast awaits you.

Lord of the Sabbath

MARK 2:23-3:6

The Son of Man is lord even of the Sabbath.
Mark 2:27

Why are car dealerships closed on Sundays? Why is Chick-fil-A closed as well? Are you honestly telling me, in our open 24/7 culture, that if a rich man with $100,000 and some spare change burning in his pocket wanted to buy a new Jaguar F-Type R Coupe and some Chick-n-minis™ on Sunday that he could not? That is right! Those shops are closed.

Why? The Sabbath command: "Remember the Sabbath day, to keep it holy. Six days you shall labor, and do all your work, but the seventh day is a Sabbath to the Lord your God. On it you shall not do any work" (Ex. 20:8–10). The reason certain companies close on Sunday is to honor that ancient command. Chick-fil-A is a Christian-owned company, and it has intentionally decided to close its doors, despite the potential loss in profit, so that its workers can rest and so as to allow them to attend, if they desire, worship services. Car dealerships in Illinois (my state), and fourteen other states, are closed due to laws enacted ages ago to enforce Christian religious standards. These laws are disapprovingly called "blue laws." The first blue law was enacted in the Virginia colony; it required that every citizen attend church on Sunday. That law is now off the books. But the repeal of such laws is not as old as you might think. Just seventy years ago, in most states there were laws forbidding leisure and sporting activities on Sundays, including clam digging and cockfighting. I cannot imagine a Sunday afternoon without a good clam dig! Can you?

Whatever we make of the old blue laws or a new company's countercultural convictions, we must admit that both the sacredness of time, a foundational ethic for ancient Israel,[1] and the authority of Scripture, the foundational

---

1 "Most of the world's religions venerate sacred places: Islam honors Mecca, Hinduism the Ganges River, and Shintoism the island of Japan. Judaism also venerated Jerusalem and especially the temple as sacred space, but it venerated something beyond it, and perhaps above it: *time,*

belief for God's people throughout the ages, are little valued by most people today. In a world where the concept of sacred time has been consumed by consumerism and the divine command to set apart one day from the rest in order to rest has been run over by our fast-paced lives, this passage before us is difficult for us to get our heads around. We might wonder, "Why are the Pharisees so upset about what happened on that particular day?" What starts with an honest question about why Jesus' disciples are plucking wheat on the Sabbath (Mark 2:23) concludes with the Pharisees' being so upset about Jesus' view of and behavior on the Sabbath that they immediately leave the synagogue and hold a counsel with their enemies—the Herodians—about how to destroy Jesus. Well, as we seek to walk from their world to ours, let us discover what all the fuss is about.

The Opposition's Next Critical Question

Like Mark 2:13–22, Mark 2:23–3:6 records another conflict story, one that features question and answer time with Jesus. Starting in **2:23–24**, we read this about Jesus and his disciples: "One Sabbath he was going through the grainfields, and as they made their way, his disciples began to pluck heads of grain. And the Pharisees were saying to him, 'Look, why are they doing what is not lawful on the Sabbath?'" The problem, from the Pharisees' perspective, is not *what* the disciples were doing but *when* they were doing it. According to OT law (Lev. 19:9; Deut. 24:19) the edges of fields were to be left unharvested so the poor or travelers could do precisely what the disciples are doing. The issue is not the eighth commandment but the fourth.

But why do the Pharisees think the disciples are breaking the Sabbath command by partaking in the original breakfast of champions? There is not a verse in the Bible that teaches that plucking the heads of grain constitutes work. The command in Exodus 20 speaks of resting from what one does for a living. The only other activities that constitute work in the OT are kindling fires in one's home (Ex. 35:3; cf. Num. 15:32), carrying burdens (Jer. 17:21–27), and buying and selling (see Neh. 10:31; 13:15–17; Amos 8:4–5). Therefore, the disciples are not breaking any God-ordained law. Rather, they are breaking a man-made law!

Before, during, and after the time of Jesus, pious Jews such as the Pharisees developed an elaborate system of religious regulations so as to build a

---

the Sabbath." James R. Edwards, *The Gospel according to Mark*, PNTC (Grand Rapids, MI: Eerdmans, 2002), 93.

hedge of protection around God's law. They categorized thirty-nine different classes of work to make sure no one came close to breaking that one commandment (see m. Šabb. 7:2). So, can one whiten wool? What does the OT say? Nothing. What do the Pharisees say? Certainly not. How about hunting gazelles? No. Extinguishing a flame? No. Tying a loose knot? No. Sewing a stitch? Fine. Two stitches? No. Writing a letter? Fine. Writing two letters. No. Separating two threads? No. Carrying any article of food larger than a dried fig? No. Plucking heads of grain? Obviously, no! The Pharisees made much work of not working.

Now, before we take a look at Jesus' rebuttal, let us first take a look at ourselves. Recently, someone came up to me after a church service and told me a joke. Three little old ladies were sitting in the worship service and the pastor was preaching on sin. He addressed stealing, he condemned lying, and so forth. On each occasion one of the women would say, "Right on, Pastor. Preach it!" And then he said, "Now, I'd next like to talk about the sin of gossip." One of the women turned to the other and said, "Well, now he has quit preaching and gone to meddling."

Let me meddle with us a little. The Pharisees took a beautiful commandment that was meant to be a blessing to people and to serve as a sign of Israel's unique relationship with God, and they buried that beauty and those blessings under dozens of unscriptural burdens. They made Sabbath keeping a heavy load to bear—so much so, as Calvin puts it, that "one could scarcely move a finger without making the conscience to tremble."[2] And in doing so they disobeyed Deuteronomy 4:2: "You shall not add to the word that I command you, nor take from it." We can easily do the same. But we ought not to. We need to hold to the line of Scripture—not adding to it or taking from it.

We are often tempted to require more than the Scriptures, venturing into religious pietism and expressing a zeal that becomes a kind of legalism. We judge others who do not maintain our extra-Biblical traditions and standards. In so doing, we add to the Scriptures. We can also be tempted to dip below the line into liberalism and pragmatism, ignoring both the content and point of Scripture. In so doing, we subtract from the Scriptures.[3]

2   John Calvin, *A Harmony of the Gospels Matthew, Mark, and Luke*, vol. 2, trans. William Pringle (repr., Grand Rapids, MI: Eerdmans, 1993), 46.
3   See David Helm, "Staying on the Line," available at https://simeontrust.org/courses/first -principles.

As God's people we must commit ourselves to believing nothing more or less than what the Scriptures say. We must hold to and live out the truth, the whole truth, and nothing but the truth.

Immanuel's Interrogative Answer: Illustrated and Explained

In Mark 2:24 the Pharisees questioned the disciples' behavior: "Look, why are they doing what is not lawful on the Sabbath?" Then in **2:25–28** Jesus answers their question by questioning their understanding of the Bible and of his identity and authority.

> And he said to them, "Have you never read what David did, when he was in need and was hungry, he and those who were with him: how he entered the house of God, in the time of Abiathar the high priest, and ate the bread of the Presence, which it is not lawful for any but the priests to eat, and also gave it to those who were with him?" And he said to them, "The Sabbath was made for man [*anthrōpos*[4]], not man for the Sabbath. So the Son of Man is lord even of the Sabbath."

Jesus makes a number of shocking statements here. His illustration, given in verses 25–26, is shocking for two reasons. First, it is shocking that he starts with the words "Have you never read?" (2:25). This is a biting critique of these so-called Bible experts. It is like asking a group of Tolkien scholars, "Have you ever read that story about Bilbo Baggins?" Of course the Pharisees have read this story about David in 1 Samuel 21:1–6. But what they have not done is read it properly, especially in light of their present judgment against Jesus. For that story clearly proves Jesus' point in Mark 2:27, namely, that the Sabbath is intended for man's benefit.

The story is this. *On the Sabbath* David went into the tabernacle at Nob to ask the priest whether he could spare some bread for him and his hungry men. The only bread available was the bread of the Presence, the twelve consecrated loaves that were placed on the table in the tabernacle each Sabbath for priests alone to consume. The priest had a choice to make. Should he let common mercy and the king's authority (1 Sam. 21:2) override sacred ritual? Seeing their need and acknowledging David's authority, he gave them the "holy bread" (1 Sam. 21:6). Then, presumably, David and his disciples devoured the loaves.

---

4   The singular form *anthrōpos*, translated "man," is "used in a representative sense: 'people.'" Rodney J. Decker, *Mark 9–16: A Handbook on the Greek Text* (Waco, TX: Baylor University Press, 2014), 66.

Jesus has put on the hat of a philosopher (Mark 2:9) and a physician (2:17); now he plays the role of attorney. He presents this story about King David as legal precedent: if David's major breach of the letter of the law was not punished by God (the showbread is not so sacred that it cannot be used to feed the starving), then the disciples' so-called violation of Sabbath law should certainly not be condemned by the Pharisees.

Now, as stated above, Jesus' illustration here is shocking for two reasons. The first is that he scolds these scribes with a story from Scripture ("Have you never read?" 2:25). He uses the sword of the Spirit to cut off the ungodly traditions that the Pharisees have attached to God's holy command. The second reason is that Jesus makes a covert but certain claim that he is on par with David. His legal precedent holds up only if he is at least as exceptional as David. In fact, we might say greater than David, because David's men could justify their actions due to near starvation, while Jesus' disciples, having recently come from Levi's banquet (2:15), were hardly famished.[5] So here Jesus is not begging the question but begging *for* the question. He wants them to ask, "Who are you?" As we shall see, blind Bartimaeus is the first to *see* Jesus as "Son of David" (10:47, 48), and then the crowd in Jerusalem will as well (11:10). Jesus himself, in his final confrontation with the scribes, will make clear that he is both David's offspring and David's Lord (see 12:35–37).

Here then is where the next shocking claim comes in. Jesus says that "the Son of Man is lord even of the Sabbath" (2:28). Throughout Mark Jesus uses various self-designations, most recently "the bridegroom" (2:19–20). Here he calls himself "the Son of Man," a reference to the divine king prophesied in Daniel 7, the one whose "dominion is an everlasting dominion" and whose kingdom, like that promised to David's offspring, "shall not be destroyed" (Dan. 7:14; cf. 2 Sam. 7:12–13).[6]

Jesus has spoken with great authority before (Mark 1:17, 25, 41; 2:5, 10–11, 14), but never like this. He claims here to have authority over a command that dates back to the genesis of the world (also the exodus of Israel). He is "clearly

---

5   "The focus of the comparison . . . is not what one might or might not do on a Sabbath, on the basis of the actions of David and his companions, but upon the parallel drawn between David and Jesus. The issue is christological. If such practices on a Sabbath were condoned for David and his companions, how much more should actions done on the Sabbath be condoned in light of the uniqueness of Jesus." Francis J. Moloney, *The Gospel of Mark: A Commentary*, SP (Peabody, MA: Hendrickson, 2002), 69.

6   In Mark, Jesus as "the Son of Man" will suffer and die (8:31; 9:12, 31; 10:33, 45; 14:21, 41), but he will also rise from the dead (8:31; 9:9, 31) and come again "with great power and glory" (13:26; cf. 8:38). He has authority both over the Sabbath (2:28) and to forgive sins (2:10).

claiming to be equal with God, who had instituted the Sabbath."[7] The point, then, is plain but profound. If Jesus says it is acceptable for his five friends to pluck some grain, then it is acceptable. He is Lord of the Sabbath! He alone determines what is lawful or unlawful. The Pharisees, therefore, misunderstand both the letter and the spirit of the law, along with its ultimate intention. The Sabbath points to the Lord of the Sabbath, the one who grants rest to all who come to him, weary and heavy laden (see Matt. 11:28–30; Heb. 4:9–11).

Having explained Mark 2:25–28, I will offer three applications. First, let us be people of the Book. That is, let us search the Scriptures constantly to discern God's will for the church. All the great reformations throughout history have started with the question, Have you never read? They have offered a critique of the religious establishment that had moved away from the Word. Churches that stop reading and teaching the Bible, no matter their size or influence, will eventually go above or below the line of Scripture. They will no longer teach the truth, the whole truth, and nothing but the truth. We need to watch out that this does not happen to us, and we need to be as bold as our Lord was to say to such churches that God will judge those who add or subtract from his revelation.

Second, let us embrace the blessings of the Sabbath. In the third chapter of Charles Dickens's novel *Little Dorrit*, Mr. Arthur Clennam recalls the dour austerity that marked the observance of the Lord's Day, a day he hated as a child because his teachers threatened damnation if he failed to follow their rigid rules. And Dickens writes of "the interminable Sunday" of Arthur's youth before he went to boarding school,

> when his mother, stern of face and unrelenting of heart, would sit all day behind a Bible—bound . . . in the hardest, barest, and straightest board, with one dinted ornament on the cover like the drag of chain, and a wrathful sprinkling of red upon the edges of the leaves—as if it, of all books! were a fortification against sweetness of temper, natural affection, and gentle intercourse.

We must understand, acknowledge, and embrace that all ten of the Ten Commandments are blessings to us. It is a blessing to live in a home where parents are loved and obeyed ("Honor your father and your mother"). It is blessing to be in a marriage where vows are kept ("You shall not commit adultery"). It is a blessing to live in community where people respect each other's property

---

7   R. Alan Cole, "Mark," in *New Bible Commentary*, ed. Gordon J. Wenham, J. A. Motyer, D. A. Carson, and R. T. France (Downers Grove, IL: InterVarsity, 1994), 955. Cf. Edwards (*Mark*, 97): "God . . . had instituted the Sabbath (Gen 2:3), and Jesus now presumes preeminence over it."

("You shall not steal") and where the legal system is just ("You shall not bear false witness"). God's laws are not buckles on a straitjacket but feathers on wings. We are most free when we follow his ways. The Sabbath, if properly observed, brings the rest we need. It is a command tied to creation, the days of creation. As God rested on the seventh day, so we rest from our work as well. God gave us the Sabbath. Take a break and reap the rewards. Oh that the contemporary church would "recapture Jesus' liberating vision of the Sabbath (Lord's Day) as a gift ([Mark] 2:27) and as a time for doing good (3:4)."[8]

Third, do not miss the point of this passage. This passage is not about whether you should eat Wheaties on Sunday or not, attend the rugby match or not, or play bridge or not. It is about who Jesus is and what authority he has. Does Jesus, who has authority over all the days of the week and all the kingdoms of the world, have authority over us? He surely does. But do we recognize it? Acknowledge it? Embrace it? Do we bow the knee before the Lord of the Sabbath? Do we prostrate ourselves before the Potentate of Time?

Immanuel's Interrogative Answer: Explained and Illustrated

In Mark 2:25–28 Jesus first illustrates his point (2:25–26) before he explains it (2:27–28). In Mark **3:1–5** he first explains his point (3:4) and then illustrates it (3:5). The story begins, however, with Jesus, as is his custom, gathering with God's people who are gathered around God's Word: "Again he entered the synagogue, and a man was there with a withered hand. And they watched Jesus, to see whether he would heal him on the Sabbath, so that they might accuse him" (3:1–2).

Jesus' rebuke and declaration have so upset the Pharisees that they decide to set a trap (bring in a man) or else find one already set (the man is inside). They think, "Let's see now whether the one who loves mercy so much will break the Sabbath to cure this cripple." Jesus readily takes the bait and lets the trap snap on him.

> And he said to the man with the withered hand, "Come here" [Gk. "Rise up into the middle"]. And he said to them, "Is it lawful on the Sabbath to do good or to do harm, to save life or to kill?" But they were silent. And he looked around at them with anger, grieved at their hardness of heart,[9] and said to the man, "Stretch out your hand." He stretched it out, and his hand was restored. (3:3–5)

8   David E. Garland, *Mark*, NIVAC (Grand Rapids, MI: Zondervan, 1996), 122–23.
9   "Their response is described in language reminiscent of Israel's response to the prophets' message (e.g., Jer 3:17; 7:24; 9:13; 11:18; 13:10; 16:12; Ps 81:13; Deut 29:18)." Robert A. Guelich, *Mark 1:1–8:27*, WBC 34A (Nashville: Nelson, 1989), 137.

Here the miracle seems secondary. But do not overlook it. Who can say to someone with a hand that is limp and shriveled, "Be restored and come to life again," and there be perfect restoration and immediate new life? The Lord of the Sabbath! The creator of the world!

But beyond the miracle is the object lesson. The scene is dramatic. Does someone ask Jesus to heal this man? No. Does the man ask? No. This the first time Jesus instigates a miracle. He motions to the man. "Who me?" "Yes, you. Come here." The man comes. They both stand center stage. How provocative! If Jesus plans on healing him, he can just wait a day. There is no urgency here. The man is not bleeding to death. He has not just broken his arm. He has a hand that does not work, which means he cannot work. A man with a withered hand (Luke tells us it is his right hand, Luke 6:6) cannot work with his hands. So what does a man, in such a situation, do? Nothing. He is unemployed. Who would hire him? He cannot make a living. He cannot provide for his family. However, Jesus seems happy to have him join his family immediately. "Come here." And he comes to Christ. He moves toward Jesus. (Faith moves toward Jesus!) Jesus could have stopped here. He could have whispered in the man's ear, "I see your issue. Can this wait a day? Let's not stir the pot." But no, he takes the boiling pot, gives it a big stir, and pours it on the synagogue floor. Everyone jumps from the shock of the heat. This is now an extremely uncomfortable situation.

Jesus turns to the Pharisees and asks, "Is it lawful on the Sabbath to do good or to do harm, to save life or to kill?" Our answer would be, "Of course. It is lawful to do good and save life, for the Sabbath was made to bless us (Mark 2:27)." Their answer is tight lips (3:4). Have they rehearsed their response? Why are they all together in their altogether silence? To give him the cold shoulder? It might be that they think the argument is about to be over. Victory is seconds away. The defendant is about to break the law. For, in their minds, and according to their traditions, it was unlawful "to set a broken limb" or "straighten a deformed body" on the Sabbath (m. Šabb. 22:6).

Whatever the reason for their silence, such a reply is deafening. Jesus has had enough of the cold shoulder from the religious snobs: "And he looked around at them [he eyes each of them?] with anger, grieved at their hardness of heart, and said to the man, 'Stretch out your hand.' He stretched it out [what obedience to the Lord of the Sabbath!], and his hand was restored" (3:5). His hand is not restored after six months of surgery and physical therapy. His hand is ready to work then and there. He can apply as a carpenter tomorrow. He can rescue his ox if it falls into a well that very day (Luke 14:5).

What angers and grieves God? When religious traditions trump love for God and neighbor, especially neighbors in need—such as widows and orphans in their affliction, or a grown man who cannot lift his hand to lower the hammer to make a living. What delights God? When we walk forward in faith, despite the possible persecution to follow, in order to acknowledge Jesus' authority and accept salvation from him. As Guelich states, "Jesus was not only healing a crippled hand, he was bringing wholeness and a new life in relationship with God befitting the age of salvation. In this sense, he was 'saving a life.'"[10]

From Conflict to Crucifixion

Our text concludes with the Pharisees' reaction. In Mark 1–2 we have seen a number of reactions to Jesus' teaching and miracles, such as obedience (1:18), amazement (1:27), and acclamation (2:12). Now, for the first but not last time, the reaction is enmity: "The Pharisees went out and immediately held counsel with the Herodians against him, how to destroy him" (**3:6**).

Athanasius speaks of the Pharisees' being "withered in their minds."[11] Indeed, for what are they thinking? Do they really think God is against someone with such supernatural powers—who can heal a man with a mere word? Do they really think Jesus has broken the Sabbath by doing good and saving a life? Do they really think Jesus' (supposedly) breaking the fourth commandment justifies their breaking the sixth commandment, along with the great commandment to love one's neighbor (Lev. 19:18)? Do they really think that Jesus has broken the Sabbath by saying a few words? Notice that Jesus does not touch the man or wrap some magical bandage around the hand. Jesus just speaks a few words (three in the Greek text, Mark 3:5). If speaking constitutes breaking the Sabbath, then their secret counsel in verse 6 (also their question in 2:24), which surely involves more than three words, is also unlawful. Blaise Pascal reflected, "Men never do evil so completely and cheerfully as when they do it from religious conviction."[12] Evil indeed.

Moreover, it takes a withered mind and an evil heart to team up with the Herodians. That is an unexpected move because the Pharisees hated the Herodians, a Jewish political party that supported Herod the Great and now Herod Antipas (8:15). They hated them because the Herodians supported the work of the immoral Herod clan (e.g., 6:18) and also Roman rule (12:13–14). So this "unexpected alliance . . . of these two otherwise antagonistic parties"

---

10 Guelich, *Mark 1:1–8:27*, 140.
11 Attributed to Athanasius (see *Homilies*, no. 28), in Thomas C. Oden and Christopher A. Hall, eds., *Mark*, ACCS NT (Downers Grove, IL: InterVarsity, 1998), 37.
12 Pascal, *Pensees*, quoted in David Tracy, *Plurality and Ambiguity: Hermeneutics, Religion, Hope* (Chicago: University of Chicago Press, 1994), 86.

demonstrates "the magnitude of their opposition to Jesus."[13] A common enemy so often makes strange bedfellows.

But why are they so against Jesus that they plot to "destroy" him? It is normal for new ideas from great persons to find some initial rejection: Pythagoras' claim that the earth is round, Galileo's view that the earth revolves around the sun, Pasteur's observation that disease spreads by germs, and hundreds of other examples. But the Pharisees' dismissal and denunciation seems extreme. Destruction! It makes sense only if we understand that, first, they view Sabbath breaking as a capital offense (Ex. 31:14–15; 35:2) and believe Jesus has legitimately and blatantly broken the law; second, that this is not the first time Jesus has played by his own rules and not theirs. There have been previous Sabbath "violations" (Mark 1:21–25; 2:23–28), disdain for their traditions (2:18–22), and socializing with sinners and tax collectors (1:40; 2:13–17). Third, and most significantly, he has threatened their authority: he has claimed the authority to forgive sins (2:5, 10–11), to eat with the "unclean" (2:13–17), "to dispense with fasting (2:18–22), [and] to supersede the Sabbath."[14] As William H. Willimon remarks, "The clash with authority is not over the rules but over *who* rules."[15]

"The Pharisees went out and immediately held counsel with the Herodians against him, how to destroy him" (3:6). Our passage ends with absolute animosity from the religious and political powers of the day. Times have not changed. Wherever the gospel is faithfully preached, opposition will arise. But the beautiful reality about the gospel is that out of such opposition rises the very purposes of God. The impure Pharisees and the unholy Herodians make a pact to kill God's pure and righteous Son (3:6), a plot that comes to fruition in Mark 15: "And Jesus uttered a loud cry and breathed his last" (15:37; esp. 15:1). But his destruction is our deliverance. Through their hostility comes hope. We "who once were alienated and hostile in mind" have been reconciled through his death (Col. 1:21–22); we who were once unreceptive "enemies . . . were reconciled to God by the death of his Son" (Rom. 5:10).

Don't Let Religion Ruin Your Life

Shortly before my grandmother died, I visited her. I had recently become a Christian. I was so excited about my faith! I shared my faith with her, but she was not receptive. In fact, these were her last words to me: "Don't let religion

---

13 Edwards, *Gospel according to Mark*, 102.
14 Edwards, *Gospel according to Mark*, 102. So the Pharisees' response to Jesus is "not the result of a single incident," but "an accumulation of incidents"; William L. Lane, *The Gospel of Mark*, NICNT (Grand Rapids, MI: Eerdmans, 1974), 122.
15 Quoted in Garland, *Mark*, 117.

ruin your life." She was right about religion. "Self-made religion" (Col. 2:23), as Paul calls it, has ruined many a life, perhaps even my own grandmother's. She grew up in Ireland at a time when every imaginable religious regulation was imposed upon people, where the teeth of religious duty penetrated the depths of her conscience.

My grandmother was right about "self-made religion," for indeed such religion ruins lives. But she was wrong about my new-found religion. She was wrong because it is so much more than some religion; it is a relationship. It is a relationship that has brought only life to my life. Man-made religion will ruin your life, but this God-made relationship with Jesus, the Lord of the Sabbath, will save it.

So come to him. Stand center stage with him before a watching, and often hostile, world. And find restoration and rest. Find goodness and salvation and life.

Five Different Reactions to the Vintage Jesus

MARK 3:7–35

When his family heard it, they went out to seize him, for
they were saying, "He is out of his mind."
Mark 3:21

Barbershops provide an authentic taste of Americana, and, sitting in a shop and listening to conversations, one gets a real feel for the people who live in the neighborhood. Once, while I was sitting in the chair, the barber asked, "What do you do for a living?" I said, "I'm a pastor." "What do you like about your job?" "The free parking spot," I joked. "No, I like helping people understand the Bible." "Hmm," he replied. "My girlfriend just went on a retreat with this new church." I interjected, "Wow, that's great. What church?" "I don't know," he said. "Do you go to church?" I asked. "No. But she wants me to."

The conversation went on from there and quickly and eventually turned to other topics and interests of his and mine. But as I was sitting there I thought, "I wonder how many people in this place have different views about Jesus." Perhaps the guy next to me, getting his beard trimmed, was thinking, "I wish this pastor would stop talking. I don't want anything to do with Jesus." Perhaps the young man cutting his hair was thinking, "I believe in Jesus. I just don't agree with Christians. I think Jesus was a holy man, but certainly not the Son of God." Perhaps the teenage girl, who came by and swept up the hair, thought, "I think Jesus was a lunatic. He said the craziest things and only crazy people follow him." And, perhaps the teenage boy across the way, getting his man-bun done, was thinking, "I don't believe in Jesus, but I have been thinking about taking my dying mother to that faith healer. I'm desperate! He might be our only hope." I have no idea what was running through the minds of the people in the barbershop that day, but I do know something of how people in my neighborhood tend to react to Jesus of Nazareth. They react a lot like the people do in Mark 3:7–35.

This text records five different reactions to Jesus from five different groups: the crowd, the unclean spirits, the apostles, Jesus' family, and the scribes. In this chapter we will examine each reaction in turn and view each reaction as a reflection of how we should or should not view Jesus.

The Crowd

First, we have the crowd. Crowds are mentioned in a few places in our text. At the tail of our text we read that "a crowd was sitting around" Jesus and that they informed him that his mother and brothers were outside, wanting a word with him (3:32). We are also informed in verse 20 that the crowd so packed the house that Jesus and his disciples had no room even to eat. Then in **3:7–10** we read,

> Jesus withdrew with his disciples to the sea, and a great crowd followed, from Galilee and Judea and Jerusalem and Idumea and from beyond the Jordan and from around Tyre and Sidon. When the great crowd heard all that he was doing, they came to him. And he told his disciples to have a boat ready for him because of the crowd, lest they crush him, for he had healed many, so that all who had diseases pressed around him to touch him.

We do not know the numbers behind the words "great" and "many"—"a great crowd" and "he had healed many." What we do know is that Jesus was extremely popular. We are told here that people from throughout the promised land ("Galilee and Judea and Jerusalem and Idumea and from beyond the Jordan") and people from outside the promised land ("from around Tyre and Sidon") "came to him" (3:7–8). Why would people as far as 60 miles away come to him? Mark's answer is that they "heard all that he was doing" (3:8). Interesting. "Doing," not "saying." Jesus' priority has been preaching. Apparently that is not their priority. What was he *doing* that made them travel so far to meet him? Verse 10 provides the answer, the same answer given elsewhere (1:32–34): he was healing the multitudes. People "who had diseases pressed around him to touch him" (3:10) so as to experience his healing touch.

With that summary of the crowd's attitudes and actions, what then are we to make of these people? We should follow the crowd in their movement toward Jesus and after him. We read in verse 8 that they "came" to Jesus and in verse 7 that they "followed" him. These are positive verbs in Mark, often associated with faith. We should also follow the crowd in its obvious trust that Jesus had the power to solve its problems. To travel from Sidon to try to touch Jesus requires a great amount of faith.

With those two positives noted, however, it is difficult to know what the crowd thought of Jesus. They certainly thought he had the power to conquer demons and disease. And they were also, as we know elsewhere, "astonished at his teaching" (11:18). But what did such crowds think of Jesus' teaching in 8:34: "If anyone would come after me, let him deny himself and take up his cross and follow me"? Did they embrace self-denial and cross bearing? Likely not. For why did a crowd, perhaps not this one, come to arrest him (14:43)? Why did a crowd, perhaps not this one, cry out for Barabbas's release rather than Jesus' (15:11)? And why do the crowds rarely acknowledge anything about Jesus' identity? Who did they think he was? Did they care? Was he just a miracle worker to them?

Well, in the Bible, as in life, the best advice is not to follow the crowd. Crowds tend to follow people, movements, and trends for selfish reasons. Crowds often ask Jesus, "What can you do for me?" Disciples of Jesus are to ask, "Lord, how can I serve you and others?" Crowds follow after personal benefits, while disciples seek first the kingdom of God and its righteousness (Matt. 6:33), no matter how popular the ruler and the rules of that kingdom might be, and no matter what it might cost them.

Sure, on the last day there will be a crowd around the throne. Unnumbered multitudes! But, as with Christian in *The Pilgrim's Progress*, for most of those saints the journey to the celestial city will be arduous and, at times, made alone or with a few. When it comes to following the crowd, be careful. "Enter by the narrow gate. For the gate is wide and the way is easy that leads to destruction, and those who enter by it are *many*. For the gate is narrow and the way is hard that leads to life, and those who find it are *few*" (Matt. 7:13–14).

The Unclean Spirits

The second group to have a perspective on Jesus is the unclean spirits. The irony here is thick, for the one group that always understands and publicly announces something of Jesus' true identity and mission are the demons. Earlier, in Mark 1:24, a demon called Jesus "the Holy One of God" and knew that Jesus' mission was to "destroy" the forces of evil. Later, in 5:7, a demon will call Jesus "Son of the Most High God" and beg him not to "torment" him. Here in **3:11–12** we read, "And *whenever* the unclean spirits saw him, they *fell down before* him and cried out, 'You are the Son of God.' And he strictly ordered them not to make him known." Jesus ordered silence not because they mistook his identity or mission but because he wanted to wait until after his resurrection for his appointed apostles to make a clear and direct proclamation of his person and purpose.

Obviously, as a point of application, I will not advocate to follow the demons' lead, at least to every extent. That is, we should understand that the demons got right the posture, person, and plan. We should bow before Jesus ("They fell down before him") and acknowledge him as the "Son of God" (3:11). But, unlike them, we should not tremble. Instead, we should rejoice that the "Holy One of God" (1:24) came to destroy the works of the devil; that the "Son of the Most High God" (5:7) descended into a hellish world to set us free from every evil. Let us fall down before him and cry out, "You are the Son of God!"

The Twelve

Mark gives us five different angles on Jesus. In Mark **3:13–19** our third view comes through the apostles' eyes.

> And he went up on the mountain and called to him those whom he desired, and they came to him. And he appointed twelve (whom he also named apostles) so that they might be with him and he might send them out to preach and have authority to cast out demons. He appointed the twelve: Simon (to whom he gave the name Peter); James the son of Zebedee and John the brother of James (to whom he gave the name Boanerges, that is, Sons of Thunder); Andrew, and Philip, and Bartholomew, and Matthew, and Thomas, and James the son of Alphaeus, and Thaddaeus, and Simon the Zealot, and Judas Iscariot, who betrayed him.

The twelve see Jesus as Lord. When he calls, they come (3:13; cf. 1:16–20; 2:14). When he commissions—here to go out and preach and exorcise demons (3:14–15)—they obey. The disciples (followers) become apostles (sent ones). Mark does not record their obedience here, but he does in 6:12–13.

With 3:13–19 before us, let me briefly ask and answer six questions. First, why did Jesus go up on a mountain and then call the twelve? It might have been to get away from the crowd. It might also have been because mountains are common places where God calls certain key servants—Moses, Elijah, and the like—so as to commission them to something grand. Second, why twelve? The number twelve corresponds to the twelve tribes of Israel, and the symbolism thus points to both an embodiment and a replacement. These men will embody what it means to be true Israel, and thus, as flawed as they are, they will replace the current ungodly religious leaders.

Third, why are they named?[1] To highlight that Jesus used ordinary men for his extraordinary mission. None of the men listed came from nobility or the upper class. Matthew was educated (he wrote a Gospel) and rich (or once was rich, as a tax collector—the only occupation named, and a very shady one at that), but the rest were tradesmen. None were politicians, although "Simon the Zealot" (3:18) may have been a part of a fringe group of militant nationalists who would do anything to take down Rome.[2] None were from the religious leaders of the day. We do not see listed St. Simon the Superhuman, Professor John von Thunder of the Tübingen Institute of Theology, or Blessed Bartholomew of the Order of the Only Elect Hermits. Rather we find the common and uncouth. Jesus selected not an all-star team to battle with the powerful devil and his mighty minions but a bunch of ragamuffins. That God would decide to change the world through ordinary men from an ordinary part of the world is just extraordinary.

Let us learn the lesson here. We do not need money, an elite education, or worldly power or prestige to be used by Jesus to do great things. "The church was built upon the faithful testimony of a bunch of rustics, as Jerome called them. God delighted in and still delights in building his church with such seemingly insufficient and slightly contorted building materials."[3]

Fourth, why are some of the twelve renamed? Only Mark records the renaming of Simon, James, and John, the first three names: "He appointed the twelve: Simon (to whom he gave the name Peter); James the son of Zebedee and John the brother of James (to whom he gave the name Boanerges, that is, Sons of Thunder)" (3:16–17). These three might be renamed because they were three of the four first disciples whom Jesus called, or because they will be with Jesus for two key moments of his ministry—the transfiguration and the garden of Gethsemane. They are obviously part of Jesus' inner circle,

<hr>

1 Mark provides "the same names that we find in Matthew and Luke, except for Thaddeus, whom Luke calls Judas, the son of Jacob. Perhaps his original name was Judas, though, after the treachery of Judas Iscariot, he decided to be called something else." Bo Giertz, *The New Testament Devotional Commentary: Volume 1: Matthew, Mark, Luke*, trans. Bror Erickson (Irving, CA: 1517 Publishing, 2021), 155.

2 Although the political party of the Zealots did not officially arise until AD 66, there were plenty of political purists in Jesus' day involved in active resistance against Rome. However, the Greek term itself (*ho Kananaios*) could simply refer to someone seeking to fulfill the Mosaic law (see *4 Macc.* 18:12; Philo, *On the Special Laws*, 2.253).

3 Douglas Sean O'Donnell, *Matthew: All Authority under Heaven*, PTW (Wheaton, IL: Crossway, 2013), 286. The quote from Jerome can be found in "Homily 14," *Homilies 1–59 on the Psalms*, FC (Washington, DC: Catholic University of America, 2001), 109.

and therefore they will bring future leadership to the twelve and the whole church. The renaming, however, might simply echo what is done in the OT, where someone important (like Jacob) is renamed because God plans on using him, despite his obvious flaws, to promote his purposes.

Fifth, why is Peter listed first and Judas last? Judas is named last for what he did: betrayed Jesus. Peter is named first here, and everywhere the list is given, because he was the first among equals. He was the first chosen by Jesus. He is the predominate disciple—in the number of lines he speaks and the role he plays—in the Four Gospels and Acts. The Acts of the Apostles focuses in part on Peter's acts (named 56x). This does not mean Peter was the first pope. However, it does mean he was just as important to the new covenant as someone like Moses was to the old.

Sixth, what of their mission is ours? Our mission is not to be the foundation of the church. In Ephesians 2:20 Paul speaks of Jesus as the "cornerstone" of the newly formed "household of God" (Eph. 2:19), a church "built on the foundation of the apostles and prophets." Our mission is also not to have the "authority to cast out demons" (Mark 3:15). If there are Christians today, or at other points in church history, who have exorcised demons, they are not the norm. Whereas for the apostles, each and every one of them, it was the norm. The Acts of the *Apostles* is a large book all about their amazing *acts*. Through the power of the Spirit given to them in a unique and unrepeatable way at Pentecost they are the ones doing the miracles. "The signs of a true apostle," Paul writes in 2 Corinthians 12:12, are "signs and wonders and mighty works." That is what they did do, not what we can do. This perhaps explains why the Great Commission does not include the command to heal sickness and cast out demons. I also believe this is why, near the end of his life, Paul writes of qualifications for elders and deacons that do not include the miraculous gifts.

What then of their mission is ours? Jesus' main thing. What we read about in Acts 8:4. Those who were scattered due to persecution "went about preaching the word." None of those who scattered preached from a pulpit. They preached to their new neighbors. They preached to their fellow countrymen—unbelieving Jews. They preached in the marketplace as they sold their goods to Jews and Gentiles alike. They wanted the world to know the good news of Jesus.

Jesus' Family

The first three views of Jesus—from the crowd, demons, and disciples—all, at points, see Jesus in a positive light. The final two views—from Jesus' family and the religious leaders—are both negative views. Let us focus first on the family, or on Jesus' family's focus on Jesus. After Jesus returns to Capernaum ("He went home," Mark **3:20**), again the crowd presses in around him. There are so many people around him that he and his disciples "could not even eat" (3:20). When his family learns he is back in town, they go to greet and em-brace him—no, that is not what we read in **3:21**. Instead we read: "And when his family heard it, they went out to seize [a strong verb!] him, for they were saying, 'He is out of his mind.'"

There are a few textual issues here. Is it Jesus' "family" (as the ESV has it) or his "friends" (as other translations have it) who do this? If it is his "family," who constitutes his family? Finally, who is the "they" in the line, "For they were saying, 'He is out of this mind'"? Is the "they" the family/friends, people, or even the scribes?

I think "family" is the correct translation and means Jesus' biological fam-ily, those named in verse 31 ("his mother and his brothers"). We learn from 6:3 that his mother's name is Mary and his half-brothers are James, Joses, Judas, and Simon. This group is the "they," those who want to take him out of the public eye because "he is out of his mind" (3:21). They likely make this statement because they are trying to protect him from the religious and political leaders who are out "to destroy him" (3:6). I also think, at this point, that Jesus' brothers do not believe that Jesus is the Messiah. I say this because of what is said in John 7:5: "For not even his [own] brothers believed in him." Mary does believe he is the Son of God, but she is struggling, as John the Baptist did (see Matt. 11:2–3), with the nature of Jesus' messianic mission.

This explains why Jesus says what he says in Mark **3:31–35**. In verse 31 Jesus' mother and brothers are standing outside the house. They send word through someone in the crowd that they are here. "Your family wants a word with you." Jesus says, "Please, bring them in!" No, that is not what he says. Rather, he says one of the most shocking statements in the Gospels: "'Who are my mother and my brothers?' And looking about at those who sat around him [the twelve], he said, 'Here are my mother and my brothers! For whoever does the will of God, he is my brother and sister and mother'" (3:33–35).[4]

Jesus was not dropped from heaven. He knows that. He knows that Mary is his mother. She birthed him. Nursed him. Raised him. Taught him. He knows that Joseph, his earthly father, has died (as scholars surmise). He

---

4 "We naturally expect the warmest affection to subsist between persons so closely allied to each other. But the love that is found among earthly relatives is but a faint image of that which both Christ and his Father feel toward all their obedient followers." Charles Simeon, *Horae Homi-leticae*, quoted in *CHSB*, 1477.

knows his brothers. The five of them trained to be carpenters. They went to Hebrew school to learn to read the ancient Scriptures. They sat together at synagogue through sermons. He also knows his sisters, who are not named here. Jesus grew up with a mother and father, and lots of brothers and sisters. Why not welcome them in, then?

The reason is that, at this point in the drama, they are acting like outsiders. The holy family is acting in an unholy way. They are on a "rescue mission to save Jesus from the ultimate rescue mission."[5] They are saying that he is out of his mind because their minds are not set "on the things of God" (Matt. 16:23). They are opposing the cross. They do not want him to die. But it is the will of God that Jesus die. And those who do the will of God follow Jesus, listen to Jesus, rest in Jesus, and believe what Jesus says about his identity and the purpose of his mission.

Recently I taught a class on the Lord's Supper. In the first lesson I pointed out how Jesus redefined the Passover meal, which he was celebrating with his disciples at the Last Supper. The Passover, according to Exodus 12, is to be celebrated with one's nuclear family. Jesus celebrates it with his new family, with a small group of disciples who have no blood relation to him. The point of that scene, and the one before us, is that "a relationship with Jesus takes priority over every other relationship, even the relationship of one's family."[6] Jesus makes this point nowhere clearer than in Mark 10:29–30, where he promises,

> Truly, I say to you, there is no one who has left house or brothers or sisters or mother or father or children or lands, for my sake and for the gospel, who will not receive a hundredfold now in this time, houses and brothers and sisters and mothers and children and lands, with persecutions, and in the age to come eternal life.

A stark reality is addressed here. The short phrase "with persecutions" stands out. Will one's own family persecute its own flesh and blood? Yes, it will. Families have done so. Read church history. Look afresh at Mark 13:12: "And brother will deliver brother over to death, and the father his child, and children will rise against parents and have them put to death." Some of us know this so deeply. Perhaps not betrayal unto death. But family divisions and derisions. Christ, whom we have put at the center of our life, has exploded the nuclear family.

---

5 O'Donnell, *Matthew*, 350.
6 O'Donnell, *Matthew*, 347.

If this is the case for you, let me offer you a word of encouragement here. Give it time and much prayer. This is not the last scene we have of Jesus' family. Mary comes around. She stands at the cross as her son dies (see John 19:26–27). She literally sees the cross. Her firstborn son dies before her eyes. Imagine the emotion. He dies with nails in his hands and feet. He dies hanging from a Roman torture device. She watches. A sword pierces her heart. But then comes the resurrection, followed by Pentecost. The breath of God breathes over the confused and doubtful. The final pieces of this terribly complex puzzle fit into place. A plan more perfect than the creation of the universe. Too brilliant to comprehend. Too great for her to grasp when she was pounding on the door and screaming, "He is out of his mind," and thinking, "Believe me. Let him live. Let him live. Please don't kill my son."

Jesus' brothers also come around. They are in the upper room on the day of Pentecost: "All these [the twelve minus Judas] . . . together with the women and *Mary the mother of Jesus, and his brothers*" (Acts 1:14). Through faith in the resurrected Christ, Jesus' mother becomes his "mother" and his brothers his "brothers." As his brother James will write in the epistle that bears his name, "James, a servant of God and of the Lord Jesus Christ" (James 1:1). Jesus' mother and brothers will spend the rest of their lives serving the suffering servant, doing the will of God. We should do the same.

The Scribes

We have one more lens to look through, that of the Jerusalem scribes. How do the experts in the Holy Bible from the holy city view Jesus? Verses 22 and 30 provide the answers: "He is possessed by Beelzebul," "By the prince of demons he casts out the demons" (**3:22**), and "He has an unclean spirit" (3:30). How do they arrive at this conclusion? They cannot deny Jesus' supernatural powers. The source behind such powers is either God or the devil. Since, to them, Jesus is a blasphemer (he has claimed the authority to forgive sins) and a lawbreaker (he has broken the Sabbath command), they deduce that he is working for the devil.

Needless to say, their perception of Jesus is not to be ours, as Jesus makes clear in verses 23–30. Starting with **3:23–27**, we read,

And he called them to him and said to them in parables, "How can Satan cast out Satan? If a kingdom is divided against itself, that kingdom cannot stand. And if a house is divided against itself, that house will not be able to stand. And if Satan has risen up against himself and is divided, he cannot stand, but is coming to an end. But no one can enter a strong man's house and plunder his goods, unless he first binds the strong man. Then indeed he may plunder his house."

Here Jesus gives a string of logical parabolic rebuttals to the scribe's false accusation. The rebuttals are a type of argument that philosophers' call a reductio ad absurdum. Basically, with the above analogies Jesus is saying, "Don't be absurd!" It would be absurd for Satan to be the source behind the casting out of demons. No kingdom or household can exist for long with such tactics. Jesus is working for God against the devil. His exorcisms are visible attestations that Jesus can, has, and will bind "the strong man" (Satan), enter his "house" (his territory), and "plunder his goods" (freed people from his dominion, 3:26–27).

Then, following that rebuttal, Jesus ends with a warning: "'Truly, I say to you, all sins will be forgiven the children of man, and whatever blasphemies they utter, but whoever blasphemes against the Holy Spirit never has forgiveness, but is guilty of an eternal sin'—for they were saying, 'He has an unclean spirit'" (**3:28–30**). The "eternal" and unforgivable sin, or blasphemy against the Holy Spirit, is to do what the scribes are doing here: "Attributing to Satan what is accomplished by the power of God."[7] It is to witness the Holy Spirit's work through Jesus and not only reject it but to denounce it as a work of the unholy spirit, Satan.

From Jesus' teaching here two questions might arise: (1) Can we still commit this sin? and (2) If so, *have* we committed this sin? Some scholars think the sin is limited to that era. The only people who committed the unforgiveable sin are men like the scribes who saw Jesus in the flesh and called good evil and evil good. Yet, because of what is said in 1 John 5:16 about the false teachers of John's day (the apostate antichrists) who have sinned a sin "that leads to death" and are thus not to be prayed for, it is possible that someone can still sin such a sin. It is a rare sin, however. It involves three phases. First, someone professes faith in the apostolic Jesus. Second, that person then denies the faith and leaves the fellowship. Third, the apostate becomes "an exponent of error, sharing his testimony of disbelief, hoping to lead others astray." So, he is "someone who has known the light but now hates and makes an earnest effort to extinguish the light."[8] That apostate becomes an apostle of darkness!

The second question follows: If someone can still commit such a sin, how does one know if he has or has not? The correct and traditional answer is,

7   J. F. Walvoord's definition, as quoted in Craig L. Blomberg, *Matthew*, NAC (Nashville: Broadman, 1992), 203.
8   Douglas Sean O'Donnell, *1–3 John: A Gospel-Transformed Life*, REC (Phillipsburg, NJ: P&R, 2015), 163.

if you have committed such a sin you would not even ask such a question, nor care about the answer. As Matthew Henry put it, "Those who fear they have committed this sin give a good sign that they have not." Those who have committed the unforgivable sin are not looking for forgiveness. Their hearts are fully hardened.

Yet, with that said, we tend to focus on the one sin that will not be forgiven and forget the amazing statement Jesus makes in Mark 3:28: "Truly, I say to you, *all* sins will be forgiven the children of man." Is the "all" here not the best word in the world? Those who believe that Jesus paid it all on the cross can have full assurance that all their sins will be forgiven on judgment day. What about cheating on a math test, stealing change from a parent's wallet, lying on a resume, having an abortion, experimenting with homosexuality, murdering a brother? All sins will be forgiven. What about greed, covetousness, breaking vows, sloth, neglecting the needy, unrighteous rage, causing dissensions within the church, looking at pornography, overcharging a customer, spreading rumors, hypocrisy, adultery, flattering, drunkenness, envy? All sins will be forgiven for those with faith in Christ.

Christ at the Center

After I left the barbershop I went to a care facility to visit Curt Daugaard, a friend with dementia. In 1993 Curt earned a PhD in philosophy with a dissertation on Jonathan Edwards. I asked Curt, "Do you remember writing your dissertation?" "Yes," he said. I said, "It was on Edwards, right?" An amazing glow came into his eyes. He stared at me, like he had discovered a new world, and said, "Yes, Jonathan Edwards." Then he tapped his head hard and said, "Where have I been?"

The time before that, when I asked him how I could pray for him, he said, "Pray that I keep Christ at the center." My brother may not have remembered much on that visit (and he has since gone to be with the Lord), but he remembered that truth, which is an excellent summary of Edwards's theology. He remembered what we need to remember today and always, and to pray for! When there are so many competing ideologies and entertainments vying for our allegiance, and so many different and false conceptions of Jesus, we need to keep the Christ presented here at the center: Jesus, the Son of God; Jesus, the compassionate healer; Jesus, the powerful Savior, who has conquered evil and forgiven all our sins.

The Secret of the Kingdom of God

MARK 4:1–20

To you has been given the secret of the kingdom of God, but
for those outside everything is in parables.
Mark 4:11

Imagine hearing the parable of the sower with its original audience. Perhaps you have experienced, or certainly witnessed, Jesus' healing powers. Perhaps you have heard him preach on repentance, faith, and the forgiveness of sins. Now you follow him "beside the sea" (Mark **4:1**), the Lake of Galilee. The crowd is so massive that Jesus gets into a boat and pushes off shore a bit. Then he begins to teach from his floating pulpit. He is teaching a number of seemingly simple, certainly short stories ("teaching them many things in parables," **4:2**), and you get close enough to hear one. He starts "Listen!" followed by "Behold." He has your attention. You are listening. You are ready to behold. Then he goes on to say,

> A sower went out to sow. And as he sowed, some seed fell along the path, and the birds came and devoured it. Other seed fell on rocky ground, where it did not have much soil, and immediately it sprang up, since it had no depth of soil. And when the sun rose, it was scorched, and since it had no root, it withered away. Other seed fell among thorns, and the thorns grew up and choked it, and it yielded no grain. And other seeds fell into good soil and produced grain, growing up and increasing and yielding thirtyfold and sixtyfold and a hundredfold. (**4:3–8**)

End of story, lesson, or whatever that was that you just heard. What would you make of it? Do you think it is an interesting story? Not especially. Do you think Jesus might be giving advice on farming? He could be. But if it is an agricultural instruction, you might question its worth. Why would a farmer intentionally waste seed on a path where people walk, on rocky surfaces where the soil is shallow, or in the thorns? And why not plow the soil and then sow the seed? What is the purpose of Jesus' rather backward and unsophisticated directions on seed sowing? Is it not obvious that a farmer should watch out for birds, avoid overexposure to the sun, and sow in good soil rather than on hard surfaces and in thorn-infested dirt?

The point I am making is that to the "very large crowd" (4:1) on the shore Jesus is not speaking simply and straightforwardly about Christianity. In fact, he uses no religious language whatsoever. So then, what do sowers, seeds, and soils have to say about God, sin, or salvation? If we were back then and there, your guess would have been as good as mine.

This is why we read in **4:10** that "when he was alone, those around him with the twelve asked him about the parables." They ask, as recorded in Matthew 13:10, "Why do you speak to them [the crowd] in parables?" Jesus' answer is given in Mark 4:11–12. Here Jesus will teach the purpose of parables; then in verses 13–20 he will explain the meaning of the parable that he told in verses 3–8.

The Purpose of Parables

First, let us examine the purpose of parables.

> And he said to them, "To you has been given the secret of the kingdom of God, but for those outside everything is in parables, so that
>
> > "'they may indeed see but not perceive,
> >   and may indeed hear but not understand,
> > lest they should turn and be forgiven.'" (Mark **4:11–12**)

According to Jesus he did not preach in parables to draw his audience's attention or to take abstract ideas and make them more concrete. Rather, he preached in parables *to* the crowds *for* his disciples. "To you," Jesus said to them, "has been given the secret to the kingdom of God." He says in essence, "God, in his sovereign election of you,[1] has graciously revealed his plan, or is slowly revealing that plan, to you. You have God-opened ears to hear (**4:9**). You understand (or, will soon understand) and act upon that understanding. You are insiders." "But for those outside everything" is concealed, told "in parables" (4:11). The reason is given in verse 12:

---

1   "The divine passive 'has been given' emphasizes divine election." Grant R. Osborne, *Mark*, TTCS (Grand Rapids, MI: Baker, 2012), 68.

so that

"'they may indeed see but not perceive,
  and may indeed hear but not understand,
 lest they should turn and be forgiven.'"

This quote is a condensed form of Isaiah 6:9–10. In Isaiah 1–5 God's people have repeatedly rebelled against God, "forsaken the LORD, . . . [and] despised the Holy One of Israel" (1:4), "defying his glorious presence" (3:8). They have rejected his offer of salvation (1:18–19), dismissed his instruction (1:10, 23–26; 3:12–15; 5:18–24), oppressed the poor and embraced injustice (1:16, 21–23; 3:15; 5:7, 23), boasted in their sin (3:9), lived in luxury (3:24; 5:9), and worshiped other gods (2:6–8, 18–20; 3:3). In doing so they have become like the idols they have worshiped—deaf and blind. In Isaiah 6 the prophet encounters the living God. He stands in the presence of the holy Lord. "Woe is me!" he declares. "For I am lost; for I am a man of unclean lips, and I dwell in the midst of a people of unclean lips" (Isa. 6:5). God forgives Isaiah's sins and then commissions him to preach to people with not only unclean lips but closed eyes and clogged ears. Here is Isaiah 6:9–10 in full. Look. Listen!

Go, and say to this people:

"'Keep on hearing, but do not understand;
 keep on seeing, but do not perceive.'
Make the heart of this people dull,
  and their ears heavy,
  and blind their eyes;
 lest they see with their eyes,
  and hear with their ears,
 and understand with their hearts,
  and turn and be healed."

Jesus is on a similar mission. Jesus' parables, like Isaiah's prophecies, will serve only to further calcify hard hearts. By God's plan and for his purposes Jesus uses parables as "anti-evangelism" devices.[2] More than that, they actually serve as words of judgment. Those, like the religious leaders, who "see"

---

2 Osborne, *Mark*, 68.

what Jesus does and "hear" what he says and yet do not understand and act are judged by God (see esp. Mark 3:29). They remain dead in their sins. Unforgiven.

On the one hand, parables conceal; on the other hand, they reveal. To those on the inside parables provide further information. They reveal the mysteries of God's rule on earth through Jesus. Parables are like stained glass. A few summers ago, when I was in Bristol, England, for a week, I walked into the Bristol Cathedral, which, like any Anglican cathedral, has lots of stained-glass windows depicting Christ's life, death, resurrection, and ascension. On the day I was there, the sun was pouring through the windows. I could see clearly all the artistic details—the vibrant mixture of colors, the twelve figures waving palm branches as they looked up to the seated Christ. However, outside on the same day and at the same time, when I looked at the glass, it was colorless. Lifeless. The windows might as well have been walls. I was able to see some of the shapes, but I could see nothing of the brilliant color or the artistry and intricacy of the images. I had to be inside to see that.

Like the outside of those stained-glass windows, Christ's parables conceal facts about his identity and mission from those who refuse to believe; like the inside of those same windows, Christ's parables reveal aspects of the kingdom to those who seek to know him and to submit to his lordship.

Explanation and Applications of the Parable of the Soils

Having looked at the purpose of parables (Mark 4:11–12), let us look at **4:13–20**: Jesus' explanation of the parable he told in verses 3–8. Let us look at the light he will shed on himself and his ministry (and ours).

In verse 13 Jesus asks the insiders, "Do you not understand this parable?" I imagine them all staring at him with confused expressions. Jesus follows up with another question: "How then will you understand all the parables?" In other words, "I need you to know the meaning of my teachings so you might eventually teach others. So, Peter, listen to lesson one on parable interpretation; then tell John Mark; then, John Mark write it down and tell the world."

> The sower sows the word. And these are the ones along the path, where the word is sown: when they hear, Satan immediately comes and takes away the word that is sown in them. And these are the ones sown on rocky ground: the ones who, when they hear the word, immediately receive it with joy. And they have no root in themselves, but endure for a while; then, when tribulation or persecution arises on account of the word, immediately they fall away. And others are the ones sown among

thorns. They are those who hear the word, but the cares of the world and the deceitfulness of riches and the desires for other things enter in and choke the word, and it proves unfruitful. But those that were sown on the good soil are the ones who hear the word and accept it and bear fruit, thirtyfold and sixtyfold and a hundredfold. (4:14–20)

Sometimes this parable is called the parable of the sower and the seeds; other times it is labeled the parable of the soils. Those titles, if put together, cover the three key details. We have a *sower* who sows *seeds* that fall on various *soils* or surfaces. Jesus does not reveal the identity of the sower, but he says that the seed is the "word." But what is the "word"? Before we get to the four soils, allow me to shed some light on the sower and the seed, starting with the seed.

The seed is the "word," namely, the message from God about Jesus as king—what Jesus calls the "gospel" of the "kingdom of God" (1:15). The sower is surely Jesus, who has been traveling from town to town, spreading the good news. But the sower, as this parable has moved beyond its original audience, is also anyone who spreads that word to others. In Mark 2:2 Jesus preached the "word" (cf. Matt. 13:37); in Acts the apostles likewise preach the "word" (e.g., Acts 6:2, 7; 13:5; 15:35). Today all Christians, to some extent, should "preach the word" (2 Tim. 4:2; cf. Acts 8:4), and we should know what will happen when we do: the same thing that happened when Jesus did. We might even say that this parable serves as an explanation of the various reactions we saw in the last chapter and will see in the chapters to come, along with what we have seen, do see, and will see in our own lives. In Mark 3:7–35 we saw five responses—two completely negative and three partially positive. Here in 4:14–20 we have four different reactions—one super positive and three various degrees of negative.

The First Three Surfaces

We start, as Jesus does, with the negative. In 4:15–19 our Lord teaches that there are internal and external reasons why people reject the gospel. The internal involve what James Boice called the hard heart, the shallow heart, and the strangled heart,[3] while the external involve Satan, trials, and temptations.

On the first surface ("the path") the seed takes no root due to both satanic swooping and human hard-heartedness. The surface here is hard. The seed stands above ground because it cannot penetrate the solid surface to get to the soil. Such hard-heartedness makes the seed easy prey. Like a hungry bird,

3   James Montgomery Boice, *The Gospel of Matthew*, 2 vols. (Grand Rapids, MI: Baker, 2001), 1:235.

Satan swoops down within seconds ("When they hear, Satan *immediately* comes and takes away the word that is sown in them," 4:15).

The scribes would be good examples of this first surface. In 2:7, after they have heard of Jesus' miracles and heard firsthand his preaching (2:2), they label him a blasphemer. Then in 3:22, after again hearing Jesus teach the otherworldly and watching him work miracles only God can perform, they conclude, "He is possessed by Beelzebul." Of course, there are thousands of other examples beyond what is recorded in the pages of Scripture. We all have our own examples of telling people the good news and having them nod along (they are listening)—and then, the moment we are done, they are done, both with us and with our gospel. They are not interested in hearing more about Jesus; some people are even antagonistic toward him and us. That is the sad reality Jesus is telling us about here.

But, that said, until Christ comes or that person dies, that sad reality is not the end of the story. The word can and should be sown again and again. When the apostle Paul first heard the gospel, he not only rejected it but hated it. Yet our gracious God had different plans for him. The Lord can lower the hammer and break even the hardest hearts. So, keep sowing the seed. Keep praying for the atheist neighbor, the disinterested boss, and the prodigal son.

The second surface is the rocky ground. "And these are the ones," Jesus explains in verses 16–17, "sown on rocky ground: the ones who, when they hear the word, immediately receive it with joy. And they have no root in themselves, but endure for a while; then, when tribulation or persecution arises on account of the word, immediately they fall away." The people described here are not the hard-hearted but the shallow-souled. The first group hears the word and immediately rejects it. This second group hears it, and they "immediately receive it with joy" (4:16). They grasp the gospel enough to understand that it is good news. They walk forward at the evangelistic meeting. They raise their hand at the church revival. They sign the prayer card after Sunday service. They are excited about the new journey they are on. But the gospel has not taken root ("And they have no root in themselves," 4:17).

What happens next is that they "endure for a while" (4:17). They start attending church. They join a small group. They even make it through the first round of their old friends' teasing them for their newfound faith and piety. They "endure for a while" (4:17). But then trouble comes, as it always does in a fallen world, a world opposed to the kingdom of God. "When tribulation or persecution arises on account of the word, immediately they fall away." When they first hear the gospel, they "immediately receive it with joy" (4:16). Now, when they lose their job or suffer from an illness (when tribulations arise), or when they are ridiculed, ousted from their family, or threatened imprisonment for follow-ing Jesus (when persecution comes), they "immediately . . . fall away" (4:17).

As I have said elsewhere,

> The true test of discipleship is not whether or not one received the gospel with joy at some datable moment in history. The true test of discipleship is whether or not one picks up his cross and follows Jesus, not for one day or two weeks or three months or four years, but until Jesus calls him home.[4]

The persevering Christian is not like a flower that a husband gives to his wife on her birthday, a red rose that is beautiful and alive for a week but quite repulsive and dead after the unrelenting sun has beaten down upon it for a month; rather, the Christian is like a deep-rooted evergreen. Or, perhaps the better analogy is that the persevering Christian is like a banana tree, a tree that produces fruit year-round—autumn, winter, spring, and summer.

So then, the first bad surface is "the path," that is, the person who cannot hold on to the gospel because he is inwardly hard and thus outwardly easy prey. The second bad surface is the "rocky ground," that is, the person who is so inwardly shallow that he outwardly cannot withstand the testing of his faith.[5] The third bad surface is the thorn-infested soil. Concerning this surface Jesus teaches, "Others are the ones sown among thorns. They are those who hear the word, but the cares of the world and the deceitfulness of riches and the desires for other things enter in and choke the word, and it proves unfruitful" (4:18–19). The image is of the seed striking the soil and eventually settling in it. The sun shines. The rain falls. The seed starts to grow. Yet, as soon as it is about to push through the surface, three thorns grow around it and choke it: "The cares of the world and the deceitfulness of riches and the desires for other things" (4:19). For example, to think that one is too busy for God now ("the cares of the world"), to think that one is not in need of God because of material prosperity ("the deceitfulness of riches"), and to want to live free from God's rules ("the desires for other things") will slowly but surely suffocate the soul.

The Fourth Surface

That is enough negative preaching for one chapter. Let us move beyond the hard heart, the shallow soul, and the strangled throat to the faithful and fruit-ful follower of Christ. Let us look at the positive surface.

---

4 Douglas Sean O'Donnell, *Matthew: All Authority under Heaven*, PTW (Wheaton, IL: Cross-way, 2013), 367.
5 See O'Donnell, *Matthew*, 368.

Cyril of Alexandria speaks of this parable as Jesus' recounting "three ways of disaster" and "three grades of glory."[6] This is a helpful summary because it gives an equal emphasis on the positive. Yes, there are typically three bad (and sad) responses to the gospel. But there is also one positive response, a response that speaks of an exceptional threefold fruitfulness for those who follow Christ: "But those that were sown on the good soil are the ones who hear the word and accept it and bear fruit, thirtyfold and sixtyfold and a hundredfold" (4:20). This ending might indeed be the pinnacle of the parable, its "climatic focus."[7] So chin up! It reminds us about the certainty of great gospel growth, which Jesus will go on to teach about in the parables in verses 26–32.

What is described here is a "superabundant harvest."[8] Palestine is not like the American Midwest. There are not rows of corn, wheat, and soybeans for miles and miles. In the Midwest seed sits well and grows well. But in certain parts of ancient Israel the land was dry and barren. There, and back then, it was hard to have consistently good harvests. If a farmer got sevenfold or eightfold what he planted, he would be thrilled. To produce tenfold the number of seed would be considered a good harvest, and twentyfold an excellent harvest; to receive thirtyfold, sixtyfold, or a hundredfold would be an unfathomable yield.

With this unthinkable harvest in mind, Jesus ends, as stated above, on a very positive note. He does not end with judgment, as in many of his other parables. He ends with unbelievable abundance. Those who follow him bear fruit. Some a lot of fruit. Others even more than a lot. Still others many bushelsful. The difference, please note, between the surfaces is not who hears and does not hear.[9] Each hears, but only one hears, accepts, and bears fruit. The good hearer, who is not hard, shallow, or self-indulgent, welcomes the word *immediately* (so that Satan cannot snatch it away), welcomes it *deeply* (so it is not withered by persecution), and welcomes it *exclusively* (so other concerns do not strangle it).[10] Then she bears fruit! She is not just a "hearer of the word" but a "doer" of the word (James 1:23). She bears fruit, a harvest of "love, joy, peace, patience, kindness, goodness, faithfulness, gentleness, self-control" (Gal. 5:22–23), as well as a harvest of humility, prayerfulness, and heavenly

6   Cyril of Alexandria, quoted in Thomas C. Oden and Christopher A. Hall, eds., *Mark*, ACCS NT (Downers Grove, IL: InterVarsity, 1998), 53.
7   Craig L. Blomberg, *Matthew*, NAC (Nashville: Broadman, 1992), 215.
8   James A. Brooks, *Mark*, NAC (Nashville: Broadman, 1991), 79.
9   On the importance that Jesus places on hearing see Mark 4:3, 9, 12, 15–16, 18, 20, 23–24, 33.
10 See Robert Gundry, *Mark: A Commentary on His Apology for the Cross* (Grand Rapids, MI: Eerdmans, 1993), 206.

mindedness. She lives a life of not yet perfect but consistent obedience to the commands of Christ.

Seven Applications

Having explained the parable of the sower, I will conclude with seven applications. First, let us show some gratitude for God's gift of grace. If you are reading this big book on the smallest Gospel because someone spoke the word of the gospel to you, you received it with joy, and you have produced fruit, praise God. You are a rare and absolutely blessed breed. Each morning I pray, "Lord, open my heart to rejoice in you, and fill me with a spirit of gratitude." May we all pray that prayer.

Second, we are to sow the "word." Mark 4:14 is our mission statement: "The sower sows *the word.*" Jesus could have said that we should bring to the world miracles. He could have said that we should provide health care. He could have said that we should bring relief to the poor. Instead, he said that his word-work is to be our world-work.

The same week I preached this sermon, a student asked me, "In your opinion, what is the most urgent problem facing the church today?" My response was the following:

Churches are *abandoning the authority of Scripture.* I'll give you an example of what I mean. Recently I attended a megachurch, one of the most influential churches in the world. In the worship service, the name of Jesus was only mentioned at the conclusion of three prayers, and the Bible was never sung, read, or preached on. The only Scriptural quotation came from a quote from Martin Luther King Jr., where Dr. King quoted Jesus on loving one's enemies. That church, and many churches like it, would state in their articles of faith that they believe the Bible to be the inspired and authoritative Word of God. However, practically, they do not demonstrate that they take seriously that claim in their Sunday morning worship or their discipleship programs. If more and more churches say one thing ("we believe in the Bible") but do another ("but we aren't going to let it dictate our philosophy of ministry"), then the church is in a world of trouble.

Third, do not be discouraged when the word is not wanted. God guarantees growth to seed that falls in the good soil. Jesus was much rejected in his preaching ministry. Know and embrace that reality. Paul was not a smashing success either, from today's standards of numerical growth. He was not speaking in stadiums to multitudes. He went from small synagogue to small synagogue. And when he preached at more important venues—as he did in Athens—he was flatly rejected. But in each city he visited, God's word took seed. The church was birthed through the tireless efforts of people like him, who made little money, received little recognition, and, in the end, died for the cause. But what a cause it is! Lives changed. Souls saved. Angels rejoicing in heaven.

Fourth, shifting gears a bit, let us help each other get to heaven. Perseverance of the saints should be done with the help of other saints. Hebrews 3:13 says, "Exhort one another every day, as long as it is called 'today,' that none of you may be hardened by the deceitfulness of sin." As we together journey toward the heavenly city (Revelation 21–22), we need to hold each other's hand and have each other's back. And sometimes we need to kick each other in the backside. Get going! Move forward! Stop backsliding! In the "strength of his might" (Eph. 6:10) we "put on the whole armor of God" (Eph. 6:11). We strive, as Paul said and modeled, to "fight the good fight of the faith," we "take hold of the eternal life to which [we] were called" (1 Tim. 6:12), and, with our eyes set on our Savior (Heb. 12:2), we finish the race (2 Tim. 4:7).

Fifth, let us make sure we do regular fruit inspections. According to the end of this parable, it should not be difficult to find fruit. And, if there is no fruit, there is no faith. But, if there is no faith, there *is* still time to repent and believe. This parable can serve even today as a wonderful wake-up call—as a call to abide in Christ. In John 15:5–6, 8 Jesus says,

> I am the vine; you are the branches. Whoever abides in me and I in him, he it is that *bears much fruit*. . . . If anyone does not abide in me he is thrown away like a branch and withers; and the branches are gathered, thrown into the fire, and burned. . . . By this my Father is glorified, that you *bear much fruit* and so *prove* to be my disciples.

Sixth, let us check the soil around us for thorns. Put differently, weed out the weeds of worldliness. A few years ago I preached through 1 John. I discovered that the word *love* is used more in that little letter than in any other book of the Bible. Fifty-one times! In all the times John speaks of love, it is positive. All but one time. In 1 John 2:15 we read, "Do not love the world or the things in the world. If anyone loves the world, the love of the Father is not in him." Cyprian famously remarked, "You cannot have God for your Father if you have not the Church for your mother."[11] As it relates to the parable of the soils,

11 St. Cyprian, *The Lapsed; the Unity of the Catholic Church*, trans. Maurice Bevenot, ACW (New York: Newman, 1956), 48–49.

we might rephrase Cyprian in this way: "You cannot have God as your spouse and still have the world as your mistress."[12] Do you love this world? If so, then you cannot love God. Do you treasure and trust your wealth? If so, then you cannot treasure and trust God. Are you anxious about everything? If so, then you cannot seek first the kingdom of God. Be not deceived. How close are the thorns to your spiritual artery? Look out for them. And look up to him.

> Turn your eyes upon Jesus,
> Look full in His wonderful face;
> And the things of earth will grow strangely dim
> In the light of His glory and grace.[13]

Seventh, and related to that old refrain, let us not only turn to Jesus, but let us be in awe of Immanuel. I call Jesus "Immanuel" here to return our focus to the storyline of Isaiah. Isaiah's message is twofold: judgment and hope. He preaches that God's judgment is coming in the form of the Assyrians and the Babylonians. Due to their idolatry and injustice and oppression, Jerusalem will fall and Israel will be led into exile (Isa. 5:13). Yet, amid this bad news is good news. God promises to fulfill his promises: a king will come from the line of David (2 Samuel 7), the covenant will be kept (Exodus 19), and all the nations will be blessed (Genesis 12). How? Or, through whom? Israel is going to be chopped down like a tree and burnt (the work of the Assyrians and the Babylonians). Yet, from that smoldering stump comes a holy seed (Isa. 6:13), a branch (Isa. 4:2), a king sprouting forth from the line of David who shall be called "Immanuel" (Isa. 7:14), which means "God with us." Empowered by God's Spirit, Immanuel will deliver his people from every evil and bring in a reign of peace and justice. And through him a redeemed people from all the nations (Isa. 2:2) will flood into the new Jerusalem to live under his rule. In Mark 4:1–20 we find a glimmer of that restoration.

---

12 Douglas Sean O'Donnell, *1–3 John: A Gospel-Transformed Life*, REC (Phillipsburg, NJ: P&R, 2015), 74.
13 Helen H. Lemmel, "Turn Your Eyes upon Jesus" (1922).

Secrets Brought to Light

MARK 4:21–34

Nothing is hidden except to be made manifest; nor is anything secret except to come to light.
Mark 4:22

Orators and writers use the tool of repetition for a number of reasons: to emphasize a point, to offer a rhythm or cadence to the flow of thought, to persuade, or even to produce laughter. Repetition can also, as in this scriptural text, be used to signal key themes, structural outlines, and even important applications. In Mark 4:21–34 "And he said" (4:21, 24, 26, 30; cf. 4:2, 13, 35), "hear" (4:23 [2x], 24, 33), and "seed/s" (4:26, 27, 31 [2x]) are used four times; "parable/s" three times (4:30, 33, 34); and "kingdom of God" (4:26, 30), "earth" (4:28, 31), "ground" (4:26, 31), and "grows" twice (4:27, 32; cf. 4:7, 8).

The clause "And he said" signals the fourfold structure (four pithy parables). The word "parable/s" signals the genre. The phrase "kingdom of God" signals the theme. The words "seed" and "earth"/"ground" and "grows" point to the basic story of the parables, and the verb "hear" indicates the main application. We are to "hear," that is, "respond to" what Jesus teaches on the nature of the kingdom. How so? Two ways. First, we are to make visible the mystery of God's rule. Second, we are to work for growth and expect growth—a slow, certain, and phenomenal harvest.

Make Visible the Mystery

First, as Jesus teaches in **4:21–25**, we are to make visible the mystery of God's rule. The first section (4:21–23), which begins, "And he said to them," uses an analogy of a lamp's carrying light into a room to refer to the message that disciples are to bring to the world. The second section (4:24–25), which also begins "And he said to them," uses an analogy of a scale to refer to the reward or punishment of the messengers. So 4:21–23 focuses on the message, and 4:24–25 on the messengers.

Jesus begins with a ridiculous rhetorical question: "Is a lamp brought in [a room] to be put under a basket, or under a bed, and not [brought in to be put] on a stand?" (4:21). No one in Jesus' day would light an oil-burning clay lamp, walk into a dark room, and take a wicker basket and place it over the lamp, or put the burning lamp under a straw and wooden bed. If someone did so, either the light would immediately go out or the house would eventually burn down. Pause here and admire the humor of Jesus. Our Lord could be quite serious and stern (see 4:24–25). But here he seeks to open his audience's ears with a dash of wit. "You can almost see the crowd smiling at the very idea" of placing a lit lamp under a basket or a bed.[1]

Jesus goes on to conclude, "For nothing is hidden except to be made manifest; nor is anything secret except to come to light" (4:22). Here our Lord seems to be speaking past his current situation, in which his identity and mission are somewhat concealed until his person and purpose are revealed more fully in the cross and resurrection. He is looking to a future time when his followers will proclaim his full message to the whole world. As he says to the twelve in Matthew 10:27, "What I tell you in the dark, say in the light, and what you hear whispered, proclaim on the housetops." Acts is a historical record of their "housetop" ministry. The apostles proclaimed the good news of Jesus literally on housetops but also in marketplaces, synagogues, palaces, and prisons.

We too, as hearers of this parable, must join in their mission. As Jesus taught both them and us, "You are the light of the world. A city on a hill cannot be hidden. Nor do people light a lamp and put it under a basket, but on a stand, and it gives light to all in the house. In the same way, let your light shine before others" (Matt. 5:14–16). Let the light of our "good works" be seen (Matt. 5:16), along with the light of the gospel itself—the message of righteous Jesus' dying for unrighteous people and rising for their justification.

This analogy and this admonition about spreading the light conclude with an exhortation, a motivation, and a warning. The exhortation is "If anyone has ears to hear, let him hear" (Mark 4:23; cf. 4:9). This is not the line from the *Saturday Night Live* comedy skit Hans and Franz, "Hear me now and listen to me later." Rather, it is "Hear me now, listen to me now, and do what I say now." Put differently, "Pay attention to what you hear" (4:24). Why? Here comes the reason, the motivation, and the warning: "With the measure you use, it will be measured to you, and still more will be added to you. For to the one who has, more will be given, and from the one who has not, even what

---

1   Sinclair B. Ferguson, *Let's Study Mark* (repr., Carlisle, PA: Banner of Truth Trust, 2016), 56.

he has will be taken away" (4:24–25). The "measure" is a marketplace analogy. In the marketplace a scoop of grain would be set on a scale. The weight of the produce on one side would be measured against weights on the other. This measurement was done to assure the buyer that the purchase price was equal to the product weight.

The point of the scale analogy is that God weighs our kingdom work, and "what we do for God [one side of the scale] we will also receive from God [the other side]."[2] If we listen to and obey Jesus' word—here about spreading the light; later about sowing seed (same command; different analogies)—he will judge us accordingly. If we bring forth the light of the gospel to others, then "by the grace of God the reward will exceed the effort."[3] He will generously recompense our labors. He will heap on the scale blessing upon blessing. So then, the point is to invest in evangelism—for the rewards will outweigh the efforts.

So we are to sow the seed, to share the good news. However, if we fail to, do not worry, it is no big deal. Wrong! Here comes the warning. Sins of omission matter to Jesus. In verse 25 Jesus teaches, "For to the one who has, more will be given, and from the one who has not, *even what he has will be taken away.*" If we take the gift of the gospel that has been given to us and hide or bury it in the ground, God will take any blessing that could have been ours and give it to someone who hears and heeds the parable of the lamp. The admonition, then and once again: invest in evangelism. The warning: or else.

Think of it this way. Pretend you learn that you have a deadly disease. There is no known cure. Then one day you discover a new doctor at the local hospital with a cure. You see her, and, sure enough, she cures you. A week later you find out your neighbor has the same ailment. One day you are both outside doing yard work and chatting. You talk about the weather, the kids, and sports. But you never talk about the cure. You never talk about the new doctor who saved your life. Would you do that? Would you keep such good news to yourself? Would you keep your dying neighbor in the dark? Of course not. Do not be ridiculous! "Is a lamp brought in to be put under a basket . . . and not [to be set] on a stand?" (4:21).

This warning about taking a possible reward away (4:25) also goes back to the parable of the soils. Those who reject God's Word do not grow. Any blessing that came to them—in the gospel preached to them—will be taken away. Put differently, and more drastically, they will die in their sin of rejection.

2 Grant R. Osborne, *Mark*, TTCS (Grand Rapids, MI: Baker, 2012), 75.
3 Osborne, *Mark*, 75.

But for those who receive what Jesus has to say, rejoice in what he has done, and work for his causes in the world, the reward is unbelievably exponential. "More will be given."

I cannot think of a truer reality in my life. I received the gospel, the wonderful news about Jesus' dying for my sins and rising so I might have eternal life with God, and I have invested my life proclaiming the good news of Jesus—and the blessings God has added are too many to count. But let me count, and recount, a few.

During my first semester in college, my girlfriend walked out of her dorm room, went to the bathroom, and took a pregnancy test. She came back, looked at me, and showed the results. She was pregnant. We were eighteen. We next quit school, moved back home, started to work, and got engaged to be married. Nine months later our son, Sean, was born. Soon after Sean was born, his mother broke off the engagement. We were never married. She broke my heart. This happened right before Christmas. I lost everything I loved and worked for. I lost her. I lost my family, in part, because they were deeply hurt. I lost my college education. But, in the words of the prophet Hosea, the Lord wounded me in order than he might heal me (see Hosea 6:1). One night I came home from work. It was one in the morning. I got down on my knees, I cried, and I cried out, "Jesus, I know you are real. I have never doubted your existence. But I have never asked for your forgiveness. Will you please forgive me? I'm full of lust and pride. And, from this day forward I promise to put you first in my life." In that moment the weight of the world fell from my shoulders. I was born from above. I was a new creation. I was given *every* spiritual blessing in Christ. The scale tipped over. But I was also given a number of earthly blessings. Through God's saving and revitalizing grace, more was given.

God gave me the gift of his church, my truest and everlasting family! "More will be given." And through the local church he gave me a wife—a spectacularly beautiful and industrious one! "More will be given." He gave us four children, including (God be praised!) a red-headed daughter. "More will be given." He gave me an education. The very summer I wrote the first draft of this commentary I was awarded a PhD from the University of Aberdeen. Unbelievable! "More will be given."

I am not saying I have lived a righteous Christian life and it is due to such good behavior that God has bestowed on me such blessings. I am not preaching the health/wealth gospel. Rather, I am preaching the gospel, a gospel that includes trials and sufferings, but also blessings untold—ten thousand and more. I am saying (and I hope you can say the same) that more has been given—"a hundredfold now in this time . . . and in the age to come eternal life" (Mark 10:30). I can say that this little parable is certainly true for me and I hope for you too.

Kingdom Growth

There are two ways in which we are to respond to what Jesus teaches here on the nature of the kingdom of God. First, we are to make visible the mystery of God's rule. Second, we are to work for growth and expect growth—a slow, certain, and phenomenal harvest.[4]

First, we are to work for growth. Our Lord taught, "The kingdom of God is as if a man should scatter seed on the ground" (Mark **4:26**). This down-to-earth analogy brings us down on our knees. Or, perhaps better phrased, it brings us down *to* our knees ("Help us, Lord!") so we might get *off* our knees and walk over and talk to our lost neighbor. To "scatter seed" means to move—to get up, walk around, and open our mouths. Also, as verse 29 records, if and when someone is "ripe" for harvest, we get to work again. We welcome in the fruit. We bring in the sheaves. We join in the harvesting of souls.

Second, we are to expect growth. Look again at our text. A person scatters seed (4:26). What does the seed represent? Back to verse 14: the "word."[5] We spread the gospel as explained in the Bible. So the seed is not a new narthex with a waterslide, touchscreens on the backs of the pews, an entertaining worship band, and a pop psychology message. It is the word from the Word. What happens next? The sower "sleeps," every night for a while ("rises night and day," **4:27**). Why sleep? Get up, you lazy fool! The sower sleeps because he trusts, as time passes, that the word will do its work. All that is needed for germination and fruit is already in that seed. The farmer does not understand how the seed actually grows ("He knows not how," 4:27), but he knows from experience that in "the earth" and "by itself" (Gk. *automatē* = without human effort or involvement, or, more broadly, without any visible cause) the seed sprouts, first into "the blade, then the ear, then the full grain in the ear" (**4:28**). The seed has an inherent power that is unstoppable!

The sower sleeps because he trusts the word will do its work. He believes Isaiah 55:11, that the word that goes out from God's mouth will not return

---

4 The repeated word in that second point is "grow," a key repeated word throughout Mark 4. The seed in the good soil grows and yields an amazing harvest—"thirtyfold and sixtyfold and a hundredfold" (4:8). The mustard seed "sprouts and grows" (4:27); indeed, it "grows up and becomes larger than all the garden plants" (4:32).

5 There is an obvious connection between the parable of the sower and the parable of the mustard seed, as both center on the theme of growth and use similar words: seeds, sowing, and the earth. Thus the latter parable should be interpreted in light of the earlier one, esp. Mark 4:8, 20.

empty but will succeed in the way God intends. He knows that God alone grants the growth (1 Cor. 3:6–7; James 1:18). Similarly, we can trust that God through his word will do his work, knowing that each stage in the growth process—the seed germinating, the stalk rising, the full kernel ready for harvest, the harvest itself—God sovereignly superintends. If we faithfully preach the word and faithfully spread the word, we should expect growth. A nongrowing church is not a kingdom-focused church. So let us all pray and sing:

> Lord, we are few, but thou art near;
> Nor short thine arm, nor deaf thine ear:
> O rend heavens, come quickly down,
> and make a thousand hearts thine own![6]

So then, the sower sleeps because he trusts the power of the seed to grow. He also sleeps because he knows *it takes time* for the seed to plant itself in the soil and days of sun and rain for it to grow. He is expectant but *patiently* expectant. Gospel growth usually takes time. If you have planted the seed, do not be discouraged by the delay.

Dick Lucas recounts a letter he received from someone who came to faith through his Tuesday lunch meetings. Each Tuesday in the London business district Lucas would give twenty-minute sermons during the lunch hour. Here is part of the letter he received:

> I came, invited by a lawyer friend, a pinstripe-clad investment banker. For several weeks I listened intently, and whilst it seemed true, I can confess to having little if any understanding, indeed recollection of anything you said. One Tuesday, however, Jesus' words in Luke hit me. What seemed right I judged as right. And *slowly*, from that Tuesday on, I came to understand what it was all about.

Later in the letter, he adds:

> Having sat for many Tuesdays under the Word of God, having invited many friends, having dug out tapes, having listened to them in the train, the tube, and in the car, here I am at Wycliffe [a theological seminary] training for full time ministry.[7]

6   William Cowper, "Jesus, Where'er Thy People Meet" (1769).
7   Dick Lucas, "Harvest Has Come," sermon, *The Gospel Coalition*, mp3 format, 26:53, https://resources.thegospelcoalition.org/library/harvest-has-come, accessed on September 9, 2021.

Every Christian, especially pastors, feels the pressure to get immediate results. Here our Lord instructs us to resist that lure. Despite unpromising appearances, we can trust that God will work through his Word.

First, we are to work for growth. Second, we are to expect growth. We are to expect *a slow, certain, and phenomenal harvest.* In **4:29** "the harvest" is referenced. How big is the harvest? When we go back to verse 20, we are reminded that the personal harvest of those who receive the gospel is plentiful (cf. Matt. 9:35)—those who "hear the word and accept it and bear fruit" do so "thirtyfold and sixtyfold and a hundredfold." Moreover, the parable of the mustard seed reinforces the idea of abundant growth. In Mark **4:30–32** Jesus compares the rule of God in the world ("the kingdom of God," 4:30) to the growth of a mustard seed. Even though the mustard seed is "the smallest of all the seeds on earth," when it "grows up" it "becomes larger than all the garden plants" (4:31–32). It is so large that birds can "make nests" in its "large branches" (4:32). So gospel growth might be gradual, but in the end it is robust. From "small and weak beginnings" comes "great increase."[8]

So be encouraged! This is the point of the parable of the mustard seed. The kingdom that Jesus announced in 1:14–15 was seemingly insignificant, as small and vulnerable as a black mustard (*Brassica nigra*) seed, a seed "one millimeter in diameter and . . . so tiny it requires from 725 to 760 seeds to equal one gram (one twenty-eighth of an ounce)."[9] That tiny seed, which we could barely see if we held it in our hand, grows into a massive plant, one that looks like a ten-foot "tree" (see Matthew's and Luke's language; Matt. 13:32; Luke 13:19) with large leaves, leaves that birds perch upon and beneath for shelter from the sun. So too Christ's kingdom.

Do you know that you, if you are a Christian, are part of the largest and longest-lasting kingdom in the history of the world? Think of the great empires. Egypt—the country is still here, but the empire is long gone. The Assyrian empire? The Babylonian empire? The Persian empire? The Han dynasty? The Roman empire? The Aztec empire? The Mongol empire? The Ottoman empire? Those realms are all gone. The Russian and British empires? Both Russia and England are still countries, but their empires are both gone. The

8   J. C. Ryle, *Mark: Expository Thoughts on the Gospels,* CCC (Wheaton, IL: Crossway, 1993), 57–58.
9   Klyne R. Snodgrass, *Stories with Intent: A Comprehensive Guide to the Parables of Jesus* (Grand Rapids, MI: Eerdmans, 2008), 220. "In both the Jewish and Greco-Roman world mustard seeds were proverbially known for their small size, even though other seeds, such as the orchid or cypress were known to be smaller. . . . Since we are dealing with proverbial use, anxiety about issues of accuracy are out of bounds" (220). The seed was superlatively small! Moreover, to Jesus' original audience the mustard seed was the smallest seed commonly planted around the Sea of Galilee.

United States of America? We are not an empire, but who knows what will become of this grand experiment. We might make America great again, but for how long? And "great" in what? Materialism? Military might?

Empires rise and fall, but Christ's kingdom is eternal. Do you know that? Rejoice in that? "His kingdom is forever." Can you sing that?

Sometimes we are tempted to wonder, "Do the teachings of Jesus have any effect at all on the world? Does the death and resurrection of Jesus really matter?" We are tempted to think that our religion is on the losing side in history. But it is not. Not only in our lives but in the history of the world this seemingly insignificant seed has produced a superabundant harvest and will continue to produce a superabundant harvest. This minuscule seed, whose gradual growth almost went unnoticed through the various eras and under various regimes, has turned into an orchard. What Jesus planted in the bloodied soil outside the holy city has spread to the whole world—from Jerusalem to Jakarta, Samaria to Shanghai, Athens to the end of the earth. Take a globe, give it a good spin, and stop it with a point of your finger. I will bet you my second-born son that there has been, is, or will be a few birds on the branch you point to—a community of Christians resting in the saving shade of God's only Son.

After the death of Christ, the earliest disciples were wondering, "What now?" (The seed went into the ground and "died.") Then came the resurrection. Hope. New life. Then came Pentecost. Immediate and amazing church growth. But what then? Will the movement survive? Will it flourish in the seedbed of Roman rule? Oh, it will. It did! A movement based on a crucified Jewish messiah (talk about small, insignificant, and seemingly insane) has flourished beyond anyone's expectations—anyone but Jesus' expectation, that is. The kingdom of God is like a grain of mustard seed, he taught, and when it grows up it is large enough to house people from every tribe and tongue and nation. How glorious! Do not be discouraged. We are on the winning side.

Missiles Launched

"The parables of Jesus," writes Sinclair Ferguson, "were like missiles launched against the kingdom of darkness in men's hearts. They were 'timed' to destroy the self-confidence of men and women, and to overcome all opposition to their conversion to Christ. They were calculated to bring people to a point of decision."[10] Ferguson is right. Jesus' parables target those currently outside the kingdom, but they also target those already in it, as **4:33–34** makes clear: "With many such parables [these four are just a sampling] he spoke the word

---

10 Ferguson, *Let's Study Mark*, 56.

to them,[11] as they were able to hear it. He did not speak to them without a parable [cf. 4:11],[12] but privately to his own disciples he explained everything." Or, as Peterson paraphrases verse 34, "When he was alone with his disciples, he went over everything, sorting out the tangles, untying the knots" (MSG).

To the crowds Jesus taught in parables to judge unbelief (see 4:12) but also to prod unbelievers. Here he wants the world to know the sure success of his kingdom, a kingdom that is the opposite of what the Jews of the day expected, a rule that began in obscurity and opposition, hidden from the headlines of the world. Here Jesus wants the world to know that his story—the story of a poor and helpless infant born in a manger who grew to be a man who would appoint a motley crew of apostles and reach out to heal and help the outcasts and then die an ignominious death between two criminals—is the greatest story ever told; and it is the truest story ever told. He wants those who are in the dark to see the light of the gospel.

Jesus wants unbelievers to believe.

And he wants believers to believe afresh. Christ wants his church to be encouraged. There has been a great harvest already: billions of believers to date. Even more to come. Soon and very soon "the earth shall be full of the knowledge of the LORD as the waters cover the sea" (Isa. 11:9) and "a great multitude that no one [can] number" will worship before the throne (Rev. 7:9).

So what then? Believe afresh. Work hard. Share the light; sow the seed. Make visible the mystery of God's rule. Work for growth. Be patient. Expectant. Confident. God is at work. Take comfort. All the growth is in God's good hands.

---

11   While the last use of the word "them" refers to the disciples (Mark 4:13, esp. 4:35, 36), these final verses (4:33–34) likely also, or more directly, indicate the crowd (4:1, 11).
12   Jesus spoke both to the disciples and the crowds more directly; that is, he spoke without parables. Thus the phrase here "without a parable" is hyperbolic, an exaggeration used to make a point.

Who Then Is This?

MARK 4:35-41

And they were filled with great fear and said to one another,
"Who then is this, that even the wind and the sea obey him?"
Mark 4:41

For three years my family lived in Brisbane, Australia. The city of Brisbane is located inland, on the Brisbane River. The river feeds into the Pacific Ocean, about 30 miles away. The beaches to the north (the Sunshine Coast) and south (the Gold Coast) of Brisbane are the most beautiful beaches I have ever seen. On the first weekend we arrived, we went to the Gold Coast. No one in our family, up to that point, had ever swum in the Pacific Ocean. So we got on our swimmers (bathing suits) and ran into the waters. We were the only people on that massive beach in the waters. This was because it was winter! Yet I will tell you that it was the warmest water we as Chicagoans have ever swum in to that point.

I miss the warm and wild waves. I miss rubbing suntan lotion on the great whites and petting box jellyfish, which is what Aussies do for fun. I miss the power and beauty and feel and even the taste of the ocean. But I am no outdoorsman. I can swim, but only the backstroke and doggie paddle, two strokes with which I have discovered saltwater crocodiles cannot keep up. I also cannot waterski. The first and only time I attempted such an inhuman sport, I could not get up after ten tries. So after being dragged through the waters of Glen Lake, Michigan, for about ten miles, I signaled the speedboat driver to bring me in and take me directly to the hospital. My first and only fishing expedition with my oldest son began and ended with my casting and tangling the line. After a morning of attempted detangling, he looked at me in dismay. "Will you ever amount to anything?" was written across his face.

A Calm Setting

When it comes to waters, the apostles were not as idiotic as I am. The first four that Jesus called were fishermen (Mark 1:16–20). All twelve lived around the Lake of Galilee. They likely all knew how to sail and fish. These experienced lake dwellers and seafaring men boarded a boat, we are told in the setting of this story, our first two verses.

> On that day, when evening had come, [Jesus] said to them, "Let us go across to the other side." And leaving the crowd, they took him with them in the boat, just as he was. And other boats were with him. (4:35–36)

"On that day" is the first phrase (**4:35**). We do not know if it was Sunday, Monday, Tuesday, Wednesday, Thursday, Friday, or Saturday (the Sabbath—likely not), but we do know what just happened "on that day." Jesus is teaching parables both to his disciples and those he is wooing to be his disciples.[1] Then our Lord notices the sun setting. "Evening had come" (4:35). When I ponder that statement, the first thought that comes to mind is "Settle down, watch a murder mystery, read a bit, and go to bed." But Jesus wants to go sailing at sundown. He says, "Let us go across to the other side" (4:35), a journey of about 6 nautical miles. Such a journey would take the average fisherman of that day on a typical boat (26.5 feet in length, 7.5 feet in width, and 4.5 feet in depth) less than two hours unless an unexpected storm arose, which was known to happen on that lake.[2]

What follows is the best part about the setting. Jesus gives the command. The disciples comply. "Yes, Lord." Then, we read, "Leaving the crowd, they took him with them in the boat, just as he was" (**4:36**). Who takes whom? The experienced fishermen take the carpenter from Nazareth aboard the boat and say something like, "No worries, mate. Leave this in our hands." This might be the greatest irony of the incarnation. We might imagine all the outdoorsmen in that boat brimming with excitement. They cannot teach with the same authority. They cannot heal to the same extent. But they can navigate, even at night, across a few miles of water. "We got this, landlubber. Take a nap. We'll get you across." Look again at the middle of verse 36: "They took him with

---

1   "The phrase 'on that day (ἡμέρα) when evening (ὀψία) had come' (4:35) introduces Jesus's calming of the storm and places it on the same day as Jesus's parabolic teaching. This connection suggests that the calming of the storm functions much like a puzzling parable that immediately exposes the imperception of those who have been given the secret (μυστήριον) of God's kingdom (4:11)." Elizabeth Evans Shively, "Mark," in *The Greek New Testament, Produced at Tyndale House, Cambridge, Guided Annotating Edition*, ed. Daniel K. Eng (Wheaton, IL: Crossway, 2023), 129.

2   "The Sea of Galilee rests at 628 feet below sea level and is surrounded by mountains gouged with deep ravines. These ravines serve as gigantic funnels to focus whirling winds down onto the lake without notice. The way is often 'greased' by a thermal build-up in the extremely low valley which, while it rises, invites the cold air to come falling violently from above." R. Kent Hughes, *Mark: Jesus, Servant and Savior*, PTW, 2 vols. (Wheaton, IL: Crossway, 1989), 1:113.

them in the boat, *just as he was.*" How was he? Exhausted. He had preached all day.

So they push off shore. Other boats follow ("and other boats were with him," 4:36). He cannot escape the eager crowd. Then what happens? We are not told about the fate of the "other boats" and their sailors, but we are told that as the sun is setting "a great windstorm arose" (4:37). Before we look at the storm, let us pause to ask and answer an important question. Where are they going? Mark 5:1 reveals the answer. They are traveling "to the country of the Gerasenes" on the northeast shore of the Sea of Galilee, a place where Gentiles live. We know this because there are pigs there. Jews do not eat pork (Lev. 11:7; Deut. 14:8). Why go there? To take a break from the Jewish crowd. To serve and save even Gentiles. But what is the rush? Why not sleep in Capernaum (Mark 2:1; 3:20), from which they likely set sail, and then, if Jesus must, sail the next day during the light of safe-sailing sunrise?

The reasons Jesus wants to travel upon the sea through some of the night, and into the heart of a storm, take us to the two lessons of our text. First, Jesus wants to teach his disciples about the nature of faith. Second, he wants to teach them something of his identity. We will return to those two lessons soon. We will first ride through the storm.

A Great Windstorm Arose

In **4:37** we read that "a great windstorm arose, and the waves were breaking into the boat, so that the boat was already filling." A few days before I preached this sermon, I was working in my upstairs office at home. In that office, as I sit behind my desk, I face a wall of large windows and some old French doors. The wind that day was wild. I could see the branches of the oak trees shaking and I could feel the wind piercing through the slight openings in the doors. Then, sure enough, the screen detached and the doors burst open. I feared all my papers would scatter across the room. So, quickly, I ran over, pushed a chair against the doors, ran downstairs, grabbed my electric screwdriver, screwed the doors shut, and got back to work!

On land, a windstorm can be scary; on the waters,[3] it can be deadly. The wind was pushing the waves over even the bow. With waves perhaps 8–10 feet high, the boat was slowly filling with water. I did not ace physics in high school, but I know that if a boat fills with water, it sinks. Imagine the twelve

---

3 The "Greek words that Mark uses to describe that storm . . . actually means a whirlwind, a storm that circles from bottom to top, like a cyclone." Bo Giertz, *The New Testament Devotional Commentary: Volume 1: Matthew, Mark, Luke*, trans. Bror Erickson (Irving, CA: 1517 Publishing, 2021), 163.

frantically bailing out the water. Then imagine Jesus. He is helping, right? Wrong. He is sleeping.[4] "But he was in the stern, asleep on the cushion" (4:38).[5] What an incredible picture of our Lord. He is asleep on the back of the boat ("the stern"). I love the detail about being "asleep on *the* cushion." There is one cushion, perhaps "a sandbag used for ballast,"[6] and Jesus has it. He is sleeping on it, and all around him his closest friends are frantically bucketing out water as the waves more frantically pour into the boat.

How could Jesus sleep through this? The answer might honestly be that he was a heavy sleeper and/or absolutely exhausted. I am a light sleeper. So if a light turns on or a noise is heard, I wake up. Also, because I am a light sleeper, I usually cannot sleep on planes. When we traveled from Brisbane to Los Angeles, I almost never slept. It was a fourteen-hour flight. Then we had a layover that lasted a few hours. I grabbed a coffee. I tried to stay awake, and I did. I most certainly cannot sleep on airport floors. But then, when we got in the plane from Los Angeles to Chicago, I almost always passed out. I was so tired. The sleeping conditions were awful. Smaller plane. Less legroom. Full flight. But my body said, "Enough is enough." The eyes close and the head leans against the tray table or window or stranger's shoulder. Out like a light.

I do not know if Jesus was a heavy sleeper or a light sleeper who was exhausted, but I do know that he likely slept for two other reasons. First, he knew that he is the Creator and that all of creation is under his control (see Col. 1:16–17). He could sleep in a storm like this because he possesses absolute authority. Second, he trusted his heavenly Father completely. We often cannot sleep because we are anxious about tomorrow. We lose sleep, in other words, because we do not trust God.

Ah, but the disciples at this point in the drama are not thinking about sleeping in their beds. They are worried about sleeping in their graves at the bottom of the sea. As the waves continue to wash over the port and starboard, they all run to the stern and push Jesus' body back and forth. "They woke

---

4   "Like Jonah's equally remarkable sleep in the storm (Jon. 1:5–6) it serves to highlight the cru-cial role of the key figure in the story where the other actors are helpless, though Jonah's role (as victim rather than victor) itself serves to emphasize Jesus' authority by contrast rather than by similarity ('something greater then Jonah is here,' Mt. 12:41). . . . Jesus, like Jonah, is awakened by the panic-stricken crew, but whereas Jonah was summoned to pray for divine intervention, Jesus is apparently expected to know what to do himself." R. T. France, *The Gospel of Mark*, NIGTC (Grand Rapids, MI: Eerdmans, 2002), 223–24.

5   "It is only in Mark that we learn that it was evening when they sailed away, that Jesus was al-ready in the boat, that other boats followed, that it was in the stern where Jesus laid down and slept, and that he slept on a pad which was undoubtedly one of the cushions from the rowing benches" (Giertz, *New Testament Devotional Commentary*, 163).

6   David E. Garland, *Mark*, NIVAC (Grand Rapids, MI: Zondervan, 1996), 191.

him." "Teacher," they yell amid the howling winds and crushing waves, "Do you not care?"

Stop there. The emotion that Jesus demonstrates most often in the Gospels is compassion. He cares! But look at the end of their question: "Teacher, do you not care *that we are perishing*?" These experienced seamen understand the dire situation. Wind + waves + too much water in the boat = boat sinking. Boat sinking = watery grave. I like how Ken Taylor in *The Living Bible* renders the apostles' actions: "Frantically they wakened him, shouting, 'Teacher, don't you even care that we are all about to drown?'" (4:38 TLB).

Faith: "Why Are You Afraid?"

Jesus does care. He wakes up. He calms the storm. The Savior saves them. "And he awoke and rebuked the wind and said to the sea, 'Peace! Be still!' And the wind ceased, and there was a great calm" (**4:39**). Matthew seems to indicate that Jesus stood up ("He rose," Matt. 8:26). Mark and Luke leave out the detail. Standing, of course, could indicate complete control. Who can stand on a boat in such a situation? But sitting, if that is in fact his first posture, might signal something similar. He has absolute authority. He sits on the stern, like a king on a throne, and speaks a word to the wind and to the sea, and they immediately heed his command. He says, "Peace! Be still!" (or a more forceful rendering, "Be quiet and keep quiet"),[7] and the wind says, "Right away, Lord." "*The wind ceased*." And the sea said, "Right away, Lord." "*And there was a great calm*." In one instant wind is blowing in their faces; in the next it is completely gone. In one instant the waves are tossing the boat back and forth, and, for as far as they can see, the sea is in a total uproar. The next instant it is completely still. A sheet of glass reflecting the moonlight.

Notice here the word "rebuked" ("And he awoke and *rebuked* the wind," Mark 4:39; cf. Ps. 106:9). This is the same word used in Mark 1:25 and 9:25 when Jesus rebukes two unclean spirits. It is the same word used when Jesus rebukes Peter by saying, "Get behind me, Satan!" (8:33). There is an exorcism-feel to this nature miracle. For, you see, to Jews the sea (notice that Mark uses the word "sea," not "lake" or "waters"), was viewed as a chaotic and even diabolic force. This is why, when John envisions the new heaven and new earth, he sees that "the sea was no more" (Rev. 21:1). There are satanic overtones here in Mark. Jesus exorcises the stormy sea. He rebukes it.

There is, of course, another rebuke here, which Jesus directs to the scared sailors in Mark **4:40**: "Why are you so afraid? Have you still no faith?" Notice

---

7 France (*Mark*, 224) speaks of Jesus' address here like that of an "unruly heckler" who says "Shut up!"

two details here. First, notice the word "still" in the question "Have you *still* no faith?" All twelve men on board have witnessed Jesus' miraculous powers (3:10) and heard his amazing teachings (4:1–32). Jesus expects more from them. He expects that by now they would trust him no matter how dire the situation looks. Perhaps, as it relates directly to the parable of the mustard seed, he expects them to make the logical deduction that, if Jesus said the kingdom of God would grow into something quite sizable, it is highly unlikely that God's plan would be for Jesus and the twelve to drown in the sea so soon into Jesus' ministry.

Second, notice the connection Jesus makes between much fear and no faith. As shown below, the phrase "so afraid" is parallel to "no faith":

Why are you	so afraid?
Have you	no faith?

This is a theme throughout Mark. For example, in 5:36 Jesus says to the ruler of the synagogue who comes to Jesus to heal his dying daughter, "Do not fear, only believe" (cf. 5:15; 6:50; 10:32; 16:8). Fearing death is natural. That father has every indication that his daughter is about to die. He is afraid she will. The disciples too had every indication that they would die. They were afraid the boat would be swamped and that they would sink with it. If I were on that boat with them, I would be afraid too. Wouldn't you?

Why then the rebuke? It is to press upon them at a poignant point in their lives, a moment they will not forget, that they can trust Jesus even when he "sleeps," that is, when he seems silent. Uncaring. Like God is snoring in the skies. The point for them and for us is this: our Lord is both concerned with our problems and capable of solving them, even if outward evidence seems to be to the contrary.

But do not miss another point, namely, that Christ is calling Christ followers here to be courageous. My wife asked me the other night when we were watching a war documentary, "How do you think you'd fare if you were drafted and had to go to war?" I assumed that she meant being drafted when I was young. I replied, "I'd die in the first battle," or something like that. She nodded in agreement. She had seen me waterski.

But I sometimes ask myself a more realistic question: "What would you do if things so changed in this country that the government started rounding up Christian leaders? Would you stand through the storm of persecution? Or, would you renounce your faith?" When I read of the heroes of faith in Hebrews 11, I am challenged. "Through faith," we are told, some "conquered kingdoms . . . stopped the mouths of lions, quenched . . . fire, escaped the edge of the sword" (Heb. 11:33–34). We are told that others, because of their faith, were destitute, distressed, mistreated, mocked, tortured, imprisoned, and killed (Heb. 11:35–37).

Who, these days, has courageous confidence in Jesus? When the curtain of Christian civilization closes in the Western world, will those of us who live there echo what Paul the prisoner says in Philippians 1:20, that with "full courage now as always Christ will be honored in [our bodies], whether by life or by death"? Paul can say this because his foundation is firm and his future certain: "To me to live is Christ, and to die is gain" (Phil. 1:21). The twelve men on that boat could not, at that point, comprehend how death equates gain. But Paul could. We can. And every Christian who has lived after the death and resurrection of Christ can.

Someone recently came into my office. He looked around at all the books. He said, "Have you read all these?" I said, "No, many of these books are resources I use. Dictionaries, commentaries, and the like." Then, as we journeyed into another area of my library, a section filled with more books, he asked, "Have you read these?" His finger pointed at a bookshelf that houses volumes on the early church. I said, "I have read half of them." If this person had continued by asking, "Tell me what you have learned" or "Tell me your favorite story from the first few centuries," I would have talked about Vibia Perpetua, a first-century Christian martyr from North Africa who died under the reign of emperor Septimius Severus.

In what became known as *Passio Sanctarum Perpetuae et Felicitatis* (*The Passion of Saints Perpetua and Felicitas*), Perpetua offers a narrative of her final days of sufferings ("passion") in prison and death at the hands of a Roman gladiator.[8] She tells us that she was in her early twenties, "well-born, educated in the manner of a free person" (2.1), and that she had a husband, "an infant son at the breast," along with a father, mother, and two brothers, one of whom was a Christian (2.2). We are not told how she and her brother became Christians, but they, along with a few other catechumens (including Felicitas), were imprisoned for their faith. While in a dark "dungeon" (3.8), facing a possible death sentence, she describes being "terrified" (3.5), hot ("the heat was intense because of the crowding," 3.6), and "tormented by

---

8   "If indeed Perpetua did write a part of the *Passio* [my view], she would be our earliest Christian female to have written in her own name and the only woman writer to give us a first-person account of her Christian experience." Barbara K Gold, *Perpetua: Athlete of God*, Women in Antiquity (Oxford: Oxford University Press, 2018), 2. The translation of *Passio Sanctarum Perpetuae et Felicitatis* is Gold's.

anxiety for [her] baby," (3.6). There she had four visions that reassured her of God's promises and strengthened her resolve to confess Christ. She was also given permission for her son to stay with her in prison until her hearing. When her pagan father learned that she would be put before a tribunal, he visited her and, hoping to "wrestle [her] away from [her] faith" (5.1), begged her to recant:

> My daughter, have pity on my grey hair; have pity on me, your father. . . . If I have raised you with these hands to this prime of your life, if I have favored you before your brothers, don't disgrace me in front of everyone. Think about your brothers, your mother and your aunt; think about your son who will not be able to live on after you die. . . . Perform the sacrifice! Pity your child. (5.2–4)

However, because she trusted in God's sovereign providence ("You should know that we are not in our own power but in God's power," 5.6), she refused to listen, and, when on trial, she replied to the procurator's plea ("Spare your father's grey head, spare your infant son. Make a sacrifice for the health of the emperors," 6.3) with the answer "No, I will not sacrifice. . . . I am a Christian" (6.4). She, along with the other confessing Christians, was "condemned . . . to the beasts" (6.6). When the day of the gladiator games came, the day they were to fight [wild beasts] in the arena" (10.1), she and her fellow martyrs "marched from the prison to the amphitheater as if they were marching to heaven—cheerful, with their faces composed, and, if they trembled, it was out of joy, not fear."[9] And, as they sang psalms, the hungry beasts wet their jaws and the great gladiators sharpened their swords. Then these "most brave and blessed martyrs!" (21.11) went to glory. Her final words, according to the *Passio*, were to her brother, who was soon to die as well: "Stand firm in your faith . . . and do not be made to lose your faith because of suffering" (20.10).

Identity: Who Then Is This?

Mark wants us to learn two lessons from this short episode about the storm at sea. The first lesson relates to discipleship. Following Jesus does not mean safety. The storms of life are natural to all fallen humans living in a fallen world, and the sufferings of Christian witness and living are part and parcel of faithfully following the suffering servant. We are to have fearless faith.

---

9 Cf. Augustine of Hippo, "The Confessions," *The Works of St. Augustine: A Translation for the 21st Century*, trans. Maria Boulding (Hyde Park, NY: New City Press, 2018), 17.

Whatever tempest we might find ourselves in, we are not to look at the bleak circumstance around us but to focus on our Savior, for he is both concerned with our problems and the only one capable of solving them. If he so wills.

The second lesson, and the one more central to the story, relates to what theologians call Christology. We are to know who Jesus is and respond appropriately to his revealed identity. Consider Mark **4:41**: "And they were filled with great fear and said to one another, 'Who then is this, that even the wind and the sea obey him?'" It is ironic that they are "filled with great fear" (4:41)[10] the moment after Jesus reprimands them for being "afraid" (4:40). But the fear here is the right response. Like Peter's reaction to the transfiguration ("He did not know what to say, for they were terrified," 9:6), here their fear fits the power, majesty, and glory that they have just witnessed. I do not know what they expected Jesus to do when they roused him from his slumber. Perhaps just help them bail water. Perhaps pray for help. I doubt they expected the wind and waves to obey his voice. Their reaction of fear is thus suitable. Likewise, their question is more than appropriate: "Who then is this, that even the wind and the sea obey him?" (4:41).

Have you ever tried to calm a storm? That is a ridiculous question; we know we have no such control over creation. Some of us cannot even get our dogs to sit. No human can do or has done what Jesus does here. At the end of Acts Paul is a prisoner on a ship heading for Italy. As they sail near Crete, "a tempestuous wind, called the northeaster" (Acts 27:14) arises and for many days "violently" tosses the ship (Acts 27:18). What does the great apostle do? Does he stand up and tell the ship's captain, "I got this. I'm a follower of Jesus. In fact, I'm an apostle. I have healed people. I have miraculous powers. I'll still this storm with a word." No, that is not what Paul says or does. Instead he helps prepare the crew for shipwreck, which then occurs.

Jesus' stilling of the storm shouts, "Jesus is acting like only God can act!" "Here," as R. T. France says, "is divine power writ large."[11] In a number of places in the Psalms we are told that God (and God alone!) controls the sea. For example, Psalm 89:8–9 says,

> O Lord God of hosts,
>> who is mighty as you are, O Lord . . . ?
> You rule the raging of the sea;
>> when its waves rise, you still them (cf. Pss. 107:23–30; 65:5–8)

10 Or "They feared a great fear," with the word "fear" in Greek repeated, one word immediately after the other (*phobeō phobos*).
11 France, *Gospel of Mark*, 221.

Also, in Job 38:8–11 God speaks about the "prescribed limits" he has put on the sea: "Thus far shall you come, and no farther, and here shall your proud waves be stayed."

Therefore, the second lesson of the stilling of the sea is for us to acknowledge Jesus' true identity: to bow before Jesus as the "Christ" and the divine "Son of God" (Mark 1:1). The title "teacher" (4:38) is insufficient. It is not only insufficient; it is borderline blasphemous. When people talk about Jesus' being just a good moral teacher, we should think to ourselves, "Well, they have never read the Gospels." When people write books like *The Jesus Diet*, *The Yoga of Jesus*, *Jesus CEO*, and the like, we should not only roll our eyes but rend our garments.

The Gospel of Mark clearly tells us, from the very start, who Jesus is. He is the "Christ [and] Son of God" (1:1). If that is not clear, Mark will make it plain with Peter's answer to Jesus' question, "Who do you say that I am?" Peter replies, "You are the Christ" (8:29). Mark will also make it plain with Jesus' answer to the high priest's question, "Are you the Christ, the Son of the Blessed?" (14:61). Jesus' reply begins, "I am" (14:62). Even the demons understand Jesus' identity. Before the calming of the sea one demon cries out, "You are the Son of God" (3:11), and afterward another demon calls him the "Son of the Most High God" (5:7). Who Jesus is matters. If we get the identity of Jesus wrong, we get the gospel wrong. If we get the gospel wrong, we die in our sins.

A Picture of the Cross

Speaking of sins, I will end with this image and idea. During the week I wrote this sermon, in preparation I researched Christian art on this famous scene of the calming of the storm. One detail I noticed in almost all works was the boat's mast. However, I did not notice any of the artists—with shading, lighting, or coloring—attempting to make a clear connection between the mast and the cross, which obviously structurally resemble each other. But I think the Evangelist Mark, with his historically realistic but theological artistic Gospel, is making a connection between what happened that day on the sea and what happened at Calvary. He makes no mention of the ship's mast. But he does make mention of the ship's master. Jesus is depicted in Mark 4:35–41 as a sovereign Savior. He saves his disciples from death. And this small salvation foreshadows the ultimate salvation accomplished on the cross, where Jesus will conquer the greatest threat that we all face: death.

So then, we must understand that "the subduing of the sea and wind was not merely a demonstration of power; it was an epiphany," through which

Jesus' identity (he is the divine Son of God) and mission (he will save us from death) are revealed to us.[12] This passage does not teach us that Jesus is here to still all the storms of life. Rather, it teaches that he has conquered the greatest storm we face—*our* deaths—through *his* death. With his outstretched arms he has saved us. Shalom. Peace with God! This is the good news we celebrate. The good news we must share with a dying world.

---

12 Paul J. Achtemeier, "Person and Deed: Jesus and the Storm-Tossed Sea," *Int* 16 (1962): 176.

Strength to Subdue an Army of Spirits

MARK 5:1-20

The unclean spirits came out and entered the pigs; and the
herd, numbering about two thousand, rushed down the
steep bank into the sea and drowned in the sea.
Mark 5:13

My oldest teenaged daughter received two text messages from a non-Christian friend. She showed them to me because she wanted some help in thinking through her response. In the first text her friend shares that she feels that she is not alone because random good things are happening to her, like turning on the radio and finding a song by the same artist she was just singing. She talks about feeling extremely happy. Then she asks whether these feelings and seemingly random occurrences have anything to do with God. "Is this a feeling you get regularly when you believe in a higher being?" She goes on to say, "Like, I don't think I've ever made a conscious effort to believe in a God but I found myself smiling up at the sky and thanking Him or Her (I'm not sure). And it's such a pleasant feeling. I really like the idea that there's someone looking out for me." In the second text she clarifies that she does not believe in a hell but *really* likes "the thought that there's a higher being and he's always looking out for everyone, regardless of religion or disposition."

My response to those two texts was threefold. First, how wonderful it is that this friend is, for the first time in her life, thinking about the possibility of a God who, in his sovereign providence, rules over even the little details of the world and cares personally for every person made in his image. Second, how easy it is to make God into our own image by, for example, dismissing the reality of hell because it does not fit our sensibilities or by embracing religious inclusivity because it is the popular position of the day. Third, and related to the second, how naive we can be to the realities of the fallen world in which we fallen people live. When we are happy and good things are happening, we might be prone to acknowledge a good God, but, when bad things happen, we tend to deny the existence of God or claim that he does not care. Rarely do we think that other supernatural forces—hellish ones—are at play, in both the happy and the unhappy experiences of life.

The Bible presents us with a world filled with sin, sickness, unexpected storms, and unexplainable and undeniable evil forces. The Bible clearly reveals our real problems, namely, that every human experiences disease, faces death, and is up against demons. And the Gospel of Mark presents us with Jesus, the higher being (the "Son of the Most High God," 5:7) who has come down in our very flesh to conquer disease, death, and demons. At various places in Mark 1–3 we have witnessed Jesus conquer disease. In the next chapter we will read about Jesus' conquering death. This text (5:1–20) focuses on Jesus' conquering of demons. These three pictures of Jesus' authority over evil instruct us that we are not alone, that God is in control of the details, and that he deeply cares for people.

The Other Side of the Sea

The previous passage began with Jesus' command to his disciples, "Let us go across to the other side" (4:35), the other side of the Sea of Galilee. We know the journey was a memorable one. A perilous storm arose. Jesus calmed the wind and waves. This passage begins: "They came to the other side of the sea" (**5:1**). The specific part of the other side of the sea is "the country of the Gerasenes" (5:1).[1] What is important about this location is that it is a predominantly Gentile region. This is the first of four missions to the Gentiles in Mark (7:24–30, 31–37; 8:1–10). It should be no surprise to us, if we know the promises of the inclusion of the Gentiles in the OT,[2] that Jesus the "Christ" would spread the gospel of the kingdom to them. But it must have been a shock to the disciples, who likely held the common anti-Gentile bias of the Jews of their time, to beach the boat on a part of the promised land that was less than promising—a region now filled with unclean Gentiles.

That is not all that is surprising. Or unclean. In **5:2**, we read, "And when Jesus had stepped out of the boat, immediately there met him out of the tombs a man with an unclean spirit."[3] Not only are the disciples entering the homeland of unclean Gentiles, but there, with Jesus' first step out the

---

1   On the debate over the location of this exorcism and a simple explanation see R. C. Sproul, *Mark*, St. Andrew's Expositional Commentary (Sanford, FL: Reformation Trust, 2015), 100.
2   E.g., Genesis 12:3; 18:18; 22:18; Psalm 22:27–28; Isaiah 9:1–2; 49:6; 56:6–8; Daniel 7:14; Hosea 2:23.
3   On the difference between the one man in Mark and the two men in Matthew and Luke see W. D. Davies and Dale C. Allison Jr., *A Critical and Exegetical Commentary on the Gospel according to Saint Matthew*, ICC (Edinburgh: T&T Clark, 1991), 2:80.

boat, they find themselves in an unclean place (a graveyard, "the tombs") approached by "a man with an unclean spirit." Yes, here we have an unclean spirit in an unclean place filled with unclean people, some of whom are herding unclean pigs. This is one unclean scene!

This is also one very heartbreaking situation. This man, we are told, "lived among the tombs" (5:3). Like Jesus' tomb (15:46), the tombs described here were caves or sections of rock cut out for burial chambers. A family would reserve such a tomb for its dead. So this poor man, for shelter from the elements, lived in either a freshly cut tomb by himself or a walk-in gravesite, surrounded by skeletons, decaying flesh, and filthy vermin. Either way, home sweet home was not so sweet.

However, the focus of Mark's graphic description of the man is not on his home but on his Herculean strength: "And *no one* could bind him anymore, not even with a chain, for he had often been bound with shackles and chains, but he wrenched the chains apart, and he broke the shackles in pieces. *No one* had the strength to subdue him" (5:3–4). This is a picture of many different people—friends, family, local authorities, perhaps soldiers, even exorcists—trying to help the man. But, sadly, they do not possess the strength to do so. *No one* does. Eventually they all give up. And perhaps they do so not only because it seems hopeless but because it has become dangerous.

The final verse in Mark's description of him is not of a strong man but of a sad and mad man: "Night and day among the tombs and on the mountains he was always crying out and cutting himself with stones" (5:5). The word "always" leaps off the page. It is bad enough that he is "crying out" (in pain and for help) and "cutting himself with stones" (to try to soften the psychological pain with physical pain, or perhaps in some ritual intended to give an exit point for the unwanted spirits), but that such crying and cutting is his daily ("night and day") pattern ("always") is terribly sad.

Now, before we see what happens next to this supernaturally strong, dreadfully unhappy, and completely unclean man, let me offer two brief applications based on these opening five verses. Both are lessons I think Jesus was seeking to teach his first disciples and, through Mark's inspired record of the event, to teach us as well.

First, let us follow Jesus' lead and go the distance for the outcast. There is only one reason Jesus journeys six nautical miles through a deadly/demonic storm to "the country of the Gerasenes" (5:1; cf. 5:21): to help this one man. This is a pattern in Jesus' ministry. He does not seek the crowds. He does not go to the palaces of princes or the shrines of holy men to announce the good news of the kingdom. Rather, he takes the message to the least and sometimes the quite unlovely. In 1 Samuel 22:2 we read of King David, "Everyone who was in distress, and everyone who was in debt, and everyone who was bitter in soul, gathered to him. And he became commander over them." Here in Mark 5:1–5 we read of a king greater than David who goes to the distraught, the poor, the depressed, and the demonized. What a beautiful picture of our beautiful Savior!

Everyone made in the image of God matters. So may we and our churches be known as those who go the distance for the outcast. Go downtown and talk to a homeless man and buy him lunch. Go to the mental health center and befriend a patient. Go to the county jail and lead a Bible study. Go to the shelter for battered women and volunteer an hour. Go to a summer camp and work with troubled teens. Visit a nursing home and speak gracious and comforting words to the dying.

Second, let us acknowledge and embrace that following Jesus sometimes means going from one difficult situation (a storm at night) to an equally difficult situation (a demon-possessed lunatic in the morning). I doubt the disciples slept that night. I am sure they were both exhausted and emotionally drained after nearly drowning. Jesus at times rests and calls them to rest. But on these two days he is making disciples by training those men in the high and hard calling of full-time Christian ministry. In Christian ministry, and at times in the Christian life, we should not be surprised when we step out of the boat with Jesus and "immediately" another stormy situation arises.

Legion vs. the Lord: When Pigs Fly!

In the second act of the drama (5:6–13) we read the dialogue between Jesus and the man, followed by an unusual exorcism:

> And when he saw Jesus from afar, he ran and fell down before him. And crying out with a loud voice, he said, "What have you to do with me, Jesus, Son of the Most High God? I adjure you by God, do not torment me." For he was saying to him, "Come out of the man, you unclean spirit!" And Jesus asked him, "What is your name?" He replied, "My name is Legion, for we are many." And he begged him earnestly not to send them out of the country. Now a great herd of pigs was feeding there on the hillside, and they begged him, saying, "Send us to the pigs; let us enter them." So he gave them permission. And the unclean spirits came out and entered the pigs; and the herd, numbering about two thousand, rushed down the steep bank into the sea and drowned in the sea.

Notice who is in control here. All the man's actions (or the demons' actions in the man) here acknowledge Jesus' authority. He sees Jesus, he runs to Jesus, and when he gets near Jesus, he drops to his knees before him (5:6). Then he confesses Jesus' rightful identity as the "Son of the Most High God" (5:7), even if he might be attempting to have authority over Jesus by knowing his name.[4] Finally, three times the demons in him beg Jesus ("adjure," 5:7; "begged," 5:10, 12) not to "torment" them (5:7),[5] not to send them out of that region (5:10), and instead to send them into the pigs (5:12).

The phrase describing this awesome exorcism—"So he gave them permission" (5:13)—sounds anticlimactic. But what is said (or not said!) here is as powerful as Jesus' "Peace. Be still" (4:39). It should remind us of the opening chapters of Job, in which God, in complete control of the cosmos, gives Satan permission to inflict Job (Job 1:12; 2:6). Here the Lord gives permission to afflict poor pigs. However, for all their begging, the demons do not actually get what they want. They do not want to be judged. They know Jesus is not going to allow them to inflict another human being, at least on his watch. So the unclean pigs seem like a safe option. What the demons do not count on is the herd's being so spooked that it would run down a steep bank into the sea.[6] The same diabolical sea that almost swallowed up Jesus and his disciples has opened its mouth to receive this stampede of swine! The unclean pigs will die; the unclean spirits will presumably return to "the abyss" (Luke 8:31; cf. Rom. 10:7),[7] there to be "committed . . . to chains of gloomy darkness to be kept until the judgment" (2 Pet. 2:4), that is, until the final judgment, when they will be cast "into the eternal fire prepared for the devil and his angels" (Matt. 25:41).

Beyond noticing who is in control here, notice also the conversation, a very curious one. Mark 5:8 takes us back before the action in verses 6–7. It could be in parentheses, the sense being that Jesus *had said*, perhaps the moment he got out of the boat, "Come out of the man, you unclean spirit!" This is why the demons, through the man's body, run to him to ask for a lighter sentence. It is

---

4   "The full address is not a confession of Jesus' dignity but a desperate attempt to gain control over him or render him harmless, in accordance with the common assumption of the period that the use of the precise name of an adversary gave one mastery over him." William L. Lane, *The Gospel of Mark*, NICNT (Grand Rapids, MI: Eerdmans, 1974), 183–84.

5   "The demons know that this is their final doom. They know that Jesus will defeat them. They know that they will be cast into a terrible place of everlasting torment (see Rev. 21:8), and so they tremble with fear. Some people may not believe in hell, but demons certainly do!" Philip Graham Ryken, *Luke: Knowing for Sure*, REC, 2 vols. (Phillipsburg, NJ: P&R, 2009), 1:399.

6   "The demons prefer the pigs to the abyss, but when the pigs rush into the lake, it becomes their abyss." Daniel M. Doriani, *Matthew*, REC, 2 vols. (Phillipsburg, NJ: P&R, 2008), 1:360.

7   "With a word, the . . . swine were off to hog heaven and the demons were howling their misery in an incorporeal existence." R. Kent Hughes, *Mark: Jesus, Servant and Savior*, PTW, 2 vols. (Wheaton, IL: Crossway, 1989), 1:121.

curious that Jesus gives the demons a hearing. When he stilled the storm, he displayed his power immediately after the command. Here, after some delay, he seems to invite a dialogue. "What is your name?" Jesus asks. The reply: "My name is Legion" (5:9). However, this brief conversation simply reinforces the first detail, namely, that Jesus is in complete control and has absolute authority over evil. A legion in the Roman army comprised six thousand foot soldiers. Maybe Jesus sent three demons into each pig. The point, in any case, of the middle of this story is not that Jesus is cruel to animals but that Jesus has power over all created beings: pigs (animals), the man (humans), and an army of unclean spirits (fallen angels). And there are three points of instruction for us: (1) Satan is at work in the world, (2) Jesus has come to destroy the works of the devil, and (3) when he does so, the effect of that destruction is revolutionary.

First, Satan is at work in the world. He is at work in obvious and in subtle ways. I have never witnessed an exorcism like the one described in our text (this exorcism has made it in the Bible because it was extraordinary), but I have witnessed people do incredibly awful acts, deeds that I would only describe with adjectives like "evil," "satanic," or "possessed." I also regularly read about events in the world that move beyond the total depravity of man to the incomprehensible corruption of otherworldly forces.

Think about it—what powers were at work in the world when a Christianized country (Germany), under the banner of a cross (Hitler's *Hakenkreuz*, "hooked cross"), promoted and allowed the extermination of over six million Jews? Was it only for human reasons that fascism and Marxism led to concentration camps and ethnic cleansing? The twentieth century, the most technologically advanced century, was the bloodiest century in world history. And how can we make sense of the sexual revolution, a movement that preached and promised "freedom" and "peace" but has led to bondage and violence—an astronomical rise in sex trafficking, sexual transmitted diseases, broken homes, abused children, aborted babies? Anti-God philosophies always lead to inhumanity. But from where do such thoughts arise if not from the "father of lies" (John 8:44)?

Satan's work is obvious, but it is also subtle. Just because we do not always see Satan at work—as we do in the newsworthy atrocities—does not mean he is not at work. For more on the subtle work of Satan in the world, I highly recommend C. S. Lewis's brilliant book *The Screwtape Letters*. In one of the letters Screwtape (the mentor demon) recalls the story to Wormwood (the demon in training) of how he successfully kept a young atheist an atheist. When the young man was thinking about exploring further the possibility of the existence of God, the demon reminded the man to first grab some lunch so he could think with a refreshed body and mind. Once the demon got him to eat, the rest was easy. He further distracted him by the events on the streets and the details he read about in the newspaper. No further thought of God.

In 2 Corinthians 4:3–4 Paul writes of the gospel's being veiled because Satan, whom he calls "the god of this world," has "blinded the minds of the unbelievers, to keep them from seeing the light of the gospel of the glory of Christ." In 1 John 5:19 John states that "the whole world lies in the power of the evil one." In Ephesians 2:2 Paul calls Satan "the prince of the power of the air," a spirit "now at work" in unbelievers ("the sons of disobedience").

Satan is at work in the world. That is the first point we should consider. Second, as well-illustrated in this Markan pericope, Jesus came to "destroy the works of the devil" (1 John 3:8). Have you ever thought of the incarnation as *destructive*?[8] It was! Jesus, the promised offspring of Eve, came to crush the serpent's head (Gen. 3:15). In Jesus' earthly ministry—with exorcisms like this one recorded in Mark—Jesus put his foot on Satan's head. At the cross he crushed it. When he returns in glory, he will eradicate all evil, tossing the devil and his minions into the "bottomless pit" (Rev. 9:2).

Third, when Jesus destroys the work of the devil in someone's life, the effect of that destruction is revolutionary. This man went from wandering around the tombs, out of his mind, to "sitting there, clothed and in his right mind" (Mark 5:15). He went from howling like an animal (5:5) to being the first evangelist, clearly communicating the gospel to others (5:20). Seeking to loosen the bondage of sin in others, he told the story of his chain-wrought and rock-pierced scars.

In my own life, and in the lives of countless other converts, I have seen people dramatically change. One day they are bound in sin. They love the world and the things in this world. They are cruel to their neighbors and co-workers. Then God gets ahold of their hearts. They love God and the things of God. Their desires change. Their behavior changes. They are new in Christ. They seek to love their neighbors. They become good spouses, parents, and employees. They want to follow Jesus and share him with others. When Jesus destroys the works of the devil, the effect is revolutionary!

Two Reactions

This passage concludes with two opposite reactions to Jesus. The first reaction, recorded in Mark **5:14–17**, is of the herdsmen, the people from the region, and the local eyewitnesses.

---

8   See Douglas Sean O'Donnell, *1–3 John: A Gospel-Transformed Life*, REC (Phillipsburg, NJ: P&R, 2015), 92.

The herdsmen fled and told it in the city and in the country. And people came to see what it was that had happened. And they came to Jesus and saw the demon-possessed man, the one who had had the legion, sitting there, clothed and in his right mind, and they were afraid. And those who had seen it described to them what had happened to the demon-possessed man and to the pigs. And they began to beg Jesus to depart from their region.

So "the swineherds spread the story"[9] throughout the region ("in the city and in the country," 5:14)! This seems like a good start. They are doing the work of evangelists. Of course, we do not know their heart motives, physical gestures, or voice inflections when they declare the news, "Jesus exorcised Legion! Lunatic finds religion. Pigs commit mass suicide."[10] What we do know is that the story seems so sensational that many people come to see for themselves (5:14–16). They arrive and see Jesus. That part of the story is true. They see the man looking and acting like a normal person. That part is true. They also see no pigs. That part is true too. They then listen afresh to the eyewitness testimony to all these events ("Those who had seen it described to them what had happened," 5:16). Herein follows an eruption of repentance and faith. A revival to rival all revivals. It makes the *Great* Awakening look *average*. Wrong!

In fact, the people of that region respond in two ways. First, "they were afraid" (5:15). The terror might be because they know they have witnessed the work of God. They are afraid just as the disciples on the boat were afraid (4:41) after witnessing Jesus calm the storm—they saw "the majesty of God [that] shone brightly in Christ."[11] However, it might be that their fear relates directly to their second response: "And they began to beg Jesus to depart from their region" (5:17). They do this because they fear what he might do with their "demons" (they are unwilling to abandon their current lifestyle), and they fear further economic damage if Jesus stays in town. Pigs today, soybeans tomorrow. Or, more likely, pigs ousted today, the casino closed tomorrow.

These people reacted to Jesus the way millions of people react to Jesus. They might witness his miraculous work in the world, but they choose staying in their sin over salvation from it, and they choose the love of money over the new life offered in Jesus Christ. They *fear* what might happen to their daily

---

9 Donald English, *The Message of Mark: The Mystery of Faith*, BST (Leicester, UK: Inter-Varsity, 1992), 111.

10 See Ryken, *Luke*, 1:401.

11 John Calvin, *Commentary on a Harmony of the Gospels*, quoted in *CHSB*, 1480.

routines, relationships, jobs, and pocketbooks. They *fear* that following Jesus might just ruin their lives. But what foolishness! As Calvin aptly summarizes,

> What could have been worse than this? They too were scattered, and here is a shepherd to collect them—or rather, it is God who stretches out his arms, through his Son, to embrace and carry to heave those who were overwhelmed by the darkness of death. They choose rather to be deprived of the salvation that is offered to them than to endure any longer the presence of Christ.[12]

Verses 14–17 record one reaction. It is a negative reaction but a popular one. Verses 18–20 record another reaction. It is a positive one and an unpopular one. But it is the one we are to emulate. Let me put it this way: Do you want Jesus to go? Or, like this man, do you want to go with Jesus?[13]

Starting in **5:18**, we read about what Jesus does after his mission is accomplished. "As he was getting into the boat, the man who had been possessed with demons begged him that he might be with him." The demons begged Jesus not to torment them. The townspeople begged Jesus to leave. This man begs Jesus to let him be a disciple. But Jesus says no ("He did not permit him," **5:19**), not because he does not want people begging to follow him but because Jesus has a special and specific commission for this man, namely, "Go home to your friends and tell them how much the Lord has done for you, and how he has had mercy on you" (5:19).[14] He is to return to his "home" and share the good news with his "friends," those who love him and have likely tried to help him.

Here Jesus models indigenous missions. He uses this Gentile man from this Gentile region to take the gospel to Gentiles. This man, of all men in the world, becomes the first apostle (cf. 6:7–12)! He is *sent out* to the Gentiles. I love this about the ending to this story. I also love, as recorded in **5:20**, that the man's obedience exceeds Christ's command: "And he went away and began to proclaim in the Decapolis how much Jesus had done for him, and everyone marveled." Jesus said to return home to do a bit of show and tell. Likely the man did so. But he does not limit his scope to his family and friends. He proclaims the good news of Jesus' mercy throughout "the Decapolis," ten different Hellenistic cities east of the Jordan.

---

12 Calvin, *Harmony of the Gospels*, quoted in *CHSB*, 1480.
13 See Sinclair B. Ferguson, *Let's Study Mark* (repr., Carlisle, PA: Banner of Truth Trust, 2016), 70.
14 In both the immediate ("Tell them how much the Lord has done for you," Mark 5:19; "He . . . began to proclaim . . . how much Jesus had done for him," 5:20) and preceding context, Jesus is the "Lord" (1:3; 2:28). Jesus is the Lord God, as Luke makes plain (Luke 8:39).

Here, with this final section, the lessons for us are twofold. First, everyone who has experienced Jesus' mercy is on mission. Like this man, we are "not only saved *from* something, but also *to* something: a life of evangelistic discipleship."[15] Second, the mission, as modeled by both Jesus and this man, should expand beyond our own community. We are to take the gospel to our homes and hometowns. We are also to take the gospel to the world.

Sharing His Testimony

Recently my teenage children encouraged me to share my testimony at youth group. Their request got me thinking about God's mercies bestowed upon this madman in Mark 5:1–20. What would be the details of his testimony? How would he specifically share "how much the Lord had done" for him (5:19)? I would imagine him sharing about his situation prior to Christ—how wretched he was and unable to free himself from the power of sin and the devil. "I was the crazy man of the cemetery. Naked. Living in a cave among the dead. Cutting myself. Screaming night and day. Desperately lonely and sad and angry. Hopeless." I imagine him speaking about how he was unable to save himself. He was "utterly indisposed" and the absolute "opposite to all that is spiritually good."[16] If there ever were a man removed from the grace of God, it was this man. But then the grace of God in the person of Jesus came to shore. "He dealt with my demons," the man shares with tears now streaming down his cheeks. "And he made my mind whole again. More than that, he renewed my mind and commissioned me (even me!) as an apostle."

What a transformation! Can you think of a better testimony? But it is, in so many ways, our testimony. We were under the dominion of the devil. Dead in our sins. Unable to escape. Hell-bent and hell-bound. Then Christ came into our lives. He destroyed the works of the devil. He forgave our sins. He gave new life. He commissioned us to service. What a glorious gospel! Let us pause to ponder afresh the good news of the grace of God in the gift of his Son to us and perhaps to those far off—but not so far from the reach of God.

---

15 Ryken, *Luke*, 1:404.
16 WLC 25.

Overcoming the Last Enemy

MARK 5:21-43

Taking her by the hand he said to her, "Talitha cumi," which
means, "Little girl, I say to you, arise."
Mark 5:41

I have a reoccurring nightmare in which something bad happens to my children, usually involving death—a disease, a car accident, a drowning, or a fire.
The sense I make of this, in my amateur psychological self-evaluation, is that
(1) it is normal for parents to fear losing children and (2) I am still affected by
the deaths of children I witnessed in my youth—a classmate in kindergarten, a
close friend in high school, and a neighbor three doors down in his late teens.

The father in our Gospel story is living through something he wishes were
a nightmare. He wishes he would just wake up and all his subconscious fears
would subside. He dreams that his daughter's imminent death were not a reality. But it is, and he knows it. He is now desperate. So he comes to Jesus for
help. The girl dies. Jesus raises his daughter to life. But his daughter is not the
only "daughter" in this text to whom Jesus gives new life. Another desperate
soul comes to Jesus. She has an incurable disease. She touches Jesus and, in
doing so, is touched by him. Saved. Granted new life.

The point of these intertwining episodes is obvious: like the man and
the woman who come to Jesus in faith, trusting that he alone has the power
over death, we too should believe that Jesus has power to overcome the "last
enemy" (1 Cor. 15:26). But, as this is a narrative, the point is made not by a
clear proposition but rather through a colorful story with interesting characters, dialogue, and plot.

The Daughter Near Death

The geographical setting is a familiar one. The action takes place around the
Sea of Galilee, likely in the town of Capernaum ("And . . . Jesus had crossed

again in the boat to the other side," Mark **5:21**). After calming the storm at sea and then tossing six thousand demons into the abyss, Jesus returns to his ministry headquarters. But there he finds no time to rest or regroup. The crowd he left (4:36) is waiting for him. The moment he steps foot off the boat ("He was beside the sea") we are told that "a great crowd gathered about him" (5:21). This is not unusual. Crowds are mentioned ten times in Mark 2–4. These crowds fill houses (2:4), make it hard for Jesus even to eat (3:20), force him to teach from a boat (4:1), and almost crush him (3:9). What is unusual is the first face that emerges from this crowd: "Then came one of the rulers of the synagogue, Jairus by name" (5:22).

What is unusual is that Jairus is a Jewish religious leader who comes not to test, accuse, or seek to plot against Jesus (the pattern thus far from the religious authorities) but rather to beg for help. What is further unusual are the details given. Rarely in his record of miracles does Mark provide us with names and occupations. But here we have the man's name ("Jairus") and his occupation, or role within the community ("one of the rulers of the synagogue," 5:22). The name tells us that this man is Jewish ("Jairus" is Hebrew for "Yahweh enlightens"), as does his occupation. To be a "ruler of the synagogue" tells us that he is respected, religious, and rich.[1] This is not the type of person who has come to Jesus for help thus far. The outcasts have flocked to him (e.g., lepers), and he has gone to the outcasts (e.g., lunatics). But it is shocking that a person of privilege and power would approach him in need.

It is more shocking what Jairus does and says. As soon as he sees Jesus, he falls at his feet (5:22). "For such a VIP to fall at Jesus' feet shows both his plight and his regard for Jesus."[2] From the feet of Jesus next comes his impassioned ("implored him earnestly," **5:23**) plea: "My little daughter is at the point of death. Come and lay your hands on her, so that she may be made well and live" (5:23). Both his posture and his petition point to his remarkable faith. In front of this large Jewish crowd, which must include some of his religious peers, he kneels before Jesus. What humility. Then he begs Jesus to do what only God can do—stop death. What confidence in the divine authority of Jesus!

We will reflect further on the nature of true Christian faith when we discuss the bleeding woman. For now, do not miss how Mark is defining faith

---

1 "Normally [a 'ruler'] was a civil community leader (there were seven of them) and the ['synagogue ruler'] was the president of the synagogue (one of three officers), but often the same person held both offices. He would be a wealthy patron and member of the synagogue board who was responsible for the order and progress of worship." Grant R. Osborne, *Matthew*, ZECNT (Grand Rapids, MI: Zondervan, 2010), 348; cf. Osborne, *Mark*, TTCS (Grand Rapids, MI: Baker, 2012), 87. For emphasis Mark repeats the man's title (Gk. *archisunagōgōn*) three times (Mark 5:35, 36, 38).
2 Osborne, *Mark*, 87.

in picture-book form. Faith acts. Faith moves toward Jesus ("Then came," 5:22—the man came to Jesus; cf. "She . . . came up behind him," 5:27; "came . . . before him," 5:33). Faith acknowledges Jesus is almighty and bows low ("He fell at [Jesus'] feet," 5:22). Faith trusts that Jesus has the authority to conquer death ("Lay your hands on her" and she will "live," 5:23).[3]

Now we return to the first scene in the story, which ends, "And [Jesus] went with him" (5:24). It is remarkable that Jesus takes the time to walk to this man's house. Jesus has proven, even in the last two miracles, that his voice can calm the wind and the waves and toss a ton of bacon into the sea. So why not speak a word? My educated guess is that the compassionate Christ does not mind, when it comes to raising little children from the dead, adding a personal touch. And, in case we get carried away by Jesus' concern for the outcast, note here that he cares also for the in-crowd. He does not care only for lepers and lunatics but for Roman centurions and synagogue rulers as well. Jesus' gospel is not the liberation gospel; it is not that he came only for the poor and oppressed and for the purpose of liberating them from despotic political systems. Rather, his gospel is the good news for all people, not just the marginalized.

When I lived in Australia, I was invited to speak at an elite boys school in Sydney that is deeply Christian in its roots but has many non-Christian students. The school paid for the whole family to fly there, and we stayed in the headmaster's beautiful house on campus. The headmaster told me that the school had recently undergone great tragedies: the death of a beloved teacher, sudden deaths of a few students, and the news of terminal illnesses. It was an unusual year, and a very sad one. So what did I share with these boys? Did I talk about how to achieve better grades? Excel in athletics? Make money? No! I talked about death. I talked about death's sad reality, and its sure conqueror.

The chaplain debriefed with me afterward. He read some of the comments on the talks, the encouraging ones. Some boys wanted to renew their commitment to Christ; others wanted to know more about him. I do not know what became of those young men. Time will tell. My prayer is that they would follow Christ and use their elite education to represent Christ to the world. My prayer is that future John Stotts will come from that week of talks.[4]

Jesus loves the privileged as much as does the poor. His special attention to the poor, so pronounced in the Gospels, is easily explained. He cares for

---

3   The ruler's plea is similar to the centurion's "Only say the word" (Matt. 8:8), because both the centurion and the ruler "had authority and recognize that of Jesus"; John Nolland, *The Gospel of Matthew*, NIGTC (Grand Rapids, MI: Eerdmans, 2005), 394. However, we should add, as Nolland (394) does, that the ruler's trust in Jesus' ability to revive the dead is "a breathtaking faith."

4   Stott, one of the most influential Christian leaders of the last century, was converted when a special speaker came to his elite boys school.

all people equally, even those for whom others do not. He makes sure that all those made in God's image get God's time and attention.

The Daughter with the Discharge

Out of the "great crowd" has come this rich, respected, and religious man (5:21). Then, all of a sudden, out of that same "great crowd" that "followed him," presumably step by step to Jairus's, pushing against him ("and thronged about him," 5:24), "there was a woman" (5:25). Her issue is an issue of blood![5] "And there was a woman who had had a discharge of blood for twelve years, and who had suffered much under many physicians, and had spent all that she had, and was no better but rather grew worse" (5:25–26). This is not as horrific a description as that of Legion (5:2–5), but it is equally graphic and sad. Notice the repetition of the small but important word "had" in English. She "*had* [still has!] a discharge of blood"; she "*had* suffered under many physicians," doctors who had no idea what to do with her peculiar problem; and she "*had* spent all that she *had*" on her problem. The result? She was no better off—she "was not better but rather grew worse" (5:26). No wealth. No health.

She is a *has-been* because she still *has* a major problem at the center of her body. Of course, women before menopause bleed each month for one week. This woman did not stop bleeding for twelve years, day after day. What does that mean? Beyond the medical issues, the implication for a Jewish woman of that time was that she was no better than a leper. Her husband, if she had one, had likely divorced her. They could not have had sexual relations or children. This is why it was her money, not his, that was spent on the dumbfounded doctors. Worse than the lack of marital relations, she was denied religious relationships. In her condition, she could not approach the priest to offer a sacrifice for her sins or be near God's people for praise and prayer (see Lev. 15:19–33). She might as well marry Legion (the man with unclean spirits) and live in the country of the Gerasenes (an unclean place) among the Gentiles (an unclean people) in the tombs (an unclean place) next to the pigs (unclean animals).

But what did this unclean dame do? She risked further banishment from her community to touch even the hem of Jesus' robe. Mark **5:27–28** reveals her reason: "She had heard the reports about Jesus and came up behind him in the crowd and touched his garment. For she said, 'If I touch even his garments,

---

5   We are not told the cause of the little girl's demise. We are told that the woman suffered from a chronic "discharge of blood" (Mark 5:25), some gynecological condition (perhaps a uterine hemorrhage).

I will be made well."[6] What a ridiculous plan. Jesus is too important to play such superstitious games. Learn from the religious ruler. Bow before Jesus. Acknowledge his power. Do not sneak up behind him, reach out amid the pressing crowd, and touch one of his four tassels. Is that the way one should approach the Lord of the universe? Certainly not. Do not be so presumptuous.

Ah, if that is how we think, we are wrong, for look at the results: "And immediately the flow of blood dried up, and she felt in her body that she was healed of her disease" (5:29). Imagine how she felt. Twelve years of discomfort and disgrace, and then "immediately" it is all over. She knows and feels it. But how does Jesus' respond? Did he approve of her approach? Yes and no. Or, we might answer, "No, but really yes." Look at 5:30–34:

> And Jesus, perceiving in himself that power had gone out from him, immediately turned about in the crowd and said, "Who touched my garments?" And his disciples said to him, "You see the crowd pressing around you, and yet you say, 'Who touched me?'" And he looked around to see who had done it. But the woman, knowing what had happened to her, came in fear and trembling and fell down before him and told him the whole truth. And he said to her, "Daughter, your faith has made you well; go in peace, and be healed of your disease."

Our Lord Jesus has this sense that something has physically happened. He perceives "that power had gone out from him" (5:30). This physical, but also metaphysical, sensation moves him to eye the crowd and ask, "Who touched my garments?" (5:30). What a seemingly silly question, as the disciples recognize: "You see the crowd pressing around you, and yet you say, 'Who touched me?'" (5:31). The disciples fail to understand their master, and in stating the obvious they rebuke him. But Jesus does not rebuke their rebuke. Rather, he "looked around to see who had done it" (5:32). His looking prompts her admission: "But the woman, knowing what had happened to her, came in fear and trembling and fell down before him and told him the whole truth" (5:33). Here Mark describes her emotional reaction (she is afraid)[7] and her physical

---

6 "This kind of conditional clause has almost a temporal meaning ('when' for 'if') and represents rather more than mere probability. There was no doubt in the woman's mind. She said to herself, 'After I have touched that garment, I shall receive my healing.'" Nigel Turner, *Grammatical Insights into the New Testament* (Edinburgh: T&T Clark, 1965), 33.

7 "Her 'fear' likely had three aspects: many in the crowd would know of her unclean state; Jesus could be displeased that an unclean woman had touched him (and made him unclean); but mostly she would feel the trembling 'awe' (cf. 4:41) of knowing that she had been miraculously healed" (Osborne, *Mark*, 88).

reaction (first, she shakes; second, she falls on her knees), followed by her confession (she "told him the whole truth"). She tells Jesus about the disease and the doctors and her plan to touch his tassel.[8] She perhaps also shares how "she had heard the reports about Jesus" (5:27) and has believed them ("Faith comes from hearing," Rom. 10:17).[9]

To her confession Jesus offers a commendation: "Daughter, your faith has made you well; go in peace, and be healed of your disease" (Mark 5:34).[10] He calls her "daughter," a tender title[11] symbolizing that through faith in Jesus she is now part of the Father's family. Then Jesus speaks of her faith: "Your faith has made you well." Some scholars think that Jesus here offers a rebuke, namely, that he makes clear to her that it is her faith, not just her touch, that is linked with the healing. But that creates a false dichotomy. Her faith is expressed in her touch.[12] Jesus is simply commending her for her courageous and determined faith. In fact, his glowing commendation is surprising in that he says "Your faith has made you well," not "I have made you well." It is also surprising that he uses such strong language. In the original Greek the word translated "well" is usually translated "saved." It is the word used for salvation. "Your faith has *saved* you!" (5:34 CSB).[13]

---

8   As visible reminders of God's covenant commands (see Num. 15:37–41; Deut. 22:12), Jesus, like other Jewish men of his day, likely would have worn a garment with four tassels sewn upon the bottom fringes.

9   Matthew Henry says it well: "The strong faith that this woman had in the power of Christ to heal her she expressed within herself, though it does not appear that she was encouraged by any preceding instance to say it. She believed that he cured not as a prophet, by virtue derived from God, but as the Son of God—by a virtue inherent in himself"; *Commentary on the Whole Bible*, quoted in *CHSB*, 1481.

10 The ESV translates *mastigos* as "disease"; it could be rendered "torment." Her persistent torment is over!

11 There are two "daughters" in this text: the ruler's (Mark 5:23, 35) and the bleeding woman (5:34, as named by Jesus). On Matthew 9:22 (// Mark 5:34) Stuart L. Love writes: "This endearing word, a tender form of recognition, is also a social metaphor that particularizes Israel (Lam 2:13; Matt 21:5)"; *Jesus and Marginal Women: The Gospel of Matthew in Social-Scientific Perspective*, Matrix: The Bible in Mediterranean Context (Eugene, OR: Cascade, 2009), 126.

12 I suggest Mark is making a striking point in connecting her faith directly to her touch (cf. Mark 6:56). The woman's faith-filled touch saves, and she is absolutely certain it will. On the words "If I touch even his garments" (5:28; cf. Matt. 9:21), some scholars say she is fulfilling Scripture. We might say that she, a Jewish woman (not "ten men from the nations"), fulfills Zechariah's prophecy by approaching Jesus to "take hold of [his] robe," because she believes that God is with him (Zech. 8:23). On Matthew 9:21 as allusion to Zechariah 8:23 see J. T. Cumming, "The Tassel of His Cloak: Mark, Luke, Matthew and Zechariah," in *Studia Biblica 1978: II. Papers on the Gospels*, ed. E. A. Livingstone, JSNTSS 2 (Sheffield: JSOT, 1980), 47–61, esp. 51–52. For a history of exegesis on this text, along with the suggestion that her touch of Jesus' tassel is a fulfillment of Malachi 4:2, see Dale C. Allison Jr., "Healing in the Wings of His Garment: The Synoptics and Malachi 4:2," in *The Word Leaps the Gap: Essays on Scripture and Theology in Honor of Richard B. Hays*, ed. J. Ross Wagner, C. Kavin Rowe, and A. Katherine Grieb (Grand Rapids, MI: Eerdmans, 2008), 132–46.

13 There are a number of parallels between the hemorrhaging woman and the ruler's daughter: both are female, called "daughter," associated with the number "twelve," and ritually unclean

Finally, at the end of verse 34, Jesus offers a promise of full restoration and ongoing wholeness: "Go in peace, and be healed of your disease." The sense is "Your suffering is over" (NLT), and "There is no more need to find a doctor to cure you of this deadly disease; the great physician has just done so. Move out. Live life again."

The Daughter Near Death, Take Two

So, with the daughter with the discharge done, what then of the other "daughter," the little girl in hospice care back home? In midsentence ("while [Jesus] was still speaking," **5:35**) another interruption occurs, taking us back to the original story. People "from the ruler's house," in a fairly straightforward and unsympathetic way, exclaim, "Your daughter is dead. Why trouble the Teacher any further?" (5:35). They might be right that the girl has died, but they are wrong that Jesus should be called a mere "teacher." The last time he was called "teacher" (4:38) he woke up and put to sleep a storm. "Teacher" is insufficient. He is Lord over of the wind and waves. This time he will do something even greater. He will teach death a lesson or two.

Here Mark does not record Jairus's response to the news. What is recorded is Jesus' response: "But overhearing what they said, Jesus said to the ruler of the synagogue, 'Do not fear, only believe'" (**5:36**). What a challenge. Will this man overcome his fear that Jesus cannot do anything more? Or will he trust that he can? The ruler does not say a word, at least none recorded by the Gospel writers. But the fact that Jesus continues to the house, and this man follows along (and does not dismiss Jesus), shows that he walks by faith, even if that walk is a limp. And, as he limps along with the Lord, I wonder if he wonders whether Jesus, who had the power to dry up blood in one woman, can get the blood flowing again in another.

So Jesus, along with his apostolic inner circle ("He allowed no one to follow him except Peter and James and John," **5:37**) and the father as well (5:40), journey to the "house of the ruler of the synagogue" (**5:38**). Once there they see and hear quite a "commotion, people weeping and wailing loudly" (5:38). Jesus enters the house and says to the mourners, "Why are you making a commotion and weeping? The child is not dead but sleeping" (**5:39**). Their response? "They"—both the professional mourners (professional flautists and wailing women; see m. Ketub. 4.4) and likely some from the extended family—think he is crazy. "And they laughed at him" (5:40). The laughter must be scoffing

---

and encounter Jesus' healing powers through touch. Some key differences, then, would be that Jesus reserves his commendation of faith (a rare thing in Mark—only here!) for the woman and also joins in the woman's language of salvation (Gk. *sōzō*).

laughs, for they know she is dead (see Luke 8:53). They misunderstand what Jesus is saying and what he has the power to do. Jesus is redefining, not denying, her death. He is redefining it as "sleep" because he is about to wake her up.

> But he put them all outside and took the child's father and mother and those who were with him and went in where the child was. Taking her by the hand he said to her, "Talitha cumi," which means, "Little girl, I say to you, arise." And immediately the girl got up and began walking (for she was twelve years of age), and they were immediately overcome with amazement. And he strictly charged them that no one should know this, and told them to give her something to eat. (Mark **5:40–43**)[14]

What an amazing and odd ending. What is not amazing is their amazement ("And they were immediately overcome with amazement," 5:42). What is not amazing is that Jesus dismisses the crowd and handpicks his eyewitnesses. He has done this and will do this for a number of key events in his ministry, including his own resurrection. What then is amazing is that Jesus touches her and that that touch wakes the dead.

According to OT law, a person becomes unclean if he touches a corpse. Jesus also becomes unclean when touched by a menstruating woman. Thus within a few hours Jesus is doubly unclean. But that is the point of the story, or part of the point. He takes on human uncleanness — our disease and our death — and comes out the other side, along with us, completely clean.

After Jesus' tender ("little girl") command ("I say to you, arise," 5:41),[15] a statement in the Aramaic ("Talitha cumi") that Peter (Mark's source) cannot get out of his mind, the girl "immediately" arises, walks (5:42), and eats (5:43). She is really alive! Absolutely amazing!

This is an amazing ending, but also an odd one. What is odd is Jesus' charge to keep quiet ("And he strictly charged them that no one should know this," 5:43). How marvelously anticlimactic. Who could keep quiet? How would they keep quiet? It would be like hiding a hippopotamus in your carry-on. Jesus knows that the news will spread, but he wants his closest followers to

---

14   It is interesting that Mark labels the "little girl" (Mark 5:41), who is "twelve" (5:42), a "child" four times (5:39, 40 [2x], 41), especially as the Greek word *paidion* is often used in the Gospels for infants or toddlers.

15   Timothy Keller labels the word *talitha* "a pet name, a diminutive term of endearment" and suggests "Honey" as translation; he renders *cumi* as "get up." Thus together he views what Jesus is doing as what "this child's parents might do on a sunny morning. He sits down, takes her hand and gently lifts her right up through it. 'Honey, get up.'" *King's Cross: The Story of the World in the Life of Jesus* (New York: Dutton, 2011), 68.

understand that his resurrection power cannot be fully understood and properly expressed until after his own resurrection.

He Is Risen, Indeed!

While these six witnesses to the miracle might have been told to keep quiet, we who live after Jesus' resurrection should not be silent. We should retell this story as we announce to the world, "He is risen! He is risen, indeed!" We have read the end of Matthew, Mark, Luke, and John. We know what happens. Jesus dies and rises. The Lord of Life defeats death.

A few years ago I watched an award-winning documentary about public education in America called *Waiting for "Superman"* (Paramount Vantage, 2010). It begins with these words from the narrator, who grew up in a rough neighborhood.

> One of the saddest days of my life was when my mother told me that Superman did not exist. I was a comic book reader. . . . And I just loved Superman because even in the depths of the ghetto you just thought, "He's coming, and I don't know when, because he always shows up, and he saves all the good people. . . . I was reading (I don't know, maybe I was in the fourth grade) . . . I said, "Ma, do you think Superman is real?" "Superman is not real." I was like, "He's not. What do you mean he's not . . ." "No he's not real." And she thought I was crying because . . . it's like Santa Claus is not real. I was crying because there was no one coming with enough power to save us.

The message of the Gospel of Mark is that someone strong enough to save has come and has saved us from the last and ultimate enemy. As Paul writes in 2 Timothy 1:10, "Our Savior Christ Jesus . . . abolished death and brought life and immortality to light." How so? Jesus died. He rose again. And since Jesus died and rose again, we who are united to him through faith will also die but arise again. As Paul phrases it 1 Thessalonians 4:13–14, "We do not want you to be uninformed, brothers, about those who are asleep, that you may not grieve as others do who have no hope. For since we believe that Jesus died and rose again, even so, through Jesus, God will bring with him those who have fallen asleep." What a Savior! What a gospel. What hope we have. And what good news to share.

Receiving or Rejecting Jesus

MARK 6:1-13

And he marveled because of their unbelief.
Mark 6:6

Sometimes when people compliment me on a sermon I say, "Well, I have good material to work with." Then usually we both laugh, smile, or nod because we acknowledge that there is no better material to work with than the inspired Word of God. However, certain passages in the inspired Word are easier to explain, illustrate, and apply than others. For example, Mark 5:21–43—the two interweaving episodes about the salvation of two "daughters"—is a text that preaches itself. That is, all the preacher needs to do is faithfully retell those two captivating stories. Mark 6:1–13 is *not* a passage that "preaches itself." There are two stories again, but they are not directly intersecting as the two in Mark 5:21–43, nor do they contain the same amount of literary artistry. There are no new intriguing characters introduced. No dramatic tension. No unexpected interruptions in the plot. No odd endings. Thus, when preaching through Mark, I wrestled with the best way to help us understand and explain the glorious truths of this text in an interesting and applicable way. Then I remembered a way forward. Each week the women's Bible study my wife then attended organized its study of the text I was preaching by asking and answering five questions. I was tempted to wait until late Wednesday night, when all their studies were done, and simply steal all their amazing insights. However, instead of stealing their answers, I simply borrowed their study method for my sermon outline. And I am glad I did, for I found it to be an effective way to cover the material in a way that was directly relevant to some in my congregation (the women doing the study) and to give the whole congregation a helpful tool for reading, understanding, and applying God's Word, even the parts that seem so distant from life today.

Question One

The first question is, How would the original audience have understood these words? This question is important because it reminds us in our reading of Scripture not to leap directly from the ancient text to our contemporary situation. That is, when we read the story about David and Goliath, for example, we might be tempted to forget the redemptive-historical setting and say something like, "This story shows that God can take care of the Goliaths—the big problems—in our lives." That may be true, but that is not why 1 Samuel 17 was originally written.

The principle behind the question is that we first must understand whom a passage was written to and what they would have made of it before we can find God's meaning and purpose for our lives. So, as it relates to Mark **6:1–13**, we need first to travel to first-century Nazareth before we can travel to twenty-first-century Chicago (or whatever city you live in).

There are all sorts of details that the original audience would have understood and that we first need to understand to make sense of this passage. For example, the "Sabbath" (6:2) was Saturday, the day Jews set apart for worship. The "synagogue" (6:2) was the Jewish gathering place for worship and other community events. The word used for "carpenter" would conjure up in their minds someone who works not just with wood but also with stones and metal. A "carpenter" is simply a tradesman or artisan, someone who makes a living with his hands. The five names mentioned here—Mary, James, Joses, Judas, and Simon (6:3)—would have made it on the list of the top ten baby names among Palestinian Jews living between 330 BC and AD 200.[1] The mention of "a prophet" in verse 4 harks back to the prophets of the OT, and the fact that Jesus says of himself, "A prophet is not without honor, except in his hometown and among his relatives and in his own household," alludes to this pattern of the prophets' being rejected by those closest to them.[2] Moreover, Jesus is provocatively claiming to be on par with such ancient holy men at a time when that last official prophetic voice would have been heard four hundred years before Jesus' birth.

So that is my answer to that question of how the original audience would have understood the words of verses 1–6. Moving on to verses 7–13, I will add that the word "twelve" in the phrase "and he called the twelve" (6:7) is a literal number (Jesus called twelve men, named in 3:13–19) symbolic of the twelve tribes of Israel. Jesus is restoring and reconstructing a new Israel around him.

---

1 See Richard Bauckham, *Jesus and the Eyewitnesses: The Gospels as Eyewitness Testimony* (Grand Rapids, MI: Eerdmans, 2006), 85. Note that four of the brothers are named after the patriarchs: James (or Jacob), Joses (or Joseph), Simon (or Simeon).

2 For example, Moses (Josephus, *Ant.* 2.327) and Jeremiah (Jer. 11:21; 12:6).

Moreover, what the twelve wear (sandals, tunics, and belts with money bags; 6:8–9), some of which they are not to wear or take (bread, bag, money) on this specific journey,[3] describes the typical attire of that day. We can picture men in long robes, with a bag of money strapped around their waists, walking with staffs (for balance and protection) in hot or temperate climate (thus the open-toed footwear). The meaning of "two tunics" refers to two garments such men usually wore, one on the outside and a longer garment near the skin.

Here, per Jesus' instruction, they are to wear only one garment because they should expect someone to house them. They will not be sleeping outside. God will provide. The mention of "bread," sometimes a word used for food in general, likely does reference literal bread here—picture a piece of bread, wrapped in a cloth and stuffed into a sack. Then picture pieces of the bread picked off to give sustenance on a long journey. But on this journey the disciples were gluten free.

The final few details I want to point out and explain under the heading of this first question (How would the original audience have understood these words?) have to do with the twelve's mission. They are sent out "two by two" (6:7) for companionship and protection and as official witnesses (see Num. 35:30; Deut. 17:6; 19:15). Their mission (each pair as it goes out) makes sense only in a culture of expected hospitality. In Israel at the time of Jesus and long before it, and still after it, if someone were on a journey and came to a town square looking for a place to stay, people usually welcomed in the traveler with no questions asked. Jesus is expecting that some hospitable host will let in his disciples for the night or many nights. This helps us understand verse 10, where Jesus says, "Whenever you enter a house, stay there until you depart from there," and also the bit about shaking off the dust (from their dust-filled sandals) if someone were inhospitable to them (6:11). The dusting off the dust is a sign of judgment.

Their mission is not just to see who does and who does not welcome them in but to mirror Jesus' work: preach repentance (6:12), cast out demons, and heal the sick (6:13). The lines about exorcisms and oil anointings are not completely removed from our century, but they are a bit removed from a missionary's usual job description.[4] This is possibly because we have wrongly removed any dealing with supernatural issues from the overseas worker and

---

3 "Beggars and itinerant philosophers who sought donations often used a traveler's bag to collect money (*Diogenes Laertius* 6.13, 22). Jesus forbade its use on this trip." Darrell Bock, *Mark*, NCBC (Cambridge: Cambridge University Press, 2015), 204.

4 "Oil was used medicinally in biblical times (Isa. 1:6; Luke 10:34), but the oil here is more likely being used to represent the healing presence of the Spirit of God." Mark L. Strauss, *Mark*, ZECNT (Grand Rapids, MI: Zondervan, 2014), 253.

local pastor's weekly work, and because what is stated here is not a directly repeatable command. Some people today come to the Bible, read about demons and exorcisms, incurable diseases and miraculous healings, and say, "I doubt that is true. That is not scientifically verifiable." Then many of those same souls glance at the horoscopes to see what lies in their futures or go to psychics to see whether their next date is their soulmate. Today we live in the land of the "materialist magician," as C. S. Lewis phrased it.

That said, I think the commission given here (cf. Matt. 9:35–11:1) to Jesus' handpicked twelve is not the commission given to all (cf. 2 Cor. 12:12). It was not given to the original audience of Mark's Gospel. It was not given to us. That said, we all should believe in the supernatural. We all should share the message of the gospel. Yet we all should recognize and appreciate that Jesus gave the unique authority to demonstrate the inauguration of the kingdom of God—the power to heal diseases and cast out evil spirits—to these twelve.

Question Two

The second question is, What surprised you in the passage? This is my favorite question. I love finding details in God's Word that teach me about him, us, and the world that I would not have known unless he had revealed it to us.

There are six surprises. First, it is surprising, at least from an American perspective, where we love our hometown heroes, that Jesus' hometown rejects him. In some ways it is not surprising, as Jesus points out in Mark 6:4, that a prophet is not welcomed in his hometown. But the extent of their unbelief is surprising. Even Jesus was surprised ("And he *marveled* because of their unbelief," 6:6).[5] They first acknowledge and are even "astonished" by his wisdom ("Where did this man get these things [insights]? What is the wisdom given to him?") and his works ("How are such mighty works done by his hands?" 6:2)—like raising the dead (5:42). At the end of 6:2 they seemed poised to put up a new town sign: "Welcome to Nazareth: Hometown of Wonderworker Jesus."[6] However, like quick-dry cement, these townspeople, who were initially soft to Jesus, grow hard. They move from astonished to offended, from quiet skepticism to outright criticism.[7] They refuse to acknowledge Jesus' heaven-sent authority and divine identity.

---

5 Only here in Mark is Jesus amazed. The Greek word *thaumazō* is reserved for the typical response to Jesus' teaching and miracles (see Mark 1:22, 27; 2:12; 5:15, 20, 42; 6:51; 12:17).
6 We can safely surmise that Jesus' "hometown" (Mark 6:1) is Nazareth (see 1:9, 24; cf. Matt. 2:23; Luke 2:4, 39).
7 Ironically, the first note of the chilling chorus "Crucify him!" (Mark 15:13, 14 // Matt. 27:22, 23) is sounded in once-safe Nazareth (see Matt. 2:19–23). In Luke's version (Luke 4:29) the townspeople want to push him off a cliff.

They reject him because they think his wisdom and his works do not align with his known identity. Nazareth was a small town, with between 500 to 1,500 people, comprising socially immobile citizens. They all know Jesus' family by name—commoners with common names. They also know Jesus' occupation. "Is not this the carpenter?" (6:3) is an ironic rhetorical question. As readers of Mark's Gospel, we think of Jesus as the Christ and Son of God. They think of him as the boy, and then man, who helped build and fix things. So, as they sift through all the resumes for messiah and come to his and read "Worked over twenty years as a carpenter in Nazareth," they quickly toss it out. It cannot be him.

The Jews of Nazareth, like most people of that time and region, did not believe a concept like the American dream. They believed that great people were born great, not made great. Just as Caesar was born great, so the Christ would be born great. He would be someone as glorious as King Solomon in all his splendor and as victorious in battle as his father David. He would *not* be from Nazareth. He would *not* be a carpenter. He would *not* be born out of wedlock—"the son of Mary" (Mark 6:3; note that they do not say, "the son of *Joseph* and Mary"). To them, Jesus was illegitimate in a number of ways. Put simply, they could not envision one of their own construction workers who lived at 205 Branch of David Drive as their Savior.

Second, it is surprising that, at this point in the story, Jesus' own family is included with the unbelievers. In verse 4 Jesus states that a prophet, such as he is (and so much more!), is not honored "among his relatives and in his own household." It is clear here that Jesus has biological siblings, four brothers and at least two sisters,[8] and it is implied here, but made clear elsewhere (3:21, 31–35), that Mary struggles at points during Jesus' ministry years to understand and embrace her son's mission.[9]

Third, it is surprising that Jesus' miraculous powers seem limited. In Mark 6:5 we read, "And he *could* do no mighty work there,[10] except that he laid his hands on a few sick people and healed them." Matthew, in his version of this story, softens the report: "And he *did* not do many mighty works there" (Matt. 13:58). Apparently Mark wants to emphasize the effects of dishonor

8 "The plain sense of v. 3, and of the NT in general, is that Jesus was the oldest of five brothers and at least two sisters, all of whom were the natural children of Joseph and Mary"; James R. Edwards, *The Gospel according to Mark*, PNTC (Grand Rapids, MI: 2002), 173. After the birth of Jesus, Mary and Joseph had children "according to natural biological processes"; Walter W. Wessel, "Mark," EBC, ed. Frank E. Gaebelein, 12 vols. (Grand Rapids, MI: Zondervan, 1984), 8:665.
9 Thus this text is proof against two important Catholic dogmas: Mary's perpetual virginity and her immaculate nature.
10 It is a double negative in Greek ("not . . . not any").

and disbelief. Those who hear and see but refuse to truly hear and see will be judged. Part of the judgment comes in a withdrawal of Christ's mercies in the form of miracles. Mark also wants to emphasize the connection made in the previous intertwining episodes, namely, that faith "untaps a fountain of miracles" and that a lack of faith greatly limits the water supply.[11] Therefore it is important for us to recognize that Jesus never throws miracles at a crowd like a clown throws candy to children during a parade. Rather, each and every miracle he performs occurs in the context of a relationship and almost always in the context of an expression of faith.[12] So we might say, as Donald English has said, that there is a divine law at work here: "As the word will not produce spiritual growth where the capacity for response is barren, choked, or scorched, so the presence of Jesus will not produce miracles in the atmosphere of total unbelief and resistance."[13]

Fourth, it is surprising that this rejection does not totally discourage Jesus. In 6:30, after the apostles tell Jesus of John the Baptist's beheading, our Lord wants to retreat from the villages and crowds for a while (6:31, 32). He is tired, hungry, and perhaps downcast. But here at the end of 6:1–6 we read, "And he went about among the villages teaching." How gracious. And before that, as just said, he healed "a few sick people" (6:5) in Nazareth. How incredibly gracious.

Fifth, it is surprising that our Lord, as we move on to the surprises in the second story, entrusts the twelve with such authority (6:7, 13, 30). I say it is surprising that he entrusts them because up to this point they have not proven to be the most reliable followers. They misunderstand Jesus' teaching (4:10), along with his identity and mission (4:35–41; cf. 5:31). So why entrust the precious gospel, and the supernatural signs that will confirm it, with such imperfect people? To answer that question is to answer the bigger question: Why is God at all gracious to sinners? Our Lord shows his grace, both then and now, by calling and commissioning saved sinners to announce the good news of salvation in Jesus.

Sixth, it is surprising that God sometimes, as is the case here with Judas, bestows spiritual gifts without bestowing saving faith. Despite all his spiritual privileges and powers, Judas does not persevere in the faith. He betrays Jesus, abandons all hope, and dies in his sin. His demise should be a warning to us, and also a wake-up call. Sometimes people are surprised when famous church leaders, whom God is obviously blessing, are caught in some grave sin

---

11 Frederick Dale Bruner, *Matthew: A Commentary, Volume 2: The Churchbook, Matthew 13–28*, rev. ed. (Grand Rapids, MI: Eerdmans, 2007), 62.

12 See Mark 2:5; 4:40; 5:34, 36; 9:23–24; 10:52; 11:22–24.

13 Donald English, *The Message of Mark: The Mystery of Faith*, BST (Leicester, UK: Inter-Varsity, 1992), 119.

or discovered to have major character flaws. We are tempted to think that, if Pastor X can heal the sick, or if people are being saved through his preaching, then he must be a Christian. Not necessarily so. Remember how Jesus ends the Sermon on the Mount:

> Not everyone who says to me, "Lord, Lord," will enter the kingdom of heaven, but the one who does the will of my Father who is in heaven. On that day *many* will say to me, "Lord, Lord, did we not prophesy in your name, and cast out demons in your name, and do many mighty works in your name?" And then will I declare to them, "I never knew you; depart from me, you workers of lawlessness." (Matt. 7:21–23)

Charismatic credentials are not sure signs of salvation. Humble reliance on the finished work of Christ and the fruits of godliness that sprout from such solely dependent faith are.

Question Three

The third question is, What is the main idea? Answer: Jesus' rejection. What the Evangelist records in Mark 6:1–13 is not all negative. People say nice things about Jesus (6:2). Jesus heals "a few sick people" (6:5), and his disciples do as well (6:13). Surely some people are hospitable to the twelve and receptive to their message (6:10–11). The disciples continue to follow and obey Jesus (6:1, 12). But beyond those positives the structure, succeeding context, and certain key words signify that rejection is the main focus.

The repeated key words center on what some people are rejecting, namely, the wisdom and works of the kingdom. Jesus and the twelve "teach" (6:2) or proclaim repentance (6:12) and work miracles: heal the sick (6:5) and exorcize demons (6:13; and perhaps "mighty work/s" in 6:2, 5). The reaction to such words and works from a hometown and presumably many homes is offense, unbelief, and rejection.

The structure of verses 1–6, with the positioning of the clauses "And they took offense at him" (6:3) and "He marveled because of their unbelief" (6:6), accentuates the negative theme (rejection followed by rejection followed by rejection), as does the clause in verse 11 "And if any place will not receive you." That line is found in the middle story of three rejection stories.

Then, beyond the key words and structure, we have the context. Immediately following these two stories Mark places a third rejection story: the horrific tale of what happens to John's head (6:14–29). If that is what happens to the greatest messenger sent to men (see Matt. 11:11), what will happen to the

Son of God? A more horrendous fate awaits him. John is rejected here; Jesus will be rejected then and there.

Question Four

The fourth question is, How does this passage point us to Christ and the gospel? The rejection Jesus receives in Nazareth and elsewhere (from those who reject the apostolic message of the kingdom throughout Galilee) foreshadows the rejection Jesus will undergo in (the big city, the holy city) Jerusalem. However, that rejection, in the form of crucifixion, is our salvation (cf. Isa. 53:3–12). As the great hymn puts it,

> Stricken, smitten, and afflicted,
> See Him dying on the tree!
> 'Tis the Christ by man *rejected;*
> Yes, my soul, 'tis He! 'tis He!
> 'Tis the long-expected *Prophet,*
> David's Son, yet David's Lord;
> By his Son, God now has spoken:
> 'Tis the true and faithful Word.

And then the final verse is the following:

> Here we have a firm foundation;
> Here the refuge of the lost;
> Christ's the Rock of our salvation,
> His the name on which we boast.
> Lamb of God, for sinners wounded,
> Sacrifice to cancel guilt!
> None shall ever be confounded
> Who on Him their hope have built.[14]

Jesus' rejection, in the form of crucifixion, is our salvation.

Question Five

The fifth question is, How should we apply this passage to our lives today? Here are four possible applications, one from the first story (Mark 6:1–6) and three from the second (6:7–13). I will start with the second story first.

---

14 Thomas Kelly, "Stricken, Smitten, and Afflicted" (1804).

First, like the twelve, we should practice a God-dependent lifestyle. Jesus asked only one person in the Gospels to sell everything and come and follow him. He only asked the twelve to leave occupations and families for three years of personal training. And he only once, here in Mark 6, commissioned his disciples to take the minimum on a short-term mission trip. So I do not think the message of verses 8–9 is "always travel light." However, there is a principle here, and that is that we should be dependent on God and his people (or God through his people) for all ministry needs.

Directly related to this first application is the second: like those who welcomed the twelve, we should practice mission-minded hospitality. The gospel goes forth only if there are goers and givers—or, as we see depicted in verse 10–11, those who evangelize and those who entertain the evangelists. Do we promote local and world missions by practicing hospitality? is the question we should ask ourselves, for, when we partner with those taking the gospel to others, then we are coworkers with them, as John writes: "We ought to support people like these [traveling missionaries], that we may be fellow workers for the truth" (3 John 8).

Third, like the twelve (cf. John 15:19–21), we should expect rejection (cf. Matt. 10:24–25), especially for proclaiming the message of repentance. In Mark 6:12 we read, "So they went out and proclaimed that people should repent." This was the message these apostles would go on to preach (see their sermons in Acts). This is the message Jesus preached (Mark 1:15). And this is the message John the Baptist preached (1:4) and that got him killed (6:17–18). This pattern—getting killed for preaching repentance—becomes the pattern throughout church history. Faithful preaching leads to persecution. Of the twelve, John was exiled and the rest were killed: Bartholomew, Matthias (who replaced Judas), and James, the son of Zebedee, were beheaded; Thomas and Matthew speared to death; Peter, Andrew, Philip, Jude, Simon the Zealot, and James, the son of Alphaeus, crucified.

While we may never face such physical persecution, we do face the prospect of spiritual persecution if we are faithful to the apostolic message. It is easy to preach that Jesus is interested in our happiness, that he wants us to be "financially comfortable, physically fit, mentally and emotionally stable."[15] It is easy to preach that God can help us find a new job or outlook on life. It is easy to preach "Jesus-lite: great taste, less demanding."[16] But to preach "Repent from your sins and trust in Christ and him crucified"—that is an open

---

15   Victor Kuligin, *Ten Things I Wish Jesus Never Said* (Wheaton, IL: Crossway, 2006), 11–12.
16   Kuligin, *Ten Things*, 11–12.

invitation to offense and animosity.[17] That message will not go over well at the neighborhood barbecue or office holiday party.

Fourth, by what Jesus' hometown was offended, we should be astonished. J. C. Ryle puts it this way:

> There is something marvelous and overwhelming in the thought! He who made heaven and earth and sea and all that is in them—without whom nothing was made that has been made—the Son of God himself, took the very nature of a servant, and by the sweat of his brow ate his food (Gen 3:19), as a working man. This is indeed the "love that surpasses knowledge" (Eph 3:19). Though he was rich, yet for our sake he became poor. Both in life and in death he humbled himself, so that sinners might live and reign forevermore through him.[18]

Something I Missed

As mentioned earlier, the women participating in the women's Bible study were looking at the same passages I had been preaching. So, oftentimes, as my wife was preparing, she would ask me my thoughts on various verses or phrases. The week before I preached on this text, and after the ladies had gathered and shared their answers to the five questions, I asked her if I could look at the results—her own notes and her compilation of others. She showed me. I learned, with their learned insights, that I am unneeded. If I may quote an unnamed source among them, "We don't need Pastor O. anymore." That was said in jest. I think. I hope.

What is no joke is that one of the ladies saw something I did not see, an insight with which I will end. On the part about Jesus' not performing many miracles in Nazareth, someone said, "That makes sense. If people in that town didn't have faith in Jesus, they wouldn't come to Jesus to heal them. You need to come to Jesus and ask for help." That is not a bad word to end on. A good summary. You need to come to Jesus and ask for help.

---

17 The Greek word translated "took offense" is *skandalizomai* (Mark 6:3), from which the English word "scandal" is derived. The NT writers often use this word to describe the Jews' reaction to Jesus' death, such as in Galatians 5:11, where Paul speaks of "the offense of the cross [the *scandal* of the cross]," or in 1 Corinthians 1:22–23, where he writes, "Jews demand signs and Greeks seek wisdom, but we preach Christ crucified, a stumbling block [a *scandal*] to Jews and folly to Gentiles."

18 J. C. Ryle, *Mark: Expository Thoughts on the Gospels*, CCC (Wheaton, IL: Crossway, 1993), 80–81.

A Hellish Tale

MARK 6:14-29

And immediately the king sent an executioner with orders to bring John's head. He went and beheaded him in the prison and brought his head on a platter and gave it to the girl, and the girl gave it to her mother.
Mark 6:27–28

In Dante's medieval masterpiece, *Divine Comedy*, the ancient Roman poet Virgil takes Dante on a tour: first of hell, then purgatory, and finally heaven. On each step of the way, at the different levels within each area, Virgil makes observations and applications. His job is to accentuate the realities of the afterlife as he reinforces the importance of right living on earth.

For this chapter, in the tradition of the *Divine Comedy*, I will serve as your guide as we walk through a hellish tale of a great prophet who lost his head. I will take you first to the king's headquarters, then to the prison. From the prison we will journey to the banquet hall. From there we will travel to the tomb. We will venture to four places, and at each place we will stop to observe (I will say "See this!") and apply (and "Learn from this") Mark's record of John the Baptist's final moments.

The King's Headquarters

Our journey begins in the king's headquarters. The first word of our text is *king*, in reference to "King Herod" (Mark 6:14). I will say more about him later. For now, just note that this is an unusual way for Mark to start a story. All his narratives thus far, and all those we will read after this,[1] feature Jesus as the protagonist. However, here in 6:14–29 Jesus is named only once (6:14), is

---

1 The closest pericope in which Jesus is not the protagonist would be Mark 1:2–8, which features John the Baptist. However, even there Jesus is the ultimate focus, as the immediate context makes clear (see 1:1, 9–11).

alluded to twice (6:14, 15), and is not presented as saying or doing anything. The focus, instead, is on Herod.[2]

Herod's relationship with Jesus is the first aspect of our text.

> King Herod heard of [Jesus' words and works], for Jesus' name had become known. Some said, "John the Baptist has been raised from the dead. That is why these miraculous powers are at work in him." But others said, "He is Elijah." And others said, "He is a prophet, like one of the prophets of old." But when Herod heard of it, he said, "John, whom I beheaded, has been raised." (**6:14–16**)

I place this scene at "the king's headquarters" in part because I am influenced by the setting of Matthew 2:1–9, in which Herod the Great, the father of the Herod of our text, assembled officials before him for the purpose of gathering information on the coming Messiah. Here I envision Herod Antipas, as he was called, calling key counselors to give their views on Jesus of Nazareth, this itinerant rabbi and miracle worker whom Herod perceives to be a possible threat to his reign. Maybe what is relayed in these verses is the talk around town. Maybe it is informed opinions based on eyewitness testimony and scholarly consensus. Herod has three options presented to him in regard to Jesus' identity: Jesus could be a reembodied Elijah, the wonder-working prophet of the OT; one of the other prophets, perhaps Elijah's double-portion-of-the-Spirit protégé, Elisha; or "John the Baptist . . . raised from the dead" (6:14). Herod, with some determination and admission of culpability, goes with the final option: "John, whom *I* beheaded, has been raised" (6:16). This is an odd choice, as resurrection from the dead was not then a widely held view. The only sense I can make of Herod's thought is that he believes that Jesus is now able to perform miracles *because* he is possessed by the spirit of John the Baptist.

The Prison

Why would Herod think this way? Is he altogether mad? I will save a psychological evaluation for later. There is another reason. "For" (**6:17**)—there

---

2   Herod is the subject of nearly every sentence. He hears of Jesus (Mark 6:14, 16); renders a judgment that Jesus is John revivified (6:16); imprisons John (6:17); marries his brother's wife (6:17); keeps John safe, temporarily, from Herod's new wife, who wanted John dead (6:19–20); fears the holy prophet (6:20); fails to process John's prophetic preaching (6:20); hosts a birthday party for himself (6:21); is pleased by his step-daughter's dance (6:22); asks the girl to offer a request under various oaths (6:22, 26); quickly learns that he has been duped by his new daughter and cunning wife (6:24–26); grieves over his idiotic vows and decides to save face rather than save John (6:26); orders John's beheading (6:16, 27); and serves his wife her expected dessert (6:28).

is our transition word to the next room—"it was Herod who had sent and seized John and bound him in prison" (6:17). He did this (keep an eye on the word "for") "for it was Herod who . . . seized John" (6:17); "for the sake of Herodias" (6:17); "for John had been saying" (**6:18**); "for Herod feared" (6:20). What a picture this simple three-letter word paints. There are four sinister strokes to the portrait. First, Herod *sent* out soldiers to *seize* John, take him to the prison cell, and *bind* him (6:17). Why? Second, "For the sake of Herodias" (6:17), who *was* Herod's "brother Philip's wife" (6:17). Here is the scandalous story. Herod Antipas had a brother named Aristobulus, who was executed by his father along with two other brothers. But before his execution, Aristobulus married and had a daughter named Herodias. Herodias married another Herod—Herod Philip. Herod Philip was Herod Antipas's half-brother. That, then, means Herodias is Herod Antipas's niece and sister-in-law. One day Herod Antipas proposed to Herodias. They were both married at the time. He was around fifty years of age; she was a good two decades younger. She accepted the proposal. Herod Antipas then divorced his wife and took his brother's wife. What did John the Baptist make of such behavior? He hated it. He hated the adultery, the divorce, the backstabbing, the deceit, and the high-handed maneuvering. As God's mouthpiece, he preached against it: "*For* [the third 'for'] John had been saying to Herod, 'It is not lawful for you to have your brother's wife'" (6:18).

The prophet's pronouncement did not sit well with Herodias. She "had a grudge against him and wanted to put him to death" (6:19). Yet Herodias could not get her way, because, or "*for*" (the fourth "for"), "Herod feared John, knowing that he was a righteous and holy man" (**6:19–20**). Therefore Herod protected John from her ("and kept him safe," 6:20). He also kept John safe because he knew, deep down, not only John but his message was righteous and holy. "When he heard him, he was greatly perplexed, and yet he heard him gladly" (6:20).

As your reliable guide, before we venture on to the banquet hall it is only appropriate that I offer you some advice on your earthly journey through life. Do not be like Herod. Do not follow Herod in repeatedly acting against your conscience. There is no doubt, as we read this portion of the Bible, that Herod had a conscience and that the man he put in his prison had pricked his conscience. Herod was a Jew. He was under the thumb of Rome, but he was under the same promises and Scriptures that Jesus and John were. Herod knew that. He knew he was a Jew. But he lived like the Romans: sex (wives and mistresses), drugs (drinking parties), and rock and roll (more mistresses).

John the Baptist loved God. He never had sex. He never drank alcohol. Within the right contexts (in marriage and at a wedding) sex and drinking are not sinful things; they just were not the Baptist's thing. This was a holy man. Set apart. No one was quite like him. But what would Herod do with him? Thank him? No. Ask him for help? No. He kept him safe and at a safe distance. He put him in prison, both for entertainment and, perhaps, in hope of finding salvation. He likely desired to repent, but he was too far gone. So what does someone who has crossed the edge of the unpardonable sin do? He edges to the edge of John's prison cell to listen to someone whose moral fortitude he wished he shared: "He heard him gladly" (6:20).

I am no John, but is that how you hear me as I preach to you through these pages? If so, I am going to challenge anyone on the edge of Herod-likeness: Get rid of your wealth. Purge your wardrobe. Come join John in the wilderness and then the cell. For, spiritually, that is a safer place to be.

The Banquet Hall

Before you do that (my point is that you may need to do something drastic), come with me again, and let us journey to the next room. We find ourselves in the banquet hall. So splendid. Fit for a king. A big party is happening. The occasion is a birthday. How many birthday celebrations are mentioned in the Bible? Two. Pharaoh's (Gen. 40:20) and Herod's. Yikes. So, should we celebrate birthdays? If we do, not like they did. Come along with me and look at Mark **6:21–26**, where, starting in verse 21, we read: "But an opportunity came when Herod on his birthday gave a banquet for his nobles and military commanders and the leading men of Galilee." The guest list is all men: those representing royalty ("nobles"), the military ("commanders" within the army), and any other important regional leaders, perhaps even religious authorities ("the leading men of Galilee").

Here in the banquet hall I want to show you not what was on the menu or who sat where or who wore what but what all the men in that room were focused on: "Herodias's daughter," called Salome in Josephus's *Antiquities* (18.136). She was somewhere between twelve and fourteen years old.[3] The men were staring at her because she "came in and danced" (6:22), an erotic and suggestive dance. I say this based on Herod's unusual reaction ("Ask me for whatever you wish, and I will give it to you") and the word "pleased"— "She pleased Herod and his guests" (6:22).[4]

---

3   The word "girl" (Gk. *korasion*) is used for Jairus's daughter, who was twelve (Mark 5:42).
4   "Herod is undone by his own sensuality. Overwhelmed by the sensual in the first place, he seduces his brother's wife. Now amid the sensual pleasures of a party, overcome again by a

She not only pleased Herod and his guests; she also pleased (in a different sense) her mother. Herod took the bait. The trap was set, and he ran right into it. Herodias knew not only that her daughter would please Herod but that Herod would then try to impress his guests with something like a foolish oath or two. He says to Salome once, "Ask me for whatever you wish, and I will give it to you" (6:22). Then he adds a vow (6:23), or a few vows ("oaths," 6:26)—something like, "May this palace be given to my enemies if I go back on my word." To say "Whatever you ask me, I will give you, up to half of my kingdom" (6:23) shows his arrogance and idiocy. He does not technically have a "kingdom," even though people dubbed him "King of the Jews."[5] He is not like Ahasuerus, the king of Persia, who thrice asked his queen Esther, "What is your request? It shall be given you, even to the half of my kingdom" (Est. 5:3, 6; 7:2). Herod is a tetrarch who rules over a quarter of *his* father's dominion. And, remember, he and his father are ruled by Rome. He is just a pawn on Caesar Augustus's chessboard. Rome has an empire. He works for them. His so-called kingdom is part of their empire. Put simply, he really does not have anything like that to give.

So his arrogance is obvious, as is his idiocy. To see this we will have to follow Salome into the hallway, where I envision Herodias poised directly outside the banquet hall. Listen to their conversation: "And she went out and said to her mother, 'For what should I ask?' And she said, 'The head of John the Baptist'" (6:24). That did not take long! "And she came in immediately with haste"—that really did not take long—"to the king and asked, saying, 'I want you to give me at once [and the next part of their plan should not take long] the head of John the Baptist'" (6:25), then she adds, "on a platter."

With this request the music stops, jaws drop, and perhaps Herod spills his wine. "What?" he must have thought. Of all the things in the world, this girl wants the prophet's severed head on a silver platter. Now, the language of speed—"immediately with haste" and "give me at once"—is important. Herodias and Salome do not want Herod to have any time to contemplate the decision. They know he has a soft spot for the saint. There is, however, a momentary pause: "And the king was exceedingly sorry" (6:26). But that pause does not lead to repentance or second thoughts. The reason is this: "Because of his oaths and his guests he did not want to break his word to her" (6:26). The case is closed. Then the deed is then done. "And *immediately* the king sent

---

pleasurable woman—this time the dancing daughter of his illegally gotten wife—he plunges again into excess." Frederick Dale Bruner, *Matthew: A Commentary, Volume 2: The Churchbook, Matthew 13–28*, rev. ed. (Grand Rapids, MI: Eerdmans, 2007), 64.

5   That noted, John Chrysostom (*Homilies on Matthew*) is right to point out the irony! "Such was the value he set upon his royal power that he was once for all made captive by his passion as to give up his kingdom for a dance" (Quoted in *CHSB*, 1483).

an executioner with orders to bring John's head. He went and beheaded him in the prison and brought his head on a platter and gave it to the girl, and the girl gave it to her mother" (**6:27–28**).

How horrific! Gruesome. Wicked. "What was a lesser sin for him [the 'lechery' of his sexual lust]," as Bede notes, "became the occasion of a greater sin ['homicide']."[6]

With that spectacle before us, what are we to make of Herod? How would you analyze his actions? I can offer an informed speculation of what Sigmund Freud would make of him. The famous psychoanalyst might say that Herod suffered from an Oedipus complex, which explains why he let two women make key decisions for him. Freud might also speak of paranoia and repression, linked to Herod's childhood. Herod the Great, Herod Antipas's father, was a ten out of ten on the dysfunctional father chart.[7] He was so insanely suspicious that he murdered many of those closest to him, including his children. A saying at the time went like this: "It is safer to be Herod's pig than Herod's son." Freud would also see Herod Antipas as the perfect example of his theory of that which accounts for all our actions, namely, *eros* and *thanatos*. *Eros*, according to Freud, is the erotic instinct that causes someone to lust after someone or covet something else, and *thanatos* is the death instinct that causes someone to be aggressive, self-destructive, and cruel. Something Freud would never do, however, is to break the first rule of his psychoanalysis, that is, to make moral judgments. So let me take it from here and make a few moral judgments of Herod and his cohort, for we need a biblically informed analysis.

How would Herod, Herodias, and Salome fare when assessed by Jesus' Sermon on the Mount? Lust? Check. Adultery? Check. Breaking vows? Check. Hatred? Check. Revenge? Check. Murder? Check. And, what if we ran the data of their deeds through Proverbs 6:16–19, "There are six things that the LORD hates, seven that are an abomination to him: haughty eyes, a lying tongue, and hands that shed innocent blood, a heart that devices wicked plans, feet that make haste to run to evil, a false witness who breathes out lies, and one who sows discord among brothers." To steal your brother's wife surely sowed some discord. Abomination seven? Check. Herodias' quickly calculated plot to kill John is surely devising wicked plans. Abomination four? Check. Herod's exaggerated offer of his kingdom surely constitutes a lying tongue, and perhaps false

---

6   Bede, *Exposition on the Gospel of Mark*, quoted in *CHSB*, 1483.

7   "Herod's last years were characterized by emotional and psychological deterioration"; H. Bond, "Herodian Dynasty," *DJG*, 380.

testimony. Abomination two? Check. Abomination six? Check. Herod's proud oaths and offer, along with his saving face rather than John's head perfectly illustrates "haughty eyes." Abomination one? Check. They are all guilty of "shedding innocent blood." Abomination three? Check. Finally, the swiftness of the whole scene sure does remind me of that line— "feet that make haste to run to evil." Abomination five? Check. Seven out of seven. This trio is perfect in their imperfections.[8]

We can learn many lessons from the ladies, such as avoiding the obvious evils: do not sexually entice men at parties and plot to kill your enemies. For most of us, however, Herod's sins are the more relatable ones. Earlier I stated something about Herod's conscience. Let me return now to that relevant and applicable theme. It is clear that Herod has a conscience, and that he repeatedly acted against it. Our lesson is *do not follow his lead.*

Herod knew the difference between right and wrong. He knew this from the Scriptures. He knew what Leviticus taught on adultery, incest, and polygamy.[9] He demonstrated as much in his assessment of John and his message. He viewed John as a "righteous and holy man" (6:20). He respected and admired him ("feared John," 6:20). This is why he protected him ("kept him safe," 6:20). We also know that Herod enjoyed hearing John (he "heard him gladly," 6:20) and that John's sermons struck a chord. The words "he was greatly perplexed" (6:20) could be translated "greatly disturbed" (NLT). In his paraphrase Eugene Peterson renders it this way: "Whenever he listened to him he was miserable with guilt" (MSG). Herod knew John's general message ("repent," 1:15), and he knew John's personal message to him ("It is not lawful for you to have your brother's wife," 6:18). Day after day he clearly heard the word of God ("heard," 6:14, 16, 20 [2x]). But whatever seed was sown was quickly swallowed up or eventually choked out. Indeed, Herod is an excellent illustration of the third soil in Jesus' parable of the sower. Herod hears the word (4:18), but the "cares of the world" (running his "kingdom" and impressing important people), the "deceitfulness of riches" (he would never give up his luxuries to live a life like John's), and the "desires for other things" (like wanton women and illicit power) "choke the word" (4:19).

---

8   Douglas Sean O'Donnell and Leland Ryken, *The Beauty and Power of Biblical Exposition: Preaching the Literary Artistry and Genres of the Bible* (Wheaton, IL: Crossway, 2022), 227–28.

9   "John was critical of the new marriage as violating OT law. It was not just the fact of divorce, but that the specific provisions of Lv. 18:16; 20:21 were being violated to be a form of incest within the family." John Nolland, *The Gospel of Matthew*, NIGTC (Grand Rapids, MI: Eerdmans, 2005), 582. On polygamy see W. D. Davies and Dale C. Allison Jr., *A Critical and Exegetical Commentary on the Gospel according to Saint Matthew*, ICC (Edinburgh: T&T Clark, 1991), 2:470.

Herod's conscience is shown also in his decision in the banquet room. He is "exceedingly sorry" (6:26). He is remorseful because he has chosen keeping his arrogant oath instead of saving John's innocent life. He still seems to be deeply regretful, as demonstrated in his ridiculous notion that John has been reincarnated as Jesus (6:14, 16). Herod's conscience is still haunted by the headless prophet.

Do not be like Herod. *Do not follow his lead.* Do not sin against your conscience. In 1 Timothy 1:18–19 Paul charges Timothy to "wage the good warfare" by holding on to the "faith" and keeping a "good conscience." He then warns that some who have rejected this charge "have made shipwreck of their faith." The image is of a man sailing along who stops holding on to "faith and a good conscience" and slowly, or perhaps quickly, veers off course into dangerous waters. The boat strikes a rock. The sharks start to circle. Hold on to "faith and a good conscience"—that is the lesson we are to learn from the banquet hall.

The Tomb

At one final destination I will point out our last few lessons. Come visit the tomb of John the Baptist. "When his disciples heard of it, they came and took his body and laid it in a tomb" (**6:29**). Here let us first bow our heads and pay our respects. We do so by looking at John's life and death and learning from these events, and by looking at the life, death, *and resurrection* of John's Lord and learning from him.

What can we learn from John? Thomas Cranmer has done the work for us. In his collect for the Nativity of John the Baptist he begins, "Almighty God, by whose providence thy servant, John the Baptist, was wonderfully born, and sent to prepare the way of thy Son our Savior, by preaching of repentance." Then the prayer shifts to these petitions: "Make us so to follow his doctrine and holy life, that we truly repent according to his preaching; and after his example constantly speak the truth, boldly rebuke vice, and patiently suffer for the truth's sake."

Let that be our prayer. First, may we truly repent of our sins. May we, as Martin Luther put it in the first of his Ninety-Five Theses, understand that when "our Lord and Master Jesus Christ . . . said 'Repent' [*poenitentiam agite*] [he] willed that the whole life of believers should be repentance." Second, may we, like John, constantly speak the truth, even and at times boldly rebuking vice. Let us not be like the false prophets of Ezekiel 13:2, 10, who deceived God's people by speaking "from their own hearts" (not from God's mind) a message of "peace" when there was coming judgment, not peace. Let us take courage from the courageous example of John. Let us speak the truth in love, but let us not be afraid to make enemies.

Years ago, when I preached on Matthew's version of this story, I remember walking over to a neighbor's house because my printer had broken. She is a Christian who attends a megachurch in the area. I had her print out my sermon for me. I titled that sermon "The Headless Prophet and the Heartless King." As the first page printed out, she looked at it. She had a puzzled expression on her face. She asked, "What topic are you preaching on this Sunday?" I said, "The beheading of John the Baptist." She replied with a smirk, "Who picks the sermon topics for your church?"

My answer now to my readers is this: with serial exposition through a book of the Bible, such as I am doing with Mark, God picks the sermon topics! And the topic for this chapter, or one of the key topics, is suffering for the truth's sake. Sermons on marriage, family, and work are all important, and the Bible occasionally addresses such topics. But a topic that can be found on nearly every page of the NT is that of suffering. Are we willing to suffer for Christ?[10] Deny ourselves? Pick up our crosses? Follow him? Follow John in following Jesus? The taglines for many Christian radio stations—positive, uplifting, and safe for the whole family—are not the taglines of the Bible. It is not that the Bible is negative and discouraging, but it *is* realistic, and realistically following Christ is not always the safest move from a worldly perspective.[11]

Another Tomb

As we stand before John's tomb, remembering his godly life and learning from it, let us conclude by focusing on another tomb. When we read Mark 6:29 ("When his disciples heard of it, they came and took his body and laid it in a tomb"), Mark wants our minds to fix upon Mark 15:46, where we read of another disciple, who took Jesus' body down from the cross "and laid him in a tomb." Surely the identical language is an intentional echo, and the point,

---

10 "As Mark interpolates John's execution between the beginning and the end of the mission of the Twelve, he underlines the fact that missionary work is dangerous and that discipleship is costly, both taking place in the context of admiration, opposition and rejection, and the real possibility of martyrdom." Eckhard J. Schnabel, *Mark: An Introduction and Commentary*, TNTC (Downers Grove, IL: IVP Academic, 2017), 148.

11 "In his Heidelberg Disputation of 1518, Luther drew a sharp contrast between theologians of glory and theologians of the cross. In typically paradoxical and challenging terms Luther argued that: '20. He deserves to be called a theologian, however, who comprehends the visible and manifest things of God seen through suffering and the cross' [and] '21. A theologian of glory calls evil good and good evil. A theologian of the cross calls the thing what it actually is.' . . . The theologian of the cross . . . sees things as they really are and calls them so." Kent Hughes, "The Scriptures: Our Life and Our Food," in *Let the Word Do the Work: Essays in Honour of Phillip Jensen*, ed. Peter G. Bolt (Camperdown, NSW: Australian Church Record, 2015), 31–32.

then, that Mark is making with the death and burial of John the Baptist is that it foreshadows the death and burial of Jesus. They would both be seized (Gk. *krateō*, 6:17; 14:46) and bound (*deō*, 6:17; 15:1). They would both suffer for righteousness' sake. They would both stand before Herod (see Luke 23:7–26). They would both die humiliating deaths. John, whom Jesus called the greatest man "born of women" (Matt. 11:11), was executed by the sword, his head severed from his body and served on a platter to a little girl at a lewd birthday party for a rash-speaking tetrarch. Where is the glory in that type of death? The only less glorious way to die would be to hang naked on a Roman cross with nails in your hands and feet and a crown of thorns pressing into your skull. What humiliation.

But we know the good news of that humiliation. We believe in the folly of the cross because we know it is the very power of God. We know that John, though he lost his head on earth, was rewarded with a crown in heaven. And we know that the grave could not hold the true King of the Jews. The tomb was empty. It is empty. Jesus is alive, alive forevermore.

A Foretaste of the Heavenly Banquet

MARK 6:30-44

And they all ate and were satisfied. And they took up twelve baskets full of broken pieces and of the fish. And those who ate the loaves were five thousand men.
Mark 6:42–44

When someone says the name "Jesus," what are some of the first thoughts that come to mind? I doubt that many of us think of a human embryo, a toddler learning to read, a little boy skipping to synagogue, a teenager falling out of a tree and twisting his ankle, or a man getting an upset stomach. Because we know Jesus as the wise teacher, wonder-working liberator, and dying and rising Savior to whom we pray and before whom we come each day to worship, we sometimes have a difficult time grasping that Jesus is truly human.

Moreover, the Gospels leave out many details of his humanity. We are not told about who taught him to read and write or if he has blue or brown eyes, is tall or short, or has straight or crooked teeth. But we are told that he was born of a woman (Gal. 4:4), grew in wisdom (Luke 2:52), walked (John 11:54), sailed the sea (Mark 6:32), got hungry (Mark 11:12) and thirsty (John 19:28), felt tired (John 4:6), and slept (Mark 4:38). We also know from Hebrews 5:7 and the Gospels that he spoke and sang and prayed. We know he grieved, even wept, over the death of a close friend (John 11:33–35). Moreover, we know that he suffered real physical pain and then died (Mark 15:37), the surest sign of his humanity.

I say all this about Jesus' humanity because the passage before us—the feeding of the five thousand—is a divinity-charged drama. Taking two fish and five pieces of bread and turning them into a meal large enough to feed a crowd packed into Veterans Memorial Stadium does not exactly shout, "This guy is one of us. He sure is human!"

Highlighting His Humanity

But that said, the beginning and end of our text (Mark 6:30–32; 6:45–46) highlight Jesus' humanity. Starting in **6:30–32** we read,

> The apostles [who had been send out][1] returned to Jesus and told him all that they had done and taught. And he said to them, "Come away by yourselves to a desolate place and rest a while." For many were coming and going, and they had no leisure even to eat. And they went away in the boat to a desolate place by themselves.

Remember, before this we read about the beheading of John the Baptist. We are not told the timeline. We do not know when that event happened. It could have been a year ago, as Mark 6:14–29 is told as a flashback. So the twelve's returning to Jesus and telling him "all that they had done and taught" (6:30) is not glossing over John's death. His execution is not the immediate historical context. The immediate historical context is Jesus' commission to the apostles to take his kingdom ministry of preaching, healing, and exorcising to the towns in Galilee.

So, that said, they return (I would imagine) quite excited about their new-found abilities. Sure, they have been rejected by some, but others have experienced the life-saving powers of heaven on earth through the apostles' own mouths and hands. So what does Jesus do? He immediately starts twelve new satellite church campuses. No. Instead, verse 31 records his next commission: "And he said to them, 'Come away by yourselves to a desolate place and rest a while.'" Jesus does not say, "We all deserve a holiday," but he does say, "Let's all take a needed break and reenergize." The humanity of Jesus is on remarkable display here. Because so many people were "coming" to them and "going" from them, "they had no leisure even to eat" (6:31; cf. 3:20), Jesus wants his disciples and himself to take a break from the crowd, even if they need to sail to a deserted seaside to do so.

Next, in verse 32 we read that they comply: "And they went away in the boat to a desolate place by themselves." Mark does not tell us the place off the Sea of Galilee to which they voyage (presumably Bethsaida Julias, Luke 9:10),[2] but he does tell us that when they arrive at this secluded location they pitch a tent on the beach, set up some hammocks, catch and cook and consume some

---

1   This is the only time the term "apostles" is used in Mark (cf. 6x in Luke; 28x in Acts).

2   The traditional site is Tabgha, south of Capernaum. Most scholars today suggest the plain of Bethsaida. Note also that three times he speaks of this place as "desolate" (Gk. *erēmos*, Mark 6:31, 32, 35), which is the common way the LXX translates "wilderness."

tilapia, and take long naps in the breeze. Not exactly. He writes, "Now many saw them going and recognized them, and they ran there on foot from all the towns and got there ahead of them" (Mark **6:33**). I love, and laugh at, this description. These crowds in Jesus' day are worse than the paparazzi in ours.

That is the top of our text, which depicts a very human Jesus: the need for rest, food, and some privacy. Then the miracle happens, of course. We will get to it soon. But, post-miracle, at the tail of our text, look at what happens:

> Immediately he made his disciples get into the boat and go before him to the other side, to Bethsaida, while he dismissed the crowd. And after he had taken leave of them, he went up on the mountain to pray. (6:45–46)

Again Mark highlights Jesus' need to revitalize. Here it is not physical but spiritual revitalization. Yet I will say that those words "He dismissed the crowd" (6:45) and "After he had taken leave of them" (6:46) are striking. They are striking because there still must be great needs in such a great crowd. They are now fully fed people, but also sick, hurting, and desperate people in need of a healing hand. What can be more important than opening a miracle medical center?

Prayer. Prayer is Jesus' priority. He desires private communion with his Father. Therefore, the crowds are dismissed. A mountain is climbed (think about the humanness of such a trek). Then a thousand unknown prayers are prayed. Or, one prayer: "Father, glorify me in your own presence with the glory that I had with you before the world existed" (John 17:5). That is the prayer, recorded in John's Gospel, that Jesus prays in the upper room before his passion. It would certainly fit what Jesus might most desire at this point in his earthly ministry, and it would fit the context of the next time in Mark when Jesus goes up a mountain: at the Mount of Transfiguration. So that prayer is a possibility. Another suggestion is that he prays something like he would pray in the garden of Gethsemane: "Remove this cup from me" (Mark 14:36). One wonders if the heaviness of the atonement weighs upon him here. As he prays on this mountain in Galilee, he might feel the hill outside of Jerusalem edging closer and closer to him. What seemed years away is now drawing near.

Jesus is human. Might he have thought and prayed here, "Father, I know what became of John the Baptist in the hands of sinful men, I don't want that, or something worse, happening to me"? Might he have thought and prayed, "Father, these twelve are as imperfect as the number thirteen. Give me someone like Joshua or Daniel to work with. What am I to do with Peter, Matthew, and John? How on earth will the kingdom of heaven be established through their witness after my death?" Of course, I only speculate on the content of his prayer. But I honestly do not understand the pause here in the action. What is Jesus up to? He is acting too human for me.

Showcasing His Divinity

After examining the top and tail of our text that highlight Jesus' humanity — the need to eat, rest, and pray — we turn our attention next to the miracle story in the middle (**6:34–44**).

Remember again the setting. The twelve have returned from their short-term mission trip. Jesus tells them to take a break and grab something to eat. So they clock out, get on a boat, and sail to an undisclosed, desert-like location. There, to their surprise, a crowd is present to meet them. "A great crowd," Mark tells us in verse 34, a crowd of "five thousand men" (6:44). Notice the word "men." Matthew's account informs us that there were "about five thousand men, besides women and children" (Matt. 14:21). So, if Jesus' nuclear family was typical (ten members), the total number present would be fifty thousand. My guess is that not every mother and child from every family was present, and thus we can safely estimate that the crowd was over ten thousand, but likely not beyond thirty thousand. Whatever the precise number, it was a substantial assembly.

Now then, what does Jesus do with such a crowd, which has crowded in on him and his disciples' day of rest and relaxation? Does he dismiss them? He will do that (6:45). But first he does something remarkable. In motive, word, and deed he shows them and us who he is. *He is the divine Son of God, the new and greater Moses, the Good Shepherd who has come to compassionately shepherd his people by providing them with a foretaste of the messianic banquet — a taste of bread from heaven on their tongues and the word of God in their ears.*

Look at the start of verse 34. "When he went ashore he saw a great crowd, and he had compassion on them, because they were like sheep without a shepherd." I say that what Jesus does here is remarkable, first in relation to his motives. When it is my day off and I run into a church member at the supermarket, pool, gym, or park who tells me about his or her need, my first reaction is consternation, not compassion. My second reaction is compassion, for the record. But my first reaction is to think first of me, my time off, and my need for rest.

The second remarkable fact recorded here is that Jesus' compassion leads to an open mouth, and then an open hand. Before he shares his food, he first shares his wisdom. "When he went ashore he saw a great crowd, and he had compassion on them, because they were like sheep without a shepherd. And he began *to teach* them many things" (6:34). Again, this is his usual pattern: word first (and of first importance), works second. If anyone believed Deuteronomy 8:3—"Man does not live by bread alone, but man lives by every word that comes from the mouth of the LORD"—it was our Lord Jesus Christ (cf. Matt. 4:4; Luke 4:4). Here in Mark we are not told the content of his teaching, but we are told that the lesson is not short (he taught them "many things") and we are given his impetus for instruction ("They were like sheep without a shepherd," Mark 6:34). With this sheep/shepherd metaphor Jesus is alluding to the OT, in which Israel's authorities were compared to bad shepherds, including the bad leaders of the wilderness generation (Num. 27:17), the corrupt kings like Ahab (1 Kings 22:17), and the false prophets that led to the exile (Ezek. 34:1–10). The Jewish leaders of Jesus' day are no better. As we saw last chapter, Herod is not exactly the role model for Israel to follow.[3] The same can be said of the religious establishment of the day, who are now out to kill Jesus, a man who we know to be the promised Davidic king who has come to shepherd his people (see Ezek. 34:23; 37:24).[4]

Finally, is it remarkable not only that Jesus' heart goes out to the crowd and his words of wisdom spill over the crowd, but also that the little food he and his disciples have, or could find, they share with the crowd. His heart, head, *and hands* reach out.

Remember, one of the reasons he and his disciples are in this desolate place is to eat, because they have been having a hard time finding time to eat because of the crowds. So the last thing on the disciples' minds is how they could somehow provide food for this massive crowd. Mark 6:35–38 records their understandable attitude. Starting in verses 35–36, we read, "And when it grew late, his disciples came to him and said, 'This is a desolate place, and the hour is now late. Send them away to go into the surrounding countryside and villages and buy themselves something to eat.'" Here, first the disciples give Jesus a command: "Send the crowd away." There might be a bit of irritation

3   "In contrast to the debauched banquet of the corrupt king Herod Antipas, which ended in the tragic murder of John the Baptist, Jesus, the great shepherd of Israel, compassionately meets the needs of God's people in a prefiguration of God's end-time messianic banquet (Isa 25:6–9). While Galilee's aristocrats feast sumptuously in Herod's ornate palace, Jesus feeds the poor and humble—the true heirs of the kingdom—in the open fields on the shores of Galilee." Mark L. Strauss, *Mark*, ZECNT (Grand Rapids, MI: Zondervan, 2014), 269.

4   "David was a successful king because he 'shepherded [Israel] with integrity of heart' (Ps 78:72; cf. 1 Kgs 9:4), and the coming Messiah from David's line was predicted to be a shepherd over God's flock (Jer 23:1–6; Ezek 34:22–23; Mic 5:2–4; Zech 13:7; *Pss. Sol.* 17:40–41" (Strauss, *Mark*, 274).

behind their words, but there is also a certain logic. The land will not provide food (it is "a desolate place," 6:35). The sun is starting to set ("The hour is now late," 6:35). So, option one, if anyone thinks it, is for everyone to fast for the night. Or, option two, as they suggest, is for people to head to the local venues and see if *Saul's Family Restaurant, In the Neighborhood Deli*, and similar establishments are still open ("go into the surrounding countryside and villages and buy . . . something to eat," 6:36).[5]

To this reasonable request, however, Jesus offers another option: "But he answered them, 'You [emphatic!] give them something to eat'" (6:37). I am not sure if he is reminding them of the lesson that they surely learned on their no-money-bag and no-bread (6:8) mission trip—namely, that God can provide. But he is definitely training these men to trust him even and especially in dire circumstances. Yet they are still a bit dense, even if their question sounds reasonable enough: "And they said to him, 'Shall we go and buy two hundred denarii worth of bread and give it to them to eat?'" (6:37). Surely not! Here they get a little snarky. They check their pockets. Everyone counts his change. James and John say, "We have one denarius." Peter says, "I have two." Judas says, "I have thirteen!" They all give him a suspicious look. "What? I'm the treasurer," he states. "Jesus," they all say, "we have some money. But not enough to cover this crowd. That would take a small fortune, seven or eight months' wages. Remember, Lord, because of your calling us, we are all unemployed. We'd be glad if we could buy enough bread to provide a day's rations for 200 people."

To their doubt, Jesus again responds. He has a better idea than buying food. He says, "Count again. Not your money but your dinner, if any is left, and see what others might have brought." Verse 38 starts, "And he said to them, 'How many loaves do you have? Go and see.'" Go to the boat and go to the people. Off they go. They gather "five [pieces of bread], and two fish" (6:39). "John 6:9 says that a young man provided the food, which was five barley loaves and probably dried or pickled fish for a bit of flavor—the food of the poor."[6] I imagine Jesus, as he looked at these scraps, thinking back to the creation of the world, especially the third and fifth days, when God said, "Let the earth sprout . . . plants yielding seed [like wheat!]" (Gen. 1:11) and "Let the waters swarm with swarms of living creatures [like fish!]" (Gen. 1:20). He looks at these two fish and fives loaves and thinks, "I've worked with a lot less."

---

5 "Villages" then, like small towns today, would have some local fare, as would *agroi* (Gk. the "countryside," or perhaps better in this context, "farms").

6 Grant R. Osborne, *Mark*, TTCS (Grand Rapids, MI: Baker, 2012), 106.

Next, look afresh to this familiar but spectacular miracle. It is recorded in all four Gospels because it is extremely important.[7] Watch how "Jesus turns a poor man's lunch into a royal feast."[8]

> Then he commanded them all to sit down in groups on the green grass. So they sat down in groups, by hundreds and by fifties. And taking the five loaves and the two fish, he looked up to heaven and said a blessing and broke the loaves and gave them to the disciples to set before the people.[9] And he divided the two fish among them all. (Mark 6:39–41)

Wherever this desolate place is, it is not a desert. The people sit down "on the green grass" (6:39), perhaps an allusion to Psalm 23 ("The LORD is my shepherd; I shall not want. He makes me lie down in green pastures") and Isaiah 35:1 LXX, where "the thirsty wilderness" will "blossom" when the Messiah comes. They are grouped "by hundreds and by fifties" (Mark 6:40), perhaps an allusion to when Moses divides the people this way (Ex. 18:21). Or perhaps the language signifies a feast is to be served—the crowd is to recline (Gk. *anaklinō*, Mark 6:39, 40) *symposia symposia* (6:39), which can be translated "dinner party by dinner party."[10]

They do as Jesus has "commanded" (6:39). But I doubt, as they sit together in their small groups, that they think it is for food distribution. Jesus surprises them. He does not surprise them by taking food in his hands and praying, likely using the traditional Jewish blessing, "Blessed are you, O Lord our God, King of the world, who brings forth bread from the earth" (m. Ber. 6:1). He surprises them by somehow turning two fish and five loaves into enough food to feed thousands of hungry people. Even if the apostles expected some sort of miracle, I doubt they expected this. Bread, bread, and more bread. One fish, two fish, red fish, blue fish, new fish, new fish, new fish, new fish. Holy mackerel!

7   Matt. 14:13–21; Mark 6:30–44; Luke 9:10–17; John 6:1–15.
8   Osborne, *Mark*, 106.
9   The miracle of the feeding of the five thousand has long been linked to the sacrament of the Lord's Supper. The four verbs—"taking" the food . . . he . . . said a blessing and broke the loaves . . . [he] gave them to the disciples"—are the same ones, in that order, that Mark uses at the Last Supper (Mark 14:22). Also, this miracle has been understood as a foreshadowing of the messianic banquet (14:25). So, when we celebrate the Lord's Supper by taking and eating of a piece of bread and drinking a portion of the fruit of the vine, we do so in remembrance of Jesus' earthly ministry and in anticipation of the consummation of salvation when he will return. As Paul puts it, when we eat and drink of this meal, we "proclaim the Lord's death until he comes" (1 Cor. 11:26).
10 Eckhard J. Schnabel, *Mark: An Introduction and Commentary*, TNTC (Downers Grove, IL: IVP Academic, 2017), 152.

The response, then, to this feast in the wilderness is full-bellied satisfaction ("And they all ate and were satisfied ["filled with food," *chortazō*"], 6:42), followed by frugality ("And they took up twelve baskets full of broken pieces and of the fish," 6:43). They are more than satisfied. There are doggy bags for a few families to take home—"twelve baskets"—perhaps to remind these sons and daughters of Abraham—the twelve tribes of Israel—that Jesus is the fulfillment of all the promises of God has given to his people.

It is surprising, here at the end of the drama, that the only reaction Mark records is their physical satisfaction. There is no questioning, "Who is this?" (Matt. 21:10) or acclamations of praise, "[And] they were all amazed and glorified God, saying, 'We never saw anything like this!'" (Mark 2:12). This toned-down reaction might be because the actual miracle was hidden from them. They never saw Jesus do anything. It was his disciples who carried a few baskets around that never ran out of food. Yet it is hard to believe that after their second helping they did not realize that something miraculous was afoot. That said, whatever the original audience thought or said during or after the meal, we can only guess. What we do know is what we should now say, having viewed this miracle from a distance. Our reaction should be something along the lines of, "Surely this is the hand of God!"

For someone to have authority over illness and demons is one thing. But to do this! This is "power on an altogether different level."[11] No first-rate faith healer or world-class magician could replicate this miracle. No such shows in some superdome ever feature the perfectly unduplicatable miracle of taking seven pieces of food and feeding the entire crowd. Moreover, while Jesus' miracle echoes God's provision of the manna and meat during Israel's wilderness wanderings (see Exodus 16; Numbers 11) and, through Elisha, the feeding of one hundred men with twenty loaves (2 Kings 4:42–44), it obviously exceeds those awesome acts.[12] Jesus' "supernatural multiplication is just that—supernatural!" And it serves as a "visible, tangible, verifiable, *edible* attestation of Jesus' identity." He is not a charlatan or false prophet but God in the flesh—the sovereign Lord of creation. "The one who spun the stars into existence and has speedily—not in one day or seven days, not one second or seven seconds, but in point seven seconds—changed the immaterial into material, the non-existent to the existing. With the blink of an eye, the passing of a loaf, one turns to two to three to four and five. This is the bread of God

---

11 Schnabel, *Mark*, 154.
12 E.g., "Jesus' miracle is two hundred times as great (Elisha multiplied the bread fivefold, Jesus a thousandfold)" (Osborne, *Mark*, 106).

from the hand of God."[13] That is what we are to see. This is God *with* us! And this is God *for* us.

Count to Eight

Frederick Dale Bruner cleverly summarizes the lesson we should learn from this miracle by saying that "disciples should always count to eight."[14] That is, when the disciples were asked to calculate the rations, they should have estimated that besides the fives loaves and two fish there was the one Jesus, the ultimate provision. We should count to eight. We should count on God through Jesus to provide our daily bread — the "bread" that is the Word of God preached (provision for our every spiritual need) and the "bread" that represents provision for our every physical need.

However, in counting to eight, we must also grasp that Jesus provides more than words for our souls and food for our stomachs; he provides himself as the "bread of life" (John 6:35), "the bread that came down from heaven" (John 6:58). Through his death on the cross and glorious resurrection from the dead he welcomes all to feed on him spiritually through faith, offering the promise that whoever "comes to [him] shall not hunger" (John 6:35) and "whoever feeds on [him] . . . will live forever" (John 6:58). If there is one thing we should understand about this passage, it is that. Yes, we need to note the compassion of Christ and the priorities of word and prayer. Yes, we are to note his full humanity and full divinity. But the one thing, the main thing, is to take and eat of him, to come to the Shepherd King, the utterly compassionate and absolutely powerful God-man, and find spiritual salvation and sustenance and satisfaction, everlasting life in him alone.

---

13 Douglas Sean O'Donnell, *Matthew: All Authority under Heaven*, PTW (Wheaton, IL: Crossway, 2013), 406–7.

14 Frederick Dale Bruner, *Matthew: A Commentary, Volume 2: The Churchbook, Matthew 13–28*, rev. ed. (Grand Rapids, MI: Eerdmans, 2004), 68.

Recognizing Him as "I Am"

MARK 6:45-56

But immediately he spoke to them and said, "Take heart;
it is I. Do not be afraid."
Mark 6:50

Recently my wife and I went to Sawyer, Michigan, for a two-day retreat on Lake Michigan. We were trying to apply my new life verse from the last chapter, "Come away by yourselves . . . and rest a while" (Mark 6:31). While there, I was reminded of the first few times I went to Lake Michigan as a boy. One of the oldest videos my dad took of me, on his vintage camera, was of me at four years old, running to the edge of the dunes near Sawyer, and from there running full steam ahead toward the lake. My pace seemed to quicken on the yellow sands the closer I got to the blue waters, and then, an inch before my toes would touch, I stopped. I walked back. I did it again. I obviously liked running. And I was very afraid of the waves.

I also remember the first time in my life when I thought I was going to die. This also happened in Sawyer. I do not remember the precise age, but I would guess that I was seven or eight. At that age, I had no fear. I jumped into the waters and started fighting the big waves. I was having the time of my life. Then I remember a wave striking me unexpectedly, lifting me off my feet, pushing me toward the shore, but then dragging me out farther than where I had started. I was underwater the whole time. I could not breathe or see, and I did not know how to swim. But then the wave gave up its ghost. It died, not me! I felt the ground. I stood up. The waters were up to my nose. I was twenty feet from shore. I ran, with all my might, step by slow step through the waterlogged sand, back to safety. Glad to be alive.

The setting for the stories God has given for us to look at in this chapter (Mark 6:45–56) is, once again, in and around a lake. Notice the words "boat" (6:45, 51, 54), "shore" (6:53), and "sea" (6:47, 48, 49, [implied] 53). The Sea of Galilee is not part of the Great Lakes, as Lake Michigan is, but its *small* size does not spare its swimmers and sailors from feeling the weight of large waves and the furious power of deadly windstorms.

Relearning the Lesson of the Loaves

Despite all that water language and analogy, I am actually calling the first half of our text (Mark **6:45–52**) "Relearning the Lesson of the Loaves." That title will make sense, in some sense, when you read this section and, in much sense, I hope, when I am done explaining it. After Mark begins again with his customary word ("immediately")—he keeps moving the action forward to the cross—the text continues, speaking of Jesus' actions:

> He made his disciples get into the boat and go before him to the other side, to Bethsaida, while he dismissed the crowd. And after he had taken leave of them, he went up on the mountain to pray. And when evening came, the boat was out on the sea, and he was alone on the land. And he saw that they were making headway painfully, for the wind was against them. And about the fourth watch of the night he came to them, walking on the sea. He meant to pass by them, but when they saw him walking on the sea they thought it was a ghost, and cried out, for they all saw him and were terrified. But immediately he spoke to them and said, "Take heart; it is I. Do not be afraid." And he got into the boat with them, and the wind ceased. And they were utterly astounded ["why?"], for [or "because"] *they did not understand about the loaves,* but [or we might add another "why?" and then "because"] their hearts were hardened.

There are nine points of interest to explore here. First, it is interesting that Jesus strongly compels (or even *forces*) the twelve into the boat. The start of verse 45 reads, "Immediately *he made* [*anankazō*] his disciples get into the boat." Why such haste? And why a forceful command, not a polite suggestion? I think Jesus gets these blokes in the boat because the crowd, after the miracle of all nature miracles (turning a poor boy's scraps into a two-course foretaste of the meal to end all meals), is in a frenzy. We know this from the Gospel of John's record on the feeding of the five thousand:

> When the people saw the sign that he had done, they said, "This is indeed the Prophet who is to come into the world!"
> Perceiving then that they were about to come and take him by force to make him king, Jesus withdrew again to the mountain by himself. (John 6:14–15)

Jesus not only withdraws, as we see in Mark 6:45, but he orders some immediate separation for the twelve from the crowd, lest they be swept up in the frenzy. (Who does not want to be popular? And who does not, in their case, as Jews living under oppressive Roman rule, want to take down the intrusive Italians?) Some people in this very crowd will fight to the death against Rome about forty years later—and to their nation's demise and the very destruction of the temple. Jesus did not come as a military king. He did not come to kill the Romans. He came to be killed by the Romans for the salvation of the nations—murderous Roman centurions, pious Jewish priests, and every type of Afghani to Zimbabwean sinner in between.

The second detail that piques my interest is the disciples' obedience. Without any delay or fuss "his disciples get into the boat" and start to push off from shore ("go before him to the other side," 6:45)—or try to. They obey this compelling but counterintuitive command as quickly as they did Jesus' counterintuitive command to feed the five thousand with five loaves and two fish. I suppose, after his feeding the crowd almost *ex nihilo*, that no one balks at his Lord's next seemingly crazy command. Off they go!

Third, it is interesting that the crowd actually backs off. We are told in verse 45 that Jesus "dismissed the crowd" ("Go home; show is over" is the sense) and that they actually go home, or at least elsewhere. If I were there, and in a sanctified state of mind (which I am occasionally), and I had just eaten manna and meat from heaven, I would have followed either the twelve on the boat or Jesus up the mountain. But this crowd, seemingly the whole thirty thousand or so, says, "Okay. We'll leave." Why would they leave? My guess is that most of those that day are like most people today. They seek after Jesus to get something from him. Then, once they have it—from a full stomach to a healed heart valve—they could not care less about him after that. They have no need for his cross. They certainly do not want to pick up their own cross and follow him. Why climb a mountain to get to him? Sounds hard. Why latch onto the back of the boat? Sounds dangerous.

Fourth, it is interesting that Jesus, who is obviously—as attested by the miracle—more than a mere man, takes time to pray. To pray means that you are truly human. Jesus, though he is truly divine, is also truly human. In the last chapter I stated that he might have prayed because he desired to return to the glory he had before the incarnation or, with the weight of the atonement weighing on his soul, might have prayed the first draft of his Gethsemane prayer. In this chapter I will add that perhaps he prayed for his disciples' endurance—that they would persevere in the faith even through the storms of life. And that he would not be tempted like he was tempted by Satan in the wilderness (1:13), to take the crown before the cross (Matt. 4:1–11)—that is, to become just the type of conquering king the Jewish crowds wanted and expected.

Fifth, it is interesting that Jesus both *sees* them in their distress and *comes to* them. After Jesus prays, he journeys down the mountain. The crowd has dispersed. The disciples are "out on the sea" (Mark 6:47). "He was alone on the land" (6:47). What does Mark record next? "And he saw that they were making headway painfully, for the wind was against them" (6:48). So they must have been near shore. Wrong. They left before Jesus had gone up the mountain. To climb that small mountain or big hill in Galilee and then pray would have taken him at least a few hours. Matthew tells us that "the boat by this time was a long way [many *stadia*] from the land" (Matt. 14:24); John says "they had rowed about three or four miles [twenty-five or thirty *stadia*]" out (John 6:19).

So what does Jesus see from the mountain? Wait! How could he see? Not only is the boat miles offshore, but the sun has set ("when evening came," Mark 6:47; or, as John more frankly phrases it, "It was now dark," John 6:17). Jesus does not have eagle eyes; and besides, even if he did, no eagle could see three miles through the dark. He has Yahweh eyes. "The LORD looks down from heaven; he sees all the children of man" (Ps. 33:13), or, to paraphrase that verse for this situation, "Jesus looks down from the mountain and across from the shore, and he sees all twelve members of his little church on a little boat in a lot of danger."

Because "the wind was against them" (Mark 6:48), they cannot use their sails. So out come the oars. With hundreds of strokes, they are slowly moving forward. Their arms ache. ("They were making headway *painfully*," 6:48).[1] They are in trouble and they know it. They know that this is a precarious place to find themselves, in the middle of the lake in the middle of the night ("about the fourth watch of the night," 6:48; between 3 and 6 a.m.),[2] with waves beating against the boat (see Matt. 14:24). I wonder whether Peter is wondering whether he should have left his brother Andrew on the shore as the designated survivor. For, if this boat sinks, this chapter in our Bibles does not exist. We have no Gospel of Mark. We do not have this eyewitness testimony about Jesus' life, death, or resurrection.

Whatever Peter might be thinking, we know what Jesus thinks. On that stormy night, as these windblown waves are pushing these sailors back like wrestler Andre the Giant lying on them for a three-second count—"One,

---

1 The translation "painfully" is of the Greek verb *basanizō*, which could be rendered "being tormented" or even "tortured." The only other time Mark uses the word is with the Gerasene demoniac: "I adjure you by God, do not torment me" (Mark 5:7).
2 Mark is using Roman (see Livy, *Annals* 36.24.1) rather than Jewish (see b. Ber. 3ab; cf. Judg. 7:19) divisions of the day.

two, . . ."—our compassionate Lord, Savior, Friend "came to them" (Mark 6:48). This battle royal is about to be over. Jesus will stay the heavyweight. How so? How does he even get there in time? A quantum leap? I have no idea how he got there. He got there, I suspect, like the next loaf got to the next hungry mouth.

I jokingly said at the start of this sermon that Mark 6:31 ("Come away . . . and rest a while") is my new life verse. But let me tell you, quite seriously, that I am considering Mark 6:48 to be my new life verse, or at least the verse that has given me life and rest of late ("And he saw that they were making headway painfully . . . [and so] he came to them"). He came to them to save them, just as he comes to me and you to save us from our sins, to save us from foolish decisions, and to save from us physical and material desperation.

Sixth, it is *extremely interesting* that Jesus "came to them, *walking on the sea*" (6:48). Question: How did he see them? Question: How did he get to them? Question: How did he get to them so fast? Question: How did he walk on water? Answer: Jesus is divine. He sees all. Answer: Jesus is divine. He knows all. Answer: Jesus is divine. He possesses wave-parting, wind-ceasing, supersonic speed. Answer: Jesus is divine. He defies gravity. Any questions? There should not be. That is what Mark is trying to make extremely clear. Here he returns to his thesis statement in 1:1, "The gospel of Jesus Christ." Underline the next phrase: "the Son of God."

Seventh, it is interesting that the disciples take the figure on the waters for a ghost. I am not surprised that they are "terrified," for it would be frightening to have violent winds pressing against you when you are miles from shore. And it would be frightening to then see a manlike figure walking on water. But I am surprised that they cry out, "Look, a ghost!" (see 6:49; cf. Matt. 14:26), because it was common for pagans in the Greco-Roman world, not Jews, to believe that ghosts of those who had drowned roamed the waters (e.g., Lucan, *Civil War* 1.11). Perhaps that is what they thought. They obviously had no category for what they saw. Humans do not walk on water. Thus some ethereal aberration of a dead person (Gk. *phantasma*) is the only option that makes sense.

Eighth, it is interesting that Jesus both declares and demonstrates his divinity. Before Jesus once again (see Mark 4:39) stills the sea (here without a word!—"And he got in the boat with them, and the wind ceased," 6:51), he first calms the disciples: "Take heart; it is I. Do not be afraid" (6:50). At face value these three lines—paraphrased as "Be courageous," "Don't worry; I'm not a ghost. It's me, Jesus," and "Stop being scared"—do not necessarily point to his divinity. Jesus might simply be trying to calm their nerves, and perhaps offer a slight rebuke ("Stop being cowards! Did I abandon you last time the waves pressed in? No, I did not!"). But the phrase between the two imperatives ("Take heart. . . . Do not be afraid"), taken literally, is the clearest admission of divinity in the Gospel of Mark. In Greek Jesus says, *egō eimi* ("I am"). They yell, "It's a ghost!" Then Jesus yells through the wind and the waves, "It . . . is . . . I . . . am." This is the closest we get in Mark to Jesus' "I am" statements in John: "I am the good shepherd" (John 10:11), "I am the bread of life" (6:35), and "I am the light of the world" (9:5)—three declarations that fit perfectly Jesus' actions in surrounding context in Mark, as does "Before Abraham was, I am" (8:58; cf. 18:6), which fits both Genesis 15:1 and our text.

Both there in John and here in Mark, Jesus, with his "I am" admission, alludes to Exodus 3:14, as well as Genesis 15:1; 26:24; and Isaiah 43:1–3. In Exodus God reveals himself to Moses as "I AM WHO I AM." In Genesis 15:1 God says to Abraham, "Fear not . . . *I am* your shield," and in 26:24, "Fear not, for *I am* with you." Five times in Isaiah Yahweh announces *egō eimi*,[3] and in a few places this divine self-identification formula is combined with the phrase "fear not." The most striking example comes from Isaiah 43, which begins, "But now thus says the LORD, he who created you . . . '*Fear not*, for I have redeemed you. . . . When you pass through the waters, I will be with you. . . . For *I am* the LORD your God, the Holy One of Israel, your Savior.'"[4]

Jesus *says* he is God ("I am") and then *shows* he is God. Immediately the wind ceases (Mark 6:51). "He caused the east wind to blow in the heavens, and by his power he led out the south wind" (Ps. 78:26). Their reaction follows. It is the right reaction. "And they were utterly astounded" (Mark 6:51). They are astounded, I surmise, both by what he has said and what he has done.

Ninth, the ending is also of interest. Mark adds this editorial, "And they were utterly astounded, for they did not understand about the loaves, but their hearts were hardened" (6:51–52). The words "their hearts were hardened" could simply mean "their brains were dull," which fits well the clause before it: "They did not understand." "Hard hearts make for blind eyes."[5] But hardness of heart in the Bible usually means more than misunderstanding. It means a heartfelt opposition to God. Here they appreciate Jesus and want to follow him. They are not opposed to the ways of God, as Pharaoh was.[6] Their hardness centers on their failure to embrace the man Jesus as more than a mere man. He is the divine Christ, the Son of the Most High God in the flesh.

---

3   Isaiah 41:4; 43:10, 25; 51:12; 52:6. Cf. Raymond E. Brown, *The Gospel according to John I–XII*, AB 29 (New York: Doubleday, 1966). Brown (537) comments on the use of *egō eimi* in the Fourth Gospel and their relationship to Isaiah: "Jesus is presented as speaking in the same manner in which Yahweh speaks [in Isaiah]."
4   Isaiah 43:1–3 LXX; *egō eimi* occurs in Isa. 43:10, with another "fear not" in Isa. 43:5.
5   Grant R. Osborne, *Mark*, TTCS (Grand Rapids, MI: Baker, 2012), 115.
6   See Exodus 7:3, 13, 22; 8:15, 32; 9:12; 10:1. Cf. Mark 3:5.

Therefore, considering these nine interesting observations, especially the last one, what is the lesson of the loaves? What do the disciples not get from it, and what should we make sure we get? What they should have learned through the miracle of the feeding of the five thousand is threefold—in fact, the precise three points reiterated by Jesus' walking on the water and stopping the winds. First, Jesus is the divine Son of God. Second, Jesus is sufficient to provide. Third, therefore, fear not. Let us take each of these in turn.

First, Jesus is the divine Son of God. I said earlier that Jesus declares and demonstrates his divinity. He called himself "I am," and he acts like only God can act. He sees through the storm, walks on the waves, and quiets the winds. That unique Markan statement "He meant to pass by them" (6:48) is used likely because it echoes the language used to describe Yahweh's passing by Moses on Mount Sinai (Ex. 33:17–23) and Elijah on Mount Horeb (1 Kings 19:9–14), as well as Job's speaking of God as "trampl[ing] the waves of the sea . . . [and] passing by" him (Job 9:8, 11).[7] Jesus' walking on water is a theophany.

Second, Jesus is sufficient to provide. Look at his track record in Mark. Does he provide for his people? Indeed. Bread from heaven, salvation from storms, and so on. In our lives, then, has he provided? The answer again is indeed. Can he provide? Certainly. Will he provide? Of course.

Third, therefore, fear not.

Fear not, I am with thee, O be not dismayed,
For I am thy God and will still give thee aid;
I'll strengthen and help thee, and cause thee to stand
Upheld by My righteous, omnipotent hand.

---

7 Following those two Christologically charged statements—"He came to them, walking on the sea"—is that odd, unexpected, and thus interesting clause "He meant to pass by them" (Mark 6:48). On these words Osborne (*Mark*, 110–11) offers three possible interpretations: that Mark (1) writes from the disciples' vantage point (they thought he was passing them by), (2) tells it from Jesus' perspective, as he expected them to trust God's provision and be comforted, or (3) means that Jesus "intended to pass their way" and describes his purpose in coming. If it is the third view, then Mark leaves the impression that Jesus knew that he was on a solo mission—to die for the sins of the elect—and thus elected to ignore the disciples for now. Moreover, Dane Ortlund suggests that Jesus' "passing by is far more significant" than passing by the way one car on the highway may bypass another and that it is "only understood against its Old Testament background. Four times in Exodus 33–34 the Lord says he will 'pass by' Moses, the Septuagint (the Greek OT) using the same word (*parerchomai*) that Mark uses. The Lord passed by Moses and revealed that his deepest glory is seen in his mercy and grace. Jesus came to do in flesh and blood what God had done only in wind and voice in the Old Testament." Dane Ortlund, *Gentle and Lowly: The Heart of Christ for Sinners and Sufferers* (Wheaton, IL: Crossway, 2020), 153. Cf. Ortlund, "The Old Testament Background and Eschatological Significance of Jesus Walking on the Sea [Mark 6:45–52]," *Neot* 46.2 (2012), 319–37.

When through the deep waters I call thee to go,
The rivers of woe shall not thee overflow;
For I will be with thee, thy troubles to bless,
And sanctify to thee thy deepest distress.

When through fiery trials thy pathways shall lie,
My grace, all sufficient, shall be thy supply;
The flame shall not hurt thee; I only design
Thy dross to consume, and thy gold to refine.[8]

As Israel of old was tested in the wilderness, so the twelve were often tested by Jesus—here on the waves, not in the wilderness—so as to refine their faith. But they failed this test. Their failure, however, has been recorded so that we might not make the same mistake (e.g., Ps. 95:8–9). How easy it is for us to focus on our predicament when we should be focusing on Jesus. When we are tempted to be terrified during our troubles, we need to trust that Christ will not abandon us.

That is the lesson of the loaves, which is retaught at the salvation at sea! First, Jesus is the divine Son of God. Second, Jesus is sufficient to provide. Therefore, third, fear not.

Recognizing Him

We are almost done. But there is a second half to our text! We will cover Mark **6:53–56** succinctly, but, I hope, completely.

> When they had crossed over, they came to land at Gennesaret and moored to the shore. And when they got out of the boat, the people immediately recognized him and ran about the whole region and began to bring the sick people on their beds to wherever they heard he was. And wherever he came, in villages, cities, or countryside, they laid the sick in the marketplaces and implored him that they might touch even the fringe of his garment. And as many as touched it were made well.

There are at least two reasons that Mark includes another brief summary passage (cf. 1:32–34; 3:7–12) after the miracle of walking on water.

First, it ties in with the theme of identity. While the disciples on the boat do not recognize Jesus (at first they think he is a ghost) and fail to understand

8 "How Firm a Foundation" (1787).

the powers he possesses (the lesson of the loaves), this crowd on the shore of Gennesaret, we are told, "immediately recognized him" (6:54). We are told not that they give the proper confession, "Lord" or "Son of God," but merely that they acknowledge his divine powers and experience them.

They bring their sick to him (6:55, 56). That takes faith. They ask ("implored") if they could "touch even the fringe of his garment" (6:56).[9] That takes faith. It takes faith because they believe, like the bleeding woman (5:28–34), that Jesus is absolutely able to help. Even one of the four strings by his feet has enough power to cure blindness, leprosy, and paralysis. Again, Mark does not present this act—the tassel-touching—as something superstitious. There is no rebuke from Jesus. And their touch is effective: "And as many as touched it were made well" (6:56), or "saved" (Gk. *sōzō*).

The second reason Mark adds these summary verses to the walking-on-the-waves narrative has to do with the salvation motif. If there is one point we are to grasp from reading verses 45–52, followed by verses 53–56, it is that Jesus is strong to save. He saves the twelve men on the boat and saves many people from the whole region of Gennesaret, people from the "villages, cities, or countryside" (6:56). Jesus is strong enough to save all who come to him and all he comes to. He can save us from our trying windstorm-like situations. (Are you in the middle of one of those at the moment?) He can save us from sickness. (Does some serious ailment ail you?)

The Power of God

But, of course, these small salvations are but anticipations of our great salvation. The one who has power to create bread and fish, tread upon the waves, settle the winds, and heal any and all ailments in a day or two will soon "empty himself" completely on the tree of Calvary (Phil. 2:7). Ah, the irony of the atonement. We are saved from all evils—sin, the devil, and death—when the powerful Son of God is deemed powerless. "And those who passed by derided him . . . 'Save yourself, and come down from the cross! . . . That we may see [your power!] and believe'" (Mark 15:29, 30, 32). But our Lord did not come down. He "uttered a loud cry and breathed his last [breath]" (15:37). And yet, in staying on that cross, he showed us the very power of God. The power to turn away divine wrath. The power to forgive sin. The power to crush the serpent's head. The power to grant eternal life.

It was a great miracle that Jesus walked on water. It was a great miracle that Jesus fed the five thousand. It was a great miracle that Jesus cast out

9   Num. 15:38–39; Deut. 22:12.

unclean spirits. It was a great miracle that Jesus cleansed a leper. It was a great miracle that Jesus healed a paralytic. It was a great miracle that Jesus raised the dead. It was a great miracle that Jesus himself rose from the dead. But perhaps the greatest miracle of all was his miraculous non-miracle: staying on the cross for our salvation.[10] The Jews demanded a miraculous sign—come down from the cross. But they missed the sign and source of our salvation: the cross of Christ!

As you finish reading this chapter, may you see that sign, and may you acknowledge and embrace that Savior afresh. May you confess, as the centurion at the foot of the cross did after witnessing the power of God on display through weakness: "Truly this man was the Son of God" (15:39).

---

10 See Douglas Sean O'Donnell, *Matthew: All Authority under Heaven*, PTW (Wheaton, IL: Crossway, 2013), 867.

What Defiles a Person

MARK 7:1-23

What comes out of a person is what defiles him. For from
within, out of the heart of man, come evil thoughts, sexual
immorality, theft, murder, adultery, coveting, wickedness,
deceit, sensuality, envy, slander, pride, foolishness. All these
evil things come from within, and they defile a person.
Mark 7:20–23

In *The Republic* Plato tells a tale of a group of prisoners who have lived together in a dark cave since early childhood. They are chained in such a way
that they are forced to sit on the ground. Their field of vision is restricted to
a wall directly in front of them. Behind them, and the wall they are leaning
against, is an elevated area where a blazing fire glows. In front of the fire men
are making noises and walking back and forth carrying various vessels, the
shapes of letters, and figures of animals. The glow from the fire casts a shadow
of the objects on the wall in front of the prisoners. Thus the prisoners hear
the echoes and see the various movements and assume that it is the shadows
themselves that both move and speak.

As the story continues, Plato (using the voice of his mentor, Socrates)
then asks what would happen if a few of the prisoners were released and allowed to walk upright and out of the cave to experience the sunlight of the
real world. The philosopher posits that they would want to return quickly to
their customary position and confine their glances to the familiar shadows.
They would do so because it would be too painful to adjust to the bright light.

That is the beginning of Plato's famous allegory of the cave, an illustration of the unenlightened man. It is a vivid image of humanity trapped in the
depths of ignorance and totally unaware of its limited perspective. In Mark's
Gospel we do not find a made-up allegory but a true story (Mark 7:1–23) about
a group of Jewish religious leaders who are so enslaved to their man-made

traditions and used to hearing echoes and seeing shadows that, when they see and hear the "true light" that has come into the world (John 1:9), they find him unbearable. But unlike the prisoners in Plato, who returned to their customary positions, these scribes and Pharisees in Scripture seek to douse the cause of their discomfort. They want to extinguish the light altogether.

Spiritual Blindness Comes to Light

Throughout Mark's Gospel the Evangelist has provided reasons for the religious leaders' desire to snuff out the Savior. As early as chapter 2, he has already shown us their subtle shift from curiosity to contempt. Thus far, they hate the heat and light that radiates from Jesus for three reasons: his claim that he could forgive sins (2:6–7), his association with tax collectors and sinners (2:16), and his disregard for their traditions surrounding the Sabbath (2:24), fasting (2:18), and now the washing of hands.

So then, look with me at Mark 7:1–5 and let us see their newest spiritual blindness come to light. Starting in 7:1–2, Mark records, "Now when the Pharisees gathered to him, with some of the scribes who had come from Jerusalem, they saw that some of [Jesus'] disciples ate with hands that were defiled, that is, unwashed." So they asked Jesus, "Why do your disciples not walk according to the tradition of the elders, but eat with defiled hands?" (7:5).

Before I explain Mark's explanation (his parenthesis in 7:3–4), first note the context in which they ask their question. In Mark 5–6 Jesus has healed the demon-possessed, raised the dead, fed five thousand plus, and walked on water. So at this point a good question might be, "Jesus, who are you?" or "We know who you must be—the divine Son of God/the I Am of our sacred Scriptures—so please accept our humble worship; and, Lord, can you please tell us how we serve you and advance your rule on earth?" But no, their question is about hand washing. Some of them (the scribes) came all the way from the holy city (Jerusalem) to ask about hand washing. This would be like a reporter from Washington, DC, flying to Boston to ask a city firefighter, just after that firefighter has rescued a baby from a burning building, "Now, sir, I've heard that your brother eats meat on Friday during Lent. Is that true?" Their question makes no sense in light of the context of Jesus' display of divine power. It is out of place. Ridiculous! It is totally the wrong question to ask. But it does make sense in light of their view of the world, the importance of their man-made traditions, and their particular beliefs about the coming Messiah. They were certain that, when the Messiah arrived, he would uphold all their religious rules. So when they saw that "some" (not all but "some"—I imagine Matthew, the former tax collector, and one or two others) of Jesus' disciples were eating without first washing, they honestly wondered why Jesus, whom people were starting to tout as the Messiah, would put up with this. Their main issue is not poor hygiene but pure religion.

As Mark explains to his Gentile readers in **7:3–4**, the inquisitors believed that, when devout Jews come from the marketplace, they "do not eat unless they wash their hands." They also wash everything associated with eating: "cups and pots and copper vessels and [even] dining couches." "All the Jews" (implied: "all law-abiding Jews") wash everything before eating. Why? Hear Tevye the Dairyman in *Fiddler on the Roof* sing. The answer is "Tradition!" They are walking "according to the tradition of the elders" (**7:5**). Does that tradition come from the OT? Yes and no. OT law dictated that priests needed to wash before entering the tabernacle.[1] "Between the tent of meeting and the altar" was a bronze basin "for washing" (Ex. 30:18). The priests were to "wash their hands" when they entered the tabernacle to offer sacrifices (Ex. 30:19); if they came in contact with anything unclean (a disease or a discharge), they would have to bathe their whole bodies (see Lev. 22:4–6). Those clear, specific (only for the Levites when they are acting as priests), and concise (given in less than ten verses) laws were then added to. What was given to a certain group of people for a certain purpose at a certain time was, over time, expanded to include all Israel before all meals.

The Mishnah, a second-century document that records the oral Jewish traditions of the first century, included a detailed summary (nearly two hundred pages) on ceremonial cleanliness. Here is a CliffsNotes version of what a *proper* (Mark 7:3) hand washing entailed. Large stone jars, filled with water, were kept in each home for the sole purpose of ceremonial washing. Before every meal the water in those jars would be poured into a smaller vessel that would then be poured over the hands. The fingertips were pointed up as the water was poured over them. Once the water hit the wrists, the fists of the opposite hand would scrub the other. Finally, the hands would be turned downward to allow the water to fall off the fingertips. All clean. Ready to eat.

Think of this tradition in view of the feeding of the five thousand. How could this elaborate ceremony possibly have been done there? Impossible. And that is why, I surmise, the purity police from Jerusalem journeyed to Galilee. Again, this washing was not about hygiene or etiquette. It was a religious ritual. To eat the food that God gave, with unclean hands, was in their eyes to be unclean before God. To them "bread eaten with unclean hands"

---

1   See Exodus 30:17–21; cf. Leviticus 22:1–6.

was no better than eating excrement.[2] (I will come back, as Jesus will come back, to that ancient saying in a page.) To be fair, their traditions, like some of our own, simply sought to apply the Bible to everyday life. However, in practice these oral interpretations of the Mosaic law so shifted the Bible's original intent that the application was now a complete perversion. It was also a burden on everyone.

The scribes and Pharisees believed that the pagan Romans would know that the Jews alone were God's holy people by their outward purity—washing hands, washing cups, washing pots, and so on. But our Lord Jesus, who in Mark's Gospel is so earthly and earthy, breaks one tradition of theirs after another. He dines with tax collectors (2:15) and Gentiles (5:1). He touches lepers (1:40–41), menstruating women (5:25), and even corpses (5:35). Our Lord obviously understands purity quite differently. The apostle Paul grasps the tenor of Jesus' position here when he asserts in Romans 14:17, "The kingdom of God is not a matter of eating and drinking but of righteousness and peace and joy in the Holy Spirit."

Shedding Light from the Scriptures

It is from this different and enlightened perspective that our Lord Jesus, as upset as his opponents, goes on the offensive, striking quite literally at the *heart* of his accusers. Making no attempt to justify his disciples' behavior, Jesus ignores their question and offers instead a one-two punch from the *written* Word of God. The first punch comes from the Prophets (an upper cut from Isaiah) and the second punch from the Law (a quick jab from Moses):

> And he said to them, "Well did Isaiah prophesy of you hypocrites, as it is written,
>
> > "'This people honors me with their lips,
> >   but their heart is far from me;
> > in vain do they worship me,
> >   teaching as doctrines the commandments of men.'
>
> You leave the commandment of God and hold to the tradition of men." (Mark 7:6–8)

2   William Barclay, *The Gospel of Mark* (Grand Rapids, MI: Philadelphia, 1956), 164–65; cf. R. Kent Hughes, *Mark: Jesus, Servant and Savior*, PTW, 2 vols. (Wheaton, IL: Crossway, 1989), 164, where Hughes provides a good summary of Barclay.

Here our Lord roars like a lion because he hates their playacting in piety. He accuses these "hypocrites" (7:6) of false and heartless worship. He dubs their traditional teachings to be man-made mockeries of divine law. He says that what Isaiah said long ago is precisely what he wants to say to them today: "You scribes and Pharisees, you 'devotees of hollow ritualism,' have it all wrong—both your attitude and your emphasis is wrong."[3]

Jesus first attacks their *attitude*:

Well did Isaiah prophesy of you hypocrites, as it is written,

> "This people honors me with their lips,
>   but their heart is far from me." (7:6; quoting Isa. 29:13)

As their lips speak God's Word and sing God's praises, their hearts are far from our pure God because their hearts are so full of everything Jesus condemns in Mark 7:21–22 and in Matthew 23:27: they are "like whitewashed tombs, which outwardly appear beautiful, but within are full of dead people's bones and all uncleanness." What an awful but accurate image of his opposition.

The point here is simple. God sees the heart. Remember that! As we listen afresh to Jesus' rebuke to them, let some of that old sting penetrate us anew. Let us remember that the bowed head, the bended knee, the raised hands, the closed eyes, the God-talk, and whatever other public or private postures we do or outward observances we keep is of no avail to the God of heaven if not done with a clean heart and a clear conscience. For "the hour is coming," Jesus said to the Samaritan woman, "and is now here, when the true worshipers will worship the Father in spirit [the whole of their inner being] and truth [the whole of God's revelation], for the Father is seeking such people to worship him" (John 4:23).

We all know what it is like to bring our bodies to church but to leave our hearts at home. Our neighbors may see us dressed bright and early, climbing into the car, and heading off to church and think us to be model Christians. Our fellow Christians, when we arrive at church, may see our smiling faces and hear our singing voices and outstretched arms and think that the joy of the Lord is our strength. But our God sees what we have truly brought to him on Sunday morning and every morning, and he alone knows whether it is gold and silver or only wood, hay, and stubble—false worship to be burned away on judgment day.

---

3   See William Hendriksen, *Exposition of the Gospel according to Mark* (Grand Rapids, MI: Baker, 1975), 274–75.

God delights in earnest adoration, unpresumptuous praise, contrite confession, and sincere supplication. Therefore, as Christians who seek to worship the Father and Son and Spirit with all our heart and strength and soul, let us not be crushed by our Lord's words here to the scribes and Pharisees. Instead, let us be encouraged to check our own attitude and, if necessary, to realign our hearts with the pulse of God's heart—and, as we shall see next, also with the plumb line of his Word.

Jesus uses two parts of the Isaiah quote to make two points. In the first part of the quote Jesus tells them that their attitude is wrong. In the second part he tells them that their *emphasis* is wrong. "In vain," Jesus declares, "do they worship me [what a "me" that is!], teaching as doctrines the commandments of men" (Mark 7:7).

The battle is not over. Three times in the next six verses Jesus reiterates that charge. He charges them with supplanting the Scriptures or uprooting the written Word. In verse 8 he says that they "*leave* the commandment of God [perhaps referring to Deut. 6:4–5] and hold to the tradition of men." In Mark 7:**9** Jesus claims that they *reject* "the commandment of God in order to establish [their own] tradition!" And at the end of verse 13 he speaks of their "*making void* the word of God by your tradition [the oral traditions that have been] handed down." Note the progression: first Jesus speaks of leaving, then of rejecting, and finally of nullifying.

So then, with the second half of the Isaiah quote Jesus answers them by accusing them of "gagging God's voice with the tattered rag of their traditions."[4] Here, to be clear, Jesus is not demonizing tradition. Jesus is not saying that all traditions are evil. He is not saying that he follows the rich and long-standing tradition of not following tradition! He is not announcing that it is his tradition not to follow tradition. His point is not whether or not God's people should have traditions. Every society has traditions. God's people hold to traditions too, for every Christian "community has to apply the word of God to situations in real life, and [thus] traditions inevitably develop from this undertaking."[5]

So from this passage we should not ask, "Should my church hold to this tradition or not?" Rather the question should be, "Does my church believe in any traditions that contradict the Bible or are detached from God's original intention?" or "Is the authority of the Scriptures deposed by man-made rituals?" For here

4   Douglas Sean O'Donnell, *Matthew: All Authority under Heaven*, PTW (Wheaton, IL: Crossway, 2013), 421.
5   David E. Garland, *Mark*, NIVAC (Grand Rapids, MI: Zondervan, 1996), 277.

Jesus is teaching against the enthronement of tradition at the expense or the dethronement of the Word of God. He is addressing traditions that immediately or inevitably force God's people to *leave, reject,* or *nullify* the written Scriptures. Thus we are taught here that those are the very traditions . . . that are to be left, rejected, and nullified.[6]

Such traditions would include forbidding clergy to marry, praying to and through anyone other than God, and worshiping images made to represent God. But they would also include issuing an altar call as a replacement for the Great Commission's command to baptize, or assuring a child of her salvation as soon as she prays the sinner's prayer and then using the recitation of that prayer as the absolute assurance that that person is going to heaven no matter how she lives the rest of her life or what she presently believes about Jesus.

These are but a few of the traditions within the contemporary Christian church that our Lord might find problematic. However, back then and there, he illustrates his point—that the religious leaders are "rejecting the commandment of God in order to establish [their] tradition!" (7:9)—by pointing out the hypocrisy of the tradition of Corban:

For Moses said, "Honor your father and your mother"; and, "Whoever reviles father or mother must surely die." But you say, "If a man tells his father or his mother, 'Whatever you would have gained from me is Corban'" (that is, given to God)—then you no longer permit him to do anything for his father or mother, thus making void the word of God by your tradition that you have handed down. (7:10–13)

Here our Lord, who regards what Moses wrote in Exodus 20:12 and 21:17 as the very "word of God" (Mark 7:13), sets up what they say ("but you say," 7:11) against what God commanded through Moses ("for Moses said," 7:10),[7] and he shows just how they set aside one of the Ten Commandments for a man-made and man-centered tradition, the tradition of Corban.

Here is how it worked. Someone could declare part of his assets "Corban"—that is, "given to God." For example, funds could be pledged to the temple that would be collected upon one's death (see m. Ned. 1:2–4; 9:7). In the meantime, these same assets could be used by the man whenever and however *he* wanted, but they could not be used for anything *else*, even

6   O'Donnell, *Matthew*, 422.
7   Francis J. Moloney, *The Gospel of Mark: A Commentary* (Peabody, MA: Hendrickson, 2002), 140.

something like funding his parents' needs in their old age if he did not want to do so. So, "under the pretense of giving God a prior claim,"[8] this lawless individual evaded his God-given duty—the command to honor his father and mother. What religious tomfoolery and trickery! Sanctioned selfishness.

Do you see the utter wickedness of this tradition? Do you see why Jesus was so disgusted with them? "A man goes through the formality of vowing something to God, not that he may give it to God, but in order to prevent" his own parents, during the time they would need it most, from ever laying claim to it.[9] This tradition of Corban and the scoundrels who taught and practiced it were (as Jesus suggests in 7:10) worthy of the death penalty, as the law declared: "Whoever reviles father or mother must surely die." And if there was ever a tradition that clearly reviled one's parents and broke both the letter and the spirit of the law, it was this one. Corban killed compassion!

So, with this "concrete expression" of the scribes' and Pharisees' hypocrisy, Jesus provides one example of a "comprehensive perversion."[10] This teaching was "not an anomaly but standard procedure" among these groups,[11] for, as the end of verse 13 states, "And many such things you do." Here with his illustration our Lord pulls not a bad apple out of an otherwise good bunch but rather a bad apple that is illustrative of the fact that the whole barrel is full of rot and worms.

A Matter of the Heart

After Jesus' knock-out punch in verses 1–13 he calls the crowd around him. He says, "Hear me, all of you, and understand" (**7:14**). He wants them (and us) to understand that the heart of the matter is the heart of man: "There is nothing outside a person that by going into him can defile him [like dirt on the hands], but the things that come out of a person are what defile him" (**7:15**). Verse 15 is his point. But what exactly does he mean? That is precisely what the disciples wonder. They want and need some private tutoring.

> And when he had entered the house and left the people, his disciples asked him about the parable [the riddle about what defiles a person]. And he said to them, "Then are you also without understanding? ["Are you still numbskulls?" serves as a good paraphrase.] Do you not see that whatever goes into a person from outside cannot defile him, since

---

8   James R. Edwards, *The Gospel according to Mark*, PNTC (Grand Rapids, MI: Eerdmans, 2002), 210.
9   T. W. Manson, quoted in Edwards, *Gospel according to Mark*, 210.
10 Edwards, *Gospel according to Mark*, 210, 211.
11 Edwards, *Gospel according to Mark*, 211.

it enters not his heart but his stomach, and is expelled?" (Thus he declared all foods clean.) And he said, "What comes out of a person is what defiles him. For from within, out of the heart of man, come evil thoughts, sexual immorality, theft, murder, adultery, coveting, wickedness, deceit, sensuality, envy, slander, pride, foolishness. All these evil things come from within, and they defile a person." (**7:17–23**)

In these verses Jesus (per Mark's insertion),[12] first, makes an important pronouncement that, as of this moment, "all foods [are] clean" (7:19), which is "an incredible thing to say" and is as though Jesus is saying, in Keller's words, "I called the world into being; I called the storm to a halt; I called a girl back from death. And now I call all foods clean." Keller continues with his clear and concise commentary:

In order to understand the magnitude of this, you have to remember that Jesus has an incredibly high regard for the Word of God. He considers it binding, even on himself. In Matthew's Gospel he says that not a jot or a tittle—that is, not a letter—will pass away from the Word of God until it is all fulfilled. Now, the cleanliness laws are a part of the Word of God. Jesus would never look at any part of it and say, "I'm abolishing this; we've gotten beyond this now." So what he is saying here is that the cleanliness laws have been fulfilled—that their purpose, to get you to move toward spiritual purification, has been carried out. The reason you don't have to follow them as you once did is that they've been fulfilled.[13]

Second, Jesus teaches that there is one place to look for spiritual purity or impurity, and it is not the hands or stomach but the heart. Every bit of dirt and food (so it does not matter whether one's diet is kosher or unkosher; see 7:19) that goes from our hands down to our stomach and out our backside does not determine before God whether we are clean or unclean. But what is in, and comes out of our heart, does.

Think here. Does Jesus think good things generally come out of the human heart? Does he have an optimistic anthropology? No! What does he say comes out of our hearts? Love? Good will towards man? Kind words? Not exactly. Not at all. What you find in a septic tank is actually cleaner than what

12 For Mark to offer an interpretive comment is rare; such rarity indicates the importance!
13 Timothy Keller, *King's Cross: The Story of the World in the Life of Jesus* (New York: Dutton, 2011), 80–81.

you would find in the human heart. The heart is desperately wicked, says the prophet Jeremiah (Jer. 17:9). So agrees Jesus.

So who is right? Jeremiah and Jesus or today's popular talking heads? Let me offer a simple test. Look at your mouth—or, better, listen to it. In the Gospel of Matthew Jesus says, "What comes out of the mouth proceeds from the heart" (Matt. 15:18). He also warns, "On the day of judgment people will give account for every careless word they speak, for by your words you will be justified, and by your words you will be condemned" (12:36–37). What better window into our hearts than our words. Do you have a pure heart? Take this fifteen-question test. Have you ever used the name of the Lord our God in vain? Gossiped? Yelled at someone in unholy anger? Offered an unjust criticism? Flattered? Lied? Boasted? Said too much? Exaggerated a story? Cursed? Slandered? Used your tongue to stir up division? Broken a confidence? Grumbled? Nagged? If America budgeted thirty billion dollars for the Environmental Protection Agency to clean up dirty words, it would be to no avail. Nothing pollutes this world more than words!

And back to the point, and the following question: What do our bad words demonstrate? They show our bad hearts. Our dirty hands are not the problem; our dirty hearts are.

Dealing with a Defiled Heart

How then does one clean an unclean heart? To get clean and circumcised hearts (Heb. 10:22; Rom. 2:29), pure hearts (1 Pet. 1:22), new hearts (Ezek. 36:26), and sincere hearts (Eph. 6:5), so that we might believe from the heart (Eph. 3:17) and obey from the heart (Deut. 11:13), we need Christ, through his Spirit, to dwell in our hearts through faith (Eph. 3:17). Through union by faith with Christ—his righteousness, his purity, his clean hands and heart in us—the old heart, with all its wicked thoughts, words, and deeds, is destroyed. And from this once sin-infested organ beats new life. Jesus. Jesus. Jesus. Christ in us. Christ in us. Christ in us. What can wash away all our sinful words? Sinful deeds? Sinful thoughts? Jesus. Jesus. Jesus. Faith in Jesus—who died for our sins and rose for our justification—turns a filthy heart into a clean heart.

I hope, as you have read this chapter, that you are not, or do not remain, unenlightened. I hope your chains are broken. I hope you arise and walk past the shadows and out of the darkness. I hope you embrace the light, the light and life found in Jesus Christ alone.

Pure Religion

MARK 7:24–37

Now the woman was a Gentile, a Syrophoenician by birth.
And she begged him to cast the demon out of her daughter.
Mark 7:26

Fingers up. Water poured. Hands scrubbed. Water dripping to the ground. All clean. It struck me as I recalled the ancient Jewish handwashing ritual how foolish it was that the scribes and Pharisees thought that a right relationship with God could be maintained based on whether or not one scrubbed off all of the perceivable dirt on one's hands. It also struck me that Mark, in his inspired brilliance, following the controversy over unclean hands,[1] takes us next to an unclean region ("Tyre and Sidon," 7:24; Gentile cities) to encounter an unclean woman (a "Gentile," 7:26) who begs Jesus to do something about her "little daughter" who has an "unclean spirit" (7:25). Not only that, but after the first unclean scene (7:24–30), Mark takes us to another unclean region ("the region of the Decapolis," 7:31; a Gentile place), where Jesus places his unwashed finger into a deaf man's unclean ears; then, with his spit on his hand, he touches the man's unclean tongue (**7:33**).

Harvard's School of Dental Medicine has discovered that it is possible for more than 615 types of bacteria to reside in the human mouth at the same time, which is more germs than found in the rectal region. Related, a trendy website published a story called "Your Tongue Is Probably Filthy, Here's How to Clean It."[2] I will not reveal their secret cleaning methods, but I will say that by any standard of modern medical research—from the prestigious to

---

1   Mark sets this encounter with the Gentile woman directly after his rebuke on the Pharisees' purity laws. He is making the point that Gentiles join Israel in God's plan of salvation (see, e.g., Acts 10:15, 28; 11:9–18). He might also be seeking to contrast the woman's purity of heart with the Pharisees' unclean mouths.

2   See Lindsey Lanquist, "Your Tongue Is Probably Filthy, Here's How to Clean It," *Self*, March 18, 2018, https://www.self.com/story/how-to-clean-your-tongue.

the popular—the tongue (and the ears) rank in the top five of unclean body parts. And our Lord Jesus, in this text that accurately records real events occurring many years ago, touches them both: the inside of an ear and the tip of a tongue.

He does so to show compassion. Christianity did not invent medicine, but it made modern medicine, hospitals, and patient care what it is. The care for the least. The gross. The rejected. The uninsured. The touch of one human being to another. A Christian nurse's loving pat on the feverish forehead to communicate, "Jesus loves you, and so do I." But it is more than that. Jesus is making a bold theological statement here. Directly following the narrative of the Jewish religious authorities' questioning our Lord about where some of his disciples' hands have been, Jesus is teaching his earliest followers, and all since, via where his hands go—on the tongue and in the ear—something about the nature of pure religion. Pure religion is a relationship with God through his one and only and perfectly pure Son, who has come to take on all our impurities so that we might, through faith (not handwashing, tongue brushing, or ear cleaning), be right with God.

Two Parallel Stories

Mark 7:24–37 presents two parallel stories that teach us three unparalleled truths about Jesus.[3] The two stories share six similar details.[4]

First, both stories share a similar structure, the common structure for healing narratives: (1) Jesus is approached, (2) a problem is presented, and (3) Jesus solves the problem—he ousts the evil or heals the sickness.

Second, both stories are set in Gentile territory. The story of the Syrophoenician woman is set in "the region of Tyre and Sidon" (7:24), two cities outside the promised land. After Jesus journeys up to Tyre, then north to Sidon, and then back to the Sea of Galilee, he goes to "the region of the Decapolis" (7:31; cf. 5:20). The region's name (*deca* is Greek for "ten," and *polis* for "city") tells us that these small cities in Syria are more Gentile than Jewish. Jesus is intentionally journeying from one Gentile village to another and yet

---

3   The miracle of Mark 7:31–37 is unique to Mark.

4   Based on M. Eugene Boring, *Mark*, NTL (Louisville: Westminster John Knox, 2006), 215, Mark L. Strauss summarizes the parallels between Mark 7:31–37 and 8:22–26: "(1) the location of each is specified as predominantly Gentile territory; (2) an unnamed group brings a person in need of healing to Jesus; (3) they 'plead' . . . with Jesus (4) to lay hands on him; (5) Jesus takes the person away privately and heals him (6) by touching him (7) on the afflicted part of his body (8) using saliva; (9) Jesus commands silence (v. 36) or tells the healed person to return home without going into the village square (8:26)"; *Mark*, ZECNT (Grand Rapids, MI: Zondervan, 2014), 320.

another. We might say that he is showing the Great Commission before he commands it (Matt. 28:19; cf. Acts 1:8).

The third similar detail in both stories has to do with the secrecy motif. Again, here, geographical movements matter. We were told in Mark 6:53 that Jesus and his disciples had docked the boat in Gennesaret and from there ministered throughout the whole region. Jesus is in Jewish territory. Then, and there, we were told next that the religious authorities from Jerusalem (7:1) had traveled all the way up there to reprimand him on the issue of handwashing. Next, Jesus goes 35 miles northwest to Tyre and then another 24 miles north to Sidon. Why travel some 50-plus miles from Gennesaret? Verse 24 informs: "And from there he arose and went away to the region of Tyre and Sidon. And he entered a house and did not want anyone to know, yet he could not be hidden." The news got out, as it always has thus far. But why does he want to hide? Why go that far away? Why go into some undisclosed location? Is it to flee the crowds so he might focus on the twelve and school them in kingdom ideas and ethics?[5] Perhaps. Is it to escape Herod's jurisdiction? Perhaps.

Jesus certainly knows what has happened to John the Baptist (Mark 6:29). He also knows that other people in high positions are out to kill him. The Pharisees (religious leaders) have gotten together with the Herodians (political leaders) and "held counsel [discussed together about] . . . how to destroy him" (3:6). They want him dead. But Jesus' time for death has not yet come. He knows that. So he leaves the Holy Land in part because Israel's unholy leaders are ready to throw stones. He is also, as said earlier, on a short-term mission trip.[6] He is showing the Great Commission before commanding it.

This secrecy motif also surfaces in the second story, when Jesus tells those who have witnessed the miracle of the healing of the deaf and dumb man not to speak. In Mark **7:36** we read, "And Jesus charged them to tell no one." However, they do not listen. "But the more he charged them [he told them repeatedly], the more zealously they proclaimed it" (7:36). This is a hard sentence to make sense of. Is this good or bad that they disobey Jesus? Part good; part bad. They cannot help but share such good news. Can you blame them?

---

5   There has been a pattern thus far of Jesus' desire to be alone with his disciples (Mark 1:35; 3:13; 4:10; 6:32).

6   "Missionary activity for the most part was restricted to going to the Diaspora synagogues in order to persuade God-fearers to become full proselytes by undergoing circumcision." Grant R. Osborne, *Mark*, TTCS (Grand Rapids, MI: Baker, 2012), 321. Jesus is not doing something unprecedented (Jonah went to the Gentiles), but he is introducing a new era, one predicted long ago, in which the Gentiles will join the Jews in experiencing the blessings of God. Perhaps the dialogue helps the first-time reader, especially those Jews who were part of Mark's original audience, to take steps toward grasping Gentile inclusion. For more on the theme of Gentile missions in Mark see 12:9; 13:9–10; 14:9.

Yet Jesus does not want them sharing such news, because people thus far (including and especially his disciples)[7] do not understand who he is and what he has come to do.

The fourth similarity between the stories is unexpected characters with exceptional dilemmas. In **7:25** we encounter "a woman," and in **7:32** "a man." The woman is not described like Queen Esther, the beautiful and heroic Jewish princess, or the Queen of Sheba, the rich and inquisitive Gentile who journeyed afar to meet with the wise King Solomon. Rather, Mark just gives us this descriptor: "A Gentile, a Syrophoenician by birth" (**7:26**), which might be paraphrased "a non-Jew—someone who is really not a Jew." In Matthew's version of this story he calls her "a Canaanite" (Matt. 15:22). He is interpreting the story to his Jewish-Christian audience in order to say to them that the clan she is from is not just distant from the promises of God to Israel but against them. She is part of the idolatrous enemies of God's people—a Canaanite!

And what is her problem? Why approach Jesus? She has a "little daughter" who has an "unclean spirit" (Mark 7:25). So she is not only, historically speaking, an enemy of God's people but a woman who has come on behalf of her young daughter (not someone of importance in the Greco-Roman world), who happens to be controlled by a powerful otherworldly force. Talk about an issue that Jesus' advisory staff is telling him to stay away from for the sake of the bad press.

Who then is the next character to encounter Christ? "A man" (7:32). The twelve are perhaps thinking, "Finally, our Lord has come to his senses. Stay away from the females—the woman and the daughter of such said woman. How will they help you bring this kingdom you have been talking about?" Who is this man? A Jewish man? No. Okay. Fine. A rich Gentile? No. An influential Gentile? No. A man who has listened to the great orators of his time, or who himself can speak in the tongues of angels? Not exactly. Instead we have "a man who was deaf and had a speech impediment" (7:32), a man who could not speak or hear well. Oh great. This is just great. Why hang out with these two people? Jesus obviously does not understand the art of effective networking.

Fifth, in both stories someone is acting on behalf of another. In the first story a mother comes to Jesus for help on behalf of her daughter (7:25); in the second people (friends, family, or both) bring ("they brought," 7:32) this man who cannot bring himself. This mother and these friends/family bring their loved one to encounter Christ because they have confidence that Jesus both cares for the lowly and has the supernatural power to help the helpless.

---

7   Note Mark 6:52; 7:18; 8:15–18.

Sixth, Jesus, seemingly effortlessly, answers these pleading people's prayers. Look and wonder at 7:29: "The demon . . . left." And then wonder again at **7:35**: "His ears were opened, his tongue was released." Remarkable. Wonderful!

Three Unparalleled Truths

Mark 7:24–37 features two parallel stories that teach us three unparalleled truths about Jesus. I could focus more on the man and the woman. For example, I could commend to you those who bring the deaf and mute man to Jesus and exhort you to bring the needs of others to the Lord in prayer, or to bring your friends to church to encounter the living God in your church's lively worship. Or I could commend to you the Syrophoenician woman and exhort you to emulate her courage, persistence, humility, and insight (her "great faith," Matt. 15:28).[8] Instead I want to focus on whom Mark focuses on, namely, Jesus.

Look at the final verse. Mark **7:37** starts, "And they were astonished beyond measure." Those who witness the second miracle, and perhaps those who witness the first as well (the twelve), are not astonished, or "over-the-top" amazed,[9] that someone expresses faith in Jesus. They are astonished by what Jesus has done. This is what I want for us to take away from this text. I want us to be astonished, and astonished at a level far higher than theirs. For we not only have these two miracle stories, but we have the full picture, recorded in the Four Gospels and throughout the Holy Scriptures.

So, here in Mark 7:24–37 I want us to be astonished that Jesus has the power to heal like this, that his mission is inclusive and universal, and that these awesome miracles are just small signposts to the renewal of all creation. Put more succinctly, let us be astonished at Jesus' extraordinary authority, the extent of his kingdom, and his eschatological salvation.

First, we have Jesus' extraordinary authority. Obviously, as we look at these two miracles, it takes a great deal of power to cast out a demon. Remember what Jesus says in 3:25–27, where he speaks about Satan as a "strong man." He says, "No one can enter a strong man's house and plunder his goods, unless he first binds the strong man" (3:27). Here in Mark 7 Jesus has tied the devil's hands and feet. He has come right into this liar's lair and has taken some valuable loot in the form of this little girl. Not only that, but he does so

---

8   For a detailed study on this theme see Douglas Sean O'Donnell, *"O Woman, Great Is Your Faith!": Faith in the Gospel of Matthew* (Eugene, OR: Pickwick, 2021).

9   Eckhard J. Schnabel, *Mark: An Introduction and Commentary*, TNTC (Downers Grove, IL: IVP Academic, 2017), 324.

in a remarkable way. He never actually travels to the house. He just speaks a word. He says, "You may go your way [go home]; the demon [right now] has left your daughter" (**7:29**). This is not the only time in the Gospels in which Jesus heals from a distance,[10] but it is the only time in Mark. What absolute power and divine authority! The woman righty calls Jesus "Lord" (**7:28**, also the only time this important title is used of Jesus in Mark), a title that fits perfectly the Lord God of the OT.[11]

Then, the healing of the deaf mute is also a display of Jesus' extraordinary authority. The moment Jesus gives a command, "Be opened" (**7:34**) — one word in Aramaic ("Ephphatha") — the man's ears and mouth instantaneously open: "And [immediately] his ears were opened, his tongue was released, and he spoke plainly,"[12] that is, he spoke without any speech impediment. This miracle echoes Exodus 4:10–12, in which Moses protests to the Lord that he should not be the mouthpiece between God and Pharaoh because he is "not eloquent" but "slow of speech and . . . tongue" (Ex. 4:10). The Lord replies, "Who has made man's mouth? Who makes him mute, or deaf, or seeing, or blind? Is it not I, the LORD? Now therefore go, and I will be with your mouth and teach you what you shall speak" (Ex. 4:11–12). By opening the man's ears and tongue Jesus is acting with the same authority as God. Who can do what Jesus does? God alone.

Also, the response to this miracle echoes Genesis 1:31. In Mark 7:37 the people say, "He has done all things well"; in Genesis 1:31 LXX God looks over his creation and, seeing "all things" he has "made" (or "done"), declares, "it was very good," with the word "good" being the same in Greek as "well." The people say of Jesus, "He has done all things well" (Mark 7:37), and Moses writes of God, "He has done/made all things well/good." Again, the point of these OT echoes is intended to remind us of God's power on display at creation.

So, first, we should be utterly astonished with Jesus' extraordinary authority. Second, we should be utterly astonished in regard to the inclusive and universal nature of Jesus' mission. I know that the words "inclusive" and "universal" are often hijacked and used to promote anti-Christian theology and ethics, such as when people say, "God's love is *universal* in that all people,

10 See Matthew 8:5–13; cf. Luke 7:1–10; John 4:46–54.
11 *Kurios* is used over six thousand times in the Greek translation of the Hebrew Scriptures. For more on this important term see Douglas Sean O'Donnell, "Insisting on Easter: Matthew's Use of the Theologically Provocative Vocative (κύριε) in the Suppliant Narratives," in *The Earliest Perceptions of Jesus in Context: Essays in Honor of John Nolland*, ed. Craig Evans, David Wenham, and Aaron W. White (Bloomsbury T&T Clark, 2018), 185–200.
12 Some NT manuscripts (e.g., P⁴⁵ A K N W Γ Θ) contain "immediately."

no matter their beliefs, will be in heaven," or, "The church is to be *inclusive* in that all types of lifestyles are acceptable." That is not what I mean by these words. I mean what Paul writes about in Galatians 3:28–29: "There is neither Jew nor Greek, there is neither slave nor free, there is no male and female, for you are all one in Christ Jesus. And if you are Christ's, then you are Abraham's offspring, heirs according to the promise." I mean what is taught clearly in Mark 7:24–29. Can a Gentile mother and daughter from "the region of Tyre and Sidon" (Mark 7:24) experience the blessings of Jesus' kingdom? Yes! They are included. The Syrophoenician woman understands this possibility. That is why she makes an effort to find Jesus (hiding away in "a house," 7:24). And once he is found, she next ("immediately") approaches Jesus (she "heard of him and came" to him) and, once there, does as anyone who wants to be part of the kingdom should do — she kneels ("fell down at his feet," 7:25) and prays ("She begged him to cast the demon out of her daughter," 7:26). Finally, when Jesus offers some resistance —"And he said to her, 'Let the children [the Jews] be fed first,[13] for it is not right to take the children's bread and throw it to the dogs ["dogs" are what Jews called "unclean" Gentiles]" (7:27)[14]— she takes his remark to be not rude or racist but right.

She likely understands that he is testing her.[15] And she passes the test. She understands Romans 3:9–10, that all, "both Jews and Greeks, are under sin," that "none is righteous, no, not one" (cf. Pss. 14:1–3; 53:1–3). She accepts the "dog" designation, this epithet for unclean people.[16] She is unclean, and her daughter is possessed by an unclean spirit. She acknowledges that she is unworthy. She also perhaps understands the theological concept expressed in Romans 1:16, that the gospel is "the power of God for salvation to everyone who believes, to the Jew first *and also* to the Greek." This is why she answers, "Yes, Lord; yet even the dogs under the table eat the children's crumbs" (Mark 7:28).

The promise to Abraham given in Genesis[17] and reiterated throughout the Psalms and Prophets[18] was that all the nations would be blessed through God's people, and ultimately through the Messiah. She might have understood that Jesus was the promised Messiah. At the very least she certainly believed that he, like Elijah, who helped raise to life a widow's son (1 Kings

---

13 Deuteronomy 14:1; Isaiah 1:2.

14 See Exodus 22:31; 1 Samuel 17:43; 1 Kings 14:11; Isaiah 56:10–11.

15 See Schnabel, *Mark*, 174; Joel Marcus, *Mark 1–8: A New Translation with Introduction and Commentary*, AB 27 (New York: Doubleday, 2000), 468.

16 See 2 Samuel 16:9; Psalm 22:16; Matthew 7:6; Philippians 3:2.

17 See Genesis 12:3; 15:5; 18:18; 22:18; cf. 26:4; 28:14; Romans 4; Galatians 3:6–9.

18 Psalm 96:3; Isaiah 2:2–5; 11:10; 14:1; 25:6; 26:2; 42:6; 49:6, 23; Zechariah 8:20–22; cf. 1 Kings 8:43.

17:8–24), could include her and her daughter in the blessings of God (Rom. 11:17). And right she was. Jesus applauds her insights and offers her and her daughter a place not under but at the table. "And he said to her, 'For this statement [because you grasp the universal and inclusive nature of my mission] you may go your way; the demon has left your daughter.' And she went home and found the child lying in bed and the demon gone" (Mark **7:29–30**).[19]

While others around her—especially the scribes and Pharisees (see 7:1–13; 8:11–13) and even the twelve (see 8:14–21)—"hear but do not understand" (4:12; citing Isa. 6:9–10), she hears and sees (Mark 4:3, 9, 23). She understands and acts. Even though she is a Gentile outcast living in enemy territory (where Jezebel was from; 1 Kings 16:31–32)[20] renowned for its paganism and materialism (see Ezekiel 28), she still believes. She knows that in Jesus "the time is fulfilled, and the kingdom of God is at hand" (Mark 1:15).

So, first, we should be astonished that Jesus has the power to heal like this and, second, that his mission is inclusive and universal. Third, we should be astonished that these two miracles are just signposts to the renewal of all creation. In Isaiah 35:5–6[21] the prophet writes about the promises Israel will receive when it is saved from their exile, an exile that comes ultimately when the Christ comes. At that time four amazing realities will come to fruition:

1. Then the eyes of the blind shall be opened (see Mark 8:25; cf. Isa. 29:18; 32:3; 42:7),
2. and the ears of the deaf unstopped (see Mark 7:35; cf. Isa. 29:18; 32:3);
3. then shall the lame man leap like a deer (see Mark 2:12),
4. and the tongue of the mute sing for joy (look again at Mark 7:35).

Jesus is compassionate in Mark 7 and has been and will be throughout Mark. He touches the untouchables. He cures the unclean. He offers a sigh on behalf of the world's sin (7:34).[22] But he is more than compassionate. He is the curse crusher. He has come to deal with the powers of Satan (the exorcism of the little girl) and the effects of the fall (the healing of the mute man). These

---

19 "The point is that the girl has been 'put to bed' and is now resting peacefully, free from the demon's power" (Strauss, *Mark*, 315).

20 Even in Josephus' day he labeled people from Tyre "our bitterest enemies" (*Ag. Ap.* 1.70). See *1 Maccabees* 5:15. Cf. Isaiah 23; Ezekiel 26–28; Amos 1:9–10; Zechariah 9:2–3. The Canaanites were known for Baal worship, arrogance, and greed.

21 The Greek word (*moglilalos*) that the ESV renders "speech impediment" (Mark 7:32) is used only here in the NT and one place in the LXX—in Isaiah 35:5!

22 The sigh is "an expression of the deep sorrow and anger our Lord felt at the ravages of the Fall in the lives of men. The sigh was the sigh of the heart of God for his needy creation." Sinclair B. Ferguson, *Let's Study Mark* (repr., Carlisle, PA: Banner of Truth Trust, 2016), 115.

miracles are signposts that Jesus places in the ground on that day to point to *that* day, the day of Christ's return, the day when creation will be fully renewed, when the kingdom of heaven will come down to earth, where we who have been "ransomed" by the Lamb shall enter the new Jerusalem "with singing," and "everlasting joy shall be upon [our] heads," and we "shall obtain gladness and joy" as "sorrow and sighing shall flee away" (Isa. 35:10).

Utterly astonishing! As the Evangelist teaches us in Mark 7:24–37, Jesus' extraordinary authority, the extent of his kingdom, and his eschatological salvation are utterly astonishing.

Singing Old Hymns

On the morning I preached the sermon that became this chapter, my congregation sang Charles Wesley's old hymn "O for a Thousand Tongues to Sing." The reason for that selection should be obvious, with lyrics such as "Hear Him, ye deaf; His praise; ye dumb, Your loosened tongues employ." After the sermon, in response to God's Word, we sang John Newton's classic "Amazing Grace." The reason for that selection was twofold. First, its final verse fits well with the theme of eschatological salvation. "When we've been there"—living on the new earth, where there are no more demons and diseases—"ten thousand years, bright shining as the sun [in God's radiance, but perhaps also an allusion to our absolute purity], we've no less days to sing God's praise than when we first begun." Praising God together will not grow old. It will not be boring. We will be in the presence of the all-joyful, awesomely interesting, and incredibly loving God. And there we will not hear what our Lord has to say to us through an inspired book and an occasionally inspiring preacher. We will know God. We will see Christ face to face. The Spirit will be the breath we breathe. And our response to the Lord will not be a stammer because we cannot hear just right. We will be in perfect pitch; we will express an eloquence beyond imagination.

The second reason we sang "Amazing Grace" is because my wife said to me earlier that week, when I asked her whether there was any song we should sing, "We should sing something that reflects well the gospel, how gracious God has been to us in Christ." She went on to talk about the one word that stood out to her in the two stories—another parallel: the word "even." The woman says, "Yes, Lord; yet *even* the dogs under the table eat the children's crumbs" (7:28). And then, of course, Jesus performs the exorcism. Even that Gentile woman and her daughter get to dine at the messianic table with Abraham, Isaac, and Jacob (and Jesus!). Then, in verse 37, those who witness the miracle of the healing of the hopeless man say of Jesus, "He *even* makes the deaf hear and the mute speak." If you are a Christian, it is because of God's amazing grace in your life. *Even* "a wretch like" you, and *even* me (a member of the wretch club as well), join our voices together, singing that sweet song, because our sweet and strong Savior has brought us into his kingdom and someday soon will bring us home — even us!

Seeing Clearly

MARK 8:1–30

And he asked them, "But who do you say that I am?" Peter
answered him, "You are the Christ."
Mark 8:29

About a decade ago I wrote a children's book called *The Dog's Dinner*. The book
retells the story of the mother and daughter we looked at in the last chapter
(Mark 7:24–30). I named the book *The Dog's Dinner* because the woman, with
absolute poverty of spirit mixed with an utter confidence in the promises of
God to the Gentiles, accepts Jesus' "dog" designation and eats the "scraps" that
fall from the messianic banquet table. Some scraps! Her daughter is healed
immediately and completely. It is as though Jesus pulls up two chairs for these
two ladies and then asks Abraham to pass the warm bread, Isaac to offer a slice
of the fattened calf, and Jacob to pour some aged wine. I called the book *The
Dog's Dinner* also because the story of that metaphorical feast—the exorcism
of the demon from the little Gentile girl—is placed between the feedings of the
five thousand and the four thousand.

I begin that book by saying, "This is a book about food. And a dog, of
course. God has always loved his people. . . . And He has shown His love in
many, many different ways. One way is through food!" I go on to talk about
the food in the garden of Eden, the wilderness, and the promised land. Then
I write, "Before Jesus was born, God's people believed a Savior was coming.
He was coming to save them from every bad thing in the world—like sin and
sickness, and death and the devil. And they knew when this Savior came,
something great would happen. They would eat!" I then walk through the two
(or three!) feeding miracles. The book concludes with these words:

When Jesus walked the earth He gave His people a sign that He was
the promised Savior and that He loves them. He fed them food! He fed

the Jews. He fed the Gentiles. He fed men, women, and children. He fed everyone who came to Him for life! And one day, when we see Him face to face, He will feed us the greatest meal in history. There will be bread and fish. There will be milk and honey. There will be every kind of fruit from the fruit trees. Oh, what a happy day that will be. We will be so full. Full of God's love for us. Full of His good food![1]

All that to say, the feeding of the four thousand, a miraculous sign that features Jesus' feeding a crowd of Gentile men, women, and children, is a foretaste of that last and everlasting meal.

But, that said, the main theme of Mark 8:1–30 is not God's provision of food for his people and others, although food is featured first and mentioned often. Rather, it is the theme of sight that ties together the feeding of the four thousand in the Decapolis (8:1–9; cf. 7:31), the Pharisees' and the twelve's reactions in Dalmanutha and on the other side of the sea (8:10–21), the healing of the blind man in Bethsaida (8:22–26), and Peter's great confession near Caesarea Philippi (8:27–30). So, in this chapter let me walk you through what I see here about sight.

As we walk at a fast pace, we see the following. A miracle happens. Jesus again multiplies the loaves and fishes. Two reactions follow. The Pharisees ask for a sign from heaven. Jesus has just turned a meal for a family of seven into a feast for four thousand. If there was ever a divine sign, it was that. The Pharisees miss it, however, because they are blind. The disciples, in the next reaction, are shortsighted. They have just dined at *Ex Nihilo*, the new restaurant Jesus opened up in downtown Decapolis. But, when Jesus cautions them to "beware of the leaven of the Pharisees and the leaven of Herod" (8:15), they think he is rebuking them for forgetting to bring enough leftovers on the journey. How shortsighted! They are too far removed from the miracle to see what they should see.

Then another miracle occurs. A blind man is healed. Jesus touches his eyes. The man sees partially. He sees people but his vision is blurred. The people look like trees. He can see only their form, not their features. Then Jesus touches the blind man's eyes again—and look what happens: "And he saw everything clearly" (8:25). This miracle then sets us up for the climax of the chapter. Next and finally, Peter sees clearly that Jesus is the Christ. To Jesus' question, "Who do people say that I am?" (8:27), Peter steps in and steps up,

1   Douglas Sean O'Donnell, *The Dog's Dinner: A Story of Great Mercy and Great Faith from Matthew 14–15* (Ross-Shire, UK: Christian Focus, 2016).

"You are the Christ" (8:29). He acknowledges that Jesus is the priestly king from David's royal line who has come to rescue God's people.

We can think of the big picture in this way. In 7:31–35 "physical ears and lips" are opened, in 8:22–25 physical eyes are opened, and in 8:27–29 "it is Peter's spiritual ears and lips [and eyes] that are opened by God to confess Jesus" as the Christ.[2] And the whole stress of these thirty verses is to get us to where Peter gets, if we are not there already. We are to see clearly that Jesus is the Christ, the promised Messiah who has come to "give his life as a ransom for many" (10:45). Peter does not yet get the second part of that sentence, but he does get the first. And we should at least start where he starts. Jesus is the Christ.

The First Miracle

That is the Google Earth perspective of the passage. Now we will click on the Street View and walk around these towns and see some of what the people who witnessed these events saw. We start in the Decapolis.

> In those days, when again a great crowd had gathered, and they had nothing to eat, he called his disciples to him and said to them, "I have compassion on the crowd, because they have been with me now three days and have nothing to eat. And if I send them away hungry to their homes, they will faint on the way. And some of them have come from far away." And his disciples answered him, "How can one feed these people with bread here in this desolate place?" And he asked them, "How many loaves do you have?" They said, "Seven." And he directed the crowd to sit down on the ground. And he took the seven loaves, and having given thanks, he broke them and gave them to his disciples to set before the people; and they set them before the crowd. And they had a few small fish. And having blessed them, he said that these also should be set before them. And they ate and were satisfied. And they took up the broken pieces left over, seven baskets full. And there were about four thousand people. And he sent them away. (**8:1–9**)

This is a familiar story that obviously echoes the feeding of the five thousand in 6:30–44. Let me quickly point out the similarities. Then I will highlight the differences. There are at least thirteen similarities. On both occasions the setting is in a "desolate place" (6:31; 8:4); there is a "great crowd" (6:34; 8:1); the crowd's number is listed at the end of each narrative (6:44; 8:9); the crowd's hunger is assumed or mentioned (6:35; 8:2–3); Jesus' "compassion"

---

2   Sinclair B. Ferguson, *Let's Study Mark* (repr., Carlisle, PA: Banner of Truth Trust, 2016), 113.

is highlighted (6:34; 8:2); the disciples offer no or poor solutions to the dilemma (6:35–36; 8:4);[3] Jesus has the twelve count the scant rations (6:38; 8:5); the sustenance comprises dried fish and flat bread (6:41; 8:6, 7); Jesus directs the crowds to "recline" on the ground (6:39; 8:6); Jesus "gives thanks" and "breaks" the bread (6:41; 8:6); the disciples "distribute" the food (6:41; 8:6); everyone eats and is "satisfied" (6:42; 8:8); and there are plenty of leftovers (6:43; 8:8).[4]

There are two main differences.[5] First, the place and people of each feeding; second, the numbers for the meal and of the leftovers. The first feeding takes place in the promised land and feeds Jews. The second feeding takes place in a group of ten cities renamed in the days of Alexander the Great as "Decapolis," which means "ten cities." Archeologists have unearthed Greek-designed theaters, temples, and coliseums in two of these ten cities, which indicates typical pagan idolatry and immorality was alive and well. Thus Gentile pagans lived in the Decapolis.[6] So, Jesus feeds the Jews, then the Gentiles.

The second difference involves the numbers. In the first story there are five loaves and two fish and "twelve baskets full of broken pieces and . . . fish" as leftovers (6:38, 43); "and those who ate . . . were five thousand men" (6:44). In the second miracle there are "seven loaves" (8:6) and "a few small fish" (8:7) and the leftovers consist of "seven baskets" of "broken pieces" (8:8), feeding "about four thousand people" (8:9). The earliest Christian commentators believed that the feeding of the five thousand with its twelve basketfuls of leftovers symbolized "Jesus' provision for the Jews" and the feeding of the four thousand with seven basketfuls of leftovers his "provision for the Gentiles." In regards to the numbers in the second mass feeding—four thousand and seven—they took the four thousand to represent "the four corners of the earth from which the Gentiles came," and the number "seven" (mentioned 5x in our text: 8:5, 6, 8, 20 [2x]) as symbolizing the perfect, "worldwide scope of Jesus' ministry."[7] It is difficult to know whether this interpretation is correct.

3   They doubt that Jesus can possibly do anything about the situation. This is understandable in the first scene but inexplicable in the second.

4   I have divided 8:1–30 by geographical references, with 8:10 thus starting the second section, not ending the first. But if we have 8:10 ending the first section, as many commentators do, then two further parallels would be added: (1) Jesus "immediately" leaves the crowds (6:45; 8:10) and (2) soon after the Pharisees challenge him (7:1–5; 8:11–12).

5   Other differences include the following: in the second account Jesus is with the crowd three days, not one (8:2; cf. 6:31, 45); there are seven not five loaves (8:5, 6; cf. 6:38, 41); there are smaller fish (Gk. *ichthudion*, the diminutive from *ichthus*; hence "small fish," 8:7); Jesus leaves with the disciples by boat (8:10; cf. 6:45); and no teaching is mentioned (cf. 6:34). We could also include that in the first story the crowd is clearly divided into set numerical groupings (6:39–40).

6   See John Nolland, *The Gospel of Matthew*, NIGTC (Grand Rapids, MI: Eerdmans, 2005), 632n187.

7   The three quotes above are from James A. Brooks, *Mark*, NAC (Nashville: Broadman, 1991), 125.

But I do think the exegetical intuitions of the earliest Christian commentators fit the pattern in Mark thus far. Jesus has welcomed both Jews and Gentiles. If this symbolism stands, then, "when the 5,000 Jews were fed and there were twelve baskets left, it was emblematic of God's full provision for the twelve tribes of Israel. And when the 4,000 Gentiles were fed and there were seven large baskets of leftovers, it symbolized the completion and fullness of Christ's mission," a mission that "extends still today throughout the world to every tongue and tribe and nation."[8]

Spiritual Blindness

After that amazing miracle our Lord does not stay in town to sign autographs and then, upon returning to Jewish territory, receive a hero's welcome. Instead, "and immediately," we read, "he got into the boat with his disciples and went to the district of Dalmanutha" (**8:10**). Scholars are not exactly sure where this place is. Educated guesses locate it near Capernaum, Jesus' ministry headquarters. If that is the case, then Jesus arrives back to home base, or near enough. And, once he returns, look who is there to greet him! It is not his family (mother and brothers) or fan club (the crowd). Rather, it is the Pharisees.

Picture the scene. Jesus has just fed five thousand, then, shortly thereafter, four thousand. The Pharisees likely know about the feedings, especially the first. What do they do with their knowledge of what Jesus has done? "The Pharisees came and began to argue with him, seeking from him a sign from heaven to test him" (**8:11**). Amazing! They want a sign greater than what Jesus has already shown. Thus far in Mark Jesus has offered many supernatural signs. For example, he has cleansed a leper (1:42), cured a paralytic (2:11–12), and healed a deaf-mute (7:35). He has also raised a young girl from the dead (5:42), stilled the storm at sea (4:39), and walked on water (6:48). What on earth did the Pharisees want Jesus to do? Hold back the sun? Curb the moon? Bring down thunderbolts? Change the direction of the wind?[9] Yes, I think so. They wanted what Pharaoh wanted of Moses and Aaron, something spectacular but something different than all the other spectacular signs already performed. However, Jesus refuses to take this "test" (8:11), or, better, fall prey to this *temptation* to turn bread into angels or raindrops into fireworks.

Instead of a *sign* he offers a *sigh*. Only two sighs are recorded in the Four Gospels. Jesus sighs right before he heals the deaf-mute. As I noted in the last

8 Douglas Sean O'Donnell, *Matthew: All Authority under Heaven*, PTW (Wheaton, IL: Crossway, 2013), 431.
9 These are Chrysostom's suggestions; see "Gospel of St. Matthew 53.3," in Thomas C. Oden and Christopher A. Hall, eds., *Mark*, ACCS NT (Downers Grove, IL: InterVarsity, 1998), 107.

chapter, that sigh is tied to his inner groanings over the consequences of the fall. The Second Adam hates Adam's first sin and that some people are therefore born deaf, mute, and blind. He comes as the curse crusher.

When, then, does he sigh again? Here in **8:12**, notice it is not just a quiet sigh but a deep one ("And he sighed deeply in his spirit"). I imagine his sigh descending almost as low as hell. I also imagine him taking a deep breath and then exhaling into his enemies' faces. For, notice that he not only sighs; he speaks. There is a limit even to divine patience. What rebuke does he offer now? In utter exasperation he says, "Why does this generation seek a sign? Truly, I say to you, no sign will be given to this generation" (8:12). Jesus' spirit will not strive with his contemporaries. "And he left them, got into the boat again, and went to the other side" (**8:13**). This confrontation is over. "Answer not a fool according to his folly, lest you be like him yourself" (Prov. 26:4).

The Pharisees are spiritually blind. Do not be like them. Please do not demand of Jesus that the promised Messiah prove himself on the grounds of something unconnected to the storyline of Scripture. Stop demanding that "God work in this world" based on your "own criteria," and instead look to his Son as set within the context of the Bible and "yield to [God's] wisdom" and the way he has chosen to reveal himself in history.[10]

Spiritual Shortsightedness

At least our Lord's closest friends understand who he is—sorry, no they do not! They are not as blind as the Pharisees, but they are, at this point in the drama, as dense as London fog. Look below at **8:14–21** and wonder at the shortsightedness of the most privileged men ever to walk the earth and sail the sea.

> Now they had forgotten to bring bread, and they had only one loaf with them in the boat. And he cautioned them, saying, "Watch out; beware of the leaven of the Pharisees and the leaven of Herod." And they began discussing with one another the fact that they had no bread. And Jesus, aware of this, said to them, "Why are you discussing the fact that you have no bread? Do you not yet perceive or understand? Are your hearts hardened? Having eyes do you not see, and having ears do you not hear? And do you not remember? When I broke the five loaves for the five thousand, how many baskets full of broken pieces did you take up?" They said to him, "Twelve." "And the seven for the four thousand, how

10 Grant R. Osborne, *Mark*, TTCS (Grand Rapids, MI: Baker, 2012), 131.

many baskets full of broken pieces did you take up?" And they said to him, "Seven." And he said to them, "Do you not yet understand?"

What a loaded last question, following a string of seven questions, most of them rhetorical and all of them basically saying, "Why, after all you have seen, are you still so dense?"

After Jesus first warns the disciples about the deceptive teachings and wicked ways of the Pharisees and the political maneuverings and false perceptions of Herod (8:15)—their evil acts are like leaven—he rebukes the twelve for their shortsightedness: "Having eyes do you not see?" (8:18); "Do you not yet understand?" (8:21; cf. 8:17). They fail to understand *whom* they are up against. Hunger is not the main issue but evil opposition to the kingdom of God. Also, they do not yet understand who Jesus is. They have forgotten what he has just done. He has multiplied the loaves and the fish. Twice! Their forgetfulness leads to their failure to see clearly the person and power of Jesus.

We can be like this as well. Shortsighted. I remember years ago when I asked God to bring a close friend into my life. I loved my wife and kids. We had a full house then. But I wanted another man in my life to talk with about life and pastoral ministry, and also to challenge me to grow spiritually and academically. Within days of that prayer God brought a friend into my life, and we have been close friends for over two decades. Praise God! But then, I also remember—it was about a month after that amazing providential provision—that some financial issue arose. We needed a new air conditioner. My first reaction was worry: "How on earth are we going to pull through the next few months?" Why did I worry? Forgetfulness! I forgot an answer to prayer. I forgot a powerful, and unexpected, answer to prayer. Back then I might have prayed the Lord's Prayer every morning, but I stopped believing that God would answer the fourth petition: "Give us this day our daily bread" (Matt. 6:11).

Let me ask you: How is your hearing? Your sight? Your memory? Your ears, eyes, heart, and mind? Do you hear and see and remember and rejoice in what God has done and is doing? Or has your heart grown hard because you have turned your eyes from Jesus?

Seeing Clearly

Next, as we are following Jesus' movements, Mark moves us from Dalmanutha on the eastern side of the Sea of Galilee (8:10–21) to Bethsaida on its northern tip (8:22–26) to Caesarea Philippi 25 miles up north (8:27–30). In Dalmanutha and on the trip to the other side we witnessed two reactions following Jesus' miracle of the feeding of the four thousand: the blindness of the

Pharisees and the shortsightedness of the disciples. In Bethsaida we witness another miracle: the healing of the blind man. Then near Caesarea Philippi we witness another reaction: Peter's confession that Jesus is the Christ. We might say that we witness two miracles: first, a physically blind man sees clearly; second, a spiritually shortsighted man sees clearly.[11]

First, as we examine **8:22–26**, we read of how our Lord heals the blind man.

> And they came to Bethsaida. And some people brought to him a blind man and begged him to touch him. And he took the blind man by the hand and led him out of the village, and when he had spit on his eyes and laid his hands on him, he asked him, "Do you see anything?" And he looked up and said, "I see people, but they look like trees, walking." Then Jesus laid his hands on his eyes again; and he opened his eyes, his sight was restored, and he saw everything clearly. And he sent him to his home, saying, "Do not even enter the village."

Two details in this narrative we have seen before. Again, we have people who are bringing a helpless person to Jesus for help (8:22). Also, we have the secrecy motif (Jesus first leads the man "out of the village" [8:23], then commands him, once healed, not to return to the village [8:26]). What is new is the ailment that is cured and Jesus' healing technique. This is the first time on record that a blind man is brought to Jesus. In the OT there is no record of someone healing a blind man. So for Jesus to do what he does is unprecedented. Once again it points to Jesus' supernatural powers. It is also a clear identity marker that Jesus is the prophesied Messiah ("Then the eyes of the blind shall be opened," Isa. 35:5).

Jesus' technique is likewise unique—and odd. It is not unique or odd that Jesus touches the untouchables ("He took the blind man by the hand," Mark 8:23; "He . . . laid his hands on him," 8:23; he "laid his hands on his eyes again," 8:25). It is unique and apparently odd that spit in the eyes and two touches upon the eyes are required. The spitting is likely a symbolic act.

---

11 "The healed man eventually sees very 'clearly' (*tēlaugōs*, Mark 8:25; an adverb used only here in the NT). It is important to note that the two-stage healing of the blind man focuses more on the blindness of the disciples' perspective, that is, their inadequate self-perception (compare 4:11; cf. 3:17), whereas the feeding miracles focus more on their inability to see who Jesus really is. Obviously, the two issues of a deficient God-perception and a deficient self-perception are closely interconnected. Note Peter's gradual progress on both accounts (cf. Mark 8:29; 14:72; Acts 2:36; 1 Pet. 2:21–25; 3:18)." Hans F. Bayer, *Mark*, in *Matthew–Luke*, vol. 8 of ESVEC (Wheaton, IL: Crossway, 2021), 576. For further exploration on this theme see Bayer's *A Theology of Mark: The Dynamic between Christology and Authentic Discipleship*, EBT (Phillipsburg, NJ: P&R, 2012), 41–98.

According to Leviticus 15:8 to be spit on rendered a person unclean. It might be, then, that there is some symbolic irony here, as Jesus uses an action associated with uncleanness as a means of cleansing a man's eyes.

The two touches are certainly symbolic. The context is key. Those touches are symbolic of the apostles' vision at this point, especially Peter's. Peter is like the blind man in two ways. First, when he first encountered Jesus, he was totally blind. However, Jesus opened his eyes enough to see that our Lord was worth leaving family and finances to follow. Yet his vision is blurred. He is following Jesus, but he does so like a man follows some large but obscure object in front of him. He sees the form but not the features. It is not until Peter's journey with Jesus to Caesarea Philippi that Peter sees clearly. There, finally, he will understand and confess that Jesus is "the Christ" (8:29). Second, even that confession does not represent perfect vision, for, when Jesus speaks next of the crosses both he and his disciples must carry, Peter rebukes him. Peter sees that Jesus is the Christ, but he needs a second touch from heaven to see that Jesus is Christ crucified and that Christ crucified is the only hope of his salvation.

But at this point in the drama let us end on a positive note as it relates to Peter. I think he is presented in 8:1–30, directly after this miracle, to demonstrate what seeing clearly means. So, next and finally, look with me at **8:27–30**:

> And Jesus went on with his disciples to the villages of Caesarea Philippi. And on the way he asked his disciples, "Who do people say that I am?" And they told him, "John the Baptist; and others say, Elijah; and others, one of the prophets." And he asked them, "But who do you say that I am?" Peter answered him, "You are the Christ." And he strictly charged them to tell no one about him.

Once again the secrecy motif ends a narrative. Jesus wants the details of his ministry to stay under wraps until the right people (properly trained eyewitnesses) say the right things about Jesus after his full mission has been accomplished and the eye-opening Holy Spirit imparted. For now, Jesus wants all his disciples to understand what Peter finally understands. He wants them and us to see clearly. And to see clearly is to see Jesus not as one of the prophets — even the greatest of the OT (Elijah) or the NT (John the Baptist) — but as more than a prophet (note esp. 10:2–8). Jesus is, as Peter confesses, "the Christ." "You are the Christ" (8:29), the anointed king who has come to save!

This is the highpoint of the Gospel, and also a hinge. It is the highpoint because readers know for certain Jesus' proper identity. It is a hinge because, as I said, it transitions us to the second half of the Gospel, which will focus on Christ and him crucified. Jesus will still heal and teach. But the focus now shifts to Jesus' journey to Jerusalem. From here on out, the shadow of the cross begins to cover each step of the way.

Life's Big Question

What then, with all these geographical movements and miracles and reactions, is the major lesson for us? It is that the proper identity of Jesus matters. The right answer to the question "Who is Jesus?" is, in fact, a matter of life or death. Your answer to Jesus' question "Who do *you* say that I am?" (8:29) matters more than your answer to the question "Whom should I marry?" or "What college should I go to?" or "What should I do for a living?" or "Should I change my profession?" or "Should I stay in this relationship?" or "Should I attend my estranged brother's funeral?" or any other question you can think of or that is currently plaguing you.

"Who do *you* say that I am?" You might not think of Jesus as a mere prophet, like Elijah or John the Baptist. But do you believe in Jesus as modern culture envisions him, or in the Jesus of the Bible? Let me encourage you to choose the real Jesus. The Jesus of history. The Jesus of the Gospel of Mark. The Jesus that Peter saw clearly. Let us join in his confession: "You are the Christ" (8:29). And, today and always, let us bow before our resurrected king, hearing afresh what Peter preached at Pentecost: "Let all the house of Israel [and all the nations as well] therefore know for certain that God has made him both Lord and Christ, *this Jesus* whom you crucified" (Acts 2:36).

Setting Your Mind on the Things of God

MARK 8:31–9:1

But turning and seeing his disciples, he rebuked Peter and
said, "Get behind me, Satan! For you are not setting your
mind on the things of God, but on the things of man."
Mark 8:33

In *Alice through the Looking Glass, and What Alice Found There* Lewis Carroll creates a mirror image of reality, where, in order to get somewhere, one
needs to think inside out. For example, to walk forward, one walks backward.
In Mark's Gospel we are introduced to Jesus, a man who lives in an upside-
down, inside-out, moving-backward-to-go-forward sort of way. For example,
although he is sinless, he is baptized by John, who was "proclaiming a baptism of repentance for the forgiveness of sins" (1:4). Then Jesus talks about
establishing a kingdom (1:15) but, instead of gathering a militia around him,
calls four fishermen, a tax collector, and seven other ordinary men (1:16–20;
2:13–14; 3:13–19). Next he does not promote himself to the people in power
at the places of power; instead he goes throughout various remote villages in
the Galilean countryside and beyond (Tyre and Sidon!), where he touches
the untouchables: a leper, a dead girl. And everywhere he goes he is received
by the rejects and rejected by the reputable. He speaks in simple parables
designed to open the ears of some but to clog the ears of others (4:12). And
he will go on to teach, here in our text and in many texts afterward, that what
is down is up and what is out is in and what seems backward is the only way
forward: the first shall be last and the last first, the greatest is the humblest,
the Christ shall be crucified, the glorious Son of Man will die, and the one
who loses his life will save it.

Well, here in Mark 8:31–9:1 we must look through the strange, peculiar, weird, and extraordinary looking glass and notice surprising realities
at which we would never arrive ourselves—two truths taught by Jesus about

kingdom realities, about seeing things the way God wants us to see them. Upside down. Inside out. Backward.

The Christ's Crucifixion

The first truth is that "the Christ" would be crucified. That is, that Jesus would suffer and die under the direction of the Sanhedrin in Jerusalem. Look at Mark **8:31–32a**: "And he began to teach them that the Son of Man must suffer many things and be rejected by the elders and the chief priests and the scribes and be killed, and after three days rise again. And he said this plainly." In other words, this statement was not another confusing parable. It was straightforward talk. Jesus will suffer and die and then, after a short period of time or "on the third day"[1] ("three days," 8:31), rise.

Jesus is not making a prediction here, like when the weatherman offers a forecast based on existing conditions and possible patterns. Instead he is laying out God's predetermined and "definite" plan (see Acts 2:23).[2] Notice the word "must"—"the Son of Man *must* suffer many things" (Mark 8:31). Jesus must follow God's will, and we know from Isaiah 53:10 that "it was the will of the LORD to crush [bruise]" his servant.

In Mark 8:29 Jesus asks, "Who do you say that I am?" and Peter correctly confesses, "You are the Christ," that is, the promised king. Here in verse 31 (also 8:38) Jesus calls himself "the Son of Man," the title used in Daniel 7:13–14 for a king whom the Ancient of Days grants a kingdom that will last forever and encompass people from all the nations. So, if Jesus is "the Christ" (the king) and "the Son of Man" (the divine king with an eternal, worldwide reign), what should the disciples expect next? The Romans routed. Pilate's head on a platter. Evil ousted from authority. Jerusalem recaptured. The promised land restored. A holy war; a whole victory. Then, after the conquest, a cavalcade and a chant, "Hosanna! Blessed is he who comes in the name of the Lord! Blessed is the coming kingdom of our father David! Hosanna in the highest!" (Mark 11:9–10). The Christ crucified? Certainly not. The Son of Man suffering and then slain? Absurd. But Christ conquering? Indeed. The Son of Man with his foot on the neck of his enemies? Amen and amen.

This is how Peter is thinking. Look at **Mark 8:32b–33**. After Jesus' plain pronouncement of the plan we read, "And Peter took him aside and began to rebuke him. But turning and seeing his disciples, he rebuked Peter and said, 'Get behind me, Satan! For you are not setting your mind on the things of

---

1   Vincent Taylor, *The Gospel according to St. Mark*, 2nd ed. (London: Macmillan, 1966), 378.
2   What are often called Jesus' passion predictions I call his "passion pronouncements." There is certainty about what he says in Mark 8:31; 9:31; 10:33–34.

God, but on the things of man.'" Jesus has said that he "*must* suffer" (8:31), and now he *must* make sure that Peter the rock does not remain Simon the stumbling stone. He does not want Peter, and those who might have overheard him, to think this way. So he rebukes Peter for Peter's rebuke.

Picture Peter before Jesus' stern and shockingly strong rebuke. Peter has just stepped forward and answered correctly the most important question in the world. He confesses that Jesus is "the Christ" (8:29). Then, after that confession (in Matthew's Gospel) Jesus commends Peter with a threefold commendation: [1] "Blessed are you. . . . [2] And I tell you, you are Peter, and on this rock I will build my church. . . . [3, Moreover,] I will give you the keys of the kingdom" (Matt. 16:17–19). Such a commendation surely gave Peter great confidence and courage. He must have felt like he had moved to the head of the class in the school of Christ. From what we know of Peter, he might have thought, "Not only have I moved to the head of the class; I think my Lord has just named me the chair of the Bible department." And, not content with that appointment, Peter appoints himself as the chairman of the psychology department as well. For, after Jesus' seemingly crazy statement about suffering and dying, we read that "Peter took [Jesus] aside" (Mark 8:32). What a telling phrase! He took the Lord of heaven and earth aside to rebuke him. "Jesus, over here. Come right here, friend. I need a word with you. How do I say this? Well, frankly, let me offer some wise counsel in regard to your foolish statement. You, who speaks like no man has ever spoken and performs miracles that no man has ever performed, are obviously the Christ. I get that. But, listen, you, as the king, are not going to Jerusalem to be killed. You are going there to conquer. And, trust me (just a final piece of advice), the last people who will oppose your campaign will be pious Jews. Rejected by the elders, priests, and scribes? Come on, Christ. All this is crazy talk."

We do not know all what Peter said, but we know that here he has once again put his foot in his mouth, followed by his arms and then legs. He might even have stuffed his torso in there. And Jesus lets him know it straight away. In verse 33 Jesus not only removes any honorary degrees that were bestowed; he puts Peter in the corner of the class with a dunce cap. But the *D* on the tall hat stands not only for *Dunce* but for *devil*. "Get behind me, Satan!" (8:33).

Jesus calls Peter "Satan" not because Peter is some embodiment of Satan or is demon-possessed but because Peter is thinking like the "ruler of this world" (John 12:31). He is thinking worldly thoughts. Peter's mind is set not "on the things of God, but on the things of man" (Mark 8:33). He is thinking like fallen people under the rule of that great fallen angel think. So here Christ's correction centers on mind renewal. "Peter, think again. Think straight. Think like God wants you to think."

Which, as we know from the end of the story of Peter's life, he does. We know from the end of John's Gospel that Peter is restored to fellowship with Jesus after his denials. We know from the end of Matthew's Gospel that he is entrusted by Jesus to take the gospel to the nations. We know from the Acts of the Apostles that he acts out that commission.[3] And we know from his own writings that he eventually understands the importance and necessity of Christ *and him crucified*. In 1 Peter 2:24 Peter writes of his Lord and Savior, "He himself bore our sins in his body on the tree, that we might die to sin and live to righteousness. By his wounds you have been healed." Once Peter sees clearly through the looking glass, he sees that what seems backward is actually frontward; what appears upside down is really right side up. He eventually sets his mind on the things of God.

Now, before we get to the second truth in our text, we should together ask and answer, "What does it mean for us to set our minds on the things of God?" First, it means that we grasp that God is gracious. Jesus might seem impatient with Peter. But, when you consider the full story, he is incredibly patient. Think about it. Does the Lord disown Peter after his brief satanic counseling session? No. How about after Peter's incredibly dumb three-tents suggestion at the transfiguration? No. After his threefold devious denials? Not even then. The first thing we should know about "the things of God" is that God is gracious and that he desires, in Peter's own words, for us to "*grow* in the grace and knowledge of our Lord and Savior Jesus Christ" (2 Peter 3:18) and that such grace shows itself clearly in God's patience. God "is patient" toward us, "not wishing that any [of us] should perish," but that we should, like Peter, "reach repentance" (2 Pet. 3:9).

Second, to set our minds on the things of God is also to understand that we are not to counsel God (cf. Rom. 11:34) but to follow his Son. Peter's pulling Jesus aside to "rebuke him" (Mark 8:32) ought to rebuke us. It ought to rebuke us when we think our ways are wiser than God's. When Peter counsels Jesus in his version of the boardgame Monopoly—to go directly to Glory and skip Gethsemane and Golgotha—he echoes Satan's temptations in the wilderness. Whenever we think that we know better than Jesus, or whenever

---

3   In Acts "he is described as the spokesperson of the Twelve (Acts 2:14; 5:1–11; 17–39), and the leader of the Jerusalem church (Acts 1:15–25; 9:32–43; 11:2–13; 15:7) and its mission in Jerusalem (Acts 3:12), Judea (Acts 9:32, 35), Samaria (Acts 8:14, 25) and Caesarea (Acts 10:5–48), who preaches at Pentecost (Acts 2:14–40), on the Temple Mount (Acts 3:11–26) and before the Jewish leaders in the Sanhedrin (Acts 4:8–12; 5:29–32)." E. J. Schnabel, "Apostles," *DJG* 39.

we want to pull him aside to offer a correction on his views—that the cross is a "must" (Mark 8:31), that he is the only way to God (John 14:6), or that marriage is between one man and one woman for life (Matt. 19:4–9)—that is the moment we have made the inside the outside, the forward the backward.

Third, to set our minds on the things of God is not to let the ways of the world determine our decisions. Some segments in the church today are possessed by satanic spirituality, by which safety and success become the goals of the Christian life. This occurs, for example, when a young, single Christian woman desires to go overseas to work with Muslim refugees but her Christian parents oppose it because, above all else, they fear for her safety. They fail to grasp that the hairs on her head are numbered, that God looks after even the lilies of the field—they fail to grasp any of what Jesus will talk about in the second half of our text (to die for Christ is gain). Or, as another example, we see this when a Christian husband receives a large and unexpected bonus at work and his gut reaction is to give it all away to support the work of the local homeless shelter, but his Christian wife convinces him that they could really use that money for their next vacation to Hawaii, the one they planned for their twenty-fifth wedding anniversary. Satanic spirituality is subtle but deadly. Watch out for it! And here is the sign of it. It always promotes physical safety and financial stability at the expense of gospel sacrifice and generosity.

Fourth, to set our minds on the things of God is fully to embrace the seemingly ridiculous—the paradox of the Christ crucified. Peter might be the first Christian leader to oppose the cross, but he is certainly not the last. We are so familiar with the symbol of the cross that we often forget that the cross was a brutal form of torture. Jesus was nailed to two wooden beams and then raised up in the heat of the day to die a slow and painful death. And, just as most pious Jews and educated Greeks of Jesus' day thought that this horrific display at Calvary was shameful, not glorious, and foolish, not wise, so most religiously sensible and intellectually sophisticated people today think the same.

Just flip on the History Channel, where you are bound to find a panel of Bible experts from prestigious universities making smart-sounding claims about Jesus. One says, "I believe that the Jesus of history was merely a Palestinian peasant with radical ideas about political reform. He made no claims to be divine. He performed no miracles. And the idea of a bodily resurrection is absurd. I do, however, believe he died on a Roman cross, but not to atone for sins. How silly." This is an example of the tame stuff out there. Another expert chimes in, "Yes, I agree fully. In fact, in my recent studies I propose the theory that the twelve apostles were all homosexuals." "Seriously?" says the moderator. "Oh, it's quite true. It is all here in my new book." "Oh, that's interesting," says his esteemed colleague on the panel. "That's especially interesting because my studies are on the correlations between the role of demons in the Gospels and the television show *Buffy the Vampire Slayer*." I exaggerate these exchanges, but only slightly.

But it is not just the crackpots from the intelligentsia whom we need to watch out for—those who deny Jesus' incarnation, substitutionary death, and bodily resurrection, plus a dozen other foundational doctrines of the Christian faith. We also need to watch out for anyone who disdains the concept of "Christ and him crucified" (1 Cor. 2:2). It might be the nice old lady next door, the friendly plumber, or the gift-giving aunt. It might even be the respectable evangelical leader. I know plenty of prominent evangelicals who believe in the cross of Christ (they are not in opposition), but rarely, if ever, do they preach on the cross of Christ (they ignore it). These days "that old rugged cross, stained with blood" is not only "so despised by the world";[4] it is so often despised by so-called "Christians" on the *New York Times* bestseller list who refuse to write about the bloody tree at Calvary. How can you write about living our best lives and the purpose-driven life without writing about the cross, which is the only means by which we live with purpose and the only means by which we live our best lives both now and forever?

Christian Cruciformity

The first topsy-turvy truth of our text is Christ crucified; the second is Christian cruciformity. The Christ must be crucified; Christians must be cruciform. That is, Christian discipleship conforms to the pattern of Christ's passion—self-denial and suffering. There is his cross and *ours*.[5] That is what Jesus teaches next in Mark 8:34–9:1. Look first at **8:34**. Soak in this Scripture. It is of absolute importance. "And calling the crowd to him with his disciples, he said to them, 'If anyone would come after me, let him deny himself and take up his cross and follow me.'"

Let me offer three observations on this key verse, mixed with a few exhortations. First, notice that Jesus' calling to cruciformity extends to the crowd ("and calling the crowd to him with his disciples," 8:34). This is not just some specific command to the hand-picked twelve, the special forces of God's kingdom. It is, as Jesus puts it here, for "anyone" ("If anyone would come after

---

4 George Bennard, "On a Hill Far Away" (1913).
5 Frederick Dale Bruner says there are two basic characteristics of a Christian: (1) "Confessing Jesus as Christ (Christo-centricity)" and (2) "Following Jesus as the suffering Christ (Crucio-christocentricity)." *Matthew: A Commentary, Volume 2: The Churchbook, Matthew 13–28*, rev. ed. (Grand Rapids, MI: Eerdmans, 2007), 119, 138.

me"). A possible application based on that observation might be that, when we preach Christ to *anyone*—both those dedicated to the mission of Christ (disciples) and those curious about it (enquirers)—we must be faithful to bring up what Jesus brings up, both here in verse 34 and in what follows. Let us not be like so many politicians who offer lots of promises without clarifying the costs: Mayor Smith says, "I promise a 50 percent tax cut," without saying, "And, just to be clear about that promise, we won't be able to plow snow, pay the police, or fill potholes until the next election." Jesus is not like that. He focuses on the costs.

Second, notice that cruciformity flows out of an understanding of the cross. His cross is first not ours, and, if we ever switch the order, we are out of order. To be clear, our Lord is suggesting not some conditions for salvation here in verse 34 and following but rather a response to it. In gratitude for what Jesus has done for us, we act. We act like him. He takes on the big cross that solves the world's biggest problem; we take up our little crosses because we believe that conformity to Christ is our highest calling. I appreciate how Isaac Watts expresses this point in his hymn "When I Survey the Wondrous Cross." He writes of, as we look upon the cross of Christ, pouring contempt upon our pride, ridding ourselves of worldly amusements (the vain things that charm us most), and giving all that we have in return:

Love so amazing, so divine,
Demands my soul, my life, my all.[6]

Dietrich Bonhoeffer, who died with a bullet in his head from Hitler's henchmen, in his book *The Cost of Discipleship* puts it a bit more bluntly: "When Christ calls a man, he bids him come and die."[7]

Third, notice how Jesus defines that sort of death. What is our cross? Is our cross enduring any kind of suffering—like losing a loved one, experiencing an injury, working under a tyrannical boss, grieving over a broken relationship, or living with a lazy husband or a nagging wife? Or is it persecutions—suffering because we publicly acknowledge Jesus under an oppressive political regime, preach the gospel to a hostile crowd, or refuse to participate in sin? It certainly is the second, but it can also be the first. Job's twofold sufferings—his friends' misunderstanding and mockery, along with his loss of health and possessions—surely constitute cross bearing.

---

6   Isaac Watts, "When I Survey the Wondrous Cross" (1765).
7   Dietrich Bonhoeffer, *The Cost of Discipleship* (repr., New York: Touchstone, 1995), 89.

However we define our cross, self-denial must be at the center of our definition, because it was at the center of Jesus'. And self-denial must preclude self-worship and self-will. Instead of worshiping self, we worship God; instead of doing whatever we want, we do whatever God wants of us. Again, look at verse 34 ("If anyone would come after me, let him deny himself and take up his cross and follow me") and notice the structure of this sentence:

> come after me
>> deny himself
>> take up his cross
> follow me.

The movements after Jesus ("come after me," which parallels "follow me") flank the admonitions to "deny" oneself and "take up" one's "cross." Are those middle admonitions also parallel? In other words, is the "cross" just a metaphorical way of speaking of self-denial? I think so. Plainly put, to "come after" or "follow" Jesus (to be a disciple of his), we must deny ourselves.

In college I took a class on John Calvin. For that class I read through Calvin's *Institutes of the Christian Religion*. Anytime I came across a line that I liked, I underlined or highlighted it. Among the thousands of underscored sentences, no sentence stood out more than this: "The sum of the Christian life is self-denial."[8] Does Calvin's summary fit yours?

Imagine you accept an overseas assignment in Dubai. You walk into the new office building and are greeted by Mustapha. Sometime that first day, as he is showing you the ropes, he asks, "Are you a Christian?" You reply, "Yes." He then asks, "How would you summarize what it means to be a follower of Jesus?" What is your answer? Is it, "Jesus demands nothing but offers us healing and happiness now"? Wrong. Is it, "To follow Jesus means perfect health and lots of wealth"? Wrong. Is it, "To follow Jesus means death to self"? Right.

Is that how you think and talk about discipleship? Have you set your mind on the things of God? Or does the world have more of a sway over you than you possibly imagined? Do you desire self-indulgent pleasures? Is that what dominates your thought life? Do you seek after ease? Do you love money—making it, spending it? Are convenience and comfort your bedfellows? Do you give ten seconds of thought per week about feeding the hungry, caring for the sick, visiting those in prison—a few of the acts, Jesus

---

8   John Calvin, *Institutes of the Christian Religion*, LCC, ed. John T. McNeill, trans. Ford Lewis Battles (Philadelphia: Westminster, 1960), 3.7.

says in Matthew 25:31–46, by which he will judge the authenticity of our Christianity? Who is your Christ? Your king? You or Jesus? Perhaps the key word in Mark 8:34 is not "cross" or "deny" but "me," in reference to Jesus: "come after me" and "follow me." Do you "belong, body and soul . . . not to [your]self but to [your] faithful Savior Jesus Christ"?[9]

Now, let me just hit the pause button here. I know that following Jesus is not easy. And I am so glad that the form of the Four Gospels is not Christ's cross (chs. 1–8) and our cross (chs. 9–16). Rather, as we keep moving to the end of each section, it is clear that the cross of Christ is bigger and heavier and that it covers more sins than we can imagine, even the sins of cross-bearing disciples who fail near the finish line.

What I find so striking about Mark's Gospel is its ending. Chapter 14 concludes with Peter's threefold denials, including that damning crescendo confession, "I do not know this man of whom you speak" (14:71). That is followed by Jesus' spectacular self-denials. Instead of defending himself in the Jewish high court, our Lord lets injustice roll over him. Instead of explaining to Pontus Pilate that he is indeed innocent of all charges against Roman law, he lets injustice roll over him. Instead of taking an iron rod and dashing to pieces (see Ps. 2:9) those soldiers who mock him, he dons silently that purple cloak and crown of thorns. He lets injustice roll over him. Instead of pushing out the nails and coming down from the cross, as his jeerers suggest, he refuses to save himself so he might save us. He let injustice roll over him so that justice—his righteousness—might become ours through faith. Jesus suffers "many things" (Mark 8:31). Arrest. Unfair trials. Brutal beatings. Mockery. Forsakenness. Pain. So much physical, psychological, and spiritual pain. Whatever we make of Christ's call to discipleship—grace is not cheap, and discipleship is certainly costly—we ought never to think that we save ourselves through cruciformity.

From that high calling (Mark 8:34) Jesus next gives us a few motivations, all tied to something bigger than us and beyond us, but also for us. Basically, in **8:35–38** Jesus says that cross bearing is worth it. In these verses Jesus provides motivations for this seemingly morbid mission. Notice the word "for." We are to live Christ-centered, cruciformed lives,

for whoever would save his life will lose it, but whoever loses his life for my sake and the gospel's will save it. *For* what does it profit a man to gain the whole world and forfeit his soul? *For* what can a man give in

9   Heidelberg Catechism 1.

return for his soul? *For* whoever is ashamed of me and of my words in this adulterous and sinful generation, of him will the Son of Man also be ashamed when he comes in the glory of his Father with the holy angels.

Notice that with these four *fors* Jesus takes us to judgment day. He has spoken about his death and resurrection, and now he talks about his return, when he will judge the whole world in righteousness. The reason we should live cruciformed lives is because it will thereby go well for us on judgment day, the day when Jesus "comes in the glory of his Father with the holy angels" (8:38). A foretaste of that great day comes at the transfiguration (9:2–8), when Peter, James, and John ("some standing here") will get a glimpse of the "power" of God's coming kingdom (9:1).[10]

So think of it this way: if you choose cross now (lose your life), you get crown then (save it), but if you choose crown now (gain the whole world), you get a cross then (forfeit your soul). If you are ashamed of Christ—his words and ways—in this life, he will be ashamed of you in the next: "Whoever is ashamed of me and of my words in this adulterous and sinful generation, of him will the Son of Man also be ashamed when he comes in the glory of his Father with the holy angels." (8:38). "At the last judgment, Jesus will not slap the wrists of those professing Christians who toyed with his teachings, who moonlighted with power and possessions, who chose self-indulgence over self-denial, who thought orthodoxy had nothing to do with orthopraxis."[11] When Jesus returns, he will judge those who prized safety and success over the gospel and those who lived for the fleeting pleasures of this world instead of longing for the eternal joys of God. At the last judgment every looking glass shall be shattered, and everyone shall see as they should have seen. We shall see that the first shall be last and the last first; that to live for self is to die and to die to self is to live; and that the crucified Christ, who rose again, will return in glory with crowns of righteousness for "all who have loved his appearing" (2 Tim. 4:8).

Alice through the Looking Glass, along with *Alice in Wonderland*, are "two beloved masterpieces of the nonsensical."[12] But the Bible, as much as its

---

10 Mark 9:1 could refer to the fall of Jerusalem, the Spirit at Pentecost, or Jesus' resurrection and return—two events of one final coming. Or it could be a general prediction of Christ's future glory, encompassing the resurrection, ascension, Pentecost, and his present heavenly session. However, I suggest that it refers to the transfiguration, upon which "some standing here"— Peter, James, and John—see "the Son of Man" (Jesus) in his kingdom glory.

11 Douglas Sean O'Donnell, *Matthew: All Authority under Heaven*, PTW (Wheaton, IL: Crossway, 2013), 463.

12 Lewis Carroll, *Alice's Adventures in Wonderland*; and *Through the Looking Glass*, Everyman's Library Children's Classics (New York: Knopf, 1992), 328.

Author turns things on their heads, is a masterpiece of the "sensical," a book designed to make sense of the world we live in and to bring us to our senses: to Jesus, the perfectly righteous king who served sinners, the everlasting God who died, so that we, who now live to serve and to die to self, might reign with him forever and ever.[13]

---

13   I am indebted to Frederick Dale Bruner for some of the ideas and language of these final two paragraphs. See Bruner, *Churchbook*, 156–157, as used in O'Donnell, *Matthew*, 463–64.

The Beloved Son of God and Son of Man Who Suffered

MARK 9:2-13

And a cloud overshadowed them, and a voice came out of
the cloud, "This is my beloved Son; listen to him."
Mark 9:7

When I was a child, one company's television commercials really stood out to me. I liked the Nike shoe commercials ("Like Mike, I want to be like Mike"), and the Wendy's fast-food commercials too ("Where's the beef?"). But it was the clever commercials by E. F. Hutton, a financial investment group, that always caught my attention. The plot for their twenty-second ads was the same. Two people are talking about investments. One man speaks of what his broker said, and then another man says, "My broker is E. F. Hutton, and Hutton says." And as soon as the actor says "says," everything stops. People in the restaurant, at the pool, or wherever the setting stop moving and talking. They all turn their ears to hear. Then, amid the stillness and silence, the slogan is said: "When E. F. Hutton talks, people listen." My favorite commercial within that series is when a schoolgirl is asked to recite the alphabet. She stands and starts: "A, B, C, D, E, F." As soon as she says, "E, F," the whole class of kindergarteners lean toward her, tilt their ears, and listen.

Mark 9:2–8 records Jesus' going up a mountain. At the top he is "transfigured" (9:2). He is changed in some dramatic way, so much so that his wardrobe shines like the sun. Mark's three descriptors highlight the point. Radiant. Intensely white. So white that "no one," not even the bleach queen of the world, "could bleach them" (9:3). He is holy, holy, holy. And at the end of this awesome event God the Father speaks. And what does he say (well, everyone please listen in)? He says, "This is my beloved Son; listen to him" (9:7).

Then Mark 9:9–13 records Jesus' going down the mountain, and, as he goes down, he speaks. And what does he say (well, everyone please listen in)?

This holy, holy, holy God-man, as he descends back into a demon-infested and faithless world (tune in for next week's episode), speaks not of his coming glory but of his seemingly inglorious mission. In Mark 9:9 he speaks of his death ("the Son of Man . . . risen from the dead"), and in verse 12 he speaks of his sufferings before his death ("that he should suffer many things and be treated with contempt").

So, at the top of the mountain, the Father speaks; near the bottom of the mountain, the Son speaks; and between those two revelations are various reactions, all which teach us what God—Father and Son, and the Spirit-inspired Word—wants to say to us. Thus our basic outline for studying Mark 9:2–13 is simple. We will ask and answer four questions. First, what does God say here about Jesus? Second, what is the proper response to that revelation? Third, what does Jesus say about his mission? Fourth, what is the proper response to that revelation?

The Father's Voice: God's Answer to Mark 8:29

First, what does God say here about Jesus? Put differently, how does God the Father answer the question that Jesus posed to his disciples: "Who do you say that I am?" (Mark 8:29).

Peter's answer ("You are the Christ," 8:29) is the right answer but not the full answer. The Father fills in the rest. After the light show of the millennia (Jesus' radiant transfiguration), the star-studded cast of the shortest but longest-aired drama of all time (Moses and Elijah conversing with Jesus), and an unusual hovering cloud that is perhaps an allusion to the glorious cloud in the wilderness, a voice is heard. God the Father speaks!

In the OT on a number of occasions God speaks directly to people. God speaks to Abraham, Moses, and Job, to name a select few. And, whenever he speaks, it is always with a revelation about his person or plan. Yet, in the NT, God rarely speaks in such a direct manner. In fact, in the Synoptic Gospels the Father speaks only twice: at Jesus' baptism we hear a voice from heaven saying, "You are my beloved Son, with you I am well pleased" (1:11); then here on the mountain we hear nearly the same opening line, "This is my beloved Son; listen to him" (9:7).[1] At the baptism it is hard to know whether anyone but Jesus hears the voice. Perhaps John does. But at the transfiguration there are five witnesses. Before two old-covenant witnesses (Moses and Elijah) and three new-covenant ones (Peter, James, and John)—the supreme

---

1 In John's Gospel the Father replies to Jesus' petition, "Father, glorify your name," with his "I have glorified it, and I will glorify it again" (John 12:28).

court of our Scriptures!—the Father says what he says about his Son, two statements that I assure you are a billion times more important than what some stockbroker has to say about money. The Father makes first a statement about Jesus' identity ("This is my beloved Son") and second a command to hear what Jesus has to say ("listen to him," 9:7).

The statement about Jesus' identity ("This is my beloved Son," 9:7) takes us back to Psalm 2:7, where God says about his anointed king, "You are my Son." It takes us back also to the opening verse of Mark's Gospel ("Jesus Christ, the *Son* of God," Mark 1:1). Peter called Jesus the "Christ" six days ago (8:29; cf. 9:2), and on the day of the transfiguration (the seventh day!) God adds the title "Son." The point of the combination of these two titles is to clarify that Jesus is more than the promised Jewish Messiah from the line of David. He is also the eternally begotten Son of the Father.

He is the begotten Son, but also the "beloved Son" (9:7). That phrase, "my be-loved Son," (9:7) speaks of God's pleasure in his Son, who has come to suffer (Isa. 42:1) and be sacrificed (Gen. 22:2). The phrase is also personal. The word *my* highlights the closeness of the relationship, and the word *beloved* the sweetness of it (Mark 9:7). God did not send some carefully designed drone, some high-ranking angel, or a half man/half alien born of the two most pious creatures in the universe to die for our sins. He sent his own beloved Son. How lovely! How loving. "God so loved the world, that he gave his only *Son*" (John 3:16).

What God means verbally by the phrase "my beloved Son" (Mark 9:7) he showcases visually. The verbal is supported by the visual. Mark **9:2** describes the setting. "And after six days Jesus took with him Peter and James and John, and led them up a high mountain by themselves." The mention of "six days" likely alludes both to the creation account (Genesis 1–2) and to Moses' expe-rience in the exodus account. In Exodus 24:15–16 we read, "Moses went up on the mountain, and the cloud covered the mountain. The glory of the LORD dwelt on Mount Sinai, and the cloud covered it six days. And on the seventh day he called to Moses out of the midst of the cloud."[2] The topography—"up a high mountain" (cf. Mark 9:9)—echoes the many important revelations from God to man that took place on mountains.[3] This is the only "high mountain"

2   Cf. David E. Garland, *Mark*, NIVAC (Grand Rapids, MI: Zondervan, 1996). Garland (342) lists the parallels between Jesus and Moses, including "Jesus takes three disciples up the mountain" (Mark 9:2) and "Moses goes with three named persons" (Ex. 24:1, 9); Jesus' "clothes become radiantly white" (Mark 9:3) and "Moses's skin shines . . . after talking with God" (Ex. 34:29); "God appears" to both Jesus and Moses "in veiled form in an overshadowing cloud" (Mark 9:7; Ex. 24:15–16, 18) and a "voice speaks from the cloud" (Mark 9:7; Ex. 24:16).
3   For a list of Scriptural references of mountains as places of divine revelation see Mark L. Strauss, *Mark*, ZECNT (Grand Rapids, MI: Zondervan, 2014), 383n10.

mentioned in Mark (cf. 5:5; 6:46; 11:23; 13:14). It is likely Mount Hermon, Syria's highest mountain, near Caesarea Philippi (8:27), a good 9,000 feet off the ground. Hermon is the nearest point to heaven in Israel. Robert Gundry calls it a "suburb of heaven."[4]

The height of Hermon itself, and the trek it must have taken to get there, tells us God is certainly about to reveal something spectacular. And indeed he does. Peter and James and John are there to witness an epiphany.[5] And a theophany! They see the light show and hear the heavenly voice. Mark **9:2–3** describe the light show, or white show. "And he was transfigured before them, and his clothes became radiant, intensely white, as no one on earth could bleach them." The focus here is not on Jesus' metamorphosis (Gk. *metamorphooami*). Jesus reverse-transfigures, that is, he changes back into his incarnate state. Or, more likely, he fast-forwards to his postresurrection glory. But the focus here is not on what that looks like but on the brightness and purity of his clothing. The language harks back to when the Son of Man in Daniel 7 stands before the Ancient of Days, whose "clothing was white as snow" (Dan. 7:9). The point, then, is, as the Nicene Creed well summarizes, that Jesus is "God of God, Light of Light, very God of very God . . . being of one substance with the Father."

Light of Light. It is like Jesus' tunic is trying to clothe the glory of God. The brightness, heat, and pure radiance shine and burn through. Here the apostles need more than BluBlocker sunglasses. They need Iron Man's shield, or NASA's MSL Thermal Protection System. Years later Peter wrote of that day, saying "we were eyewitnesses of his majesty" (2 Pet. 1:16). John, as he meditated on the incarnation, but perhaps also alluding specifically to this event, wrote, "And the Word became flesh and dwelt among us, and *we have seen his glory*, glory as of the only Son from the Father, full of grace and truth" (John 1:14). They saw the Shekinah glory, the glory that filled the tabernacle and temple in the OT (Ex. 40:34–35; 2 Chron. 7:1–3). Jesus reveals that he is the light of the world.

We do not know what James thought of that moment, but we can surmise that he would agree with his brother John's depiction of the risen and exalted Jesus in Revelation 1:12–17. There Jesus is surrounded by light ("seven golden lampstands," Rev. 1:12); his hair is light, "like white wool, like snow"

---

4   Robert H. Gundry, *Mark: A Commentary on His Apology for the Cross* (Grand Rapids, MI: Eerdmans, 1993), 457.

5   Jesus selected these three men to establish proper legal evidence (see Deut. 19:15). Moreover, Peter, James, and John would become the pillars of the church (see Gal. 2:9)—instrumental parts of growing the future church.

(1:14). His eyes are light ("like a flame of fire," 1:14); in his right hand is light ("he held seven stars," 1:16), and his face is light ("like the sun shining in full strength," 1:16; cf. Matt. 17:2). And, having seen Jesus on the high mount of holy transfiguration, James would agree with John both that "God is light, and in him is no darkness at all" (1 John 1:5) and that the Son of God is also light, and in him is no darkness at all. What these eyewitnesses see that day is "the light of the knowledge of the glory of God *in the face* of Jesus Christ" (2 Cor. 4:6). God showed Moses a glimpse of his glory (Ex. 34:6). Elijah rode on a chariot of fire into heaven (2 Kings 2:11). But here these two prophets and three apostles see an unprecedented revelation—God the Son face to face. And, by God's grace, they live to preach about it.

Responding to the Father's Voice

What I have detailed above we might call Peter's, James's, and John's mature response, a response that came years later and from further revelation (after Jesus' resurrection, appearances, and ascension) and inspiration (after the Spirit's power at Pentecost and the permanence of his indwelling throughout their lives). Their first response, however, is less than mature. Let us pick up the story in Mark **9:4–8**:

> And there appeared to them Elijah with Moses, and they were talking with Jesus. And Peter said to Jesus, "Rabbi, it is good that we are here. Let us make three tents, one for you and one for Moses and one for Elijah." For he did not know what to say, for they were terrified. And a cloud overshadowed them [a divine interruption],[6] and a voice came out of the cloud, "This is my beloved Son; listen to him." And suddenly, looking around, they no longer saw anyone with them but Jesus only.

Notice here two wrong reactions. The first wrong reaction is to call Jesus what Peter called him, "Rabbi" (9:5). If there was ever a day to recognize that Jesus is more than a teacher, it was that day. "Lord" or "Christ," two words in Peter's vocabulary, would have been preferable, or, even better, "Son of Man," Jesus' favorite designation for himself (9:9, 12). It would have been better, if Peter were to say anything at all, that he say something like, "Jesus, Son of Man and Son of God, it is both amazing and humbling to be here. Shall I shut my mouth now and get on my knees?"

---

6   For a list of Scriptural references to the correspondence between clouds and God's presence see Strauss, *Mark*, 385n28.

The second wrong reaction is Peter's impulsive suggestion to pop up a few pup tents. "Let us make three tents, one for you and one for Moses and one for Elijah" (9:5). It is not necessarily wrong that Peter wants to erect little tabernacles, as was done at the Feast of Tabernacles and originally out in the wilderness after the exodus. There and then God asked his people to house him in a tent or tabernacle, so they might worship him. What is wrong, however, is that Peter places Moses and Elijah on par with Jesus.[7] Moses and Elijah do not deserve minitemples, and certainly not on the same level and of the same dimensions as Jesus'.

Moses and Elijah seem to understand this. That is why they do not stick around. They have been speaking with Jesus, but now they know it is time for him, and him alone, to speak. They embrace Hebrews 1:1–3. They know both that Jesus is the "radiance of the glory of God" and that he is God's last word. They likely represent the Law and the Prophets (the Scriptures of the old covenant; see Matt. 11:13; Luke 16:16), but they know that Jesus alone is the fulfillment of the Law and the Prophets (see Matt. 5:17). They have been with him, and even shared in something of his glory (Luke tells us that they light up too; Luke 9:30–31), but now they know that he alone is worthy of worship. They are not there to have their latest and last earthly appearance commemorated, and they are certainly not there to be worshiped alongside Jesus. The last two words of the transfiguration account are of utmost importance: "Jesus only" (Mark 9:8).[8]

The astrophysicist Michael Hart, in his book *The 100: A Ranking of the Most Influential Persons in History*, ranks Jesus third behind Mohammad and Isaac Newton. Then follow Buddha, Confucius, and Paul. On the Mount of Transfiguration Mark does not line up the Jewish heroes of the past and present and rank them: Jesus, Moses, Peter, Elijah, John, and James. Rather, he says of Jesus that there are no equals. Jesus alone stands alone, for he alone is God's beloved Son.

So when people say to you something like, "I respect all religions. Jesus, Mohammad, Buddha, and Confucius are all on the same plane. They are all wise men. Top ten teachers who all taught the truth," Christian, you must say

7 "Do not set up tents equally for the Lord and his servants. 'This is my beloved Son, hear him'—my Son, not Moses or Elijah. They are servants; this is the Son." Jerome, "Homily 80," quoted in *CHSB*, 1488.
8 Christians who venerate holy places (e.g., the unnamed mountain in Mark) and holy people (Saints Peter, James, and John) more than they revere the holy Son of God are wholly mistaken. In fact, they are wholly unholy. On the Mount of Transfiguration, six of the most prominent figures in the Bible are gathered in one place, and the Father acknowledges only his Son. Moreover, Jesus rebukes Peter for his suggested building project. If Jesus rebuked Peter then and there and for that—his holy shrine for holy people in the Holy Land—one wonders what he made of the building of St. Peter's Basilica in Rome.

in a kind tone, "I disagree. That is not what the Gospel writers say about Jesus. It is not what Jesus says about himself. It is not the testimony of the Father about his Son."

There are two wrong reactions to the transfigured Jesus. First is to call him "rabbi," a mere teacher. He is more than a carpenter and more than a good teacher. He is the divine Son of God. Second is to think of him as being on par with any other human being, be it Moses or Mohammad. He alone is worthy of our worship. "Worthy is the Lamb . . . to receive power and wealth and wisdom and might and honor and glory and blessing!" (Rev. 5:12).

So, with this in mind, I invite you to come to that mountain with Peter, James, and John and to see afresh something of Christ's glory. Oh that our personal and corporate worship would be filled with gratitude, reverence, and awe (Heb. 12:28), worship that is befitting the transfigured Son of God. "Jesus was not merely a great leader (Heavenly CEO) or a profound moralist (What Would Jesus Do?), but he was/is the glorious Son of God, *and* thus he deserves our acknowledgement ('You are Son of God and Son of Man'), our adoration ('We fall before you and worship you'), and our obedience ('We will listen to what you have to say')."[9]

Listen to Him: The Son's Sayings

There are two wrong reactions to the Father's testimony about Jesus and there are two right reactions. First, worship Jesus and him alone; second, listen to him. We turn our attention next to that second reaction—to the Father's command to hear what Jesus has to say, which takes us to the second half of our text (Mark **9:9–13**).

I advocate that the command "listen to him" (9:7) incorporates everything Jesus taught. So it includes the Great Commission, namely, knowing and obeying all his commandments. It also includes his talk on the road to Emmaus, where he taught his disciples to read the whole of the OT in light of his life, death, and resurrection.[10] He has come not to abolish the Law (Moses) and the Prophets (Elijah) but to fulfill the Hebrew Scriptures (Matt. 5:17). Finally, it certainly includes what he taught directly after the Father's command to "listen to him" (Mark 9:7).

And as they were coming down the mountain, he charged them to tell no one what they had seen, until the Son of Man had risen from the

---

9   Douglas Sean O'Donnell, *Matthew: All Authority under Heaven*, PTW (Wheaton, IL: Crossway, 2013), 471.
10 See Richard B. Hays, *Echoes of Scripture in the Gospels* (Waco, TX: Baylor University Press, 2016).

dead. So they kept the matter to themselves, questioning what this rising from the dead might mean. And they asked him, "Why do the scribes say that first Elijah must come?" And he said to them, "Elijah does come first to restore all things. And how is it written of the Son of Man that he should suffer many things and be treated with contempt? But I tell you that Elijah has come, and they did to him whatever they pleased, as it is written of him." (9:9–13)

There are a number of important details here. We should notice the topological shift. Jesus and the three apostles come "down the mountain" (9:9), a journey that would have taken many hours. We should also notice Jesus' now familiar command to keep quiet about his true identity until the right time. The three are told "to tell no one what they had seen, until the Son of Man had risen from the dead" (9:9). Finally, we should notice that Jesus here focuses on his cross. He has just had a crown-like moment, but he has now taken off that crown—the coming crown of vindication and the crown he wore before the incarnation—for the cross.

As stated earlier, Jesus speaks of his passion in two places (rising "from the dead," 9:9; suffering "many things" and being "treated with contempt," 9:12). He speaks also of the John the Baptist's cruel sufferings and brutal death in verse 13, a passion that prefigures his own ("They did to him whatever they pleased"). I will also add here an important cross-reference on the cross. In Luke's account of the transfiguration Luke writes of Moses and Elijah appearing "in glory" (Luke 9:31). But he also tells his readers something of the specifics of their conversation with Jesus. Luke writes that they "spoke of his *departure* [an idiom for his death, cf. 2 Pet. 1:15], which he was about to *accomplish* in Jerusalem" (Luke 9:31). The Greek word for "departure" is *exodus*. Jesus' death will be our exodus. His exodus is an *accomplishment*! His exodus will accomplish our redemption. We will be set free from the penalty and power and, soon and very soon, the presence of sin.

Responding to the Son's Voice

With all that said, how do the three apostles respond to the news of Jesus' passion and resurrection, and how should we? Their response is confusion. They do not understand what Jesus means by "rising from the dead" (Mark 9:10), nor they do understand the timeline of his messianic mission. They believe, as the scribes of the time teach (based on Mal. 4:5–6; cf. Mark 15:35–36), that Elijah must come before the kingdom does. They are confused by what Jesus has just said, considering the backdrop of what they have likely been taught their whole lives. It is like they are talking to each other, and trying to hear each other, from two sides of a large river. My quick-witted Irish father e-mails me jokes all the time, occasionally funny ones. Recently he sent this one. A good one.

> A guy yells across the Fox River, "Hey, how do you get to the other side of this river?"
> A guy on the other side yells back, "You *are* on the other side!"

Verses 9–13 are a bit like that joke. Jesus is on one side; the apostles the other. The apostles think Elijah is still to come. Jesus knows that Elijah has already come, both literally at the transfiguration and symbolically in the person of John the Baptist. And, just as the apostles do not grasp that, they do not grasp the bigger and more important revelation—the centrality of the death and resurrection of Jesus in the plan of salvation. They are afraid to question Jesus about that (see 9:10). So again Peter, James, and John offer the wrong reaction. They ask about Elijah when they should have asked Jesus to clarify his mission. "Are you really the Son of Man, the glorious figure mentioned in Daniel? If so, how can you die? We do not understand. And, what do you mean by resurrection from the dead? We believe that there will be a resurrection from the dead at the final judgment (Dan. 12:2–3) but not before it. We do not have a category for dead people three days after death rolling away stones. So please explain yourself. Rabbi, we are here to learn and listen to you."

If their reaction here is the wrong reaction (which it is), what then are the right reactions to the revelation of Jesus' death and resurrection? There are at least three right reactions: first, we should understand the mystery; second, give thanks for it; and third, anticipate our future.

First, we should understand the mystery, namely, how the transfiguration connects with the cross, a mystery that Paul describes clearly in Colossians 1:19–20. Writing of Jesus, Paul says, "In him all the fullness of God was pleased to dwell [we must grasp the incarnation at the transfiguration—Jesus is God's beloved Son], and through him to reconcile to himself all things, whether on earth or in heaven, making peace by the blood of his cross [the cross—the sufferings of the Son of Man for world restoration]." The transfiguration and the crucifixion are connected. We must hold the paradoxical parallels together: the high mountain and the lowly hill, Jesus' standing between two saints and dying between two sinners, the bright clothing and divided rags, the light and the darkness, and the voice of our holy God ("This is my beloved Son," Mark 9:7) and the confession from the pagan centurion who crucifies him ("Truly this man was the Son of God!" 15:39).

Second, we should give thanks. We should give thanks that we cannot have one without the other. John Chrysostom wrote that Jesus was "transfigured to manifest the glory of the cross."[11] Indeed! Who went to the cross for us? The glorious Son of God. Who died for our sins? The glorious Son of God. Who bore the shame? The glorious Son of God. What a savior! Each morning, as I have stated earlier, one of the short prayers I pray is this: "Lord, open my heart to rejoice in you, and fill me with a spirit of gratitude." That should be our constant prayer. We should give thanks that the transfiguration is not the end of the Jesus story. Our hearts should be filled with thankfulness,

> To Him who bore [our] pain;
> [to him] who plumbed the depths of [our] disgrace
> And gave [us] life again;
> [to him] Who crushed [our] curse of sinfulness
> And cloth[es us] in His light.[12]

Third, we should anticipate our future. Before the transfiguration, Moses and Elijah had been dead for a long time. Luke, in his account of this story, says that they then "appeared in glory" (Luke 9:31). However they got there and wherever they returned to, on that day both they and the apostles got a glimpse of their future glory and ours. In Philippians 3:20–21 Paul writes that "our citizenship is in heaven," and, because that is true, we should eagerly "await [our] Savior, the Lord Jesus Christ." Why? What will happen when he returns? He "will transform our lowly body to be like his glorious body." In 2 Corinthians 3:18 Paul writes of the work of the Spirit: as we behold "the glory of the Lord, [we, through the Spirit] are being transformed into the same image [the image of Jesus!] from one degree of glory to another"—the glory that the Father gave the Son, the Son through the Spirit (John 17:22) gives to us. At the transfiguration we are given a glimpse not just into the nature of our Savior but also a glimpse into our own glorious eternal condition. In heaven we will forever reflect the glory of the glorious Son of God. That is our future. That is our purpose for existing. God made us to glorify him forever.

---

11 Chrysostom, "The Gospel of Matthew" (Homily 56.2), quoted in *Matthew 14–28*, ed. Manlio Simonetti, ACCS NT 1B (Downers Grove, IL: InterVarsity Press, 2001), 54.

12 "My Heart Is Filled with Thankfulness." Words and music by Keith Getty and Keith Townend copyright © 2003 Thankyou Music Ltd (PRS) (adm. worldwide at CapitalCMGPublishing.com excluding the UK and Europe which is adm. by IntegratedRights.com). All rights reserved. Used by permission.

In his brilliant book *The Weight of Glory*, C. S. Lewis dwells on that purpose and these scriptural promises. He observes that "there are no *ordinary* people." He states that we "have never talked to a mere mortal." All those we "joke with, work with, marry, snub, and exploit" are destined to either "immortal horror or everlasting splendours." Of the latter he says we should "remember that the dullest and most uninteresting person you can talk to may one day be a creature which, if you saw it now, you would be strongly tempted to worship."[13]

So, to summarize, we should understand the mystery, give thanks for it, and anticipate our future. What a future! Whatever trials and troubles we face, remember that the transformed Jesus, through his Spirit, will one day transform us into his likeness. So press on. Look up. Long for that day.

---

13 C. S. Lewis, *The Weight of Glory* (Grand Rapids, MI: Eerdmans, 1977), 14–15.

Into a Demon-Infested World

MARK 9:14-29

And when Jesus saw that a crowd came running together, he re-
buked the unclean spirit, saying to it, "You mute and deaf spirit,
I command you, come out of him and never enter him again."
Mark 9:25

As recorded in an earlier chapter, I told a joke when I preached on Mark
9:2–13. It was the second joke I have ever told in a sermon. After twenty-six
years of preaching, it was my second joke! That said, I think I am getting
pretty good at joke-telling. So here is a third, and perhaps final, joke of my
calling. (You be the judge and executioner.)

> How many Irishmen does it take to change a lightbulb?
> Five. One to hold the bulb and four to drink whiskey till the room
> starts to spin.

For all its inappropriate humor (ethnic stereotyping, allusions to excessive
drinking), I use that joke because it, and the thousands of others in the "how-
many-does-it-take" genre, has a simple structure. A problem is raised and a
solution is offered. That same twofold structure is found in all the miracle
stories in the Gospels, including the one we find in Mark 9:14–29. Verses
14–24 describe the problem (a problem a bit more difficult than screwing in
a lightbulb), and verses 25–29 the solution (it takes only one man, the right
man for the job—our very sober Savior). So, with Bibles open and our hearts
slowly adjusting back to a pious disposition, let us look first at the problem
presented to our Lord Jesus and second at his solution to it.

The Problem

Before we look at the problem, let me remind us briefly of the context, which
is addressed in the opening clause, "And when they came to the disciples"

(9:14). The "they" are Jesus, Peter, James, and John, who have just been up a mountain and are returning back down after the transfiguration. "The disciples" are the nine remaining apostles, those who stood at the foot of the mountain.

What seems to be the problem? As verse 14 continues, "And when they came to the disciples, they saw a great crowd around them, and scribes arguing with them." What are they arguing about? That is Jesus' precise question (**9:16**). In **9:15** the crowd sees him and is excited to see him, so "greatly amazed" that they "ran up to him and greeted him." It is possible they are "greatly amazed" or "overwhelmed with wonder" (NIV) because something of God's glory is still visible on his clothing or body. Or perhaps they were "greatly amazed" by the timing of his arrival, or that he has arrived at all as he had recently trekked up a large mountain. At this point, they did not expect him to be in the equation, to offer a possible solution to the problem. I also think he likely had some of "the lingering effects of the transfiguration," like "a radiant face,"[1] just as Moses did when he encountered God on Mount Sinai (see Ex. 34:29–30).

And the problem? We have not gotten there yet. Let us look at that now. What is the answer to Jesus' question, "What are you [the scribes] arguing about with them [nine disciples]?" Mark **9:17–19** provides the details.

> And someone from the crowd answered him [here is the problem], "Teacher, I brought my son to you, for he has a spirit that makes him mute. And whenever it seizes him, it throws him down, and he foams and grinds his teeth and becomes rigid. So [since you were not around] I asked your disciples to cast it out, and they were not able [lit., strong enough]."

The problem is twofold. This man's son is demon possessed. That is the first and main problem. And the effects of that possession are severe. The boy cannot speak (the spirit "makes him mute," 9:17) or hear (he is "deaf," 9:25). This seems to be a permanent problem. And then at certain times ("whenever it seizes him") the demon drives the boy to the ground, where he first foams at the mouth and then grinds his teeth. Finally, when the boy has lost all strength, his body becomes like a corpse ("rigid," 9:18). This epileptic-like convulsion Jesus will witness himself (see 9:20), and he will learn that this has been a problem for a while ("from childhood," 9:21). He will also be told that

---

1   Mark L. Strauss, *Mark*, ZECNT (Grand Rapids, MI: Zondervan, 2014), 395–96.

the demon "often" ("often" is an awful word here, and a sad one, too) seeks to kill the child ("destroy him"), casting him "into fire [perhaps the hearth in the home] and into water [perhaps the well outside it]" (9:22).[2]

This is a big problem.

But it is not the only one. The second problem is apostolic impotence. The nine disciples cannot solve the first problem. The father says, "I asked your disciples to cast it out, and they were not able" (9:18; cf. 9:28). Their inability, then, seems to have led to an argument. The scribes (9:14), the professional Bible scholars, are arguing with the disciples. Perhaps they are arguing over the issue of authority, the sense being, "By what authority do you even claim to have the ability to do exorcisms?" Or the argument might be over the disciples' failure. The disciples know they have failed (they will admit so in 9:28), but they are arguing their case. They are defending their credentials and recounting their past successes. They boast, "We do have the power to solve this problem." The scribes say, "Sure you do. Prove it!" The nine cannot wait until Mark's Gospel gets published so that they can read to all those who oppose them, "And [Jesus] called the twelve . . . and gave them authority over the unclean spirits. . . . And they [all of them] cast out *many* demons" (Mark 6:7, 13). Or the argument might be over technique. The scribes are suggesting the right way to do an exorcism. Whatever the argument is about, Jesus has had enough of it.

Having heard the two problems and overhearing the banter about it, Jesus offers two answers. The second answer will be the exorcism. The first will be a prophetic exasperation. "And he answered them, 'O faithless generation, how long am I to be with you? How long am I to bear with you? Bring him to me'" (9:19). Like Moses' descending the mountain, where atop it he glimpsed God's glory and heard his voice, to find God's people worshiping a golden calf (Exodus 32), Jesus descends the mountain to find not idolatry but unbelief, even once again in his own apostles (cf. Mark 6:52; 8:17).

"At the top of the mountain," Bruner writes, "Jesus had shone and glowed; at the foot of the mountain he moans and groans. There we saw his deity; here his humanity."[3] It is true that we see Jesus' humanity as he wears his emotions on his sleeve. Just as he shows his human emotions elsewhere—sorrow, joy, zeal, grief, and compassion—so here he shows "righteous exasperation."[4] But

---

2   Mark's description is vivid. He uses 272 words to tell a story that Matthew will shorten to 110 words and Luke to 144.

3   Frederick Dale Bruner, *Matthew: A Commentary, Volume 2: The Churchbook, Matthew 13–28*, rev. ed. (Grand Rapids, MI: Eerdmans, 2007), 188.

4   Daniel M. Doriani, *Matthew*, REC, 2 vols. (Phillipsburg, NJ: P&R, 2008), 2:119.

his deity is shown here as well. Here our Lord Jesus echoes the Lord God of the Hebrew Bible: "And the LORD said to Moses, 'How long will this people despise me? And how long will they *not believe* in me, in spite of all the signs that I have done among them?'" (Num. 14:11; cf. Num. 14:26–27; Deut. 32:20; Ps. 78:8).

Why is Jesus so upset, with a God-like holy wrath? He is angry because unbelief is no small failure. Some people think unbelief to be like a white lie. "What's the big deal?" Jesus thinks unbelief to be like the great white shark in the movie *Jaws*. Unbelief is a dangerous reality, something that pulls people down—not into the raging sea but into the pit of hell. Some people think other people go to hell because they act like Joseph Stalin, Pol Pot, or Osama bin Laden. Those men are in hell, but they are not in hell simply because of all the wicked ideologies they advocated and ruthless commands they gave. They are in hell because they were unbelievers. The one Savior God sent to save the world was not enough for them to cling to.

Jesus is upset because unbelief is a dangerous and damnable offense. Jesus is also upset because this whole scene is a reminder of how far he is from home. "How long am I to be with you? How long am I to bear with you?" (Mark 9:19). Jesus is going to the cross, but he is also, soon after the cross, returning home to heaven. He has been so patient—thirty-three-years patient. Moments ago, on the Mount of Transfiguration, he had a taste of the fellowship he had had with the Father before his earthly mission. Then, hours later, he is confronted afresh with the evil of this fallen world. He is up against a demon. His own fallen disciples fail him and this poor man's son. The scribes, experts in God's sacred Word, are not only gathered to take Jesus down when he gets down the mount but are in the middle of a cage match with nine of Jesus' hand-picked leaders. Jesus has descended into a dark, demon-infested, sinner-rebellious world.

At the bottom half of Raphael's painting of the transfiguration, the artist (1483–1520) depicts well the sharp contrast between the glorious Jesus on the mountain and the chaos and confusion, along with the opposition and arguments confronting our Lord as soon as he reaches the foot of the mountain. Raphael shows the demon-possessed boy on the right. He is flailing, with his hand reaching out to heaven. The boy's father is attempting to hold him up. He is right beside him, holding on to him. The nine apostles, who are on the left side, look confused. Shadowing and shadows are everywhere. All those details on the bottom half highlight not only their confusion but also the darkness to which Jesus has just reentered.

Let us pause here and ponder afresh the wonder of the incarnation. Think about it: what a sacrifice it was for the beloved Son of God to become a man!

What a sacrifice to move from the high mountain to the low valley, from the transfiguration to this—from his Father's voice of approval to this father's plea for mercy, from pure light to pure darkness, from a taste of heaven to confrontation with hell. Yet (think about this too) what compassion here ("Bring him to me," 9:19). I would have said, "Get him away from me," or, "Get me out of here. Time for another hike up the heaven-near mountain."

Appreciate afresh the incarnation. Bow low. Jesus could have gone back up the mountain to commune with his Father. He could have ordered angels to take him home. But he refused to do so. He stayed the course. What condescension for our salvation; and here what a descent on that day for this boy's deliverance.

The Solution

Let us look next at Jesus' compassion in action—his solution to the problem. In **9:20** we read that "*they* brought the boy to him." (It took a group of people to handle him.) Then the real battle—the main event—begins. The demon puts up a fight. When the demon eyes who he is about to be in the ring with ("when the spirit saw him"), he displays his power over the child. The boy "convulsed" and then "fell on the ground and rolled about, foaming at the mouth," as he had done "from childhood" (**9:20–21**). The father steps in and begs Jesus to "have compassion . . . and help" (**9:22**). The action is building. Can you feel the tension? Next the crowd senses a dramatic confrontation between the beloved Son and this loathsome beast. Like a fight that breaks out in the schoolyard, they come to him "running together" to witness firsthand the face-off (9:25). Then the knockout punch (Jesus' first and only punch) strikes its target. The solution!

> Jesus . . . rebuked the unclean spirit, saying to it, "You mute and deaf spirit [or, "You spirit that keeps this boy from speaking and hearing," NRSV], I command you, come out of him and never enter him again." And after crying out and convulsing him terribly, it came out, and the boy was like a corpse, so that most of them said, "He is dead." But Jesus took him by the hand and lifted him up, and he arose. (**9:25–27**)

In verse 29 Jesus will say, "This kind cannot be driven out by anything but prayer." That is a teaching for the twelve to take to heart, and we will take it to heart too. Soon. But for now just notice the first part of that sentence and the phrase "this kind." That implies that there are different degrees of demons, which of course makes sense. The devil is a demon, the overlord of a vast arsenal of evil spirits. This "spirit" here is not the devil but a fallen angel not far down in the hierarchy. But how well does this high-ranking spirit from the underworld fare against the Son of the Most High God? Not well at all. Jesus gives a swift twofold command, which can be paraphrased, "Get out and never come back." The demon punches back. The demon cries out. The boy convulses, this time "terribly" (9:26), but also for the final time. "It came out" (9:26). It. This is no Stephen King horror novel.[5] This *it* is it. The real thing. A real demon really ousted.

Victory! But one that, at first, looks like a failure. The boy is still. There is no expression on his face. "The boy was like a corpse" (9:26). People wonder, "Is he breathing?" It does not appear so. From the great crowd comes the chorus, "He is dead" (9:26). He is not, but the consensus is that he is. But what does it matter? The one whose life will look like a failure to most (Jesus never defeated the Romans in his lifetime), and whose death will make for a good laugh (ha—some "Son of God," hanging from a Roman cross), takes the boy "by the hand" (the ever-compassionate Christ—hand-holding love!) and lifts him up. Look at the last phrase of verse 27 and marvel. "And he arose." Death. Resurrection. It might just be a pattern to look out for in the Gospel of Mark. Indeed. As Sinclair Ferguson says, "Jesus's actions pointed to the time when he would conquer all the powers of darkness—in the weakness of the cross and the triumph of his own resurrection."[6] Indeed and amen.

Let us pause again, shall we? And what shall we say? Something simple but profound. Be in awe of the resurrection power of Jesus. Soak in the supremacy of the Son. Who can do what Jesus does here? What authority! What power! What authority and power mixed with compassion! Have you ever met a world leader like that? Humble greatness. Great compassion.

Now, there is something more here, something designed especially for us. There is what we might call a second solution Jesus offers to another problem that was under the surface of much of what happened in verses 14–19. That problem was a lack of faith. Jesus labels most, if not all, of the people at the foot of the mountain as "faithless" ("O faithless generation," 9:19). The father of the boy might not be included in this rebuke, because he did, after all, trust that Jesus, and even Jesus' disciples, could do something about the demon. That takes a ton of trust. But his trust is imperfect in a few ways. As we learned last chapter, Jesus should not be called "teacher" or merely "teacher." The man wants Jesus to move a mountain, and yet he calls Jesus

---

5   *It* is the name of a famous horror novel (published 1986) by American author Stephen King. "It" is evil embodied most often in the form of Pennywise the Clown, who preys on young children.
6   Sinclair B. Ferguson, *Let's Study Mark* (repr., Carlisle, PA: Banner of Truth Trust, 2016), 145.

"teacher" (9:17). Bad choice of available titles. Go with "Lord," "Son of God," "Son of Man," or "Son of David." Those are the titles to use.

Also, this father's petition is weak. Look again at the dialogue in verses 22–24. The man says to Jesus, "But if you can do anything, have compassion on us and help us" (9:22). This is very different than what the leper said in 1:40, "If you will, you can make me clean." That leper's "you can" and the father's "if you can" are worlds apart. And Jesus tells him so; he responds with a rebuke: "If you can!" (9:23). It is like asking the 7-foot, 7-inch center whether he can touch the 9-foot basketball net. *Jesus can!* Jesus continues, moving from a stern rebuke to a kind correction: "All things are possible for one who believes" (9:23). Then what happens? I love this. "Immediately the father of the child cried out [he did not care who was listening and what they would think of him] and said, 'I believe; help my unbelief!'" (9:24). This again is an admission of weak or "little" faith, but I wonder how little it is. Mustard-seed sized? That is all that is needed, as Jesus teaches elsewhere, to move a mountain.

"I believe; help my unbelief!" What a prayer. Is there any more human moment, totally relatable moment, than this? What raw authenticity and beautiful honesty. What faith. For all his imperfections, what the man says here is actually a model of faith, one of the greatest models of faith in the Bible. I say that because right before this man's admission Jesus says, "All things are possible for the one who believes" (9:23). Is this man one of the ones? Look at what happens! He *immediately* responds. How? With a prayer, an honest and sincere one. What then? His son is restored. Resurrected! The power of prayer. That prayer. "All things are possible for the one who believes."

What then is the lesson for us? It is the same lesson Jesus gives to the nine—and I am sure he roped in Peter, James, and John as well. He is roping us in now. We are brought into this inner circle to hear what is said in the huddle: "And when he had entered the house, his disciples asked him privately, 'Why could we not cast it out?'" (9:28). It is good they want to learn. A bud of faith here bursts onto the limb. Jesus continues: "And he said to them, 'This kind cannot be driven out by anything but prayer'" (9:29).[7]

Prayer. Wow, after all these fireworks, is this whole passage a little lesson on the simplest thing? What my mother taught me as a boy? Pray? I think so.

7   "The textual variant ['by prayer and fasting'] . . . reflects a common association in the minds of many early Christians. Although apparently originating fairly early in the transmission of the text . . . , the shorter reading ['by prayer'] . . . is supported by early external evidence . . . , and is also most consistent with internal evidence (viz., Jesus' attitude toward fasting as expressed in 2:18–22)." Rodney J. Decker, *Mark 9–16: A Handbook on the Greek Text* (Waco, TX: Baylor University Press, 2014), 24.

And again, how great of our humble Lord. He is heading to Jerusalem, where he will die like a common criminal. And what here does he do? He gives instruction to his earliest followers and all who will come after. What then is the word? Have faith in faith? No. It is the object not the subject of faith that matters most. Learn that. Is it, "Have enough faith within yourself to move the hand of God to give you whatever you want, even if it is against his revealed and sovereign will?" God forbid! That is the wicked teaching of the health-wealth gospel. The satanic stuff you most often see on "Christian" television.

What then is the stuff that makes our soul's longings rise to transfiguration heights? It is prayer like this, prayer like the short two-part prayer the father of the boy prays. It is belief in Jesus. It is, specifically, belief in Jesus' power to do something about your problem. There is limitless power in his hands. "I believe." It is that. But it is also admitting our weakness and impotence and humbly begging for Christ's help. "I believe. Help my unbelief."

Compare that prayer with what the disciples say to Jesus in verse 28. "Why could *we* not cast it out?" There is one really wrong word there. "We." They believed in themselves, so much so that it never dawned on any of them (nine of them, and likely after nine tries—"Me first. Stand aside, my turn. Mine.") to stop and pray. Why? Prayer requires humility. They are not yet humble men. It will take a few more lessons, perhaps the greatest lesson of all—the humble sufferings and death of the beloved Son of God—for them to learn that lesson. In the next scene in Mark we will read that "on the way they had argued with one another about who was the greatest" (9:34). The human ego is amazing, is it not? Like Narcissus the twelve loved looking at their reflections in the water. Thankfully, only one of them (not all twelve!) would fall in and drown. There is some hope for even the remaining eleven, and for us as well.

The lesson here is so important. It is to learn, in Christ's own words, that apart from him we "can do nothing" (John 15:5). A little something? No. Add something to our justification? No. Add something to our sanctification? Wrong again. Faith is trust in Christ and his finished work alone. It is not peppered with a dash of self-reliance.

But, that said, faith is not dead. It is active. It works. Apart from Jesus' work in us we "can do nothing" (John 15:5). But "through him who gives [us] strength" (NIV), as Paul puts it in Philippians 4:13, we "can do all things." That is not a slogan to hang on the wall of a Christian college weight room. "I can bench press five hundred pounds if I just pray hard enough." But it is a life verse that should hang in our homes and within our hearts.

What is the nature of genuine Christian faith? Simple. We have it here in story form. Faith is humble reliance on Jesus. More specifically, as it relates to the details of this specific text, faith is prayerful reliance on Jesus and his ability to overthrow evil. And then, as it relates to the connection between faith and prayer, and to put the theme taught here more metaphorically: "Prayer is simply faith breathing."[8]

Get in Shape

How is your breathing? When I am not writing sermons, and learning new jokes for sermons, I exercise. Well, a bit. I do a ten-minute core workout three times a week. After about thirty-seconds into it, I start to breathe heavily. Whew. Whew. Whew. Every half-second. That breathing technique, along with the exercise, for those few minutes has become my routine. A habit. A good habit. How is your prayer life? I have a simple starter workout routine for you. I am still serious now. Get up every morning and pray one simple prayer for one month. A five second workout. Pray, "I believe. Help my unbelief." Breathe. Let me say it again. "I believe. Help my unbelief."

8   Bruner, *Churchbook*, 191.

Three Major Misunderstandings

MARK 9:30-41

They went on from there and passed through Galilee. And he did not want anyone to know, for he was teaching his disciples, saying to them, "The Son of Man is going to be delivered into the hands of men, and they will kill him. And when he is killed, after three days he will rise." But they did not understand the saying, and were afraid to ask him.
Mark 9:30–32

Have you ever been misunderstood?

Deborah Tannen, professor of linguistics at Georgetown University, has written a number of books on communication, including titles such as *That's Not What I Meant* and *You Just Don't Understand*. With those titles in mind, I imagined myself at the local library asking the librarian for those two books. "Excuse me. I'm looking for two books. I don't see them anywhere in your database. Perhaps I can get them through interlibrary loan. Can you help with that?"

"Sure," she says. "What's the first title?"

I respond, "*That's Not What I Meant.*"

She says, "Okay, what then do you mean?"

I laugh. "No, *That's Not What I Meant* is the title of the first book I want."

She looks confused. "Okay. I'm not sure I'm following. Let's just try the second book. What's the title of the other book you are looking for?"

I reply, "*You Just Don't Understand.*"

She slams down her fist on the computer keys. "What do you mean, 'I don't understand'? I'm trying to help."

"No, no, no," I say. "*That's Not What I Meant* and *You Just Don't Understand*—those are the titles of the books. Honestly."

She rolls her eyes and thinks, "Men."

No one likes to be misunderstood. I do not like it when I make a point in a sermon about trusting fully in Christ and him alone and then someone comes up to me afterward and says, "You're right, pastor. I do need to believe in myself. I liked it when you suggested that." For the record, that specific example did not happen, but something like it does happen from time to time. And I am sure you have your long list of times you might have said to the leaders of your church, the boss at work, or a family member at home, "That's not what I meant," or "You just don't understand."

In the Gospel of Mark we see in black and white all the times that the disciples misunderstand their Lord and ours. When Jesus speaks in parables, they do not understand (Mark 4:13). When he multiplies the loaves (twice!), after both miracles "they did not understand" the significance of the events (6:52; cf. 8:17–18, 21). They misunderstand the nature of true purity, thinking outward purity, like a clean hand, is more important than inward purity, like a clean heart (7:18). They do not understand the transfiguration, wanting to build a tabernacle for the divine *logos*, who himself tabernacles among us and cannot be housed in some twig temple (9:5–6). They misunderstand their dependence on God, as highlighted last chapter in their lack of prayer (9:28–29). And they misunderstand the mission of the cross, be it Peter's bad counsel after the first passion prediction ("Peter took him aside and began to rebuke him," 8:32) or here in our text, in which Jesus again speaks of being "killed" (9:31) and they do not speak. They remain silent because "they did not understand" (9:32).

As you can see from the title of this chapter, there are three misunderstandings here, major misunderstandings. The first centers on Jesus' death and resurrection. The second on the nature of true greatness. The third on the scope of the kingdom. We will take each of these in turn.

The First Misunderstanding

The first misunderstanding centers on Jesus' death and resurrection (**9:30–32**). The scene starts with a shift in locations, the twenty-second shift we have seen thus far. Jesus is not sitting still. One reason he is on the move is to spread the good news of the kingdom. Another reason is that the religious authorities are seeking to find ways to track him down and take him out. A final reason Jesus is on the move is that he wants to pound into the heads of his dimwitted disciples the most foundational truths of the Christian faith.

Verse 30 begins with their movement ("They went on from there and passed through Galilee"—they are heading southwest again), followed by his motive ("and he did not want anyone [but these twelve] to know" where he was headed). Why? He wants to be alone with them. He wants to school them in the salvation story, along with the attitude and actions that must accompany godly leadership—those who share that story with the world. If they are to represent him on earth, they better get the message and medium down and then give it straight as they live straight.

So look at verse 31, where we read, "For he was teaching, . . . 'The Son of Man is going to be delivered into the hands of men, and they will kill him. And when he is killed, after three days he will rise." The verb "he was teaching" implies a continuous action. He is teaching the same lesson repeatedly. For part of the 27 miles—the distance from Caesarea Philippi (8:27) to Capernaum (9:33)—he delivers the same short sermon. Imagine that. A marathon with the Messiah in which he gives, along the way, a three-point sermon: (point one) "The Son of Man [point two] is going to be delivered into the hands of men, and they will kill him. And [point three] when he is killed, after three days he will rise."

What then is their response to Jesus' short, repetitive, three-point sermon? Silence. What! Not a single "Amen"? None. No words. No words from anyone. Not even Peter? Even Peter is silent. (This might be the greatest miracle recorded in Mark!) But why? Why are they all silent? They are silent because twelve out of the twelve have no idea what he is talking about ("They did not understand the saying," 9:32), and they obviously think this time, instead of offending Jesus or saying something imprudent (e.g., Peter's recent three tents for three great guys proposal), they will just listen. I imagine them nodding along with each point, like mindless bobblehead dolls when you press the head. Mark tells us that they are "afraid to ask" (9:32) because to do so (to say, "None of us understands a word you are talking about") might upset Jesus yet again. The last thing they want to hear is what they heard quite recently, Jesus' "Do you not *yet* understand?" (8:21). That "yet" is hanging over their heads.

What should we make of their misunderstanding? That is, how might we apply their mistake here? Simple. If there is any message we need to understand, it is the details of Jesus' three-point sermon, summarized in verse 31.

Point one: it was the Son of Man who was killed at Calvary.

Fourteen times the title "the Son of Man" is used in Mark, each time on the lips of Jesus. Jesus alone calls himself "the Son of Man." What else does he call himself? What other titles does he use? Here in verse 41 he labels himself "Christ," as in 12:35 (cf. 13:21; 14:61–62), where he speaks of "the Christ" as the "son of David." But that is it. "The Son of Man" is who he says he is. But who is "the Son of Man?" I have said this before, but it is worth repeating, as there might still be some dullness among the disciples reading this commentary. The title, as Jesus uses it, is "linked to Daniel 7:13, where 'one like a son of man' is brought on the clouds of heaven to 'the Ancient of Days,' being vindicated after a period of suffering, and is given kingly power."[1] We know this is how Jesus thinks of himself, because at his trial the high priest asks, "Are you the Christ, the Son of the Blessed?" (Mark 14:61), and Jesus replies, "I am, and you will see the Son of Man seated at the right hand of power, and coming with the clouds of heaven" (14:62). Jesus uses the title "the Son of Man" because the story of Daniel 7 is played out perfectly in his life. He suffers. He is vindicated. He comes again to judge. He rules a forever kingdom forevermore.

That is point one. I hope you have got it lodged into your cranium. Point two is that this holy and glorious and powerful being (here is the paradox of our faith) "is going to be delivered into the hands of men, and they will kill him." Notice the grammar here. The verb "going to be delivered" (or "will be handed over") is what Greek scholars call a futuristic present. That is, Jesus is not speculating here. "I might die. Maybe not." He is certain. He will die, sometime in the near future. Also notice the subject, or lack thereof, of that verb. Who is going to hand Jesus over? Jesus might mean Judas, as Judas indeed will hand Jesus over to the Jewish authorities (14:44). Or our Lord might mean those Jews who hand him over to Pilate (15:1, 10), or Pilate, who also hands him over to the soldiers to be crucified (15:15). However, I think it is best to think of God as the subject of the verb. This is what is called a divine passive. God will deliver up his own Son as a sacrifice to save us from our sins. This idea is certainly supported elsewhere in the Bible. For example, in the Greek translation of the Hebrew Scriptures Isaiah writes of the suffering servant, "The LORD has laid on [same verb] him the iniquity of us all" (Isa. 53:6 LXX). And Paul uses this same verb in Romans 4:25, where he writes that Jesus "was delivered up [same verb] for our trespasses and raised for our justification."

Speaking of Jesus' resurrection, let us move on to point three. Point three is that the Son of Man, after three days in the grave, will rise from the dead.

The disciples here struggled to comprehend this statement about Jesus' personal resurrection because they believed, as Jews of their time did, that there would be a final resurrection of the dead. But that would be on the day of the Lord, when God would raise all the dead and judge all people. So, for Jesus to speak of a personal resurrection—his midhistory resurrection, no less—makes little sense. They do not have an intellectual category for it. Also,

---

1   N. T. Wright, *Matthew for Everyone: Chapters 1–15* (London: SPCK, 2004), 221.

they have witnessed Jesus raise the dead (5:41–42). But, if he himself was dead, who would raise him?

We, of course, live after the fact. We know Jesus rose from the dead. These same men, then the dumbfounded doubters, soon after became the very eyewitness testimony we trust. I believe in the resurrection, as you should believe in the resurrection, because these men saw, heard, touched, and then proclaimed, "Christ has died; Christ has risen."

The Second Misunderstanding

The first misunderstanding centers on Jesus' death and resurrection. The disciples do not yet get the gospel. Let us make sure we do get it. The second misunderstanding centers on the nature of true greatness (**9:33–37**). Mark begins with their arrival to their ministry headquarters: "And they came to Capernaum" and entered into "the house," likely a reference to Peter and Andrew's house (9:33; cf. 1:29).

Imagine Peter and Andrew's wives and children embracing them when they finally arrive home. Then imagine, later that day, the men standing on the flat rooftop, looking out across the Sea of Galilee as the sun starts to set. Peter's mother-in-law climbs the back stairs and serves them some refreshments. This is so like her. A servant (1:31)! Then Jesus eyes his closest companions, each one of them (in her presence, I imagine), and asks, "So, men, I'm just curious, before we hit the hay, 'What were you discussing on the way?'" (9:33). That question is a conversation killer. Silence. Dead silence, again. "Peter? Nothing to say? Matthew? Thaddeus? Come on Thaddeus, you'll get a line in the NT if you say something now." They all "kept silent" (9:34a). The reason given is this: "For on the way they had argued with one another about who was the greatest" (9:34b). They are silent because they know they should not have been arguing about that topic. Great shame makes for great silence.

Can you imagine the conversation on the way? I can. I would imagine that it started with James and John, the sons of thunder, who will later ask Jesus if they can sit on the thrones next to his throne when he comes to power (10:37). So they say to the nine who were not asked to journey with Jesus up the mountain and witness the transfiguration, "Expel any demons lately?" Simon the Zealot throws a punch. "We're just teasing," they say. "But listen, guys, it is time we come to an understanding of who ranks where in this newly established kingdom Jesus has been talking about. If he is the king, who is next in line?" Peter says, "I am, obviously." That might be the logical deduction at this point, if ranking is to be done. Peter was called first. Peter alone gave the great confession. Peter witnessed the transfiguration. But that obvious answer obviously did not go over well. For their discussion—which covered 27 miles of terrain—did not end there. I am sure all Peter's flaws were pointed out. I am sure that others gave the grounds for their high ranking. I am sure no one suggested that they be ranked number twelve.

It might seem curious to us why they would argue over the question, Who is the greatest? in the first place. Their timing, as I mentioned last chapter, is awful.[2] Jesus has just reprimanded them, along with the scribes and crowd, in his pronouncement, "O faithless generation!" (9:19). He has also taught them about the power of prayer. Humble reliance on Jesus' authority over evil through prayer is to be their constant disposition. Then, of course, just days before that, he had taught them that great lesson on self-denial ("If anyone would come after me, let him deny himself," 8:34).

Jesus knows, after they have broken their silence, that another lesson is, sadly and obviously, necessary. He knows that he needs, once again, to turn upside down the foundational values of their honor/shame culture, where ranking and boasting about such ranking are the norms of everyday life. Verses 35–37 record the CliffsNotes for that session in the school of Christ:

> And he sat down and called the twelve. And he said to them, "If anyone would be first, he must be last of all and servant of all." And he took a child and put him in the midst of them, and taking him in his arms, he said to them, "Whoever receives one such child in my name receives me, and whoever receives me, receives not me but him who sent me."

Notice Jesus' posture. He sits. That is a position of authority. A king sits on a throne. A rabbi sits to teach. Think of the times in the Gospels when Jesus sits: when he delivers the Sermon on the Mount, the Olivet Discourse, and here—for a smaller but no less important sermon. Notice also the formal calling. "And he sat down and *called* the twelve." The last time he called each and every one of them was when he said, "Follow me," and they all left everything and followed. He is about to call them to something important, or perhaps he is re-calling them. "Men, let's start over. Your calling to me, take two."

Then follows the instruction: "If anyone would be first, he must be last of all and servant of all" (9:35). To Jesus, success in God's kingdom demands both the attitude (I am willing to be last and thought of as a nobody) and the

---

2   We might also add, as J. C. Ryle does, this observation: "Who would have thought that a few fishermen and publicans could have been overcome by emulation and the desire of supremacy?" *Expository Thoughts on Mark*, quoted in *CHSB*, 1489.

actions of humility (I am willing to serve everybody, even those below my status). In the ancient Near East every aspect of life fell under the question, Who is the greatest? Whether one was a Jew living in Jerusalem or a Gentile in Rome, one could not walk into a court of law, the marketplace, a temple, or any home without knowing or soon learning who was who and where everyone ranked. A servant was not above his master, the poor above the rich, or a child above his parents. So, you see, what Jesus is teaching here is radical. It is radically countercultural.

And, it is radically counternatural.[3]

Why did so many Americans like Donald Trump's successful 2016 presidential campaign slogan, "Make America Great Again"? People liked it likely because they agreed that America was losing its place among the ranks of other countries. They liked it also because Americans like being first—atop the world. The best universities. The best military. The best technology. We like America to be first because we like being first. I doubt any political candidate these days could ever win a campaign, even at the local level, on any of Jesus' slogans. Why? Because what our Lord says is strange to us. It is counternatural. R. C. Sproul said of Jesus' saying here in Mark 9:35,

> He turned the values and the aspirations of all human beings upside down. Every one of us is born with an aspiration for significance. We want our lives to count. We do not want to fail to achieve the goals we pursue in our lives. The last thing we want to do is to come in last. We are not satisfied with mediocrity. We dream of glory, of winning, of reaching the pinnacle of success, of getting to the top, of attaining greatness, of being the best. What Friedrich Nietzsche called "the will to power" beats in the heart of every human being.[4]

"Make America Great" sounds as good to us as "Make Me Great." We naturally love what the Reformers called a "theology of glory" and disdain Jesus' "theology of the cross"—that death leads to resurrection, servanthood to exaltation. "Whoever exalts himself will be humbled, and whoever humbles himself will be exalted" (Matt. 23:12).

Next, to illustrate his point, our Lord offers an object lesson. What does it mean to be a servant leader? It is to do what Jesus does next. "And he took

---

3 See R. Kent Hughes, *Mark: Jesus, Servant and Savior*, PTW, 2 vols. (Wheaton, IL: Crossway, 1989), 2:31.

4 R. C. Sproul, *Mark*, St. Andrew's Expositional Commentary (Sanford, FL: Reformation Trust, 2015), 230.

a child and put him in the midst of them, and taking him in his arms, he said to them, 'Whoever receives one such child in my name receives me, and whoever receives me, receives not me but him who sent me'" (Mark 9:36–37). Imagine here Peter's youngest son. He climbs up the stairs to listen in on the conversation. Jesus sees him. He motions to him. The boy runs to Jesus. Our Lord then picks him up and places him on his lap. The boy laughs. The disciples wonder. No great man in their society would do this. What a strange spectacle.

The point of this visual parable is that even those on the lowest end of the social spectrum—like a little Jewish boy from a small town within the vast Roman Empire—matters. The disciples here, and disciples from here on out, will always be tempted to think ministry to those who matter matters most—the influential, the accomplished, the acclaimed, the affluent. Here Jesus teaches that what matters most is accepting all, especially those least accepted by the world. For to welcome anyone who is like a child (What influence do they have in the world?) is to welcome Jesus himself. And to welcome Jesus is to welcome God the Father (cf. John 13:20).

I know that some Christians believe that being a pastor is the greatest thing a Christian can do to serve God. I do think the calling to preach God's Word, administer his sacraments, and shepherd his people is a high calling. But I also know that those who sacrifice their time to watch and teach children, those who teach Sunday school to the mentally disabled, those who clean up after everyone is gone—often thankless, seemingly insignificant tasks—are doing something great. Who is going to interview them for that? Who is going to offer them a book contract? Ah, but who is going to reward them? I will tell you who. Jesus will reward them on the last day. So, for all of us, the lesson is plain: chin up and head down. Keep following our cross-bearing Lord's lead into eternal glory.

The Third Misunderstanding

In Mark 9:30–41 the Evangelist highlights three major misunderstandings: the disciples misunderstand, first, the gospel of Jesus' death and resurrection; second, the nature of true greatness (that down is the way up); and third, the scope of the kingdom. We turn to **9:38–41**. Perhaps feeling something of the sting of what Jesus has just said, the apostle John offers a confession, or, more likely, he displays a total misunderstanding of what Jesus has just said:

> John said to him, "Teacher, we saw someone casting out demons in your name, and we tried to stop him, because he was not following us"

[underline "us"; shouldn't it be "you"—Jesus?]. But Jesus said, "Do not stop him, for no one who does a mighty work in my name will be able soon afterward to speak evil of me. For the one who is not against us is for us. For truly, I say to you, whoever gives you a cup of water to drink because you belong to Christ will by no means lose his reward."

John's comment and commentary unearth a spirit of proud exclusivism. He basically says, "We saw someone doing what you gave just us the power to do—cast out demons (even though nine of us did not fare so well the other day). So we told him to stop acting like an apostle. There is one true church, and it is we twelve. Please wait for a satellite campus of St. John the Apostle's to come to your town, and then we might allow you to do something for Jesus."

Intolerance and envy—what amazing vices! Such vices will make even the wisest leaders say the most foolish things. Do you remember what Joshua said to Moses when he heard of two other men's prophesying? He said, "Moses, stop them" (Num. 11:28). Moses' response is brilliant: "Are you jealous for my sake? Would that all of the LORD's people were prophets, that the LORD would put his Spirit on them!" (Num. 11:29). Do you have Moses' attitude? More importantly, do you have Jesus' attitude when he says (and I paraphrase), "Don't be dumb. If someone is doing something pro-Jesus (like ousting evil), he cannot at the same time be anti-Christ. Anyone who belongs to me (is in our camp, which is [Luke 10:1–17], and certainly will be, bigger than you twelve) and does something great (an exorcism) or seemingly not so great (bringing a cup of cold water to someone who is thirsty, or simply identifying with me) will be, should be, praised.[5] His reward will be great (see Matt. 25:34–40). Or, at the very least, he should not be excluded from Christian ministry."

Let me ask you: Do you think that "the advancement of the kingdom of God is more important than personal ambition?"[6] Or what about denominational distinctions? I am a Presbyterian minister because I believe that the Westminster Standards offer the church the clearest and best summary of biblical doctrine. Yet from time to time I honestly struggle to treat the other gospel-preaching churches in town like branches of the same business—hoping we all prosper together for the good of the company. I treat them like, I would imagine, one bank treats another: "So glad you are doing well. We hope and pray that we will soon shut you down and take you over." If the church down the road, the one next door, or any of the churches in town prospers in true

5   Sproul, *Mark*, 34.
6   Mark L. Strauss, *Mark*, ZECNT (Grand Rapids, MI: Zondervan, 2014), 410.

gospel conversions, we should offer to throw the angel-rejoicing celebration. One of the evilest things in the world is when true believers, and true believing churches, compete against each other. Let us not spend a dime from our annual budgets building a wall. Instead let us fly the flag, "In essentials unity, in non-essentials liberty, in all things charity."[7] You might say I am a lover, not a fighter, but, let me tell you, I am a lover of truth and a fighter for it, and the truth here is that those Christians and those churches that are not against us are for us, and we for them. Competition for power and people, attendance and influence, is how the world works, not how the church should work.

I am reminded of the time I set out to plant a church in Naperville, Illinois. I met with the pastor of a vibrant and large church there. We had a good conversation about the demographics of the community. At the end I said, "Can I ask you an honest question?" He said, "Sure." I asked, "Are you at all bothered that I'm thinking about planting a church in Naperville?" He said, "Absolutely not." He leaned over and whispered, "There are one hundred thousand people in this town that don't go to church. One hundred thousand! There is plenty of room for more churches here."

Let us not misunderstand the scope, the generous scope, of Christ's kingdom.

Misunderstandings in the Kitchen

In the O'Donnell home our kitchen features a large chalkboard. My wife often writes a verse of Scripture on the board or sticks little cards on the kitchen windows. She has done that, or something like that, throughout our marriage. I remember, years ago, waking up in the morning and finding a verse from Proverbs posted on the coffeemaker. I usually get up first and make coffee. It was Proverbs 25:27, "It is not good to eat much honey, nor it is glorious to seek one's own glory."

"Ouch," I thought.

When she got up and I humbly served her some coffee, I said, "Thanks for the subtle rebuke." She said, "What are you talking about?" I said, "The Proverbs verse over there." She laughed and replied, "That isn't for you. It is for me and the kids to memorize." I said, "Well, then, it is for the whole family to memorize." Indeed, it is for the whole church family to memorize. "It is not . . . glorious to seek one's own glory." Whatever misunderstandings we might have with each other, let us not misunderstand the gospel, the nature of true greatness, and the scope of God's reign.

---

7   This famous saying, often attributed to Augustine, was penned by Rupertus Meldenius, a German Lutheran theologian in a tract on Christian unity that was written during (c. 1627) the Thirty Years War (1618–1648).

Two Tough Teachings

HELL AND DIVORCE

MARK 9:42–10:12

And he left there and went to the region of Judea and
beyond the Jordan, and crowds gathered to him again. And
again, as was his custom, he taught them.
Mark 10:1

A recent article in the news attracted my attention. The headline read, "Monty Python's 'Always Look on the Bright Side of Life' has become the most popular tune to play at a UK funeral."[1] That song, from the sacrilegious comedy *Life of Brian*, is a ballad that Brian, who was mistakenly taken for Jesus of Nazareth, sings while dying on the cross. Trying to cheer up all those on crosses around him, he sings lines such as "Forget about your sin; give the audience a grin." Eventually, in the tradition of musicals, the other cross-bearing criminals join in the chorus, "Always look on the bright side of life." They are swinging back and forth on their crosses, smiling and singing. The scene is funny to many. Absurd to most. Wicked to me, and hopefully to you as well. It is not a song to be sung at all, least of all at a funeral.

That song's popularity, the article further reports, passed Frank Sinatra's "My Way" as the favorite selection. We can be glad that "My Way" is moving down the list. But how do we explain how the song "Always Look on the Bright Side of Life" has moved up, even to the top? The article offers this motive: "David Collingwood, of the co-operative Funeralcare, suggested the findings represented 'a generational shift in attitudes towards funerals.'" That is true and obvious enough. But we might suggest a deeper motive. In the United Kingdom, as in most parts of the Western world, people do not know

1   "Monty Python Tune Tops Funeral Songs," Entertainment & Arts, *BBC*, November, 21, 2014,
    https://www.bbc.com/news/entertainment-arts-30143250.

what to do with death. So why not laugh at it? Why not mock what Christianity has to say about it? Why not treat it like a sitcom or a classic comedy? I think there is also a darker motive, namely, subtle suggestions from the underworld to not take seriously the question of what to do with death.

Triviality is perhaps Satan's greatest weapon in the modern world. Take something serious like death and laugh at it. Take something serious like hell and have brilliant comedians (cf. George Carlin's famous routine "The Difference between Heaven and Hell") and comic strip writers (Gary Larson's *The Far Side*) make us fall over laughing so that, in the end, we think the concept itself is laughable. Well, in this chapter, God forbid if we laugh about our text's two topics: hell and divorce. Instead let us listen soberly to what our Lord has to teach, and let us let his teaching stem the tide of triviality in our own lives.

An Eternal Hell

The first tough topic is hell, which Jesus introduces in Mark **9:42–50**. Jesus brings up the doctrine of hell not because he is teaching a class on systematic theology and it happens to be the next topic in the syllabus. Rather he turns to the topic because a new, but related, thought is triggered in his mind. In Mark 9:41 he spoke of a simple and seemingly insignificant act of kindness: someone's bringing a cup of water to someone who is on his side. That person, he says, "will by no means lose his reward" (9:41). Two thoughts—the prospect of eternal reward and the reality of our need for water—seem to press our Lord to talk about not just eternal rewards but eternal punishments. I also think that the child in his arms (9:36) presses against his pure soul all the wicked acts perpetrated against children—and against those like children, the lowly and vulnerable. What will happen to those who abuse and exploit the weak? Moreover, what will happen to those who oppose Jesus, those who will not bow the knee before the humble and sacrificial Son of Man? It will not be a slap on the wrist. It will not be a time-out for ten minutes. In graphic language our loving Lord tells us, and all in the world who will listen, that hell is a place no one wants to occupy:

> Whoever causes one of these little ones who believe in me to sin, it would be better for him if a great millstone were hung around his neck and he were thrown into the sea. And if your hand causes you to sin, cut it off. It is better for you to enter life crippled than with two hands to go to hell, to the unquenchable fire. And if your foot causes you to sin, cut it off. It is better for you to enter life lame than with two feet to be thrown into hell. And if your eye causes you to sin, tear it out. It is better for you to enter the kingdom of God with one eye than with two eyes to be thrown

into hell, "where their worm does not die and the fire is not quenched."
For everyone will be salted with fire. (9:42–49)

Notice, first, that our Lord speaks of hell (3x) in the same breath as fire (3x).
Hellfire.[2] In verse 49 he says that "everyone" in hell "will be salted with fire."
The image of salt and fire is a common image in the Bible of divine judgment,
such as God's judgment on Sodom in Genesis (see Gen. 19:24–26; cf. Isa.
43:2) and his judgment of all evildoers in Revelation (Rev. 19:20). Earlier, in
Mark 9:43, 48, Jesus speaks of hell as an "unquenchable fire," a place where
"the fire is not quenched."

Second, to speak of "unquenchable fire" (9:43) and of a place where living
things (grotesque things, like worms) will "not die" (9:48; quoting Isa. 66:24)
is to speak of eternal and ongoing punishment. That unquenchable fire (in
Mark 9:44, 48; cf. 9:49) is contrasted with what comes before it, an image of
certain death (9:42). The contrast is shocking between an immediate earthly
death and an eternal "second death" (Rev. 20:14).

Imagine the worst possible earthly death. How about this: Somehow "a
great millstone" (Gk. "a millstone of a donkey") is hung around your neck.
Then you are taken out to the middle of a deep lake and dropped in. It would
not take you long, with that dense concrete collar, to hit the bottom. What a
horrific way to go. Yet that death "would be better" (Mark 9:42), Jesus teaches,
than the unquenchable fire of hell.

Third, Jesus speaks of being "thrown into hell" (9:45, 47), which parallels
the idea of being "thrown into the sea" (9:42). Jesus does not say who is doing
the throwing, but God is the implied subject, as he is the ultimate judge (cf.
Matt. 10:28). In Revelation he sends out his angels to judge evildoers. The
beast, the false prophet, and all those they have deceived are "thrown alive
into the lake of fire" (Rev. 19:20), where "they will be tormented day and night
forever and ever" (Rev. 20:10). These are sober thoughts. Our Lord "knows
nothing of an easy universalism or of a 'second chance' after death, or even of
a limited period of punishment."[3] He does not water down hell.

Fourth, Jesus presents all these awful images of the afterlife to his disciples
so that they might avoid hell,[4] but also so they might live godly lives on earth.

---

2   The Greek word for "hell" is *Gehenna*. "Gehenna, the eternally smouldering rubbish-dump
    outside Jerusalem, is the symbol of the final fate of those who have rebelled against God."
    R. Alan Cole, *Mark*, TNTC (Downers Grove, IL: IVP Academic, 1989), 228.

3   Cole, *Mark*, 228–29.

4   "Jesus . . . spoke of hell to professed saints, and of heaven to acknowledged sinners, unlike
    many other preachers" (Cole, *Mark*, 228). The disciples are his audience—believers, not unbe-
    lievers!

Ethics are actually his emphasis. He begins, "Whoever causes one of these little ones who believe in me to sin . . ." (Mark 9:42) and quickly moves to "And if your hand causes you to sin, cut it off" (9:43). Notice the link between one believer's sin being the cause of another believer's sin. The "your" and "you" ("if your hand cause you to sin") in the original context is the twelve, those men who have walked with Jesus for almost three years. We can call them, for all their faults, committed followers. The "little ones who believe in" Jesus (9:42), in the original context, are the children present in the house that day. Today (and this was the intent of what Jesus taught then, not only today) the "little ones" represent any of his disciples, including children, who might be susceptible to spiritual shipwreck. Thus the point is that the committed ought to cut off sin in their lives so as not to cause the susceptible to stumble.

Jesus does not name the specific sin the committed Christian needs to cut off. It could be sexual sin, as in the Sermon on the Mount (see Matt. 5:27–30). However, in light of the last chapter (and obviously Mark 9:42–50 follows right on the heels of 9:33–41) there are additional possibilities. The sin could be misunderstanding or miscommunicating the gospel. You will often find spiritual failures and backsliding in "little ones" when pastors and parents fail to teach faithfully and repeatedly that the Son of Man died and rose for our salvation. The sin could be pride. When Christian leaders argue over who is the greatest (like the twelve did), it does great harm to new believers and those struggling to keep the faith. The sin could be narrow-mindedness and a lack of charity toward other Christians. When churches are run like private country clubs or, worse, business monopolies, those young in the faith, who have just *escaped* the world, wonder why in the world the church is acting so much *like* the world.

Or, related to that specific sin and all the sins mentioned thus far, and also related to what is said in verse 50, Jesus could be referencing division within the church. "Salt is good," says Jesus, "but if the salt has lost its saltiness, how will you make it salty again? Have salt in yourselves, and be at peace with one another." The ambiguous command "Have salt in yourselves" is interpreted by the unambiguous command "Be at peace with one another." The twelve were arguing among themselves (9:34) and were arguing with those who were doing kingdom work (9:38). When such division happens, the church loses its pure witness to the world and within the church — its saltiness. It is like the salt around the Dead Sea, a salt that, when the water evaporates, looks like salt and has some of the chemical characteristics of salt but has no life to it. That is, the salt flavor cannot be tasted nor used to preserve food. It is useless.

Against that sin, or any of the sins listed above, Jesus next calls for decisive, immediate, and absolute action. Whatever the cause of the sin—be it "your hand," "your foot," or "your eye" (fairly important body parts)[5]—"cut it off" or "tear it out" (9:43, 45, 47). These three parallel imperatives are hyperbolic; that is, Jesus is speaking metaphorically, not literally.[6] So put the knife down, please! Call off the surgery. But do not call off serious urgency. "Be killing sin or it will be killing you."[7] Self-denial should feel like self-mutilation. Cutting off sin hurts.

But the action here, remember, is not just that of self-preservation—to avoid hellfire. It is that we help the "little ones" to avoid it too. We are in this together. We help each other persevere. So, committed Christian, let me ask you, are you willing to cut off sin in your lives (lust, pride, a spirit of division, teaching an incomplete gospel) so as not be a hindrance to others and so as to be a model of Christian discipleship (self-denial and cross-bearing)? Let us "decide [now!] never to put a stumbling block or hindrance in the way of" another (Rom. 14:13; cf. 1 Cor. 9:12).

That is what Jesus in Mark 9:42–50 teaches about hell.

Dick Lucas's excellent twenty-minute evangelistic talk on these verses ends with a short story in which a new pastor was called to an old church. This old, established church had long moved away from the great truths of the gospel, but they still had their annual "revival" meetings where they brought in an itinerant evangelist to give talks for four straight nights. When the evangelist arrived, the pastor told him that the congregation was a bit touchy when it came to any talk on judgment, hell, and damnation; and, if he would be so kind, please to avoid such subjects. The visiting minister said, "I have a solution. What if I just preach on John 3:16? Would that be alright?" "Certainly," said the pastor. "An excellent idea." So, on the first night he preached on "For God so loved the world." The second night he preached on "that he gave his only Son." The third night he preached on "that whoever believes in him." Then, the fourth night, he asked the pastor, "Is it alright that I continue on?" The pastor said, "Certainly; everyone is enjoying your messages on God's love." So, he gave his final sermon, which began, "For God so loved the world that he gave his only Son that whoever believes in him *should not perish*."[8] Jesus saved us from perishing. Divine judgment. Damnation. Hellfire.

---

5   It is possible that a person's *hand* and *foot* are references to sinful actions (sins we commit) and the *eye* to sinful thoughts (sins we desire to commit).

6   This is a common enough genre in Jesus' teaching ministry (e.g., Mark 10:25; Matt. 7:3–5; 18:9).

7   John Owen, *The Mortification of Sin in Believers* (London: The Religious Tract Society, 1799), 9.

8   For the full talk see Dick Lucas, "Time & Eternity 6," sermon, The Gospel Coalition, mp3 format, 26:35, https://www.thegospelcoalition.org/sermon/time-eternity-6/, accessed on June 14, 2023.

My older brother, a churchgoer, often calls me on Sunday afternoon. We have a wonderful relationship. I love my brother. Yet he will sometimes say, sarcastically, "So, did you give them the fire and brimstone this morning?" I will usually think, "Well, if there is fire and brimstone, or salt and millstones for that matter, in the biblical text, then, yes, I did." I will also think, "If you mean, did you give them the truth, the whole truth, and nothing but the truth, so help me God," I hope so. So help me God if I didn't.

Now then, the whole truth and nothing but the truth requires that we look at a second, often pushed aside, truth—Jesus' teaching on divorce.

Divorce

In Mark 9:42–50 Jesus teaches on the tough topic of hell. Then in **10:1–12** he teaches on the tough topic of divorce. As with the first topic, this second topic surfaces within a certain historical context.[9] Jesus did not decide to first talk on hell and then go to the next town and talk on divorce. Instead, as he journeyed from Capernaum through "the region of Judea and beyond the Jordan," teaching the crowds wherever he went ("crowds gathered to him . . . and . . . as was his custom, he taught them," 10:1), he was presented with a question: "And Pharisees [in one of these towns] came up and in order to test him asked, 'Is it lawful for a man to divorce his wife?'" (10:2).[10] The context of Jesus' teaching on divorce is a test, a theological test, intended to trip him up. He talks about divorce only because they ask about divorce.

His answer comes in verses 3–9. It is a twofold response that takes them back to the Bible—first to Deuteronomy and then to Genesis. He begins his answer with a question. "He answered them, 'What did Moses command you?'" (10:3). They might think they are testing him. However, he is testing them on their knowledge of Scripture. As verse 4 records, they pass the first round. They say, "Moses *allowed* a man to write a certificate of divorce and to send her away." They are partly right and partly wrong here. They are right that Moses spoke of a "certificate of divorce" (Deut. 24:1), but the context is a command of what to do after someone has *already* divorced his wife. The command is that, if a man serves her papers and she later marries another man and that second man also divorces her or dies, the first husband cannot

---

9   Jesus' teaching on divorce is "only of a skeleton nature" and is "by no means a full treatment of the difficult" doctrine (Cole, *Mark*, 234).

10   Notice that they do not ask important questions, those in line with what Jesus has been teaching. They do not ask about the nature of the kingdom or about the source of his wisdom and works. They ask about divorce!

remarry her (see Deut. 24:1–4). Moses did not declare any grounds for divorce, and he certainly did not mandate or sanction it.

I honestly think that Jesus, with his opening question, has won the debate. It is like a chess match between me and a grandmaster. I move my pawn here, then there, and he looks at me and offers his hand: "Checkmate." And I say, "What? How?" He then explains each move he will take to take out my pawns, rooks, knights, bishops, queen, and king. The Pharisees, however, are still blind to who is the winner and to who is the King who will allow himself to be killed only because the Father has so willed.

What then is the next move? The King moves forward. Jesus says to them, "Because of your hardness of heart he wrote you this commandment" (Mark 10:5). The words "your" and "you" are jabs at them. The men in Moses' day, and obviously those in Jesus', were not treating their wives well. The sense is, "You might be having problems with your wife, but the biggest problem, if you are contemplating divorcing her for unlawful reasons, is you. You are the problem. Your hard heart is the problem. It was true then, and it is true now."

Jesus' next move is to take them back to Genesis. In Mark 10:6–8 Jesus quotes from Genesis 1:27; 2:24: "But from the beginning of creation, 'God made them male and female.' 'Therefore a man shall leave his father and mother and hold fast to his wife, and the two shall become one flesh.'" God's intention for marriage, Jesus teaches, was laid out on the sixth day of creation. Marriage is between one man and one woman. Marriage creates a new allegiance, a new nuclear family. A man leaves his parents and cleaves to his wife. Marriage is an act of unity ("The two . . . become one"). Through the covenant (marriage vows) and consummation (the marriage bed) the man and the woman are spiritually and physically united. How long are they united? Jesus offers the briefest but most important commentary on Genesis: "So they are no longer two but one flesh. What therefore God has joined together, let not man separate" (Mark 10:8–9). Notice how Jesus' comment on the phrase "The two . . . become one flesh" ("They are no longer two but one flesh," 10:8) teaches that "this new entity takes priority over . . . individual rights."[11] It is as Paul teaches in 1 Corinthians 7:4. Speaking of the marriage bed he writes, "the wife does not have authority over her own body, but the husband does. Likewise the husband does not have authority over his own body, but the wife does." As the bride in the Song of Solomon sings, "My beloved is mine, and I am his" (Song 2:16). The two become one.

So then, if the two are one, should they ever be separated? Ideally, no. "What therefore God has joined together, let not man separate" (Mark 10:9). The

---

11 Mark L. Strauss, *Mark*, ZECNT (Grand Rapids, MI: Zondervan, 2014), 425.

foundational reason they should stay together is not because their parents think it is a good idea, it is in the best interest of the kids, or they took vows but because God in his providence brought them together and bound them together.

Whenever I preach on this text at a wedding, I make this application to the couple: remember who brought you together.[12] I tell them that, as important as it is to focus on the present and future—what Scripture teaches husbands and wives to do in Ephesians, Colossians, and 1 Peter (for husbands to love, be understanding, and not be harsh to their wives, and for wives to submit and respect their husbands)—it is just as important to focus on the past, on what God has done in his providence to bring a couple together. When my wife and I have had difficulties and disagreements, that clause "What God has joined together" often settles my soul, calms my temper, and reassures me of God's will for our lives.

Our Lord at this point is finished with the Pharisees, but he is not yet finished with his disciples. Jesus next moves into a "house" to tutor his twelve once again on the touchy matter. They ask for clarification ("The disciples asked him again about this matter," 10:10), and he adds this further instruction: "Whoever divorces his wife and marries another commits adultery against her, and if she divorces her husband and marries another [remember Herodias and Herod], she commits adultery" (10:11–12). Jesus' logic here goes like this: if God brings together a man and a woman in the mystical bond of holy matrimony, then for a man to offer a piece of paper (a certificate of divorce) to his wife and then marry another woman is the same as having an affair with that other woman. The reason is that the marriage bond, in God's eyes, has not been broken. Both Jesus and Paul speak of times when the marriage bond is broken—"sexual immorality" (Matt. 5:32) and desertion (1 Cor. 7:15)—but here our Lord offers no exception clause. Likely he offers no exception clause because he is simply trying to reset his disciples' values in regard to marriage. He wants them to think of Genesis first. He wants them to embrace God's original intention for marriage.

The disciples lived in a culture like ours in regard to marriage and divorce. It was easy to get a divorce. Some of the rabbis of their time taught that the clause in Deuteronomy 24:1 about a man's divorcing his wife "because he has found some indecency in her" was as broad as the man's imagination. A man could divorce his wife for burning a meal. How archaic. A man could divorce his wife because he has found a woman who is "prettier than she" (Rabbi Akiva, m. Giṭ. 9:10). How contemporary.

---

12 For a full wedding sermon on this text see R. Kent Hughes and Douglas Sean O'Donnell, eds., *The Pastor's Book: A Comprehensive and Practical Guide to Pastoral Ministry* (Wheaton, IL: Crossway, 2015), 163–65.

Jesus knows that, in a postfall world, sinners get married. Sinners, soon after the "I do," sin against each other. Some sins cause irreconcilable separation. He knows that. He knows that divorce happens. He knows it is always heartbreaking. A tragedy of high order. What can be a more hellish experience than to live through the tearing apart of two people who once were one? He knows that. But he wants here, before they and we rush to any and all the ways we can get out of a marriage, to remind us of God's prefall plan for it. The covenant vows are not something to be entered into lightly. And they certainly should not be broken over burnt toast.

My Way or God's Way?

Kent Hughes tells the story about the time he learned that his old college roommate had decided he was going to leave his wife of twenty-two years. He says that as soon as he heard the news he got on the next plane—the red-eye special from Chicago to California. At 7 a.m. he was knocking on his friend's front door. The man had no choice but to let him in and talk to him. Kent spent that day trying to convince him of what the Bible had to say about marriage and that he had no grounds for leaving his wife whatsoever. Kent headed back to Chicago optimistic that his friend was convicted of biblical truth. Yet, several weeks later, his friend informed him that he was indeed leaving his wife. He gave this tenuous theological justification. He said that he knew that the Bible did not condone what he was doing, but he was under grace and was going to do it anyway because God was going to forgive him.

What a hell-bent thought.

A year after the man left his wife, Kent received an invitation to attend this man's wedding. What audacity! According to the invitation the wedding was to take place on the yacht *Mia Vita*, which means "my life." As Kent looked at the invitation, his mind turned to the lyrics of Frank Sinatra's song, in which the singer boasts of living a full life, traveling many highways, and doing everything "My Way."

Kent's friend did it his way. But what had he done? Kent went on to say. This man quickly created a trail of broken relationships—with his wife, children, grandchildren, friends, and church. He sinned against God. He sinned against the leadership of his church. He sinned against his wife. He sinned against his "little ones," his children, and eventually his grandchildren (who were born long after the divorce). He broke what God had brought together, and the pieces of that separation are too many to pick up and put together. Kent concludes by saying of this man's ungodly decision,

It's been devastating to his wife and it's been devastating to his now adult children. He thought that since his children were essentially raised, it wouldn't make any difference. What a mistake he made. It has devastated their lives. And so I say . . . that the primrose path to self-fulfillment that so many believers trip merrily down, is strewn with the bones of people who have walked down that path and the bones of many of the people that they loved the most.[13]

How different that man's course is from my in-laws'. On a business trip to Hong Kong, my wife's father was convicted by the Holy Spirit. He confessed to his wife that he had been unfaithful for many years with many different women. She was devastated, as anyone would be. She had biblical grounds for divorce. But she decided to forgive him. It was not an easy road ahead. But he was truly repentant, and her attitude through it all was "I'm married to Christ first and my husband second. But, because I'm married to a perfect heavenly husband, I can forgive my imperfect earthly husband." They have been married nearly fifty years. What is their legacy? No broken relationships—with God, his people, or their "little ones." Peace. Love. Forgiveness. The goodness of the gospel lived out.

I do not know your story. You might be divorced, contemplating a divorce, in a terrible and difficult marriage, in a wonderful and joyful marriage, about to be married, or never to be married. But I know there is always hope and always blessings (if not in this life, then in the next) to be had when we obey our Lord Jesus. In Revelation 21:5 Jesus says, "Behold, I am making all things new." The verb is present tense. He is right now making all things new. He is offering hope. Newness of life. A fresh start. Be part of his plan. Listen to his words, as tough as they may be to hear, and flourish. Grow in the grace of the gospel.

---

13 Audio is available at R. Kent Hughes, "The Sacredness of Marriage," sermon, The Gospel Coalition, mp3 format, 44:18, https://resources.thegospelcoalition.org/library/the-sacredness-of -marriage, accessed November 5, 2021.

Childlike Faith

MARK 10:13-31

Truly, I say to you, whoever does not receive the kingdom of
God like a child shall not enter it.
Mark 10:15

You might be wondering why I chose to preach Mark 10:13–31 as a unit, rather than present one sermon on Jesus' interaction with the children (10:13–16) and another sermon on the rich man's encounter with Jesus (10:17–31). I chose to teach these texts together because Mark uses three key terms to connect the two stories: "child/ren" (10:13, 14, 15, 24, 29, 30),[1] "enter" (10:15, 23, 24, 25), and "kingdom of God" (10:14, 15, 23, 24, 25; cf. "gospel" of the kingdom, 10:29; cf. Matt. 4:23).[2] Yet more important than these three key terms are the shared themes found in these two stories, told in three scenes.

In scene one children come to Jesus. He receives them.[3] He blesses them. He offers an object lesson: "Truly, I say to you, whoever does not receive the kingdom of God like a child shall not enter it" (10:15). This lesson is then played out in the next two scenes.

In scene two a rich man approaches Jesus. Does he receive the kingdom like a little child? Put differently, is he willing to be totally dependent on Jesus, a dependence that, in his case, would show itself in absolute self-denial in regard to his great possessions? No, he is not willing.

---

1 Mark uses two Greek words for "children" (*teknon* and *paidion*); the latter usually refers to "infants" or "young children."

2 Entering the kingdom is synonymous with eschatological salvation ("Then who can be saved?" Mark 10:26), the "eternal life" the rich man seeks to obtain (10:17; cf. 10:30).

3 "Christ stands with the arms of his love open to receive all children. It would be a great thing for some great man to enter into communion with some poor child. But Christ is ready to receive little children into communion with him, and that, even the poor children of poor parents. Those that are despised in the world, Christ does not despise them." Jonathan Edwards, *Works of Jonathan Edwards*, vol. 22, quoted in *CHSB*, 1490.

Then in scene three Jesus instructs his disciples on the dangers of wealth: "How difficult," he says, "it will be for those who have wealth to enter the kingdom of God!" (10:23). He reiterates his point, "*Children* [he calls his disciples], how difficult it is to enter the kingdom of God!" (10:24). Then he gives an exaggerated metaphor to explain just how difficult it is: "It is easier for a camel to go through the eye of a needle than for a rich person to enter the kingdom of God" (10:25). Wow! The disciples are astonished. They wonder whether anyone can enter the kingdom and experience eternal life, ultimate salvation. Next Jesus talks about the possibility of an impossibility. God alone can save people! Then Peter makes an interesting statement to Jesus: "See, we have left everything" (10:28). Is this statement (which represents a reality) an expression of childlike faith? And are these three scenes simply a dramatic retelling of Jesus' final line, "But many who are first will be last, and the last first" (10:31)? Let us find out.[4]

Scene One: Coming to Christ

Before we get to the end (10:31), we start with the beginning. Look at Mark **10:13–16**. This scene starts with parents from the "crowds" (see 10:1) "bringing children" to Jesus (10:13; Luke labels the children "infants," Luke 18:15). Perhaps these parents approach Jesus, child in hand, because they want a blessing from him in the form of a "touch" (Mark 10:13), which Jesus in fact offers: "And he took them in his arms and blessed them, laying his hands on them" (10:16). But why do these parents want Jesus to bless their children? They must hold him in high regard, viewing him as a great teacher, miracle worker, and compassionate man. The disciples also have a high regard for Jesus but, as we learn next, not for these children. In verse 13 we read that, when the parents were bringing their children to Jesus, the "disciples rebuked them." The disciples did not rebuke the Pharisees when they "came up" to Jesus (10:2). Why then stop the children? Easy answer: the Pharisees were important and influential men; the children unimportant and uninfluential. How could children advance the cause of their king? The disciples do not want screaming babies wasting Jesus' precious time. However, as the story continues, we see that Jesus disagrees with their mindset. Strongly. Our gracious Lord steps in with a rebuke of his own, an emotional one. "But when Jesus saw [what the disciples did], he was indignant" (10:14). What upsets Jesus? When members and royal heirs of his kingdom are treated like second-class citizens; when the least are treated lousily.

---

4   This introduction is also listed as an example in Table 1.2 of Douglas Sean O'Donnell and Leland Ryken, *The Beauty and Power of Biblical Exposition: Preaching the Literary Artistry and Genres of the Bible* (Wheaton, IL: Crossway, 2022), 60.

Our Lord's indignation is followed by two culturally counterintuitive pronouncements. First, Jesus says, "Let the children come to me; do not hinder them, for to such belongs the kingdom of God" (10:14). Put differently, the reason it is more than appropriate for even children to come to him is because children are and will be a part of the kingdom. Second, Jesus explains the reason: "Truly, I say to you [he is doubly emphatic about what he is saying here], whoever does not receive the kingdom of God like a child shall not enter it" (10:15). Kingdom entrance demands childlike status (lowliness) or disposition (poverty of spirit) and childlike faith (a trust in Jesus and a dependence on him).

So will social position gain entrance? No. Influence over others? No. Worldly power? No. How about wealth? Let us see next. Your guess is as obvious as mine.

Scene Two: Walking Away From Christ

Before Jesus answers "No" we find a rich man who, at first, appears childlike enough. Mark **10:17** records, "And as [Jesus] was setting out on his journey, a man ran up and knelt before him and asked him, 'Good Teacher, what must I do to inherit eternal life?'" Because we know the negative end of the story, we often fail to notice the positive start. This man comes to Jesus, the right person to come to with a physical problem or spiritual need. And the way in which he approaches him is remarkable. He *runs* to Jesus. Like a child. Then, once he gets near to Jesus, he "knelt before him" (10:17). How humble. And odd! How often have you seen a rich man bow before a poor one?

This great man is off to a great start. Even his question, with its obvious flaws, is commendable. It is commendable in that he asks the right person life's biggest question. In my children's book on this biblical narrative I start the story like this:

> Once there was a rich man. He lived in a big stone house. He rode a fast white horse. He wore a long purple robe. He had everything—everything, except for an answer to the world's biggest question. "Is the moon really made of cheese?" No. That's not the world's biggest question. "Why can't I hit my sister if she hit me first?" No. That's not the world's biggest question. "Why do I have to brush my baby teeth if they're just going to fall out?" No. That's not the world's biggest question. "What must I do to inherit eternal life?" Yes! Yes, that's the world's biggest question. "How do I get to heaven? How do I live with God forever and ever and ever?— that's what the rich man wanted to know.[5]

---

5   Douglas Sean O'Donnell, *Two Fat Camels: The Story of Two Rich Men from Luke 18–19* (Ross-shire, Scotland: Christian Focus, 2015), 6.

This man does not ask an earthbound question. He is not simply and superficially focused on his earthly life. Rather, he is genuinely concerned about life after death. So this rich man's question is the right question in that it asks "*the* essential question."[6]

His question is a good question, but it is not the perfect question, and its imperfections are revealed in the word "good" and the clause "what must I do" (10:17). The word "good" is problematic because he thinks some people, like Rabbi Jesus, are good and that that goodness translates to God's blessing. The clause "What must I do" is also problematic, as it implies a piety of achievement and as it stands in contrast to what Jesus has just taught his disciples—that the kingdom must be received like a child would. Receiving is the only way to find eternal life. Personal merit matters not when it comes to salvation. No one does enough to earn entrance to paradise.

This second scene, along with Jesus' later analogy about the eye of the needle, reminds me of a scene near the beginning of *Alice in Wonderland*, in which Alice "found herself in a long, low hall, which was lit up by a row of lamps." She walked up and down the hallway and tried to open all the doors, "but they were all locked." She started to fear that she would be trapped. Then "suddenly she came upon" a glass table with a tiny golden key on it. Alice took the key and tried it on all the doors. But it did not open any of them. Then, as she was trying the locks a second time, "she came upon a low curtain she had not noticed before, and behind it was a little door about fifteen inches high: she tried the little golden key in the lock, and to her great delight it fit!" Alice then opened the door, knelt down, and saw through the tiny opening that outside the door, through a small passage, was "the loveliest garden [she] ever saw." Oh,

> how she longed to get out of that dark hall, and wander about among those beds of bright flowers and those cool fountains, but she could not even get her head though the doorway. There seemed to be no use in waiting by the little door, so she went back to the table, half hoping she might find another key on it. This time she found a little bottle on it . . . and round the neck of the bottle was a paper label, with the words "DRINK ME" beautifully printed on it in large letters.

Alice hesitated. She checked to see if the bottle was marked "poison." When she saw that it was not, she drank it. "'What a curious feeling!' said Alice [as she began to shrink]; 'I must be [closing up] like a telescope.' And

---

6   James R. Edwards, *The Gospel according to Mark*, PNTC (Grand Rapids, MI: Eerdmans, 2002), 309.

so she was indeed: she was now only ten inches high, and her face brightened up at the thought that she was now the right size for going through the little door into that lovely garden." Sure enough, she walked through.[7]

That part of Alice's story is a fitting illustration of the choice before the rich man. For here in Mark 10 we see a man inches away from eternal life but locked out from experiencing it. His issue is not whether he has the right key. He knows and loves, and seeks to live out, the law. His issue is size. He is too big to fit through the entrance into the kingdom of God. He is like a 2,000-pound camel trying to squeeze its way through the tip of a tiny sewing needle.

Jesus knows that. So he next gives this too big man a special potion. His words! And, if the man drinks them in, he will get small enough to squeeze through the entrance. Our Lord starts with a question and statement about goodness. "And Jesus said to him, 'Why do you call *me* good? No one is good except God alone'" (**10:18**). What is our Lord saying here? Is he denying that he is morally good? No. He is the sinless Son. Is he denying that he is God, one with the Father and Spirit? No. He is very God of very God. What he is doing here is setting up what follows. He is turning the mirror not on himself (in essence saying, "Let me explain to this man that I am more than a mere man") but on this man. Jesus wants this man to see himself in light of a perfectly good God. If God alone is good, then is anyone else?

"Are you good?" Jesus asks him, and he tests this man's self-perceived goodness by means of God's good law. "What must [you] *do* to inherit eternal life?" (10:17)? Here is what. Let us start the test. "You know the commandments: '*Do* not murder, *Do* not commit adultery, *Do* not steal, *Do* not bear false witness, *Do* not defraud, Honor your father and mother'" (**10:19**). Jesus takes this man back to the Ten Commandments, the heart of God's law, in the hope that this man would remember that the law is "holy and righteous and good" (Rom. 7:12) but also that he would learn what Paul taught and discovered for himself, that "through the law comes the knowledge of sin" (Rom. 3:20; cf. Gal. 3:24). Jesus wanted this man to see himself as a sinner in need of a Savior.

But notice that Jesus does not list all ten. He focuses on the second half of the law: the love of neighbor. The best way to know whether you are keeping the first half of the law (loving God) is to see how well you do with the second (loving neighbor; see 1 John 4:20). Also notice here in Mark that Jesus does not quote the tenth commandment, "You shall not covet" (Ex. 20:17). It might be that "do not defraud" (Mark 10:19) is a direct application of the command.

---

7 Lewis Carroll, *Alice's Adventures in Wonderland*; and *Through the Looking Glass*, Everyman's Library Children's Classics (New York: Knopf, 1992), 15–18.

It might also be that Jesus' fivefold command in verse 21 is a custom-made test directed at this man's specific, but likely hidden, vice. He covets money more than God. He so desires it (having it and making more of it) that he might defraud others in order to amass his fortune.[8]

However, if the rich man's reply in **10:20** ("And he said to him, 'Teacher, all these I have kept from my youth'") is honest then that is not true of him. Has he murdered? No. Has he committed adultery? No. Has he stolen from his neighbor? No. Has he, in a court of law, borne false witness? No. Has he defrauded his investors or employees? Not as far as he knows. Has he honored his father and mother? Indeed. He might even be providing for them now. I think this man is sincere and that his sincerity is what induces Jesus' positive response: "And Jesus, looking at him, loved him" (**10:21**). I think our loving Lord loved him in that he loved that he was honest, or sought to be honest. He loved that this man so loved the law that he sought to live his life by it. He loved that this man came to him and desired to make the necessary change. I think he also loved him in what follows. Tough love. He gives him a tough command to expose a "good" man with a bad heart, the same heart we all have.

The shock of the story comes in verse 21. Our Lord says to him, "You lack one thing: go, sell all that you have and give to the poor, and you will have treasure in heaven; and come, follow me." To our Lord, this "good" man lacks something—loving his neighbor as much as he loves himself. Go. Sell. Give. He lacks loving God more than money. Come. Follow. He lacks childlike dependence on Christ.

What then is the man's reaction to Jesus' call to become like a child? He is supposed to cut off both his dependence on his possessions ("go, sell . . . give") and his self-dependence ("come, follow me"). However, he refuses to repent and believe: "Disheartened by the saying, he went away sorrowful, for he had great possessions" (**10:22**). So sad. The spirit of the law, that of the Tenth Command-ment, has exposed his soul. This exemplary man is an idolatrous man. This man on bended knee gets up and walks away. The one reason given is that "he had great possessions" (10:22)—or, we might say, great possessions had him.[9]

Scene Three: Leaving Everything for Christ

In what follows (**10:23–25**) Jesus makes the previous point abundantly clear:

---

8   See Craig A. Evans, *Mark 8:27–16:20*, WBC 34B (Nashville: Nelson, 1988), 96.

9   "It is true, indeed, that riches do not, in their own nature, hinder us from following God, but, in consequence of the depravity of the human mind, it is scarcely possible for those who have a great abundance to avoid being intoxicated by them." John Calvin, *Commentary on a Harmony of the Gospels*, quoted in *CHSB*, 1491.

And Jesus looked around and said to his disciples, "How difficult it will be for those who have wealth to enter the kingdom of God!" And the disciples were amazed at his words. But Jesus said to them again, "Children, how difficult it is to enter the kingdom of God! It is easier for a camel to go through the eye of a needle than for a rich person to enter the kingdom of God."

Mark Twain once wrote, "It ain't those parts of the Bible that I can't understand that bother me, it is the parts that I do understand."[10] Twice Jesus says, quite clearly, that is it difficult for the rich to enter the kingdom. And the analogy that follows is not that complex. As it is impossible for the largest animal from that region to fit through a tiny sewing needle, so the chances of a rich person's entering the kingdom and experiencing eternal life are slim. We understand the teaching. We get the absurd analogy. But it is bothersome, is it not?

We are bothered that Jesus does not say perhaps what we expect him to say, "How difficult it will be for those who *love money* to get to heaven!" We might be as "amazed" as the disciples (10:24),[11] and amazed for the same reasons. We think of wealth not as something inherently dangerous but as a generous sign of God's provision. We think of the wealthy not as the spiritual underprivileged but as those outwardly blessed by God. But Jesus wants us to think differently. He warns us about wealth.[12]

Jesus warns us because wealth has a way of making people too large and too adult. Wealth often "deadens the instinct for self-sacrifice,"[13] fosters the ungodly idea that this world has much to offer, lures us into believing that everything can be had for a price, and numbs our spiritual sensibilities to the joys of heaven and the torments of hell. When one has wealth, there is always something more on earth to look forward to. Wealth is often a bedfellow with the harem of self-indulgence, self-reliance, self-importance, and self-security. Wealth often rules our time, commitments, and concerns. And the whole point of Jesus' "colorful hyperbole" about the camel and the eye of the needle

10 Mark Twain, quoted in *The Wit and Wisdom of Mark Twain* (New York: Harper Perennial, 2005), 24.

11 The Greek word *thambeō* (translated "amazed") is a unique word to Mark, only here and in 1:27; 10:32.

12 In the Synoptic Gospels Jesus has nothing positive to say about money (e.g., Matt. 6:24; 13:22; Mark 4:19; Luke 12:13–32; 16:1–5, 19–31; 19:1–10). Moreover, he never speaks of wealth as a blessing. Instead, he repeatedly uses illustrations that regard the abundance of possessions to be "toxic to the soul." David E. Garland, *Mark*, NIVAC (Grand Rapids, MI: Zondervan, 1996), 402.

13 Garland, *Mark*, 403.

288 | *Childlike Faith*

underlines the fact that "those who are ruled by money cannot be ruled by God."[14] Thus, while it is true that "it is not so much the having of money, as the trusting in it, which ruins the soul,"[15] it is also true that if one has money it is easier to trust in it. And what is required by Christ here is a childlike faith in his heavenly Father.

At this point, if you are offended or aghast, you are not alone, for the disciples cannot believe their ears. They move from amazement ("And the disciples were amazed at his words," 10:24) to astonishment ("And they were exceedingly astonished, and said to him, 'Then who can be saved?'" (**10:26**).[16] If a law-abiding rich man cannot be saved, who can? Great question. Jesus loves this question as much as he loves the man. What is Jesus' response? "Jesus looked at them and said, 'With man it is impossible, but not with God. For all things are possible with God'" (**10:27**). Put differently, no one qualifies. The great will not be let in because they are great, the good because they are good, or the rich because they are rich. Salvation is impossible for man. Jonathan Edwards once wrote, "To take upon yourself the task of earning your own salvation, is a greater work than if you had taken upon yourself to create the entire material universe."[17] Salvation is a work of God from start to finish. It is possible only if he makes it possible. And he does make it possible!

In Mark 10:32–34 Jesus explains the possibility of the impossible. Here we discover just how Jesus will get even a large beast through the impossible eye of a needle. Here is the answer to how any sinful person is able to enter into the kingdom of God. Jesus says,

> See, we are going up to Jerusalem, and the Son of Man will be delivered over to the chief priests and the scribes, and they will condemn him to death and deliver him over to the Gentiles. And they will mock him and spit on him, and flog him and kill him. And after three days he will rise. (10:33–34)

There is the only way in: Jesus suffers, dies, and rises again. It is only through Jesus' giving his "life as a ransom" (10:45) that we are granted eternal life. We believe that. And we trust in him like little children trust their parents for food, clothing, shelter, and love. For everything! We trust that his death and

---

14 Garland, *Mark*, 399.
15 J. C. Ryle, *Mark: Expository Thoughts on the Gospels*, CCC (Wheaton, IL: Crossway, 1993), 153.
16 The rich man was "disheartened by the saying" (Mark 10:22; lit., "having become shocking at the word"); the disciples "were amazed at his words" (10:24) and "exceedingly astonished" (10:26).
17 Jonathan Edwards, *The Works of Jonathan Edwards*, ed. Edward Hickman, 2 vols. (repr., Carlisle, PA: Banner of Truth, 1992), 1:581.

resurrection provide salvation for us. We trust that he alone has opened the door to paradise.

The disciples have heard Jesus talk about his death and resurrection, but they have yet to make sense of it. For now, however, they are trying to make sense of Jesus' teaching on wealth after the aftermath of the rich man's refusal to obey Jesus. So Peter announces to Jesus, "See, we have left everything and followed you" (**10:28**).

What is going on here? Is Peter trying to self-justify the twelve? Is he missing the point? He may not have all his theological ducks in a row, but notice that Jesus does not rebuke Peter, as he has done repeatedly in the past. Instead he emphatically offers a twofold promise:

> Truly, I say to you, there is no one who has left house or brothers or sisters or mother or father or children or lands, for my sake and for the gospel, who will not receive a hundredfold now in this time, houses and brothers and sisters and mothers and children and lands, with persecutions, and in the age to come eternal life. But many who are first will be last, and the last first. (**10:29–31**)

Jesus first promises earthly blessings. For those who have left everything—anti-gospel people and possessions—for Christ and his kingdom ("for my sake and for the gospel," 10:29) life will not always be easy (note the word "persecutions" in 10:30), but they will receive in the here and now ("now in this time," 10:30) a hundred times more ("a hundredfold," 10:30). This is likely a reference to the Spirit-united brothers and sisters Jesus spoke of in 3:33–34. Christ promises a new, better, and eternal family. And how true this is! I have worshiped with brothers and sisters in Australia, Canada, Cuba, England, Ireland, Japan, Malawi, New Zealand, Scotland, and Wales. My new family has been more than a hundredfold larger. It has been a thousandfold!

Second, Jesus promises heavenly blessings. "In the age to come" he guarantees "eternal life," what the rich man was after (10:30).[18] Imagine that. Imagine what is prophesied in Daniel 12:2 one day happening to us: "Those who sleep in the dust of the earth shall awake . . . to everlasting life." Imagine what is envisioned in Revelation 21–22 becoming reality. No more pain or death or tears (Rev. 21:4). No more sin (Rev. 21:27; 22:14). I cannot wait not to be

---

18 Matthew makes this point clearer, also recording Jesus' amazing promise: "Truly, I say to you, in the new world, when the Son of Man will sit on his glorious throne, *you* who have followed me will also sit on twelve thrones, judging the twelve tribes of Israel" (Matt. 19:28).

able to sin! Perfect order and beauty (e.g., Rev. 21:16–21). Perfect fellowship with God (Rev. 21:3) and worship of him (Rev. 22:3).

So, based on this positive response to Peter, Jesus views Peter's statement "we have left everything and followed you" (Mark 10:28) not as childish but childlike. Those who, like the disciples, "have demonstrated that they have been poor in spirit and rich in faith, so much so as to subordinate all their allegiances—occupation, income, real estate, family, religion—to their Lord"[19] will enter the kingdom and experience eternal life even now.

And the lesson, then, of all three scenes taken together is Jesus' last line: "But many who are first will be last, and the last first" (10:31). Those like the rich man (those "who are first" in this life) will be, in the life to come, "last," and those who are perceived to be "last" on earth (like those believing children and fully trusting disciples) will be "first."

An early edition of *Webster's Dictionary* defined a Christian as "a decent, civilized, or presentable person." The rich man would qualify under that faulty definition. The *Random House Dictionary* definition is slightly better: a Christian is one who demonstrates "a spirit proper to a follower of Jesus Christ, as in having a loving regard for other persons." That definition is incomplete, but not completely off. Here then is a more complete and accurate definition, one that comes from my summary of Jesus' teaching here: a Christian is simply "someone who is *last* but places Jesus *first*," that is, someone who is humble and trusting enough to subordinate all allegiances to the crucified and risen Christ.[20] That is what a Christian is.

Drink of Christ!

It was thirty years ago that God, in his infinite and irresistible grace, used this very story as one of his means of converting me to Christ. For the first half of my life I was told and believed the most common religious lie, that I was basically a good person who occasionally sinned but that nothing would ultimately disqualify me from one day entering the joys of eternal life. I was not saved until the Holy Spirit taught me what should have been obvious: that I was a sinner. Not that I was a good person who occasionally sinned but that I was a sinner (at root a very bad person) in a continual state of rebellion against a good God and his good law. I did not love God or love others, and I certainly loved self.

19 See Douglas Sean O'Donnell, *"O Woman, Great Is Your Faith!" Faith in the Gospel of Matthew* (Eugene, OR: Pickwick, 2021), 170.
20 This definition above, and part of the personal testimony below, can be found also in Douglas Sean O'Donnell, *Matthew: All Authority under Heaven*, PTW (Wheaton, IL: Crossway, 2013), 554.

But it was not just the first half of this passage but also the second half that the Lord used to change my mind and heart and will. I knew that God alone was perfectly good. I believed that Jesus was indeed the Son of God and the Savior of the world. But at that time in my life he was never my Savior. He was never my Lord. And as I prayed to Christ those many years ago and asked him to forgive me and to clean me up on the inside, I also (with this passage in mind) told him (in so many words) that I would "sell everything," that I would put him first in my life—first above self, family, career, education, sports; first above every aspect and every love of my life. I told him I would be last and he would be first.

Dear Alice may have unexpectedly entered Wonderland by drinking from that bottle. However, we are given a sure promise that, if we drink of Christ, we gain that which is most refreshing in the here and now (real life) and that which makes us small enough to enter the kingdom of heaven, where there is indeed (so we are told) an ever so lovely garden and life everlasting. May we one day—by God's grace and goodness alone—find ourselves there.

Why the Son of Man Came

MARK 10:32-45

For even the Son of Man came not to be served but to serve,
and to give his life as a ransom for many.
Mark 10:45

I recently read about a rich man who stood up during a church service and testified about how God had blessed him through his sacrificial giving. He talked about the time he received his first paycheck and how he was so excited to have some money of his own. Then he recounted how he was in church the Sunday after he received the check, and, as the offering plate was being passed, he was deeply convicted. God was tugging at his heart. It was as though God were saying to him, "Give it all. Give it all." He gave in to God and gave it all to God. He signed over that first check to the church. Then this man went on to explain how, from that time on, God has blessed him financially. He became, as the years passed, a wealthy man. After he shared, he sat down. Everyone in the congregation was so encouraged by his amazing testimony. Everyone but the old lady who sat behind him, who leaned over and whispered in his ear, "I dare you to do it again!"[1]

In our last chapter our Lord taught us, as we listened in on what he had to teach his first followers, about the dangers of possessions. The rich man who approached Jesus to find enteral life walked away sad because he had "great possessions" and great possessions had him. He was not willing to heed Jesus fivefold command to love his neighbor (go, sell, give) and put God first (come, follow). It is easy to give away $100 of a $100 first paycheck, but not so easy to give away $2,000,000 of a $2,000,000 estate.

Earlier in Mark 10 our Lord taught about the dangers of possessions. Here, later in the chapter, he will teach a lesson on the dangers of pride. We move from possessions to pride. James and John will ask Jesus whether they can

---

1   See Mark L. Strauss, *Mark*, ZECNT (Grand Rapids, MI: Zondervan, 2014), 447.

sit on his right and left hands when he rules in glory. Jesus will correct their false perceptions of glory and greatness: to be great is to be servant of all; to be glorious is to suffer for the kingdom.

Going up to Jerusalem

That theme of glorious suffering, or suffering as the way to glory, is introduced after James and John's request, but also before it. In Mark **10:32–34** Jesus makes his third and final passion prediction (cf. 8:31; 9:31).[2]

> And they were on the road, going up to Jerusalem, and Jesus was walking ahead of them. And they were amazed, and those who followed were afraid. And taking the twelve again, he began to tell them what was to happen to him, saying, "See, we are going up to Jerusalem, and the Son of Man will be delivered over to the chief priests and the scribes, and they will condemn him to death and deliver him over to the Gentiles. And they will mock him and spit on him, and flog him and kill him. And after three days he will rise." (10:32–34)

Let me ask and answer four questions here. First, where are they headed next? Jerusalem. This is an easy answer but also an important one. This geographical shift is important.[3] Mark includes three major geographical movements. In 1:14–8:26 Jesus ministers in and around Galilee, moving in and out of Jewish and Gentile territories. In 8:27–10:52 he journeys from Caesarea Philippi in the north straight south, through Galilee, toward Jerusalem. Finally, in 11:1–16:8 Jesus enters Jerusalem. He goes "*up* to Jerusalem" (10:32, 33) because the holy city is set upon a hill, Mount Zion.

2   In all three passion predictions Jesus identifies himself as the "Son of Man" and speaks of his death as being "killed" and his resurrection as occurring "after three days." Those who reject him in the first two predictions are the Jewish religious authorities (the elders, ruling priests, and experts in the law), and Gentiles (the Romans) are included in the third. As Timothy Keller notes: "Jesus gives us more details about his death than he had previously. For the first time, we are told that his death will be in Jerusalem, and that both Jews and Gentiles will reject him. Chapter 8 speaks only of the Jewish religious leaders, and 9 speaks more generally about being delivered into the hands of 'men.' In chapter 8 he had said he would be 'rejected' by the priests and scribes, but now he reveals that they will 'condemn him to death.' This legal term indicates that he will be tried and executed within the criminal justice system. His depiction of his final days also becomes more graphic and violent: They will 'mock . . . spit . . . flog' him." *King's Cross: The Story of the World in the Life of Jesus* (New York: Dutton, 2011), 139.

3   "The 'way,' or travel narrative, has been emphasized throughout this journey from Caesarea Philippi (8:27; 9:33; 10:17, 32). Jesus 'leading [*proagō*] the way' looks forward to 14:28; 16:7 (the same verb as here and Jesus 'going ahead' of the disciples to Galilee). Jesus determines the path that believers follow." Grant R. Osborne, *Mark*, TTCS (Grand Rapids, MI: Baker, 2012), 182.

Second, why does Jesus want to journey to Jerusalem? Another obvious and important answer. He tells us in verses 33–34: he is going there to suffer and die and rise. His mission is the cross and resurrection.[4]

The third question follows: What is unusual about his mission? The brutality is unusual. Innocent and nonviolent Jesus will first be doubly delivered over—denied and condemned by both Jews and Gentiles: he will be "delivered over" first to the Jewish authorities ("the chief priests and the scribes") and then, after they sentence him to death, will be "delivered . . . over" next to the Romans ("the Gentiles," 10:33). The Gentiles, however, will not strap Jesus into an electric chair and pull the switch, a quick thus relatively painless death. Rather, "they will mock him and spit on him, and flog him and kill him" (10:34).[5] After they torture him mentally (the mocking and spitting) and physically (the lashes on the back), he will die the most painful and humiliating of deaths: crucifixion.[6]

Beyond the brutality, it is also unusual that someone who suffers and dies, as Jesus will suffer and die, will, just a short time later ("after three days," 10:34), rise from the dead.[7] Dead people do not rise from the dead. The Jews did not have a category for what Jesus predicts here. The Romans did not either. No one in the ancient world talked about rising again the way Jesus talks about it. People might rise again as ghosts (as Romans thought) or on the final day of judgment (as some Jews thought), but no one thought anyone could rise again on Sunday morning if buried on a Friday afternoon. This is why, even after three clear predictions of his resurrection, the disciples do not believe in that resurrection until they see, hear, and touch their resurrected Lord.

Then, beyond the brutality and the resurrection, perhaps the most unusual part of Jesus' mission is *who* he says will suffer, die, and rise. "See, we are going up to Jerusalem, and *the Son of Man* will be delivered over" and "condemn[ed] . . . to death" and tortured and killed (10:33). Fourteen times in Mark Jesus calls himself the "Son of Man." It is his favorite self-designation and an allusion to the glorious king depicted in Daniel 7:13–14:

---

4   Notice also Jesus' resolution: "Jesus was walking ahead of them" (Mark 10:32; cf. Luke 9:51).

5   The Jews will also mock Jesus (Mark 15:31–32), spit on him (14:65), and beat him (14:65).

6   In *The Cross of Christ* (Downers Grove, IL: InterVarsity Press, 1986), 23–24, John Stott writes of the cross: "It is probably the most cruel method of execution ever practised, for it deliberately delayed death until maximum torture had been inflicted. . . . Cicero in one of his speeches [*Against Verres* II.v.64, para. 165] condemned it as *crudelissimum taeterrimumque supplicium*, 'a most cruel and disgusting punishment.'"

7   "The resurrection is the ultimate reality that overrules Jesus' suffering and death, without superseding or canceling it." M. Eugene Boring, *Mark*, NTL (Louisville: Westminster John Knox, 2006), 299.

I saw in the night visions,

and behold, with the clouds of heaven
  there came one like a son of man [looks like a human],
and he came to the Ancient of Days [God]
  and was presented before him.
And to him was given dominion
  and glory and a kingdom,
that all peoples, nations, and languages
  should serve him;
his dominion is an everlasting dominion,
  which shall not pass away,
and his kingdom one
  that shall not be destroyed.

In light of Daniel 7, it is not unusual that the Son of Man should rise from the dead. He would have to rise from the dead in order to rule an everlasting and indestructible kingdom. But it is unusual that the Son of Man would die first.

When we read the opening words "See, we are going up to Jerusalem, and the Son of Man . . ." (Mark 10:33), we expect to read next ". . . will overthrow his enemies," not be delivered over to them. We expect to read that the "Son of Man" will shut the mouths of evildoers, not that evildoers will open their mouths to mock him and spit on him. We expect to read that the "Son of Man" will then rule over Jerusalem—sitting on his throne and receiving honor and glory from all the nations—not that he will receive thirty-nine lashes on his back and nails in his hands and feet. Surely the "Son of Man," to allude to what our Lord says in Mark 10:45, came to rule, not "to serve," and to live forever, not "give his life." However, this is the paradox of the passion of the Christ, a paradox we will explore further when we return to verse 45 at the end of this chapter.

Fourth, how do the disciples react to Jesus' actions and predictions? Verse 32 records their reactions to what Jesus has said in verses 13–31. They are "amazed" and "afraid" (10:32).[8] I grasp that they are amazed by what Jesus has said about receiving the kingdom like children, the dangers of riches, the impossibility of salvation, and his climactic pronouncement of his upside-down afterlife: "But many who are first [in this life] will be last [in the next life], and the last first" (10:31). But it surprises me that "those who followed him were [also] afraid" (10:32).

---

8 I take "they" and "those who followed" to be the twelve (see Mark 10:23, 32).

Perhaps they are afraid that they do not qualify for kingdom entrance. Perhaps they are afraid that Jesus is not the Messiah for whom they hope. Perhaps they are afraid they have sacrificed everything for a lost cause. Perhaps they are afraid because they fear what Jesus will talk about next and what he has mentioned in verse 30 ("persecutions"). Yes, perhaps they are afraid that Jesus is heading to Jerusalem for a holy war, something they will have to fight in against the well-trained and well-equipped Roman military. We do not know why they are afraid, and we do not know how they all respond to Jesus' final passion prediction, other than what we see next in the second half of our text, verses 35–45. Next let us look there, and let us together learn a few lessons.

Going up Is Going Down

Look first at **10:35**: "And James and John, the sons of Zebedee, came up to him and said to him, 'Teacher, we want you to do for us whatever we ask of you.'" In the last chapter we looked at what was commendable and condemnable about the rich man's question. James and John's smug statement is outright condemnable. Even the title "Teacher," which could be appropriate for Jesus in the right context, is inappropriate here. Jesus has just called himself the "Son of Man." To label him "Teacher" would be like an American tourist in the throne room of Buckingham Palace calling the king of England "Chuck." However, what is really inappropriate and condemnable, as it relates to Jesus, is the presumptuous attitude expressed in their statement: "*We* want <u>you</u> to do for *us* whatever *we* ask of <u>you</u>." I am not sure if the words "We want you to do for us" are worse than "Whatever we ask of you," but put together they are quite awful. After three years they are close to graduating from the School of Christ, but they have forgotten the ABCs of discipleship.

That said, I love what our loving Lord says in response. Here he does not say, "Get behind me, Satan." Instead he plays along: "And he said to them, 'What do you want me to do for you?'" (**10:36**). Put differently, "I'm curious just how spiritually shallow you are. What might you want from me? Help in the art of self-denial? Lessons on cross bearing?" Not exactly. Out of the heart the mouth speaks. "And they said to him [here's want we want], 'Grant us to sit, one at your right hand and one at your left, in your glory'" (**10:37**). What audacious ambition! Jesus has just told them about the cross, and these two want to be crowned. Jesus will soon be lifted up on a tree, and these two are scurrying to see who will sit upon thrones numbers two and three. Also (think about this!), what about Peter? James and John *and Peter* constitute the apostolic inner circle. I doubt they have told poor Peter what they are up to here. These two are up to no good.

Well, maybe some.

For, you see, as condemnable as this request in verse 37 is, there is actually something quite commendable about it. Their entreaty, "Grant us to sit, one at your right hand and one at your left, in your glory," implies that they believe that Jesus will reign in glory and that believers will reign with Jesus in glory.[9] Charles Spurgeon wisely noted, "We may question ourselves as to whether we think as much of our Lord as [they] did."[10] Indeed. They believed Jesus would reign in glory. They wanted a share in that glory. Do we?

However, it is not their high view of Jesus that Jesus will address next but their high view of self and their misunderstanding of the mission—both his and theirs. Look next at the interesting dialogue that ensues:

> Jesus said to them, "You do not know what you are asking. Are you able to drink the cup that I drink, or to be baptized with the baptism with which I am baptized?" And they said to him, "We are able." And Jesus said to them, "The cup that I drink you will drink, and with the baptism with which I am baptized, you will be baptized, but to sit at my right hand or at my left is not mine to grant, but it is for those for whom it has been prepared." (**10:38–40**)

Put simply, we see here that their "thoughtless self-confident spirit" does not persuade Jesus to give in to their demands.[11] Jesus is not buying their placard for the fireplace mantle ("We are able") or buying into their overconfident attitude. He offers three corrections.

First, he tells them that they are ignorant ("You do not know what you are asking," 10:38).

Second, he attacks their arrogance. They claim to be able to face whatever fate awaits them, as "the cup" (cf. Isa. 51:17) and "the baptism" (cf. Ps. 69:15) are both symbols of suffering, "especially for enduring the wrath of God."[12] But these two here have no idea of what actually awaits them. They might be thinking that "the cup" is a golden chalice of wine they will drink from in the throne room and their "baptism" some sort of special anointing for their new positions of power. Or they might be thinking like soldiers in an army:

---

9   Their thoughts are likely prompted by Jesus' teaching on glory (see 8:38; cf. 9:2–8; 13:26) and the event of the transfiguration (9:3). However, they have an overrealized eschatology. Jesus always links glory (Gk. *doxa*) to his return and his suffering, death, and resurrection (see 8:31; 9:31; 10:33–34). Also, in Matthew's and Luke's accounts Jesus speaks of the twelve's sitting on thrones (see Matt. 19:28; Luke 22:30).

10   C. H. Spurgeon, *The Gospel of the Kingdom* (Pasadena, TX: Pilgrim Publications, 1996), 171.

11   R. Alan Cole, *Mark*, TNTC (Downers Grove, IL: IVP Academic, 1989), 247.

12   Cole, *Mark*, 236.

"We may suffer in the battle, but we will be greatly rewarded on the day of victory." But, whatever thoughts be in their minds, Jesus wants them to think like cross-bearing soldiers in his self-sacrificial army.

They will indeed sip from Christ's chalice, but only he will drink in the full wrath of God on the cross (Mark 14:36). They will suffer, though, for Christ: James will be beheaded by Herod (Acts 12:2) in the early 40s, and John will be exiled to Patmos (Rev. 1:9) to die in the late 90s. James's cup contains a lethal dose of cyanide (a brutal but quick death); John's cup contains small doses of a subtle poison (a long life of long suffering). They certainly share in the sufferings of Christ (Col. 1:24). They are baptized into his mission.

Finally, Jesus denies their request. He says that thrones two and three are not his to give: "To sit at my right hand or at my left is not mine to grant, but it is for those for whom it has been prepared" (Mark 10:40). Here Jesus is not denying his divinity but clarifying his role and highlighting his humility. He has come to suffer, die, and rise. God the Father's role will be to raise him from the dead and also to determine who sits where at the messianic banquet. James and John might be surprised at the seating arrangements. They will be at that table. Jesus has promised that. But it might be Peter and Paul next to Jesus, or perhaps the daughter of the Syrophoenician woman and the widow who gives away her savings.

After Jesus' threefold correction the other ten disciples want in on the action. "And when the ten heard it, they began to be indignant at James and John" (**10:41**). They are angry not because James and John are failing to act like mature Christ-followers but because those two have gotten to the king of the kingdom first. They are mad that the lightning-fast "sons of thunder" (3:17) have struck first. We know this because Jesus addresses them all in **10:42–44**. He tosses the ten angry men into the pride pool, along with the two arrogant brothers. All twelve are ruled by a desire for preference and promotion.[13]

Our Lord, however, will not let them drown in this pool of pride. He will rescue them. He tosses in his life-saving teaching, found in verses 42–44:

> And Jesus called them to him and said to them, "You know [there is something I want you to know] that those who are considered rulers of the Gentiles lord it over them, and their great ones exercise authority over them. But it shall not be so among you. But whoever would be great among you must be your servant, and whoever would be first among you must be slave of all.

---

13 They have not moved beyond their argument in 9:34.

Jesus once again calls the twelve into a holy huddle. Unbelieving leaders (the "rulers of the Gentiles," 10:42), he tells them, have their game plan for winning in life. They "maneuver themselves into the favored places"[14]—they coerce and cajole to get to the top—and from there treat everyone below them in social status as inferior, as their servants and slaves.[15]

| Rulers of the Gentiles | lord it | over them |
| their great ones | exercise authority | over them. (10:42) |

"This is not our game plan," Jesus says. The inspired version reads: "But it shall not be so among you" (10:43). Below are the Xs and Os our Lord draws up.

| Whoever | would be great among you | must be your servant, and |
| whoever | would be first among you | must be slave of all. (10:43–44) |

Throughout Mark 10 Jesus has taught that cultural norms in relation to marriage, divorce, children, and wealth are not to be the norm in his kingdom. Here he adds a lesson on Christian leadership. He reverses the norms. A Christian leader is "great" and "first" if he is "servant" (Gk. *diakonos*) and "slave" (*doulos*).[16]

In those days a man's position within his community was measured by his manpower. The man who had one thousand slaves was more important than the man with ten. The man with ten slaves was more important than the man with none. Or, in our context, we would say that the CEO with one thousand employees is more important than the local business owner with only a secretary, a salesman, and a part-time cleaner.[17] Jesus says, "Think differently. I will estimate your greatness based on your service to others. First place goes to the one who serves the most."

14 Boring, *Mark*, 301.
15 In Plato's *Gorgias* (491E) Callicles says, "How can anyone be happy when he is the slave of anyone else at all?"
16 Note the focusing parallelism. Jesus moves from a "servant" of some to a "slave of all" (10:43–44). Also, the term "slave" (Gk. *doulos*) is a humbler designation than "servant" (*diakonos*). A servant might serve an owner in his house, while a slave is owned by him (part of his household). A slave is someone "who has no right or existence on his own, who lives solely for others." W. D. Davies and Dale C. Allison, *A Critical and Exegetical Commentary on the Gospel according to Saint Matthew*, ICC (Edinburgh: T&T Clark, 1988–1997), 93–94.
17 "In ancient times, the world measured greatness by the number of servants, even the number of slaves, one possessed. . . . Things have changed over the centuries, yet they remain much the same. People commonly consider other people successful if they have a large staff, if their name sits atop the organization chart, if many people report to them or take their orders." Daniel M. Doriani, *Matthew*, REC, 2 vols. (Phillipsburg, NJ: P&R, 2008), 2:228.

I do not know whether it is just me or the Spirit of God's working within me as we walk through the Gospel of Mark, but with each step closer to Calvary Jesus' teaching seems more difficult and more convicting. I waited tables for a year after college. From that experience I know that I would much rather be waited on than wait on others. Call it my natural disposition. Call it original sin. Call it total depravity. How hard it is to want to serve others. How hard it is to serve others. How hard it is to delight in serving others. We need God's help, do we not? God, help us. Serve us afresh with your Spirit. Thankfully, our Lord himself in his very teaching here gives us help. Here is the grand motivation to Christian service. Jesus is the ultimate example of what he has been talking about. Look at **10:45**. Underline it. "For even the Son of Man came not to be served but to serve, and to give his life as a ransom for many." Proverbs 25:11 says, "A word fitly spoken is like apples of gold in a setting of silver." Here we might say that Jesus' words are like watermelons of diamonds set on a platinum platter. Whatever the analogy (Solomon's is surely better than mine), every word here is to be treasured.

The word "for" (the first "for"), as I just said, gives us the motive for our mission. The word "even," as it comes before "the Son of Man," once again reminds us of the paradox of the divine plan. "No one would expect the One destined to receive eternal glory, worship, honor, and rule to come as a lowly servant. Still less would [one] expect him" to die for others.[18] The verb "came" tells us not only that "Jesus knew that the purpose of his incarnation was his death" but that he preexisted.[19] He came from somewhere. John 1:1–2 tells us where: "In the beginning was the Word, and the Word was *with* God, and the Word was God. He was in the beginning *with* God." That is where he came from! He came from the everlasting presence of the Father and Spirit. In the popular 1980s chorus "Lord I Lift Your Name on High" the refrain speaks of Jesus' coming from heaven to earth to "show the way" (Jesus models servant leadership: "He came not to be served but to serve," Mark 10:45) and then journey from the earth to the cross so as to pay our debt. Jesus is our example to imitate. But what we cannot imitate is the ultimate act of service: the cross, where he gave "his life as a ransom" (10:45).

These words tell us why Jesus came ("to give his life"), what his death accomplished (it was "a ransom"), and to whom it applies (the "many," 10:45). "A ransom (or redemption—the terms are interchangeable) is a purchase price paid to obtain the release of a captive."[20] The picture given here, and

18   Strauss, *Mark*, 458.
19   Osborne, *Mark*, 185.
20   Doriani, *Matthew*, 2:229.

elsewhere in the NT, is of Jesus' offering himself in order to release us from the slavery of our sins. As Peter says in 1 Peter 1:18–19, "It was not with perishable things such as silver or gold that you were redeemed . . . but with the precious blood of Christ" (NIV). Jesus offers himself in our place: Jesus "came . . . to give his life as a ransom *for* many" (10:45). The word "for" is a preposition of substitution. It means "in place of" or "instead of." With his blood (see Rom. 3:25) Jesus pays the price of our redemption. He goes to the grave; we go free and rise to new life.

The object of this redemption is the "many": Jesus "came . . . to give his life as a ransom for *many*" (Mark 10:45). The term "many" might mean "all" people (see "all" in 10:44) and embrace "the whole human race," or it might mean "the elect," not all people around the world but some people out of the world. I take the term to mean "the elect" or "God's chosen people" because Jesus here is borrowing from the language of Isaiah 53.[21] In Isaiah 53:12 the prophet speaks of the suffering servant, who "bore the sin of *many*, and makes intercession for the transgressors," and in verse 8 we read that he was "stricken for the transgression of *my people*." In Isaiah 53 the "many" are God's "people," those he has chosen out of this world and for whom the servant suffers in their place.

Children's Church

When I pastored at Westminster in Elgin, Illinois, every Sunday the church offered Children's Church for children aged 4 to 2nd grade. Children's Church was dismissed from the service for the sermon; the children learned, at an age-appropriate level, the same message from the same text I preached. On Thursday I sent a draft of my sermon to the teacher, and she changed it into a short and simple message. However, on the week I preached this sermon, I was late getting the sermon draft to Marcia, the teacher. So she simply studied the text herself and came up with a lesson. When I read it the day before I preached, I thought not only that she had done a great job but that she had written the perfect summary for *my* sermon's conclusion. Here is how she ended her lesson to the little ones:

> James and John—and the other disciples—had an ugly sin in their hearts called PRIDE. Pride is thinking too highly of yourself. Thinking you are always right and best.

---

21 "It is possible that in Jesus' eucharistic words as given in Matthew and Mark the term is employed with reference to the band of disciples." James C. VanderKam, *The Dead Sea Scrolls Today*, 2nd ed. (Grand Rapids, MI: Eerdmans, 2010), 202.

Thinking that you deserve to be first. Pride is a sin. We are not to think of ourselves first but others first. That is called HUMILITY. Someone who is humble is quick to think of others first. Someone who is humble is someone who serves.

Jesus was completely humble. Jesus was the perfect example of serving others. Even when he was tired or hungry, he served others. He always chose other people's needs over his own. His whole life—and death—was for other people. For us!

Seeing the Son of David

MARK 10:46–52

And when he heard that it was Jesus of Nazareth, he began
to cry out and say, "Jesus, Son of David, have mercy on me!"
Mark 10:47

In front of Evelyn (my middle daughter) I asked Charlotte (my youngest), "Do you trust me?" She smiled and said, "Yes." I then asked, "Have you ever done a trust fall?" She smiled and said, "Yes." I said, "Will you do one with me now?" She smiled and said, "Yes." I walked behind her and said, "Okay. Fall back." She trusted me. She fell back. I caught her. I said, "Now, keep your eyes closed." I motioned to Evelyn to walk behind her. I moved in front of Charlotte. Standing directly in front of her I asked again, "Do you still trust me?" She did not smile but gave a reluctant, "Yes." I said, "Well then, fall backward." She immediately opened her eyes. She looked behind her. Evelyn smiled. I said, "Charlotte, you didn't trust me!" I did the same to my son Simeon later that day. The same results. I obviously have a lot of work to do as a father to regain, or gain, my children's absolute trust.

I begin this way because the climax of this miracle story is Jesus' statement to blind Bartimaeus, "Your faith has made you well," or, as it could be rendered (the Gk. verb is *sōzō*), "Your faith has saved you." Saving faith is a key theme here. But there are other themes and other lessons to be learned in this short but theologically charged text. And one way to learn all the lessons is to review the three characters in the story: the "blind beggar" who cries out for help, those who at first oppose him (the "disciples and a great crowd," 10:46), and "Jesus of Nazareth" (10:47), the Savior who restores the man's sight.

The Disciples and the Great Crowd

We start with those who at first oppose the plea of this poor man. That is, we start by highlighting in the text the actions and lines of the disciples and the crowd. The story begins with Jesus' leaving Jericho. Why is he leaving Jericho? Is it because a historical reenactment of the walls of Jericho falling down has just ended?[1] No. Is it because Jericho is not a welcomed destination? No. Jericho was, and still is, an oasis in the desert. It is well watered ("well watered everywhere like the garden of the LORD," Gen. 13:10) and thus teeming with life ("the city of palm trees," Deut. 34:3). Jesus is leaving lovely Jericho because he is on a mission—the mission of the cross. He is heading down and then up to Jerusalem to suffer and die.

Pause here and ponder. Think about how difficult this move must have been. Colossians 1:16 tells us that Jesus created the world: "By him all things were created, in heaven and on earth." Imagine creating beautiful Jericho and then having to leave it. If I were the creator of the world, I would spend a good summer holiday there. But Jesus, our totally sacrificial Savior, walks away from it. He walks away from a taste of heaven to walk toward Jerusalem, where he will taste hell for us. He will drink the cup of God's wrath in our place.

With the salvation of the world at stake, as our Lord begins the long 17-mile walk to Jerusalem, "sitting by the roadside" is a "blind beggar" (Mark **10:46**). He is a smart beggar. If I were a beggar, I would station myself outside a city with a nice climate, strong economy, and thus plenty of rich people taking the route from the suburbs (Jericho) to the big city (Jerusalem). We will learn more about this blind man soon enough. For now, as our focus is on the disciples and the crowd, notice that, after the man asks Jesus to help, those following Jesus are not thrilled about his interruption.

What is their response to Bartimaeus's plea, "Jesus, Son of David, have mercy on me!" (**10:47**)?[2] They offer a public scolding. "And many rebuked him, telling him to be silent" (**10:48**). The "many" here are likely both the twelve and what we might call the adherents of the ancient version of the health-wealth gospel, the I'm-willing-to-follow-Jesus-if-he-will-do-something-for-me followers. This crowd will not crowd around Jesus for long.

Imagine the sting of what they say. Pretend that you are the blind man. You get word that the greatest miracle worker since Elijah is walking by. You cannot see. You just hear and feel the buzz of the biggest crowd you have ever known. You shout over the crowd—"Son of David, Son of David"—perhaps

---

1 "There were two Jerichos in Jesus' day. The old city, which was now either uninhabited or sparsely settled, was the first city conquered by Joshua and the Israelites when they entered the Promised Land (Josh 5). The new city, located a mile to the south, had been built by the Hasmoneans and expanded by Herod the Great." Mark L. Strauss, *Mark*, ZECNT (Grand Rapids, MI: Zondervan, 2014), 467.

2 This same faith-filled expression is found in the Psalms (see Pss. 6:2; 9:13; 30:10; 41:4, 10; 86:3 LXX). What the psalmists prayed to Yahweh, the blind man says to Jesus!

a hundred times, only to be told, "Be quiet, beggar." Who says this to you? "Many" from the crowd, but also some of those closest to Jesus. In the last chapter we learned that all twelve apostles wanted to be great by this world's standards. The next thing we know is that they have not exactly understood and applied Jesus' teaching on the first as last and the last as first. They push aside a blind beggar, the lowest of the low and the last of the losers. Perhaps they say to him, "We must get Jesus to Jerusalem. Our king has important matters to attend to. He doesn't have time to help a dirty, rotten, sinner like you."

Again the disciples disappoint. But they are not total imbeciles. They offer an ounce of compassion. Or, at the very least, they are willing still to obey orders. Look at verse 49. The blind man yells out his same line, "Son of David, have mercy on me!"[3] Then what happens? Jesus moves on? No. He stops. He stops to save. He stopped to save me. He stopped to save you. Jesus still stops to save sinners. But here he not only stops; he commands. Jesus says, "Call him" (**10:49**), the sense being "Bring him to me now." And they (the crowd, the disciples, some in the crowd who want to be disciples) actually obey. Notice how Mark phrases this act of obedience. Jesus issues an order, "*Call* him." What happens? "And they *called* the blind man, saying to him, 'Take heart.' Get up; he is calling you" (10:49). Here I imagine Peter, Andrew, James, and John, along with Matthew, issuing this summons. And I wonder whether their hearts are softened when they say these words, remembering their own call to come to Christ. "Get up; he is calling even you."

Blind Bartimaeus

Let us next look at the man Jesus calls, the blind man, and notice three aspects of this second character. First, notice that he is named. This might seem like an insignificant detail, but it is not. Major characters in Mark are always named (e.g., Peter). Important characters are also often named (e.g., John the Baptist). Minor characters are usually unnamed, even if they are influential people in that culture. For example, we are not told the name of the rich man in 10:17. In fact, this blind man is the only person in the miracle stories who is both named and healed. We are not told the names of the man with the unclean spirit (1:23), the leper (1:40), the paralytic (2:3), the man with the withered hand (3:1), the demon-possessed man (5:2), the bleeding woman (5:25), the little girl who died (5:23, although her father, Jairus, is named,

---

3   "That is prayer, when the poor soul in some weighty trouble, fainting and athirst, lifts up its streaming eyes, and wrings its hands, and beats its bosom, and then cries, 'Son of David, have mercy on me.'" Charles Spurgeon, *Sermons*, vol. 5, sermon 266, quoted in *CHSB*, 1492.

5:22), the Syrophoenician woman (7:26), the deaf man (7:32), another blind man (8:22), or the boy with the unclean spirit (9:17). And notice also that not only is he named, but his father is named as well. Bartimaeus is the "son of Timaeus" (10:46), which is redundant (*bar* is Hebrew for "son," and "Timaeus" is a common Greek name).[4]

Mark does not tell us why he records the blind beggar's name. Perhaps it is to give him the dignity that the disciples do not. To them he is a no-name, but to Mark (and Jesus, of course) even this blind beggar is a real person with a real name who has a real father and mother. Or perhaps he is named because he becomes a leader within the early Christian church. Some claim that Bartimaeus was a prominent leader in the church in Jerusalem. So, just as Mark recorded how Peter came to know Jesus (leader of the church in the eternal city), he records how Bartimaeus (a leader in the holy city) did as well. Perhaps. Whatever the reason, we should be assured that Jesus knows our names. We should, in fact, rejoice that our "names are written in heaven" (Luke 10:20). Jesus knows us, saves us, and will greet us by name when we enter the eternal kingdom.

The second aspect of this second character is that blind Bartimaeus understands Jesus' true identity. Or, we might say, he sees before he sees! Look again at Mark 10:46–48. After we read about Bartimaeus's "sitting by the roadside," Mark adds, "And when he heard that it was Jesus of Nazareth, he began to cry out and say, 'Jesus, Son of David, have mercy on me!' And many rebuked him, telling him to be silent. But he cried out all the more, 'Son of David, have mercy on me!'"

Historians still call Jesus what Mark calls Jesus here, "Jesus of Nazareth." It is a safe designation: the man's name (Jesus) and where he is from (Nazareth). There is no theological commitment with that title. But that is not what the blind man calls Jesus. He calls him "Son of David" (10:47, 48). Twice! No one else in Mark's Gospel calls Jesus the "Son of David"![5] So by calling Jesus "Son of David" the blind man is making a unique and important claim.

Just as the title "Son of Man" is linked to the prophets, so the title "Son of David" is linked to the OT, especially to the promise given to David in 2 Samuel 7. And those two titles are tied together tightly in the person of Jesus Christ. In 2 Samuel 7:12–13, 16 God promises that from Israel's king (David) shall come a future king through whom God will establish a forever kingdom.

4 This might be added to emphasize who Jesus is, namely, the "son of David," or to aid Mark's Gentile readers.
5 Jesus will refer to himself in this way in his question "How can the scribes say that the Christ is the son of David?" (Mark 12:35).

In Daniel 7:14, as we were reminded last chapter, the Son of Man is granted a forever kingdom, "an everlasting dominion, which shall not pass away." And with the story of the blind man coming right after Jesus' self-declaration of his identity ("the Son of Man," Mark 10:45) and mission (the cross and resurrection), the point that Mark makes here is that Jesus is the Son of Man and the Son of David and that we are to see what the blind man saw.

Recently I was with a Christian couple who shared with me about their relationship with a Jewish couple. At some point in their conversation with this couple, when they were talking about my sermons, the husband from this Jewish couple asked, "So does he preach from the Hebrew Scriptures?" The Christian couple replied, "He sure does!" To that I will add this: "More than that. I preach on the OT even when I am in the NT." I do so because the story of Jesus is the fulfillment of the story of the Hebrew Scriptures.

Now, let us say you corner me in a dark alley and say, "Pastor, you have two minutes to tell me the ten most important chapters of the OT or else," I would quickly reply, "Can I have one minute and give you twelve chapters?" Then, after you say, "Sure. I guess so. I will put down the knife and start to tithe regularly." I would say, "Great. No problem."

1. Genesis 1 (creation)
2. Genesis 3 (fall)
3. Genesis 12 (the Abrahamic covenant—through Abraham's offspring God will bless all the nations)
4. Exodus 12 (the final plague of the Passover; Israel's exodus from Egypt)
5. Exodus 20 (the Ten Commandments)
6. Leviticus 16 (the priesthood and Day of Atonement)
7. Deuteronomy 18 (the promise of "the prophet"; see John 1:21, 25; 6:14; 7:40)
8. 2 Samuel 7 (the Davidic covenant—through David's offspring God will establish a forever kingdom)
9. Psalm 110 (the divine Davidic king, by means of his resurrection, will rule over the nations)
10. Isaiah 53 (the suffering servant)
11. Jeremiah 31 (the new covenant)
12. Daniel 7 (the bestowal of the forever kingdom on the Son of Man)

Who is the Jesus we believe in? Hopefully, it is the Jesus presented in the Bible. And who is that Jesus? He is the creator of the world (Genesis 1). He is the curse crusher (Genesis 3). He is a Jew, offspring of Abraham, who has brought salvation to the nations (Genesis 12). He is the only man to ever keep the law perfectly (Exodus 20). He is the prophet greater than Moses (Deuteronomy 18). He is the one "pierced for our transgressions" (Isa. 53:5). He is the "great high priest" (Heb. 4:14) who has made "propitiation for the sins of the people" (Heb. 2:17) and who with his blood ushers in the new covenant (Leviticus 16; Jeremiah 31). He is the resurrected king who has conquered his enemies (Psalm 110). He is the forever king of the forever kingdom from the line of David (2 Samuel 7; Daniel 7). He is the Son of David! Of course, the blind man did not know or believe all this about Jesus. But we can and should. And we should be grateful for this beggar who points us in the right direction, the blind man who helps us see.

So, as we are looking at the blind beggar, we are noticing three aspects. First, we notice that he is named, and, second, that Bartimaeus understands a central component of Jesus' true identity, namely, that Jesus is the "Son of David." Third, Bartimaeus trusts that Jesus can do the impossible. Put simply, notice the blind man's great faith.

As I said earlier, the climactic moment in this story is when Jesus says, "Your faith has *saved* you" (Mark 10:52 CSB). What is the nature of saving faith? Well, this story explains the doctrine of Christian faith in story form. First, saving faith is in Jesus. The object of faith is Jesus. It is not faith in self. It is not faith in faith. It is not faith in Jesus plus anything or anyone else.

Second, saving faith is in the Jesus of the Bible, the Jesus I just explained, the good news about Jesus that Paul describes in this way: "Remember Jesus Christ, raised from the dead, descended from David. This is my gospel" (2 Tim. 2:8 NIV; cf. Rom. 1:3–4). Is that the gospel you believe about Jesus?

Third, saving faith acknowledges a need for salvation. For what does the blind man ask?[6] He asks for mercy. He cries out, "Jesus, Son of David, have mercy on me!" (Mark 10:47). He is told to keep quiet. He perseveres in faith.[7] He cries out again, "Son of David, have mercy on me!" (10:48). He begs for mercy. At one level he wants Jesus to pity his physical position. He is blind. When Jesus asks, "What do you want me to do for you?" the man replies, "Let me recover my sight" (10:51). But at another level he might be asking Jesus to have mercy on his *body and soul*, to forgive him his sins—perhaps specifically to forgive him of the sin or sins that had led to his blindness. We learn from John 9 that there is not always

---

6   "He was not asking for glory. He was not asking to be exalted in Jesus' kingdom. He was not even asking to be delivered from poverty." R. C. Sproul, *Mark*, St. Andrew's Expositional Commentary (Sanford, FL: Reformation Trust, 2015), 275.

7   This is a trait often associated with faith in Mark (see Mark 2:5; 5:23, 34; 7:27–29, 32; 8:22; 9:24).

a direct correspondence between some sin and certain blindness. But in other places in the Bible blindness is related to sin. For example, Paul, deep in his sin of persecuting the church, is blinded on the road to Damascus (Acts 9:8–9; cf. 13:11). God also blinds the men pounding on Lot's door in Sodom (Gen. 19:11).

Whatever the possible relationship between blindness and sin as it relates to blind Bartimaeus, we know that this man, like all people, is a sinner and that his deepest need, like that of the paralytic, is not physical restoration but spiritual restoration. Thus we know that we, along with King David himself, can and should pray,

> Have mercy on me, O God,
>   according to your steadfast love;
> according to your abundant *mercy*
>   blot out my transgressions. (Ps. 51:1)

We should call out, knowing that whoever "calls on the name of the Lord shall be saved" (Joel 2:32; cf. Rom. 10:13; Acts 2:21).

Fourth, saving faith trusts that Jesus has the power to save. Look again at Mark **10:51–52**, where we read:

> And Jesus said to him, "What do you want me to do for you?" And the blind man said to him, "Rabbi,[8] let me recover my sight." And Jesus said to him, "Go your way; your faith has made you well." And immediately he recovered his sight and followed him on the way.

This man believed that Jesus had the ability to cure blindness. Where did such confidence come from? It could be that he had heard about the healing of the blind man in Bethsaida (8:25), although Bethsaida is a good distance from Jericho, and news did not travel fast in those days. It could be that he believed that Jesus, as the Messiah ("Son of David") and as part of his ministry, would open the eyes of the blind. Isaiah had predicted, "The eyes of the blind shall be opened" (Isa. 35:5) and that the Christ would care for the poor (see Isa. 11:4; cf. Ps. 72:12). That said, this man had no precedent to work with. If he were somehow educated in the Bible, or had attended synagogue to hear the Bible explained, he never would have heard a story about a blind man's

---

8 The Greek word here is *rabbouni*, used only one other time in the NT (John 20:16), when Mary addresses the resurrected Jesus outside the tomb.

receiving his sight. No prophet (not even Elijah),[9] priest (not even Aaron), or king (not even Solomon) had brought sight to the blind. So, what amazing faith in Jesus to believe that Jesus had the power to do what had never been done in world history.

Fifth, saving faith is active: it heeds Jesus' call to come and follow. This man's active faith is shown from start to finish. He hears that Jesus is walking by ("and when he heard") and immediately takes action ("he began to cry out," 10:47). He is told by the crowd to cut out the crying out. "But he cried out all the more" (10:48). Jesus stops. He asks his disciples to call the man to him. They say, "Take heart. Get up; he is calling you" (10:49). And does the man move? Yes. He acts in faith! Look at the language: "And throwing off his cloak, he sprang up and came to Jesus" (**10:50**). How marvelous! What a picture of *pistis* (faith)! He throws off his outer garment, which keeps him warm at night but might hold him back in getting to Jesus in time. Or, he thinks, "I won't be needing this rag anymore. I'll be healed. A new life is ahead of me." The jumping up is also great. There is no hesitation here. He springs up. He is like a jack-in-the-box just waiting for the lid to open. Then, after the healing, notice his final action. Jesus says, "Go your way; your faith has made you well" (10:52). Jesus says in effect, "You are free to walk wherever you want to walk and on whatever path you desire." And what does this man do? "And immediately he recovered his sight and [immediately] *followed him on the way*" (10:52).

When someone comes to Jesus when Jesus calls him, as this man did, it always has a positive connotation. It is a good thing to do. Also, whenever someone follows Jesus, especially after Jesus has just done something for him, it is a really good sign. Do you remember what Jesus said to the rich man? "Come, follow me" (10:21). That rich man did not. He would not. But this poor beggar, he would. He did. He came to Jesus; he followed Jesus. Not only that, he followed Jesus "on the way" (10:52).[10] That is a loaded phrase, for what is "the way"? Put differently, where is Jesus going? Jerusalem. "See, we are going up to Jerusalem" (10:33a). Why? "And the Son of Man will be delivered over" to suffer and die (10:33b). This once blind man is going to walk with Jesus to the cross.

9   Yahweh, through Elisha's prayer, restored sight to the once-blinded Arameans (see 2 Kings 6:18–20). But there it is clear that God, not the prophet, has the power to take away and give sight.
10   Mark indicates the nature of discipleship by repeating the Greek words κολουθέω ("follow," 18x) and ὁδός ("way," 16x), "with a concentration in 8:27–10:52." Elizabeth Shively, "Mark," in *The Greek New Testament, Produced at Tyndale House, Cambridge, Guided Annotating Edition*, ed. Daniel K. Eng (Wheaton, IL: Crossway, 2023), 129. Cf. Hans F. Bayer, *A Theology of Mark: The Dynamic between Christology and Authentic Discipleship*, EBT (Phillipsburg, NJ: P&R, 2012), 96, "Fig. 1. Eight core characteristics of discipleship in Mark."

With that in mind we come to a sixth feature of faith. Cruciformity. A willingness to follow Jesus into a life of suffering. Faith knows the way to glory is through the pain of persecution. Down in this life is up in the next.

So, with all that said, let me ask you the following questions. As you look at this blind man as he shows us the nature of saving faith, do you have such faith? Is your faith *in* Jesus, the Jesus of the Bible? Does your faith acknowledge a need for mercy, for salvation from sin? Does your faith trust that Jesus, and he alone, has the power to save? And is your faith alive and active, willing to come to Jesus and continue to follow after him, even if that following after him means suffering for identifying with the humble king and his counter-cultural kingdom?

Jesus of Nazareth

In this chapter, as we have been exploring all the interesting and applicable facets of Mark 10:46–52, we turn our attention from the "blind beggar" who cries out for help to "Jesus of Nazareth" (10:47), the Savior from the highest heavens who restores the sight of the least of men on earth. Of course, we have had our eyes on Jesus from the start and have noticed a number of things he has said and done. I want us now, however, to tighten the focus.

I wrote of how Jesus was not sidetracked from his mission. He was headed to Jerusalem. No stopping in Jericho for a spa day. I also wrote of the power of Jesus' call. But let me now highlight four other details of this miracle story that should make us love and want to continue to follow Jesus.

First, notice that out of the "great crowd" Jesus stops for one man, a "blind beggar" (10:46). He does not stop here because a rich man asks him an important question. He does not stop here because a religious leader wants to debate with him a point of theology. He stops here to help the helpless. He stops here to touch (see Matt. 20:34) an untouchable.

Second, notice that Jesus does not deny the designation "Son of David." Many people from the crowds, and perhaps the disciples too, rebuke Bartimaeus. "Be quiet!" But not Jesus. In Matthew, when the children cry out, "Hosanna to the Son of David!" the chief priests and the scribes are "indignant" (Matt. 21:15). But Jesus is not upset here in Mark with that same title. Why? Because the blind man, in his childlike faith, understands who Jesus is.

Third, notice the irony of what Jesus asks. As we saw in the last chapter, James and John had said to Jesus, "We want you to do for us whatever we ask of you" (Mark 10:35). Here Jesus asks the blind man, "What do you want me to do for you?" (10:51; cf. 10:36). Of course, such a question fits perfectly what Jesus had said in verse 45: that he came to serve not to be served. "What do you want me to do for you?" What an utterly humble question. Can you imagine being invited to the Oval Office, where the president greets you, invites to you take a seat, and grabs a tray of coffee and cakes, brings it to you, and then, as he is serving, asks, "Is there anything you'd like for me to do for you?" Oh, the humility of Christ! May we never get over it or take it for granted. "You know the grace of our Lord Jesus Christ," Paul writes in 2 Corinthians 8:9, "that though he was rich, yet for your sake he became poor, so that you by his poverty might become rich."

Fourth, notice Jesus' creative, or re-creative, power, featured in Mark 10:51–52:

> And Jesus said to him, "What do you want me to do for you?" And the blind man said to him, "Rabbi, let me recover my sight." And Jesus said to him, "Go your way; your faith has made you well." And immediately he recovered his sight and followed him on the way.

I do not know whether the sun stood still again in Jericho when Jesus said, "Go your way; your faith has made you well" (10:52), but I do know that from the time it takes Jesus to say, "Go"—what Mark labels "immediately"— this blind man's eyes are opened. The speed is impressive. The "immediately" here is awesome, and it highlights Jesus' awesome authority. Jesus does not conjure up a special potion or recite a magical incantation. He uses no props, such as a rod sent from God. He does not even pray to heaven, as far as we know. He just acts. He acts like God (Ps. 146:8). He creates with a word ("Let there be light," Gen. 1:3), and this man sees light and all that the sunlight around brings to light. He sees Jericho. His eyes are opened just outside this Edenic city. Imagine seeing the colors of the fruits dangling from the trees— the green leaves filled with orange, red, and yellow. He sees his own hands (brown), those dirty hands that had held out each day hoping for a coin to be dropped into them. He sees the blue sky. The white clouds. The tropical birds. I imagine a rainbow trout jumping from the fresh waters on such an occasion. He sees people. He sees the beggar he had begged next to for years. "Joe, wow, you look worse than me. I thought I was bad off." He sees rich people riding by him in such beautiful purple robes and bleached-white turbans. Then he sees Jesus. He literally sees "the light of the knowledge of the glory of God in the face of Jesus Christ" (2 Cor. 4:6).

Do you see Jesus? Do you see that light? Do you see Jesus for who he is and what he has come to do, has already done, and someday soon will do? And do you long to see your own resurrected body? New? Fresh? Not plagued with the side effects of sin? Do you long to see the new heavens and new earth? To run in the green fields? To leap into the fresh waters? To taste the milk and honey? To run your fingers through a lion's mane? To ask an asp over for tea? To hug a loved one? To see your Savior? To see the "light of the world" after living in a dark one?

A Parable of Our Salvation

Once Helen Keller was asked, "Isn't it terrible to be blind?" She replied, "Better to be blind and see with your heart than to have two good eyes and see nothing." In this final miracle in Mark we have more than a miracle story. We have a parable of saving faith. Like this blind man, we are all born into darkness, spiritual darkness. Also like him, we need to acknowledge our condition, come to Jesus, understand his identity, believe in his power, beg for mercy, receive salvation, and follow him. Have you done that yet? If not, I invite you to do so. For Jesus is passing by today and is more than willing to stop to save.

Blessed Is the Coming Kingdom of David!

MARK 11:1-11

Hosanna! Blessed is he who comes in the name of the Lord!
Blessed is the coming kingdom of our father David! Hosanna
in the highest!
Mark 11:9–10

I remember the day that President Jimmy Carter came to my hometown. A large crowd was gathered to see Marine One land in the open field near my house. A red carpet was rolled out. Two marines stood at attention as the stairs were lowered. When the president walked out, the soldiers saluted, a high school band played "Hail to the Chief," the large crowd cheered, and a plethora of photographers clicked their cameras. President Carter waved at the top of the stairs and walked down. Then, surrounded by the Secret Service, he entered a black stretch limousine. Led by dozens of police cars in their squad cars with lights ablaze, he rode slowly through town. All streets were closed. All traffic stopped. Someone important had come to town. I knew it. Everyone knew it.

In the days of Jesus a certain protocol existed for important world leaders. For example, when Julius Caesar entered Rome after a military victory, he rode through the Triumphal Arch on a chariot pulled by four white stallions. The thousand-plus crowd erupted in praise as it waved tree branches. Red banners with golden phoenixes lined his way. The Roman military, garbed in its red and white gear, marched before and after him. Soldiers. Archers. Trumpeters. Caesar wore golden armor and a red sash, with a golden garland held above his head like a halo.

Mark 11:1–11 depicts a royal entrance, but one unlike any other in history. There is a parade of sorts, a crowd eager to draw near and offer shouts of acclamation. But this king rides into town on a colt, not on a chariot pulled by warhorses or in a five-hundred-horsepower limo. He moves slowly toward Jerusalem. Low to the ground. Step by slow step. Imagine a full-grown man riding on a newly born donkey! It is an odd and ironic scene, one I want to help us make sense of and one I want to help us understand so we might rightly acknowledge the glorious king of creation who came to save us (hosanna!) and who came also to call us to follow in his humble ways.

Near to Jerusalem

In order to understand and apply this odd, ironic, and extraordinary scene, I want us first to walk through the text verse by verse and then, second, to pause and think about how what happened nearly two thousand years ago is relevant today, more relevant than the latest news flash that interrupts our regularly scheduled broadcast.

We will get at understanding this text by following the three movements Jesus makes. First, in Mark 11:1–7, after Jesus has zigzagged through Galilee, then Samaria, then Perea, and finally Judea, ministering in at least thirty-five localities,[1] he now draws near to Jerusalem ("They drew near to Jerusalem," 11:1). Traveling southwest from Jericho, he comes to Bethphage and Bethany, villages less than 2 miles outside the holy city. Then, second (11:8–10), as he makes his way around the eastern slopes of the Mount of Olives,[2] he is "on the road" (11:8), an old Roman road that goes into Jerusalem. Finally, he arrives at his ultimate destination ("And he entered Jerusalem," 11:11).

Let us start, then, where Marks starts. Look with me at **11:1–7**. Look at what Jesus does first outside of Jerusalem and notice the detailed preparations for his entrance.

> Now when they drew near to Jerusalem, to Bethphage and Bethany, at the Mount of Olives, Jesus sent two of his disciples and said to them, "Go into the village in front of you, and immediately as you enter it you will find a colt tied, on which no one has ever sat. Untie it and bring it. If anyone says to you, 'Why are you doing this?' say, 'The Lord has need of it and will send it back here immediately.'" And they went away and found a colt tied at a door outside in the street, and they untied it. And some of those standing there said to them, "What are you doing, untying the colt?" And they told them what Jesus had said, and they let them go. And they brought the colt to Jesus and threw their cloaks on it, and he sat on it.

---

1 R. Kent Hughes, *Mark: Jesus, Servant and Savior*, PTW, 2 vols. (Wheaton, IL: Crossway, 1989), 2:78.

2 "The Mount of Olives lies east of Jerusalem and overlooks the city. It consists of a mountain ridge two miles long, and its northern summit is 2,963 feet above sea level." Robert H. Stein, *Mark*, BECNT (Grand Rapids, MI: Baker Academic, 2008), 503.

Before I preached this sermon I met with my youth-ministry intern, and we talked about the text. I asked him to come with a homiletical outline. What I really liked about his outline was a subpoint he made under an accurate but unexciting heading: "Jesus sends two disciples into a village to commandeer a colt." Great summary of these verses, but a bit dull for coming off the tongue, staying in the head, and moving the soul. But here is what I liked: the first subpoint under that, which reads, "The explicit and detailed instruction of such seemingly insignificant acts indicates the special significance of the event." I like the alliterative qualities. But I also like the precise summary of the irony. Why does Mark spend seven verses on Jesus' instructions about how he is to enter Jerusalem? We will find out soon enough. But the observation stands, one that my intern noticed well: there must be something important about all the specific instructions we find before the main event. So then, what specific instructions, and other specific details, do we find?

First, the town of Bethany should leap off the page. This is the place, as recorded in John's Gospel, where Jesus has recently raised Lazarus from the dead (John 11). No wonder people want to hail Jesus as king when he comes to town or is traveling through one town into the big city.

Second, notice that Jesus sends "two of his disciples" into the village (Mark 11:1). I imagine he sent James and John because those two, who wanted to be great (10:37), needed to be taught a lesson. That lesson for them, or whomever Jesus sent, was to learn *the importance of going on a seemingly ordinary mission.* For their mission was just that! "Go into the village in front of you, and immediately as you enter it you will find a colt tied, on which no one has ever sat. Untie it and bring it. If anyone says to you, 'Why are you doing this?' say, 'The Lord has need of it and will send it back here immediately'" (11:2–3).

Imagine what they are thinking to themselves. Perhaps something like, "Okay, we are to go into some unnamed village, the next Podunk town we come upon. Then we are to look left as soon as we pass the sign that reads, 'Welcome to Nowhereville, population under twenty,' and there will we find something spectacular! A stolen Roman battle steed? No. There we will see the baby of a dumb ass. We are to steal this little stupid creature. Then, after we are running away with this baby donkey, we should expect to be targeted by some locals, who shout, 'Hey, what are you two youngsters up to?' Then (Is this for real?) our next line is to be, 'The Lord has need of it and will send it back to you this very day' (see 11:3). Put differently, 'Jesus is borrowing, not stealing. So, can we go?'"

Third, notice that Jesus is accurate in his predictions:

And they went away [They actually obeyed this odd order!] and found a colt tied at a door outside in the [main or possibly only] street, and they untied it [Did they believe Jesus' predictive powers now?]. And some of those standing there said to them, "What are you doing, untying the colt?" And they [astonished, I imagine] told them what Jesus had said, and they [the locals] let them go. (11:4–6)

The only way this could have all worked out the way it did is either if Jesus had prearranged everything or if he had predictive powers[3] and those townsmen had some sort of divine revelation. I favor the more supernatural explanation because, if Jesus can restore sight to a blind man, then he can find a way to communicate a simple plan to procure a simple-minded creature. Also, in Luke's account the owner of the colt has no knowledge of any earlier agreement (see Luke 19:33).

So, how did Jesus know the precise location of the colt? He is the omniscient Son of God. And why did these few townspeople let the two disciples take the colt? My theory is that they were in on this plot, a righteous and divine conspiracy, one as suspicious and nearly as spectacular as what Gabriel had announced to Mary. They knew the Lord. They knew that Jesus was Lord. And so they did what their Lord had said to do, directions perhaps given to them in a dream or through an angelic encounter. When they heard the line, "The Lord has need of it" (Mark 11:3, cf. 11:6), they knew their mission was accomplished as soon as they said, "Please, then, take the animal."

Fourth, notice the two disciples also accomplish their mission ("And they brought the colt to Jesus"), even making a makeshift saddle for him ("And [they] threw their cloaks on it," 11:7).

On the Road to Jerusalem

Once Jesus straddles this beast of burden ("And he sat on it," 11:7) the action moves forward as he—their Lord and ours—moves forward. We follow. We are moving from being "near to Jerusalem" (11:1) to being "on the road" to Jerusalem (11:8).

And many spread their cloaks on the road, and others spread leafy branches that they had cut from the fields. And those who went before

3 See Mark 2:8; 3:5; 5:30, 32; 8:17, 31; 9:31; 10:33–34; 12:15; 13:3–36; 14:7–9, 18–21, 27–30.

and those who followed were shouting, "Hosanna! Blessed is he who comes in the name of the Lord! Blessed is the coming kingdom of our father David! Hosanna in the highest!" (**11:8–10**)

Jesus gets the green-carpet treatment. Tall grasses, branches from palm trees (see John 12:13), and other green leaves are used to line the road. Shouts of praise echo in the air. This is a spontaneous celebration. They treat Jesus like a king because they hope he is journeying to Jerusalem for a holy war against the occupant Romans and oppressive Jewish authorities. They hope that what he has done to demons, disease, and death he will do to evildoers. Just as Simon Maccabeus entered Jerusalem over a century before Jesus, with people "singing hymns of praise and thanksgiving"; "playing harps, cymbals, and lyres"; and "waving palm branches" (*1 Macc.* 13:51), so this crowd cries out in hope that a military savior has arrived, one who, like Simon, will oust the enemies of God's people.

They shout "Hosanna!" which means "Save us now." I imagine the crowd walking closely before him, yelling, "Hosanna! Blessed is he who comes in the name of the Lord!" (Mark 11:9), while the crowd pressing closely behind him echoes and advances the idea, "Blessed is the coming kingdom of our father David! Hosanna in the highest!" (11:10). The first part of this antiphonal arrangement comes from Psalm 118:26, the last of the Hillel psalms (Psalms 113–118), the six psalms that pilgrims sang as they went up to Jerusalem for the Passover.[4] The second part, which focuses on the promise of the coming of David's eternal kingdom (2 Sam. 7:14–16), likely corresponds to the coronation parade of King Solomon, in which Solomon rode into town on David's mule and the people shouted, "Long live King Solomon!" and "rejoiced with great joy" (see 1 Kings 1:32–48). After that experience, Solomon introduced the breeding of horses. From then on, he would ride tall and proud.

Entering Jerusalem

So, as we are journeying along with Jesus, we have seen him "near to Jerusalem" (Mark 11:1) and "on the road" to Jerusalem (11:8), and now he finally enters Jerusalem: "And he entered Jerusalem and went into the temple. And when he had looked around at everything, as it was already late, he went out to Bethany with the twelve" (**11:11**).

---

4   The pattern is ABBA, A containing "Hosanna" and B "blessed." It could also be that one group says the A lines and the other the B lines.

In Mark this is the first and only record of Jesus' entering the holy city. With all the pomp and circumstance that precedes verse 11, we expect something dramatic to happen next. Instead, this episode has an "odd and anticlimactic ending."[5] Jesus enters the holy city. He even goes into the holy temple. Yet Jesus says nothing; he does nothing else. And where has the crowd gone? Why is no one here to greet him? Has everyone gone to sleep? How late is it? Why is the temple complex like a ghost town? Instead of a cloud of glory descending on the Most Holy Place when the King of kings enters, a shadow of darkness covers the temple mount. It is the shadow of the cross. It is in less than a week from that day when the Lord will hang lifeless on a dead tree.

The point, then, of verse 11 is this: Jesus has come not as "a gawking tourist, marveling at the magnificent temple, nor [as] a pious worshiper offering prayer or sacrifice"[6] but rather as the Son of David, the Son of Man, and the Son of God, who will render judgment on God's people (stay tuned for the next day) and allow God's people,[7] as the week will close, to render judgment upon him. Oh, the mystery of the marvelous cross!

The colt has been returned.[8] The owner is glad to see that Jesus keeps his word. The eager crowd has dispersed to find a room for the night. Jesus stands alone, I imagine, for a moment: "And *he* entered Jerusalem and [he] went into the temple. And when *he* had looked around at everything, as it was already late, *he* went out to Bethany with the twelve." He dried his tears (Luke tells us that Jesus "wept over" the city, Luke 19:41). Then he woke up the twelve. "Okay, men, let's walk to Mary, Martha, and the resurrected Lazarus's house for a rest. Tomorrow, I have some table turning to do."

From Three Geographical Shifts to Two Theological Truths

As we have been working our way through this familiar but fascinating passage, we have made three geographical shifts. We have walked with Jesus outside of Jerusalem, on the road to Jerusalem, and then into Jerusalem. Let us conclude by continuing the walk. What does this ancient journey to Jerusalem teach us today? Two theological truths. Two applications and admonitions. First, know the coming king—or, from our perspective, know the

---

5   Mark L. Strauss, *Mark*, ZECNT (Grand Rapids, MI: Zondervan, 2014), 478.

6   David E. Garland, *Mark*, NIVAC (Grand Rapids, MI: Zondervan, 1996), 428–29, in Strauss, *Mark*, 483.

7   "Jesus declared himself to be both king and high priest, who presided over the temple and the worship of God." John Calvin, *Commentary on a Harmony of the Gospels*, quoted in *CHSB*, 1493.

8   "Jesus, unlike plundering kings, returns the colt when finished." Grant R. Osborne, *Mark*, TTCS (Grand Rapids, MI: Baker, 2012), 189.

king who has come and will come again. Second, live under the rule of his kingdom. We will tackle each truth in turn.

Know the King Who Has Come

First, let us know the king who has come.

In the last chapter we looked at Jesus' identity. The blind man calls Jesus the "Son of David." I explained how that title is the proper title for Jesus, one he accepts for himself, because he is the promised descendant of David who has come to establish and rule the everlasting kingdom. Here in Mark 11:9–10, after people declare that Jesus is the one "who comes in the name of the Lord," they say, "Blessed is the coming kingdom of our father David!" They say this because here Jesus makes his first public declaration of his identity. Before this day, and after many incredible miracles, he has asked people who have rightly announced his identity to keep quiet.[9] But here, as Jesus enters the holy city, the secret is out! Jesus himself announces his identity through a bold action. He rides into Jerusalem on a colt, which is what Zechariah (Zech. 9:9) said the Messiah would do:[10]

> Rejoice greatly, O daughter of Zion!
>> Shout aloud, O daughter of Jerusalem!
> Behold, your king is coming to you;
>> righteous and having salvation is he,
> humble and mounted on a donkey,
>> on a colt, the foal of a donkey.

Do you see the audacity of Jesus' intentions? He procures a colt. He sits on it. He rides into town. And in doing so he sets the stage for a conflict of kingdoms: Jesus versus the Roman Empire; Jesus versus the Jewish religious establishment. Jesus waits until this moment to announce his identity. He waits for the right moment. He knows the plan. He obeys the plan. He rides into Jerusalem as the humble promised king, the king from the line of David.

First, let us know the king who came. Jesus is the Son of David. But he is more. He is the Son of Man and Son of God. Biologically, he is an actual descendant of David; ontologically, he is the second person of the Trinity.

---

9 The messianic secret. See Mark 1:25, 34, 44; 3:11–12; 5:43; 7:36; 8:26, 30; 9:9.

10 The "minor" prophet Zechariah is of major importance to the authors of the NT (quoted or alluded to over 80x). In chapter 9 he speaks of the coming of a human king and in chapter 14 of a divine king. In the coming of Jesus these two kings are combined in him. Jesus is both the Son of David and David's Lord. The Davidic king will come both as the humble and suffering king and as the king who forever reigns in perfect righteousness and glory.

Moreover, notice what Jesus calls himself. In verse 9 the people speak of Jesus' coming on God's behalf ("in the name of the Lord"), but in verse 3 Jesus labels himself "the Lord"—"The Lord has need of it."[11]

The label "Lord" is a loaded label.[12] Is Jesus claiming to be the Lord God of the OT? I answer in the affirmative, for five reasons. First, as pointed out, in the immediate context Jesus uses the same word for himself that the people use for God. Second, *kurios* is used of Yahweh over six thousand times in the Greek translation of the Hebrew Scriptures. Third, in Mark 12:35–37 Jesus tests the scribes with his riddle from Psalm 110. How can David write, "The Lord said to my Lord?" The only plausible answer is that the Son of David is also David's Lord. Fourth, the word is used elsewhere in the NT in reference to Christ (see Acts 2:36; Rom. 10:9; Phil. 2:11). Fifth, Jesus here rides on a colt, an animal "on which no one has ever sat" (Mark 11:2). "The idea," as Strauss points out, "seems to be one of purity. In the OT animals that had never been yoked were used in sacrifices (Num 19:2; Deut. 21:3) and for pulling the ark of the covenant (1 Sam 6:7). The Mishnah [m. Sanh. 2:5] says that a king's horse cannot be ridden by anyone except the king."[13] Jesus' sitting also demonstrates his control of creation. A colt takes months to be broken in. Even the most experienced rider cannot just mount a colt without being shortly thereafter tossed off. The colt needs to get to know its rider. The two need to interact on the ground first. So, what does it say that Jesus can so easily tame this beast? Why is the colt not scared? Why does it not buck him off and then take off? This creature knows its Creator. This is similar to what happened to Jesus in the wilderness. In Mark 1:13 we read that after his temptation Jesus "was with the wild animals"; implied in that is that the wild animals, such as lions, were not tearing him limb from limb. Just as Jesus

---

11 "The word *kurios* could reference, as used elsewhere in Mark, God (11:9; 12:11, 29–30, 36; 13:20) or the colt's master/owner (12:9; 13:35). However, the most natural referent in the immediate context, and the content of the Gospel as a whole, is Jesus (see 1:3; 2:28; 5:19; 7:28; 12:36, 37). Also the theme of Jesus' authority is prominent throughout the narrative of the triumphal entry. It is clear from as early as 1:3—where the evangelist applies the term for the sacred tetragrammaton to Jesus, as John the Baptist references the coming of Jesus—that Mark does hesitate to make the connection between Jesus and Yahweh, or Jesus as Yahweh. Mark intentionally blurs the lordly identity of Jesus and Yahweh of the OT." Simon J. Gathercole, *The Preexistent Son: Recovering the Christologies of Matthew, Mark, and Luke* (Grand Rapids, MI: Eerdmans, 2006), 245. This is said in reference to Matthew 22:43–45 (parallel Mark 12:36–37), but it could also be said of Mark 1:3.
12 See Douglas Sean O'Donnell, "Insisting on Easter: Matthew's Use of the Theologically Provocative Vocative (κύριε) in the Suppliant Narratives," in *The Earliest Perceptions of Jesus in Context: Essays in Honour of John Nolland on His 70th Birthday*, ed. Aaron W. White, Craig A. Evans, David Wenham (Bloomsbury T&T Clark, 2018).
13 Strauss, *Mark*, 479.

tamed the lions in the wilderness and waves at sea, so he tames this beast of burden. He is the king of creation!

We need to know the king who came. We need to know that he is the Son of David. We need to know that he is the Son of Man. We need to know that he is the Son of God. We need to know that he is the Lord. We need to know that he is the king of creation.

Live under the Rule of His Kingdom

Second, we need to live under the rule of his kingdom.

We do that, according to this text, through an allegiance demonstrated in three ways. First, we worship Jesus as Lord. The homage shown to Jesus as he enters Jerusalem—the spreading of cloaks and branches on the road and the shouts of praise (Mark 11:8–10)—gets us in tune for the song we should be singing now and will be singing forever. Their hosanna leads into our hallelujah: "Hallelujah! Salvation and glory and power belong to our God" (Rev. 19:1). We sing now and forever hallelujah ("praise the Lord") because of the salvation that has been granted to us in Christ and also because of the justice that will come when Christ comes again (see Rev. 19:1–2). When Jesus returns, we will witness the real triumphal entry!

> I saw heaven opened, and behold, a white horse! The one sitting on it is called Faithful and True, and in righteousness he judges and makes war. . . . From his mouth comes a sharp sword with which to strike down the nations, and he will rule them with a rod of iron. He will tread the winepress of the fury of the wrath of God the Almighty. On his robe and on his thigh he has a name written, King of kings and Lord of lords. (Rev. 19:11, 15–16)

There is a time and place for a holy war. That is on the day of the Lord. So from our time until that time we must rehearse our lines. We must worship. "Worthy is the Lamb who was slain to receive power and wealth and wisdom and might and honor and glory and blessing!" (Rev. 5:12); "Hallelujah! Salvation and glory and power belong to our God" (19:1).

So to live under his rule is, first, to worship the king. Second, it is to obey his orders. This is the second way in which we demonstrate our allegiance. Again, the characters in this story showcase what obedience sometimes looks like. The two disciples are ordered to carry out an odd and ordinary task. Go to a small town. Untie a small creature. When confronted, say your line. Bring the beast back. They carry out each part of that fourfold command. Obedience to Christ often looks like that. We do not always know what Jesus is up to, but we obey because we trust that he is wiser and greater than we are.

For example, take Jesus' teaching on sexual ethics. He suggests that sexual activity outside of marriage is a serious sin (see Matt. 19:9). How often today are we told and shown just the opposite. Why remain sexually pure? Why not experiment and explore? Two reasons come to mind. First, sin always has consequences. Today's fleeting pleasure is tomorrow's enduring pain. Second, Jesus said so. We obey Jesus because we trust that he is wiser and greater than we are. We trust that the Creator knows what is best for his creatures. Refraining from sexual immorality, in this day and age, might seem as silly as being told to untie a colt in a remote Judean village. But with obedience comes true blessing. "God blesses those who obey him" (Prov. 16:20 TLB). So "Trust in the LORD with all your heart, and do not lean on your own understanding" (Prov. 3:5).

Finally, the third way in which we demonstrate our allegiance is by embracing the values of the kingdom of God. Jesus was born a Jew in Palestine, a province among many other provinces that was part of the Roman Empire. Caesar Augustus reigned from 27 BC until his death in AD 14. He was emperor when Jesus was born and into his teens. Augustus ushered in what is called the Pax Romana ("Roman peace"), creating an "unprecedented period of stability."[14] But this "peace" came at a cost for everyone the Romans conquered. It went like this. The Roman army came to town. They told people to surrender or be killed, imprisoned, or enslaved. Surrender was the usual and understandable decision. Then, those now under Roman rule paid taxes to Rome. Rome provided services for those taxes—roads, aqueducts, and military protection. Peace was kept. And if anyone did not like the "peace," if there was any dissent or rebellion, it was quickly squashed. Rome ruled through military might.

The kingdom of God is so different. It is a kingdom established and ruled through humility. It is ruled by a king who rode into Jerusalem on a colt and died outside Jerusalem on a cross. He brings the peace—the peace of Christ—to those whose hearts the Spirit has conquered, a peace made possible through his death. As Colossians 1:20 states, through Jesus God has reconciled "to himself all things . . . making peace by the blood of his cross" (cf. Rom. 5:1; Eph. 2:13–17). Jesus is the "Prince of Peace" (Isa. 9:6). So, as part of this peaceful spiritual kingdom, we follow his pattern. We live in humility. Engraved upon our shields is Philippians 2, lines such as "Do nothing from selfish ambition or conceit, but in humility count others more significant than

14 Strauss, *Mark*, 484.

yourselves" (Phil. 2:3) and "Let each of you look not only to his own interests, but also to the interests of others" (Phil. 2:4). And the banner above us reads, "Have this mind among yourselves, which is yours in Christ Jesus" (Phil. 2:5). We know that the way up is down.

By God's grace and through Christ's example[15] we seek to live in humility, knowing that as God ushers in the kingdom we invite others to be part of it by living like the last for the least. We donate time and money to organizations like Administer Justice, which offers legal help for the poor and shares the good news of Jesus in doing so. We serve meals and teach the Bible at ministries like Wayside Cross, giving what we have been given to the homeless.

The Wheel of History

Albert Schweitzer, a critic of orthodox Christianity, "portrayed Jesus as attempting to turn the wheel of history, only to be crushed himself."[16] How wrong that estimation and illustration is. In the whole of this week before his death, from the colt to the cross, Jesus is in total sovereign control. He pushes the wheel of history forward. He freely lays down his life. He takes it up again (see John 10:18). And the only people crushed by the wheel of history (take a sneak peek at Mark 14) are those people and kingdoms who do not acknowledge him as king, worship him, obey him, and seek to live like him.

15 "Jesus' choice of the donkey told the whole world who he was, but it also proclaimed what he was like" (Hughes, *Mark*, 2:80).
16 Albert Schweitzer, *The Quest for the Historical Jesus* (New York: Macmillan, 1959), 370–71, as summarized in Hughes, *Mark*, 2:81.

The Barren Temple and the Withered Tree

MARK 11:12–25

May no one ever eat fruit from you again.
Mark 11:14

Have you ever been to St. Paul's in London or St. Peter's in Rome? Most people who enter those large, ornate, and beautifully designed churches experience an inexplicable architectural euphoria. What is seen with the eyes is felt in the soul.

For Jesus' disciples, as it would be for most first-century Jews, entering the temple produced that same sense of elation. By any standards, Herod's temple was a magnificent complex, a building that took ten thousand carpenters and masons laboring over four decades to build. The boundary walls of this immense and extravagant edifice had meticulously engraved and painstakingly painted cedar roofs supported by massive pure marble colonnades. Some of these columns were 30 feet high and others 100 feet high. At the heart of the temple was the Most Holy Place behind the Holy Place. The doors to that sacred sanctuary were 60–100 feet high. That was the center of the divine design. The Holy Place was surrounded by the Court of the Priests, where the altar was housed and the sacrifices were made. The next ring was the Court of Israel (for Jewish men), followed by the Court of the Women (for Jewish women). Surrounding these center structures was the Court of the Gentiles, a place for non-Jewish converts to Judaism. This outside ring, of course, is essential to not only the setting but the theology of our text.

Worship in the Temple[1]

With all that in mind, when we read in Mark **11:15** (cf. 11:11) that Jesus "entered the temple"—first into the Court of the Gentiles, the 35-acre, open-air

---

1   The outline for this sermon, and some of the language, has been borrowed from Douglas Sean O'Donnell, *Matthew: All Authority under Heaven*, PTW (Wheaton, IL: Crossway, 2013), 599–609.

courtyard—and then eyed the glorious heart of the complex before him, we may expect to read about Jesus' euphoric experience. Perhaps he would say, as his disciples will in 13:1, "What wonderful stones!" Or perhaps, with the entrance of the one touted as "the Son of David" (10:47, 48) who would usher in the "coming kingdom of . . . David" (11:10), we may well expect the Shekinah glory that filled Solomon's temple to return now. However, such expectations are surely squelched when we read about the shockingly unexpected actions of our Lord: "And he entered the temple and began to drive out those who sold and those who bought in the temple, and he overturned the tables of the money-changers and the seats of those who sold pigeons. And he would not allow anyone to carry anything through the temple" (**11:15–16**). What Jesus saw upon entrance into this supposedly holy place was none other than a "huge religious circus!"[2] Although God's people were commanded to bring sacrifices from their *own* flocks (Deut. 12:5–7), Jesus noticed that that law was disregarded and replaced by a convenient and profitable marketplace wherein travelers could purchase an onsite and authorized animal. And, for the sake of expediency, the site was inside the immense Court of the Gentiles. The problem here, as Jesus saw it, was that this court was part of the temple and was the only place where Gentile converts could worship. Imagine, then, the experience of someone like the Ethiopian eunuch, who would have traveled hundreds of miles to worship the living God during the Passover. He would have found his sanctuary crammed with livestock and loose change, resembling a mix between a county fair and the pit of a stock exchange.[3]

That is what Jesus *saw*.[4] What Jesus *did* was overturn the tables and drive out the salesmen. He was, of course, overturning more than tables; he was also overturning these newly implemented anti-Abrahamic-covenant traditions. By driving out the spiritual swindlers and the currency-exchange racketeers he was decreeing their behavior to be unlawful and unloving.

Why did he do this? Verse 17 records Jesus' motives. But before we go there let us talk about this unusual fig tree incident in **11:12–14**, which happens right before Jesus enters the temple.

> On the following day, when they came from Bethany, he was hungry. And seeing in the distance a fig tree in leaf, he went to see if he could find

---

2   R. Kent Hughes, *Mark: Jesus, Servant and Savior*, PTW, 2 vols. (Wheaton, IL: Crossway, 2001), 2:87.
3   Hughes, *Mark*, 2:87. Cf. Alan R. Culpepper, *Mark*, SHBC (Macon, GA: Smyth & Helwys, 2007), 389: "When he cleansed the temple, therefore, Jesus purged it of the poison of worship for profit, for convenience, or for any other end besides the praise of God."
4   When the night before "he . . . looked around at everything" (Mark 11:11), part of that "everything" was perhaps all the trade tables.

anything on it. When he came to it, he found nothing but leaves, for it was not the season for figs. And he said to it, "May no one ever eat fruit from you again." And his disciples heard it.

Here we are not surprised by Jesus' hunger. The divine Son of God is fully human. He got hungry and needed food. But we are perhaps surprised by Jesus' irritable, and seemingly irrational, behavior. Bertrand Russell, as he examined this episode, accused Jesus of "vindictive fury." He wrote, "I cannot myself feel that either in the matter of wisdom or in the matter of virtue Christ stands quite as high as some other people known to history."[5] Russell is not alone his critique; others suggest that Jesus was "acting like a spoiled child who did not get his way."[6] Such readings are understandable but ill-informed.

Jesus did not, with supernatural spite, take out his frustrations on some innocent shrub because he was hungry. He could do without food. Let us remember that he was without food for forty days in the wilderness, resisting the temptation to turn stones into bread. Let us also remember that he multiplied the loaves and fish. He could surely make himself a salmon sandwich if he wanted, or turn a green leaf into a chopped salad. Jesus was not stymied by a little fruit tree. Then why do what he did? If Jesus was not acting like a spoiled child endowed with supernatural powers, what was he up to?

Our explanation starts with a brief lesson in horticulture. In Israel during the month of March fig trees produce small edible green buds called *paggim* ("early fruit," Song 2:13 NIV). In April large green leaves sprout forth. In May these buds fall off and are replaced by figs. We know from the time in which Passover was celebrated and the mention of the leaves ("a fig tree in leaf," Mark 11:13) that this incident occurred in April. Thus, when our Lord saw from a distance the green leaves, he did not expect to find ripe, full-grown figs (for "it was not the season for figs," 11:13). But he did expect to find something: either *paggim* or figs that have ripened earlier than expected.[7] However,

---

5 Bertrand Russell, *Why I Am Not a Christian, and Other Essays on Religion and Related Subjects* (New York: Carion, 1957), 17–19. Cf. also his article "The Cleansing of the Temple," *BJRL* 33 (1951): 259.

6 The words, not sentiment, are Hughes's (*Mark*, 2:85).

7 James W. Voelz offers a different idea but similar conclusion: "The fig in the Mediterranean world is a deciduous tree ten to twenty feet tall with irregular, curved branches and large leaves. It bears two crops per year, the winter, with inedible fruit on leafless twigs, and the summer, after it has leafed out, with fruit in the middle of the end of summer, which is edible. Billerbeck [Str-B 1:857], considering the rabbinic sources, agrees, as it were, with this understanding, asserting that Jesus could have not expected *edible* fruit. He proceeds to assert, however, that the Tosefta knows of two *edible* crops, the first with a stunted growth that begins in the prior year and resumes in the spring with the production of leaves." Cf. Christopher W. Mitchell. *Mark 8:27–16:20*, Concordia Commentary (St. Louis: Concordia Publishing House, 2019), 825.

this particular tree was deceptive. With all its green foliage, there should have been fruit. Something. Anything. A little bud! However, there was nothing. This fruit tree, which had the signs of fruit, was fruitless.

Thus Jesus did not curse the tree because he was distraught over its current food supply. Rather, he cursed it to provide his disciples (those who "heard," 11:14, and "saw," Matt. 21:20, this curse) with a visible parable of what was happening to Israel. Like this green tree, Israel (often compared to a fig tree in the OT; Jer. 8:13; Mic. 7:1–6; cf. Luke 13:6–9) was fruitful in appearance alone. Spiritually, many from God's covenant people were barren. From a distance their house of worship looked inspiring, but upon closer examination—within the temple's gates—it was fruitless. The Passover activities within the Court of the Gentiles and even within the Most Holy Place were but hollow rituals and futile exercises.

When Jesus entered the temple, he expected to see fruit—expressions of love for God and others. He expected to witness devout songs and sacrifices to God, accompanied by a demonstration of humility, kindness, and justice for all God's people. Instead he discovered merciless injustices, as the poor were being extorted and the Gentiles pushed out. That is why Jesus quoted Isaiah 56:7, "Is it not written, 'My house shall be called a house of prayer for all the nations'?" (Mark 11:17).

According to the popular Jewish literature of this time many Jews expected that the coming messiah would purge Jerusalem and the temple of Gentiles and foreigners (see m. Kel. 1:6–9). Jesus' attitude and actions, however, express "exactly the reverse."[8] As the true Christ, the one who came to fulfill the Scriptures, Jesus "does not clear the temple of Gentiles, but *for* them."[9] He clears the temple so that Gentiles might worship God in spirit and in truth. In Isaiah 56, the text that Jesus references, the prophet "speaks of the extension of God's salvation to people who formerly were excluded from it."[10] To Jesus, as it was for Isaiah, the temple is not Israel's exclusively but a house of prayer for both Jews and Gentiles. It is a place for all from among the nations who seek to worship Yahweh.

As Jesus turns over tables, he turns his audience's attention to Israel's prophets—first to Isaiah and then to Jeremiah. In the second half of Mark

---

8   James R. Edwards, *The Gospel according to Mark*, PNTC (Grand Rapids, MI: Eerdmans, 2002), 343–44.
9   Edwards, *Gospel according to Mark*, 343–44.
10 Edwards, *Gospel according to Mark*, 343–44. In Matthew's record of this event Jesus ousts the evildoers and invites in the poor: "The blind and lame came to him *in the temple*, and he healed them" (Matt. 21:14). Jesus opens the temple gates to those normally excluded from entrance (see 2 Sam. 5:8).

11:17, where Jesus says, "But you have made it a den of robbers," he quotes from part of Jeremiah 7:11, with the whole of Jeremiah 7:1–11 in mind when he gives his stinging rebuke:

> The word that came to Jeremiah from the LORD: "Stand in the gate of the LORD's house [the temple], and proclaim there this word, and say, Hear the word of the LORD, all you men of Judah who enter these gates to worship the LORD. Thus says the LORD of hosts, the God of Israel: Amend your ways and your deeds, and I will let you dwell in this place. Do not trust in these deceptive words: 'This is the temple of the LORD, the temple of the LORD, the temple of the LORD.'
>
> "For if you truly amend your ways and your deeds, if you truly execute justice one with another, if you do not oppress the sojourner, the fatherless, or the widow, or shed innocent blood in this place, and if you do not go after other gods to your own harm, then I will let you dwell in this place, in the land that I gave of old to your fathers forever.
>
> "Behold, you trust in deceptive words to no avail. Will you steal, murder, commit adultery, swear falsely, make offerings to Baal, and go after other gods that you have not known, and then come and stand before me in this house, which is called by my name, and say, 'We are delivered!'—only to go on doing all these abominations? Has this house, which is called by my name, become a den of robbers in your eyes? Behold, *I myself have seen it*, declares the LORD."

This is exactly what Jesus *himself* has seen and now judges—to him the temple has become a "den of robbers." The den is not where thieves steal but where they hide out after they acquire the loot. Here our Lord's denouncement focuses less on the unlawful buying and selling in the Court of the Gentiles[11] and more on the false security people procure through the animal sacrifices

---

11 That is not to ignore, as Jerome notes, that "it often happened that those who came from far away [and who suffered from 'habitual poverty'] did not have sacrificial victims. So, the priests thought of a way that they could obtain plunder from the people. They sold all kinds of animals that were needed for sacrifice, so that they might both sell to those who lacked and also receive back what was purchased. . . . The Lord, seeing this kind of business [what Jerome earlier calls, 'This scam of theirs'], or rather robbery, in his Father's house, was roused to action by the ardor of his spirit in accordance with what is written in the sixty-ninth Psalm: 'The zeal of your house has consumed me' [Ps. 69:9]." D. Hurst and M. Adriaen, eds., *S. Hieronymi Presbyteri Opera, Commentariorum in Mattheum Libri IV*, Corpus Christianorum Series Latin 77 (Turnhout, Belgium: Brepols, 1969), 186–88, as translated by Michael Graves, *How Scripture Interprets Scripture: What Biblical Writers Can Teach Us about Reading the Bible* (Grand Rapids, MI: Baker Academic, 2021), 182–83.

in the Most Holy Place. Jesus teaches that those who enter the temple and offer a sacrifice for sin without the fruits of repentance are as cursed as the withered fruit tree. That the temple has degenerated into a hideout where Jews think that they experience God's fellowship and forgiveness no matter how they live is an abomination in Christ's sight.

Do you see what Jesus saw? Hypocrisy! He saw faithless and fruitless brethren disregarding God's holy law (stealing, murdering, committing adultery, lying under oath, and worshiping idols), journeying to Jerusalem, purchasing an animal, having the priest sacrifice it, and standing before God in his holy sanctuary and announcing, "We are delivered!" They were treating the temple like an oversized confessional booth, where, if they went through the motions, they would have assurance that their sins were completely absolved, even if they had every intention of returning to those same sins the day after the Passover.

This same hypocrisy, of course, can be found in the Christian church, where some churchgoers, through their sinful actions, rob God during the week and then enter the church building to find "sanctuary," a hiding place for a guilty conscience. But no religious practice can cover a fruitless life—not the leaf of baptism, the leaf of church membership, or the leaf of praying a prayer of confession. These things cannot hide sin from the eye of an all-seeing God. And, as Jesus entered the temple to check for fruit, so now he enters into our lives, looking for the fruit of repentance and holiness of life. And, if there is no fruit, then there is only one thing to expect—judgment!

Such judgment is displayed vividly in our text. For here we see that Jesus will have none of their playacting in piety. Those in the temple on that Passover can shout, "We are delivered. We are saved!" Like thieves after their robbing, they can return to their hideout, and rejoice: "We're safe! We're safe! This is the temple of the Lord, the temple of the Lord, the temple of the Lord." But the Lord (cf. Mark 11:3) has come suddenly into his temple (see Mal. 3:1). And there and then the *Lord* Jesus, standing in the midst of their hideout, tells them the game is over. By overturning the tables, driving out those who sell the animals *necessary for sacrifice*, our Lord is doing something radical.[12] He is making a prophetic protest and pronouncement. He is not cleansing the temple; he is *cursing* it! He is withering Israel's fig tree.

And of course that is the significance of what is recorded in Mark **11:20–21**, where we read that Jesus has not merely condemned the tree but has totally destroyed it: "As they passed by in the morning, they saw the fig tree withered away

---

12 For a brief and excellent summary of thoughts regarding Jesus' temple action see the first paragraph of Nicholas Perrin, *Jesus the Temple* (Grand Rapids, MI: Baker Academic, 2010), 80.

to its roots [that tree is deep-down dead]. And Peter remembered and said to him, 'Rabbi, look! The fig tree that you cursed has withered.'" The first disciples may not have understood the symbolic significance of this day with its many strange events, but we as readers of Mark's Gospel are able to fill in the theological gaps. Throughout Jesus' ministry we are able to see that he has been subtly taking the place of the temple: he announces forgiveness, brings sinners into a saving relationship with God, and is the very presence of God in the world.

With that in mind, circle back to **11:18–19**: "And the chief priests and the scribes heard it and were seeking a way to destroy him, for they feared him, because all the crowd was astonished at his teaching. And when evening came they [Jesus and his disciples] went out of the city." At the end of the day Jesus makes it safely back to Bethany, but only by the skin of his teeth. The religious rulers do not like what they have seen (the tables turned) or heard (Jesus' prophetic judgments). They want him dead, and they would have moved in that direction that day if not for the people, who are "astonished" (not offended at this point) by Jesus (11:18). But why are the religious leaders so offended? Why such indignation (see Matt. 22:15)? The reasons likely include that their livelihood, religion, and workplace are at stake.

According to the Gospels there were *two times* Jesus "cleared" the temple: once at the beginning of his ministry and once at the end.[13] The first time "the Jews said to him, 'What sign do you show us for doing these things?'" (John 2:18) And Jesus replied, "Destroy this temple, and in three days I will raise it up" (2:19). The Jews were quite baffled by this response, and so they said, "It has taken forty-six years to build this temple, and will you raise it up in three days?" (2:20). Thankfully John helps us by inserting his commentary: "But [Jesus] was speaking about the temple of his body" (2:21).

For what crime is Jesus condemned to death? Insurrection. Rome condemns him to death for claiming to be a king and thus a rival of Caesar. Above the cross reads Jesus' sentence, "The King of the Jews" (Mark 15:26). But the Jewish Sanhedrin, which comprises "all the chief priests and the elders and the scribes" (14:53), condemns him to death, in part, because of his anti-temple antics and *rhetoric*: "We heard him say," some witnesses testified, "'I will destroy this temple that is made with hands, and in three days I will build another, not made with hands'" (14:58). Jesus will be sentenced to death for such claims and others (for the blasphemy of claiming to be the Son of the Blessed God and the coming Son of Man, see 14:62–64).

---

13 For a defense of two temple cleansings see Leon Morris, *The Gospel of John* (Grand Rapids, MI: Eerdmans, 1971), 167n55.

Yet here is the irony of these attitudes and actions. Their desire to destroy Jesus in chapter 11 and their destruction of him in chapter 15 brings about what they fear and what Jesus has so clearly prophesied. When the temple of Jesus' body is destroyed (i.e., he dies) it is at that very moment that the temple in Jerusalem (the building itself, which will be destroyed just a few decades later) is symbolically destroyed. It has theologically gone out of business.

This very point is made by Mark in his record of the crucifixion. That scene starts in this way:

> And those who passed by derided him, wagging their heads and saying, "Aha! You who would destroy the temple and rebuild it in three days, save yourself, and come down from the cross!" So also [Guess who else is there?] the chief priests with the scribes mocked him to one another, saying, "He saved others; he cannot save himself." (15:29–31)

Later, in verse 37, we read, "And Jesus uttered a loud cry and breathed his last." Then what happened at the moment of his death? "And the curtain of the temple was torn in two, from top to bottom" (15:38). Out of business. Permanently closed. There is a new access point to God.

The curtain that divided the Most Holy Place from the Court of the Priests, from the Court of Israel, from the Court of the Women, and from the Court of the Gentiles was torn asunder. This symbolized that through Christ's sacrificial death the earthly temple is replaced by the one who said of himself, "I tell you, something greater than the temple is here" (Matt. 12:6). Through Jesus' death the curtain has been torn in two, so that all those who believe in Israel's Messiah ("Hosanna to the Son of David!" Matt. 21:9) might be sewn together into one body, the church—slave and free, male and female, Jew and *Gentile* (see Gal. 3:28).

This is the precise point the Evangelist makes in Mark 15:39. In that verse we find this remarkable response to the crucifixion: "When the centurion, who stood facing him, saw that in this way he breathed his last, he said, 'Truly this man was the Son of God!'" Do you get what is happening? At the foot of the cross a Gentile confesses Jesus as the Christ. A Roman solider acknowledges Jesus as God's Son. Amazing. Amazing grace. And what wonderful worship.

The Worship of the Temple

James McCosh (1811–1894), a prominent philosopher and president of Princeton University, once said, "The book to read is not the one which thinks for you, but the one which makes you think. No book in the world equals the Bible for that."[14] Here in Mark the Bible has once again made us think. As we have looked at these ten verses of our passage, we have *thought* about the temple: the purpose of the temple, Jesus' relationship to the temple, and Jesus' reaction to what was going on in the temple. But we are not done thinking just yet. As we move on to **11:22–25** we move into a section of application, a set of exhortations that I want you to see are directly connected to the preceding context. Think of verses 12–21 as "The Worship *in* the Temple: Faithless and Fruitless"; then think of verses 22–25 as "The Worship *of* the Temple: Faithful and Fruitful."

The phrase "the worship *of* the temple" picks up on the language of the NT epistles, where Paul calls Christians "God's temple." In 1 Corinthians 3:16–17 Paul says to believers, "Do you not know you are God's temple and that God's Spirit dwells in you? . . . God's temple is holy, and *you* are that temple." Such language would be sacrilegious if the Second Temple were still the one and only place where people met God and sins were forgiven. But if this earthly temple on Mount Zion has been "taken up and thrown into the sea" (Mark 11:23),[15] and if Christ is the new and everlasting temple, the one and only person in whom we meet God and have our sins forgiven, and if his Spirit dwells in those who now believe, then what Jesus calls his followers to in verses 22–25 makes perfect sense. Outside of Jerusalem and the temple (near the destroyed fig tree) Jesus calls his church to worship.

What then does our worship—the worship *of* the temple—look like? It resembles Mark 11:22–25:

> And Jesus answered them, "Have faith in God. Truly, I say to you, who- ever says to this mountain, 'Be taken up and thrown into the sea,' and does not doubt in his heart, but believes that what he says will come to pass, it will be done for him. Therefore I tell you, whatever you ask in prayer, believe that you have received it, and it will be yours. And when- ever you stand praying, forgive, if you have anything against anyone, so that your Father also who is in heaven may forgive you your trespasses."

Our worship—the worship *of* the temple—can be summarized in the sim- ple command, "Have faith in God" (11:22). And the nature of that faith is expressed in two ways: prayer to God and forgiveness of others. There is a vertical dimension. Our prayers upward should be confident in God's power,

---

a power than can move even mountains.[16] Our prayers should be unwavering, not doubting God's ability to do the impossible—to remove the place of worship on one mountain into the hearts of many people spread throughout all the hills and valleys and plains of the world. Do not let the stupidities and heresies of how the health-wealth movement applies this verse (name it and claim it) hinder your boldness before the throne of grace.[17] Pray big prayers. Pray for the cancer to be gone. Pray for the prodigal to come home. Pray for a Third Great Awakening.

And there is a horizontal dimension. As we "stand" (the context might be in corporate worship, 11:25) to pray, we must be in a right relationship with our neighbor: "And whenever you stand praying, forgive, if you have anything against anyone, so that your Father also who is in heaven may forgive you your trespasses" (11:25).[18] Jesus teaches the same truth in the Sermon on the Mount, when he says, "If you are offering your gift at the altar and there remember that your brother has something against you, leave your gift there before the altar and go. First be reconciled to your brother, and then come and offer your gift" (Matt. 5:23–24). The point of both passages is plain: to be in a right relationship with God is to be in a right relationship with people. To have faith is to love God and neighbor. Put differently, faith is not acting like a hypocrite—expressing love for God with your lips while you hold bitterness in your heart against others.

Here is how this teaching fits within the context of what Jesus said and did in the temple. The temple had become a moneymaking marketplace, a hideout for hypocrites, and an exclusive religious club—the sign outside read "Gentiles need not apply." But it was designed to be a "house of prayer" for all people (Mark 11:17)—rich and poor, men and women, Jews and Gentiles. So what does Jesus teach his people gathered around him outside the temple? He teaches them to pray, which is what they should have been doing in the temple.

Then, as I am tying the themes in the first part of this passage with those in the second, why did people come to the temple each year at Passover? They

16 "Prayer is an all-efficient panoply, a treasure undiminished, a mine never exhausted, a sky unobstructed by clouds, a haven unruffled by storm. It is the root, the fountain, and the mother of a thousand blessings. It exceeds a monarch's power." John Chrysostom, *On the Incomprehensible Nature of God*, sermon 5, quoted in *CHSB*, 1494.

17 "There are a number of qualifications to this promise. Most importantly, we must ask according to God's will (1 John 5:14); we must ask in Jesus' name (John 14:13–14; 15:16; 16:23–24, 26), that is, in accord with the person and work of Christ; we must ask from a position of obedience (1 John 3:21–22) and having forgiven others in the same way God has forgiven us (Mark 11:25)." Mark L. Strauss, *Mark*, ZECNT (Grand Rapids, MI: Zondervan, 2014), 501.

18 Some manuscripts add Mark 11:26: "But if you do not forgive, neither will your Father who is in heaven forgive your trespasses."

came to have their sins forgiven. So what does Jesus teach his people outside the temple? He teaches forgiveness. God can forgive us not through a pigeon or ox (that is not how it works anymore) but through Jesus (the ultimate atoning sacrifice, the one to whom those pigeons and oxen pointed to all along), and thus the forgiven are to forgive.

Outside of the temple Jesus teaches his people—God's new temple—how to worship. Have faith. Pray to God. Forgive others.

The Lion Becomes the Lamb

In C. S. Lewis's *The Voyage of the Dawn Treader* there is a scene in which Edmund and Lucy came upon a large grassy area, where they spied from a distance "a white spot in the middle of the green expanse," a spot "so white . . . they could hardly look at it." As they ventured closer, they saw that it was a lamb. This lamb, like all the animals in the Chronicles of Narnia, talked. Not only did the lamb talk; he cooked! "'Come and have breakfast,' said the Lamb in its sweet milky voice." They sat down on the grass and ate. He fed them roasted fish. They feasted. "And it was the most delicious food they had ever tasted." Then, as they struck up a conversation about "the way to Aslan's country" (heaven), the gentle and generous lamb miraculously transformed into a grand and glorious lion. "As he spoke, his snowy white flushed into tawny gold and his size changed and he was Aslan himself, towering above them and scattering light from his mane."[19]

In this scene Lewis is describing what happens after Jesus' death and resurrection: the Lamb of God who was sacrificed for the sins of the world rose again, and he, in a sense, has now transformed from the sacrificial lamb into the ruling lion. He is the lion of the tribe of Judah. The promised and powerful king. In Mark 11–15, however, Jesus is portrayed first as the lion and second as the lamb. When he enters the temple, he roars! The temple cleansing and cursing is the first of a few showdowns between Jerusalem's religious hierarchy and the Son of the Most High God. Here in Mark 11:12–25 Jesus has let out his first battle cry. In the next chapter, as we shall see, the battle will only intensify.

---

19 C. S. Lewis, *The Voyage of the Dawn Treader* (New York: HarperCollins, 1994), 269.

Authority over the Temple Authorities

MARK 11:27–12:12

By what authority are you doing these things, or who gave
you this authority to do them?
Mark 11:28

After I preached on Mark 11:12–25 someone from the congregation told me, "That is not the usual picture we have of Jesus." True. We do not usually think of Jesus as standing before a 25-foot fig tree, pronouncing a judgment, and walking by the next day to observe the total destruction—a curse that caused a tree to wither down to its very roots. Moreover, we do not usually envision Jesus coming into the holiest place (the temple) of God's holy people (the Jews) in the holy city (Jerusalem) and making a complete commotion, wholly upsetting the exchange of money and purchase of animals necessary to conduct the Passover sacrifices. Can you picture Jesus' running around the Court of the Gentiles, an area "the length of three football fields and some 250 yards wide,"[1] turning over every table and chair he could get his hands on? This is no Jesus meek and mild! This is not the picture of Jesus we are used to.

What pictures, then, are we used to? Well, I did my research. As a serious scholar, I did what serious scholars do. I went to Google Images and typed in *Jesus*. And I saw pictures of the baby Jesus, the carpenter Jesus, the baptized Jesus, the gentle Jesus (holding a lamb and sitting with a child), the smiling Jesus, the praying Jesus, the teaching Jesus, and the healing Jesus. I also saw pictures featuring the sacred heart of Jesus, the dying, rising, ascending, and sitting-atop-a-throne-in-heaven Jesus. Sadly, I also saw pictures of the make-Jesus-whatever-you-want Jesus: the married Jesus, the gay Jesus, the black Jesus, the blond-haired/blue-eyed Jesus, the Buddha-sitting Jesus,

---

1   R. Kent Hughes, *Mark: Jesus, Servant and Savior*, PTW, 2 vols. (Wheaton, IL: Crossway, 1989), 2:87.

the dope-smoking Jesus, the Green Bay Packers Jesus (with a piece of cheese as his crown). No joke, and no laughing matter.

However, what I did not see on the popular webpages was any "negative" image. That is, there was no image of Jesus' turning over tables, killing trees, arguing with the scribes, or judging the world. Yet, what we have seen in Mark 11:12–25 and will see again till the end of chapter 11 and into chapter 12 is that same Jesus: Jesus as judge, especially over those who oppose his heaven-endowed authority.

Opposition to Jesus' Authority

That opposition comes again on the next journey Jesus makes to Jerusalem. As he travels from Bethany, we read in **11:27–28**,

> They came again to Jerusalem. And as he was walking in the temple, the chief priests and the scribes and the elders came to him, and they said to him, "By what authority are you doing these things, or who gave you this authority to do them?"

Think about it. What a bold move for Jesus to return to the temple. Imagine him walking through the gates into the Court of the Gentiles, the very place he had made a mess the day before. Did all the money changers cuff their coins? Did the pigeon salesmen hide their birds? Picture it this way. Pretend I walked into Hobby Lobby and knocked down a few displays, pushed over all the cash registers, untangled 10,000 yards of yarn, and yet somehow escaped without anyone's handcuffing me. How well would I be received if I decided to return the next day? Not well. As soon as the security spotted me, they would either arrest me or forcefully escort me out.

Jesus is bold here. He walks into the temple a second time after a controversial first appearance the day before. And who is there to greet him? The temple authorities! Perhaps all seventy members of the Sanhedrin. The way Mark writes verse 28 gives the impression that, as soon as Jesus stepped foot into the temple, immediately "the chief priests and the scribes and the elders came to him."[2] Imagine them running in their robes. Imagine them as mad as Hades at the heaven-sent Son. Out of breath, and breathing a sigh of relief that the tables are still on all fours, "they said to him, 'By what authority are you doing these things, or who gave you this authority to do them?'" What a great question. I will paraphrase it: "Jesus, who on earth do you think you are,

---

2   Notice the addition of "the elders" (Mark 11:27; cf. 11:18).

and who in heaven do you think sent you? Explain your anti-temple antics and accusations."

And how does Jesus respond? We enter now into question/answer time with Jesus. This is one of my favorite parts of the Bible. In 11:27–12:37 we find four tough questions posed to Jesus (11:28; 12:14, 19–23, 28), followed by a showstopping question asked by Jesus. So here at the end of chapter 11 a question is asked to Jesus, followed by not a showstopping question but a scene-stopping one, asked by Jesus in return. He answers their question with a counterquestion. Look at **11:29**. "Jesus said to them, 'I will ask you one question; answer me, and I will tell you by what authority I do these things.'" Stop there.

What audacity. And what authority. What Jesus does is so not the norm! I recall the time when Judge Kavanaugh, in his hearing to sit on the bench of the US Supreme Court, replied to a question with a question of his own, and this power play did not go over well. He asked for a break. It was granted. And, when he returned, he apologized. Here Jesus does not back down. He does not recant his boldness. He does not admit a misstep. Our Lord questions his questioners, "Was the baptism of John[3] from heaven or from man? Answer me" (**11:30**). It is the "answer me" here that lights up like a firecracker, an M-80 exploding in a hand. If I were one of the chief priests of Herod's marvelous temple, one of the world's most prestigious edifices, I would have said, "What! Answer you? You, O man of Galilee, will answer me."

But what do they do? They search for an answer. They hold an ecumenical council. "And they discussed it with one another" (11:31). Historians label it "The First Unholy Council of AD 33." No, they do not. But they should. The Sanhedrin reasons, "If we say, 'From heaven,' he will say, 'Why then did you not believe him?'" (**11:31**). So they cannot say that. But they also cannot say he was not sent from God, that he was not a prophet. Why? "Shall we say, 'From man'?—they were afraid of the people,[4] for [the people] all held that John really was a prophet" (**11:32**). The Sanhedrin would have made great politicians because they based their decision on the polls. They were pleasing people rather than giving an honest answer. They lacked moral courage. "So they answered Jesus, 'We do not know'" (**11:33**).

And, because they refuse to reply to his question, Jesus refuses to reply to theirs. "And Jesus said to them, 'Neither will I tell you by what authority

---

3   "The phrase 'the baptism of John' is shorthand for John's whole ministry—his call to repent and be baptized for the forgiveness of sins in preparation for the coming of the Lord (1:2–8)." Mark L. Strauss, *Mark*, ZECNT (Grand Rapids, MI: Zondervan, 2014), 505.

4   Luke adds a further motive: fear of death ("All the people will stone us to death," Luke 20:6).

I do these things'" (11:33). Or paraphrased: "Listen, if this theological brain trust is unable to discern that John the Baptist was sent from God, then you are certainly not capable to judge if I am sent from God. Moreover, how can you possibly shepherd God's flock if you cannot discern his will on such an obvious matter?"

Jesus' Opposition "to Them"

Jesus is not done. While he has their ear, he instructs them. He next challenges their authority. "And he began to speak to them in parables" (12:1). Mark records one of those parables.[5]

Do you remember when Jesus explained that to some parables reveal and to others they conceal (4:10–12)? They are like stained-glass windows: to those on the inside the shapes and colors and sense are seen, but to those on the outside the glass is gray, lifeless, and meaningless. The chief priests, scribes, and elders of Israel are standing on the outside. They correctly perceive that the parable is about them (12:12), but they likely do not understand the extent of the judgment Jesus renders against them. "For those outside," Jesus taught in 4:11–12, "everything is [told] in parables, so that 'they may indeed see but not perceive, and may indeed hear but not understand, lest they should turn and be forgiven'" (cf. Deut. 29:4; Jer. 5:21; Ezek. 12:2). The religious authorities see and hear that the parable is about them, but they do not perceive and understand that it should lead them to repentance from their hostile rejection of Jesus and to faith in him as their Messiah and Savior.

Explaining the Parable of the Wicked Tenants

So the parable of the wicked tenants is a parable of judgment, a story-form pronouncement of judgment by Jesus against those who reject Jesus. Starting in Mark 12:1, and borrowing language and ideas from Isaiah 5:1–7, Jesus shares,

> A man planted a vineyard and put a fence around it and dug a pit for the winepress and built a tower, and leased it to tenants and went into another country. When the season came, he sent a servant to the tenants to get from them some of the fruit of the vineyard. And they took him and beat him and sent him away empty-handed. Again he sent to them another servant, and they struck him on the head and treated him shamefully. And he sent another, and him they killed. And so with many

5 For another parable Jesus told see Matthew 21:28–32.

others: some they beat, and some they killed. He had still one other, a beloved son. Finally he sent him to them, saying, "They will respect my son." But those tenants said to one another, "This is the heir. Come, let us kill him, and the inheritance will be ours." And they took him and killed him and threw him out of the vineyard. What will the owner of the vineyard do? He will come and destroy the tenants and give the vineyard to others. (**Mark 12:1–9**)

What do we make of this parable? How do we interpret it?

When I was a professor in Australia, I taught a class on the Synoptic Gospels. As part of that class, I came up with a lecture humorously titled "Doug O's Amazing Ten Steps for Mastering Parable Interpretation and Finding Meaning in Life."[6] Let us walk through those steps now. I promise this will be both enlightening and enthralling. The first three steps have to do with context.

Step One

First, within the context of the whole narrative of Mark's Gospel, where is this parable found?

The parable is found in the last section, set in Jerusalem, which depicts the week prior to Jesus' death and resurrection. This is the second of only two narrative parables in Mark, and its placement is purposeful. Jesus tells this parable to foreshadow his fate.

Step Two

Second, what is the preceding context, and does it shed any light on the motive and/or content of the parable? Put differently, was there an issue, teaching, or action that prompted this parable?

Indeed. Before this parable Jesus has cleansed the temple, returned to the temple, and refused to answer the religious authorities' question on the source of Jesus' authority.

Step Three

Third, look at what happens after the parable is told. Is there any reaction to the parable?

There is. **Mark 12:12** records a hostile reaction. The authorities "were seeking to arrest him . . . for they perceived that he had told the parable

6 Part of the section below was first published in Douglas Sean O'Donnell and Leland Ryken, *The Beauty and Power of Biblical Exposition: Preaching the Literary Artistry and Genres of the Bible* (Wheaton, IL: Crossway, 2022), 82–99.

against them." They did not immediately arrest him because, once again, they "feared the people" (12:12). The crowd was still pro-Jesus at this time. "So they [for now] left him and went away" (12:12). They needed to regroup. They needed a better plan to take down Jesus.

Step Four

From those questions about the context we move to further instruction based on observations. The fourth step is to look to see whether a major contrast is made in the parable. If so, note what it is. Also, see whether there is any direct discourse. If so, also note it. These two details often provide clues for unraveling the parable's meaning.

There a major contrast between the owner of the vineyard and the wicked tenants. There is no dialogue between those two major characters, but there is self-reflective processing. The owner thinks to himself, "They will respect my son" (12:6); the tenants think to themselves, "This is the heir. Come, let us kill him, and the inheritance will be ours" (12:7). These are two key lines, lines to which we will return later.

Step Five

Fifth, what would have surprised or shocked the original hearers and readers?

The two actions expressed in those two lines above. It is shocking that the owner, after what has happened to his three servants and more ("with many others," 12:5), would risk sending his own "beloved son" (12:6).[7] Also, the tenants' rationale for killing the son—that they would somehow inherit the vineyards if the son were out of the equation—makes no sense.[8] This is a senseless murder.

Step Six

Sixth, list every person, place, thing, and action in the parable.

The *people* mentioned are the owner of the vineyard, his servants (plus the "many others," 12:5), his son, and the tenants. Also note the "others" in verse 9. The only *place* is the vineyard, mentioned five times. Most of the

---

7   "The 'unrealistic' behavior of the landowner and the tenants in the parable corresponds exactly with the 'unrealistic,' but true behavior of the God of Israel [e.g., Heb. 11:35–37]. . . . What some scholars criticize as absurd and unrealistic is in reality the inconceivable 'amazing grace' of God!" Robert H. Stein, *Mark*, BECNT (Grand Rapids, MI: Baker Academic, 2008), 531–32.

8   For answers to the question, How could the tenants expect to inherit the vineyard? see Strauss, *Mark*, 516. For example, "Under Jewish law the possession of the property without the payment of rent for four years could result in a claim to ownership," and therefore "the tenants may be thinking that if they kill the son, they will be able to possess the land long enough to claim it."

things detailed revolve around the vineyard: a fence, pit, winepress, tower, and fruit (12:1–2). Two other things include the "country" to which the owner went away (12:1) and the "season," indicating the time for harvest or the appointed time to collect the rent (12:2).

The *actions* include the owner's planting, securing, and leasing out his vineyard ("A man . . . planted . . . put . . . dug . . . built . . . leased . . . went" away, 12:1). The owner then sends his servants and son to collect payment or produce from the tenants ("He sent a servant," 12:2; "He sent . . . another servant," 12:4; "He sent another" servant, 12:5; "He sent" his son "to them," 12:6). Next, the tenants act violently toward the sent ones ("They took . . . and beat him and sent him away empty-handed," 12:3; "They struck him . . . and treated him shamefully," 12:4; "They killed" him, 12:5; "They took him and killed him and threw him out of the vineyard," 12:8). The final action, as detailed by the narrator, is the owner's coming retribution: "He will *come* and *destroy* the tenants and *give* the vineyard to others" (12:9).

Steps Seven and Eight

Here now is where the fun begins. After those six steps come the seventh and eighth. We move from context to observations to meaning. Step seven is, in that list, from whom, what, where, and/or when has come a likely *second level* of meaning? In other words, the "beloved son" certainly symbolizes someone, and the "fence" likely does not. The son is more than a son, but the fence is just a fence.

Step eight follows. Work out the meaning.

Here is my stab at the symbolism. The owner is God the Father. His servants are the prophets.[9] The servant that is killed is possibly John the Baptist (6:14–29). The son is Jesus (see 1:11; 9:7; 14:61; cf. Gen. 22:2), the Father's last entreaty or God's "final emissary" to rebellious Israel, and the one "to whom the vineyard rightly belonged."[10] The vineyard is Israel ("The vineyard . . . is the house of Israel," Isa. 5:7).[11] The tenants are the temple authorities—

9   For the prophets as "servants" see Jeremiah 7:25–26; 25:4; Amos 3:7; Zechariah 1:6. On their rejection see 2 Samuel 10:2–5; 2 Kings 17:7–20; 2 Chronicles 24:20–22; 36:15–16; Isaiah 3:14; Jeremiah 12:10; 25:3–7; 26:20–23. See also R. T. France, *The Gospel of Mark*, NIGTC (Grand Rapids, MI: Eerdmans, 2002), 460.
10 Klyne Snodgrass, *The Parable of the Wicked Tenants: An Inquiry into Parable Interpretation*, WUNT 27 (1983; repr., Eugene, OR: Wipf & Stock, 2011), 86.
11 "The metaphorical vineyard in the Old Testament does not designate the nation so much as the elect of God and all the privileges that go with this election. . . . Logically it is necessary to understand the vineyard as the privileges entrusted to the people, i.e., the law, the promises, and the working of God in past and present, or as the vineyard is interpreted in Matthew 21,43, the kingdom of God" (Snodgrass, *Parable of the Wicked Tenants*, 75, 76).

the chief priests, scribes, and elders. The fruit symbolizes the fruit of repentance that John preached, the fruits that sprout from faith, namely, a life of prayer to God and forgiveness of others (Mark 11:22–25). The many acts of violence represent persecutions for righteousness, for obeying God's orders. The murder of the son is the cross of Christ. The throwing his body "out of the vineyard" (12:8) is likely a reference to Jesus' burial. If not for Joseph of Arimathea, Jesus' body would have rotted outside. The "others" mentioned in verse 9—the vineyard will be given "to others"—could be limited to the new godly leaders of the early church, who have replaced the bad shepherds of Israel, or it could have a wider scope representing the elect from among the nations, Jews and Gentiles, those who hear God's Word, respond to the gospel in faith, and bear fruit for the kingdom. As Klyne Snodgrass suggests, this group is "the true Israel and will replace those who are bound up in the hypocritical established religion and are Israel in name only."[12]

The whole parable, then, is a short summary of the grand story of the Bible. God chose Israel out of the world to be his own people. He cared for and protected them. He sent his prophets to proclaim his word, offer his promises, render his judgments, and predict the future. But so often throughout Israel's history the leaders of God's people rejected, persecuted, and even killed the prophets. Finally, God thus loved his people, even though they had rebelled against him, that he sent his own beloved Son. But then the unthinkable happened. The irrational. The inexplicable. God's people killed God's own Son. "They took him and killed him and threw him out of the vineyard" (12:8). He is buried in a borrowed tomb outside of Jerusalem. How then does the story end? Vindication of the rejected but now risen son! Judgment and salvation. Those who reject Jesus will be destroyed (both in AD 70 and forever),[13] while those who accept him will share in his inheritance (both now and forever).

That is the meaning of the parable, and here is Jesus' final metaphoric summary to the Bible experts of his day:

Have you not read this Scripture:

"'The stone that the builders rejected
has become the cornerstone;
this was the Lord's doing,
and it is marvelous in our eyes'?" (Mark **12:10–11**)

12 Snodgrass, *Parable of the Wicked Tenants*, 93.
13 Note that the tenants "kill" (Mark 12:5, 7, 8) God's servant and son, but God "destroys" them (12:9, likely indicating "a more comprehensive and devastating judgment"; Strauss, *Mark*, 516).

Here Jesus quotes from Psalm 118:22–23, the same poem on the lips of the people as Jesus journeyed up to Jerusalem on the colt. In its original context the poem is about Israel. Yet here in Mark Jesus applies it to himself as the ultimate fulfillment of all the promises to and about Israel. He is the stone that the builders (or wicked "tenants") rejected. To them he was a useless stone that did not fit properly into their design. But that stone, upon his death and then formally when every stone of Herod's temple was turned over and destroyed, became the cornerstone—the part that holds everything together—to a new and everlasting structure. This is the permanent foundation stone (1 Cor. 3:11; Eph. 2:20). But, while an immovable foundation, it is also a living stone, a rock that trips up and crushes down those who oppose him but saves all who are willing to build upon it (see 1 Pet. 2:6–8). "As it is written [in Isa. 8:14], 'Behold, I am laying in Zion [Jerusalem] a stone of stumbling, and a rock of offense; and whoever believes in him will not be put to shame'" (Rom. 9:33; cf. 1 Peter 2:6).

There is, then, an important connection between the two halves of our text. Jesus does not answer the religious leaders' question at the end of Mark 11 ("By what authority are you doing these things?" 11:28), but he does, in a sense, answer it with his parable at the start of chapter 12. His authority comes from God, his Father. He is his beloved Son. He is the beloved Son that they want to kill, the promised stone of which they want to dispose. He is the heaven-sent Son and stone.[14]

Step Nine

From meaning we move to applications, the final two steps of C (context), O (observation), M (meaning), and A (application). I hope you are not, by now, in a coma!

Step nine answers the questions, Who are the main characters?, and, What is the point of application for each that Jesus is making? We can discern the main characters from their actions. Who acts in this parable? The servants and son do what they are told. They are sent by the owner, and they go. They obey. But it is the owner and the tenants who have all the verbs attached to them. The important, and repeated, verb for the owner is the word "sent" (4x). The important, and repeated, verb for the tenants is "killed" (3x). What then are the two points of application? I will make it three, two related to the owner of the vineyard (God) and one to those who reject those he sends.

---

14 "The parable may . . . be seen as an implicit answer to the question about the source of his authority in the previous episode, which Jesus refused to answer (11:33). His authority comes from his Father, who is the vineyard's owner, and he has been sent to claim what is rightfully his" (Strauss, *Mark*, 509).

First, know and appreciate that God is longsuffering. Think again about what Jesus teaches about his Father in this parable. God cultivates this vineyard carefully. Then his chosen people take care of it. When he sends his select servants, the holy prophets, to see how the work is going, those whom he first sends are brutally beaten. At this point, if I were God, I would stop there. My patience would be exhausted. The day of retribution is now at hand! But this is not what God does. Here the Lord is patient toward them. The God of the universe is lovingly longsuffering. He sends more servants. What a demonstration of patience! The clauses from the parable, "He sent to them another servant" (12:4) and "He sent another" (12:5), and then the little detail that he sent "many others" (12:5), write in large print—like a banner following the Goodyear blimp—"God Is Patient." And just when you think his people have exhausted his patience, he sends and sacrifices his own beloved Son. Oh the loving longsuffering of God. Know it. Appreciate it. Praise God for being a patient God.

Second, grasp, and be saddened by, human depravity. Due to Adam's sin we are all born spiritually blind, ignorant, and wicked. Totally depraved. We are not as bad as we could be, but we are tainted in every part of our being— our minds (we do not think rightly), our hearts (we do not feel rightly), and our wills (we do not do what is right).[15] We are not too different from the religious leaders in our passage.

"There but for the grace of God, go I." For some that popular saying can be trite, but for us it should not be. We should rejoice in the grace of God, knowing and appreciating what we have been saved from—from thinking, feeling, and acting against God the way the Sanhedrin thought, felt, and acted.

Third, rejoice that God is just. I label this parable not the parable of the wicked tenants but the parable of the patient but just master. I do so because the focus of Jesus' teaching is not on the rebels but on his righteous Father. God judges those who do not receive his Son. God judges those who reject his Son.[16]

---

15   As Michael Horton, *For Calvinism* (Grand Rapids, MI: Zondervan, 2011), 41 states: "The 'total' in total depravity refers to its extensiveness, not intensiveness: that is, to the all-encompassing scope of our fallenness. It does not mean that we are as bad as we can possibly be, but that we are all guilty and corrupt to such an extent that there is no hope of pulling ourselves together, brushing ourselves off, and striving (with the help of grace) to overcome God's judgment and our own rebellion." Stated in traditional confessional language, our nature is "so poisoned" and "so corrupt" that all humans are both "inclined toward all evil" and "totally unable to do any good" without help from God. See the Heidelberg Catechism 7–8. By "any good" is meant "what indeed is truly good, such as saving faith in the first place" (*The Remonstrance*, Article III).

16   This is a "judgment parable" that "asserts that, contrary to appearances, God will judge and will achieve his purposes, and people will be held accountable." Klyne R. Snodgrass, *Stories with Intent: A Comprehensive Guide to the Parables of Jesus* (Grand Rapids, MI: Eerdmans, 2008), 297–98.

As with the fruitless fig tree and the spiritually barren temple,[17] in Jesus the old regime is over. God has come. In his justice he has destroyed the temple and its wicked leaders. And he has given his vineyard to others, believers from among the nations.

My Final Step, My Central Application

We come finally to the tenth step, where we seek to explain how the ideas embedded in the story apply both then (in Jesus' day) and now (to us today), and the question we seek to answer is, If you had to summarize the central application of this parable, what would it be? Remember, it must be related in some way to Jesus and his kingdom—its coming, its proclamation, participation in it, how to get in, the kind of things that keep one out, encouragement to persevere in it, and the like. So look to see whether Jesus features as one of the characters. Also, look at the end to see whether Jesus gives the answer, as our Lord often gives the punch of the parable at the end.

Jesus is one of the characters. And what is the picture of him here? He is the "son," who faithfully obeyed the will of his Father and died upon the cross. So what? The final and main application, found in Jesus' own summary of the parable (12:10–11), is twofold. First, we are not to reject the Son/stone but to receive him. We are to welcome him, build upon him, give him the fruits of our labors. Second, we should not only receive him but marvel in the whole grand plan of salvation. With humility and joy we should say and sing, "This was the Lord's doing [this whole plan that is played out here], and it is marvelous in our eyes" (12:11).

---

17 "The parable of the vineyard was, in fact, the spoken form of the parable of the fig-tree which Jesus had 'told' in the previous chapter." Sinclair B. Ferguson, *Let's Study Mark* (repr., Carlisle, PA: Banner of Truth Trust, 2016), 188.

Render to God

Jesus said to them, "Render to Caesar the things that are
Caesar's, and to God the things that are God's." And they
marveled at him.
Mark 12:17

The Babylon Bee is a satirical online news site featuring fictional stories that poke fun at political and church leaders, the Christian life, and the world in which we live but are formatted like authentic news stories and told with that objective anchorman voice of traditional news organizations. Here are some recent headlines: "Woman Graciously Submits to Husband by Allowing Him to Pick Which Episode of 'Gilmore Girls' to Watch"; "Banned from Playing Violent Video Games, Local Kid Settles for Reading Old Testament"; "Worship Leader Commits 47 Heresies in 30-Second Prayer." One headline, a story directly related to our text, reads, "Youth Pastor Questioned for Rendering Half His Budget unto Little Caesars," and the short article reported on how youth pastor Troy "Turnt" Hatley, after a semiannual budget audit, was called in for questioning by the elder board at Lake Michigan Bible Fellowship over the fact that he had rendered half his budget unto Little Caesars. When questioned, Hatley claimed that he was simply following Jesus' command to "render unto Little Caesars" by giving the firstfruits of his annual budget to the discount pizza chain.[1]

Of course, when our Lord Jesus gave his famous answer, "Render to Caesar [big Caesar—the Roman emperor] the things that are Caesar's" (12:17), it was no laughing matter. At the time Jesus was being questioned by the Jewish temple authorities, who were deliberately trying to catch him in his words

---

1 "Youth Pastor Questioned for Rendering Half His Budget unto Little Caesars," Church, *Babylon Bee*, August 13, 2018, https://babylonbee.com/news/youth-pastor-questioned-for-rendering -half-his-budget-unto-little-caesars, accessed November 1, 2021.

because they wanted him arrested (12:12) and sentenced to death (11:18). They wanted him dead because, in the last forty-eight hours, he had ridden into Jerusalem on a colt (thus deliberately claiming to be the promised King), cleansed the temple, and told a parable of judgment against them. Put simply, for the last two days he had been claiming to be in a position of great authority, all the while strongly questioning their authority.

The chief priests, scribes, and the elders did not like that. So they arranged for two other groups of Jewish leaders to attempt to "trap him in his talk" (12:13). In verses 13–14 some of the Pharisees and Herodians approach Jesus and ask him a question. This is the first half our text, which we can call "the trap." Then in verses 15–17 we have the second half, which we might label "the great escape." Youth Pastor Hatley, with a misquote from the Bible, escaped the wrath of the pizza expenditure committee. Let us see how Jesus, with a true understanding of the Scriptures and the will of God, escapes his accusers.

The Trap

First, we have the trap.

> And they sent to him some of the Pharisees and some of the Herodians, to trap him in his talk. And they came and said to him, "Teacher, we know that you are true and do not care about anyone's opinion. For you are not swayed by appearances, but truly teach the way of God. Is it lawful to pay taxes to Caesar, or not? Should we pay them, or should we not?" (**12:13–14**)

Perhaps the best way to organize and understand all the details recorded above is to ask the questions where, who, and what.

First, notice *where* this question is asked. Jesus and his accusers are in the temple. Mark 11:27 makes clear that Jesus had entered the temple. Mark 12:35, 41 make clear that Jesus is still in the temple. Mark 13:1 reveals a shift in locations ("And as he came out of the temple"). So the temple is the setting of this question and the two that will follow. This detail is important, and we will make sense of it later.

Second, notice *who* is involved in this question. Three groups are involved. The "they" are the temple authorities, "the chief priests and the scribes and the elders" to whom we were introduced in 11:27. They are also called the Sanhedrin, the seventy men who ruled the affairs of the temple. We might even say that they are the three branches of Jewish government: the priests are the clergy, the scribes are the scholars, and the elders are the lay leaders. This influential group, as we saw at the end of the last chapter, was stumped by Jesus' clever answer to their question and dumbfounded by his public, but parable-hidden, denouncement of them. Mark 12:12 ends with the Sanhedrin's leaving Jesus with the sense that it is plotting its next move. And Mark 12:13 tells us what that next move is. They "sent to [Jesus] some of the Pharisees and some of the Herodians" (12:13). Their mission is clear. They are to "trap him in his talk" (12:13), or, as Matthew puts it, "entangle him in his words" (Matt. 22:15). Like the sly reporter today, they are looking for a sound bite, a sacrilegious and treasonous one, that they can use in an official Roman trial to sign and seal Jesus' death sentence.

But who were the Pharisees and the Herodians? The Pharisees were religious purists, men who sought to obey God's law perfectly. They were zealous for the purification of Jerusalem, and thus for Roman occupation to come to an end. The Herodians were quite different. They were "friendly to the Herodian rule and consequently to the Roman rule upon which it rested."[2] Put differently, they were pro-Herod Antipas and pro-Caesar Tiberius. They were Jews who sided with Roman rule. The Herodians, we might say, were men of the world, while the Pharisees were separate from it.[3]

So, when we read that "some of the Pharisees and some of the Herodians" (Mark 12:13) came together to challenge Jesus, we are reading about an unlikely union. It would be like the most conservative senator agreeing to be the running mate for a liberal vice president the next presidential election. The only reason those two would come together today is the same reason these two groups came together then: a common enemy makes for temporary allegiances. The Pharisees and Herodians were both out to get Jesus. They wanted to kill him because he challenged their authority.

Third, notice *what* is said. Before they ask their ensnaring interrogative, the accusers try to soften Jesus' resistance to them with some flattery. They call him "teacher," an honorific title but one they use insincerely.[4] They are there not to learn from him but to ensnare him. Then, after they call him "teacher," they spread on another layer of thick butter. "Teacher, we know that you are true and do not care about anyone's opinion. For you are not swayed by appearances, but truly teach the way of God" (12:14). Everything they say here is correct. Unlike the members of the Sanhedrin, who lack moral courage and are totally swayed by the opinions of the crowds (see 11:32; 12:12), Jesus is unaffected by the latest popular poll. He is absolutely courageous. He

2 H. W. Hoehner, "Herodian Dynasties," in *DNTB*, ed. Craig A. Evans and Stanley E. Porter (Downers Grove, IL: InterVarsity Press, 2000), 493.
3 Daniel M. Doriani, *Matthew*, REC, 2 vols. (Phillipsburg, NJ: P&R, 2008), 2:291.
4 Also, as careful readers of Mark's Gospel we are reminded that, while Jesus is a teacher, it is better to call him, "Son of David," "Son of Man," or "Son of God." "Teacher" is too lowly a title for our great Lord.

boldly announces God's kingdom. He boldly preaches repentance and faith. He boldly challenges the evil authorities and their religious sham. For, you see, these men would not be asking their question (in 12:14b) if they truly believed that Jesus "truly [taught] the way of God" (12:14a).

Ah, the "hypocrisy," which Jesus will point out at the very start of his reply (12:15).

But first the question, then the answer. Their question is clever. And it is admirable in the sense that one admires the smarts and skills of the first engineer to design a time-delay bomb. Here it is! "Is it lawful to pay taxes to Caesar, or not? Should we pay them, or should we not?" (12:14b). They set the timer and stand back.

The Great Escape

But, as Mark records in **12:15–17**, Jesus answers and easily escapes.

> But, knowing their hypocrisy, he said to them, "Why put me to the test? Bring me a denarius and let me look at it." And they brought one. And he said to them, "Whose likeness and inscription is this?" They said to him, "Caesar's." Jesus said to them, "Render to Caesar the things that are Caesar's, and to God the things that are God's." And they marveled at him.

In the first part of Mark's narrative and Jesus' reply our Lord exposes his opposition's sinister motives ("aware of their malice," Matt. 22:18; "he perceived their craftiness," Luke 20:23). Because Jesus sees their trickery, he once again questions his questioners: "Why put me to the test?" (Mark 12:15). This rhetorical question gets at the subtle mistake that would trip the trap. If Jesus says "It is not" to the question "Is it lawful to pay taxes to Caesar, or not?" (12:14), then he admits that he is an insurrectionist. Those who refuse to pay taxes to Rome do not fare so well. Political sedition is taken seriously. But if Jesus answers "It is"—that taxes should be paid to Caesar—then he admits the truths of the accusations against him, namely, that he is not only a friend of Gentile sinners but also a comrade of tax collectors. He might also admit, in their minds, that he is no true king and that his kingdom has no earthly authority. What king pays taxes? At this point, as I have stated elsewhere,

> Some scholars think the Pharisees would have answered the question no (it is not lawful) but the Herodians yes (it is lawful). Whether the Pharisees represent one horn of the dilemma and the Herodians the other, we don't know for certain. What we do know is that those are the two horns

of the dilemma—revolution against Rome or collaboration with it. If Jesus moves too far this way or that way, he is nicked or cut or killed.[5]

Their question is clever. But Jesus' answer, as he stands between the horns of this dilemma, is far more brilliant. He takes the horns and snaps them with his careful and concise words. They called Jesus a straight shooter. Now he loads and locks the gun. His first shot hits the target—them. "Bring me a denarius," Jesus commands, "and let me look at it." And they bring one. And he says to them, "Whose likeness and inscription is this?" They say to him, "Caesar's." They seek to trap him, but he has just destroyed the base of their attack.

How so? Let us remember the setting of this scene. They are standing in the *temple*. What did Jesus do in the temple the day before? He overturned the tables. Why? Because the Jewish religious authorities authorized the Court of the Gentiles—the place where pilgrims from among the nations came to worship—as the place where people exchanged their money so they might buy the proper animal for the Passover sacrifice. What money did they exchange? All sorts of currency, from the silver denarius of the Roman Empire to Jewish coins, which were locally minted, image-free copper coins.[6]

So then, with all that in mind, here is the irony. Jesus apparently has no Roman coinage. He does not have a denarius. So he asks for a coin. I imagine—and perhaps I exaggerate—that the Herodians reach down into their pockets, which are filled with pagan coins. Or perhaps the Pharisees grab one off a table and bring it to him. "Here you go."

They thought they had a good trap. However, Jesus' trap is better. The first claw of our Lord's trap snaps. He has gotten them. Who has the pagan coin? They do, not he. What are they doing with a pagan coin in the holy temple? Here comes the second claw. "Whose likeness and inscription," Jesus asks, "is this?" They said to him, "Caesar's" (12:16). What are they doing with a pagan coin *that has an image on it* in the holy temple?

On one side of this coin was the image of Caesar, with the inscription *TI CAESAR DIVI AVG F AVGVSTVS* ("Ti[berius] Caesar Divi Aug[gusti] F[ilius] Augustus"), which translated means "Tiberius Caesar Augustus, son of the divine Augustus." On the other side was the emperor's wife, Livia, or a picture of some woman seated. She likely symbolized the Pax Romana. The inscription on this side of the coin read *PONTIF MAXIM* (Pontif[ex] Maxim[us]), which means "High Priest." They are holding and eying a coin

5 Douglas Sean O'Donnell, *Matthew: All Authority under Heaven*, PTW (Wheaton, IL: Crossway, 2013), 636.

6 R. T. France, *The Gospel of Mark*, NIGTC (Grand Rapids, MI: Eerdmans, 2002), 466.

with idolatrous images and blasphemous inscriptions. Jesus has caught them red-handed in their hypocrisy. They hold the idolatrous and blasphemous coin in their hands, a coin that should never be found in the temple.

Render to Caesar

Next our Lord takes them down with his pithy perfect answer. "Jesus said to them, 'Render to Caesar the things that are Caesar's, and to God the things that are God's'" (Mark 12:17). The word "render" (Gk. *apodidomi*) can be translated "give back." So the first part of his short twofold answer is to "Give back the emperor's coin to the emperor." If Caesar has created and circulated the coin, then it is his. If he, in the form of taxes, asks for it back, then give it back.

Why does Jesus say this? Why does he condone and command that pious Jews pay taxes to Roman pagans? Two reasons. First, the tax in question was not an unreasonable tax for the services rendered. The tax was a denarius, one silver coin. The coin equaled a day's wages for an unskilled laborer (Matt. 20:2) and a common soldier. So a common soldier in the Roman army received about 300 to 400 denarii a year, while a centurion could receive up to 15,000 denarii. Once a year, in the province of Judea, everyone under Roman rule paid the poll tax. For most people this was not an excessive tax. I pay the city of Elgin ten times more each year in property taxes, most of which goes to the public schools, which has no direct benefit to my family, as my four children are in a private Christian school. Do I complain? No. Well, only passive-aggressively in commentaries.

The Roman poll tax was not an excessive tax, and it was a tax of which a taxpayer saw its returns. Throughout the empire Rome provided water, sanitation, roads, law and order, and police protection. They offered legal, political, and economic stability. They also offered advancements in agriculture, education, and architecture.

Years ago I remember my daughter Evelyn having to do a report on the Roman Empire. Her project was a write a letter to the Romans. This was perhaps in second or third grade. Here is what she wrote:

Dear Romans,

Thank you for starting a democracy, creating Roman numerals, making beautiful architecture, inventing concrete, making bathhouses, teaching us how to build roads, and building aqueducts.

Sincerely,
Thankful Evelyn

Of course, it is one thing for a little American girl two thousand years removed from the situation to write what she wrote, but for a Jew in Jesus' day no man, woman, or child would ever write a thank-you note to Rome. In fact, when this tax was introduced in AD 6, it was met with violent opposition. Judas of Galilee (named after the revolutionary Judas Maccabeus) refused to pay that tax. He, and those he led, thought it ridiculous that Jews should pay Caesar to live in their own land. So they revolted against Rome. They wanted Rome to leave them alone. They wanted back their Holy Land. And how successful was their campaign? The powerful Roman army quickly and ruthlessly squashed their hopes (read Josephus, *J.W.* 2.118). Thousands of Jewish insurrectionists were crucified.[7] So, please understand, there was a recent history behind this question posed to Jesus, a history that would have touched personally many Jews in the temple that day. Many had lost fathers and brothers due, indirectly, to the Roman poll tax. A small imperial tax that led to a major loss of life.

But, that said, I still think one reason, the first reason, Jesus condones and commands that pious Jews pay this pagan tax is because the tax in question was not an unreasonable tax for the services rendered.

Second, and more foundationally, Jesus believes the Roman Empire to be the legitimate governing authority. "Let every person be subject to the governing authorities," Paul writes in Romans 13:1, "For there is no authority except from God, and those that exist have been instituted by God." Jesus believed that. He promoted that theology. Paul goes on to say, "For because of this you also pay taxes [to Rome!], for the authorities are ministers of God. . . . Pay to all what is owed to them: taxes to whom taxes are owed, revenue to whom revenue is owed, respect to whom respect is owed, honor to whom honor is owed" (Rom. 13:6–7).

In God's providence, and at this time in history, God's people lived under Roman rule. And any legitimate government was to be honored, respected, and prayed for. Look at what Jesus' apostles wrote on this theme. In 1 Timothy 2:1–2 Paul penned, "First of all, then, I urge that supplications, prayers, intercessions, and thanksgivings be made for all people, for kings and all who are in high positions, that we may lead a peaceful and quiet life, godly and dignified in every way." In Titus 3:1–2 he said, "Remind [the church] to be submissive to rulers and authorities, to be obedient, to be ready for every good work, to speak evil of no one, to avoid quarreling, to be gentle, and to

7   For a graphic depiction of this see José Saramago's novel *The Gospel according to Jesus Christ* (New York: Harcourt Brace & Company, 1994).

show perfect courtesy toward all people." Christians, then and now, are not antigovernment. Christians are good citizens and kind neighbors.

In 1 Peter 2:13–14, 17 Peter issues these commands: "Be subject for the Lord's sake to every human institution, whether it be to the emperor as supreme, or to governors as sent by him to punish those who do evil and to praise those who do good. . . . Honor everyone. Love the brotherhood. Fear God. Honor the emperor." Those exhortations were all written to Christians living under Roman rule, sometimes oppressive Roman rule. Those exhortations are all built upon Jesus' teaching in Mark 12:17, and they are theologically undergirded with the principle that "respect for government is an important form of respect for God."[8]

God's people have rarely lived under a Christian theocracy. We have been, are, and will be exiles on this earth. We will not be free of the yoke of godless governments until heaven. But, because we believe God is sovereign, we trust that we can submit to the government he has providentially placed over us, whether we live in Babylon in the days of Daniel or in Jamestown, Virginia, 1607.

There are times for revolution. There are times when serious critiques must be made. And "if Caesar coins a new Gospel, he is not to be obeyed."[9] Acts and Revelation detail acts of civil disobedience and the persecution that followed. If the government tells us that our babies are to be aborted, we must disobey. If the government tells us that our Christian schools must employ transgendered teachers, we must disobey. If the government tells us to stop preaching that Jesus Christ is the only way to God, we must disobey. But if the government tells us to pay a certain tax in which certain services are expected in return, then we pay that tax. We render to Jefferson the things of Jefferson; we give back our Benjamins to Benjamin. "In this era of exile (1 Peter 1:1), as we long for the city of God (cf. Hebrews 11:10), Christians pay taxes to the glory of God and for the welfare of the city (Jeremiah 29:7)."[10]

Render to God

Jesus answers their tax question in the first part of his answer, "Render to Caesar the things that are Caesar's" (Mark 12:17a). But then he adds to it. He expounds further: "And [render] to God the things that are God's'" (12:17b), which is an obvious poetic parallelism:

8 Frederick Dale Bruner, *Matthew: A Commentary, Volume 2: The Churchbook, Matthew 13–28*, rev. ed. (Grand Rapids, MI: Eerdmans, 2007), 399.
9 J. C. Ryle, *Matthew: Expository Thoughts on the Gospels*, CCC (Wheaton, IL: Crossway, 1993), 207.
10 O'Donnell, *Matthew*, 641.

Render	to Caesar	the things that are	Caesar's, and
[Render]	to God	the things that are	God's

So, to render to Caesar includes paying taxes, and it also means praying for our leaders (from the president of the United States to the small-town mayor), practicing civil obedience (even when our views are different than our elected or appointed officials), and participating in public life (we are free to vote, serve in the military, hold office, speak on public issues, and pursue and offer political solutions).[11]

To render to Caesar involves all that. But what do we render to God? The answer is not merely a 10 percent tithe. The answer is *everything*. If the whole earth and everything in it—all created matter and all the creatures roaming on it, flying above it, and swimming within it—is the Lord's (which it is, according to Psalm 24:1: "The earth is the LORD's and the fullness thereof, the world and those who dwell therein"), then the answer to what we render back to God is *everything*.

The theologian and prime minister of the Netherlands Abraham Kuyper once wrote, "There is not a square inch in the whole domain of our human existence over which Christ, who is Sovereign over *all*, does not cry: 'Mine!'" Christ says, "Mine" to our bodies, houses, families, time, work, and money. This sentence ("[Render] to God the things that are God's," 12:17b) is, as Ryken notes,

> not just one of the most important things [Jesus] said about religion and politics; it is one of the most important things Jesus ever said about anything: give to God what belongs to God. This includes absolutely everything. Our bodies belong to God. Our eyes, our ears, and our hands are instruments to use in the service of God as we see the needs around us, listen to God's voice, and reach out with the compassion of Christ. Our homes belong to God. They are places that God has set apart for us to rest in his goodness and practice hospitality for people in need. Our time belongs to God. It is the most precious resource we have—the canvas we have for painting his grace. Our work belongs to God; it is service we offer to the Lord of all masters. Our money belongs to God, to be held loosely until we have the next golden opportunity to invest it in the kingdom of God. It all belongs to God![12]

---

11 These are Ryken's four ways to render unto Caesar. See *Luke: Knowing for Sure*, REC, 2 vols. (Phillipsburg, NJ: P&R, 2009), 2:366–70.

12 Ryken, *Luke*, 2:373.

So, think of the point this way. If the so-called divine Roman emperor should get a denarius once a year, how much should the truly divine Creator God get every day of our lives? The answer, again, is everything. Give back to God! To him "who has given us life and breath, salvation and sanctification, his Son and his Spirit, we are to give back our adoration and allegiance, our treasures and talents, our hearts and heads and bodies and souls."[13]

Amazed at Him

Our passage ends with a reaction: the Jewish authorities' amazement. "And they marveled at him" (Mark 12:17). They are amazed either in recognizing a brilliant answer that silenced their accusations[14] or in Jesus' admission. To say that something, even taxes, should be given back to Caesar makes clear that Jesus is not the messiah many Jews were waiting for, especially the Pharisees. They expected that the Son of David would come as a conquering king (see *Pss. Sol.* 17:21–25), and first on his list of kingdoms to conquer would be the Roman Empire. However, Jesus' kingdom (as he makes plain both here and before Pontus Pilate; see John 18:36) is not of this world. He is not the conquering king in that way. Instead, he is the conquering king in the sense that he came to conquer sin and hell and the devil and death by dying on a Roman tree.

Whatever its nature, amazement is the correct application of this short conflict story. But our amazement, the nature of it, should be that of awe in the authority and wisdom of Jesus Christ. Jesus answers an incredibly complex question on religion and politics in one simple statement, a statement that echoes throughout history and has been discussed and applied, in various ways, to every political system in the western world, and perhaps in every nation in the world. What wisdom!

Isaiah prophesied in Isaiah 11:2 that, when the offspring of David came, "the Spirit of the LORD shall rest upon him," and he would have "the Spirit of wisdom and of understanding, . . . [and] knowledge." What the Pharisees and Herodians said in deceptive flattery we say in honest worship: "Teacher [and Lord!], we know that you are true and do not care about anyone's opinion. For you are not swayed by appearances, but truly teach the way of God" (Mark 12:14). Jesus is a truthteller. Jesus is a man of integrity and impartiality. Jesus is not swayed by public opinion. And, perhaps most importantly, Jesus not only teaches the way of God; he *is* the way to God.

13 O'Donnell, *Matthew*, 642.
14 Luke records their silence ("But marveling at his answer they became silent," Luke 20:26).

Jesus is wiser than Solomon. Jesus is not easily tripped up by tough riddles. Jesus is greater than Solomon. He is the Son of David who came to die and rise for our salvation.

"And they marveled at him" (12:17). Let us marvel too. Let us pause and ponder the one, who in the ultimate act of wisdom (see 1 Cor. 1:18–25), went to the cross for us. Let us shout, "Worthy is the Lamb who was slain, to receive power and wealth and [ever more!] *wisdom*" (Rev. 5:12), and "Amen! Blessing and glory and *wisdom* . . . be to our God forever and ever! Amen" (Rev. 7:12).

The God of the Living

MARK 12:18-27

And as for the dead being raised, have you not read in the
book of Moses, in the passage about the bush, how God
spoke to him, saying, "I am the God of Abraham, and the
God of Isaac, and the God of Jacob"? He is not God of the
dead, but of the living. You are quite wrong.
Mark 12:26–27

James Joyce's novel *A Portrait of the Artist as a Young Man* has a scene in which Stephen Dedalus, the main character, is dropped off at boarding school. There Stephen encounters some of his new classmates. Wells, one of the boys there, asks Stephen,

> "Tell, us Dedalus, do you kiss your mother before you go to bed?"
> Stephen answered: "I do."
> Wells turned to the other fellows and said: "O, I say, here's a fellow says he kisses his mother every night before he goes to bed."
> The other fellows stopped their game and turned around, laughing. Stephen blushed under their eyes and said: "I do not."
> Wells said: "O, I say, here's a fellow says he doesn't kiss his mother before he goes to bed."
> They all laughed again. Stephen tried to laugh with them. He felt his whole body hot and confused in a moment. What was the right answer to the question? . . . Was it right to kiss his mother or wrong to kiss his mother?[1]

"What was the right answer to the question?" was not the question Jesus was asking in Mark 11:27–33 when he was asked by the Sanhedrin their

---

1   James Joyce, *A Portrait of the Artist as a Young Man* (Norwalk, CT: Easton, 1977), 8–9.

serious question, "By what authority are you doing these things?" (11:28). It was not the question Jesus was asking in 12:13–17, when the Pharisees and Herodians asked their entrapping question, "Is it lawful to pay taxes to Caesar, or not?" (12:14). And it is not the question Jesus is asking in 12:18–27, when the Sadducees, like sassy schoolchildren, try to fool him with their sophisticated but sophomoric riddle. To their question, "Whose wife will she be?" (12:23), Jesus is not thinking, "What was the right answer to the question?" As we shall see, he plainly, promptly, and properly answers their complex and cunning question.

The Questioner

Before we get to the Sadducees' question and Jesus' answer, let us set the stage by understanding who the Sadducees were and what they believed. Mark **12:18** provides their key theological distinctive (the "Sadducees" claimed "that there is no resurrection"). They held this view because they were convinced that the Torah taught nothing on the resurrection from the dead. Those five books of the Hebrew Scriptures were their canon. They did not view the other thirty-four books in our canon, the traditional Jewish canon, as authoritative.

Mark speaks of the Sadducees only once, in verse 18. The other inspired authors of the NT give us thirteen more verses. Those verses affirm what Mark says about their denial of the resurrection, but they also expand the picture of this religious group. We learn, for example, that the Sadducees also denied, expectedly, any activity after death—a final judgment or an everlasting soul (see Acts 23:6–10). This view, along with denying the existence of angels (Acts 23:8), was the opposite view of the Pharisees. The Pharisees believed in angels, life after death, and a final judgment.

We learn also that the Sadducees were as political as they were religious, perhaps more political than religious.[2] They, like the Pharisees, and possibly other religious groups (the Essenes and the Zealots), served on Israel's high court, the Sanhedrin (Acts 4:1; 5:17; 23:6–7). In fact they had the most clout because they, unlike those other groups, came from the nobility, likely the priestly aristocracy dating back to the time of King Solomon. Also, they were

---

2 As Bo Giertz well summarizes, "The Sadducees represented the secularized national church in Israel. As a rule, they were wealthy and conservative. The core of their party was the noble temple priesthood. They had ill regard for the pietistic zeal supported by the Pharisees. They were theologically conservative for reasons of convenience. For them, the measure of pious customs that had always been the convention was sufficient." *The New Testament Devotional Commentary: Volume 1: Matthew, Mark, Luke*, trans. Bror Erickson (Irving, CA: 1517 Publishing, 2021), 200.

pro-Roman. They embraced the status quo and practiced quid pro quo. They liked the way things were and they expected something in return for political and religious favors.

Now, here is a question that came to my mind the other night: "Why might the Sadducees have rejected the prophets as part of their Scripture?" Ah, it came to me as in a dream. Simple. The prophets contain a lot of prophecies against those who warm up to worldly powers. Also, some of the prophets talk about judgment after death. For example, Daniel 12:2 reads: "Many of those who sleep in the dust of the earth shall awake, some to everlasting life, and some to shame and everlasting contempt." Everlasting contempt—that is what was coming to these worldly religious leaders, whether they believed it or not. A dose of their condemnation came shortly after Jesus' death and *resurrection*. This powerful religious and political party disappeared from history shortly after the first Easter and the complete destruction of their power source—the temple. After AD 70 we have no historical record of the Sadducees—which is sad, you see. They are extinct but not annihilated. They have met their Maker, the very man they questioned that spring day before the Passover. These well-bred and well-read men know more fully than we know just how real the resurrection is and how real the final resurrection of ultimate judgment will be.

So, all that to say, the upper class from the temple hierarchy, the most aloof among the religious parties thus far, approaches Jesus. They have a question too. The Pharisees, their rivals, and the Herodians, their peers in political perspective but not position, have failed. The Sadducees approach Jesus with confidence. They think they are so smart. They cannot wait to show off their elite education. And Jesus cannot wait to put down their pride.

Their Question

That is who Jesus is up against. The Sadducees are our Lord's next question-ers. They are an important opponent, and an ingenious and inventive one as well. Next, let us look at their question. They begin, "Teacher, Moses wrote for us that if a man's brother dies and leaves a wife, but leaves no child, the man must take the widow and raise up offspring for his brother" (**12:19**). Before we examine the rest of their question, stop and notice here that they set the theological foundation for their question and debate with the words "Moses wrote." "We," they are saying, "are pro-Moses. We believe what he wrote on the resurrection. What did he write? Nothing! But he did write about remar-riage. So let's eye that command. Let's see, teacher, if what Moses taught fits with what you have taught about some resurrection."

With their question and reference to Moses, they allude to the levirate law. This is a law that God, through Moses, gave to his people, recorded in Deuteronomy 25:5–10. The gist of the law was that if a man married and then died, his brother must marry his wife. This was done to keep the family name and to ensure the household inheritance was passed on to someone in the family. These are not as important issues for us today, but they were the bedrock of the ancient world.[3] Deuteronomy 25:5–10, put simply, is the Sadducees' biblical proof text that Jesus was wrong about the resurrection.

But they have more in their arsenal of "rationalistic religiosity" than a proof text.[4] They have a great story attached to it. They have a story problem that would make those who manage a perfect score on the math portion of the SAT (Scholastic Aptitude Test) scratch their heads. Here it is. It is brilliant. I love their question; I hate that they seek to entrap Jesus with it. They say,

> There were seven brothers; the first took a wife, and when he died left no offspring. And the second took her, and died, leaving no offspring. And the third likewise. And the seven left no offspring. Last of all the woman also died. In the resurrection,[5] when they rise again, whose wife will she be? For the seven had her as wife. (**12:20–23**)

This must have been *the* question of theirs. It is logically sound and seemingly biblically tight. I can imagine that, every time a pious Pharisee approached them, they asked their brilliant question and heard silence. "What! No answer? I thought not." They expected that Jesus would have no response as well. But they were wrong. A theological genius stood before them. Their Creator too. But, someone who, as a man, was never educated as they were. He was educated on his mother's lap and at the local synagogue. But he also was the one, as I said (the Creator!), who created words, riddles, and the story of salvation history. The Educator would now educate them. "Sit and learn, rich boys. The carpenter and Creator will now school you."

The Awesome Answer

Mark **12:24–27** records Jesus' awesome answer. "Jesus said to them, 'Is this not the reason you are wrong?" Stop again there. What do we do with this?

3 See Genesis 38:8–10 and m. Yebam. "To die childless so that the lineage died out, that was the greatest misfortune an Israelite could imagine" (Giertz, *New Testament Devotional Commentary*, 200).
4 Giertz, *New Testament Devotional Commentary*, 200.
5 The phrase "in the resurrection" was, as Mark Strauss notes, "shorthand for the end-time resurrection of the dead, the final judgment, and eternal life with God (Luke 14:14; John 11:25; Acts 17:32; 23:6, 8; 24:15; 26:8)." *Mark*, ZECNT (Grand Rapids, MI: Zondervan, 2014), 533.

The boldness here. The gravity. The authority. The correctness, without the political correctness. Look at our Lord's response:

> Jesus said to them, "Is this not the reason you are wrong, because you know neither the Scriptures nor the power of God? For when they rise from the dead, they neither marry nor are given in marriage, but are like angels in heaven. And as for the dead being raised, have you not read in the book of Moses, in the passage about the bush, how God spoke to him, saying, 'I am the God of Abraham, and the God of Isaac, and the God of Jacob'? He is not God of the dead, but of the living. You are quite wrong." (12:24–27)

Notice that Jesus starts with a rhetorical question ("Is this not the reason you are wrong?" 12:24), and ends with a condemnation ("You are quite wrong," 12:27). What is wrong with their logic and their interpretation of the Bible? Two things are wrong, "wrong" both in the sense of "incorrect" and in the sense of "immoral." Their thinking is both erroneous and evil.

Knowledge of God's Word

First, their knowledge of God's Word is wrong.

When Jesus says that they are wrong because they do not know the Scriptures, does he mean that they have failed to understand that the canon includes Joshua to Malachi, as well as Genesis, Exodus, Leviticus, Numbers, and Deuteronomy? Perhaps. Jesus' canon does include all those books. His Bible contains not just the Law but the Law, the Psalms, and the Prophets.[6] But I think, based on how he answers in verse 26, that he is willing to deal with them based on their own "Scriptures," the first five books.

He is correcting what I often call a flat reading of the Bible. Question: Should we baptize infants? Let me check my Bible concordance for all the times "baptism" is mentioned. Here are all the verses. I do not find one verse that commands that we should baptize babies. Question. Is God triune? Let me check my Bible concordance for all the times "trinity" is mentioned. I do not find one verse that contains the word "trinity." Thus, God is not triune, and we should not baptize babies into the name of the Father, Son, and Spirit. That is a flat reading of the Bible. Someone searches the Scriptures without understanding the story of the Scriptures, or how all the stories, commands,

6 For example, related to his own ministry, Jesus speaks of its fulfilling "the Law of Moses and the Prophets and the Psalms" (Luke 24:44; cf. 24:27). He also quotes most often from Exodus (7x), Deuteronomy (10x), Isaiah (8x), and the Psalms (11x).

covenants, discourses, proverbs, parables, and prophecies fit together into one grand narrative and theological proclamation.

So, for example, when Jesus reads the whole of their canon and the start of his (the first five books), he too finds no mention of the resurrection. But what does he find? Exodus 3:6, the John 3:16 of old-covenant believers. At the Bethlehem Bulldogs' football games some devout Jew always held up Exodus 3:6 during field goals and extra-point attempts. What does that verse say? It says what Jesus says, if you share his same biblical inclinations, if you get how the whole of God's revelation fits together.

Look again at Mark 12:26–27. There our Lord answers and admonishes: "As for the dead being raised, have you not read in the book of Moses, in the passage about the bush, how God spoke to him, saying, 'I am the God of Abraham, and the God of Isaac, and the God of Jacob'? He is not God of the dead, but of the living. You are quite wrong." Why are they "quite wrong" (or "badly mistaken," NIV; or "You're way, way off base," MSG; or, my favorite translation and the oldest one, "Ye err much," Wycliffe)? They "err much" concerning the resurrection because the patriarchs are not dead. Sure, they died. But they are not dead. You see, the nature of God's covenant promises to them and personal relationship with them (real people in a real relationship with a real God) assures us that they are not annihilated. Or, as Jesus summarizes, "[God] is not God of the dead, but [he *is* (present tense) the God] of the living" (12:27). If Yahweh is "I am who I am"—an ever-existing and ever-living God—then those whom he has covenanted with will not be left for dead. There is a living and lasting relationship between all those he has called and covenanted with. To read the first five books of the Bible and think of death as extinction is to miss the story and one very key verse that starts the story of God's relationship with Moses (Ex. 3:6). If Abraham, Isaac, and Jacob were forever dead, then God's promises to them have been broken and what God was about to say to Moses about the exodus would be meaningless. Our God is a God of the living!

I wish that Jesus had not stopped there. I wish he had corrected their view of the canon of Scripture (it is more than five books) and then quoted from the rest of the OT: from Psalms 16, 68, 110 or Isaiah 26:19: "Your dead shall live; their bodies shall rise. You who dwell in the dust, awake and sing for joy!"[7] I wish he then asked them, "What do you make of those texts?" I also wish that Jesus had done a bit of show-and-tell. I wish he had said, "You should ask Peter about what happened on the Mount of Transfiguration.

---

7   For other examples see Isaiah 25:7–8; Hosea 13:14; and, of course, Daniel 12:1–2, cited earlier.

Ask him whether he saw Moses and Elijah alive and in person. Then ask him whether they had aged well. Moses died 1,480 years before, and Elijah went away in the whirlwind about 900 years before. Did they look like skeletons or men with real flesh and bones?" Or I really wish his show-and-tell had included the greatest event in history—his own resurrection. I wish he had said, "Stop with your smart but sophomoric question. Will you allow me just a few days before I answer? If it is okay with you, can I first die, be buried, and then rise again in front of five hundred-plus witnesses (1 Cor. 15:6) before I answer your silly question about a woman, her seven husbands, and the possibility of a resurrection?" And yet our humble, not haughty Lord gave what he gave: a simple but profound answer to their slick, satanic question.

Knowledge of the Power of God

So, back to the logic of Jesus' rebuttal of their question. Their thinking is erroneous and evil in two ways. First, their knowledge of God's Word is wrong. Second, their knowledge of God's resurrection power is wrong:

> Jesus said to them, "Is this not the reason you are wrong, because you know neither the Scriptures nor the power of God? For when [human beings] rise from the dead, they neither marry nor are given in marriage, but are like angels in heaven." (12:24–25)

Jesus rejects their denial of the resurrection because he both understands and, of course, embodies the power of God. He himself has raised the dead. He himself will be raised from the dead. He knows and trusts that God will raise all his covenant people to be with him forever.

When Jesus corrects their perception of God's power, he also exposes their faulty presumptions. Their clever question hangs on the conjecture that marriage is a permanent institution. Is it? Jesus says no.[8] Is that shocking to you? It was to them. I imagine their jaws dropping to their tassels when Jesus said these words.

Imagine further with me. Imagine these important and educated men at a dinner party a year before their encounter with Jesus. After the meal Saul the Sadducee says, "Who's up for a game of *Stump the Rabbi*?" They all raise their hands. They are all in. They clink their glasses of expensive Pinot Grigio imported from Italy. The year is AD 32, an excellent year. The first question read

---

8   This does not necessarily mean that God erases the oneness. It may be that those married on earth will have a very close relationship in heaven.

from the game *Stump the Rabbi* is this: "Create a question to prove that the resurrection from the dead is not true. You cannot use Genesis through Deuteronomy. You must use a later book, what the Pharisees consider part of the canon. Extra points if you use something from the apocryphal books." Judas the Just starts the ten-minute timer, but not before writing down a few ideas for an answer. The time passes. Aaron the Erudite offers, after much debate and discussion, the best answer. Turning to the book of Tobit, he offers the story of the seven husbands and one wife. In that apocryphal book a woman named Sarah marries seven men from the same family line (*Tob.* 7:11). Each husband, one after the other, is strangled by a demon after the wedding ceremony and before the wedding night (*Tob.* 3:7–8; 6:14–15). Tobias, the last and longest-lasting husband, makes it through both the ceremony and the consummation. He is not killed in the bedchamber because he had prayed and had angelic help with the demon (*Tob.* 8:1–18). (That is too close to my honeymoon to comment on.) So Aaron the Erudite offers, in some form, the question recorded in Mark 12:20–23.

The presumption that holds together the logic of the Sadducees' question is that the relationship structures of earth must be precisely the same as those in the afterlife. So, if Sarah marries Joseph and he dies, for Sarah to marry another man would be to mess up the relational structures of heaven. If she marries and buries seven men, the mess is even greater. Will she be married to Joe or John, Tim or Tom, Simeon or Simon or Sam? Will she be married to her first or her favorite husband? But if there is no marriage in the resurrected state (if, when people "rise from the dead, they neither marry nor are given in marriage," 12:25), then it is possible for Sarah, Joe, John, Tim, Tom, Simeon, Simon, and Sam to coexist without any conflict. They can coexist without conflict not just because those marriages have been dissolved but because those marriages have been surpassed. They—the eight of them, and eight million more—will be a part of the greatest wedding and marriage in history! Those temporary marriages, which all have symbolized to the couple and the world the marriage of God with his people, have reached their goal. They can coexist without conflict—Tom wrestling Tim over Sarah to see who wins their earthly wife for eternal life—because everyone in heaven, those who were single or married on earth, those who were married once or a dozen times, will have the same purpose and mission. They, and we with them, will be "like angels in heaven" (12:25).

If that sounds boring to you, think again. If that sounds sad, think again. We do not know a lot about the angels in heaven, but the Bible does tell us that they are without sin, that they worship God perfectly and perpetually, and that they accomplish his mission. Sounds wonderful! We often think that we will be most satisfied if we can have the right romantic relationship with another human being. That is simply not true. We will be most satisfied when we are living without sin, worshiping God in the presence of God, and obeying all the orders he has for us. Do we honestly think that "the infinitely creative God of the universe, who has given us a glimpse of his creative genius in this marvelously diverse planet, is preparing" a place that is dull and drab for us, and work and worship that we will consider tedious and tiresome?[9] To be "like angels in heaven" will be awesome. To be "like angels" but remain human (the pinnacle of God's creation, even above the angels; the only creature made in God's image) will be totally awesome. To see our Lord Jesus, fully man forever, and the millions of other men, women, and children from around the nations and throughout history in their glorious and perfect resurrected bodies will be to see not only something awesome but the power of God. The resurrection power of God!

You see, the Sadducees cannot see what the Scriptures say and cannot imagine what God can and will do. They do not understand the Bible, and they do not grasp the power of God.

No Eye Has Seen

Many years ago I heard the story of when historian Martin Marty of the University of Chicago addressed the Society of Biblical Literature at its annual meeting. The Society of Biblical Literature comprises thousands of Bible scholars from around the world. Professor Marty began his address by stating, "Never in the last few hundred years has there been such a gathering of theological intelligence since Jonathan Edwards sat alone in his study in Northampton." When we look at Mark 12:18–27, alongside Mark 11:27–12:12 and 12:13–17, we see a man far more brilliant than Edwards and certainly more brilliant than the Bible scholars and temple authorities of Jesus' day— the chief priests, the scribes, the elders, the Pharisees, the Herodians, and the Sadducees. But this passage, and what Jesus teaches in it, teaches us more than that Jesus is wise. It does teach us that! Do not miss the wisdom of Jesus. Challenge your unbelieving friends to read the question/answer time with Jesus in the Gospels. But it teaches us also that all who are in Christ have such a great hope. Great hope. Real hope. We are all facing challenges right now. Some of us are facing unemployment. Some of us are facing sickness. Some of us are facing financial troubles. Some of us are facing the ache of separation

9   Strauss, *Mark*, 537.

from loved ones. But the greatest challenge that awaits us all is death. How will we fare against death?

Our Lord Jesus holds out to us here the promise of life after death. He gives us hope. He gives us a hope that should make us join Paul in confessing, "I am sure that neither death nor life, nor angels nor rulers, nor things present nor things to come, nor powers, nor height nor depth, nor anything else in all creation, will be able to separate us from the love of God in Christ Jesus our Lord" (Rom. 8:38–39). Our Lord Jesus holds out to us here more than the promise of life after death; he holds out life to the fullest after death. Again, as Paul writes, "No eye has seen, nor ear heard, nor the heart of man imagined, what God has prepared for those who love him" (1 Cor. 2:9). We have the promise of life after death. We have the promise of a great life after death. We have the promise of a never-ending wedding celebration.

Most Important of All

MARK 12:28-34

Jesus answered, "The most important is, 'Hear, O Israel: The Lord our God, the Lord is one. And you shall love the Lord your God with all your heart and with all your soul and with all your mind and with all your strength.' The second is this: 'You shall love your neighbor as yourself.' There is no other commandment greater than these."
Mark 12:29–31

One of the most memorable scenes in cinematic history is the final trial scene in *A Few Good Men*. Jack Nicholson, playing the high-ranking Colonel Nathan R. Jessup, is questioned by Tom Cruise, playing Lieutenant Daniel Kaffee, a young and inexperienced naval lawyer. Lieutenant Kaffee calls Colonel Jessup as a witness. His goal is to get Jessup to admit that he called a "code red," an unofficial and illegal order to discipline violently a soldier who was causing trouble or not pulling his weight. Kaffee believes that US Marines Lance Corporal Harold Dawson and Private First Class Louden Downey, who are facing a court-martial, were ordered to strike Private William Santiago violently, a beating that killed him.

After Kaffee unnerves Jessup by pointing out a contradiction in his testimony, Jessup is irate. He is upset that Kaffee has caught him in a lie and that the young lawyer has no respect for his high position and crucial job. Feeling that he has gotten under his skin enough, Kaffee asks point blank, "Colonel Jessup, did you order the Code Red?" The judge interrupts, "You don't have to answer that question." "I'll answer the question," Jessup replies. "You want answers?" Kaffee says, "I think I'm entitled to them." "You want answers?" Jessup says again. "I want the truth!" shouts Kaffee. "You can't handle the truth!" replies the colonel. Then the colonel goes on to talk about his role in maintaining national security, stating at the end of his personal defense that

"Santiago's death, while tragic, probably saved lives." The prosecutor returns to his question, "Did you order the Code Red?" "I did the job," is the answer. He asks again, "Did you order the Code Red?" And then Jessup finally admits that he had ordered it.

Case closed. The colonel is arrested and led out of the courtroom.

Throughout Mark 11:27–12:27 the Jewish religious authorities have been asking questions hoping that they would break Jesus, get an admission of guilt, and thus have enough evidence to arrest and condemn him. Case closed. But, instead of tripping, Jesus has tied their tongues. After being asked four difficult questions from seven different sets of religious leaders, we read, "And after that no one dared to ask him any more questions" (12:34). But before their silence we have the privilege in this chapter, as we cover Mark 12:28–34, of listening to another beautiful answer from our brilliant Lord.

A Final Question

The scene starts with a final question. Mark **12:28** reads,

> And one of the scribes came up and heard them [likely the Sadducees] disputing with one another [over Jesus' answer in 12:24–27], and seeing that he answered them well [*kalōs*, or "beautifully"], asked him, "Which commandment is the most important [*protos*] of all [i.e., first among all the commandments]?"

A scribe is an expert in the written law and oral history around it, someone skilled in reading and interpreting the Bible. What stands out here, set within the context of the other questions and questioners, is that, first, this man comes by himself, not as part of a religious posse, and, second, his motives are apparently pure.[1] He does not approach Jesus to trip him up or because he was sent by some higher authority on a mission to destroy Jesus. He approaches Jesus because he is impressed by Jesus' answer to the Sadducees' question. He likely agrees with Jesus' view on the resurrection and is impressed by his clear and concise answer to their unanswerable riddle.

Thus the scribe's question ("Which commandment is the most important of all?") is an honest one. He has studied the matter. He has an answer to the question. He has perhaps heard other rabbis on the matter. But he is genuinely interested in how Jesus will answer it. He grasps that Jesus is wise and worth

---

1   "The experts in the law appear frequently in Mark's gospel [1:22; 2:6, 16; 3:22; 7:1, 5; 8:31; 9:11, 14; 10:33; 11:18, 27; 12:35, 38; 14:1, 43, 53; 15:1, 31], often with the Pharisees and almost always in an adversarial role." Mark L. Strauss, *Mark*, ZECNT (Grand Rapids, MI: Zondervan, 2014), 540.

listening to. He calls Jesus "teacher," but this is the first and only character in Mark 12 who calls him that and is actually willing to listen and to be taught. So, amid the noise of the temple bustle and the heat of the battle between the temple authorities and Jesus, there is something serene about this scene.

With that said, let me clarify *what* he was asking. According to rabbinic tradition there are 613 commands in the Hebrew Scriptures, 248 positive (e.g., "Honor your father and mother") and 365 prohibitive (e.g., "You shall not steal"). This man is not asking, "Which laws from the Scriptures need to be obeyed and which can safely be ignored?" Rather he is asking, "What is the fundamental premise of the law on which all the individual commands depend?"[2]

This was a common question asked and answered by rabbis. Some rabbis would take what they thought was the key commandment and state in it a slightly different way, perhaps a more provocative way. For example, Rabbi Hillel, who was asked to summarize the law while the questioner stood on one leg (i.e., quickly), answered with a version of the Golden Rule from Leviticus 19:18, "What you yourself hate, do not do to your neighbor; this is the whole law—the rest is commentary."[3] Other rabbis would select a verse that had one, two, or three central commands.[4] For example, Amos 5:4: "Thus says the LORD to the house of Israel: 'Seek me and live.'" Or Proverbs 3:6: "In all your ways acknowledge him, and he will make straight your paths."

A Twofold Response to One Question

So then, Mark 12:28 presents us with another questioner ("a scribe") and his important question ("Which commandment is the most important [or 'first'] of all?"). What is the fundamental premise of the law on which all the individual commands depend? Mark **12:29–31** provides Jesus' ready answer. He is happy to reply. He will soon chide the scribes as a group in verses 38–40, which begin with Jesus' "Beware of the scribes" and end with a word about their "greater condemnation." But here he is open to an important discussion with this learned but teachable man.

---

2   David E. Garland, *Mark*, NIVAC (Grand Rapids, MI: Zondervan, 1996), 476.

3   B. Šabb. 31a, quoted in William L. Lane, *The Gospel of Mark*, NICNT (Grand Rapids, MI: Eerdmans, 1974), 432.

4   In b. Mak. 24A-B we read that Rabbi Simelai expounded, "Six hundred and thirteen commandments were given to Moses. . . . David came and reduced them to eleven [Psalm 15]. . . . Isaiah came a reduced them to six [Isaiah 33:25–26]. . . . Micah came and reduced them to three [Micah 6:8]. . . . Isaiah again came and reduced them to two [Isaiah 56:1]. . . . Amos came and reduced them to one, as it is said, 'For thus says the Lord to the house of Israel. Seek Me and live' [Amos 5:4]. Habakkuk further came and based them on one, as it is said, 'But the righteous shall live by his faith' [Hab 2:4]." As summarized in Jacob Neusner, *A Rabbi Talks with Jesus: An Intermillennial, Interfaith Exchange* (New York: Doubleday, 1993), 95–96.

Jesus answered, "The most important is, 'Hear, O Israel: The Lord our God, the Lord is one. And you shall love the Lord your God with all your heart and with all your soul and with all your mind and with all your strength.' The second is this: 'You shall love your neighbor as yourself.' There is no other commandment greater than these." (12:29–31)

At the heart of the Jewish faith is the Shema, Deuteronomy 6:4–5, which Jesus quotes in Mark 12:29–30. The words of the Shema would hang in a mezuzah, a little rounded box, on the doors of Jewish homes. The Shema was also worn by many Jewish men in a phylactery or tefillin, a leather box worn on the forehead and tied around the wrist during weekday morning prayers. Every morning and evening a devout Jewish household would recite those words (see m. Ber. 2:2; m. ʾAbot 2:13). The synagogue service would begin with this oral creed, and "it was often the last words on a martyr's lips."[5]

Among the polytheistic pagans in the Greco-Roman world in which the Jews of Jesus' day lived, Israel alone held to monotheism. They worshiped one God, not many gods. The Shema starts with a confession, followed by a command. The confession is that God is one, and the command involves the whole of who we are to the one and only God. Deuteronomy 6:5 speaks of three parts of the whole of who we are—heart (our emotions, but also our intellects), soul (our entire being), and strength (our abilities and actions)—and Jesus of the four parts, adding "mind," perhaps emphasizing the intellect.[6] Both lists make the same point: if Yahweh is one, then our complete ("all," 4x—all of who we are) adoration and allegiance is to him. Total Godward devotion. "Love," this all-encompassing word, involves all of us—our attitudes, affections, and actions. We will see in the next chapter what such love looks like in the widow who gives "all she had to live on" to the temple treasury (see Mark 12:41–44). In giving all her money to God she shows that she loves him with her "heart" or "mind" (the core of who she is intellectually and emotionally), her "soul" (her whole person), and her "strength" (her resources, all she owns).[7] She loves God with all she is and has.

But, in addition to that first and greatest command (12:30), and tied hand in hand with it, is the second, which comes from Leviticus 19:18. In context,

5   Strauss, *Mark*, 542.
6   Jesus' mention of the heart, soul, mind, and strength is not "a breakdown or a psychological analysis of human personality"; R. Kent Hughes, *Mark: Jesus, Servant and Savior*, PTW, 2 vols. (Wheaton, IL: Crossway, 1989), 2:115. Instead it is a listing of "overlapping categories [for] our every faculty and capacity"; D. A. Carson, "Matthew," in EBC, vol. 9, rev. ed. (Grand Rapids, MI: Zondervan, 2010), 523.
7   On Deuteronomy 6:4–5 see Daniel I. Block, *For the Glory of God: Recovering a Biblical Theology of Worship* (Grand Rapids, MI: Baker, 2014), 100–2.

"loving one's neighbor means . . . not harboring anger in your heart, or seeking vengeance, or bearing a grudge, and yet frankly reasoning or kindly rebuking him or her if necessary."[8] Elsewhere, in the parable of the good Samaritan (Luke 10:25–37), Jesus teaches that our neighbors include more than the people around us of the same race and religion. He also states, in the Sermon on the Mount, that we are to love even our enemies (Matt. 5:44). We are to love God with all we are, and we are to love all people.

Jesus adds this second commandment because the first cannot exist without the second.[9] This is why Jesus says, "The second is this: 'You shall love your neighbor as yourself.' There is no other commandment [singular] greater than these [plural]" (Mark 12:31). The two are one great commandment. As the apostle John writes, "If anyone says, 'I love God,' and hates his brother, he is a liar; for he who does not love his brother whom he has seen cannot love God whom he has not seen" (1 John 4:20).[10] To love God is to love people; to love people is to love God. In this way the Christian life mirrors Christ's cross. There is a vertical dimension (love for God) that connects with a horizontal (love for others). Christian love is not humanism (we should love people without reference to God) nor mysticism (we should love God without reference to humans). We love both God and people.

And here in Mark 12:31 Jesus makes clear that the litmus test of our love for people is self-love. At times we might struggle with self-esteem, but we rarely struggle with self-love. We all naturally love ourselves. And, as much as we love ourselves, that is the standard for how we should love others.

We are to (1) love God and (2) love others. Matthew's version of Jesus' answer records an additional line. After Jesus quotes from Deuteronomy 6:4–5

---

8   Douglas Sean O'Donnell, *Matthew: All Authority under Heaven*, PTW (Wheaton, IL: Crossway, 2013), 659.

9   Matthew adds, "And a second is like it" (Matt. 22:39). The phrase "like it" takes on the sense of both origin (the second command grows out of the first) and equal importance (the second, by itself, is a valid summary of all the OT commands; see Rom. 13:9; Gal. 5:14). The first great command is both complemented and completed by the second.

10 Cf. Douglas Sean O'Donnell, *1–3 John: A Gospel-Transformed Life*, REC (Phillipsburg, NJ: P&R, 2015), 138: "As God's love is manifested to us in Christ (4:9; cf. John 1:18; 6:46), our love for God is manifested in our love for others. In this way our love for the *invisible* God is made *visible*. The one who truly 'love[s] God' will love 'his brother' (1 John 4:20)—sacrificially and compassionately. That is God's 'love . . . perfected in us' (4:12). God's love for us is completed, is made whole, or 'reaches its extended goal' when we actively extend it to others, or, as Thompson put it, 'when it flows from God, through us, to our fellow believers.'" Cf. Marianne Meye Thompson, *1–3 John*, IVP New Testament Commentary (Downers Grove, IL: IVP, 2011), 123. Thompson (126–27) goes on to say: "The shape of perfect love is triangular: love comes as a gift from God that enables us to love each other and so return to God the gift that is given to us. . . . Where any one leg of the triangle is missing, love remains incomplete and immature. But where the triangle is whole, love is complete."

as the first great commandment and Leviticus 19:18 as the second, he gives this helpful image: "On these two commandments depend all the Law and the Prophets" (Matt. 22:40). Put differently, the whole of the OT—the "commandments and covenants, prophecies and promises, types and testimonies, invitations and exhortations"—hang upon the double love command.[11]

A Right Response to the Right Answer

The scribe, as we see next in Mark **12:32–33**, is delighted with Jesus' answer. Before his peers (thus with great courage and offering an independent assessment) he compliments, reiterates, and expounds.

> And the scribe said to him, "You are right, Teacher. You have truly said that he is one, and there is no other besides him. And to love him with all the heart and with all the understanding and with all the strength, and to love one's neighbor as oneself, is much more than all whole burnt offerings and sacrifices." (12:32–33)

After the scribe commends Jesus' answer ("You are right, Teacher," 12:32; "You have truly said," 12:32), he both reiterates what Jesus has said and adds to it. He agrees that God "is one" (12:32). He affirms the Shema. He then adds an allusion to the first of the Ten Commandments: "and there is no other besides him" (cf. Ex. 20:3), a command reiterated throughout the OT (Deut. 4:35; Ps. 86:8; Isa. 45:6, 21; 46:9; 47:8, 10). His allusion reminds us of the division of the Ten Commandments, with the first four focusing on loving God and the second six on loving others. He affirms that God should be loved with all that we are—with "all the heart and with all the understanding [his summary of Jesus' "mind"] and with all the strength" (Mark 12:33). He agrees that the second-greatest command, paired perfectly with the first, is to love others ("and to love one's neighbor as oneself," 12:33). He adds that this command, or perhaps the two of them together, "is much more than all whole burnt offerings and sacrifices" (12:33).

To make that statement in the temple in Passover week is extremely bold. Yet here the scribe reiterates a theme found in various places in the OT. Sacrifices—from the least costly to the most ("whole burnt offerings," literally a "holocaust," in which every part of the animal is consumed by the flames)—matter less than love. As the Lord God said through Hosea, "I desire steadfast

---

11 William Hendriksen, *Exposition of the Gospel according to Matthew* (Grand Rapids, MI: Baker, 2002), 810.

love and not sacrifice, the knowledge of God rather than burnt offerings" (Hos. 6:6).[12] Or, to bring it into a Christian context, Paul echoes in 1 Corinthians 13:13 what the scribe says here in Mark: love is "the greatest." Loving God and loving others are even more important than every bull and bird sacrificed on the altar in the temple.

The Last Word

Mark **12:34** records that Jesus has the last word. He has the last word as "no one dared to ask him any more questions" and as he comments on the scribe's wise response, announcing to him, "You are not far from the kingdom of God." The man is close to kingdom entrance because he understands that love of God and others supersedes temple sacrifices. But he likely, at this point, does not yet understand fully the nature of his own sin or the mission of Jesus. He could not conceive how Jesus' full body sacrifice—his holocaust on the cross—would not only atone for sins but demonstrate the only time any human being fully loved both God and man. So he could not possibly grasp that entrance into the kingdom requires repentance of sin and faith in Jesus.

But the optimistic tone of Mark 12:34 makes me optimistic about this man's future. We read in Acts 6:7, "The word of God continued to increase, and the number of the disciples multiplied greatly in Jerusalem, and a great many of the priests became obedient to the faith." If "a great many of the priests" in Jerusalem came to saving faith, why not a good number of scribes, some of whom were priests?

Now, before I offer some final thoughts and applications on this whole passage, let me dig down deeper into the statement, "You are not far from the kingdom of God." What is striking about these words is that Jesus does not say to this devout and learned Jew, "Congratulations, with your reaffirmation on my excellent answer, you are *in* the kingdom of God." Our Lord says that he is "near," not "in." With that Jesus is encouraging him to continue his journey. "You are moving in the right direction." But he is also warning him (and us) that "near" is not "in." That teaches us what I said above, that faith in Jesus Christ is the only way in. Love of God and love of others is not the double-serrated key to unlock the narrow gate into the kingdom. Love of God and love of others is the response of those who, through faith in Christ, have entered through the narrow gate. Why is the love of God and love of others not the way in? Because no one but Jesus has ever loved God and others perfectly.

---

12 On the similar theme of "to obey is better than sacrifice" (1 Sam. 15:22) see Psalm 40:6; Isaiah 1:11–17; Jeremiah 7:21–23. In Psalm 51:16–17 David speaks of God's delighting more in "the sacrifices of . . . a broken and contrite heart" than mere "sacrifice."

We all sin against God, and we all sin against others. Our holy and loving God demands perfect holiness and love. No one but Jesus ever perfectly loved God (obeying his will) and perfectly loved people (he came, lived, and died, even for some of his enemies).

So Jesus' "near"-not-"in" comment teaches us that knowing the right answer to the question (i.e., What is the greatest commandment?) and attempting to live out the answer (i.e., loving God and people the best we can) is not the way "in." Moreover, Jesus' "near"-not-"in" comment teaches us that some people, like the scribe, can be "near" the kingdom, but that does not mean they are "in." To stand on one side of the Colorado River at the Grand Canyon, to be propelled to the other side, but to fall two inches short is to hit the side and fall to one's death. "Being almost there, is not being there," as Kent Hughes puts it. "It is possible to be within an inch near heaven, yet go to Hell!"[13]

When I was in graduate school, I took an independent study on the famous eighteenth-century evangelist John Wesley (1703–1791). John, along with eighteen other children, grew up in a pastor's home. John's father served as the rector at the Anglican church in Epworth. John was raised in a Christian home with two fine Christian parents. He was educated at Charterhouse School and Christ Church, Oxford, both distinctly Christian schools at the time. While at Oxford, he started the "Holy Club," a group of men who gathered regularly for study of the Greek NT, prayer, and other devotional exercises and who were committed to partaking regularly of Holy Communion, rigorous self-denial, works of charity, and other spiritual disciplines. After lecturing as a professor of Greek and logic Wesley was ordained to Christian ministry. He was a brilliant Bible scholar and teacher.

A few years later John came to Savannah, Georgia, as a missionary to Native Americans. He worked for the Society of the Propagation of the Gospel. He was in his early thirties. Yet for all his Christian upbringing, commitments, and acts of service he began to see that something was amiss. On his way back to England he encountered the Moravians, a group of German Christians who seemed alive to Christ in a way he never experienced. Upon his return he wrote, "I went to America to convert the Indians; but, oh, who shall convert me?"

On the morning of May 24, 1738, Wesley randomly turned in his Bible. He opened to Mark 12:34 and read Jesus' words to the scribe, "You are not far from the kingdom." He then realized that he, like the scribe, was deeply religious but sadly lost. He was an almost Christian, a good but unconverted and

---

13 R. Kent Hughes, *Mark: Jesus, Servant and Savior*, PTW, 2 vols. (Wheaton, IL: Crossway, 1989), 2:117, 118.

unregenerate man. But Wesley was also journeying in the right direction. He was turning to Jesus for help. That evening he gathered with a Christian group in Aldersgate Street, a short walk from St. Paul's Cathedral in London. There he heard someone read Martin Luther's preface to the Epistle of Romans. In his *Journal* Wesley wrote of his conversion: "About quarter before nine, while [Luther] was describing the change which God works in the heart through faith in Christ, I felt my heart strangely warmed. I felt I did trust in Christ, *Christ alone*, for salvation; and an assurance was given me, that He had taken away my sins, *even mine*, and saved me from the law of sin and death."[14]

From then and there the rest is history. Wesley wrote, planted, and preached. He was perhaps the greatest evangelist of all time. It is estimated that he traveled 200,000 miles on horseback and preached over 42,000 sermons in the UK, Ireland, and America for the last fifty years of his life. All the while, Mark 12:34 remained his life verse. He preached to men and women and children, many like himself—those who grew up knowing the truths of the Christian faith but not the reality of a personal relationship with Jesus wrought by the life-changing power of the Holy Spirit in the heart.

Some professing Christians (and professional preachers!) are like Wesley before he encountered the saving power of the living God. Christian in name, attitudes, affirmations, convictions, values, education, and family. But not yet a Christian. It is possible to be near the kingdom but not yet in it. If that is you, now is the time to admit that this scribe in this text mirrors your relationship with Christ. Now is the moment also to cry out to God: "God, work in my heart. Hear my confession. Take away my sins. Save me from the law of sin and death. Give me saving faith in Christ. Help me trust in Christ, *Christ alone*, for salvation. Warm my heart toward you. Give me the assurance that you are mine and I am yours." And, if you have prayed that, take the next step. Repent and believe in the gospel (Mark 1:15) and watch the gates of paradise open wide.

Some Final Thoughts

Recently, on a drive home from Detroit to Chicago, after listening for two hours to a hundred or so of the thousand channels of Sirius XM radio I turned off the noise. I often like to drive in silence. I really do. I like to drive in silence because I like to see where my mind wanders. I might think about the family, the church, or the future. I might think about my childhood, my to-do list, the sermon for Sunday, or food. It is good to just stop and think. Do you do that?

---

14 I was inspired by Kent Hughes's retelling of the story; see *Mark*, 113–14, 117, 119. See *The Works of the Rev. John Wesley* (London: Methodist Conference Office, 1809), 1:280.

When in my short commute home I stopped to think about this text before us, a few thoughts came to mind. I thought about how grounded Jesus' ministry and teaching was in the OT. Yet I also thought about how original and innovative he was. Do you know that what is recorded in Mark 12:29–30, 32–33—Jesus' answer and the scribes' reiteration of it—is the first time in Jewish literature that the double love commands were paired together? Jesus was unoriginal in quoting the Bible for his answer but quite original in affirming the "love of God and neighbor as the center and sum of the law."[15]

From there a number of thoughts came to mind the more I meditated on these verses. I asked myself, "Why are these two the greatest?" I surmised that they are the greatest both because, as I said earlier, all the other commandments attach themselves to them (e.g., not to commit adultery is to love your spouse; to rest and worship on the Sabbath day is to demonstrate that God is more important than work or money) and because they reflect perfectly the essence of God. "God is light" (1 John 1:5). "God is love" (4:8, 16). God is holy and abounds in steadfast love. And, speaking of and thinking about the person and attributes of God, I was reminded afresh (my final thought) from this text—from the Shema ("God is one")—that our God stands alone. Our God stands alone! In a world of religious diversity and plurality there is no god like our God. Who alone created this world? Our God. Who alone has created us in his image? Our God. Who alone became man and dwelled among us? Our God Immanuel. Who alone perfectly kept the law? Our God Immanuel. Who alone conquered disease and demons and death? Our God Immanuel. Who alone offers us heaven, a place to abide with him, and worship alongside the multitude of heavenly hosts? A place of perfect love! Our great God—Father, Son, and Spirit.

Who then calls us to put him first? Our God. Who then commands us to love him with all we are and have? Our God. Who then commands us to love our neighbors to the same degree we naturally love ourselves? Our God. Our great God does!

What a great commandment! What a great God!

---

15 As James R. Edwards claims, "Although love of God and love of humanity were occasionally affirmed separately in Israel, there is no evidence that before Jesus they were ever combined. It does not appear that any rabbi before Jesus regarded love of God and neighbor as the center and sum of the law"; *The Gospel according to Mark*, PNTC (Grand Rapids, MI: Eerdmans, 2002), 372–73). In the Babylonian Talmud, which consists of documents compiled in Late Antiquity (3rd–5th centuries AD), two sources also contain the double love command: "Love the Lord and your neighbor" (t. Iss. 5:2); "Throughout all your life love the Lord and one another" (t. Dan. 5:3). Note that those statements are not direct combinations of Deuteronomy 6:5 and Leviticus 19:18. Also, some scholars argue that these Jewish texts were edited (added to) by Christians in the Middle Ages: cf. H. C. Kee, "The Testaments of the Twelve Patriarchs," in *Old Testament Pseudepigrapha*, ed. James Charlesworth, 2 vols. (Peabody, MA: Hendrickson, 2016), 1:776–80.

Three Last Lessons in the Temple

MARK 12:35-44

How can the scribes say that the Christ is the son of David?
Mark 12:35

One Sunday afternoon my son Simeon had a friend over. After they played outside in the snow, they came inside and talked for a while. When they got bored (we have a "no electronic device" policy on Sundays), they walked over to the bookshelves in the living room. Imagine that. Books! Simeon asked, "Dad, out of all these books, which is your favorite?" I walked over. I eyed bookcase one, then two, and finally three. I pulled a volume off a shelf. I said, "G. K. Chesterton's *Everlasting Man*."

I thought then, as I am always looking for providential sermon illustrations, that Chesterton might have just the word to attract your attention and turn on your brains, one that actually (in God's kind providence) relates to the key themes of our text. So I randomly flipped through the book, which I had thoroughly marked up years ago. I read Chesterton's witty insight on pagan idolatry: "Just as they became unnatural by worshipping nature, so they actually became unmanly by worshipping man." I flipped further and read, "The figure in the Gospels [Jesus] does indeed utter in words of almost heart-breaking beauty his pity for our broken hearts." I flipped further and read, "Whatever else is true, it is emphatically not true that the ideas of Jesus of Nazareth were suitable to his time, but are no longer suitable to our time."[1] Put differently (and here is how that quote connects with our text), it is extraordinary how Jesus' timeless words (words relevant for two thousand years and still relevant this very day) were words so unexpected, so original, and at times so defiantly countercultural in his own day.

---

1   The quotes above are found in G. K. Chesterton, *The Everlasting Man* (London: Dodd, Mead, & Company, 1925; repr., San Francisco: Ignatius, 1993), 153, 187, 194.

That fact is perhaps no truer than in Mark 12:35–44, where Jesus teaches three lessons: "And as Jesus taught" (12:35); "And in his teaching he said" (12:38); "And he called his disciples to him and said to them" (12:43). He taught them! First Jesus teaches monotheistic Jews, who daily recite the Shema, that the "God [who] is one" (Deut. 6:4) has a "son" (Mark 12:35–37). Then in the holy temple he reprimands the revered Bible scholars (12:38–40). Finally, he contrasts these most privileged hypocrites with the most destitute but sincere believer, a poor, no-name widow whose two-coin contribution has served the church throughout the ages as an example of love and liberality (12:41–44). Such radical teachings would have amazed the average pilgrim in Jerusalem on that Passover week almost as much as they still amaze us.

With those three teachings before us perhaps we can summarize what we are to learn in this text from the timeless countercultural Christ: in contrast with the ostentatious, attention-seeking, proud, and greedy scribes, who are the opposite of the quiet, humble, and generous widow, we are to acknowledge and worship Jesus as the divine Lord from David's line.

The First Lesson

The first and most foundational lesson can also be phrased in this way: the man who is Israel's Messiah is also the Lord of heaven and earth. Or, the King of the Jews is the King of the cosmos! This truth is expressed in **12:35–37**:

> And as Jesus taught in the temple, he said, "How can the scribes say that the Christ is the son of David? David himself, in the Holy Spirit, declared,
>
> > "'The Lord said to my Lord,
> > "Sit at my right hand,
> >   until I put your enemies under your feet.'"
>
> David himself calls him Lord. So how is he his son?" And the great throng heard him gladly.

We start with the last clause first: "And the great throng [crowd] heard him gladly" (12:37). The sense of the word "gladly" is not that of a joyful understanding and acceptance of what Jesus has just taught. It is the sense of entertainment. Jesus of Nazareth has once again stumped the scribes. The unofficial rabbi has just silenced the rabbis who finished first in their class. And the crowd loves it. "Tell us another riddle. Give the experts in the Law, Prophets, and Psalms another question that makes them scratch their heads."

Remember that Jesus, because of his mighty works and otherworldly wisdom, always attracted a crowd. So a number from this "throng" had likely been near him for each and every question posed to him. They had watched from the stands, we might say, as Jesus knocked the Pharisees' fastball about Roman taxes out of the park. They had applauded as the Sadducees' curveball about the resurrection hit the rooftops in Bethesda, a few miles away. They stood in awe as the scribe's easy lob about the greatest commandment landed in Illinois among the Illini tribe.

After all that Jesus takes the mount, the temple mount (he "taught in the temple," 12:35), and he only needs one pitch to strike out his opponents. It is a curveball thrown faster than the speed of light, but it looks to the batter like a changeup. The ball curves with each question. "How can the scribes say that the Christ is the son of David?" (12:35) is the first question. This is a rhetorical question that sets up his second question. The scribes correctly affirm what God had said in 2 Samuel 7:12–16 and elsewhere,[2] that the Messiah would come from David's offspring and would liberate and restore Israel. He would be a "son of David." Jesus, who was born from David's royal bloodline,[3] agrees and even accepts this designation for himself (see Mark 10:47–48). But he presses them, with his second question, to think whether there be more to the Messiah than his bloodline and mission. Might the Messiah, according to one of David's own Spirit-inspired songs, be more than a mere man?

David himself, in the Holy Spirit [cf. Acts 2:30–31[4]], declared,

"The Lord said to my Lord,
'Sit at my right hand,
until I put your enemies under your feet.'"

David himself calls him Lord. So how is he his son? (Mark 12:36–37)

Here once again Jesus returns to the OT to support his position and to make his point. The quote is from Psalm 110:1.[5] In it David speaks of two

---

2   E.g., Psalm 89:4, 36–37; Isaiah 9:6–7; 11:1–16; Jeremiah 23:5; 33:15–16; cf. *Sirach* 47:11; 48:15; *Psalms of Solomon* 17:21; 4QFlor 1:11–13.
3   See Matthew 1:20; Luke 1:27, 32, 69; 2:4, 11; Romans 1:3–4; 2 Timothy 2:8; Revelation 5:5; 22:16.
4   "Being therefore a prophet, and knowing that God had sworn with an oath to him that he would set one of his descendants on his throne, he foresaw and spoke about the resurrection of the Christ, that he was not abandoned to Hades, nor did his flesh see corruption."
5   "This is . . . the most frequently quoted Old Testament text in the New Testament, quoted or alluded to some thirty-three times. . . . This [text] becomes the preeminent proof text for the

Lords. The first "Lord" must be the Lord God and the second "Lord" the promised Messiah, the King who would come after David and from David. So the psalmist says that "the Lord" (God) had promised the Messiah ("said to my [David's] Lord") that the Messiah would be granted co-regency ("sit at my right hand") and dominion over his enemies ("until I put your enemies under your feet," 12:36). That truth, then, raises a question: If "the Lord is one" (12:29) and "there is no other besides him" (12:32), what is this second Lord doing sitting at God's right hand? Or, as Jesus puts it, "David himself calls him Lord. So how is he his son?" (12:37). What father would call his son "Lord"?

Next, watch the ball move out of the temple, back in, and right across home plate.

The only answer that makes any sense is that David's son, the one enthroned next to Yahweh, is also David's "Lord," that "David's son as man [is] David's Lord as God."[6] The human son of David is also the divine Son of God.[7]

Whenever I interview people for church membership, I ask them to define the gospel. My hope is that that person takes me to Romans 1:1–5, because there Paul summarizes well what Jesus teaches here in his first lesson in Mark 12:35–44. Paul writes that the gospel is what God "promised beforehand through his prophets in the holy Scriptures, concerning his Son, who was *descended from David* according to the flesh [a real man from David's lineage] and was declared to be the *Son of God* [a real man who is also God's eternally begotten Son] in power according to the Spirit of holiness by his resurrection from the dead, Jesus Christ our *Lord*." The man who is Israel's Messiah is also the Lord of heaven and earth!

The throne upon which the English monarch sits at his or her coronation is called King Edward's Chair. The chair was built in 1296. Originally it was ornately decorated, with gold paint and other royal colors. Today—due to the touch of tourist traffic and choir-boy carvings—the chair is quite plain looking. If you walked into Westminster Abbey, you would see simply a bare, natural oak colored, wooden chair. That is one aspect of this throne that is unusual. The other is that this chair is huge, ten feet high and four feet wide.

---

exaltation of Jesus (e.g., Acts 2:33–35; Rom. 8:34; 1 Cor. 15:25; Col. 3:1; Heb. 1:3, 13)." Grant R. Osborne, *Mark*, TTCS (Grand Rapids, MI: Baker, 2012), 225.

6   Frederick Dale Bruner, *Matthew: A Commentary, Volume 2: The Churchbook, Matthew 13–28*, rev. ed. (Grand Rapids, MI: Eerdmans, 2007), 425.

7   On Mark's Son of God language see Mark 1:1, 11; 3:11; 5:7; 9:7; 14:61–62; 15:39. Note esp. the Father's declarations of Jesus' identity at Jesus' baptism (1:11) and transfiguration (9:7). "The Messiah is Lord, God's co-regent and thus Lord of all, even David, indeed of the whole earth (Phil. 2:11; Rev. 19:16). He is the messianic son of David and he is the Son of God ([Mark] 1:1, 11; 9:7; 14:62)." Eckhard J. Schnabel, *Mark: An Introduction and Commentary*, TNTC (Downers Grove, IL: IVP Academic, 2017), 308.

Needless to say, when Elizabeth, who was about five feet high and two feet wide, sat on the throne, she looked small. Yet that is the point. Each monarch is too small when compared to the monarchy. The greatness of the realm is too vast for any one monarch to fill.[8]

The kingdom that God promised to David is an everlasting empire, a kingdom that has dominion over all kingdoms of the world. In Psalm 2, a psalm of King David, we read of the nations as the inheritance of the Messiah (the Lord's "Anointed," Ps. 2:2) and "the ends of the earth" as his possession (Ps. 2:8). In Psalm 72, a psalm of King Solomon, we read that this anointed one will have "dominion from sea to sea" (Ps. 72:8) and that "all kings" will "fall down before him" and "all nations" will "serve him" (Ps. 72:11). Imagine how large that throne must be! Even King Solomon in all his glory must have looked like a gnat sitting in a child's high chair. Together Solomon and the twenty heirs who followed him could not have covered the four corners of that chair. But here is the point of Mark 12:35–37: Jesus fills the seat! That throne is built for him alone. When Jesus sits at the right hand of the Father (cf. 16:19), every inch of the throne is filled by the exalted Son. As Paul speaks in Ephesians 1:17–23, "The Father of glory," after he raised Jesus from the dead,

> seated him at his right hand in the heavenly places, far above all rule and authority and power and dominion, and above every name that is named, not only in this age but also in the one to come. And he put all things under his feet and gave him as head over all things to the church, which is his body, the fullness of him who fills all in all.

I hope our vision of Jesus is not too small. I also hope we acknowledge him, bow before him, and serve him. Love him!

With all that said, here now is the connection I am making between this chapter and the previous one. In Mark 12:28–34 Jesus taught clearly that the greatest commandment is to "love the Lord" with all that we are and have— our heart, soul, mind, and strength (12:30). Here in 12:35–37 Jesus teaches clearly that he is the Lord. He does not define or explain the mystery of the Trinity, but he mentions the work of the Spirit and quietly introduces the idea of the Father and the Son.[9] So, if Jesus is the Lord God, then he rightly

---

8   For this illustration I am indebted to Michael LeFebvre, *Singing the Songs of Jesus: Revisiting the Psalms* (Fearn, Ross-shire, UK: Christian Focus, 2010), 59–60.

9   In a subtle way Jesus affirms the Trinity here. He mentions God the Father (the first "Lord"), God the Son (called both "son" and "Lord"), and the Holy Spirit.

deserves our love (see Matt. 10:37). We are to love the Lord with all that we are and have. And what does such love look like? As I said in the last chapter,

> [It] looks like in the widow who gives "all she had to live on" to the temple treasury (see Mark 12:41–44). In giving all her money to God she shows that she loves him with her "heart" or "mind" (the core of who she is intellectually and emotionally), her "soul" (her whole person), and her "strength" (her resources, all she owns).

It also looks like another woman, the woman who anoints Jesus. Shortly before Judas betrays Jesus, we read in Mark 14:3–9 of this woman's incredible actions. She interrupts a dinner party to open an "alabaster flask of ointment" containing very expensive oil (in the amount of a full year's wages) and "poured [the ointment] over his head" (14:3). She does this to anoint Jesus for his burial, as he states (14:8), and/or, in her mind, to anoint him because she views him as her king (cf. 1 Sam. 9:16). Whatever the motive, her "beautiful thing," as Jesus labels her act (Mark 14:6), is a perfect illustration of love. Loving the Lord looks like "wasting" (see 14:4) the best of what we have on Jesus because we believe that Jesus is Lord, the one seated at the right hand of God in power, ruling over all things for all time.

The Second Lesson

The first lesson, taught in Mark 12:35–37, is that the man who is Israel's Messiah is also the Lord of heaven and earth. The second and third lessons relate to that first and foundational lesson. Here is the big picture again: in contrast to the ostentatious, attention-seeking, proud, and greedy scribes (we will read about them next in **12:38–40**)—who are the opposite of the quiet, humble, and generous widow (we will read about her in 12:41–44)—we are to acknowledge Jesus as the King of the cosmos.

The second lesson then involves two contrasts. The scribes are contrasted with the widow, but also with Jesus. He is the good shepherd; they are the wolves in sheep's clothing. The second lesson is precisely what Jesus says at the start of verse 38: "Beware of the scribes." Beware of being ostentatious (they "like to walk around in long robes and like greetings in the marketplaces," 12:38), privileged and proud (they "like to . . . have the best seats in the synagogues and the places of honor at feasts," 12:39), and greedy and malicious scam artists (they "devour widows' houses and for a pretense make long prayers," 12:40). The lesson might be stated like this: watch out for narcissistic religious leaders who know and teach the Bible but use God's people for their own personal gain.

When I was a newborn Christian, I thought the world was black and white. If a Christian leader said he loved God and believed the Bible, I assumed he was a good, honest, and solid believer, because those are now such countercultural commitments in America. But now, over thirty years later, I know the world of Christian leadership to be a thousand variations of gray. I have met "Christian" leaders who do not know Christ. I have met other genuine Christian leaders who are so caught up in self-love and self-promotion that they have left their first love. The commandment to love God first is not first on their list. Some of these leaders are eventually exposed. But all of them, if you look carefully, can be spotted, and Jesus tells us here what to look for.

First, look at their wardrobes. Do they regularly don expensive religious garbs, similar to the "long robes" of the scribes (12:38)?

Second, and related, notice whether they like to be noticed. One's clothing gets one noticed if one wears a certain attire. In walks a man dressed in all black with a white collar. "Good morning, Father. Please have my seat on the train." Or, "Ah, you must be the new youth pastor. I can tell by your designer black t-shirt, expensive tattoos, and well-trimmed beard. Let me buy you a ten-dollar latte."

Third, see where they sit. The scribes liked having the seats on the platform during the worship service ("the best seats in the synagogue," 12:38, the "seats of Moses," which faced the congregation), perhaps so people could worship them as they pretended to worship God. "Oh, look how pious Pastor Talkative is![10] His hands are in the air when he sings, his head is bowed to his knees when he prays, and he always cries when the collection plate is passed." Then, when these leaders get out of the church into the public sphere, look to see whether they are seated at the local diner with a refugee family or at Morton's The Steakhouse with the CEO of Bank of America. The scribes loved the "best seats in the synagogues *and* the places of honor at feasts" (12:39).

Fourth, examine the source of their incomes. Verse 40 tells us that many of the scribes of Jesus' day, per our Lord's perfect estimation, took advantage of the poor and susceptible (they "devour widows' houses"—that is how they

---

10 In Bunyan's *Pilgrim's Progress* Christian encounters Talkative, a man who talks about "the vanity of earthly things, and the benefit of things above . . . the necessity of the New-birth, the insufficiency of our works, the need of Christ's righteousness . . . [about] what it is to repent, to believe, to pray, to suffer." But, as Christian soon learns, Talkative's Christian confession is all talk. Christian says to his companion, Faithful, "He talketh of Prayer, of Repentance, of Faith, and of the New-birth: but he knows but only to *talk* of them. . . . Religion hath no place in his heart. . . . All he hath lieth in his *tongue*." *The Pilgrim's Progress*, World's Classics (Oxford: Oxford University Press, 1984), 63–65.

make their money!),[11] all while they pray prayers as long as a drive through Nebraska. I applaud how J. B. Phillips and Ken Taylor paraphrase this verse. Phillips writes, "These are the men who grow fat on widow's property and cover up what they are doing by making lengthy prayers" (PHILLIPS). Taylor renders for the modern ear, "They shamelessly cheat widows out of their homes and then, to cover up the kind of men they really are, they pretend to be pious by praying long prayers in public" (TLB).

A scribe was paid by his community to study and teach the Bible. Those who funded him could be rich patrons, like a widow whose husband had left her a fortune. Or they could be poor, like a widow whose husband's death meant that her source of income had dried up. The scribes of Jesus' day preyed on both types of widows. But, as with the health-wealth preachers today, it was often the destitute who gave a dollar in hope that these mighty men who sit in front at church and have dinner at the chophouse could commune with God so the poor patron might experience a miracle or simply catch a break in life.

Discernment is what was needed then and is needed ever so much now. "Beware of the scribes" (12:38). Watch out for narcissistic religious leaders who know and teach the Bible but use God's people to their own personal gain. To gain a reputation. To gain more money. To gain the praise of people.

But also know that Jesus Christ is Lord. He will put his enemies under his feet (Mark 12:36). He will judge evildoers.[12] He will judge teachers and preachers with a stricter judgment (James 3:1; Heb. 13:7). And those whose wardrobes resemble a prince of Saudi Arabia, who love to be noticed and greeted with great titles, who crave and often have the nice seats both in the religious assembly and at the city's top restaurant next to the city's top people, and whose income is generated by feeding off the poor—be assured that they will get theirs. On judgment day, among the hoard of the damned, "they will receive the greater condemnation" (12:40).[13]

---

11   "This ['devouring' = 'appropriating their houses in an unethical manner'] could happen through charging excessive legal fees when they worked as probate lawyers, deliberate mismanagement of a widow's estate of which they had been made trustees, taking their houses as pledges for unpayable debts, prompting them to support the temple with recourses they could not really afford, or exploiting their hospitality and trust" (Schnabel, *Mark*, 310).

12   "Jesus' verdict corresponds to the prophets' condemnation of people who defraud widows. . . . In Ezekiel 22:7, 15 and Zechariah 7:10–14 the threatened punishment for defrauding widows, orphans and the poor is the dispersion of Israel among the nations; in Jeremiah 22:3–6 it is the destruction of the king's place; in Deuteronomy 27:19, the loss of fortune in this life" (Schnabel, *Mark*, 311).

13   God will avenge the exploitation of the poor (see Ex. 22:22; Deut. 10:18; 24:17; 27:19), especially the wicked crime of defrauding widows (see Isa. 10:1–4; Jer. 7:6–7; Ezek. 22:7; Zech. 7:10–14; Mal. 3:5).

The Third Lesson

The first lesson is that Jesus is the cosmic king. The second lesson is to watch out for narcissistic religious leaders who know and teach the Bible but use God's people for their own personal gain. The third lesson is to sacrificially surrender everything to the purposes of God. Jesus teaches this lesson in Mark **12:41–44**.

Taking the posture of a teacher in the ancient world ("And he sat down," 12:41; cf. Matt. 5:1), Jesus, before he taught, first noticed the activity related to "the treasury" (Mark 12:41). Within the outer court of the temple "many rich people" came up to the "offering box" (12:41; there were thirteen brass boxes in the shape of trumpets) and "put in large sums" (12:41). Jesus could see and *hear* their dropping their gold and silver coins. They were not tooting their own horns, but they were making some noise. He also noticed a "poor widow" (12:42). He knew she was a poor widow by her tattered black widow's garb and the amount of her donation. She dropped in two lepta, "two small copper coins," an offering that, in our currency equals a "penny" (12:42, *quadrans*), or enough loose change in that day to buy a meager meal. No big deal, right? If the office staff told a pastor that the collection for last week was $10,000 and then the church treasurer later came into his office and said, "Sorry, we made a mistake; it was $10,000.01," he would likely say, "Why bother me about that?"

Jesus did not have my attitude. This penny was a big deal to him. For next he holds a Christian Conference on "Divine Accounting" and offers the opening lecture, "A Penny for My Thoughts on a Penny."

> He called his disciples to him and said to them, "Truly, I say to you, this poor widow has put in more than all those who are contributing to the offering box. For they all contributed out of their abundance, but she out of her poverty has put in everything she had, all she had to live on." (12:43–44)

I do not know what, if any, relationship this particular widow had to the scribes. But as Jesus is making a direct contrast between those widows whose wealth had been devoured by the scribes and this widow, I imagine that she was either a rich woman whose savings had been swindled or a poor woman whose pittance had been regularly purged. But here and now she turns as directly to God as she can. She does not want to give to those men, so she gives to God. She drops her coins in the temple coin box because she believes in the sacrificial system. She believes that when the priest,[14] whose salary is

---

14 Some scribes were priests. However, if my conjecture is true, then the scribes just denounced here, like the Pharisees in Matthew 23, would not be priests but those who advise them.

paid in small part by her coins, sacrifices an animal for her sins, God deems her forgiven. She looks to the cross, we might say, without yet knowing Jesus and what he will do for her. The ultimate sacrifice for sin. A sacrifice whose benefits are free to all who come in faith.

But the point here is not so much about her relationship with the sacrificial system as her love for God and trust in God. She renders to God the things of God (12:17). She gives all that she has to him, literally "her entire life" (Gk. *holon ton biov autēs*). Those two coins might be her daily income that she has given away, or even all that she has left (her whole savings). Either way, at this moment she gives all that she has this day back to God in worship. She is "rich toward God" (Luke 12:21) because she trusts that God will provide her daily bread.

In this way she is not only a dramatic contrast to the slick and superficial scribes but an example to be emulated. Are we like her? Do we sacrificially surrender everything to the purposes of God? Look, "our giving is always in the sight of Jesus Christ."[15] We may fool the person next to us when we pull out a big wallet and stuff a few hundred-dollar bills in the plate, but we will not fool Jesus. And to Jesus our giving is measured not by the amount but by the sacrifice (the proportion of our income that is given).[16] God delights in a cheerful giver, but also a generous one. The person who gives $2,000 a year out of her $20,000 salary (out of her relative "poverty") gives far more than the person who gives $2,000 out of $200,000. As Grant Osborne puts it, "Which is better . . . to give all of the little we have to God or a little of all we have to God?"[17] Freely we have received; let us freely give (see Matt. 10:8).

The Everlasting Man

With those three lessons learned—the King of the Jews is the King of the cosmos; beware of the scribes; sacrificially surrender everything to the purposes of God—I will conclude by returning to the first lesson, and also to where we started—with a quote from Chesterton's *The Everlasting Man*: "Mahomedans [Muslims] did not misunderstand Mahomet and suppose he was Allah. Jews did not misinterpret Moses and identify him with Jehovah. Why was this claim [of Jesus' divinity] alone exaggerated unless this alone was made? Even if Christianity was one vast universal blunder, it is still a blunder as solitary as the Incarnation."[18]

---

15   Sinclair B. Ferguson, *Let's Study Mark* (repr., Carlisle, PA: Banner of Truth Trust, 2016), 209.
16   Ferguson, *Let's Study Mark*, 209.
17   Osborne, *Mark*, 227.
18   Chesterton, *Everlasting Man*, 202.

Jesus alone claimed to be God. Christianity alone holds him up as Christ and Lord, Son of David and Son of God. And Mark 12:35–44 teaches that, in contrast to the ostentatious, attention-seeking, proud, and greedy scribes, who are the opposite of the quiet, humble, and generous widow, we are to acknowledge and even worship Jesus as the divine Lord from David's line, as the incarnate Immanuel.

The Imperatives of the Olivet Discourse
MARK 13:1–23

If anyone says to you, "Look, here is the Christ!" or "Look, there he is!" do not believe it.
Mark 13:21

Where were you when the Twin Towers fell?

I was at home in my bedroom. I was sick that day. So I slept in and then did what I never do in the morning: I turned on the television. We had this little black-and-white television set that we kept in the closet. I pulled it out and plugged it in the wall and sat on the floor. I sat on the floor because the cord did not reach the bed and there was no stand on which to place the television.

Almost immediately after I turned on the set American Airlines Flight 11 crashed through floors 93–99 of the North Tower of the World Trade Center. That was at 8:46 a.m. Minutes later a news alert came on. The amazing footage was shown. I didn't know what to make of it. An accident, I presumed. Then at 9:03 a.m. United Airlines Flight 175 flew into floors 75–85 of the South Tower. This was a terrorist attack. I knew it, but I could not believe it. Then at 9:59 a.m. and 10:28 a.m. the unthinkable happened. Both massive towers, one after the other, collapsed. Total destruction. Like nothing I had ever seen, or likely will ever see. My friends Nick and Rebecca lived in New York City at the time. The collapse of the Twin Towers, followed by the eerie silence throughout the world's most significant city, made Rebecca wonder, "Is this the end of the world?" It obviously was not, but you could understand why she and millions of others thought the same way.

When Jesus told his disciples that the temple complex would be completely leveled ("There will not be left here one stone upon another that will not be thrown down," Mark 13:2), their immediate reaction was to think that he was talking about the end of the world, the day, as the prophets foretold, when God would "make Jerusalem a heap of ruins" (Jer. 9:11; cf. 22:5; 26:6) and plow "Zion . . . as a field" (Mic. 3:12).

Besides these prophecies that might have come to mind, why did the disciples think this way—that the temple's destruction would signal the end of the world? Three reasons come to mind. First, they knew that it had taken "forty-six years to build" (John 2:20) the Second Temple, this fortress-like structure made of precious stone and metals. For this strong citadel to fall to the ground would have been unthinkable because it would have been so improbable. Twin Towers improbable. How could that happen unless the end was at hand?

Second, the temple not only had an architectural permanence about it; it was also awesome and iconic. It was a man-made wonder, "probably the most awesome building in the ancient world."[1] The first-century Jewish historian Josephus said that "the building wanted nothing that could astound either mind or eye" and that with its gold-plated, white-marbled exterior it appeared "from a distance like a snow-clad mountain."[2] Others said, "He who has not seen the temple of Herod has never seen a beautiful building in his life."[3] For such a symbol of Israel's greatness to be leveled would surely indicate the end of all things.

Third, the temple was the God-appointed place on earth where God's presence was to be found. So then, if the temple were destroyed, many thought there would be no way for God's people to keep covenant with God. What would happen to the Levitical priesthood, the sacrifices, the forgiveness of sins? Without the temple, Israel's relationship with Yahweh would be over. And if that were over, then everything must be over.

The View from Atop

But here in Mark 13:1–23 Jesus corrects their view. While Jesus does prophesy about the most cataclysmic event in Israel's history, his foundational advice about the event is not to mistake it for the end. After the temple is destroyed, followed with or preceded by other disastrous occurrences—wars, earthquakes, and famines (13:7–8)—he knows that his earliest followers will be tempted to think this is the end. But it is not. "Do not be alarmed. This must take place, but *the end is not yet*. . . . These are but *the beginning of the birth pains*" (13:7–8). Jesus' foundational advice about the amazing events that will occur shortly after his resurrection is not to equate the end of the

1 George R. Beasely-Murray, *Jesus and the Last Days: The Interpretation of the Olivet Discourse* (Peabody, MA: Hendrickson, 1993), 383.
2 See Josephus, *Ant.* 15.11.5; *J.W.* 5.5.6.
3 B. Bat. 4a; b. Sukk. 41b.

temple with the end of the world and, related to that, not to be led astray by those who would say otherwise (13:5–6), claiming to be Jesus or another messiah ("saying, 'I am he!'" 13:6; cf. Matt. 24:5) and gaining quite a following ("They will lead many astray," Mark 13:6).

The big picture of the Olivet Discourse unfolds in four movements. First, Jesus, with his disciples, journeys to the top of Mount Olivet.[4] There they look down upon the temple complex west of them, "opposite" them (13:3). There one of the disciples says, "Look, Teacher, what wonderful stones and what wonderful buildings!" (**13:1**). Second, Jesus predicts the destruction of the temple complex: "Do you see these great buildings? There will not be left here one stone upon another that will not be thrown down" (**13:2**). Third, the two sets of brothers ("Peter and James and John and Andrew," **13:3**), those Jesus had called to be his first four disciples (1:16–20), muster up the courage to ask him about his amazing prediction: "Tell us, when will these things be, and what will be the sign when all these things are about to be accomplished?" (**13:4**). They believe what he has said, but here they seek to make sense of it. They think, as already stated, that the destruction of the temple must coincide with the end of the world. So they ask for inside information on what apocalyptic signs will accompany that fateful day. Fourth, Jesus clarifies in the rest of his short sermon that what they think of as one event he knows to be two. And in what follows in verses 5–37 he prepares them for both.

Jesus answers the first part of their question (When will "these things" happen, or when will the temple be destroyed?) by saying in effect, "When you witness false prophets and messiahs, large-scale apostasy, wars, earthquakes, and famines (see 13:6–7), 'the end' of the world 'is not yet' at hand (13:7). I will not tell you when the temple will be destroyed, only that it will occur. And, 'when you see these things taking place,' know that the Son of Man 'is near' (soon to return, or able to return at any moment after that, 13:29). You can count on my words (13:31). These labor pains (13:8) will happen in your lifetime (13:30). In the meantime here is what is going to happen and here is how you are to respond. Rome will desecrate ('the abomination of desolation,' 13:14) and destroy (stone upon stone overturned, see 13:2) the temple. Do not journey to Jerusalem to fight against Rome and this divinely determined historical event. Instead, flee. Get out of the region as fast as you

---

4   "The Mount of Olives is an appropriate setting, since the hill plays a prominent role in eschatological expectations in Judaism (cf. 11:1). Zechariah describes the final eschatological battle when the Lord will go out to fight against the nations, his feet touching down on the Mount of Olives, splitting it in two from east to west (Zech 1:1–9)." Mark L. Strauss, *Mark*, ZECNT (Grand Rapids, MI: Zondervan, 2014), 571.

can. Run for your lives. Then, know that those days will be tumultuous. False christs and prophets will appear. Do not be fooled by them. Do not believe a word they say. Do not be led astray. And do not be alarmed by the most alarming man-made conflicts (wars) and God-made disasters (earthquakes, famines). Expect persecutions. Endure them. Bear witness during them."

Understand, then, that Jesus answers the second part of their question ("What will be the sign" [13:4] that the world is coming to an end and that you are returning?) by saying, first, what are *not* the signs (e.g., a regional earthquake) and, second, that the signs will be unmistakable: "The sun will be darkened, and the moon will not give its light, and the stars will be falling from heaven, and the powers in the heavens will be shaken. And then they [the whole world] will see the Son of Man coming in clouds with great power and glory" (13:24–26). When Jesus returns, "he will send out the angels and gather his elect from the four winds, from the ends of the earth to the ends of heaven" (13:27). No one on earth that day will miss that event, and Jesus will not miss finding each and every person, no matter where he or she is.

In the meantime, should God's people try to figure out the precise date for this final event in world history? God forbid! Jesus forbids. Only God knows when this will happen ("But concerning that day or that hour, no one knows, . . . but only the Father," 13:32). What then should Christians do? Be on guard. Keep awake. Do the work we have been called to do. This is because Christ may return suddenly (13:36), and, when he returns, Christians must be waiting and working while they wait.

The View from the Valley

All that has been said above we might label "the view from the top." As we look over the 37 verses of the Olivet Discourse that is what we should see. Next, and for the rest of the chapter, let us view the prophecies on the ground—through the valleys, onto the plains, and up the Judean hillside. Let us see what the original audience was to see and do, for the "you" in **13:5–23** is not you or me. Jesus' command, "See that no one leads *you* astray" (13:5), is addressed directly to his earliest disciples. But what they were to think and do, as we shall see, has much to teach us today. That is, while the imperatives to them ("Do not be alarmed," 13:7; "Be on your guard," 13:9, 23; "Do not be anxious," 13:11; "Flee to the mountains," 13:14, and do so quickly; "Let the one who is on the housetop not go down, nor enter his house, to take anything out, and let the one who is in the field not turn back to take his cloak," 13:15–16; "Pray" for the timing, "that it may not happen in winter," 13:18; and "do not believe" those who claim Jesus has returned, 13:21) and assumptions of them (that they would proclaim the testimony of Jesus, 13:9–10, and endure to the end, 13:13) are not made directly to us or of us, these commands nevertheless have as much to say to us as they do to them. In fact, the three lessons that Jesus taught them he now teaches us. The exhortations found in these ancient prophecies, which have already been fulfilled, are still relevant. In particular, Jesus provides three timeless lessons to his church. First, discern the times and teachers. Second, trust God's sometimes counterintuitive commands. Third, persevere through persecutions.

Discern the Times and Teachers

First, discern the times and teachers. Knowing the times and knowing whom to listen to during the time before, during, and after the destruction of the temple is the main emphasis of Mark **13:5–23**. Jesus' first and final commands are crucial: "See that no one leads you astray" (13:5); "Be on guard" (13:23; cf. 13:9). The disciples are not to believe (13:21) that Jesus has returned during these tumultuous times, even if these self-professed messiahs and prophets "perform signs and wonders" (13:22). It will be tempting to follow the announcements: "'Look, here is the Christ!' or 'Look, there he is!'" (13:21). It will be tempting to follow those who confidently assert, "I am he!" (13:6), especially when so many follow their falsehoods ("And they will lead *many* astray," 13:6).

Obviously the circumstances are different for us, but the same lesson applies. Let us be discerning when it comes to the times. Let us be discerning about those to whom we listen. The church today, as it was then, is filled with false teachers. Know what to look out for. In Mark 13 the clear sign of a false teacher is someone who goes against Christ's clear word. If Jesus says that localized earthquakes are not signs of his return,[5] then we should not believe the TV evangelist who says the earthquake in Japan last month is the first of ten steps to happen before Christ's return and that, if you just give him $100, he will tell you the next nine. If Jesus says that no one knows the hour of his return but God, then, when someone says he knows the hour, we know he is a false teacher.

Then, beyond that first and foundational way to discern a false teacher (namely, that he contradicts Christ), let us remember what Jesus taught in Mark 12:38–40: watch out for narcissistic religious leaders who know and teach the Bible but use God's people for their own personal gain. Do they love to be noticed? Are they making money off their end-time predictions?

---

5   This does not mean there are no other biblical texts that describe "the coming day of the Lord ... with earthquakes." Strauss (*Mark*, 573n36) lists Isaiah 2:19, 21; 13:13; 24:18; 29:5–6; Ezekiel 38:19; Joel 2:10.

Are they the focus? Whose kingdom are they building? False teachers do not listen to Jesus' words—about money, the end times, and glory.

Trust God's Sometimes Counterintuitive Commands

First, discern the times and teachers. Second, trust God's sometimes counter-intuitive commands. The five commands in Mark 13:14–20 would have been hard for any first-century Jewish Christian disciple to follow. The first few commands, found in verses 14–17, center on reactions to the Roman army's entering the Most Holy Place:

> But when you see the abomination of desolation standing where he ought not to be (let the reader understand), then let those who are in Judea flee to the mountains. Let the one who is on the housetop not go down, nor enter his house, to take anything out, and let the one who is in the field not turn back to take his cloak. And alas for women who are pregnant and for those who are nursing infants in those days!

The readers then (pre-AD 70) need to "understand"[6] that the "abomination of desolation" (13:14)[7] is about to happen, and the readers now need to know it already happened and what it was. This "abomination" refers to what the prophet Daniel foretold (see Matt. 24:15), a time when after the exile seven years (seventy "weeks") would elapse and then two key events would occur: first, the Christ (the "anointed one," Dan. 9:25) would die (be "cut off," Dan. 9:26); second, in the middle of the last "week" an "appalling sacrilege" (Matt. 24:15 AMP) would cause temple worship and sacrifices to cease ("He shall put an end to sacrifice and offering," Dan. 9:27). When the Romans, led by commander Titus,[8] captured and conquered Jerusalem in AD 70, they marched

---

6 Following the scholarly consensus, I take this sentence as "an insertion by the Gospel writer himself"; Hans F. Bayer, *Mark*, in *Matthew–Luke*, vol. 8 of ESVEC (Wheaton, IL: Crossway, 2021), 957. Following Adela Yarbro Collins, *Mark*, Hermeneia (Minneapolis: Fortress, 2007), 608, I take the clause "as an aside from the evangelist to the individual who read the Gospel aloud to a group of assembled followers of Jesus (directly) and to his audience (indirectly), a hypothesis supported by the concluding statement in v. 37 ["what I say to you all"], which makes clear that the speech is directed to a broader audience than the four disciples named in v. 3."

7 "The distinctive phrase combines religious and political allusions: 'abomination' is a term that is often used in the Hebrew writings in reference to idolatry (Deut 29:17; 1 Kgs 11:5, 7; 2 Kgs 23:13; 2 Chr 15:8; Isa 66:3; Jer 4:1; 7:30; Ezek 5:11; Zech 9:7), and 'desolation' often occurs in contexts that refer to the ravages of war and utter destruction (Lev 26:34–35; 2 Chr 30:7; 36:21; Jer 4:7; 7:34; 22:5)." Alan R. Culpepper, R. Alan, *Mark*, SHBC (Macon, GA: Smyth & Helwys, 2007), 459.

8 "The Markan insistence that the sacrilege will be a male human figure 'standing where he ought not' determines my acceptance of the suggestion that the 'he' is the Roman commander Titus himself, amid the planting of Roman standards, accompanied by his idolatrous acclamation

into the temple with their idolatrous images on their military banners and sacrificed to the Roman gods in the Most Holy Place.[9] Luke makes clear the connection: "When you see Jerusalem surrounded by armies, then know that its *desolation* has come near" (Luke 21:20; cf. Josephus, *J. W.*, 4.486–90).[10]

But we as readers also need to understand that, when this happened, *fleeing from*, not *running toward*, Jerusalem would have been terribly difficult for any patriotic Jew. On 9/11, when Americans heard that the White House was a possible target, some Americans wanted to drive to Washington and do something to protect our nation's emblem. For a pious Jew, even if he became a Christian, to learn that Caesar had ordered "the whole city and the temple to [be leveled] to the ground,"[11] and that soon after "the wall encompassing the city [had been] . . . completely leveled,"[12] and that the Roman troops were headed to the temple to break through barriers of everything pure and sacred, into the Court of the Jews and through to the Holy Place, the natural impulse would have been to do everything for the cause. For example, it would have taken every moral muscle in pious Peter's body to put down his sword and run away from the wicked pagans who were slowly overturning every stone of the burnt temple and stealing the massive amounts of melted gold.

But Jesus commanded his followers not only to run away from some of their nationalistic impulses and heartfelt allegiances, but also to do so immediately. He told them, as soon as the Romans broke through the city wall, to get to a secure location ("Flee to the mountains," 13:14). They were not to waste a minute. "Let's say," Jesus commanded, "that you are on the flat-roofed housetop hanging the laundry; don't take the stairs or ladder down into the house to collect a few valuables" ("Let the one who is on the housetop not go down, nor enter his house, to take anything out," 13:15). "Or let's say," directed Jesus, "that you are seeding the soil for next year's crops and you hear the news; don't waste a second to get your outer garment" ("And let the one who is in the field not turn back to take his cloak," 13:16).

---

as *imperator* (*autokratora*) within the temple area." Francis J. Moloney, *The Gospel of Mark: A Commentary*, SP (Peabody, MA: Hendrickson, 2002), 258–59.

9 See Josephus, *J. W.* 6.4.7; 6.6.1. It is also possible that the "abomination" describes the desecration of the temple (e.g., they entered with unwashed feet and appointed their own high priest) by Jewish Zealots (see 4.3.6; 4.3.7–8), which would have occurred earlier than AD 70 (likely AD 67/68) and would better explain why Jesus encouraged his disciples to flee before the Romans arrived and leveled the temple.

10 So here Jesus echoes Daniel's prediction ("Forces from him shall appear and profane the temple and fortress, and shall take away the regular burnt offering. And they shall set up the abomination that makes desolate," Dan. 11:31; "The regular burnt offering is taken away and the abomination that makes desolate is set up," Dan. 12:11).

11 Josephus, *J. W.* 7.1.

12 Josephus, *J. W.* 5.12.4.

Then there is Jesus' "and alas"—a pause in his prophecy: "And alas for women who are pregnant and for those who are nursing infants in those days!" (13:17). It is one thing to run to the hills if you can run, but imagine being nine months pregnant or having a baby at breast. I know that Mark does not include the words "And Jesus wept," but I imagine Jesus did. And then, with tears running down his cheeks, he offered this next command to his new church: "Pray that it may not happen in winter" (13:18). Pray, in other words, that the weather conditions for those with child will be favorable.

As a theological aside, let me ask a question: If God is in absolute control of history (as is nowhere plainer than here), why pray? What a counterintuitive command! God loves when we pray because it shows our dependence, that we believe that he alone has the power, and he loves to use our simple prayers to fulfill his grand plans for world history. Read verses 19–20. Weep. Then rejoice.

> For in those days [weep] there will be such tribulation as has not been from the beginning of the creation that God created until now, and never will be. And if the Lord had not cut short the days, no human being would be saved. But [rejoice] for the sake of the elect, whom he chose, he shortened the days.

Picture the scene. This is 9/11 times three hundred or four hundred. Josephus tells us the gory details of slaughter and starvation: over a million Jews died; nearly one million were enslaved.[13] That is fewer bodies than the Holocaust, but the German abomination was slow and methodical, not brutal and quick. This was truly "Israel's darkest hour . . . a time of tribulation unsurpassed in Israel's history."[14] We can believe this promise: "There will be such tribulation [a world-changing ordeal] as has not been from the beginning of the creation that God created until now, and never will be," 13:19). So, if we think worse things are coming for Israel, think again. Do we actually trust Jesus' words, or are we listening to the wrong news sources?

But I have what I think is a more important question than that question about prayer, namely: Why did God "shorten the days" (13:20)—make the defeat quick? Most military campaigns took years (the Punic Wars between

---

13 See Josephus, *J. W.* 6.9.3.
14 Kim Riddlebarger, *A Case for Amillennialism: Understanding the End Times* (Grand Rapids, MI: Baker, 2013), 206.

Rome and Carthage took 118 years); this struggle took the Romans only five months to win. The answer is the elect. God loves his elect.

So imagine dear Judith, daughter of James and wife of Joshua. She and her family came to believe in Jesus when he came to Bethany. She is now with child in an eight-pound way. James and Joshua hear about a massive Roman legion marching south. Their first response is to fight. But they remember Jesus' words. So, instead of fighting, they gather to pray. They pray to Jesus, "Help us, Lord." They pray for traveling mercies, "Lord, help Judith to move across the plains and up to safety." They pray, "O Lord, please make this happen in the spring or summer, not the winter, when the conditions will be too cold and brutal." They bow low, "Spare her life. Spare the baby!" And what happens is that their prayers are answered. The Romans come and conquer in summer. The Jewish Christian refugees flee when the weather is warm and the roads walkable. Those who have obeyed Jesus—prayed and fled—are spared. Saved.

Do we really believe that God is absolutely sovereign over history? If so, then we must pray. Trusting that he is in control of local and world politics, we must pray. Letters to public officials, voting for wise candidates, and denouncing wicked leaders are all important activities. But at the end of the day prayer is more important. Pray for those in power. Pray that God's will be done. And trust that your pithy but powerful prayers matter most in the most important matters of world history.

Persevere through Persecutions

The third lesson is to persevere through persecutions. Mark touches on the theme earlier with Jesus' declaration, "If anyone would come after me, let him deny himself and take up his cross and follow me" (Mark 8:34), and here with his prediction (13:9–13):

> But be on your guard. For they will deliver you over to councils, and you will be beaten in synagogues, and you will stand before governors and kings for my sake, to bear witness before them. And the gospel must first be proclaimed to all nations. And when they bring you to trial and deliver you over, do not be anxious beforehand what you are to say, but say whatever is given you in that hour, for it is not you who speak, but the Holy Spirit. And brother will deliver brother over to death, and the father his child, and children will rise against parents and have them put to death. And you will be hated by all for my name's sake. But the one who endures to the end will be saved.

Here Jesus teaches the church how to persevere through persecutions. He is teaching them then, but he is also teaching us now.

Recently at my church the prayer requests from missionaries Emad and Michelle, who serve in the Middle East, were, first, a praise for some Sudanese refuges who came to faith and, second, a petition for these refugees' protection and perseverance, as their Muslim family and friends have not only alienated them but threatened them. As a church, we were asked to pray for twenty-four-year-old J, whose cousin in Libya had threatened to find him and cut off his head. We are also asked to pray for M, a twenty-eight-year-old whose roommates had found Christian materials in his room and planned to seriously harm him. He barely escaped the situation and found himself living on the street until a dear Christian brother, who was recently imprisoned unjustly last summer, welcomed him into his home. Emad and Michelle ended their monthly update by saying, "We stand in awe at the price these dear people pay for their faith. Please pray for them." We ought also, with these dear brothers in mind, to pray for ourselves, for "indeed all who desire to live a godly life in Christ Jesus will be persecuted" (2 Tim. 3:12). We too must be prepared.

And we too must listen afresh to Jesus' instructions. If and when the time comes, we are to be careful. Do not try to get caught. "Be on your guard" (Mark 13:9). But, if you get arrested, do not be surprised by it. In fact, do not be surprised that your own people, perhaps even your own religious community, physically beat you, hand you over to the civil authorities, and testify against you (13:9). Do not be surprised if your own family rises up against you, turns you in, and condemns you to death (13:12). Do not be surprised if everyone around you hates you because you follow Jesus ("You will be hated by all for my name's sake," 13:13). But also, do not be surprised if you find God closest to you in your darkest hour. The Paraclete will be your personal attorney: "And when they bring you to trial and deliver you over, do not be anxious beforehand what you are to say, but say whatever is given you in that hour, for it is not you who speak, but the Holy Spirit" (13:11). That is the verse to give not the unprepared preacher courage but the defenseless Christian hope.

Here in Mark 13 Jesus teaches us *how* to persevere through persecutions. He also teaches us *why*. First, this is how the gospel will spread. On trial, Christians are to "bear witness" (13:9). When then happens, then and now—when Christians testify faithfully no matter the personal cost—the good news spreads, just as Jesus promised it would ("And the gospel must first be proclaimed to all nations," 13:10). In the NT how did the gospel grow,[15] reaching

---

15 E.g., see Acts 8:1–4.

even the ends of the earth (the edges of the Roman Empire) in Peter and Paul's days? Here is God's formula for church growth: power plus preaching plus persecution equal gospel growth. When the power of the Spirit came upon the apostles, they preached a message that always led to persecution. Read the Acts of the Apostles.[16] Yet the gospel was received, even at times by the apostles' persecutors (see Phil. 1:12–13; 4:22). Paul's imprisonment promoted the gospel. He shared the good news with the imperial guard, and they shared it with others, even Caesar's household. Though Paul was chained, the word was not.

Second, the eternal reward outweighs the temporary troubles. It is cross now. The normal Christian life, between Christ's resurrection and return, is one of adversity and anguish. "Through many tribulations we must enter the kingdom of God" (Acts 14:22; cf. John 16:33). But there is a crown soon! Labor pains now; delivery date forthcoming. Breathe in; breathe out. And look up and long for the future. As Paul writes in Romans 8:18, "I consider that the sufferings of this present time are not worth comparing with the glory that is to be revealed to us." In 2 Corinthians 4:17 he speaks of our "momentary affliction [that] is preparing for us an eternal weight of glory beyond all comparison." What an amazing future. Salvation for those who endure! "If we endure, we will also reign with him" (2 Tim. 2:12). Or in Jesus' own words: "The one who endures to the end will be saved" (Mark 13:13). Whoever loses her life for Christ will save it (8:35).

Discern the times and teachers, trust God's sometime counterintuitive commands, and persevere through persecutions—that is the start of the Olivet Discourse, Jesus' timeless imperatives to them and to us.

The End of the Bible

Last year I read through the Bible in a year, something I had not done in years. I found it a refreshing challenge and an encouraging accomplishment. What is wonderful about reading through the Bible in a year is that one ends each year with Revelation. In Revelation 21, we are given a picture that helps us to persevere. The picture is of God's victory and our share in that victory, a victory that culminates with this vision:

> I saw the holy city, new Jerusalem [imagine that!], coming down out of heaven from God, prepared as a bride adorned for her husband. And I heard a loud voice from the throne saying, "Behold, the dwelling place

---

16 E.g., Acts 4:3; 5:40–41; 7:57–60; 12:1–12; 14:19; 16:22; 21:30–32. Acts also illustrates how the church rapidly grew (6:1) after the apostles proclaimed the gospel and suffered for it (Acts 4–5).

of God is with man. He will dwell with them, and they will be his people, and God himself will be with them as their God. He will wipe away every tear from their eyes, and death shall be no more, neither shall there be mourning, nor crying, nor pain anymore, for the former things have passed away. (Rev. 21:2–4)

I saw no temple in the city [no temple? no need!], for its temple is the Lord God the Almighty and the Lamb. And the city has no need of sun or moon to shine on it, for the glory of God gives it light, and its lamp is the Lamb. By its light will the nations walk, and the kings of the earth will bring their glory into it, and its gates will never be shut by day—and there will be no night there. They will bring into it the glory and the honor of the nations. (Rev. 21:22–26)

What a vision! What a reality to come. What a vision and reality to live by today. To walk forward in courageous confidence. To press on to victory.

Stay Awake! The Son Is Coming

MARK 13:24-37

What I say to you I say to all: Stay awake.
Mark 13:37

A second- and third-century Roman clergyman calculated that Jesus would return in AD 500. His prediction was based on the dimensions of Noah's ark. Christ did not return. After that, many Christians in Europe predicted the end of the world would be on January 1, 1000. Sadly, some reacted to that millennial mark in a military fashion. As the first of the year fast approached, Christian armies traveled to some of the pagan countries in northern Europe in order to make converts by force, if necessary, before Christ returned. Christ did not return. In the Middle Ages, Pope Innocent III took the number 618 (the year Islam was founded) and added the number 666 (the number of the beast) to get 1284 as the year of Christ's final judgment. Christ did not return. On February 14, 1835, Joseph Smith called a meeting of Mormon leaders. He announced that Jesus would return within fifty-six years. Earlier, Smith had written, "I prophesy in the name of the Lord God, and let it be written— the Son of Man will not come in the clouds till I am eighty-five years old" (*Doctrines and Covenants* 130.17). A mob murdered him before his thirty-ninth birthday. Christ did not return. In 1874 Charles Taze Russell, founder of the Bible Student movement, from which came the Jehovah's Witnesses, predicted the rapture in 1910, followed by the end of the world and Christ's *invisible* return in 1914. Christ did not return (or, at least no one saw him).

In 1998—a good year for such prophecies, as 666 times three equals 1998—psychic Edgar Cayce taught that a secret underground chamber would be discovered between the paws of the Great Sphinx in Egypt. Within that chamber would be documents about the history of the lost city of Atlantis. This new revelation would activate the second coming of Christ. Christ did not return. In more recent days Harold Camping predicted the end of the world. He advertised on his fifty-five radio stations and on six thousand billboards: "Judgment Day is coming/May 21 [2011]. The Bible guarantees it!" Christ did not return. Camping then, without apology for his first false prediction, named October 21, 2011, as the right date for Christ's return. Again, Christ did not return.

We might snicker at some of these scenarios. But of course all these false predictions are no laughing matter. Those who made them brought Christ and Christianity into disrepute. And those who made them were either ignorant of or disobedient to Jesus' clearest sentence in the often-unclear Olivet Discourse: "But concerning that day or that hour, no one knows, not even the angels in heaven, nor the Son, but only the Father" (Mark 13:32). While admittedly there is some chronological cloudiness to some of what Jesus teaches in Mark 13, what he says in this verse is crystal clear.

So then, as we return to our study of Mark 13, we will begin with verse 32 and the straightforward point of that verse, which we shall label "What Is Not Known" about the end of the world. Then we will look at "What Is Known" and, finally, "What to Do in Light of Such Knowledge."[1]

What Is Not Known

We begin with what is not known about what Jesus calls "that day or that hour" (13:32). The conjunction "or" between "that day" and "that hour" tells us that the terms are synonymous. They are also synonymous with the phrase "the day of the Lord," used twenty times in the OT and five times in the NT. The "day of the Lord" is also called the *parousia*, the Greek word for "coming,"[2] what Christians call the "second coming." Also note the term "those days," found in **13:24**: "But in those days, after that tribulation." The phrase "that tribulation" refers to what the Romans did to the Jews and their temple in or around AD 70 (the phrase "these things" describes that time as well; 13:4, 29, 30); the phrase "those days" ("But in those days, after that tribulation") is the language used by the prophets to speak of the eschaton,[3] the time before the end. Put simply, "those days" and "that day" mean the end times. We know that when Jesus speaks of "that day or that hour," along with "those days," he is referring to the time of his return—his second advent/the day of the Lord, the time when he will come to judge and save.

---

1   The outline, and part of the introduction, for this chapter come from chapter 72 of Douglas Sean O'Donnell, *Matthew: All Authority under Heaven*, PTW (Wheaton, IL: Crossway, 2013).

2   See its use in Matthew 24:39, 42, 43, 44, 46, 50; 25:10, 19, 27. Also note the use of *parousia* in Matthew 24:3; 2 Thessalonians 2:1, 8; James 5:7; 2 Peter 3:4.

3   Jeremiah 3:16, 18; 31:29; 33:15; Joel 3:1; Zechariah 8:23.

Concerning *when* that moment in history will be, Jesus says, "No one knows . . . but only the Father" (13:32). So do "the angels in heaven" know? Even though they have a major role in this event, they do not know. Does the heaven-sent Son know? Even though "the day of the Lord" is his day, he did not know at the time he said this. I do not know, now that Jesus has completed his earthly ministry, where for our sake and salvation he "emptied himself, by taking the form of a servant, being born in the likeness of men" (Phil. 2:7),[4] whether the Father and *the Son* know. I would imagine so. But what I know for certain is that no created being in heaven or earth, not the purest angel in heaven nor the most righteous man on earth, knows when Jesus will return. So, if you think that you know, or you believe that someone else knows, then you need to repent.

This is precisely what Camping did a few months before he died. In a letter to the listeners of his Family Radio network he admitted that his predictions were "sinful," that he had not heeded what Jesus taught in the Olivet Discourse, and that he was now studying his Bible "even more fervently . . . not to find dates, but to be more faithful in [his] understanding [of it]."[5] Praise God. Camping also stated in a private interview what Jesus clearly stated here in Mark 13:32, that no human being can know the day the world will end.[6] Precisely. That is our first point. The second follows.

What Is Known

Let us turn our attention from what is not known to what is known. What is known about "that day" can be summarized under five headings.

First, Jesus' second coming will be obvious. When Christ returns, all "the powers in the heavens will be shaken" (Mark **13:25**): the sun ("The sun will be darkened") and the moon ("The moon will not give its light") will turn off, followed by the stars' "falling from heaven" (13:25). These are all *obvious* indications that something important is afoot.

So too is the new and spectacular light show that will fill the universal dark void: "And then they will see the Son of Man coming in the clouds" (**13:26**). The darkness is set in contrast to the heavenly "sign" of the Son of Man (Matt. 24:30).[7] We are told that Jesus will descend from heaven ("coming

4   On Jesus' choosing to limit his divine powers when he became man see Daniel M. Doriani, *Matthew*, REC, 2 vols. (Phillipsburg, NJ: P&R, 2008), 2:381–82.
5   "Letter from Harold Camping to the 'Faith Radio Family,'" *Charisma News*, March 7, 2012.
6   "Harold Camping Exclusive: Family Radio Founder Retires," *Christian Post*, October 24, 2011.
7   "The supernatural darkness of the consummation is richly symbolic. Not only does it belong to the correlation of beginning and end, but it is a sign of both divine judgment and mourning and becomes the velvet background for the Son of man's splendor (24.27, 30). Moreover, on the literary level it foreshadows the darkness of Jesus' death (27.45) while that darkness in turn

in clouds") and that this coming will be "with great power and glory" (Mark 13:26). Mark states, "And then they will see" (13:26); Matthew tells us that the "they" are "all the tribes of the earth" (Matt. 24:30), everyone from every nation who is alive on that day.[8]

But how will everyone alive then, from different parts of the globe, see Jesus at the same time? Perhaps our Lord is speaking metaphorically.[9] If so, the point still stands. His return will be obvious. No one will miss it. But if he is speaking literally, then the scene is more remarkable. Think about it. How will everyone see him in the dark—without the light of the sun, moon, or stars? The answer is that the "light of the world" (John 8:12) needs no lesser lights to line his way (cf. Rev. 22:5).

Another detail that highlights the obvious nature of Jesus' return concerns the mission of the angels. Jesus, we are told, "will send out the angels and gather his elect from the four winds, from the ends of the earth to the ends of heaven" (Mark 13:27). If the number of the elect is, as Revelation 7:9 states, "a great multitude that no one could number, from every nation, from all tribes and peoples and languages," then what is described in Mark 13:27 is unimaginable. I cannot imagine how many angels it would take to gather a countless multitude. And whatever this angelic gathering will look like, it will be obvious. In Matthew's record those angels accompany a "loud trumpet call" (Matt. 24:31).[10] The second coming will be really obvious. Sights. Sounds. Visible. Universal. No one alive on that day will miss it.

Second, Jesus' second coming will be awesome. Notice that Jesus uses his favorite title for himself in relation to his second coming. It is the "Son of Man" (Mark 13:26) who will be riding upon the clouds. This title is linked to Daniel 7:13–14 and relates to Jesus' divinely bestowed authority. In that chapter the Ancient of Days grants the Son of Man a glorious and everlasting kingdom. That is awesome. Jesus will return as the Son of Man, the one who has been granted all authority over all creation (Mark 2:10, 28; cf. Matt. 28:18).

---

presages the world's assize." W. D. Davies and Dale C. Allison Jr., *A Critical and Exegetical Commentary on the Gospel according to Saint Matthew*, ICC (Edinburgh: T&T Clark, 1991), 3:358.

8   "The first coming of Christ the Lord, God's Son and our God, was in obscurity. The second will be in sight of the whole world." Augustine, *Sermons on Selected Lessons of the New Testament*, quoted in *CHSB*, 1499.

9   While many commentators take Jesus' words as metaphors (i.e., he is not giving a literal or scientific explanation of future events), I am not completely convinced. Certainly from time to time Jesus speaks prophetically, and like the prophets he uses vivid and metaphorical language. However, might he here be explaining how he will usher in the new creation in a way that resembles the creation of the universe? It will be spectacular—literally!

10   Paul adds more sound to the second coming: "The Lord himself will descend from heaven with *a cry of command*, with *the voice of an archangel*, and with *the sound of the trumpet* of God" (1 Thess. 4:16; cf. 1 Cor. 15:52).

Other details also highlight the awesomeness of Christ's return. In fact, nearly every phrase of Mark 13:24–27 is brimming with this theme. When Jesus says, in verse 24, "But in those days . . . the sun will be darkened, and the moon will not give its light," he is not talking about a double eclipse; when he mentions in verse 25 "the stars . . . falling from heaven," he is not talking about a divine firework show that starts with a few shooting stars. Rather he is talking about all the great lights created on day four of creation turning off for good. They will turn off because, as I said, a new and spectacular light show fills the universal dark void: "The Son of Man coming in the clouds" (13:26). Whatever that awesome cosmic upheaval will look like, it will make Haley's Comet look like two Boy Scouts rubbing sticks together to make a spark.

Verse 26 provides another image of the awesomeness of the second coming. Not only will the appearing and arriving of this everlasting ruler be witnessed by the world ("They will see"), but what the world will see will be amazing. Our Lord will arrive in style ("coming in clouds") and strength ("with great power") and splendor ("and glory"), a strength that will show itself in what is recorded in verse 27. Look for Jesus' absolute authority. Notice the pronouns that announce his parousia power: "And then *he* will send out the angels . . . and gather *his* elect . . . from the ends of the earth to the ends of heaven." He's got the whole world in his hands, *and* he's got the whole heavens in his hands too. He will soon have all his elect in his hands as well.

The second coming will be awesome.

> He came the first time as a "man of sorrows, and acquainted with grief" (Isaiah 53:3): he was born in the manger of Bethlehem, in lowliness and humiliation; he took the very nature of a servant, and was despised and not esteemed; he was betrayed into the hands of wicked men, condemned by an unjust judgment, mocked, flogged, crowned with thorns and at last crucified between two thieves. [In his second coming] he will come . . . as the King of all the earth, with royal majesty: the princes and great men of this world will themselves stand before his throne to receive an eternal sentence: before him every mouth shall be silenced, and every knee bow, and every tongue shall confess that Jesus Christ is Lord.[11]

Totally awesome!

---

11   J. C. Ryle, *Matthew: Expository Thoughts on the Gospels*, CCC (Wheaton, IL: Crossway, 1993), 232.

Third, Jesus' second coming will bring relief to the righteous; it will be a day of vindication for God's people. The image of God's messengers' ("the angels") gathering God's people ("his elect") from the whole earth ("from the ends of the earth") and throughout the highest heavens ("to the ends of heaven," Mark 13:27) is an image not only of God's power but of his grace. For those who have persevered through persecution (see 13:9–13) final vindication will come with the coming Son.

I began the last chapter by asking us to think about where we were when we heard or saw the news of 9/11. My first sermon as a pastor was on September 16, 2001, five days after 9/11. My preselected passage was Revelation 19:11–21. I preached a sermon on Jesus' coming as savior and judge, and it was precisely the message that God's people on that Sunday needed to hear. I prefaced the sermon by saying,

> The events of this week are indeed shocking, sickening, and sorrowful. That the rules of the kingdom of God have been violated is of little surprise, but that the soil of America has now been raped is revolutionary. We have witnessed this week acts of war against both God and man, episodes of evil that are too incredible to fully comprehend. But in God's great providence he has a word for us today. I am neither a prophet nor the son of a prophet but I must confess that it was months ago that I selected Revelation 19:11–21. At that time, I was obviously unaware of the future, and when I wrote most of it (before September 11) I was apprehensive about how well it would be received, due to the graphic nature of the text. Yet, in light of the events of this week I can think of no passage in the entire Bible more relevant, appropriate, and practical. I am convinced that it will do us well this morning to meditate on the great sovereignty of our God and the glorious return of his Son.

Then I read the text. We prayed. And I began the sermon like this:

> Vengeance has its place in the Christian faith. And it holds not an insignificant, unnecessary, or minor role in our salvation. It is as foundational and as crucial as the biblical concepts of grace, mercy, love, and forgiveness because at its center stands our Lord Jesus Christ. When most of us think of Jesus we rarely picture him, as the book of Revelation does, as a holy king, righteous judge, and victorious warrior. In our minds, we have little trouble imagining him as a baby wrapped in swaddling clothes, as a child teaching in the temple, as a man miraculously walking on water,

and as a dying savior. But we struggle to envision Jesus as a mighty conquering king—muscular, fierce, relentless, and vengeful. One reason we may have this difficulty is due either to our ignorance or to our misunderstandings concerning Christ and his second coming. On the one hand, we may simply be uninformed of the details of Christ's return; on the other hand, we may be able to recite some of the facts of the second coming, yet fail to comprehend its ultimate objective.[12]

I will stop there, since I do not want to give you two sermons in one chapter. So let us return to Mark, but obviously in relation to what I once said, as recorded above. The objective of Jesus' second coming is salvation. Jesus comes to save his people, and he does so in part by judging those who are not his people. Salvation and judgment are linked.

What the angels are doing in gathering the elect is sparing them from the coming judgment. "Christ's return . . . will deliver his people from suffering (2 Thess 1:6–7; 1 Pet 4:13) and will rescue them from wrath (1 Thess 1:10), bringing reward to those who have persevered (Matt 16:27; 2 Tim 4:8 Heb 9:28)."[13] It will prove to be the "vindication of his faithful followers."[14] We need to know that Jesus' second coming will bring relief to the righteous, and we need to praise God for that.

Fourth, Jesus' second coming is certain, as he makes clear in Mark **13:30–31**: "Truly, I say to you, this generation will not pass away until all these things take place. Heaven and earth will pass away, but my words will not pass away." In the immediate context (see 13:5–23) Jesus predicts the destruction of the temple emphatically ("Truly, I say to you," 13:30), and sure enough the temple is toppled. Of course, what Jesus says in verses 30–31 we can apply to every word Jesus said.

A number of times in the last five years I have given a talk titled "Why I Am a Christian." I give four reasons. I talk about Jesus' irresistible call on my life, the alluring paradox of Jesus' claims and character, and how Jesus has

---

12 This section in Mark was first preached at Westminster Presbyterian Church in Elgin, Illinois, and first published in Douglas Sean O'Donnell and Leland Ryken, *The Beauty and Power of Biblical Exposition: Preaching the Literary Artistry and Genres of the Bible* (Wheaton, IL: Crossway, 2022), 267–68.

13 Mark L. Strauss, *Mark*, ZECNT (Grand Rapids, MI: Zondervan, 2014), 598. He also notes (598–99), "It will be accompanied by the resurrection of those who have died 'in Christ' (1 Cor 15:22–23; 1 Thess 4:16) into glorified, imperishable bodies (1 Cor 15:42–44, 51–54; Col 3:4) and will initiate the permanent dwelling of Christ with this people (John 14:2–3; 1 Thess 4:17; 2 Thess 2:1)."

14 Strauss, *Mark*, 599.

dealt with and will deal with the three universal problems humans face: sin, death, and injustice. I also talk about the power of his words.

Nearly two thousand years ago Jesus said, "Heaven and earth will pass away, but my words will not pass away" (13:31). What does history make of this bold statement? Is it true or false? It is true. It is historically verifiable. Let us say there are forty million local churches around the world where over two billion Christians gather each Sunday. In most of those churches, even the unorthodox ones, the words of Jesus are being read and taught. Christians, and some non-Christians, each Sunday morning seek afresh to understand and apply what Jesus said. Can we say this of the words of Socrates, Cicero, Julius Caesar, or Winston Churchill? No! This is not true of any philosopher or politician, and it certainly is not true of celebrities. People are not gathering together each week to try to understand and apply what John Lennon sang or said.

Back to the point. If Jesus' words are more permanent than the ground below or the sky above ("Heaven and earth will pass away, but my words will not pass away," 13:31), and if Jesus has a proven track record on a massive prediction in world history—the destruction of the temple ("This generation," that of his apostles, "will not pass away until all these things take place," 13:30)—then we can trust that what he says about his return, and the events surrounding it, will likewise occur.

That certainty takes us to the fifth fact. We know the second coming will be (1) obvious, (2) awesome, (3) a day of vindication for God's people, and (4) certain. The fifth fact follows: (5) since the temple has been destroyed, we must know that Jesus' return is imminent. This is what our Lord says with his parabolic teaching in **13:28–29**: "From the fig tree learn its lesson: as soon as its branch becomes tender and puts out its leaves, you know that summer is near. So also, when you see these things taking place, you know that he is near, at the very gates."

Here either Jesus is talking indirectly about his second coming, saying in effect, "As soon as the temple falls, know that there is a possibility, at any time, for my return." Or, more likely, in these verses Jesus returns to speaking directly about the destruction of the temple and what his earliest followers should do. As soon as they hear the rumble of the Roman troops as they shake the foundation of the holy city (a sign as obvious as a fig tree in spring spouting leaves), they need to do everything Jesus has taught in verses 5–23. So here is how I understand verse 29: "When you see these things taking place [the desolation and destruction of the temple], know that he [or "it," i.e., "that tribulation"] is near, at the very gates."

Whatever the case, what Jesus is doing throughout the Olivet Discourse is what scholars call "prophetic foreshortening." What that means is that Jesus, like the prophets, speaks of two events—one in the near future and another in the distant future—as though they will happen close to each other. For example, Isaiah speaks of the destruction of Babylon in the same breath as he does the final day of the Lord, as though there were one day of divine judgment ("the day of the Lord") when we know there will be two.

The analogy often used to explain this teaching technique or unique genre is that of a mountain range. If we looked at a mountain range from a distance, it might appear that two peaks were close to each other when in fact they were miles apart. Likewise, Jesus speaks of two mountaintops—the destruction of the temple and his return—as though they were close together when, in reality, they are thousands of years apart.[15]

Let me flesh this further out. In AD 33 Jesus makes a number of prophecies. For example, he predicts that false prophets will come. And sure enough before AD 70 a number of false prophets predicted that God would grant the Jews of Jerusalem victory over the Romans. Many people were deceived. But that was only the first mountain. Come down off that mountain and walk many miles (a journey that we know has taken many years and will perhaps take many more) to the next mountain, and someday soon we will witness the final fulfillment of Jesus' prophecy, when the "man of lawlessness" (2 Thess. 2:3) or "antichrist" (1 John 2:18) through his words and works deceives multitudes. So understand, then, that the cataclysmic events surrounding the destruction of the temple foreshadow the events that will surround the end of the world.

What to Do in Light of Such Knowledge

In light of those five facts, especially the last one, what are we to do? Jesus tells his disciples and us in Mark **13:33–36**. He begins with two similar exhortations: "Be on guard" and "Keep awake" (13:33). He then says why, reiterating the point of **13:32**: "For you do not know when the time will come" (13:33). Next, he illustrates, "It is like a man going on a journey, when he leaves home and puts his servants in charge, each with his work, and commands the doorkeeper to stay awake" (13:34). That story then morphs into an admonition, one we have heard before: "Therefore stay awake—for you do not know when the master of the house will come, in the evening, or at midnight, or when the

---

15 Jesus' teaching here resembles the way the prophets spoke of the near and distant future. Like in much of OT prophecy, Jesus predicts both near and distant events without putting them in chronological order (see Joel 2:28–32, quoted in Acts 2:16–21; cf. Zechariah 14).

rooster crows, or in the morning—lest he come suddenly and find you asleep" (13:35–36). This admonition is universal, given to both Jesus' first followers and all since: "And what I say to you I say to all: Stay awake" (**13:37**). Here then is the logic to Jesus' call to vigilance: if no one knows the time of Christ's return ("Concerning that day or that hour, no one knows," 13:32; "You do not know when the time will come," 13:33), then the hour-by-hour application should be readiness ("Be on guard," 13:33) and wakefulness ("Keep awake," 13:33; "Stay awake," 13:34, 35, 37).

That then raises the question, what does readiness resemble? The answer is that it looks like work. To "be on guard," like a soldier's guarding a base, is strenuous work. To "stay awake" on the night watch requires commitment. To be one of the many servants in charge of the estate while the master is gone ("on a journey")—especially the "doorkeeper" commanded "to stay awake" so everyone in the household will know the moment the master has arrived—is hard work. Watching means working; waiting means working—doing the job, whatever it is, that God has called you to do.[16]

And what Mark hints at—each "servant" has his or her "work" (13:34)—Matthew vividly emphasizes. In Matthew 24–25 we find a fuller version of the Olivet Discourse, which concludes in 24:37–25:46 with illustration after illustration of the necessity of kingdom industry.

Starting in Matthew 24:37–39, Jesus first speaks of what happened before the great flood. Jesus tells the story from the perspective of those who were judged. But, if we view that story from Noah's perspective, we see that Noah worked for decades on that big boat. He had both the attitude and the actions of attentiveness and expectancy. He must have reasoned that (1) God's word is true, namely, that (2) judgment is coming, and therefore (3) he should obey God's word by getting to work on the ark.

Next Jesus gives the illustration of four workers—two in the field and two at the mill. Two are "taken" and two "left." It is not clear if "taken" is a sign of being saved (cf. 1 Thess. 4:17) and "left" a sign of judgment. However, since most people in Noah's generation were "taken" away by the flood of God's judgment, to be "left behind" likely symbolizes salvation. Either way, the people saved are working. They are accomplishing their ordinary and everyday tasks in the field or at the mill.

Then Jesus speaks of the thief in the night. As it relates to the theme of work, the point is this: if you knew a thief was going to target your house

---

16 "Try your daily occupations, your daily state of feeling, your daily enjoyments—try them by this test: Am I doing as I would wish to do on the day of his coming?" Robert Murray M'Cheyne, "Second Advent," quoted in *CHSB*, 1498–99.

tonight, you would *do* something about it, such as securing the entranceways, calling the police, or borrowing a guard dog. You "would not have let [your] house be broken into" (Matt. 24:43).

The final illustration in Matthew 24 is of the "faithful and wise servant," who is contrasted with the "wicked servant:" "Who then is the faithful and wise servant, whom his master has set over his household, to give them their food at the proper time? Blessed is that servant whom his master will find so *doing* when he comes" (Matt. 24:45–46). Doing!—doing "good" unto others (Matt. 7:12; cf. 25:35–40).

So then, with all that is detailed above, to "stay awake" or to "be ready" involves both the attitude and the actions of attentiveness. We wait expectantly by working expectantly. Readiness resembles work.

Readiness also resembles resting. How do I get "resting" from the five exhortations to "stay awake?" I said "resting," not "sleeping." I mean resting in the sense of resting on the finished work of Christ and the promises associated with his return. And I justify this final suggestion because of how Mark's narrative unfolds. His Gospel ends not with Jesus' Olivet Discourse (prepare for the end!) but with his cross and resurrection (dwell on Christ's end). The Gospel concludes by focusing our attention not on what we must do but on what Christ alone has done for us. So, as much as we should work as we wait, we should rest as well. We should rest in the perfect finished work of Jesus and trust that he will hold us fast.

Last Things First

Throughout church history Jesus' clear teaching on the end times has been ignored. We do not know the day or hour. Yet what is also sadly ignored is that the last things should be first. We may not know *when* Jesus will return, but we do know *that* he will return. And that reality should keep us actively serving the kingdom as we rest moment by moment in Christ.

Yes, we need level heads when evangelical oddballs offer their strange speculations and when ecclesial eccentrics claim that the Bible informs us of all we need to know about modern science, American politics, and the end-of-the-world calendar. But we also need warm hearts that resolve to "live," as Luther put it, "as if Jesus had died this morning, risen this afternoon, and was coming this evening."[17] We need voices that cut through all the false apocalyptic fervor with true apocalyptic enthusiasm: "Come, Lord Jesus!" (Rev. 22:20).

17 Luther, quoted in Frederick Dale Bruner, *Matthew: A Commentary, Volume 2: The Churchbook, Matthew 13–28*, rev. ed. (Grand Rapids, MI: Eerdmans, 2007), 523.

A Beautiful Thing

MARK 14:1-11

Jesus said, "Leave her alone. Why do you trouble her? She has done a beautiful thing to me."
Mark 14:6

As a parent there are certain stories from your children's childhoods that are ingrained in your mind. For me, I can remember my son Sean's visit to the ER when he was a baby, fighting an uncontrollable fever. I can remember one-year-old Lily's nightly escapes from the crib. I called her Poudini because she would escape from the crib, unzip her pajamas (which we had on backward—the zipper in back), and tear off her diaper. Total freedom. And sometimes a total mess. Then, from my more dignified middle daughter, I can remember the early mornings when, as a toddler, Evelyn would come down the stairs and sit next to me for my morning devotions; I drank my coffee and she sipped her chocolate milk. I can remember six-year-old Simeon's running out into the street in front of our house and my chasing after him, hoping and praying that a car would not strike him before I caught him. Finally, with Charlotte, my youngest, I remember the time when she was four and I turned to her after reading her a book and asked, "Lotte, do you know how much Daddy loves you?" She stared at me in anticipation. I asked, "This much?"—opening the space between my thumb and pointer finger. She laughed and shook her head. She jumped off the couch and stood in front of me. "No!" she answered. "This much, this much, this much!" as she waved her arms wider and wider between each "this much." Then she paused and began to count as the arm-flailing restarted. "One, two, three, four, five, six, seven, eight, nine, one hundred this much!" she shouted.

What was especially sweet and memorable about that moment was that I had played the "how much/this much" game with her only a few times before that. Also, when I did so, I used only three extremes—this much (showing the space between two fingers), this much (half of the space of full-hand extension), and this much (full extension). She added the arm-flapping and the counting to a hundred. That *exercise* in love demonstrated her high, and correct, view of my love for her.

Mark 14:1–11, if I were to summarize it with one word, is a text about love. Of course, it is not about a father's love for a child or a child's love for her father. Rather, it is about a disciple's love for Jesus and his love for her. It is specifically about how much she loved him and how much he loved her.

The Passover Plot

But before we look at the *how* we need to begin with *when* and *where*. That is, we begin with the significant setting of our story. After the Olivet Discourse in Mark 13—in which Jesus predicts the tragedy of the destruction of the temple, followed by the triumph of his second coming—Mark 14 begins with another foretold tragedy, which we, of course, know turns out to be the triumph of our faith:[1]

> It was now two days before the Passover and the Feast of Unleavened Bread. And the chief priests and the scribes were seeking how to arrest him by stealth and kill him, for they said, "Not during the feast, lest there be an uproar from the people." (**14:1–2**)

The setting is not yet fully set. Mark **14:3** changes the camera angle so as to focus on a seemingly ordinary meal in the home of an unexpected host: "And while [Jesus] was at Bethany in the house of Simon the leper, as he was reclining at table." Stop midsentence and notice here two different camera angles and their significance.

In one room is the temple aristocracy ("the chief priests and the scribes," 14:1). In Jerusalem at Caiaphas's luxury accommodations (his "palace," Matt. 26:3) the Jewish religious leaders are devising a shrewd plan to do away with a man who they think is a nuisance and a blasphemer (they "were seeking how to arrest him by stealth and kill him," Mark 14:1). They are hoping to wait for a time *after* the great festival, when the quarter of a million pilgrims will return home and the religious expectations and fervor will die down. As they discuss the dilemma, that is the consensus: not to arrest Jesus "during the feast, lest there be an uproar from the people"

---

1   Mark L. Strauss summarizes Mark 14–16 well: "Despite all appearances, the dreadful events about to unfold in Jerusalem represent the sovereign purposes of God, the good news of salvation, and the inauguration of the kingdom of God." *Mark*, ZECNT (Grand Rapids, MI: Zondervan, 2014), 601.

(14:2). A wise move, they think. However, God has his own more brilliant countermove.

In a second room we find the man they want to kill. Where is the Son of Man who will return in glory (see 13:26) sitting—or reclining, as the case may be? Jesus is two miles outside the holy city in the town of Bethany, a rather humble place to be for the one who will come with the clouds beneath his feet as his angels gather the billion-plus elect from every edge of the earth (13:26–27). He is "reclining at table" (14:3); that is, his face is toward the food at the middle of the table with his sandal-free feet hanging over the edge of the sofa. He is quite exposed if a hired assassin wanted to make his move. But Jesus is not anxious. He trusts that his Father's plan, not the Sanhedrin's scheme, will come to fruition. Jesus will not be killed after the Passover week, as they originally planned, but during the Passover.[2] In fact, we are told in Mark 15:25—as we fast-forward to the crucifixion—that "it was the third hour" (9:00 a.m.) when the soldiers lifted Jesus on the cross. At this same time, on the temple altar, the first lamb of the daily sacrifice was sacrificed. Then we are told in Mark 15:34 that Jesus died "at the ninth hour," the hour of the second daily sacrifice. Per God's divinely orchestrated plan, Jesus will not be killed after the Passover, as they planned, but during the Passover.

Let me pause here to allow for an amen (a praise God for his remarkable providence!) but also to expand the panoramic view as it relates to the Passover. For we are to see more than the correlation between the Temple Mount and Golgotha. There are two other details in our text that we should notice and appreciate. Days before the Passover Jews would "purify themselves" (John 11:55) by ritually cleaning themselves. So we can assume that the Jewish religious leaders, Jesus, and his disciples are doing that. But notice *where* and *with whom* Jesus decides to do so: "And . . . he was . . . in the house of Simon the leper" (14:3). Note the irony. As all the Jews in Jerusalem are cleaning their impure bodies, Jesus' pure body reclines at the most impure setting imaginable—a leper's house.

There is irony here, but also mystery. Who is this Simon? Is he still a leper, or was he cured of his disease but has taken on the designation "Simon the Leper" to remind him and others of his deliverance? If he was cured, did Jesus cure him? Was he the leper mentioned in Mark 1:40–45, to whom Jesus said, "Be clean" (1:41), and "immediately . . . he was made clean" (1:42)? We do not know. I think Simon might still be a leper (or have some sort of serious skin

---

2 Once Judas approaches it (Mark 14:10–11) the Sanhedrin will advance its plans to the Passover week.

disease). I say this because in John's version of this story we are told that Jesus could no longer appear in public (John 11:54) because the authorities wanted him dead. So it may be that Jesus chose a hideout that no pious Jew would suspect—the lair of a leper. If this is the case, then Jesus is violating Leviticus 13:45–46, which outlawed dwelling with lepers. Why would he do this? The same reason he would break—or better, *fulfill*—the law in Mark 1:41, when he touched a leper and *by touching him* made him clean. Somehow there, like here, Jesus transcends the law without breaking the law. Moreover, that touch, like this short stay with Simon, serves as a visual of the gospel message on the eve of Passover: on the cross Jesus takes on all our impurities—"our Passover lamb" (1 Cor. 5:7; cf. John 1:29) pours out his blood (Mark 14:24) so we might be "cleansed . . . from all sin" (1 John 1:7). Indeed, God through Jesus' sacrifice says to us, "Be clean," and we are "immediately . . . made clean" (Mark 1:41–42).

Her Love for Him

Between the Passover plot (14:1–2) and Judas' scheme to betray Jesus (14:10–11) Mark records a love story—"One of the greatest love stories in the Greatest Love Story ever told."[3] It is a short story (told in one verse), but also a spectacular one: "And while he was at Bethany in the house of Simon the leper, as he was reclining at table, a woman came with an alabaster flask of ointment of pure nard, very costly, and she broke the flask and poured it over his head" (14:3).

Mark's description of this woman is vague. We are not given her name or motives. We do not know whether she was a notorious sinner, like the woman featured in Luke's Gospel who likewise anointed Jesus (Luke 7:37, 38) and came to repent.[4] We are not told whether she was in need of a miracle, like the great majority of people who approached Jesus, or whether she approached Jesus for purely devotional purposes, like the magi, who came bearing gifts. She could have viewed herself in a priestly role, offering a messianic anointing—giving her personal acknowledgement that Jesus is king, the Christ, the now anointed one.[5] We do not know. Mark's description is vague. However, his description of what she did and how both the disciples and Jesus reacted

---

3   Douglas Sean O'Donnell, *Matthew: All Authority under Heaven*, PTW (Wheaton, IL: Crossway, 2013), 764.

4   Matthew 26:6–13, Mark 14:3–9, and John 12:1–8 record the same event, whereas Luke 7:36–50 records a similar but different event. Luke's story has a different setting (Galilee), features a *sinful* woman, and records different responses.

5   It is possible, as Grant R. Osborne, *Mark*, TTCS (Grand Rapids, MI: Baker, 2012), 254 suggests, that Mark records "two anointings, one by the Holy Spirit at Jesus' baptism (1:9–11), the other by the woman here. The first anointed Jesus as God's Messiah for his earthly ministry (introducing the new age of the Spirit), the other for his death as the suffering Messiah and sacrificial Lamb."

is quite detailed. She came into the house. She approached Jesus with a "very costly" perfume (made of "pure nard") contained in an ornate bottle ("an alabaster flask," 14:3). She then "broke" the seal and poured all the ointment over Jesus' head.

Next the disciples, or "some" of the men around the dinner table, reacted in two ways. First, in hushed anger ("There were some who said to themselves indignantly") they questioned her action: "Why was the ointment wasted like that? For this ointment could have been sold for more than three hundred denarii and given to the poor" (14:4–5a). That quiet buzz around the table quickly led to a public rebuke: "And they scolded her" (14:5b).

Picture the scene. The ointment is poured over Jesus' head. He is a mess. The couch and floor are likely a mess as well. Judas turns to James and James to John and down the line. "What a waste." "Agreed." "Perfume like that could have been sold for a ton of money. The poor could have been provided for." "This is the time of year to give gifts to those in need."[6] "Yes." "Yes." "What was she thinking?" Then finally the noise stops, and I picture Simon the host or Simon Peter the apostle turning to her and summarizing the chatter: "What were you thinking, woman! Do you know how much this ointment costs? Don't you care about the poor? What a waste! Shame on you."

But Jesus quickly quiets the storm. He rebukes those who have rebuked her: "But Jesus said, 'Leave her alone. Why do you trouble her? She has done a beautiful thing to me. For you always have the poor with you, and whenever you want, you can do good for them. But you will not always have me'" (14:6–7). Jesus knows they are right: she could have sold this filled flask for "more than three hundred denarii" (14:5), which equals a full year's wages for a common laborer (Matt. 20:2). To give some perspective, in Mark 6 the disciples estimate that it would take two hundred denarii (Mark 6:37) to feed the five thousand plus people (6:44). So, if we use the median wage for US workers in 2021, then she dropped five hundred liquid Benjamins on Jesus' head: $50,000!

Seems wasteful. Ah, but what they call "wasteful" Jesus calls "beautiful" (14:6). He labels this lavish act "beautiful" because she grasps that a love for Jesus should be our first and greatest love. Put differently, Jesus corrects the disciples' poor theology about the poor by clarifying that our relationship with him ought not to be on the same level as our relationship with others, even those most in need. It is not that widows and orphans do not matter; it is that Jesus matters more. Jesus first; everyone else second (see Matt. 10:37).

---

6 See John 13:29; m. Pesaḥ. 9:11–10:1.

Jesus' "me," you see, in Mark 14:6–7 is key: "She has done a beautiful thing to *me*. For you always have the poor with you. . . . But you will not always have *me*.'"

We are told in John's Gospel that Mary of the Mary, Martha, and Lazarus clan was the woman in this story. (Perhaps Simon the leper was their father.) What we have to admire about Mary, something Jesus surely admires, is that she puts Jesus first. She gets that the "me" is the key to the Christian life. Unlike her sister and the disciples, who suffer from "shortsighted utilitarianism,"[7] Mary shows the better way (see Luke 10:42). The better way is not to put off serving others and feeding the hungry; it is simply acknowledging that Jesus deserves our highest outpouring of love and acting upon that acknowledgement.

So what are we to make of Mary's ointment-spilling antic? We are to see it, as Jesus saw it, as an act of love. We are to see it as the first characteristic of three characteristics of her love for Jesus. The first characteristic is that she loved Jesus above all.

The second characteristic is that she loved Jesus with costly love. What openhandedness and self-sacrifice is pictured here! In John's version of this event Martha is serving Jesus, Lazarus, and the apostles as they recline at table (John 12:2). We are not told Mary's whereabouts—whether she was serving alongside her sister or cooking in the kitchen. Whatever tasks she was busy accomplishing, a Spirit-wrought spontaneous idea came upon her. Instead of bringing in cups of wine, she carried in an alabaster flask of perfume, perhaps a family heirloom. She broke the flask. They gasped. She gasped! But she also, wasting no time, began to pour it over Jesus' head. Again, can you picture that? How strangely extravagant and shockingly costly!

The extravagance and shock of her action is especially seen when set against Judas' decisions. "Then Judas Iscariot, who was one of the twelve, went to the chief priests in order to betray him to them" (Mark **14:10**). Matthew adds Judas' question, "What will you give me if I deliver him over to you?" (Matt. 26:15). Both Matthew and Mark record the religious leaders' happy willingness to team up: "And when they heard it, they were glad and promised to give him money. And he sought an opportunity to betray him" (Mark **14:11**; cf. Matt. 26:14–15).

While one group of men plots (Mark 14:1–2), another man ("one of the twelve" no less, 14:10–11)[8] makes that plot possible. Amazingly, after Judas

---

7   H. B. Swete, *The Gospel according to Mark*, 3rd ed. (London: MacMillan, 1927), 323, quoted in W. D. Davies and Dale C. Allision Jr., *A Critical and Exegetical Commentary on the Gospel according to Saint Matthew*, ICC, 3 vols. (Edinburgh: T&T Clark, 1988–1997): 3:445.

8   "The identification of Judas Iscariot . . . as 'one of the Twelve' (cf. 14:20) shows that the betrayal comes from Jesus' closest followers, magnifying the crime" (Strauss, *Mark*, 609).

has just witnessed this woman waste a year's salary on Jesus, he accepts about four months' wages for his Lord's life, thirty pieces of silver (Matt. 26:15; cf. John 12:6). Once again we have a remarkable contrast of characters and their character: while the woman gives generously, Judas seeks to gain greedily, and "whereas her sacrifice is costly, Judas settles his bargain for a relatively paltry sum."[9]

The question we are to ask ourselves as we witness afresh this odd act is not, How can I be more reckless in my weekly tithe? (Although regular, impulsive check writing in the range of $50K will always be warmly welcomed by the church treasurer.) Rather the question is, Am I willing to love Jesus with what is most valuable to me? Loving Christ is costly. Think about that. And think about something you love that you will sacrifice even now for Christ and his kingdom.

The third characteristic is that she loved Jesus for who he said he was. Here is where Mark **14:8–9** comes into play. Jesus teaches his disciples, saying, "She has done what she could; she has anointed my body beforehand for burial. And truly, I say to you, wherever the gospel is proclaimed in the whole world, what she has done will be told in memory of her." One way to read verse 8 (we will return to verse 9 later) is to say that, while her actions demonstrated that she loved Jesus above all and in a costly and sacrificial way, she did not necessarily grasp the symbolic value Jesus now attaches to her actions. She is acting better than she knows. As a dead body for a Jewish burial would be drenched in oil to conceal the smell (see Mark 16:1; m. Šabb. 23:5), she unwittingly perfumes his body for his impending death.

Another way to read Mark 14:8 is to say not that she acted better than she knew but that, while she knew little, she acted as best she could. This more positive reading would fit with the theme in Mark's Gospel that the outcasts (like lepers) and the unexpected (like Jewish women) understand Jesus' mission before others do. It would also fit with what we know about Mary and her family. We know from John 11 that her family was extremely close to Jesus and that her sister Martha was theologically informed and her mind teachable about new theological truths. We also know from Mark that Jesus gave three public predictions about his death (8:31; 9:30–31; 10:33–34), one of which Mary must have heard first- or secondhand.

So perhaps this woman (Mary of Bethany), whom Mark places at the beginning of his passion narrative, grasped something of what was said to the

---

9   Davies and Allison, *Matthew*, 3:450. According to Exodus 21:32 thirty pieces of silver (Matt. 26:15) is the price paid by the owners of an ox that gored a slave to death. To Judas, Jesus is worth no more than a slave.

first woman who begins the birth narrative (Mary of Nazareth), namely, that Jesus came to "save his people from their sins" (Matt. 1:21). In fact, maybe she understood far more. Maybe she knew something of how that salvation would be accomplished. Maybe she even grasped that the cross of the "Christ" (Mark 1:1) would be his coronation—that the crown is the cross.

But whether we are reading too much or too little into her motives, our vision of the post-crucified, buried, and resurrected Jesus should be clear. We are to take Mark's Gospel as a discipleship manual, and her passion here is to be ours now. We are to love Jesus above all, with a costly love, and for who he says he is, namely, the Son of Man who came to die and be buried for the forgiveness of our sins.

His Love for Us

Think back to the story of Lazarus' resurrection. When he became extremely sick, his sisters sent word to Jesus, "Lord he whom you *love* is ill" (John 11:3). What remarkable language. Then, when Jesus received the message, we read, "Now Jesus *loved* Martha and her sister and Lazarus" (John 11:5). Put simply, Jesus loved that family.

I want to end by expanding upon that thought here in Mark. We have focused on Mary's love for Jesus; next we will focus on Jesus' love for her. There are three ways he showed his love. First, he protected her. When the men were in a huff and puffed out, "What waste!" Jesus showed a simple but sadly rare male sensitivity. He came to her defense. Let those with both the X and the Y chromosome learn from this act. When a woman is being yelled at by a group of men, stand up for her. Be bold. Be brave. You can even use Jesus' line, "Leave her alone" (Mark 14:6).

Second, as part of his defense, Jesus commended her. He protected her not only because the boys were being brutish but because the boys were wrong and the girl was right. He told them, "She has done a beautiful thing [or "good work," as it can be translated] to me" (14:6). We might say that he said, "Well done, good and faithful servant" (Matt. 25:21). Then his commendation continued with a remarkable prophecy: "And truly, I say to you, wherever the gospel is proclaimed in the whole world, what she has done will be told in memory of her" (Mark 14:9). Whether the phrase "the gospel" refers to the Gospel of Mark (as it is read or recited aloud)[10] or to the passion narrative—

---

10 "The term εὐαγγέλιον ["gospel"] is repeated from beginning to end to convey the 'nature of the subject matter' of the narrative (France, 4). The author begins his work proclaiming the εὐαγγέλιον (1:1), and then Jesus begins his ministry proclaiming it (1:14–15). Jesus expects his disciples and future followers to live boldly for the sake of the εὐαγγέλιον (8:35; 10:29) and to

the death and resurrection of Jesus—"her sweet perfume that filled this leper's house now fills the four corners and seven continents of the world."[11]

Here it is remarkable that what is about to happen to Jesus—his capture and sufferings and death and burial—constitutes "good news." It is also remarkable that his prediction has come true. When we read of Jesus' burial in 15:42–47 and then the final line of the Gospel—"And [the women] went out and fled from the tomb, for trembling and astonishment had seized them, and they said nothing to anyone, for they were afraid" (16:8)—we might be tempted to think, "How exactly will this good news about Jesus, let alone this one-verse story about an unnamed woman, spread to the whole world?" Ah, but that is the beautiful thing about this "beautiful thing" (14:6). I am glad you are reading this chapter today, for a prophecy has been fulfilled in your reading.

Together we have walked through her story. And we are not alone. Every day around the world this prophecy is fulfilled. In the millions of local churches and among nearly two billion Christians someone somewhere is reading or hearing read and explained Mark 14:3. As J. C. Ryle said, "The deeds and titles of many a king and emperor and general are as completely forgotten as though written in the sand; but the grateful act of one humble Christian woman is recorded in" over fifteen hundred different languages "and is known all over the globe." Ryle continues,

On that great day [judgment day] no honor done to Christ on earth will be found to have been forgotten. The speeches of parliamentary orators, the exploits of warriors, the works of poets and painters, will not be mentioned on that day; but the least work that the weakest Christian woman has done for Christ, or his members, will be found written in the book of everlasting remembrance. Not a single kind word or deed, not a cup of cold water, or a jar of perfume, will be omitted from the record. Silver and gold she may not have had; rank, power and influence she may not have possessed; but if she loved Christ, confessed Christ and worked for Christ her memorial will be found on high: she will be commended before assembled worlds.[12]

proclaim it to all nations (13:10; 16:15). And the perpetual proclamation of the εὐαγγελιον is tied to the recognition of the secret of Jesus's death (14:9)." Elizabeth Evans Shively, "Mark," in *The Greek New Testament, Produced at Tyndale House, Cambridge, Guided Annotating Edition,* ed. Daniel K. Eng (Wheaton, IL: Crossway, 2023), 129.

11 O'Donnell, *Matthew,* 770.

12 J. C. Ryle, *Matthew: Expository Thoughts on the Gospels,* CCC (Wheaton, IL: Crossway, 1993), 251–52.

Jesus commended her. He praised her act as a "good work," or "beautiful thing," and he announced it as a timeless treasure that the world would know of and rejoice in. Finally, he praised the "extraordinary nature of her sacrifice."[13] The disciples told her what she should have done with the money; Jesus responded, saying, "She has done what she could" (14:8). What a great line! The sense of the saying is this: "She couldn't have done more or less than what she did." Like the widow of 12:41–44,[14] who gave away "all she had to live on" (12:44), this woman sacrificed perhaps her greatest possession.

So Jesus demonstrated his love for her by protecting her and commending her. He also, third and finally (and ultimately!), showed his love for her by dying for her. Her passion (devotional love) for him cannot be compared to his passion (dying love) for her. The Passion of the Christ, we might say, far surpasses the Passion of the Church.

This Much!

Mark's Gospel has been called "a Passion Story with a long introduction."[15] That is a helpful and true statement. For it is now in this Gospel, starting here in chapter 14, that we come to the heart of the matter. As much as Jesus' birth, miracles, parables, prophecies, and second coming matters, the matter that matters most is the cross of Christ. In the same way that Jesus loved Mary, so he loves all who are his. He loves his beloved church with both undying and *dying* love. What strangely extravagant love! Shockingly sacrificial! Costly! He loves us (How shall I phrase it?)—arms wide on the cross, one, two, three, four, five, six, seven, eight, nine, one hundred times one hundred zillion this much!

---

13 Strauss, *Mark*, 608.
14 And standing "in stark contrast . . . to the greedy and exploitive scribes (12:38–40) and the scheming religious leaders (14:1–2, 10–11)" (Strauss, *Mark*, 608–9).
15 Martin Kähler, quoted in Frederick Dale Bruner, *Matthew: A Commentary, Volume 2: The Churchbook, Matthew 13–28*, rev. ed. (Grand Rapids, MI: Eerdmans, 2007), 586.

The Passover Lamb

MARK 14:12-31

This is my blood of the covenant, which is poured out for many.
Mark 14:24

People have many motives for attending a church service. Some people come because it is a rough season of life and they want a soothing balm for their souls. Others come because they are stuck in a difficult situation and seek some practical wisdom on their next move. Still others come with thankful hearts to praise God for some unexpected blessing. Whatever the motives, everyone's deepest need is the same. Our deepest need is not a cure for cancer, the blessing of a new job, or even the joy of Christian fellowship but God himself. Christian and non-Christian alike are all starving for God. We crave, we need, and we cannot properly function without him.

And so in this chapter as God's servant I will serve you the gracious salvation that is found only in the one who invites us to take and eat and to take and drink. From the Word of God I will feed you the incarnate God, our Lord Jesus Christ, who came from heaven to earth to suffer the forsakenness first of his friends (here in our text) and second of his Father so that we—though sinners who daily deny him in our thoughts, words, and actions—might sup with the King of kings for eternity. So let us open up Mark 14:12–31 and dig in. I want us here to digest three key themes: (1) Jesus' sovereignty over the story of salvation, (2) Jesus' sacrifice for sinners, and (3) Jesus' summons to sinners to sup of his salvation.

Jesus' Sovereignty

The theme of Jesus' sovereignty is seen in two ways. First, it is seen in the timing of his passion. He will be denied, betrayed, and killed during the Passover week ("Passover," 4x in 14:12–16). Recall that the Sanhedrin plotted to capture and kill Jesus after the Passover (14:1–2). However here Jesus in his sovereignty assures his first disciples and Mark's readers that his passion will not be postponed until after the Passover. Look at verse 12: "And on the first day of Unleavened Bread,[1] when they sacrificed the Passover lamb." Stop here midsentence.

"They sacrificed the Passover lamb" is the perfect summary sentence of 14:12–15:41. As Jesus and the twelve are celebrating and commemorating the final plague before the exodus from Egypt, when the Lord passed over the houses that had the blood of the lamb on the doorposts but killed the firstborn sons of all the Egyptians (Ex. 12:1–13, 23, 27), the scene is set for Jesus' own Passover story, in which God's people will be saved when the Lord does *not* pass over his own firstborn Son—when Jesus, as "our Passover lamb" (1 Cor. 5:7; cf. John 1:29), will pour out his blood (Mark 14:24) to atone for our sins. "Even the Son of Man," Jesus taught, "came not to be served but to serve, and to give his life as a ransom for many" (Mark 10:45). Indeed, we "were ransomed," Peter writes in 1 Peter 1:18–19, "with the precious blood of Christ, like that of a lamb without blemish or spot."

The timing of Jesus' passion demonstrates his sovereignty. Many powers are at play in the passion narrative—the Jewish religious and political leaders, the large crowd, and the Roman authorities and soldiers. But, as Mark makes clear, Jesus is king over the whims of the crowd and the wills of any and every worldly ruler.

Second, Jesus demonstrates his sovereignty through his fulfilled predictions. In our passage Jesus makes four predictions, all of which come true. First, as recorded in **14:12–16**, he predicts that two of his disciples will encounter two mysterious men—the "man carrying a jar of water" (14:13) and "the master of the house" (14:14).

> And on the first day of Unleavened Bread, when they sacrificed the Passover lamb, his disciples said to him, "Where will you have us go and prepare for you to eat the Passover?" And he sent two of his disciples and said to them, "Go into the city, and a man carrying a jar of water will meet you. Follow him, and wherever he enters, say to the master of the house, 'The Teacher says, Where is my guest room, where I may eat the Passover with my disciples?' And he will show you a large upper room furnished

---

1 "By the first century, Passover had merged with the Feast of Unleavened Bread until the two were commingled. . . . Luke, writing to a Greek audience, reflects the *de facto* merging of the feasts when he writes, 'now the Feast of Unleavened Bread, called the Passover, was approaching' [Luke 22:1 NIV]." John R. Sittema, *Meeting Jesus at the Feast: Israel's Festivals and the Gospel* (Grandville, MI: Reformed Fellowship, 2012), 37.

and ready; there prepare for us." And the disciples set out and went to the city and found it just as he had told them, and they prepared the Passover.

What is described above is a bit like an escape room.[2] Recently my family went to a place that was designed like a prison cell. As a team we had thirty minutes to find the clues and escape the cell. Here in Mark 14:12–16 two disciples have the morning and afternoon not to escape a room but to find one. And they do! They find the clues and follow Jesus' directions. The first prediction comes true: "And the disciples set out and went to the city and found it just as he had told them, and they prepared the Passover" (14:16). Such preparation ("prepare," 3x) would involve removing all leaven from the room, securing a properly sacrificed lamb from the temple, and setting the table with the lamb, a sauce for dipping (*haroseth*), bitter herbs, wine, and unleavened bread.

As an aside, you have to admire the obedience and effort of these two disciples. If I were asked to do this, I would have been tempted to offer an objection: "Lord, I do love you, but finding these two clues sounds awfully strange. If this has all been prearranged between you and the master of the house, can we just have a name and address?" However, the reality is that sometimes our Lord asks his disciples to do seemingly strange things—such as Isaiah, who was asked to preach to a people who could hear but would not listen, or Jonah, who was asked to preach to his enemies who would listen, or Peter, who was asked to go fishing to find the coin to pay a Roman tax and later to venture to a Gentile's house to eat a non-kosher meal with a Roman centurion (Acts 10:1–11:18). In such cases it is best that we not argue but obey. These disciples in Mark 14 had no idea that they were the two men in history who would set up the Last Supper. I cannot think of a more privileged meal in world history to be asked to prepare. Sometimes we miss out on the big things of God when we disobey the small and seemingly senseless commands of Christ.

The other three predictions follow. First, Jesus predicts that two of his disciples will encounter two mysterious men. This comes true. They find the men, then the house. Next they secure the room and prepare the meal. This would have taken place on Thursday afternoon (14 Nisan), the first day of the eight-day feast.

2 "A game in which participants confined to a room or other enclosed setting (such as a prison cell) are given a set amount of time to find a way to escape (as by discovering hidden clues and solving a series of riddles or puzzles)." *Merriam-Webster.com Dictionary*, s.v. "escape room," accessed September 20, 2022, https://www.merriam-webster.com/dictionary/escape%20room.

Second, Jesus predicts his betrayal. During the Passover meal (now Thursday evening, 15 Nisan; **14:17**), Jesus says to the twelve, "Truly, I say to you, one of you will betray me" (**14:18**). They all deny it (**14:19**). But we already know from verses 10–11 that Judas has offered himself as the traitor and is waiting for the right opportunity to betray Jesus, which he finds that very night while Jesus is praying in the Garden of Gethsemane (see 14:32–45).

Third, Jesus predicts that the remaining eleven will not remain. Every man around that table, including and especially Peter, will deny Jesus. Mark **14:26** describes the geographical shift: "And when they had sung a hymn [one of the final Hallel Psalms, Psalms 115–118]," they went out from Jerusalem ("the city," Mark 14:13), where preparation (14:12–16) and then celebration (14:17–25) of the Passover took place in a "large upper room" (14:15), to the Mount of Olives, the mountain east of the city. There Jesus gave a second Olivet Discourse, not about the fall of Jerusalem but about the failure of the twelve:

> And Jesus said to them, "You will all fall away,[3] for it is written, 'I will strike the shepherd, and the sheep will be scattered.' But after I am raised up, I will go before you to Galilee." Peter said to him, "Even though they all fall away, I will not." And Jesus said to him, "Truly, I tell you, this very night, before the rooster crows twice, you will deny me three times." But he said emphatically, "If I must die with you, I will not deny you." And they all said the same. (**14:27–31**)

"And they all said the same" (14:31b). One by one they all echoed Peter's brave but presumptuous battle cry, "If I must die with you, I will not deny you" (14:31a).

But look then at verse 50. What happens when Jesus is arrested? What happens is what he had predicted: "And they all left him and fled" (14:50). Peter obviously circled back, but only to make matters worse, only to deny thrice his Lord (14:66–72). After Peter's final denial of Jesus—"I do not know the man" (14:71)—the rooster crows. Despite all Peter's confident assertions and efforts Jesus' prediction comes true. What sovereignty!

Fourth, Jesus predicts his death and resurrection. Earlier Jesus had made three straightforward predictions of his death and resurrection (8:31;

---

3 The verb "you will . . . fall away" (Mark 14:27, 29), which can be rendered "let oneself be led into sin" (so Joel Williams, *Mark*, EGGNT [Nashville: B&H Academic, 2020], 239), refers to "a serious but temporary loss of faith." Raymond E. Brown, *The Death of the Messiah: From Gethsemane to the Grave; A Commentary on the Passion Narratives in the Four Gospels*, 2 vols. (New York: Doubleday, 1994), 1:127n24.

9:30–31; 10:33–34). Here he makes subtle allusions to those amazing events. He speaks of his death in 14:21, 24, and 27, where he says that his "blood" will be "poured out for many" (14:24, an allusion to the suffering servant of Isa. 53:11–12) and that he, as the shepherd, will be struck ("strike the shepherd," Mark 14:27, a quotation from Zech. 13:7). His prediction, as Jesus states in Mark 14:21, is based on OT predictions ("as it is written of him"): the sufferings (Isa. 53:6, 10) of the Son of Man (Dan. 7:13–14).

Then Jesus speaks of his resurrection in Mark 14:25, 28. In verse 28 he clearly states, "After I am raised up, I will go before you to Galilee." Next in verse 25 he alludes to his resurrected state and his promise to his disciples. He speaks of drinking wine ("the fruit of a vine") with his disciples ("with you," Matt. 26:29), presumably at some eschatological banquet ("in the kingdom of God," Mark 14:25), "the marriage supper of the Lamb" (Rev. 19:9). For a human being to drink requires, of course, both a body and breath. Jesus' resurrection is a bodily resurrection.

Of course, the fulfillments of Jesus' fourth and final prediction is as evident as the three others. In Mark 15 Jesus' death is recorded in detail (e.g., "And Jesus . . . breathed his last" breath, 15:37), and in chapter 16 his resurrection is recorded: the stone of the tomb is rolled away (16:4) and an announcement is made, "You seek Jesus of Nazareth, who *was* crucified. He has risen" (16:6).[4]

What does this all mean? These four fulfilled predictions make clear to us that Jesus knew, accepted, and even helped design his earthly mission. Put simply, his death was not a sad foible of history; it was, rather, part of a predetermined plan that was perfectly executed on the Passover Week in the holy city nearly two thousand years ago. Moreover, it means that "God is sovereignly at work, even through those who oppose [e.g., Judas and the Sanhedrin] and fail [the disciples] him."[5] What some people meant for "evil . . . God meant . . . for good" (Gen. 50:20). "Lawless men," Peter preaches in Acts 2:23, "crucified and killed" Jesus, but it was all "according to the definite plan and foreknowledge of God."

What it also means is that we can trust God today. We can and should believe that God is in complete control of the world and has your life under his eye and in his hands. He's got the whole world in his hands, but also your issues and problems and hopes and dreams. In Philippians 4:5 Paul writes that "the Lord is at hand," and in verse 6 he says that he has you in his hands: "Do not be anxious about anything [even terminal cancer, an unwanted divorce, a

4   Matthew records Jesus' reuniting with the eleven in Galilee (see Matt. 28:16–17).
5   Mark L. Strauss, *Mark*, ZECNT (Grand Rapids, MI: Zondervan, 2014), 628.

rebellious child, unemployment], but in everything by prayer and supplication [pray about it!] with thanksgiving let your requests be made known to God."

Jesus' Sacrifice

The first theme is Jesus' sovereignty. From the blood of the lamb on the door-post at the original exodus to the Lamb of God's not being passed over in the new exodus, Jesus is sovereign over the story of salvation. The second theme is Jesus' sacrifice for sinners.

Note that the first verse of this section speaks of the Passover lamb's being sacrificed. An unblemished one-year-old male lamb was slaughtered (Ex. 12:5). Its blood was shed as a reminder of God's salvation when he spared Israel. However, note in Mark 14:22–25 that there is no mention of a lamb. That, of course, does not mean that they did not eat a lamb, as would be the tradition. But it means that the focus has shifted. Jesus is the lamb ("This is my blood of the covenant"),[6] and his followers are now, in his institution of the Lord's Supper, to eat bread to symbolize his body and to drink the wine in the cup to symbolize his shed blood. The Lamb of God sacrificed his body and blood for our salvation.

This language of being "poured out for many" (14:24), an allusion to Isaiah 53:11–12, signifies this. Jesus sacrificed himself so that "many"[7] people might be saved ("By your blood you ransomed people for God from every tribe and language and people and nation," Rev. 5:9; "a great multitude that no one could number," Rev. 7:9). That salvation involves the forgiveness of sin, as is made clear elsewhere in the NT, notably in Mark 10:45. But that salvation also has future promises and blessings—what Jesus speaks of in Mark 14:25. Those who are saved by his body and blood and who partake of that salvation through faith will someday feast with their Savior.[8]

So the theme of Jesus' sacrifice is obvious, and obviously important. But note too that his sacrifice is for sinners. He offers the bread and cup to

---

6   "Given the recurring themes of (new) exodus in Mark's narrative, the ominous intimations of Jesus' death punctuating Mark's Gospel (e.g., Mk 3:6; 8:31; 9:31; 10:32–34) and Jesus' self-identification as a 'ransom for many' (Mk 10:45), the reader is prepared for Jesus' symbolically revealing himself through the meal as a Paschal lamb" (Nicholas Perrin, "Last Supper," *DJG* 493).

7   For a brief but helpful argument that the term "many" refers to "a particular people," namely, "the eschatological people of God, composed of Jews and Gentiles who believe in him," see Matthew S. Harmon, "For the Glory of the Father and the Salvation of His People," in *From Heaven He Came and Sought Her: Definite Atonement in Historical, Biblical, Theological, and Pastoral Perspective*, ed. David Gibson and Jonathan Gibson (Wheaton, IL: Crossway, 2013), 276–77.

8   Note the structural inclusio: The Last Supper (Mark 14:22–25) is sandwiched by Jesus' predictions of the twelve's denial and betrayal (14:17–21; 14:27–31). Mark does this to emphasize the importance of what comes in the middle—Jesus' words about his sacrifice and the benefits of that sacrifice.

sinners: Judas will betray him; the eleven will deny him. This does not mean that Judas is saved just because he partakes of the first Holy Communion. When Judas dips his bread into the bowl at the same time Jesus does (**14:20**), Jesus announces not a final warning but a final condemnation of him: "Woe to that man by whom the Son of Man is betrayed! It would have been better for that man if he had not been born" (**14:21**).[9] That said, regarding the other eleven, we can safely say based on what we know from the book of Acts, after these "sheep [were] scattered" (14:27), they returned to the great shepherd (see 14:28).

Let us be wooed and warned here.

First, let us be wooed. "It is a trustworthy statement, deserving full acceptance, that Christ Jesus came into the world to save sinners" (1 Tim. 1:15 NASB). His sacrifice was for sinners. What unwavering commitment to the glory of God and what steadfast love for us it must have taken to stay the course. How difficult it must have been to sit around a table with friends, one of whom would soon betray him and all of whom would deny knowing him. Yet, as Jesus loved his disciples, so he loves us. Let him now woo you with that love.

Second, let us be warned. Apostasy is real. We read about it here within Jesus' twelve closest companions. We read about it in Paul's letters, about one-time traveling companions who denied the truth and turned against the gospel. We know it, some of us, from life experience—friends or family members who have shipwrecked their faith. And throughout Christian history most often it is "the cares of the world and the deceitfulness of riches" (Mark 4:19), as Jesus labeled them in the parable of the sower and the seed, that cause apostasy. Worldliness takes hold of one's spiritual life and chokes it.

While those who are truly in Christ need not fear apostasy (the seed that God has sown will produce fruit), we should fear falling into the temptation of publicly denying our Lord. In Bach's *St. Matthew Passion*, after the line "Is it I, Lord?" is sung, the composer has the congregation sing this confessional chorale: "I'm the one; I should repent." Indeed! We are all prone to wander, to leave the God we love. We are all tempted to boast in our own spiritual strength. We are all prone to presumption.

So, with Judas' betrayal and the eleven's denials, let us be warned here. "Let anyone who thinks that he stands take heed lest he fall" (1 Cor. 10:12).

---

9 "Jesus is alluding to Psalm 41:9 (quoted in John 13:18), a lament psalm where David decries the fact that a 'close friend, someone I trusted, one who shared my bread, has turned against me' and joined his enemies." Grant R. Osborne, *Mark*, TTCS (Grand Rapids, MI: Baker, 2012), 258. Osborne also notes how "woe" is "used in prophetic judgment oracles (e.g., Isa. 10:5; Jer. 23:1; Hosea 7:13)" (259).

Let us "examine" ourselves, not only before we "eat of the bread and drink of the cup" of the Lord's Supper (1 Cor. 11:28) but each day. May we daily pray Luther's morning prayer, "Keep me this day . . . from sin and every evil" (cf. Matt. 6:13), and sing Lowry's hymn, "I Need Thee Every Hour."

Jesus' Summons

There are three themes in this text: (1) Jesus' sovereignty over the salvation story, (2) Jesus' sacrifice for sinners, and (3) Jesus' summons to sinners to sup of his salvation. Here we come to Mark **14:22–25**.

> And as they were eating, he took bread, and after blessing it broke it and gave it to them, and said, "Take; this is my body." And he took a cup, and when he had given thanks [*eucharistēsas*] he gave it to them, and they all drank of it. And he said to them, "This is my blood of the covenant, which is poured out for many. Truly, I say to you, I will not drink again of the fruit of the vine until that day when I drink it new in the kingdom of God."

According to the OT the Passover celebration included lamb (the "slaughter [of] the Passover lamb," 2 Chron. 35:6; also called the "Passover sacrifice," Deut. 16:5–6) and "unleavened bread" (Ezek. 45:21), followed by an explanation of Passover (see Ex. 12:26–27).[10] From the Mishnah, a record of Jewish oral traditions compiled around 170 years after Jesus' life, we have a detailed account of the Passover seder:

> The Passover meal had eight stages: (1) the blessing of the wine is followed by the first cup; (2) the bread, herbs, stewed fruit, and lamb are brought in; (3) after the son . . . asks why this night is important, the father tells the exodus story and praises God's redemption via the first part of the Hallel (Psalms 113–114); (4) the second cup of wine is drunk; (5) the unleavened bread is blessed ("Blessed are you, O Lord our God, king of the universe, who brings forth bread from the earth," see m. Ber. 6:1), broken, distributed, and eaten with the herbs and fruit as the father explains the meaning of the bread; (6) the meal proper is eaten; (7) at the

---

10 Note the connections not only with the Passover meal recorded in Exodus 12 but with the feeding miracles in Mark. As Nicholas Perrin ("Last Supper," 493) notes, "Upon examining Jesus' actions in Mark 14:22, the careful reader finds that his taking (*labōn*), blessing (*eulogēsa*), breaking (*eklasen*), and giving (*edōken*) of the bread follow the pattern established in the feeding of the five thousand ('taking' [*labōn*] . . . 'blessed' [*eulogēsen*] . . . 'broke' [*kateklasen*] . . . 'gave' [*eddidou*]) at Mark 6:41 and in the feeding of the four thousand ('taking' [*labōn*] . . . 'blessed' [*eucharistēsa*] . . . 'broke' [*eklasen*] . . . 'gave' [*eddidou*] at Mark 8:6."

end of the meal the father blesses a third cup ("Blessed are you, O Lord our God, king of the universe, creator of the fruit of the vine," see m. Ber. 6:1) and the family sings the second part of the Hallel (Psalms. 115–118); (8) a final cup concludes the celebration.[11]

In Mark's account, however, the details of the meal are sparse. We read only of a piece of bread and a shared cup of wine.[12] We also read of blessings made and a song sung. So it is highly probable that they are celebrating the Passover, but we cannot be certain that they are celebrating a seder, the meal described in later rabbinic testimony.

That said, oftentimes when the Passover seder is assumed and thus read into Mark's record, we miss what Mark actually says and emphasizes. Instead of the father of the house recalling the Passover and exodus, Jesus speaks to his spiritual, not biological, brothers (his disciples) and focuses not on the blood of the lamb but on his own body and blood. The unleavened bread now symbolizes not the haste by which Israel fled Egypt but his body sacrificed, and wine symbolizes not the blood on the doorpost but his atoning blood that ushers in both a new covenant ("Blood of the covenant, which is poured out for many," 14:24)[13] and the promise of eternal fellowship at a future celebration (drinking the cup "new in the kingdom of God," 14:25).[14] It is no wonder that, when Paul writes of the Lord's Supper, he says, "As often as you eat this bread and drink the cup [present], you proclaim the Lord's death [past] until he comes [future]" (1 Cor. 11:26).

With all that explanation in place, I have called this final theme "Jesus' summons" because he offers an invitation to his followers to partake of the salvation offered in him. His "take" (Mark 14:22) is an invitation open to every sinner who acknowledges the need for Jesus' saving body and blood:

11 As summarized by Osborne, *Mark*, 257–58.
12 "We can . . . be reasonably confident that Jesus' offer of a common cup was an innovation. This creativity may have been part of an attempt to attach new significance to the gesture, perhaps emphasizing its socially integrative character (cf. 1 Cor 10:17)" (Perrin, "Last Supper," 493).
13 "Just as a blood sacrifice sealed the first covenant, so Christ's death seals or ratifies the new covenant" (Strauss, *Mark*, 625). Strauss (629) clarifies, "Jesus' death represents the 'blood of the covenant' (v. 24; Exod 24:8), the blood sacrifice that inaugurates and ratifies the new covenant (Jer 31:31). Though Jer 31 is not explicitly cited, conceptually it lies behind Jesus' words and is highlighted by both Luke (Luke 22:20—assuming the longer reading) and Paul (1 Cor 11:25) in their versions of the eucharistic words."
14 The Roman Catholic view of transubstantiation does not fit the historical context. That is, when Jesus broke the bread and called it his "body" and lifted the cup and labeled it his "blood," the twelve did not understand the bread and wine to be literal extensions of his physical body. Moreover, it is a denial of the bodily ascension of Jesus to claim that the elements for the meal are actually his body and blood. How can Jesus' body be both in heaven and on earth at the same time?

"The power of the passion drama lies precisely in . . . invitations for the reader to participate."[15] When we ask the apostles' question—"Is it I?"—we participate. So too when we take seriously Jesus' command to "take."

In February 2014 Nabeel Qureshi wrote a book that became a *New York Times* bestseller. A few months later he announced that he was in the advanced stages of stomach cancer. On September 16, 2017, at the age of 34, he died. That book was called *Seeking Allah, Finding Jesus: A Devout Muslim Encounters Christianity*. In it Nabeel recounts his conversion to Christ.[16] He grew up in a devout Muslim family. By age five he had recited the entire Qur'an in Arabic and memorized the last seven chapters. Throughout his childhood he viewed Christians as immoral, ignorant, and uncommitted. To him Christians did not own their faith, as their faith did not seem to affect the way they thought and lived. Throughout high school he said that there was no Christian whom he encountered that could defend his faith. Then, as a freshman in college, he met David, a committed Christian who knew what he believed and why. The two became friends, and for years they debated over the central differences of the two faiths.

As Nabeel was seeking to disprove that Jesus was the divine Son of God, that he did not die on the cross, and that he did not rise again, Nabeel realized that the evidence for Jesus' deity, death, and resurrection was incredibly convincing. At that point he was an "almost Christian," to use George Whitefield's description of Agrippa in Acts 26:28. He was willing to leave his Muslim faith but not yet willing to embrace the actual person of Jesus Christ as revealed in the NT.

Then one day he had a dream. In the dream he was standing at the threshold of a narrow door, a door just wide enough for him to fit through. At the other side of the door was a room set for a wedding feast. But his friend David was standing in the way. He could not get through the door. "David," he said, "I thought we were going to eat together." David replied, "You haven't responded." Nabeel had not yet responded to David's invitation to receive Christ.

After he woke up, he told David the dream. David told Nabeel to read Luke 13, where Jesus speaks of people's coming from "east and west, and from north and south" to "recline at table in the kingdom of God" (Luke 13:29) and our Lord invites, "Strive to enter through the narrow door" (Luke 13:24).

---

15 Donald Senior, *The Passion of Jesus in the Gospel of Mark* (Collegeville, MN: Liturgical Press, 1992), 53.

16 My summary is taken from "NABEEL QURESHI 'Seeking Allah, Finding Jesus' Muslim Converts to Christianity," interview by Robbie Symons, 100huntley, February 24, 2014, video, 13:13, https://www.youtube.com/watch?v=NGJzkm8lZjU.

Nabeel read the passage, and it was clear now what he should do. He decided to leave behind his family and his family's faith and to enter through the narrow door. That is, he decided to trust in Christ and in him alone for salvation.

Now in heaven, what is Nabeel doing? I imagine he is preparing the table for the wedding supper of the Lamb. Perhaps he is preparing a seat for his friend David, next to King David himself, or perhaps near King David's "Lord."

Behold, the Lamb of God!

Jesus summons us to take and eat. But before we join him at the feast we must first acknowledge him as the way, the truth, and the life (John 14:6). But also as the lamb of God! We must "Behold, the Lamb of God, who takes away the sin of the world!" (John 1:29, cf. 1:36). We must behold his body sacrificed for us and blood poured out for us. We must behold the sacrificed lamb who has redeemed us from our bondage to sin and freed us to worship God—to forever feast with him.

Go to Gethsemane

MARK 14:32-42

Abba, Father, all things are possible for you. Remove this
cup from me. Yet not what I will, but what you will.
Mark 14:36

When I was eight, my father, older brother, and I traveled to Connemara, Ireland. There we visited relatives, viewed family headstones, survived traditional Irish culinary offerings, and explored my father's acreage. On his land, atop the rolling hills, sits the house in which he grew up. What I remember most about the small stone structure was that the loft was full of hay and my brother and I had a wonderful time hiding and jumping around in it.

Years later, when I returned with my son Sean, I had a very different view of my father's house, land, and life. I realized that he grew up in extreme poverty. The small cottage has only two rooms with dirt floors, with no bathroom, electricity, or running water. Even the picturesque landscape—stone walls line each plot—indicated to me, on this second visit, the land's barrenness. The land cannot sustain most crops. It is full of rocks.

My father rarely talks about his childhood. But recently he shared with me a story about the poverty he experienced. One day he stole two shillings from his father's wallet, walked over to the McGillicuddys, and bought a few apples. When he returned home, my grandmother interrogated him, "Where did you get those apples?" He lied, "Oh, Mrs. McGillicuddy is giving them away. She thought you'd like to make an apple pie." As my grandmother discovered the truth when she went to thank Mrs. McGillicuddy, so my grandfather discovered the missing coins. Needless to say, such behavior did not fare well for my father's *an dara leath* ("bottom half").

My father, Padraic, also shared about a Christmas Eve when he stayed up late. He wanted to meet St. Nicholas and know immediately what gift he would receive in his stocking. Each Christmas he received only one gift. That year he was hoping for a penny. A penny! For a few hours he kept climbing down from the loft where he slept to feel the stocking. After a few unsuccessful attempts he fell asleep. When he awoke, he ran to the stocking. He felt something. He reached down and pulled out a penny! "Thank you! Santa," he said aloud as he looked up to heaven.

In Mark 14:36 Jesus prays, "Abba, Father" (also implied in 14:39: "He . . . prayed, saying the same words"). With this obvious observation I seek not to demonstrate some thematic connection between my father and Jesus' Father but rather to highlight the importance of perspective. For, just as it took a second visit to my father's homeland, and a few decades of normal human maturity, for me to recognize his childhood poverty, likewise, when we understand who Jesus is (the beloved Son of the Father, 1:11) and where he comes from (his Father's eternal and glorious presence; cf. 9:2–3; 14:25), we then hopefully will gain a better understanding of and appreciation for the incarnation, the prayers of Gethsemane, and the significance of Jesus' sacrifice.

To give us the proper perspective on what we read in Mark 14:32–42 we will ask and answer eight questions. As each question will build upon the preceding one, and in some ways grow in complexity as well as in significance, the final two questions and answers will be the most important ones for us to comprehend, value, and apply.

The First Question

The first question is, What and where is Gethsemane? Gethsemane is a "place" (Mark **14:32**) located on the western slopes of the Mount of Olives, where Jesus preached his recent Olivet Discourse (Mark 13) and made the final prediction of his resurrection (14:28). Since the word "Gethsemane" means "olive press," it was likely an olive orchard, a *garden* of olive trees.[1]

The Second Question

The second question is, Whom did Jesus take with him to the garden of Gethsemane? Mark **14:32–33** provides the answer: "[Then] they went to a place called Gethsemane. And [Jesus] said to his disciples, 'Sit here while I pray.' And he took with him Peter and James and John." Jesus took "his disciples," a reference to those with him in the upper room: the twelve minus Judas, his "betrayer" (14:42), who would arrive with his evil entourage in verse 43. But

---

1   John labels it a "garden" (John 18:1). He is perhaps making a theological connection between the first Adam and second Adam, namely, how Adam in the garden of Eden failed to obey and how Jesus in the garden of Gethsemane perfectly submits to God's will.

out of the eleven who came with Jesus to the olive orchard, Jesus selected Peter, James, and John to join him.

Why these three? Jesus might have chosen Peter to humble him and ready him for his coming trial. At the Last Supper Peter boasted of his fidelity ("Even though they all fall away, I will not," 14:29) and bravery ("If I must die with you, I will not deny you," 14:31). Jesus might have wondered, "Well, let's see how this loyal, courageous, unmovable 'rock' fares against the seductive power of sleep." Of course, we know that the weight of heavy eyes (**14:40**) will soon be his demise. It is also possible that Jesus included the sons of Zebedee because they "strongly expressed their willingness to suffer for him (10:38–39),"[2]—to drink their own "cup"—only after they expressed a desire to partake of the greatness of the coming kingdom, wanting seats at the right and left hand of his throne (10:37). They need some humility as well.

All that is possible. What is more certain is that Jesus once again (cf. 5:37; 9:2; 13:3) selected his inner circle to serve as his official witnesses (cf. Deut. 19:15). These three saw Jesus raise the dead (Mark 5:37, 42). They viewed his transfiguration (9:2). They had also just heard his prophecy about his glorious return (13:3ff.). They have beheld and will behold his glory. But now they would witness (when they were not sleeping)[3] something seemingly inglorious. They would see and hear, in the words of a great medieval hymn, the "sacred head . . . wounded," the paleness of his anguish, and how Jesus "with grief [would be] weighed down." Here they would witness not the heavenly Father's voice but instead loud moans, distressful cries, and silence from heaven. At Gethsemane the Spirit's assuring presence did not descend like a dove; the Father did not offer a word of comfort and commendation.

The Third Question

The third question is, Why did Jesus go to Gethsemane? Or, what was he there to do? I think he went there because it was a place to which he often took his disciples and a place to which Judas would thus come to see whether he was there (see John 18:1–2). In Mark 14:43 Jesus shows no surprise at Judas' arrival ("And immediately, while he was still speaking, Judas came"), for as soon as he sees Judas he says, "Rise, let us be going; see, my betrayer is at hand" (Mark 14:42). His "communion with his *Abba* [has] soothed Jesus' lament

---

2   Mark L. Strauss, *Mark*, ZECNT (Grand Rapids, MI: Zondervan, 2014), 633.
3   "Since normally one prayed out loud, the three disciples probably overheard Jesus praying. One should not assume that the disciples fell asleep from the moment Jesus left them to the moment he returned. They would have heard bits and pieces of Jesus' prayer (France 2002; 583)." Robert H. Stein, *Mark*, BECNT (Grand Rapids, MI: Baker Academic, 2008), 661.

and steeled him for the crisis."[4] So perhaps Gethsemane was the twelve's secret place of prayer, their hideout (cf. 11:17)—an open-aired house of prayer.

Jesus went to Gethsemane to make his arrest easy for his enemies. But also, and most obviously, he went there to pray. "Sit here," Jesus told the disciples, "while I *pray*" (14:32); "And going a little farther, he fell on the ground and *prayed*" (**14:35**); "And again he went away and *prayed*" (14:39). Then, as Jesus prayed, the disciples slept. So he offered his reproach to the tired trio: "Watch and *pray*" (14:38). Jesus went to Gethsemane to pray; he went there to pray *with* his disciples.

The Fourth Question

The fourth question follows: How did the prayer meeting go? Four men showed up. Ah, but, only one man prayed. While the pillars of the church counted sheep ("sleeping," "asleep," 14:37; "sleeping," 14:40; "sleeping," 14:41; cf. "taking your rest," 14:41), the shepherd of our souls bowed low and cried out. They slept, slept, slept, slept; he prayed, prayed, prayed. Jesus alone prayed. And, as the perfect praying God-man's interceding continually for God's people (e.g., John 17) might be all that the church needs, Jesus here does not clear the trio of their sinful negligence. It was very late. Jesus knew that. Everyone was physically and emotionally exhausted ("sleeping for sorrow," Luke 22:45). Jesus certainly felt that too. However, our Lord gave an order, "Sit here while I pray" (Mark 14:32), and he made clear that "to sit" meant not "to sleep" but "to be watchful" ("Remain here and watch," **14:34**). And in **14:37–38**, when he returned from a round of praying, he made absolutely clear that "to watch" included prayer— "Simon, are you asleep? Could you not watch one hour? Watch and pray."[5]

Peter was singled out (by his "pre-called name" no less)[6] in part because his temptation to deny Christ was but hours away. Instead of sleeping, he should have been praying, "Lord, I'm so fearful that I might fall into temptation; please strengthen my resolve." Like all disciples, past and present, Peter needed to remember that even when our "spirit" (our inner spiritual desire) is "willing" to obey, "temptation" is difficult to resist when the body (our "flesh") is "weak" (14:38). Human attentiveness ("watch") and divine assistance ("pray," 14:38) are both necessary for victory.

---

4   Donald Senior, *The Passion of Jesus in the Gospel of Mark* (Collegeville, MN: Liturgical Press, 1992), 80.

5   "Watching and praying, a constant staying awake for prayer, is often enjoined on Christians (Luke 21:36; Eph. 6:18; Col. 4:2; 1 Pet. 4:7; cf. with 5:8)." Rudolf Schnackenburg, *The Gospel of Matthew*, trans. Robert R. Barr (Grand Rapids, MI: Eerdmans, 2002), 271.

6   Strauss, *Mark*, 635: "'Peter' is used elsewhere in contexts critical of Peter (8:32–33; 9:5–6; 14:29, 31)—most significantly in the denial that follows (14:54, 66, 67)."

Besides the need for alertness (which they all clearly disobeyed—to "watch" does not mean to close one's eyes), Jesus also wanted human companionship and empathy. He wanted his closest friends to be friends. Like anyone facing dreadful things, he needed people to lift up his spirits and to lift up to heaven (with him) his deepest needs. When Jesus said to his three close friends, "My soul is very sorrowful, even to death" (14:34), he was calling out *to them* for help and support. He wanted vigilant solidarity.

While today Jesus does not need our prayers for him, it is advisable that we stop in the middle of this chapter, as Jesus did in the middle of his solo prayer meeting, to learn from Jesus on the topic of prayer. That is, as our Lord and Savior agonized, wrestled, lamented, groaned, and persevered in prayer to his Father at Gethsemane, so we must learn to come to our Father in our hour of greatest need. Moreover, as Jesus pleaded boldly for what he earnestly desired, so we should embrace emptying our hearts before the Lord—our inner struggles, personal battles, and soul-felt wishes. Do we feel the ground beneath us giving way? If so, where do we go? We go to Gethsemane. We join Jesus in the deep distress, the gut-wrenching agony, the unstoppable tears. We join hearts and hands together for that type of prayer meeting.

The Fifth Question

The fifth question is, Why did the Lord Jesus pray?

When we speak or sing of our triune God, the words on our lips are usually not about the depression, tears, and prayers of the second person of the Trinity. We do not think that way. But let me help you think that way; that is, let me help you grasp the humanity of Jesus.[7]

Do you think of Jesus as experiencing fatigue? He did. Read Mark 4:38. How about hunger? He got hungry. Read Mark 11:12. But did he ever express anger or frustration? Yes, he did. Read Mark 1:43–44; 3:5; 8:17, 21; and 10:14. Has he "felt the emotional weight of betrayal and abandonment by his closest friends"?[8] Absolutely. Read Mark 14:18–21, 27–31. Was our Lord overwhelmed with grief? Certainly. That is our text (see esp. 14:33–34). Read it too!

Many summers ago, my family vacationed in Clear Lake, Iowa. Half of our time we spent in the water—whether it was the lake or the pool. One afternoon I was sitting poolside, supervising four O'Donnell children, especially Charlotte, who was four at the time. She was swimming in the shallow end. She was throwing a floating foam noodle in front of her and swimming toward

---

7 Citing Matthew 26:38, Irenaeus names Jesus' soul being exceedingly sorrowful as one of the "tokens of the flesh" (*Haer.* 3.22.2).

8 Strauss, *Mark*, 638. Strauss lists all the references above.

it. Time after time. She was so happy! But suddenly everything stopped. The motion in the water. Something changed. When my eyes looked up, I saw her eyes. She had a desperate look. She could not move to safety. The noodle was too far away. The side was as well. She started to sink. I immediately jumped in the water, clothes and all. I pulled up her head.

This might sound sacrilegious, but at Gethsemane our sovereign Savior felt as distressed as a drowning child. So he looked up. He cried out. He asked his Father to jump in, hold him up, and save his life. That does not easily register in our minds because, as readers of this great Gospel, we have witnessed Jesus' standing up to the religious authorities. We have seen the God-powered miracles: he raised the dead; he fed the thousands with scraps of bread. We have heard the bold claims.

What now? What is this? Jesus is like Superman with kryptonite around his neck. Here Christ the King is so feeble. But that is the point. Jesus is not superman. He is human. "And the Word became flesh" (John 1:14). Human flesh. Human blood. Human bones. Human intellect. Human emotions. Human needs. "Jesus' divinity chose to share humanity *completely*."[9] Do we grasp, believe, and embrace that reality?

In this garden we cannot dilute Jesus' humanity. But why would we? For Jesus' humanness is indispensable to our salvation. As Gregory of Nazianzus summarized, "What was not assumed was not redeemed."[10] That is, if Jesus was not completely human, then he could not stand as our substitute for sin and as our representative before the Father. Jesus' humanity is something for us to ponder, and be in awe of.

The Sixth Question

The sixth question is, How did Jesus pray?

First, note his posture, a posture of submission. "Jews normally prayed with face uplifted and hands raised to heaven."[11] But here Mark writes of Jesus, "He fell on the ground and prayed" (Mark 14:35); Matthew adds, "He fell on his face and prayed" (Matt. 26:39). That is likely not how most of us most often pray. Yet, with Jesus' lying face down before the Father, I wonder whether his example is something we should more often emulate. Hebrews 5:7–8 records: "In the days of his flesh, Jesus offered up prayers and supplications, with loud

9   Frederick Dale Bruner, *Matthew: A Commentary, Volume 2: The Churchbook, Matthew 13–28*, rev. ed. (Grand Rapids, MI: Eerdmans, 2007), 648.
10 See Edward R. Hardy, ed., *Christology of the Later Fathers*, LCC (Louisville: Westminster John Knox, 1954), 31.
11 Grant R. Osborne, *Mark*, TTCS (Grand Rapids, MI: Baker, 2012), 269.

cries and tears, to him who was able to save him from death, and he was heard because of his reverence. Although he was a son, he learned obedience through what he suffered." I wonder whether we should learn such reverence for God and obedience to God through the type of suffering that affects the posture of our praying. Here in the garden Jesus prayed prostrate. Find a prayer closet. Lock the door. Lie full-body, facedown. And pray.

Second, note his petition. He prayed, "Abba, Father,[12] all things are possible for you [God is absolutely almighty]. Remove this cup from me. Yet not what I will, but what you will" (Mark **14:36**). That is a prayer of submission.

Verse 41 tells us that Jesus had three separate seasons of prayer, and **14:39** tells us that the content of the prayers was identical: he "prayed . . . the same words." He certainly prayed more than the three sentences recorded in verse 36, but that record serves as a perfect summary of his heartfelt desperation and resolution. Here Jesus did not question God or his will. He did not ask or accuse—"Why me and why this way?" Instead, he became the living embodiment of the first three petitions of the Lord's Prayer, "Our Father in heaven, hallowed be your name. Your kingdom come, your will be done" (Matt. 6:9–10). Jesus' temperament was that of the refrain of Psalm 42–43, "Why are you cast down, O my soul, and why are you in turmoil within me?" (Pss. 42:5, 11; 43:5), but his actual petition was part of what he taught his own disciples to pray.[13]

I admire greatly how one of my seminary professors speaks of this point. "Here," Grant Osborne comments, "we see a true philosophy of prayer, the exact meaning of intercession. We confidently place our needs before God in the expectation that he will act, yet at all times that his will takes precedence over our own."[14] He adds, "Prayer is not only pouring our heart out to God but also an act of surrendering our will to the will of God."[15] Precisely.

Third, note the period of prayer. After Jesus found the three sleeping saints, he rebuked all of them through Peter, saying, "Simon, are you asleep? Could you not watch one hour?" (Mark 14:37). From this rebuke we ascertain that beseeching heaven for "one hour"—whether this refers to sixty minutes or simply a period of time that lasted about an hour—was, at least in this

12 In Mark Jesus teaches on prayer (9:29; 11:24–25; 13:18) and prays (1:35; 6:46), but only here, on the cross (15:34), and in the upper room (John 17) do we have record of the content of his prayers. In every prayer in the Four Gospels, except in that cry from the cross (cf. Matt. 27:46), Jesus calls God "Father."
13 This is a son's, not a stoic's, prayer. When Socrates faced death, he drank the poison and told his friends to wipe their tears, assuring them that he was journeying to a better life in the afterlife (see *Phaedo* 58E). Jesus did not face death in that way.
14 Osborne, *Mark*, 270.
15 Osborne, *Mark*, 273.

situation, not too long to pray. And, since Jesus prayed three times and three times returned to his sleepy disciples, we can safely estimate he prayed for an extended period, perhaps even three or four hours.

Again, Jesus models the praying life to his disciples both then and now: he prayed standing and on his face; he prayed short and long prayers; he prayed during the day and at night; he prayed alone and with others; he prayed his set daily prayers and he prayed extemporaneously when he was sad and desperate; he prayed with reverence and yet with childlike trust in God's will for his life; and he prayed by pouring out his petition and then accepting God's "No" without grumbling or complaining.[16]

Let us imitate our Lord.

The Seventh Question

The seventh question is, What is the "cup"?[17]

At the heart of Jesus' hours-long prayers is the plea, "Father,. . . . Remove this cup from me" (14:36). The cup is a metaphor for his awful sufferings (cf. 10:38–39). Jesus knows what lies ahead. He knows he will suffer betrayal, denial, an official sentence of condemnation from his own people, brutal torture from the Romans, and a slow and embarrassing death (see 10:33–34; 14:18, 27, 30). He eyes "the hour" (14:41, the last moments of his life, including crucifixion) ahead[18] and knows it is paved with unspeakable agony. He knows he has to die and how he will die. This is why he is "greatly distressed and troubled" (14:33); at the core of his being the "sorrow is so deep that it feels as if he is dying"[19] ("My soul is very sorrowful, even to death," 14:34).

He must drink that cup of pain. But there is more to the "cup" than those horrific sufferings. There is one particular detail of his death that has him sweating ("His sweat became like great drops of blood falling down to the ground," Luke 22:44). And that is that he will bear our sins ("He himself bore our sins in his body on the tree," 1 Pet. 2:24), and, more than that, that he will become in some inexplicable way sin for us—"For our sake [God] made [Christ] to *be sin* who knew no sin, so that in him we might become

---

16 See Douglas Sean O'Donnell, *Matthew: All Authority under Heaven*, PTW (Wheaton, IL: Crossway, 2013), 799.

17 Some of the content of this answer is taken from the section "God-Forsakenness," in Douglas Sean O'Donnell, "'If You, Then, Who Are Evil': Sin in the Synoptic Gospels and Acts," in *Ruined Sinners to Reclaim: Human Corruption in Historical, Biblical, Theological, and Pastoral Perspective*, eds. David Gibson and Jonathan Gibson (Wheaton, IL: Crossway, forthcoming).

18 "The 'hour' is not merely one moment in time but connotes that critical and definitive hour when the salvation of the world would be decided" (Senior, *Passion of Jesus in the Gospel of Mark*, 79).

19 Strauss, *Mark*, 633.

the righteousness of God" (2 Cor. 5:21). He will become the object of God's judgment for our transgressions.

Jesus is not a martyr facing death. Like Stephen in Acts 7:54–60, "most martyrs face death with courage and confidence, expressing steadfast faith in God and hope for the resurrection."[20] Jesus is not a martyr. He is a propitiatory sacrifice. He will drink "the cup" of "the wine of [God's] wrath" (see Jer. 25:15–28; cf. Isa. 51:17, 22).[21] That is what is causing him to tremble, tremble, tremble. May we too tremble, tremble, tremble.

How are sins forgiven and the judgment of a holy God appeased? Jesus is "betrayed into the hands of sinners" (Mark 14:41) for sinners. How are sins forgiven and the judgment of a holy God appeased? Jesus gives his "life as a ransom" (10:45), that is, he pours "out [his blood] for many for the forgiveness of sins" (Matt. 26:28; cf. Mark 14:24). How are sins forgiven and the judgment of a holy God appeased? Jesus endures the silence and seemingly inexplicable separation from his Father: "My God, my God, why have you forsaken me?'" (15:34).[22] How are sins forgiven and the judgment of a holy God appeased? Jesus drinks the cup. "The whole of the punishment of his people," Charles Spurgeon wrote,

> was distilled into one cup; no [mere] mortal lip might give it so much as a solitary sip. When he put it to his own lips, it was so bitter, he well nigh spurned it: 'Let this cup pass from me.' But his love for his people was so strong, that he took the cup in both his hands, and at one tremendous draught of love, He drank damnation dry.[23]

That was the cup.

The Eighth Question

The final question focuses especially on the theme of perception. The eighth question is, Who drank the cup? Of course Jesus drank the cup. But who is Jesus?

---

20 Strauss, *Mark*, 637.

21 "In the prophets, it is the evil nations—from Edom or Babylonian—that drink the cup due to their sin. But here holy Jesus drinks the cup. How inexplicable and ironic! Does he drink their cup *for the nations*? Another mysterious irony relates to the title 'Son of Man.' In Daniel the Son of Man is this future figure who is supposed to come to judge sinners [see Dan. 7:13–14, 26–27; cf. Matt. 13:41; 24:30–51; 26:64]. But here, Jesus, as the self-professed Son of Man has come to be judged by sinners" (O'Donnell, *Matthew*, 800).

22 For more on this verse and the nature of Jesus' God-forsakenness see the chapter on Mark 15:33–47.

23 Charles Haddon Spurgeon, *Sermons of the Rev. C. H. Spurgeon of London*, third series (New York: Sheldon, Blakeman, & Company. 1858), 298.

Does Jesus hold to Chalcedonian Christology—that "our Lord Jesus Christ" is "at once complete in Godhead and complete in manhood, truly God and truly man"[24]—and Paul's Colossae Christology—that "in him the whole fullness of deity dwells bodily" (Col. 2:9)? Indeed, he does. Here he firmly establishes such theological perceptions. He finishes his time in the garden with these profound words: "The hour has come. The Son of Man is betrayed into the hands of sinners. Rise, let us be going; see, my betrayer is at hand" (Mark 14:41–42). Jesus calls himself "the Son of Man." Others call him "Teacher" or "Lord," but he most often calls himself "the Son of Man." Why? What does this title signify? With this title Jesus is claiming that he is the divine king prophesied in Daniel 7:13–14, the ruler to whom "the Ancient of Days" (God) bestows an everlasting kingdom. This is why Jesus can say that he as "the Son of Man has authority on earth to forgive sins" (Mark 2:10); that he as "the Son of Man is lord even of the Sabbath" (2:28); that he as "the Son of Man" will rise from the dead (9:9; cf. 8:31; 9:31); that he as "the Son of Man," who will be "seated at the right hand of Power" (14:62), will come again "with great power and glory" (13:26; cf. 8:38); but also that he as "the Son of Man" will be "betrayed" (14:21, 41), delivered over to "suffer many things and be rejected . . . and be killed" (8:31; cf. 9:12, 31; 10:33), so as to "give his life as a ransom for many" (10:45).

So who drank the cup? What an important interrogative. The answer is that the Son of Man drank it. Jesus here highlights his divinity. He further highlights his divinity and unique and intimate relationship with God with his language, "Abba, Father." "Abba" is Aramaic for "Father" [*'abba*], a relational but respectable term. "Abba" is not "Daddy,"[25] as is so often claimed. So Jesus said "Father" in Aramaic, followed by "Father" in Greek [*patēr*]. For anyone

24 Here is more of the language of the Council of Chalcedon (AD 451): "Our Lord Jesus Christ" is "at once complete in Godhead and complete in manhood, truly God and truly man, consisting also of a reasonable soul and body; of one substance with the Father as regards his Godhead, and at the same time of one substance with us as regards his manhood; like us in all respects, apart from sin . . . recognized in two natures, without confusion, without change, without division, without separation; the distinction of natures being in no way annulled by the union, but rather the characteristics of each nature being preserved and coming together to form one person and subsistence, not as parted or separated into two persons, but one and the same Son and Only-begotten God the Word, Lord Jesus Christ."
25 For a defense of this position see James Barr, "Abba Isn't Daddy," *JTS* 39 (1988): 28–47. "In the Mishnah and Targums, it is used primarily by adult children . . . as an address to their fathers" (Stein, *Mark*, 662). "At the time, the Aram. [Aramaic] word αββα belonged to the familiar language of family, and, although it was certainly used by children, it was not a childish expression. Adults would also use αββα, since it was the appropriate and adult way to address one's father. . . . Therefore, αββα is a family word that communicates a close relationship with God, as with one's Father." Joel Williams, *Mark*, EGGNT (Nashville: B&H Academic, 2020), 242.

who is bilingual (Jesus was trilingual; he spoke Aramaic first and Greek second and knew how to read the Hebrew Scriptures) it is not uncommon to pray in two tongues. I think, however, that the duplication—Father/Father—highlights the unique and beautiful relationship between the Father and the Son,[26] something that we in Christ now share: "You did not receive the spirit of slavery," Paul writes, "to fall back into fear, but you have received the Spirit of adoption as sons, by whom we cry, 'Abba! Father!'" (Rom. 8:15; cf. Gal. 4:6).

Who drank the cup? We can give a good answer by quoting from the two key verses in Mark's Gospel: the "Son of God" (1:1) and the "Son of Man" (10:45). And to that final theological truth what should be our response? Put differently, how do we respond to Gethsemane? Praise! Adoration! Glory! Honor! The closing lines in "Fairest Lord Jesus" come to mind and should stick in our minds:

Beautiful Savior! Lord of the nations!
Son of God and Son of Man!
Glory and honor, Praise, adoration,
Now and forevermore be Thine.

---

26 "What is of signal importance . . . is that the Son-Father/Father-Son relationship characterized by the use of the term αββα is not principally one of intimacy . . . , but, rather, as seen clearly in the argumentation of Gal 4:3–7, one of 'privileged status,' that of an 'adult son (not daughter) and heir,' in the words of Mary Rose D'Angelo." James W. Voelz, *Mark 8:27–16:8*; Christopher W. Mitchell, *Mark 8:27–16:20*, Concordia Commentary (St. Louis: Concordia Publishing House, 2019), 825, quoting D'Angelo, "*ABBA* and 'Father': Imperial Theology and the Jesus Traditions," *JBL* 111 (1992): 616.

Naked and Ashamed

MARK 14:43-52

And a young man followed him, with nothing but a linen
cloth about his body. And they seized him, but he left the
linen cloth and ran away naked.
Mark 14:51–52

> When the woman saw that the tree was good for food, and that it was a
> delight to the eyes, and that the tree was to be desired to make one wise,
> she took of its fruit and ate, and she also gave some to her husband who
> was with her, and he ate. Then the eyes of both were opened, and they
> knew that they were naked. And they sewed fig leaves together and made
> themselves loincloths. (Gen. 3:6–7)

Genesis 3:6–7 is far removed from Genesis 2:25: "The man and his wife were
both naked and were not ashamed." But it is not far removed from Mark
14:52, where we read of a man who was so ashamed of aligning himself with
Jesus that he "ran away naked" when the guards grabbed his garment. And
Genesis 3:6–7, along with that unusual action in Mark 14:52, is not far removed from what we read in Mark 14:43–52.

This naked man is not alone in his Adam-and-Eve-like sin and shame. The
Jewish religious leaders will send a "crowd with swords and clubs" (14:43) that
will successfully seize their true Messiah and lead him off to his death sentence
(14:46). Judas, "one of the twelve" apostles (14:43), will betray Jesus with a sinister sign (14:45). Another apostle will try to kill a man to save Jesus from the
mission of the cross (14:47). And all eleven remaining apostles (minus Judas)
will abandon Jesus and run for their lives (14:50). How nakedly shameful!

One man will stand out, stand alone, and stay the course. Jesus, the sinless
one, will willingly be betrayed into the hands of sinners[1] in accordance with

---

1   On this theme of being delivered into human hands see Mark 9:31; cf. 8:31; 10:33; 14:18.

God's divine plan (14:49). Jesus, who will die on the tree as soldiers gamble for his clothing (15:24), will bring God's covering—his forgiveness—to all who, through repentance and faith, acknowledge that they are naked and ashamed of their sin and in need of a Savior.

Do you see the beautiful theological artistry here? Each story that Mark tells is more than a historical record of an event in Jesus' life. Each narrative, and often each character within a narrative, teaches the church lessons. And the lessons here in Mark 14:43–52 are fivefold, a lesson for each character. In this chapter we will learn from the sinners and the Savior.

The Religious Leaders Have Jesus Arrested

We start with the sinners.

First are the men who put into motion this next movement in "the greatest drama ever staged"[2]—the Jewish religious authorities. In **14:43** we read of the Sanhedrin, "the chief priests and the scribes and the elders." These were not just the religious ruling class but the political ruling class. The Sanhedrin was Israel's supreme court. We know that some men from this group of seventy (plus the high priest, m. Sanh. 1:6) were secretly Jesus' disciples. But we also know that most of these men hated Jesus and wanted him dead.

Why? At least four reasons. *Jealousy.* The crowds flocked to hear Jesus' wisdom and to witness (or experience!) his miracles. *Philosophy.* The Jews wanted a military messiah who would hold Rome accountable, not one who would call Jews to repent and believe. *Theology.* Jesus made seemingly blasphemous claims—such as that he was "the Son of Man" who had "authority on earth to forgive sins" (2:10, cf. 2:5) and would return after his resurrection from the dead to judge the world and gather his elect (13:26–27; 14:62). *Rebellion.* Jesus overturned the tables in the temple, told parables of judgment against the leaders, and called them hypocrites.

For these four reasons it is "the chief priests and the scribes and the elders" who had Jesus arrested. But notice that Mark makes no mention of the religious leaders' being present at Gethsemane, the site of Jesus' arrest. Instead they sent "a crowd" (14:43), or, as John records, a "band of soldiers and their captain," along with the "officers of the Jews" (the temple police, John 18:12; see Luke 22:47, 52). The captain and the cohort (600–1,000 men) were likely Romans, as Roman military terms are used here. Mark does not mention the Romans perhaps because he is making the same theological point John makes at the start of his Gospel: Jesus "came to his own [the Jewish people], and his

2 Dorothy Sayers, *Creed or Chaos?* (New York: Harcourt, Brace, and Co., 1949), 5.

own people did not receive him" (John 1:11). They did more, of course, than reject him: they detained him, handed him over to the enemy occupiers, and publicly denied and reviled him.

Here in Mark 14:43–52 notice *who* arrested Jesus: his own people did. Also notice the details of their dirty deed: Jesus rebuked them because they came out against him like he was a common criminal, a thug who might need a few clubs to the head and swords to the knees in order to back down and come with them (**14:48**; cf. "swords and clubs," 14:43). Jesus reminded them that he was not a thug but their teacher: "Have you come out as against a robber [an insurrectionist leading an armed rebellion], with swords and clubs to capture me? Day after day I was with *you* in the temple teaching, and you did not seize me" (14:48–49). Although he had taught them day after day (11:27–12:37), this day this throng decided to listen to the voice of the false teachers, the Sanhedrin who sent them there.

So notice the "swords and clubs" (Mark 14:43, 48) the crowd carried. But also notice their main action. Judas said that as soon as he kissed Jesus they were to "seize him and lead him away under guard." What did they do? "And they laid hands on him and seized him" (**14:46**), the same word ("seized") Jesus will use in verse 49 (also in 14:51 of the young man). "They Seized Him" would serve as a good title for this text, although "They Laid Hands on Him" might also serve as an appropriate title for this motion picture, or picture of ironic motion. Our Lord Jesus, who had laid his hands upon people from the crowd to heal them and welcome them into the kingdom,[3] was now captured by "the crowd."

With all that said, what would serve as a good lesson for us? What is Mark's point as it relates to this first character? Jesus tells us at the end of verse 49: "Day after day," he says to them, "I was with you in the temple teaching, and you did not seize me. But let the Scriptures be fulfilled." The lesson is that we need to know that God has so orchestrated history that even evil people and events, like the arrest of Jesus by God's chosen people (the Jews), are used by him to bring about good—in this case the salvation of the world, grace extended to both Jews and Gentiles. His plan cannot be thwarted (see Job 42:2)!

Judas Betrays Jesus

The first characters are the Jewish people of Jesus' day, those from the highest level (the Sanhedrin) to the lowest (the face in the crowd with a club in hand). They organized the arrest of their very own messiah. So shameful!

3   Mark 5:23; 6:5; 7:32; 8:25.

The second character is Judas. (Shame has no limits.) He executed the first part of the plan. Look at **14:43–45**, which record the depths of human degeneracy:

> And immediately, while [Jesus] was still speaking, Judas came, one of the twelve, and with him a crowd with swords and clubs, from the chief priests and the scribes and the elders. Now the betrayer had given them a sign, saying, "The one I will kiss is the man. Seize him and lead him away under guard." And when he came, he went up to him at once and said, "Rabbi!" And he kissed him.

Mark records four sad ironies. The first is Judas's name. Judas Iscariot was likely named after Judas Maccabeus, the Jewish priest who led a successful revolt (the Maccabean Revolt) against the Greeks, the Seleucid Empire (167–160 BC). The holiday Hanukkah celebrates his greatest achievement, when he restored Jewish worship in the temple after removing the statues of the Greek gods and goddesses and then purified the Holy Place. The name "Judas" is also another way to say "Judah." Judah was, of course, the tribe from which the promised Messiah would, and did, come (Gen. 49:10; Matt. 1:2). So the name Judas cannot get any more Jewish. But Judas, sadly, does not act like a pious Jew should. He not only rejects the Messiah; he is willing to betray him for thirty silver coins.

The second sad irony is that Judas is "one of the twelve" (Mark 14:43). This highlights his privileged position. Chosen apostle. Companion of Christ. Eyewitness. Judas is both "one of the twelve" (14:43) and "the betrayer" (14:44; "my betrayer," 14:42).

The third sad irony is the title Judas uses for Jesus ("Rabbi," 14:45). Judas has been taught by Jesus daily, and yet here Judas makes clear that not one of Jesus' lessons on loyalty or warnings against the love of money has been heard and heeded. Or, Judas has unlearned all such lessons.

Last and certainly least, this false greeting is followed by a false act of loving friendship: the kiss.[4] The Greek word is *kataphileō* and means a loving kiss,[5] usually given on the hand or cheek. The word is used of the father of the prodigal son (Luke 15:20) and the woman who kissed Jesus' feet (Luke 7:45). Why this kind of kiss? An unholy kiss. A sickening "sign" (Mark 14:44).

---

4   "Judas twists a greeting of friendship . . . into a death sign." Donald Senior, *The Passion of Jesus in the Gospel of Matthew* (Collegeville, MN: Liturgical Press, 1985), 84.
5   "To kiss is to love." Philip Graham Ryken, *Luke: Knowing for Sure*, REC, 2 vols. (Phillipsburg, NJ: P&R, 2009), 2:510.

In Luke's record Jesus, with an element of surprise in his voice, asks, "Judas, would you betray the Son of Man with a kiss?" (Luke 22:48).

Step back and think about this low moment in history. How could Judas do this after living side by side with Jesus for three years? He did not just hear Jesus teach in the temple for one week; he *heard* Jesus teach day after day, from the time of "the baptism of John [nearly] until the day" of Jesus' death (Acts 1:22). Imagine hearing with your own ears: "If anyone would be first, he must be last of all" (Mark 9:35); "Truly, I say to you, whoever does not receive the kingdom of God like a child shall not enter it" (10:15); "You shall love your neighbor as yourself" (12:31).

Judas *saw* the miracles firsthand. Imagine seeing with your own eyes a leper cleansed, a paralytic walk, the sea stilled, a dead child raised to life, the multiplication of the loaves and fish, the walking on water, the eyes of the blind made to see.[6] Judas *touched* Jesus with his own hands; Jesus touched him. Just the night of this betrayal Jesus washed his feet (John 13). That same night Judas tasted the bread and wine of the Last Supper. Imagine sharing the Passover with the Lamb of God. Judas even *smelled* Jesus' body odor. He knew what Jesus smelled like after they had walked a few miles together, day after day, year after year. With all five senses he fully encountered the incarnate Christ.

How then could Judas betray his Lord?[7]

The only motive Mark hints at is greed. Judas did it for the money. After the incident of the woman who "wasted" a year's wages of perfume, making a mess of Jesus' body and the dinner table, Judas "then" (Mark 14:10) made an offer of betrayal to the Jewish authorities, who were more than willing to pay him half a year's wages. "They . . . promised to give him money" (14:11). So he turned in Jesus, to use a somewhat contemporary analogy, for a 1971 Ford Pinto. What a foolish deal. What a Satanic covenant. He too ate from the fruit. Luke makes it plain that "Satan entered into Judas" at the Last Supper (Luke 22:3). But human greed and Satanic sway go hand in hand. John records that Judas spoke against the woman's wasteful anointing "not because

---

6   Judas also personally experienced Jesus' healing power through his calling to be an apostle. Judas was given "authority over unclean . . . spirits" (Mark 6:7), and he "cast out many demons and anointed with oil many who were sick and healed them" (6:13).

7   This is the last we hear of Judas in Mark, Luke, and John. Matthew writes of Judas' remorse and suicide (Matt. 27:3–10; cf. Acts 1:18–19). The NT is somewhat silent on Judas' final fate. It gives no graphic depiction of him in the lowest level of hell. In Dante's *Inferno*, Judas is one of three sinners (Brutus and Cassius—Julius Caesar's assassins) forever chewed to eternal death by the triple-headed Satan (see Dante, *Inferno*, canto XXXIV). However, Jesus' pronouncement "Woe to that man. . . . It would have been better for that man if he had not been born" (Mark 14:21) cannot mean annihilation. It implies some kind of conscious punishment in the afterlife.

he cared about the poor, but because he was a thief, and having charge of the moneybag he used to help himself to what was put into it" (John 12:6).[8]

A lesson here for us is to take to heart Paul's warning in 1 Timothy 6:10 that "the love of money is a root of all kinds of evils" and that through that "craving . . . some have wandered away from the faith and pierced themselves with many pangs." Another lesson is to embrace what James says in James 4:7, to "submit . . . to God" and to "resist the devil," knowing that, if you submit to God and resist the devil, then the devil "will flee from you."

The Swordsman Strikes!

The third character we learn from is the unnamed swordsman: "But one of those who stood by drew his sword and struck the servant of the high priest and cut off his ear" (Mark **14:47**).

Rewind the tape. Jesus is praying at Gethsemane. The eleven are near him. Peter, James, and John are closest to him. They have been sleeping. Jesus wakes them and tells them that the time of his betrayal has arrived: "Rise, . . . see, my betrayer is at hand" (14:42). Picture a crowd with torches in the distance and the glow of the moon lighting the landscape. Judas arrives with an armed "crowd" (14:43), certainly more than eleven men. Judas greets Jesus. The guards grab Jesus. Then we arrive at what is recorded in verse 47. John tells us that it was Peter who did this and that Malchus was the servant's name (John 18:10). Luke, the physician, tells us that Jesus shouted, "No more of this!" and then "touched [the man's right] ear and healed him" (Luke 22:51). Mark provides no such details. Perhaps he does not record Peter's name, or his own (if he is the fleeing naked man),[9] to protect their reputations. Or perhaps it is because his focus is on two characters, the only two named: Judas and Jesus. Whatever the reason for Mark's sparsity, the two rebukes Jesus gives, as recorded in Matthew and John's accounts, fit well as lessons for us to learn.

The earliest commentators on Mark find in impetuous Peter's action some important applications. Why did Peter do this? In part because he had said he would. Just a few hours before this event Peter had declared to Jesus, "If I must die with you, I will not deny you" (Mark 14:31). He was ready to fight to the death. Peter was not trying to cut off this man's ear. He was attempting

---

8   "Judas, the Devil was also of this Religion, he was religious for the bag, that he might be possessed of what was therein, but he was lost, cast away, the very Son of perdition." John Bunyan, *The Pilgrim's Progress*, World's Classics (Oxford: Oxford University Press, 1984), 86.

9   Scholars give over a dozen options of the identity of the naked man. The most popular position is that it is John Mark, the author of the Gospel of Mark.

either to cut off his head or to slice his throat. Malchus should have been glad Peter was a fisherman, not a soldier.

Another reason Peter did this was because he, once again, misunderstood Jesus' mission. He might have overheard Jesus pray, "Father, . . . remove this cup from me," but had fallen asleep during the next line, "Yet not what I will, but what you will" (14:36). This explains why Jesus said, as John records, "Put your sword into its sheath; shall I not drink the cup that the Father has given me?" (John 18:11). Matthew notes that Jesus also said, "Put your sword back into its place. For all who take the sword will perish by the sword. Do you think that I cannot appeal to my Father, and he will at once send me more than twelve legions of angels?" (Matt. 26:52–53). Brave but impetuous Peter forgot both who Jesus was and why Jesus had come. He forgot the person of Jesus and the plan of God. He forgot that Jesus had about 72,000 angels ("twelve legions of angels," Matt. 26:53) at his beck and call. In 2 Kings 19:35 one angel "stuck down 185,000 in the camp of the Assyrians." Imagine what an arsenal of angels would do to a mob of mere mortals! Peter misunderstood the person of Jesus. Peter misunderstood the plan of God. Jesus had come to drink the cup. His time was at hand. The cross was now his to bear. So what place does the sword have in God's strategy of salvation—of peace between God and man through the cross?

Of course, there is a place for the sword. Just war, law enforcement, and self-defense are such places.[10] Jesus does not say, "Peter, what's with the sword? Christians are pacifists! Throw that sword away." He says to put it back in "its place" (Matt. 26:52). It has a place. But there is no place for the sword in advancing the kingdom of God. "Where Christians have used violence to promote . . . Christianity, those regions of the world are . . . least receptive to the gospel. Having no ears, they cannot hear!"[11]

The lesson here, then, can be stated in a few different ways. In broad categories it is this: know God's plan and stick with the plan. More narrowly, understand that Christianity advances by faith, not force. Or, to add to that, do not oppose the mission of the cross through political or military maneuverings. If you think, as Peter here thought, that the best way to oppose the powers that be is through the sword, you know nothing of the power of the cross. On the cross Jesus "disarmed the rulers and authorities and put them to

---

10 See Luke 22:36. "There is a time and place for the proper use of the sword. In the case of an unprovoked attack by an unlawful aggressor, we have a legitimate right to self-defense. The sword also has a divinely approved authority in the hands of the state, including its lawful use by a legitimate army in the prosecution of a just war" (Ryken, *Luke*, 2:515).

11 Douglas Sean O'Donnell, *Matthew: All Authority under Heaven*, PTW (Wheaton, IL: Crossway, 2013), 807.

open shame, by triumphing over them" (Col. 2:15). The power of the church is still the power of the cross. When the church suffers with Christ (Phil. 3:10), it grows into Christ. When the church unashamedly preaches "Christ and him crucified" (1 Cor. 2:2), persecution arises, but so too are people drawn unto Jesus.

The Eleven Flee from Jesus

As we continue in our character study, we come to Jesus' disciples. In Mark **14:50** we read one of the saddest verses of the Bible: "And they all left him and fled." The word "all" springs off the sheet. The word "left" is also striking, for in the first chapter of this Gospel some of Jesus' disciples had left (Gk. *aphiēmi*) their livelihoods to follow Jesus (1:18, 20); now near the end of the Gospel they leave (*aphiēmi*, 14:50) Jesus to save their own lives.[12] Not one of the twelve will heed Mark 8:34 and "deny himself and take up his cross and follow." If Jesus felt abandoned by his friends when he prayed at Gethsemane, how must he feel now? Like the scapegoat on the Day of Atonement?

That abandonment is illustrated further in **14:51–52**, where we read of an unnamed man who had the courage to follow an arrested Jesus ("A young man followed him," 14:51). The detail about his donning only a "linen cloth about his body" (14:51) tells us that he was in his pajamas. Jewish men slept with a thin layer of cloth that covered their bodies from shoulder to toe. This man's sleepwear was made of "linen" (14:51). He was upper class.

So this rich man was likely sleeping in his house on or near the grounds of the olive press called Gethsemane when he heard the voices and the drama created by Peter's poor swordsmanship. While all the disciples fled, he followed from a distance. Following Jesus is what Christian disciples do! Yet, when he got too close and was discovered, the guards "seized him" (14:51, the same verb used for Jesus' arrest), and this man followed Jesus no more. Like the eleven, he too left (same verb, *aphiēmi*)—he left his linen clothing (it was obviously pulled off him as he "ran away," 14:52).[13] The eleven "fled" (14:50); this man "ran away" (14:52).

The last word of our English text is "naked" (14:52). It is used only once in Mark: here! The only other time it is used in the Gospels is by Jesus in his parable of the sheep and the goats ("I was *naked* and you clothed me," Matt. 25:36). Elsewhere in the Bible from Genesis 3 to Revelation 17 the word

---

12 Raymond E. Brown, *The Death of the Messiah: From Gethsemane to the Grave; A Commentary on the Passion Narratives in the Four Gospels*, 2 vols. (New York: Doubleday, 1994), 1:287.

13 This is perhaps an allusion to Amos 2:16: "Even the bravest warriors will flee naked on that day" (NIV). Although this man is more curious, I think, than brave.

symbolizes human unholiness and shame in light of God's judgment.[14] After Adam and Eve ate of the forbidden fruit they found themselves exposed to divine wrath. That is why God clothed them. In Exodus 28:42 we read that part of the priestly attire for Aaron and his sons included "linen undergarments to cover their naked flesh." Even the holy priests could not stand before God as Adam and Eve did before the fall.

What then, as we look at the fleeing disciples (including this naked young man), is the lesson? It is not simply that our flesh is weak (Mark 14:38). Rather, it is that our whole selves are fallen. As Calvin says, "We are so entirely controlled by the power of sin, that the whole mind, the whole heart, and all our actions are under its influence."[15] Our whole selves—mind, heart, and will—are like a glass of water into which ten drops of red dye have been dropped. Adam's original sin is pervasive.

What we have here, however, is total depravity in the form of "total undependability."[16] As the Lamb of God is led away to slaughter (see Isa. 53:6, 7), the darkest sheep—Judas—betrays Jesus, while the others from the apostolic flock not only stray. They run! Even a would-be disciple joins them in their sprint to safety. All have gone astray; all have run away. Literally.

But that is precisely the lesson here. The lesson is Isaiah 53:6.

> All we like sheep have gone astray;
>> we have turned—every one—to his own way;
> and [meanwhile] the LORD has laid on him
>> the iniquity of us all.

We must have self-knowledge and Savior-knowledge. We must know our sinful nature and see our need for a Savior.

Jesus Stays the Scriptural Course

It is to that Savior that we turn next and finally. The final character of our study is the key character. Notice Jesus in this narrative. There is only one dependable one. Notice that.[17] But also notice four other characteristics of

---

14 See Isaiah 20:4; Ezekiel 16:26; 23:10; Revelation 3:17; 16:15.

15 John Calvin, *Commentaries on the Epistle of Paul the Apostle to the Romans*, trans. John Owen, vol. 19 of *Calvin's Commentaries* (Edinburgh: Calvin Translation Society, 1849), 261.

16 Frederick Dale Bruner, *Matthew: A Commentary, Volume 2: The Churchbook, Matthew 13–28*, rev. ed. (Grand Rapids, MI: Eerdmans, 2007), 655. "One of the purposes of the Trial Stories in the Passion Narrative is to teach the sinfulness of all strata of the human race" (668).

17 Unlike the people of Israel, including the twelve, Jesus alone remains faithful unto the end—obedient to the Father even unto death. He will fulfill his Gethsemane prayer by faithfully

this character: total humanity, absolute authority, steely determination, and scriptural compliance.

First, notice Jesus' humanity. Some may wish to paint this scene with a halo over Jesus, representing his divine holiness. But that night I assure you there was no visible halo over Jesus' head. Not because he is not holy but because he is human. He looked human, so much like the other eleven men with him that Judas needed to signal which of these young bearded Jewish men was Jesus. In Gethsemane, from Jesus' honest prayers to his Father to this singling out with the kiss, do not miss that a totally human Jesus is arrested, condemned, flogged, teased, beaten, and crucified.

Second, although Jesus is totally human, he is totally in control. He does not give up his divine authority in the passion narrative; he shows it. For example, do not overlook his speech here. Other than Judas' lines, only Jesus speaks. Near the end of our text Jesus rebukes his arrestors. And at the start of our text Mark speaks about Jesus' speech: "While he was still speaking" (Mark 14:43). It is almost like Jesus' words have drawn his betrayer. And remember, Judas arrives as Jesus is saying, "Rise, let us be going [to the cross]; see, my betrayer is at hand" (14:42). Jesus knows what is happening. He has predicted it (8:31; 9:31; 10:33–34; 14:21, 27).

He moves forward with the plan. That is the third characteristic. Notice his steely determination to obey the will of the Father. The Father has answered no to Jesus' repeated plea to remove the cup, but somehow, even in that no, Jesus feels reassured and reinvigorated to accomplish the task before him. Here Jesus offers no resistance. He does not resist Judas's kiss. He does not resist the crowd's hands upon him. Our "great high priest" (Heb. 4:14) now in heaven, then on earth, lets them lead him "to the high priest" (Mark 14:53) in Jerusalem.

Fourth, notice that Jesus allows this tragedy to happen to him because he knows that the details of his life are in line with his Father's will as revealed *in Scripture*. Although Jesus is in control and could wield control in a military fashion (asking the angels to defend and free him), he refuses to use his divine power to thwart the divine plan. "But let the Scripture be fulfilled" (**14:49**). Jesus chooses the way of sacrificial love and not sword-drawn revolt because he believes in his Bible. He not only believes in his Bible; he knows that his Bible, and that of his captors, finds its greatest prophecies fulfilled in

---

submitting "to the dreadful consequences required by the will of God for the redemption of the world." Peter G. Bolt, "The Faith of Jesus Christ in the Synoptics Gospels and Acts," in *Faith of Jesus Christ: Exegetical, Biblical, and Theological Studies*, ed. Michael F. Bird and Preston M. Sprinkle (Grand Rapids, MI: Baker Academic, 2010), 221.

him.[18] He knows that "all the promises of God"—like that of the Son of Man of Daniel 7, the suffering servant of Isaiah 53, the mocked and forsaken king in Psalm 22, and the new covenant of Jeremiah 31—"find their Yes in him" (2 Cor. 1:20; cf. Matt. 5:17).

So what is the lesson to learn—believe your Bible? Sure. But more than that: believe that the story of Jesus is the unfolding of the story of Scripture. We must grasp that the good news we believe is not some de-storified truth claim. Rather, the gospel is a story that began with creation and ends with new creation, a story that began with a man and a woman naked and unashamed and will end with shameless, fallen creatures clothed in "the righteousness of God through faith in Jesus Christ" (Rom. 3:22; cf. Rev. 3:5; 7:9, 13), who is "clothed in a robe dipped in blood" (Rev. 19:13).

---

18 Jesus likely also found the prophecy of his betrayal in his Bible (see Pss. 41:9; 55:12–13; Matt. 27:3–10; Acts 1:15–22). We can certainly say, with Paul, that Jesus "died . . . according to the Scriptures" (1 Cor. 15:3 NIV).

Can I Get a Witness?

MARK 14:53–72

Are you the Christ, the Son of the Blessed?
Mark 14:61

A famous Bible scholar once wrote, "Mark's gospel is relatively artless."[1] What he meant was that, compared to the other Gospels, certain stylistic details—such as John's poetic prologue, Luke's carefully crafted parables, or Matthew's record of Jesus' brilliant Sermon on the Mount—are not found in Mark's sparse and succinct narrative. Yet, as we saw in the last chapter, Mark is not without his metaphors, repeated key words, ironies, or carefully structured stories. In fact, Mark 14:53–72 is a work of high literary art. Mark carefully weaves together the stories of two trials—that of Jesus and that of Peter. These two trials are filled with a number of contrasts and ironies, which I will point out.

But the structural design is not merely that of one trial following another.[2] A theme ties every sentence of the 347 Greek words: the theme of "testimony," or "witness." That word (and it is the same root in Greek, *martyreō*) is used seven times in our text,[3] almost always of the false testimonies against Jesus. And, while the word is not used of Peter in verses 66–72, he certainly fits the pattern. He adds his own false testimony.

At the theological and structural heart of our text is the only true testimony: Jesus' answer to Caiaphas's question, "Are you the Christ, the Son of the Blessed?" (Mark 14:61). As Jesus ends his true testimony about himself, saying, "I am, and you will see the Son of Man seated at the right hand of Power, and coming with the clouds of heaven" (14:62), we have covered 172

---

1   Robert H. Gundry, *Matthew: A Commentary on His Literary and Theological Art* (Grand Rapids, MI: Eerdmans, 1982), 628.
2   Also note the Markan intercalation, or "sandwich"; see Mark 14:54, 66.
3   Mark 14:55, 56 [2x], 57, 59, 60, 63.

words in Greek, and then in verses 64–72 we find 175 more. Yet surrounding that true testimony is one false testimony after another, including Peter's threefold denial of Jesus.[4]

I have titled this chapter "Can I Get a Witness?" both because I am playing off the popular use of that phrase in African-American churches, in which the preacher calls for a witness (an "Amen") after some truth has been proclaimed, and also because that question summarizes well the tragedy of this text. For, by the time the rooster crows a second time, Jesus could ask literally, "Can I get a witness?" Peter will deny knowing him. Others will offer false testimonies about him. Only Jesus will speak on his own behalf, making a statement that brings about his condemnation by the Jewish supreme court. The high priest asks, "What further witnesses do we need?" (14:63). The Sanhedrin gives its verdict: "They all condemned him as deserving death" (14:64).

Since I see this text as an accurate historical account that is also a literary and theological work of art, I think it only fitting to use an artistic outline to cover the material. I want you to think of Mark 14:53–72 as an abstract painting in which the brushstrokes of red, black, gold, and blue are used to show us what Mark wants us to see about the four main characters of Jesus' trial: red (the Sanhedrin), black (the false witnesses), gold (Jesus), and blue (Peter).

Painted Red: The Chief Priests, Elders, and Scribes Condemn Jesus

I have selected the color red for the Sanhedrin, those "chief priests and the elders and the scribes [who] came together" to render a judgment upon Jesus (Mark 14:53), because they will "condemn him" to "death" (14:64), death by crucifixion (15:13–15). Jesus' "blood" will be "poured out" (14:24) on the cross.

It will also be poured out before that. Here in Mark 14:65 is just the start of his bloody beatings. Here our Lord's face is covered (with a sack or blindfold) as some of the religious leaders slap and punch him ("And some began . . . to strike him," 14:65). Also, the temple police, or the household guards, "received him with blows" (14:65; "beat him," NIV, NET). Later that day the Romans will whip him ("having scourged Jesus," 15:15),[5] place a crown of thorns upon his brow (15:7), and nail him to a cross (Matt. 27:35; Luke 23:33; cf. John 20:25). Mark does not highlight the bloodiness of Jesus' passion narrative, but each step from the high priest's house to the hill called Golgotha must have been lined with blood.

---

4 The language of a courtroom, however, is not missing: "He denied it" (Mark 14:68, 70); "He began . . . to swear" (14:71).
5 A scourging was "a Roman judicial penalty, consisting of a severe beating with a multi-lashed whip containing embedded pieces of bone and metal" (Mark 15:15 ESV mg.).

Thus I color not only the Sanhedrin's actions red but also their murderous motives. When Jesus is received into the Roman governor's headquarters, Pilate perceives that "it was out of envy that the chief priests had delivered him up" (15:10). If this is true—and it is likely—then how quickly being green with envy turns to a thirst for blood. It also blurs into black.[6]

Painted Black: False Witnesses Testify against Jesus

Let me show you what I mean as we walk through the entirely of Jesus' trial, focusing on his accusers. Mark **14:53** tells us that the guards who arrest Jesus in Gethsemane lead him to the high priest, Caiaphas (Matt. 26:3).[7] At his "palace" (Matt. 26:3) "all the chief priests and the elders and the scribes came together" (Mark 14:53). This means either that every member of the San-hedrin is there or simply that a quorum is established.[8] Twenty-three of the seventy-one members would be needed to hear a capital punishment trial (see m. Sanh. 4:1).

Mark **14:54** sets the stage for Peter's trial. We learn that Peter, after fleeing, has regained his courage, even enough courage to circle back to see what is happening to Jesus. As Peter sits with "the guards" and warms "himself at the fire" in the outside "courtyard of the high priest" on that cold spring night (14:54), the "whole council" gathers inside (**14:55**). Jesus stands before them on trial. Their purpose is clear: they are "seeking testimony against Jesus to put him to death" (14:55). There is only one problem: "They found none" (14:55).

This kangaroo court cannot find a joey (British slang for a fool) who does not contradict the next dupe brought before him. We are told that "many bore false witness against him, but their testimony did not agree" (**14:56, 59**).[9] How they get "many" people to testify in the middle of the night is uncertain. Are

6 I mean nothing racial about the term "black." I am using it as Scripture uses various colors to represent realities: "The white garments of the saints (Rev. 3:18; 19:14) symbolize spiritual purity. A red horse (Rev. 6:4) symbolizes slaughter in warfare and a black horse (Rev. 6:5) death. The purple and scarlet cloth of the world empire 'Babylon' (actually Rome) in Revelation 18:12 represents affluence and mercantile prosperity." Leland Ryken, *Symbols and Reality: A Guided Study of Prophecy, Apocalypse, and Visionary Literature* (Wooster, OH: Weaver, 2016), 98.

7 John tells us that the guards first brought Jesus to Caiaphas's father-in-law, Annas (John 18:13), the former high priest, and then to Caiaphas (John 18:24). The Evangelist also tells us that the apostle John, who must have circled back with Peter, granted Peter access to Caiaphas's court-yard (John 18:15–16).

8 Mark 15:1 reads: "And as soon as it was morning, the chief priests held a consultation with the elders and scribes and the whole council." So, likely just some of the members are there for the trial detailed in Mark 14 ("the whole council," 14:55 = the entire quorum), and then all of them are in attendance the next day.

9 "Twice Mark describes their testimony as 'false' (vv. 56, 57) and twice he says that they 'did not agree' (vv. 56, 59)." Grant R. Osborne, *Mark*, TTCS (Grand Rapids, MI: Baker, 2012), 282.

these witnesses from the crowd that has arrested Jesus? Are they the guards? Whoever they are, they prove unreliable. The high priest needs just two reliable witnesses to testify against Jesus for a crime that deserves the death penalty in Roman law. The closest they can get is what Jesus says about Herod's temple in Jerusalem.

It was a capital offense to desecrate a holy place, including a pagan shrine or the Jewish temple. Some took what Jesus said about the temple's destruction as an act of sedition. Jesus had said, "Destroy this temple, and in three days I will raise it up" (John 2:19). As John makes clear, however, "He was speaking about the temple of his body" (John 2:21). In other words, Jesus was talking metaphorically about his death and resurrection. He also mentioned, in private to his disciples, that the temple would be destroyed by the Romans in the near future (see Mark 13:2). But that is all he had said about that matter. He never said he would destroy the temple. So it is no wonder that Mark calls the testimony—"We heard him say, 'I will destroy this temple that is made with hands, and in three days I will build another, not made with hands'" (**14:58**)—false ("Some . . . bore false witness against him," **14:57**) and points out that it was not only false but contradictory ("Yet even about this their testimony did not agree," 14:59).

Let me pause here and highlight the thick darkness of this midnight meeting. To bear false witness is to break the ninth commandment. It is a serious offense. To lie in a court of law and to lie before the eyes of God about the Son of God is high treason. This courtroom, which is colored "Dusty Dim" (to create a new Benjamin Moore color), needs a darker shade of onyx ("Pure Gloom" or something).

These people who testified against Jesus might have thought, since they were standing before their religious leaders, that they were on God's side. How wrong they were.[10] As Jesus said to the Pharisees in John 8:44, so he could have said to his accusers in Mark 14:53–65: "You are of your father the devil, and your will is to do your father's desires. He was a murderer from the beginning, and does not stand in the truth, because there is no truth in him. When he lies, he speaks out of his own character, for he is a liar and the father of lies." And Jesus could have added the warning John issues in Revelation 21:8: "As for the cowardly, the faithless, the detestable, as for murderers, the sexually immoral, sorcerers, idolaters, and *all liars*, their portion will be in the lake that burns with fire and sulfur, which is the second death."

---

10 "The very ones who were supposedly God's people and should have witnessed for God sought false witness to kill his Son" (Osborne, *Mark*, 284).

At this point in the trial the high priest is almost at an impasse. Based on the change in his line of accusation in Mark **14:61**, he knows that these witnesses have provided poor testimonies. Yet, like a clever lawyer who is losing his case, he tries to sway the jury with antics (standing and walking to the middle) and rhetoric: "And the high priest stood up in the midst and asked Jesus, 'Have you no answer to make? What is it that these men testify against you?'" (**14:60**).

Jesus, however, does not take the bait. "He remained silent and made no answer" (14:61). He remains silent to "show contempt for the hostile proceedings,"[11] to make clear he does not consent to the false witnesses' claims, and simply because silence is often the wisest defense. Why risk incrimination? Why "answer . . . a fool according to his folly"? You might end up sounding "like him yourself" (Prov. 26:4). Perhaps Jesus keeps quiet because he sees no need to defend himself legally, no more than he feels the need to defend himself physically. And, related to that, he can hold such a disposition because, once again, he trusts in God and his Word. I can picture him mouthing to himself, "[Just] let the Scriptures be fulfilled" (Mark 14:49), as he meditates on Isaiah 53:7:

> He was oppressed, and he was afflicted,
>> yet he opened not his mouth;
> like a lamb that is led to the slaughter,
>> and like a sheep that before its shearers *is silent*,
>> so he opened not his mouth.

Next the high priest breaks the silence with another question, "Are you the Christ, the Son of the Blessed?" (Mark 14:61). We will explore Jesus' golden answer later. For now note that Jesus answers in the affirmative. He is "the Christ, the Son of the Blessed," with "the Blessed" being a veiled name for God. "I am," he replies (**14:62**). I imagine Caiaphas as being stunned for a second, thinking to himself, "Wait, did Jesus just say yes?" Then, once he realizes that he has done so, Caiaphas knows this trial is over, because in his mind Jesus is obviously guilty of blasphemy. Look at what follows. The speed of the proceedings is incredible. There are no counterquestions or calls for further explanation or defense. Instead, in outrage "the high priest tore his garments" (**14:63**).[12] He gives a declaration of victory: "What further witnesses do we

---

11 Raymond E. Brown, *The Death of the Messiah: From Gethsemane to the Grave: A Commentary on the Passion Narratives in the Four Gospels*, ABRL, 2 vols. (New York: Doubleday, 1994), 1:464.

12 "Caiaphas's rending of his own clothes signifies the rending of the priesthood from him." Matthew Henry, *Commentary on the Whole Bible*, quoted in *CHSB*, 1501.

need? You have heard his blasphemy" (14:63–64; cf. m. Sanh. 7:5).[13] He calls for a vote: "What is your decision?" Then the votes are tallied: "And they all condemned him as deserving death" (**14:64**).

Jesus has claimed to be the Son of God and the Son of Man—the divine King. Leviticus 24:16 reads (cf. m. Sanh. 7:4–5), "Whoever blasphemes the name of the LORD shall surely be put to death." Case closed. But, sadly, court still in session. "And some began to spit on him and to cover his face and to strike him, saying to him, 'Prophesy!'[14] And the guards received him with blows" (**14:65**).

It is not just the violent mockery with which this trial ends that is disturbing. The whole trial from beginning to end is disturbing. This scene is painted "Pure Gloom" because of the injustice, the cruel brutality, the uncensored lies, and the blatant breaking of both God's law and the religious leaders' own laws. They have "neglected the weightier matters of the law," such as "justice and mercy" (Matt. 23:23), and failed to uphold God's clear command: "You shall not bear false witness" (Ex. 20:16).

More than that, their own rules for criminal court cases require that such trials be heard in the temple precincts, only during the day, and never over the Passover week. "All the evidence of innocence of the accused" must come prior to accusations against the defendant, and a guilty verdict must take at least two days to arrive at, "so that feelings of mercy might have time to arise."[15] Jesus' trial takes place at night in a private residence on the Passover week, with no defense offered on his behalf, and a guilty verdict is reached in likely less than an hour. This is a dark night in the soul of human civilization. Painted black.

Painted Gold: Jesus Confesses That He Is King

However, it is in this darkness that the light of the world reveals something of his glory. Jesus' confession that he is king (Mark 15:2) is painted gold—gold for glory. When Jesus answers, "I am, and you will see the Son of Man seated at the right hand of Power, and coming with the clouds of heaven" (14:62), he tells the world precisely who he is. In Mark 8:29 Jesus asked his disciples,

---

13 According to m. Sanh. 7:5 it was only using the divine name that was considered blasphemy. However, D. L. Bock has shown that the charge of "blasphemy" could embody "a whole range of actions offensive to God." *Blasphemy and Exaltation in Judaism: The Charge against Jesus in Mark 14:53–65* (Grand Rapids, MI: Baker, 1988), 111.

14 In their treatment of Jesus they actually fulfill both Isaiah's prophecy about the suffering servant (Isa. 50:6) and Jesus' own prophecy about himself (Mark 10:34).

15 Sections of m. Sanh. 4–7, as summarized by William Barclay, *The Gospel of Matthew*, 2 vols., rev. ed. (Philadelphia: Westminster, 1975), 2:353–54.

"Who do you say that I am?" Now on trial he will give his own answer to that question. First, he agrees that the title "Christ, Son of the Blessed" (14:61) is a correct designation. He is the Jewish Messiah who is also the divine Son of God (1:1; cf. 15:39), the divine Son—being both "the son of David" and David's "Lord" (see 12:35–37). His unique relationship with God was shown when he prayed "Abba, Father" (14:36) at Gethsemane and earlier when the Father—at Jesus' baptism and during his transfiguration—called him his "beloved Son" (1:11; 9:7). Jesus is, as earlier announced, "Jesus, Son of the Most High God" (5:7; cf. 3:11).

To Caiaphas's question, "Are you the Christ, the Son of the Blessed?" (14:61), Jesus first offers a clear reply: "I am" (14:62). He is the Christ. To claim as much is not blasphemous. What is blasphemous, according to this Jewish council, is to agree that "the Son of the Blessed" should be attached to it.[16] You see, with Jesus' "I am" he is basically claiming oneness with "I AM." That divine designation is made absolutely clear when he adds, "And you [plural] will see the Son of Man seated at the right hand of Power,[17] and coming with the clouds of heaven" (14:62).

This short sentence, following the admission before it, is enough to condemn Jesus of the crime of blasphemy, because Jesus claims not only to be the Son of Man of Daniel 7:13–14, this royal being who will rule over an everlasting kingdom (an extravagant claim!),[18] but to be equal to Yahweh, who is depicted as the judge of the world in Daniel 7:10. When Jesus speaks of himself as "the Son of Man seated at the right hand of Power," he is claiming equality with God (Ps. 110:1)—a share in God's reign. When he speaks of "coming with the clouds of heaven," he is speaking of himself as the Son of Man (Dan. 7:13), coming as the final judge. As Jesus said in Mark 8:38, when "he comes in the glory of his Father with the holy angels" he will judge that "adulterous and sinful generation" based on whether someone was for or against him and his words. The judged will be the Judge. Ah, the irony! "Jesus places his judges under the judgment of God, a judgment soon to descend upon them and entrusted to himself (cf. Matt. 23:39)."[19] No wonder Caiaphas needs a change of clothes.

Jesus is the high priest too. Mark makes that clear in Mark 14:53–65. Five times the phrase "the high priest" is used of Jesus' earthly judge (14:53, 54,

---

16 Jesus is not less than the Messiah, but he is more than the Messiah.
17 The ESV capitalizes "Power" to indicate that Jesus is speaking about God.
18 Remember, this would be the first time the high priest would have heard Jesus call himself by this title. He must have been as shocked as the scribes in Capernaum who heard Jesus say, "That you may know that the Son of Man has authority on earth to forgive sins" (Mark 2:10).
19 Rudolf Schnackenburg, *The Gospel of Matthew*, trans. Robert R. Barr (Grand Rapids, MI: Eerdmans, 2002), 277.

60, 61, 63). But, as Mark will make clear in chapter 15, Jesus is not only the highest priest imaginable; he is the greatest sacrifice ever made. He is the culmination of a million bulls, oxen, goats, lambs, and turtledoves.

Here the Jewish leaders scorn him as prophet and are oblivious to his office of priest. In the next scene the Roman soldiers will mock him as king. But Jesus is the prophet, priest, and king. As prophet, he fulfills the very predictions he made about his own passion: Judas' betrayal (14:18, 20–21; cf. 14:43–45), the disciples' desertion (14:27; cf. 14:50–52), Peter's denials (14:30; cf. 14:66–72), Jesus' deliverance into the hands of those who will sentence him to die (9:31; 10:33; 14:64; cf. 15:15), his contemptuous treatment (spitting, flogging, mocking; 9:12; 10:34; 14:65; cf. 15:15), and his rejection by the Jewish religious authorities (8:31; 12:1–12; cf. 14:53–65).

As prophet, he testifies to God's truth. As priest, he embodies the whole sacrificial system—temple, priest, altar, sacrifice. As king, he will return as cosmic ruler and judge of all.

So in this scene see the gold! The glory of Jesus. This trial is contemptible. Legally, all is out of order. But in God's grand providential plan of salvation all is perfectly in place. "The Deliverer in bonds; the Judge attained; the Prince of Glory scorned; the Holy One condemned for sin; the Son of God as a blasphemer; the Resurrection and the Life sentenced to die!"[20]

Painted Blue: Peter Denies Jesus

From that fine line of gold—the glory of Christ—that streaks through this dark portrait of the trial of Jesus, Mark adds another dark color. Blue. I say blue because Peter's trial ends in sorrow: "And he broke down and wept" (14:72).

But Peter is not just blue (sad); he is yellow (chicken). He is blue because he was yellow. But at first he wears a red badge of courage.[21] That is, Mark 14:66–72 begins by detailing Peter's presence at the trial of Jesus. As Jesus is on trial in a room above him, "Peter was below in the courtyard" (14:66). It takes courage for Peter, who ran for his life at Gethsemane (14:50), to sneak back into Jerusalem to be near Jesus. With his presence there he perhaps becomes the church's earwitness to the legal proceedings. Certainly he stands as the church's representative, not of fearless faith in the face of persecution but of this mixture of courage and fear, boldness and weakness, faith and doubt,

---

20 See Frederick Dale Bruner, *Matthew: A Commentary, Volume 2: The Churchbook, Matthew 13–28*, rev. ed. (Grand Rapids, MI: Eerdmans, 2007), 691.

21 Peter's "badge" of bravery is not a bloody wound, as in Stephen Crane's famous novel, but a bold statement.

loyalty and treason. By the time that rooster crows again, we should all see ourselves with Peter. Tearful. Remorseful. Blue. We can all sing that penetrating line from that great hymn of the faith:

> Who was the guilty? Who brought this upon Thee?
> Alas, my treason, Jesus, hath undone Thee;
> I crucified Thee.[22]

Let us look at that temporary treason, Peter's threefold denial. I will walk us through the text, pointing out a few key details (including Mark's literary artistry), and then we will conclude with a lesson we should learn and live out.

Peter's trial is set in "the *court*yard." The first witness against him is "one of the servant girls of the high priest" (**14:66**). Perhaps her duty is to add more charcoal into the fire. John tells us that she serves as a doorkeeper (she "kept watch at the door," John 18:16–17). Whatever her task that night, she comes into the courtyard (she "came") and notices a man "warming himself" by the fire (she sees Peter, Mark **14:67**). Then she does a double take ("She looked [stared] at him") and immediately announces, "You also were with the Nazarene, Jesus" (14:67). Peter's face gives him away. She likely saw him with Jesus when Jesus taught in the temple (11:15–12:44). By calling Jesus "the Nazarene" she is identifying which Jesus, of the thousands throughout Jerusalem, she is referencing. She is likely also maligning Jesus' homeland. It would be like a New Yorker' calling someone from Arkansas a "redneck."

Peter emphatically denies her declaration about him: "I neither know nor understand what you mean" (Mark **14:68**). Peter's denial is both dumbfounding and dumb. Why say that you do not understand the question? Whom are you fooling? Are you the only person in Jerusalem to know nothing of the buzz surrounding Jesus of Nazareth, the very man on trial in the house?

Peter wants out of this interrogation. He walks toward the exit ("And he went out into the gateway," 14:68). He is moving farther away from Jesus (both geographically and spiritually), but he has already moved closer to Jesus' prediction (14:30). The rooster's crow (14:68) should have jogged Peter's memory. Now would be the time to stop and pray.

However, this servant girl will not go away. She calls more witnesses to the stand. "And the servant girl saw him and began again to say to the bystanders, 'This man is one of them'" (**14:69**). Mark does not record what the bystanders think or say. But we know that Peter once "again . . . denied" (**14:70**) her

---

22 Robert Bridges, trans., "Ah, Holy Jesus, How Hast Thou Offended?" (1989).

accusation. If some of these "bystanders" are the men who arrested Jesus, one of whom Peter cut with his sword (John calls the bystanders "servants and officers" and mentions that one of them saw Peter "in the garden" and was related to "the man whose ear Peter had cut off"; John 18:18, 26), then he has every reason to fear. Matthew tells us the words of Peter's second denial. Peter says, "I do not know the man" (Matt. 26:72), similar to what he will say in the third denial (in both Matthew and Mark). Peter has moved farther away from Jesus. Instead of saying what he said a few months before (that Jesus is the Christ; see Mark 8:29), he denies the fact that he knows him. He has moved from pretended ignorance to complete disavowal.

Peter's trial continues. His refutation does not get him out of the dock. While a short recess (or reprieve!) is given, verses 70–71 tell us that court is back in session: "And after a little while the bystanders again said to Peter, 'Certainly you are one of them, for you are a Galilean.' But he began to invoke a curse on himself[23] and to swear, 'I do not know this man of whom you speak.'" It is remarkable that Peter will not even put Jesus' name to his lips. He does not say, "I don't know this Jesus of whom you speak." He calls Jesus "this man" (**14:71**). It is also remarkable that Peter invokes a curse upon himself. He says something like "I swear to God, I'm telling the truth. If I'm lying, may lightning strike me dead." Finally, it is remarkable that Peter, whose accent tells his accusers that he is from Galilee, claims he does not know the most popular man in Galilee. But he fools no one. His "accent betrays" him (Matt. 26:73).

Peter's third denial is "immediately" met with the fulfillment of Jesus' Last Supper prediction: "The rooster crowed a second time" (Mark **14:72**). Only then is Peter's mind jogged: "And Peter remembered how Jesus had said to him, 'Before the rooster crows twice, you will deny me three times.' And he broke down and wept" (14:72). How fitting that a rooster, a creature known for its "cocky" strutting, reminds Peter of his own foolish boast (14:29).

Notice the irony. While Jesus stands strong and "calm in the midst of terrible opposition" from Israel's leading men, Peter cowardly collapses under the "flimsiest of pressures" from a servant girl and some bystanders.[24] While Jesus is being slapped and spit upon and mocked as a false prophet, his prophecy about Peter is fulfilled. As Jesus, who will soon be lifted up on a tree (and will

---

23 The phrase "on himself" is not in the Greek. Thus it is possible that Peter is cursing them, something along the lines of "Go to hell for making such accusations against me! I swear to you I do not know the man."

24 Osborne, *Mark*, 280–81.

one day come in the clouds!), testifies to the truth, so Peter, the rock (with all his lies), reaches rock bottom.

Capturing the Final Color

Having seen all the details of Peter's denials, let us conclude with four lessons from this sad moment in his life. First, we should take Proverbs 16:18 to heart: "Pride goes before destruction, and a haughty spirit before a fall." At the Last Supper Peter boasted in his bravery and resilience: "Even though they all fall away, I will not" (Mark 14:29). What a sad line. In one packed-with-pride pronouncement he contradicts Jesus, is condescending toward his friends, and is overly self-confident. Here, before the rooster gives its first morning crow, "Peter hollers like a high-pitched peacock."[25] In front of the disciples he builds himself up by cutting them down. "They might fall away. But I most certainly won't!" Then, a short time later, they all are emphatic about their allegiance to Jesus, but it is Peter who is the first to say, "If I must die with you, I will not deny you" (14:31). Watch out for pride. It is Peter's downfall here; it can be our undoing as well.

Second, let us remember that discipleship is demanding. The servant girl accuses Peter of being "with . . . Jesus" (Mark 14:67). What a wonderful thing for which to be known (Acts 4:13). But Peter gets cold feet while he warms his hands, just as many of us cower at the watercooler. Let us help one another to stand strong. Let us not be "ashamed of the gospel, *for* it is the power of God for salvation to everyone who believes" (Rom. 1:16). The life-changing power of God can come to someone only if a preacher is sent and that preacher (even at the watercooler or around the firepit) speaks up for Jesus. Be bold. Identify yourself as a disciple of Jesus. Share your faith. Defend your faith. And be willing to suffer for your faith. To share Christ's sufferings is the call of the Christian disciple (Mark 8:34; Col. 1:24).

Third, true repentance brings genuine restoration. With the description of Peter's tears ("And he broke down and wept," Mark 14:72) Mark speaks of Peter's sorrowful repentance and also hints at Peter's restoration. Both Matthew and Luke add the details that Peter bolted for the gate, ran off into the night, found a quiet place, and bawled his eyes out ("And he went out and wept bitterly," Matt. 26:75; Luke 22:62), and Luke adds Jesus' glare from feet away ("He turned and looked at Peter," Luke 22:61) as the likely impetus to Peter's remembrance, remorse, and future repentance. Mark leaves his readers with

---

25 Douglas Sean O'Donnell, *Matthew: All Authority under Heaven*, PTW (Wheaton, IL: Crossway, 2013), 786.

the impression that Peter might have offered a public repentance, namely that, as soon as the rooster crowed a second time, Peter remembered and then repented then and there in front of his accusers.

Whatever camera lens we take on Peter at this point, here with his tears he returns to Jesus' first words in the Gospel of Mark: "Repent and believe in the gospel" (Mark 1:15). Jesus knew Peter would do this. He promised his disciples that, after his resurrection, he would return to them and they to him. He would meet with them again in Galilee (14:28). This is why the angel in the empty tomb tells the women, "Go, tell his disciples *and Peter* that [Jesus] is going before you to Galilee" (16:7). Moreover, we know from the end of John's Gospel that Peter is personally restored and from the book of Acts that God will use Peter's public proclamations about Jesus, despite all the persecutions he endures, to spread the good news and establish the church. "Filled with the Holy Spirit," Peter speaks "the word of God with boldness" (Acts 4:31; cf. Acts 4:13). Look, if you have denied Jesus, not only is there hope for a restored relationship with God; there is the hope of future years of fruitful ministry. If God can use Peter, he can use ragamuffins like us as well.

The fourth and final lesson is the most important. Mark's candid retelling of Peter's personal testimony[26] of temporary apostasy clearly teaches us the absolute need for Jesus' atoning death. Peter's last line in the Gospel of Mark is "I do not know this man" (Mark 14:71). If you walk away from this Gospel thinking, "I'm so glad I have St. Peter to welcome me into heaven and help me find the path there," you are not reading the same Gospel I am reading. Peter might have come to Caiaphas's palace because he hoped to save Jesus, but that very night he would learn what he would preach till his death: "There is salvation in *no one else*, for there is *no other name* under heaven given among men by which we must be saved" (Acts 4:12).

Please note that in the final chapter of Jesus' life everyone around him acts so evilly: his own people reject and condemn him, the Romans torture him, one of the twelve betrays him, the chief apostle denies him, not one friend will stick by him till the end. Why? Because he alone will atone for the sins of "many" (Mark 10:45), even most of his "apostate apostles" and some of those "blasphemous bystanders, taunting thieves, and . . . flesh-whipping Roman soldiers."[27]

---

26   If the tradition is true that Peter was the primary source for Mark's Gospel, then he must have told this story of his failure to the Evangelist.
27   O'Donnell, *Matthew*, 790.

The Condemnation of the King

MARK 15:1-15

Pilate asked him, "Are you the King of the Jews?" And he
answered him, "You have said so."
Mark 15:2

Pastor Paul is the chairman of our Shepherding Committee, a group that provides care and accountability for all the pastors in the Chicago Metro Presbytery of my denomination. Each Sunday morning he sends to this group of
pastors an encouraging text message. When I preached on part of the Olivet
Discourse, he sent this:

> Brother, here's a morning riddle for you. What is the only global and
> historical institution that has and still causes Satan and the demonic
> realm to tremble? It meets all around the globe today. Some meet in
> grand cathedrals and others in secret locations. Some are found in urban
> areas and others in rural areas. Last clue, all answer the question of the
> unclean spirit to Jesus, "Have you come to destroy us?" (Mark 1:24) with
> an emphatic, "Yes! You got it!"

Before I preached on Mark 14:53–72, Pastor Paul sent a quote from Robert
Capon: "The Gospel—the Good News of our Lord and Savior, Jesus Christ, is
the astonishing announcement that God has done the whole work of reconciliation without a scrap of human assistance." That morning, as I prepared
to preach, I thought, "What a perfect summary!" For who left last chapter
thinking that Peter was the hero? Who thought, "If I am to be acceptable before God, I need to obey Jesus' commands perfectly"? No one, I hope. Rather,
I hope we walked away with gratitude for Jesus. I hope we are thankful that
the coming judge would be arrested and falsely accused for us, that the glorious Son of God would be condemned as a blasphemer for us, and that the

creator of all life would be sentenced to die for us. And I hope, as we come to this chapter, that we will walk away with an even deeper sense of gratitude for Jesus, who (as we shall see) is the true king, the innocent king, and yet the suffering king who suffers in our place to set us free from our sin and God's holy judgment against sinners.

The True King

I am homing in on this theme of Jesus as king because three times in our text Pilate calls Jesus "the King of the Jews" (Mark 15:2, 9, 12)[1] and because, as we saw last chapter, Jesus said he was "the Christ" and not only called himself "the Son of Man" (14:62) in reference to the divine king featured in Daniel's prophecy (Dan. 7:13–14) but also claimed that he would be "seated at the right hand of Power," an allusion to sitting on the throne next to God (Ps. 110:1) on judgment day.

So obviously the Sanhedrin took Jesus' religious claims of being the Christ, the Son of Man, and also the Son of God and turned them into a political pronouncement. To Pilate, the Roman governor of Judea, they said something simple like, "Jesus claims that he is the King of the Jews." Rome would take such a claim quite seriously, for anyone claiming to be a king in light of Caesar's lordship would be considered treasonous or seditious. In light of those facts, Pilate was willing to take an early wake-up call: "And as soon as it was morning, the chief priests held a consultation with the elders and scribes and the whole council. And they bound Jesus and led him away and delivered him over to Pilate" (**15:1**).

I get tired just reading this verse. I rarely miss a night of sleep. I do not, and never did, pull all-nighters. I would not be able to function the next day. The quorum that made this ungodly and unlawful decision to condemn Jesus must have stayed up all night. Jesus certainly stayed up all night, likely on his feet for most of it. Remember when he fell asleep on the boat because he was so tired. I imagine he was so tired here as well. (Oh how he loved us!) Then, as the cocks were crowing at the morning sunlight ("and as soon as it was morning," 15:1; "early morning," John 18:28), the most powerful man in town got a knock on his bedroom door.[2] Pilate, who was appointed directly by the emperor

1 In the next pericope Jesus is also mocked as "the Christ" (15:32) and "the King of the Jews" (15:18, 26, 32). "Though the titles are meant to mock and deride Jesus, ironically they are true, since Jesus is the messianic King who will enter into his royal glory through suffering and death." Mark L. Strauss, *Mark*, ZECNT (Grand Rapids, MI: Zondervan, 2014), 675.

2 It is possible that Pilate's headquarters were stationed in Herod Antipas's palace. This would be a safe and fitting place and would explain how both Pilate and Herod could see Jesus in the same morning (see Luke 23:6–12).

Tiberius Caesar, served as the prefect of Judea from AD 26 to 36. He governed a volatile region of the world. Likely one of his servants informed him that the high priest, sometime around midnight, had held a trial in his home and that a guilty verdict had been rendered against Jesus of Nazareth. Then this servant also informed him that "the chief priests held a consultation with the elders and scribes and the whole council" (every member of the Sanhedrin)[3] and had collectively decided to handcuff Jesus ("And they bound Jesus") and take him from Caiaphas's house to Pilate's headquarters ("And [they] led him away and delivered him over to Pilate," Mark 15:1). Jesus was delivered to Pilate because, at this point in Jewish history, "it [was] unlawful for [them] to put anyone to death" (John 18:31). He was also delivered to Pilate because Jesus had predicted that his own people would deliver him over to the Gentiles (Mark 10:33; cf. 9:31).

This is a nightmare for Pilate. His job in Jerusalem is to care about the Jews' religious squabbles. So he will take the Sanhedrin seriously. "But what is the big problem today?" he must be wondering in these early hours. What on earth could be so important as to wake him now? Jesus is the problem, and their problem is now his problem.

But what is the problem with Jesus? Pilate will find out. Picture the scene. Pilate has changed from his overnight attire into his military garb. He looks powerful and regal. He walks "outside" of the headquarters because Jews would not enter a Gentile's house lest they "be defiled" (John 18:28–29). He sees a commoner who has been dressed "in splendid clothing" (Luke 23:11), something Herod did to mock Jesus as king. (According to Luke's Gospel Jesus first went to Herod, then Pilate.) Pilate asks the Jewish leaders, "What accusation do you bring against this man?" (John 18:29). They detail the crime of sedition.

Now read along with me in Mark's account and see what really wakes him up!

> And Pilate asked him, "Are you the King of the Jews?" And he answered him, "You have said so." And the chief priests accused him of many things. And Pilate again asked him, "Have you no answer to make? See how many charges they bring against you." But Jesus made no further answer, so that Pilate was amazed. (Mark **15:2–5**)

Pilate does not rend his garments, but I imagine he adjusts them.

---

3 The word "their" in the phrase "after making their plans" (Mark 15:1) likely refers to the smaller council that met the night before.

Again, picture this. Pilate walks into the room. He asks an adviser, "What is the crime?" His adviser whispers, "This Jew claims to be a king." "Very well," says Pilate. "Let me see this king." Jesus is brought to him. Our Lord's face is bruised with blows to the head. He has dark skin from walking so much in the sun, a common black beard, and perhaps long, disheveled hair. Imagine him short like David, not tall like Saul. He looks harmless. He looks tired too. He does not look like a king. He is not an apparent threat to Rome or Pilate's personal power. So Pilate sits down in his chair of judgment. He asks his question. He wants to be official. He also wants to mock Jesus and embarrass the Jewish leaders. "Are *you* the King of the Jews?" (15:2). This question is so ridiculous to him. He, a king?

Unexpectedly, Jesus actually answers! "You have said so" (15:2). What a twist this is. Pilate sits up in his chair. Jesus tells him that he has unwittingly declared the truth: "You, governor, on your own lips, said the word 'king' in relation to me. That is right." Our Lord might also be thinking, "That is close to calling me by the right name. Next time use 'Son of God' and 'Son of Man' when you address me."[4] No wonder Pilate is "amazed" (15:5) at the end of this discussion. He is likely amazed here and now in this drama.

Next, to get Pilate's mind back on track—on his essential duty to keep the peace—the chief priests chime in. They "accused [Jesus] of many things" (15:3). They have their accusations prepared: "This man said he wants to destroy the temple; he claims that he is a king; he teaches that he, not Caesar, is Lord."[5] Pilate takes these accusations seriously, in addition to whatever other ones they drum up ("many charges," 15:4). His main task is to keep the peace—the peace that then exists between Rome and the Jews who live under Roman occupation. So a second question arises: "And Pilate again asked him, 'Have you no answer to make? See how many charges they bring against you'" (15:4).

Picture a long pause here. Perhaps a repeated authoritative question: "Have you no answer to make?" (15:4). But Jesus does not budge. He makes "no further answer," something that absolutely astonishes Pilate ("so that Pilate

---

4   John tells us that at some point in their discussion Jesus offers this jaw-dropping declaration to Pilate: "You would have no authority over me at all unless it had been given you from above" (John 19:11).

5   In Luke's version we read: "And they began to accuse him, saying, 'We found this man misleading our nation and forbidding us to give tribute to Caesar, and saying that he himself is Christ, a king'" (Luke 23:2), and later, "He stirs up the people, teaching throughout all Judea, from Galilee even to this place" (Luke 23:5). John adds the accusation that Jesus "has made himself the Son of God" (John 19:7). "In the larger context of Mark's gospel, we can think of other possible charges: violating the law of Moses ([Mark] 3:2, 6) and encouraging others to do so (2:24), disrupting and defiling temple worship (11:18, 28), threatening the temple's destruction (13:2; 15:38), and undermining religious authority (12:1–12)" (Strauss, *Mark*, 675–76).

was amazed," 15:5).[6] Pilate is likely amazed that Jesus offers no defense.[7] He will remain amazed, I imagine, later, as he will offer Jesus' freedom, "Do you want me to release for you the King of the Jews?" (15:9), only to hear that the Jewish crowd prefers the violent criminal "Barabbas instead" (15:11). Then he will be utterly amazed to hear them twice chant "Crucify him" (15:13, 14) to his question, "What shall I do with the man you call the King of the Jews?" (15:12). Now, at this point let us just say that Pilate is having a bad day at the office, and he has not even had his morning coffee.

Pilate does not really believe that Jesus is a king. He mocks Jesus with the title here, and he will mock him again when "the inscription" above Jesus' head on the cross reads "The King of the Jews" (15:26). The Jews here will not accept that title for Jesus. They will not acknowledge him, especially in his present condition, as their Christ. But, here, as the rulers of the Romans and the Jews rage against God's anointed and plot to have him killed (Ps. 2:1–2), we should stop and pause to bow before Jesus—to kiss God's only begotten Son (Ps. 2:7, 12) and to seek to serve him "with fear, and [to] rejoice with trembling" (Ps. 2:11) as we "take refuge in him" (Ps. 2:12) from God's coming wrath against all who oppose his anointed (Ps. 2:5).

The Innocent King

Jesus is the true king. He is king of the Jews. He is King of kings and Lord of lords. He is the one to whom "every knee should bow, in heaven and on earth and under the earth, and every tongue confess that Jesus Christ is Lord" (Phil. 2:10–11). Do you believe that? And do you live right now like he is Lord of all?[8]

Jesus is the true king. He is also the innocent king.

Pilate knows that Jesus is innocent of all criminal charges. This is why he seeks Jesus' release (John 19:4, 12). It is clear that he offers the crowd Jesus over Barabbas. He thinks "that it was out of envy that the chief priests had delivered him up" (Mark 15:10). He thinks, in other words, that the religious leaders' personal issues will not be shared by the people. The leaders are jealous of Jesus, but the people, as far as he knows,[9] esteem Jesus. Surely they

---

6   Elsewhere (Mark 1:22, 27; 2:12; 5:15, 20, 42; 6:2, 51; 7:37; 11:18; 12:17, 37) Mark records *amazement* as the response to Jesus' teachings or miracles.

7   "Great is the contrast between the second Adam and the first! Our first father Adam was guilty, and yet tried to excuse himself. The second Adam was guiltless, and yet made no defense at all." J. C. Ryle, *Expository Thoughts on Mark*, quoted in *CHSB*, 1502.

8   As Strauss (*Mark*, 680) exhorts, if we are "to acknowledge Jesus as our [true] king . . . [we must] place ourselves in absolute submission to his will, to turn our lives over to his service, and to make him Lord of our lives."

9   As readers of Mark's Gospel, we can safely assume that news of Jesus has reached the highest authorities in Jerusalem (see Luke 23:8; cf. Mark 6:14). He is so popular (on the theme see esp. 1:33; 2:2, 4; 3:7–9; 4:1; 5:21, 24; 11:8) that even slave girls know of him (14:67).

will want their relatable rabbi and miracle worker returned to them, for there are so many new teachings to learn and bodies to be healed.[10] But Pilate underestimates two things: (1) the chief priests are working the crowds ("But the chief priests stirred up the crowd to have him release for them Barabbas instead," 15:11) and (2) the people now see the rebel Barabbas, someone "who had committed murder in the insurrection" (15:7), as the type of leader they desire most. Like Barabbas and his band of rebels, here we see Israel edging toward its near future—a military rebellion against Rome.

Pilate testifies to Jesus' innocence in that he seeks Jesus' release. Pilate testifies to Jesus' innocence also when he says to the crowd that calls for Jesus' crucifixion, "Why? What evil has he done?" Strauss is right in suggesting that the verb "[Pilate] said" in verse 14 takes on "an iterative imperfect" sense,[11] meaning, "Pilate kept asking." He kept asking, "Why? What evil has he done?" Thus imagine the crowd's voice is growing louder and louder, "Crucify him!" while Pilate's voice grows quieter and quieter, "Why? What evil has he done?"

In the other Gospels this theme of Jesus' innocence is even more pronounced. For example, in Matthew's record of this event, as Pilate is sitting on the judgment seat and offering to release one of the two criminals (Matt. 27:17, 19), Pilate's wife sends him word, "Have nothing to do with that righteous man" (Matt. 27:19). Pilate also washes "his hands before the crowd, saying, 'I am innocent of this man's blood'" (Matt. 27:24) to shift the legal blame from himself to the crowd, a culpability that the crowd readily embraces. In Luke and John Pilate declares, "I find no guilt in this man" (Luke 23:4; "I find no guilt in him," John 18:38; 19:4, 6) and also "After examining him before you, behold, I did not find this man guilty of any of your charges against him. . . . Look, nothing deserving death has been done by him" (Luke 23:14–15).

As all the Gospels attest, Pilate knows Jesus is innocent of all criminal charges. And we, of course, know that Jesus is completely innocent of all sin. We believe the biblical testimony of Hebrews 4:15, 1 Peter 2:22, and 2 Corinthians 5:21, where we read that Jesus who was "in every respect . . . tempted as we are, yet without sin," that "he committed no sin," and that he "knew no sin."

We also have the doctrine of Jesus' sinless life in story form in the Gospels. In Mark, for example, we see John the Baptist's hesitancy to baptize Jesus prefaced by his statement that he is unworthy even to "stoop down and untie" a strap from Jesus' sandals (Mark 1:7) and followed by God's voice of approval,

---

10 When Jesus first arrived in Jerusalem the religious authorities wanted to arrest him, but they did not because they "feared the people" (Mark 12:12), namely, that the crowd was on Jesus' side.

11 Strauss, *Mark*, 679.

"You are my beloved Son; with you I am well pleased" (1:11). Jesus alone pleases God perfectly. Jesus alone resisted the devil perfectly, from his early temptation in the wilderness (1:12) to his later temptations to take the crown without the cross (8:32). Jesus alone obeyed both God's law and his own new commandments perfectly. He loved God. He loved his neighbor. He loved even his enemies.

Finally, at the transfiguration Jesus' holiness literally came to light. On the mountain his body "transfigured" so that something of his inward divine nature shown forth outwardly: "His clothes became radiant, intensely white, as no one on earth could bleach them" (9:2–3). As "God is light, and in him is no darkness at all" (1 John 1:5), so that day Jesus showed that the light shared only by the Father and Spirit was shared by him in bodily form. "He is the radiance of the glory of God and the exact imprint of his nature" (Heb. 1:3). He is holy, holy, holy. He is the absolutely innocent king.

The Suffering King

First, Jesus is the true king. Second, he is the innocent king. Third, he is the suffering king.

In Mark 8–9 Jesus predicted that he "must suffer many things" (8:31; 9:12). In chapters 14–15 those sufferings take center stage. He is betrayed, denied, and abandoned by the twelve. Imagine the internal angst of such infidelity. He is also arrested, falsely accused, rejected, condemned, mocked, spit on, and hit by the Jewish authorities. Imagine him "treated with [such] contempt" (9:12). Then he was teased, scourged, and crucified by the Romans. Imagine enduring such horrific pain. He was forsaken even by his Father: "My God, my God, why have you forsaken me?" (15:34). Imagine the unimaginable.

Jesus is the suffering king.

But his sufferings are not in vain. And that is nowhere more plain than after he breathes his last breath "and the curtain of the temple was torn in two, from top to bottom" (15:38), and here in **15:6–15** as a notorious criminal is released and, in his place, innocent Jesus is sentenced to death.

The Jews think that a released Barabbas could help their cause—the hope of freedom from the bondage of Roman oppression. That backfires as that generation and the next, some thirty years later, is nearly obliterated by the Roman army when Jerusalem's temple is destroyed. Those who live by the sword die by it. But we know, both now and then, that those who call out to Jesus for their emancipation from their slavery to sin will find their salvation through his sufferings. Jesus suffers in our place to set us free from the judgment we truly deserve due to our sins against God.

Let me show you that great doctrine of the great exchange here in story form. Read verses 6–15, then I will explain this text and apply it.

> Now at the feast [Passover] he [Pilate] used to release for them [the Jews] one prisoner for whom they asked. And among the rebels in prison, who had committed murder in the insurrection, there was a man called Barabbas. And the crowd came up and began to ask Pilate to do as he usually did for them. And he answered them, saying, "Do you want me to release for you the King of the Jews?" For he perceived that it was out of envy that the chief priests had delivered him up. But the chief priests stirred up the crowd to have him release for them Barabbas instead. And Pilate again said to them, "Then what shall I do with the man you call the King of the Jews?" And they cried out again, "Crucify him." And Pilate said to them, "Why? What evil has he done?" But they shouted all the more, "Crucify him." So Pilate, wishing to satisfy the crowd, released for them Barabbas, and having scourged Jesus, he delivered him to be crucified.

Notice two key details. First, these verses feature some major sinners. Pilate is cruel. He is not threatened by Jesus. He does not actually believe that Jesus is a king who threatens Roman rule. So why execute an innocent man by means of scourging (what a terrible thing to do) and crucifixion (even more terrible)? Pilate is also an unscrupulous people pleaser. Instead of upholding Roman law and common sense he agrees to release a criminal and sentences an innocent man to death. May that phrase "wishing to satisfy the crowd" (15:15) never be said of us. We might finally say that Pilate is "a ruthless pragmatist, who sees the direction of the tide and rides along."[12] That is, he thinks to himself as the crowd screams its verdict at him, "What is the death of yet another self-professing Jewish messiah? It is far better to kill this commoner than to aggravate the Jewish establishment and face a riot during the Passover." This, he thinks, can be a political win in two ways: (1) the crowd will be pleased if he gives it its zealot warrior, and (2) the religious elite will be thrilled to know that, with Jesus soon dead and gone, they will quickly resume their proper authoritative place in the lives of their parishioners.

Pilate is not alone in his crimes. The crowd sins as well. *Sin* seems too weak a word. When Jesus first arrived in Jerusalem, the religious authorities wanted to arrest Jesus, but they did not because they "feared the people"

---

12 Strauss, *Mark*, 679.

(12:12), namely, that the crowd was on Jesus' side. How quickly the populace has turned on Jesus. To go from shouting "Hosanna! Blessed is he who comes in the name of the Lord!" (11:9) to their horrific repetition, "Crucify him" (15:13, 14) is remarkable.[13] Where does this change of mind come from? From their own religious leaders—those who "out of envy . . . delivered" Jesus to Pilate (15:10) and who out of hatred and hardness of heart "stirred up the crowd" to turn on Jesus (15:11). But it also came from the pit of hell. The father of lies! To want a fellow Jew—someone who taught new and life-changing truths about God's kingdom and performed signs to validate his teachings, including opening the eyes of the blind and raising the dead to life—to die by Roman crucifixion can come only from the darkest underbelly of the underworld.

Then, joining the Roman governor and the Jewish crowd and its leaders in the lineup of sinners that stand before us in this story is Barabbas. Mark describes him as a "rebel" (15:7; "a notorious prisoner," Matt. 27:16). Barabbas' crime is detailed in Mark 15:7: he "committed murder in the insurrection." He was a freedom fighter, or what we usually call a "terrorist." The two men crucified next to Jesus were called "robbers" (15:27), but they would be better labeled—as, for example, the NLT renders the term—"revolutionaries."[14] They, like Barabbas, were violent insurrectionists who wanted to overthrow Roman rule.[15] In fact, it is possible that Barabbas was the ringleader and that the very cross that Jesus will hang on, between these two men, was intended for Barabbas.

First, notice that these verses feature some major sinners. Do you see these sinners?

Second, with that said, notice Jesus dies *in the place of* an infamous sinner. "So Pilate . . . released for them Barabbas, and. . . . delivered [Jesus] to be crucified" (15:15).

With angry shouts they have my dear Lord done away;
A murderer they save, the Prince of Life they slay!

13 It is likely that the crowd who shouted "Hosanna!" at the triumphal entry were Galileans and that the majority of the crowd who shouted "Crucify him" were Judeans. However, it is unlikely that there were no Galilean Jews in that crowd before Pilate.
14 "Barabbas is also called a λῃστάς in John 18:10, as are the two men crucified with Jesus in Mark 15:27." Rodney J. Decker, *Mark 9–16: A Handbook on the Greek Text* (Waco, TX: Baylor University Press, 2014), 239.
15 We might say that these men were both robbers (street thieves) and rebels (armed political fighters) and that they did anything they could—kill and steal from the rich Romans and pro-Roman Jews as they traveled to and from Jerusalem to Jericho, as well as literally fight against Roman soldiers—to topple the enemy.

Yet willingly He bears the shame
That through His name all might be free.[16]

Jesus dies in the stead of "Barabbas," an Aramaic name that means "son [bar] of a father [abbas]." Embrace the sweet irony. Jesus the Son of the Father dies in the place of this other son of a father. But also embrace the gospel in story form. Barabbas's Passover amnesty is now ours! Listen to the apostolic chorus. Paul writes, "While we were still weak, at the right time Christ died for the ungodly. For one will scarcely die for a righteous person—though perhaps for a good person one would dare even to die—but God shows his love for us in that while we were still sinners, Christ died for us" (Rom. 5:6–8). And Peter echoes, "Christ also suffered once for sins, the righteous for the unrighteous, that he might bring us to God" (1 Pet. 3:18). Or listen to words from the Gospel of Mark mixed with those from Isaiah 53: Jesus was scourged and crucified ("despised," "rejected," "stricken," "smitten," "afflicted," Isa. 53:3–10) "for our transgressions . . . for our iniquities" (Isa. 53:5). His scourging brought us healing, his crucifixion "peace" (Isa. 53:5). The guilty man was released, the innocent condemned because God's judgment for sinners fell on Jesus: "The LORD has laid on him the iniquity of us all" (Isa. 53:6; cf. Isa. 53:11–12). The true and innocent King through his sufferings for the guilty sets us free—free from the power and punishment due our sin. Let us not only listen to these gospel declarations but sing them:

My song is love unknown,
My Savior's love to me;
Love to the loveless show,
That they might lovely be.

O who am I,
That for my sake
My Lord should take
Frail flesh, and die?[17]

Be Reconciled to God!

This chapter began with my sharing what my friend Paul texts to all the pastors in our presbytery. I shared only the first part of what he sent the week

16 Samuel Crossman, "My Song Is Love Unknown" (1584).
17 Crossman, "My Song Is Love Unknown."

I preached this text: "The Gospel—the Good News of our Lord and Savior, Jesus Christ, is the astonishing announcement that God has done the whole work of reconciliation without a scrap of human assistance." Following that quote he ended with his own exhortation: "Brother, make a passionate and clear appeal to your listeners to be reconciled to God (2 Cor. 5:14–21). As you do this, announce this Good News with the punctuation of the exclamation point of praise!"

My appeal to you is just that, an appeal mixed with praise, or an appeal founded upon praise. I will preach to you the good news because it is good news! If you are not now reconciled to God, you can be. How? Through acknowledging that you are a sinner in need of a Savior and by bowing before the King—the true king, the innocent king, the suffering king—who rules like a lion because he gave himself for us as a sacrificial lamb (see Rev. 5:5–6) and who thus deserves our loudest praise. Let us shout,

> Worthy is the Lamb who was slain,
> to receive power and wealth and wisdom and might
> and honor and glory and blessing! (Rev. 5:12)

Perfect Mockery

MARK 15:16–32

And the soldiers led him away inside the palace (that is, the governor's headquarters), and they called together the whole battalion. And they clothed him in a purple cloak, and twisting together a crown of thorns, they put it on him. And they began to salute him, "Hail, King of the Jews!"
Mark 15:16–18

Often when I preach I create "Sermon Notes for Children." I know that some adults in the congregation, who seek to enter the kingdom by becoming like little children, use the notes as well. The notes are to help the young—and old—follow along with the sermon, to provide the structure of my outline, and to make sure the main points are understood and embraced.

For example, in my sermon on Mark 15:1–15 I divided the text into three sections: "The True King," "The Innocent King," and "The Suffering King." Under the heading "The True King" I asked a few questions, such as, "In what three verses in Mark 15:1–15 does Pilate call Jesus a king?" The answer is verses 2, 9, and 12. Under the heading "The Innocent King" I gave this multiple choice: "We know that Pilate thinks that Jesus is innocent because (a) he seeks to release Jesus; (b) he says to the crowd, "What evil has he done?"; (c) in John's Gospel, Pilate says, "I find no guilt in him"; or (d) all of the above. What is the right answer? All of the above. Under the heading "The Suffering King" the first question I asked was this: "Jesus suffered much! What is the one thing below he did *not* suffer?" I listed arrest, betrayal, denial, false accusation, teasing, broken bones, spit on his face, hitting, whipping, forsakenness by God, crucifixion. The answer is broken bones. Jesus' bones were not broken—which means that Jesus was arrested, betrayed, denied, falsely accused, teased, spit upon, hit, whipped, God-forsaken, and crucified.

The final questions I asked were, "Is Jesus your personal Savior? Is he your King?" I do not know what everyone wrote down. But I did look at what my youngest daughter wrote. In capital letters (the only capitals in all her notes) she wrote "YES," followed by an exclamation point (which, of course, made my heart brim with joy).

My primary goal in preaching is that each and every man, woman, and child would say "YES!" to Jesus as his or her personal Savior and Lord. My other regular goal is that we would all—congregants and commentary readers alike—know whom we are saying yes to. Who is Jesus, what has he done for us, and what does it mean to call him Savior and Lord? Mark once again helps us. Building on this theme of Jesus as king, as well as narrowing in on one part of Jesus' sufferings—his mockery—Mark uses irony to paint a picture of the only king worthy of our bowing before and embracing.

The Roman Soldiers Mocked Him

I have titled this sermon "Perfect Mockery" because Jesus is mocked by four groups of people in twelve different ways.[1] He is "mocked" (15:20) by the Roman soldiers (15:16–27), "derided" by "those who passed by" (15:29) beneath the foot of the cross (15:29–30), "mocked" (15:31) by "the chief priests with the scribes" (15:31–32a), and even "reviled" by "those who were crucified with him" (15:32b).

The first to mock Jesus are the Roman soldiers. They mock him as king in nine different ways. Read **15:16–27** along with me and notice (I will help you notice) that the soldiers are the subject of each sentence.

> And *the soldiers* led [Jesus] away inside the palace (that is, the governor's headquarters), and *they* called together the whole battalion. And *they* [1] clothed him in a purple cloak, and twisting together a crown of thorns, *they* [2] put it on him. And *they* began to [3] salute him, "Hail, King of the Jews!" And *they* were [4] striking his head with a reed and spitting on him and [5] kneeling down in homage to him. And when *they* had mocked him, they stripped him of the purple cloak and put his own clothes on him. And *they* led him out to crucify him.

1   The soldiers mock Jesus by (1) clothing him in purple, (2) placing a crown of thorns upon his head, (3) saluting him, (4) striking him with a reed-made scepter, (5) bowing before him, (6) offering him mixed wine, (7) dividing his clothing/crucifying him without his clothing, (8) placing the inscription "The King of the Jews" above his cross, and (9) placing his cross between two criminals. Then (10) those passing by the cross deride him, (11) the Jewish religious authorities mock him, and (12) those crucified beside Jesus revile him.

And *they* compelled a passerby, Simon of Cyrene, who was coming in
from the country, the father of Alexander and Rufus, to carry his cross.
And *they* brought him to the place called Golgotha (which means Place
of a Skull). And *they* [6] offered him wine mixed with myrrh, but he did
not take it. And *they* crucified him and [7] divided his garments among
them, casting lots for them, to decide what each should take. And it was
the third hour when *they* crucified him. And [8] the inscription of the
charge against him read, "The King of the Jews." And with him *they* [9]
crucified two robbers, one on his right and one on his left.

Other than one subject/verb (the clause "But he did not take it," 15:23, related
to Jesus' refusing to drink the mixed wine), every verb has as its subject the
Roman soldiers, and nearly every action involves their mocking Jesus.

After Jesus is sentenced "to be crucified" (15:15), a few Roman soldiers take
Jesus back inside Pilate's headquarters. Their task is to crucify him. To expedite
death by crucifixion the Romans would first scourge criminals. Mark does not
give the gruesome details, but we know from other historical documents that
victims "would be stripped and their hands tied above their head," and "a whip
of leather cords with pieces of bone, lead, or glass imbedded in them would be
used," thus causing "severe lacerations not only to the skin but also to muscle
tissue and bone." We also know that "such scourging was [so] incredibly severe" that it could even result in death. We do not know how many times Jesus
was whipped. "The Jews limited scourges to forty lashes, but the Romans had
no such limitations."[2] But we do know that he must have been near death, as he
was unable to carry his own cross for long (see John 19:17), and he died after
only six hours (Mark 15:25, 33, 34). Mark may have some symbolic meaning
attached to Simon the Cyrene's carrying Jesus' cross; in Jesus' own teaching, all
who want to follow him must pick up the cross. But Mark certainly attaches
historical value to what is recorded in verse 21. A real man from the crowd,
someone named Simon—who was from Cyrene (near modern-day Shahhat,
Libya) and came to Jerusalem with his sons, Alexander and Rufus—carried
Jesus' crossbeam[3] "to the place called Golgotha" (15:22), less than a mile from
Pilate's headquarters. If Simon traveled from his North African country, he
would have walked over 1,100 miles to get to Jerusalem for the Passover, an
estimated 360 hours of travel. I doubt, on that day before the holy day, that he
could have ever imagined that he would add this extra leg to his long journey.

2   Mark L. Strauss, *Mark*, ZECNT (Grand Rapids, MI: Zondervan, 2014), 679–80.
3   Likely Simon carried the *patibulum* (a crossbeam) that would then be attached to the *palus* (a
    vertical pole) at the crucifixion site.

Before that happened (before the soldiers "lead [Jesus] out [of the head-quarters] to crucify him," 15:20) Jesus was first mocked inside Pilate's palace. We are told in verse 16 that a Roman battalion used the criminal charge against Jesus to mock him. Not only did they kneel down before him (15:19) and "salute him" (15:18) with both their spit and their scoffing, "Hail, King of the Jews!" (15:18); they also clad him like a king (with "a purple cloak"[4] as his royal robe and a tiara of thorns as his crown, 15:17). Finally "they . . . mocked him" (15:20) by putting "a reed in his right hand" (Matt. 27:29) and then taking that handmade scepter from his hand and "striking his head" (Mark 15:19) with it, surely causing the crown of thorns to pierce his skin and perhaps his skull.

The soldiers' scorn did not cease once they arrived at "Golgotha" (15:22), the second setting of our text. There "they crucified him" (15:24). That clause "They crucified him" appears twice (15:24, 25) in verses 22–27, yet here the act of crucifixion is not Mark's focus.[5] He does not mention the nails, the blood, or the cries of pain. Instead his focus in all 15:16–32 is on the theme of mockery. Surely sticks and stones—or thorns and nails, as the case was—hurt Jesus' body and bones, but a major part of Jesus' excruciating pain was this consistent and persistent ridicule he received in his last hours.

Here the soldiers were relentless in their malicious mockery. First, "they offered him wine mixed with myrrh," a gesture he refused ("But he did not take it," 15:23). Jesus might have refused it because they were offering him an anesthetic, medicine to lessen the agony, or an ancient version of an assisted suicide solution. If this was the case, then Jesus' rejection is commendable in that he consciously chose to bear the full effects of death by crucifixion and was determined to drink only the cup his Father offered him. However, it is more likely, as Matthew depicts Jesus' tasting the wine ("When he tasted it, he would not drink it," Matt. 27:34) and both Matthew and Mark tell us that the wine was mixed with something ("gall," Matt. 27:34; "myrrh," Mark 15:23), that this was a cruel joke, like offering a thirsty man lemon juice and calling it lemonade or granting this "king" some "fine" (rancorous!) wine.[6]

---

4   Matthew says the cloak was "scarlet" (Matt. 27:28). It could be the fabric was "a faded scarlet military cloak" (Strauss, *Mark*, 687) that looked purplish or that Mark uses "purple" for the reddish/blue cloak to emphasize the theme of Jesus' royalty.
5   For details of Roman crucifixion see Cicero, *Verr.* 5.64.165; Seneca, *Ira* 2.2; Josephus, *J.W.* 5.11.1, 7.6.4; cf. Martin Hengel, *Crucifixion in the Ancient Word and the Folly of the Cross*, trans. John Bowden (Philadelphia: Fortress, 1977), 30–31. Josephus calls crucifixion "the most miserable of deaths."
6   See Craig A. Evans, *Mark 8:27–16:20*, WBC 34B (Nashville: Nelson, 1988), 501.

The next way the soldiers mocked Jesus was by dividing his clothing. We read that "they . . . divided his garments among them, casting lots for them, to decide what each should take" (15:24). What this temporary casino at the foot of the cross shows—they gamble for his garments—is just how insensitive they were to a dying man and how oblivious they were to who Jesus is and what he was doing right above them. It also once again shows that there are no limits to their mockery. They have nailed Jesus to a tree without his clothes on, or very little (perhaps a loincloth). How embarrassing. Shameful.

> O sacred Head, now wounded,
> With grief and *shame* weighed down,
> Now scornfully surrounded
> With thorns, Thine only crown.[7]

The soldiers were not done. Above Jesus' head they wrote "the charge against him," which was that he was or claimed to be "The King of the Jews" (15:26). They obviously did not believe that "inscription" (15:26), but they wanted to make sure everyone who passed by could read Rome's ridicule of Jewish opposition. The inscription was written in Aramaic, Latin, and Greek (see John 19:20) so all who could read could either have a good laugh or get riled up.

Their final act of mockery was the placement of Jesus' cross. The soldiers "crucified two robbers, one on his right and one on his left" (Mark 15:27). This adds to innocent Jesus' indignity. He was numbered among the transgressors (Isa. 53:12). He was crowned king between two captured terrorists, men who, we are told at the end of the text, "also reviled him" (Mark 15:32). Even the insurrectionists rejected him! Mark does not detail the later change of mind (the repentance and faith of one of the two; see Luke 23:40–43), and I surmise that he does this to highlight the total humility of Jesus, the absolute rejection, and the perfect mockery.

With all that said, Mark obviously does not want us to follow the soldiers' evil intentions and their awful actions. But he does want us to follow something of their posture and praise, to see in their mockery one of the most profound and foundational truths of our faith, namely, that Jesus' coronation as king happens on the cross. The charge that he is "The King of the Jews" (Mark 15:26; cf. 15:32) is true. Their salute, "Hail, King of the Jews!" (15:18), is both accurate and appropriate.

---

7   Bernard of Clairvaux, trans. James W. Alexander, "O Sacred Head Now Wounded" (1829).

I love how Mark makes sure that we do not miss this truth and that we do not fail to embrace the irony! In Mark 14:53–15:15, which records Jesus' two trials, Mark uses a repetition of royal titles—"Christ" (14:61), "Son of Man" (14:62), and "king" (15:2, 9, 12; cf. 15:18, 26, 32)—to help us recognize who Jesus is. Here in 15:16–20 Mark uses a chiasm to make his point that Jesus reigns as king through his sufferings.

> And the soldiers *led* him away inside the palace (that is, the governor's
>   headquarters), and they called together the whole battalion.
>   And they clothed him in a purple cloak,
>   and twisting together *a crown of thorns*, they put it on him.
>   And they began to salute him, "Hail, King of the Jews!"
>   And they were striking *his head* with a reed and spitting on him
>   and kneeling down in homage to him.
>   And when they had mocked him, *they stripped him of the purple cloak*
>   and put his own clothes on him.
> And they *led* him out to crucify him.

Do you see how Mark takes several similar words and actions and, starting from both ends, works his way to the center? In verses 16a and 20c the soldiers *lead* Jesus somewhere ("They led him"); in verses 17a and 20 they put on and take off a *purple cloak*; in verses 17b and 19 they do something to Jesus' *head* (put a crown of thorns on it/strike it with a reed). But then, as we finally arrive at the center, there is no parallel because we have arrived at the point, poetically and thematically. The point is that these soldiers pay homage to Jesus as king: "Hail, King of the Jews!" (15:18).

Of course, as we know, the soldiers' adoration and enthronement is a farce. They are mocking him. Yet, if we remove their appalling attitudes from their actions—take away the parody of the wreath of thorns as golden garland, a soldier's cloak as royal robe, a reed as scepter, and the adulation due Caesar conferred upon Christ—then we have the truth set before us. As these joking Gentiles bow before Jesus, so all the nations in every imaginable tongue are to give to the true king of the kingdom of God the veneration due his majestic name.[8]

Yes, even (and especially) the escalating mockery of the "whole battalion" (15:16)—picture six hundred men kneeling before Jesus—is the ironic image

---

8   For parts of this paragraph see Douglas Sean O'Donnell, *Matthew: All Authority under Heaven*, PTW (Wheaton, IL: Crossway, 2013), 852.

of what the 7.9 billion men, women, and children of the world today should do: acknowledge Jesus as their king, a crucified king, a king who reigns through his sufferings, a king who "receives his 'glory' (10:37) not through conquest but through suffering and sacrifice."[9]

More Mockery, Additional Ironies

Jesus' coronation as king happens on the cross. This is the first ironic instruction. This is what Mark seeks to teach us in Mark 15:16–27. But there are two further ironic instructions that can be found in the final mockeries, recorded in verses 29–32.

Look first at **15:29–30**, where we read: "And those who passed by derided him, wagging their heads and saying, 'Aha! You who would destroy the temple and rebuild it in three days, save yourself, and come down from the cross!'" Each line is dripping with irony. It is ironic that their derision against a man who they think is surely cursed of God (he is dying on a tree; see Deut. 21:23) is a fulfillment of Scripture. Psalm 22:1 will soon be on Jesus' mouth, "My God, my God, why have you forsaken me?" but other portions of the psalm come to light before that. Psalm 22:18 reads, "They divided my garments among them, and for my clothing they cast lots," and verses 6–7 speak of the suffering king "scorned . . . and despised" as "all who see [him] mock [him]" and "wag their heads."

Another irony is what they say Jesus said about the temple. Jesus did predict the destruction of the temple. He did also speak symbolically about his death and resurrection: the temple of his body would be destroyed and then rebuilt. But these bystanders completely miss that in Jesus' death and resurrection he will hang an out-of-business sign on the doors of the Most Holy Place; by doing the opposite of what they ask—to "save [himself], and come down from the cross!" (Mark 15:30)—he actually saves people.

I will put it this way. Here is the headline for the second ironic instruction: Our Salvation Comes Only Because Jesus Stays on the Cross and Dies for Sinners. Jesus' death saves (10:45)! Through his death our Lord destroys the need for a man-made temple. Look again at Mark 15:25, and do not overlook the timing of the crucifixion: "And it was the third hour [around 9 a.m.] when they crucified him," that is, when they first lifted him to the cross. Jesus died, Mark tells us in verse 34, at "the ninth hour" (around 3 p.m.). So from roughly 9 a.m. to 3 p.m. what was happening in the temple? The high priest was preparing and then shedding the blood of the innocent Passover lambs

---

9 Strauss, *Mark*, 693.

to secure the forgiveness of sins. So by staying on the cross and dying on the cross Jesus, as the innocent Lamb of God, took away the sins of the world. He "put away sin by the sacrifice of himself" (Heb. 9:26). He is the perfect priest who offers the perfect sacrifice and grants God's perfect forgiveness for imperfect people.

The final taunts against Jesus come from an unlikely combination—the religious elite and the criminal class. Members of the Sanhedrin, who had declared Jesus guilty of blasphemy, now blaspheme the holy Son of God: "So also the chief priests with the scribes mocked him to one another, saying, 'He saved others; he cannot save himself. Let the Christ, the King of Israel, come down now from the cross that we may see and believe'" (Mark **15:31–32a**).[10] Joining in their chorus are "those who were crucified with him." They "also reviled him" (**15:32b**).[11]

What greater shame is there than this? We are not surprised that Roman soldiers would mock a self-professed Jewish messiah, or even that the Jewish leaders, who have long wanted Jesus dead,[12] would do the same. But for these two men struggling for each last breath themselves to use some of their last words to condemn a fellow "criminal" is criminal itself. "Even those suffering the same fate as Jesus have nothing but derision for him and his apparently deluded messianic claims."[13] Oh the depths of human depravity!

However, it is in the very words of these final mockeries that Mark offers us another ironic instruction: only through faith in Christ and him crucified is salvation applied.

It is natural to think like the chief priests, scribes, and criminals; that is, to think that if Jesus would show his superpowers—push the nails out of his hands and feet, fly off the cross, heal himself in the front of the gawkers, and then destroy the Roman battalion with fire from his eyes—then after such marvels we would believe. That is a savior to believe in!

Yet the greatest sign of Jesus' supernatural powers is that he stays on the cross. That nonmiracle is most miraculous. The crucified Christ conquers our greatest enemies—sin, death, and the devil. He loses his life but saves all who believe in this unbelievable nonmiracle, this sign as seemingly silly as Jonah's being swallowed by a big fish and spat out again. Of course, Jesus has saved others, and he can save himself. He has the power. But he understands

10 With the repetition of the word "king"—"King of the Jews" (Mark 15:2, 9, 12, 18, 26) and "King of Israel" (15:32)—Mark is making his point.
11 Those crucified "also reviled him in the same way" (Matt. 27:44), namely (and in part) by saying, "Let him come down now from the cross, and we will believe in him" (Matt. 27:42).
12 See Mark 3:6; 11:18; 12:12; 14:1–2, 10–11, 64; 15:1, 3, 11.
13 Strauss, *Mark*, 695.

now that the "real power is the control of power, the rejection of power, the willingness to express power in weak-seeming ways."[14]

Jesus' death saves! Is it not ironic? Is it not awesome! His death saves all who believe in his death as the only means of salvation. That is ironic and awesome too. His mockers say that they will believe in him only if he comes down from the cross. Christians say that we believe in him because he did not come down from the cross.[15] "We believe in Jesus as Savior because he stayed up there to die, came down only to be buried, and rose up again three days later."[16] God saves only those who trust in the folly of the cross, "those who believe" that Christ and "Christ crucified" is "the power . . . and the wisdom of God" (see 1 Cor. 1:20–24).

The Place of a Skull

The Romans brought Jesus outside of the city to the designated place for capital punishment, a place that in the local Hebrew vernacular (Aramaic) was called "Golgotha," translated "Place of a Skull" (15:22). In Latin it is *Calvariæ*; in English "Calvary." This nickname, "Place of a Skull," could have been given because the shape of the hill resembled a human skull or because that was the site where many men met their death by crucifixion. Yet, because "a skull" is used, not "the skulls," some church fathers took this to be a reference to the place where Adam was buried. Genesis 5:5 does say that "Adam lived . . . and he died." The Bible does not say where he was buried. But he was buried somewhere, perhaps in a cave-like tomb in the land of Canaan that would someday be a skull-shaped hill outside of Jerusalem.

Many Christian medieval artists certainly believed this to be the case, as in their paintings of the crucifixion we often see Adam's skull at the foot of the cross (e.g., Salimbeni's *The Crucifixion*, 1416). I do not know whether they have correctly captured the historical facts. But they certainly have captured some theological truth, for in the death of Jesus the curse of Adam is broken. Jesus' death destroys death. Jesus' death offers new life to all those living east of Eden. Jesus' death saves those who believe in him as the Christ and know that his crucifixion is more than his momentary coronation—it is an eternal shout of victory.

---

14 Frederick Dale Bruner, *Matthew: A Commentary, Volume 2: The Churchbook, Matthew 13–28*, rev. ed. (Grand Rapids, MI: Eerdmans, 2007), 738–39.

15 General William Booth, the founder of the Salvation Army, put it this way: "It is precisely because he would not come down that we believe in him." Quoted in William Barclay, *The Gospel of Matthew*, 2 vols. (Louisville: Westminster John Knox, 1975): 2:367.

16 O'Donnell, *Matthew*, 869.

Crown him with many crowns,
The Lamb upon his throne.
Hark! How the heavenly anthem drowns
All music but its own.
Awake, my soul, and sing
Of him who died for thee,
And hail him as thy matchless king
Through all eternity.[17]

17　Matthew Bridges, "Crown Him with Many Crowns" (1851).

The Power of the Cross

MARK 15:33-47

My God, my God, why have you forsaken me?
Mark 15:34

The ancient acronym INRI stands for *Iesvs Nazarenvs Rex Ivdaeorvm*, "Jesus of Nazarene, King of the Jews"—the Latin inscription that hung above Jesus on the cross. Over a decade ago the Yale Daily News recorded that, during Holy Week, a student affixed a cross on Yale's campus with an inscription that read not INRI but ROFL, the modern acronym for Rolling On the Floor Laughing.[1] Such ridicule of the Christian faith should come as no surprise, for, as Paul wrote nearly two thousand years ago, "the word of the cross is folly to those who are perishing" (1 Cor. 1:18). It is folly to many Ivy League students today as much as it was folly to the first-century Jewish religious elite, Roman officials, and even condemned criminals.

In the last chapter, as we examined and applied Mark 15:16–32, we saw what we read about in the news headlines: Jesus Is Mocked. Four sets of people mocked him in twelve different ways. In Mark 15:33–47, however, something has changed. Jesus is still on the cross. In fact, we will read about his last breath. Yet something of the power of the cross can be felt here. As Mark, through his narrative of Jesus' final moments, preaches "Christ crucified," which is indeed a "stumbling block" to many, it is also, "to those who are being called, both Jews [even Jewish religious leaders!] and Greeks [even Roman centurions!], . . . the power of God" (1 Cor. 1:23–24).

Here in Mark we will see that power at work in four different ways as the power of the cross is seen to do the impossible, to soften the hardest hearts,

---

1   See Jordon Walker, "Walker: An Insulting Prank and Hypocritical Response," *Yale Daily News*, April 21, 2011, https://yaledailynews.com/blog/2011/04/21/walker-an-insulting-prank-and-hypocritical -response/; Garrett Fiddler, "Fiddler: Good Friday and the ROFL Cross," *Yale Daily News*, April 21, 2011, https://yaledailynews.com/blog/2011/04/21/fiddler-good-friday-and-the-rofl-cross/.

to use the "weak" to witness effectively to the world, and to turn scared, secret disciples into courageous servants.

The Seemingly Powerless Jesus

But before we get to the powerful effects of the cross we stop, as Mark does, to witness the seemingly powerless Jesus die. It is a holy moment, and a literally and spiritually dark moment as well, in Mark **15:33–37**:

> And when the sixth hour had come, there was darkness over the whole land until the ninth hour. And at the ninth hour Jesus cried with a loud voice, "Eloi, Eloi, lema sabachthani?" which means, "My God, my God, why have you forsaken me?" And some of the bystanders hearing it said, "Behold, he is calling Elijah." And someone ran and filled a sponge with sour wine, put it on a reed and gave it to him to drink, saying, "Wait, let us see whether Elijah will come to take him down." And Jesus uttered a loud cry and breathed his last.

Notice the artist's details. First, notice the timing. Mark mentions the "sixth hour" (15:33) and the "ninth hour" (15:34). In verse 25 the evangelist-artist had also mentioned the "third hour." Around nine in the morning Jesus is nailed to the cross and lifted up; around three in the afternoon he dies. But at midday, when the sun is at its zenith, God turns off the lights. Darkness covers the land. This is the second detail to notice. This is a supernatural sign. The darkness signifies judgment.[2] Just as God judged the land of Egypt with the plague of darkness (Ex. 10:22), so he judges his own promised land. The light of the holy city is eclipsed because God's people are killing God's anointed! The darkness also signifies sorrow. "The Cross is draped in the mourning sackcloth of darkness."[3] The prophet Amos' language of apocalyptic upheaval matches the moment:

> "On that day," declares the Lord GOD,
>   "I will make the sun go down at noon
>   and darken the earth in broad daylight. . . .
> I will make it like the mourning for an only son." (Amos 8:9–10)

---

2   "Darkness symbolized divine judgment, a cosmic sign of God's anger that will take place at the Day of the Lord (Isa. 13:9–10; Jer. 4:28; 13:16; Ezek. 32:7–8; Amos 8:9; Zeph. 1:15). So the darkness at the crucifixion is a harbinger of the judgment to come, first in the destruction of Jerusalem in AD 70 and then in the eschaton, the destruction of the world of evil, at the end of history." Grant R. Osborne, *Mark*, TTCS (Grand Rapids, MI: Baker, 2012), 308.

3   R. Kent Hughes, *Mark: Jesus, Servant and Savior*, PTW, 2 vols. (Wheaton, IL: Crossway, 1989), 2:206.

That outer darkness is next, in our third detail to notice, met by Jesus' inner darkness.[4] Mark 15:33–34 is painted black. Jesus' shout of abandonment matches the color scheme. His dark cry of dereliction is the darkest moment in world history! "At the ninth hour," the very light of the world and the Creator who brought light into the world "cried with a loud voice, 'Eloi, Eloi, lema sabachthani?' which means, 'My God, my God, why have you forsaken me?'" (15:34).

Ponder the beauty of the incarnation. God became a child, born in Bethlehem, raised by godly Jewish parents, living in a Greek-speaking but Latin-ruled world. Mary and Joseph taught Jesus how to speak Aramaic, a Hebrew dialect.[5] He learned Psalm 22:1a by heart in his own heart language, "Eloi, Eloi, lema sabachthani?" On the cross he cries out in his own native tongue, and his last words are God's word. The Bible in his own language.

Jesus is so raw here and so remarkable, so ordinary and so extraordinary, so human and so divine. But why then, as the divine Son of God, does he not say what he said at the dawn of creation: "Let there be light" (Gen. 1:3)? This dark landscape needs some light. Or, if he wants to recite a psalm, why not the start of Psalm 23, "The LORD is my shepherd; I shall not want"? Jesus selects the dark words of Psalm 22 because it fits the dark setting. But also, and more importantly, because it fits what is happening to him on the cross.[6] He has been forsaken by his own people, the Jews. He has been forsaken by his closest friends, the apostles. And now he is forsaken by his own Father.

What then is the nature of this God-forsakenness? Does Jesus just feel forsaken or is he really forsaken? Can the Trinity experience, even for a moment, a divine divorce? The mystery of the atonement is as mysterious as the mystery of the incarnation! Yet, as we believe that Jesus, very God of very God, was born of a woman and died, so we believe that Jesus, on the cross, experienced some separation from his Father. As Charles Cranfield says, Jesus experienced "not merely a felt, but a real, abandonment by his Father," and "the paradox [is] that, while this God-forsakenness was utterly real, the unity of the Blessed Trinity was even then unbroken."[7]

---

4   "Mark's entire focus is on the gloomy darkness of the scene, the agonizing suffering and aloneness of the Son of God." Mark L. Strauss, *Mark*, ZECNT (Grand Rapids, MI: Zondervan, 2014), 702.

5   There are only four times when Mark records words in Aramaic (Mark 5:41; 7:34; 14:36; 15:34). The first two uses are in Jesus' healing ministry, the last two in his prayer to his Father.

6   "Jesus expresses this horror of great darkness, this God-forsakenness, by quoting the only verse of Scripture which actually described it and which he had perfectly fulfilled." John Calvin, *A Harmony of the Gospels Matthew, Mark and Luke and the Epistles of James and Jude*, vol. 3, trans. A. W. Morrison (Grand Rapids, MI: Eerdmans, 1975), 81.

7   Cranfield, quoted in John R. W. Stott, *The Cross of Christ* (Downers Grove, IL: InterVarsity Press, 1996), 82.

The best sense I can make of the meaning of Jesus' cry is in its connection to Jesus' prayers in Gethsemane. The "cup" of God's wrath (Mark 14:36; cf. Isa. 53:4–6) that Jesus wanted removed is now felt on his lips and into the pit of his stomach.[8] The "Son of Man" is giving "his life as a ransom for many" (Mark 10:45); he is pouring out his blood for many (14:24). And the best summary, then, of what Mark shows here in story form is what Paul says propositionally in 2 Corinthians 5:18–21: God made sinless Jesus "to be sin" so that all who believe in him might be forgiven of sin. As I explain elsewhere in greater detail:

> Calvin (*Institutes*, 2.16.11) summarizes it in this way: Jesus "bore the weight of divine severity, since he was 'stricken and afflicted' (cf. Isa. 53:5) by God's hand and experienced all the signs of a wrathful and avenging God." Earlier Calvin (2.16.10) states that Christ "suffered the death that God in his wrath had inflicted upon the wicked . . . that invisible and incomprehensible judgment which he underwent in the sight of God in order that we might know not only that Christ's body was given as the price of our redemption, but that he paid a greater and more excellent price in suffering in his soul the terrible torments of a condemned and forsaken man." Thus, Jesus's forsakenness was "an objective reality as well as a subjective experience."[9] The Father forsook the Son in that his wrath was upon him in his *profession* as mediator, but not in his *person* as Son. As Arthur Pink explains: "Never was God more 'well-pleased' with his beloved Son than when he hung on the cross in obedience to him (Phil. 2:10), yet he withdrew from him every effect or manifestation of his love during those three hours of awful darkness, yea, poured out his wrath upon him as our sin-bearer, so that he exclaimed 'Your wrath lies hard upon me, and you have afflicted me with all Your waves' (Ps. 88:7)."[10] The forsakenness is that God left him to die, and in that death he suffered the punishment for sin. Jonty Rhodes uses the analogy of Jesus having a blocked view of the Father's smiling face. "Just as darkness covered the land but the sun didn't cease to shine, so the experience of bearing the covenant curse overwhelmed Jesus in his human nature, clouding his view of his Father's love, steadfast though he remained. . . .

---

8 "The cry of dereliction is best understood as the moment when Jesus experienced God's wrath and the sense of forsakenness that came with it" (Strauss, *Mark*, 712).

9 Jonty Rhodes, *Man of Sorrows, King of Glory: What the Humiliation and Exaltation of Jesus Mean for Us* (Wheaton, IL: Crossway, 2021), 84. Note original.

10 Arthur W. Pink, *The Doctrine of Reconciliation* (Lafayette, IN: Sovereign Grace, 2006), 91. Note original.

Christ felt the anger of God . . . on account of our sin," and "for a short while," the Father "suspended Christ's enjoyment of the grace, happiness, and consolation that he normally enjoyed."[11] . . . Thus, Jesus is not a martyr facing death. Like Stephen in Acts 7:54–60, "most martyrs face death with courage and confidence, expressing steadfast faith in God and hope for the resurrection."[12] Jesus is a propitiatory sacrifice. He will drink "the cup" of "the wine of [God's] wrath" (see Jer. 25:15–28; cf. Isa. 51:17, 22).[13]

It is one thing to think about, and comprehend something of, the nature of Jesus' God-forsakenness. But it is another thing altogether to feel something of his pain and to have genuine heartfelt love to him for his love for us.

In his novel *The Heart of the Matter* Graham Greene describes a police lieutenant's overhearing a conversation between two officers describing a man's suicide. The conversation was sterile and far removed from the pain that that dead man must have felt and his family must have now felt. As the lieutenant himself examined the corpse, he thought to himself, "Through two thousand years . . . we have discussed Christ's agony in just this disinterested way."[14] When we see a cross atop a gravestone or hanging around someone's neck, do we feel anything? It is easy to see a cross, or hear a sermon on the cross, and still experience and express no emotion. It is easy to be dispassionate.

Going into preaching the passion narrative, I did not pray that I might feel something of Jesus' pain, but in God's providence I experienced both physical and emotional pain when I preached on Christ's passion. I was having in-need-of-a-root-canal pain as I preached on Jesus' trial before Pilate (Mark 15:1–15), which ends with the crowd's shouting, "Crucify him" (15:13, 14), Pilate's granting their wish, and his having his soldiers scourge Jesus before he is delivered over to be crucified (15:15). That bad tooth caused me great pain for six days. But it also kept me, in a small way, connected to the king of pain. It made me thankful for his physical sufferings on my behalf.

During this same time, as I preached through Mark 14–15, I had two nightmares. In one I was climbing a pillar of stones. As I climbed higher, I assured myself that there was something—my freedom, a way out—at the top. So I kept climbing. But I never reached anywhere. And I only became more and more frightened the higher I climbed. In the other dream I was dressed in my

11 Rhodes, *Man of Sorrows*, 81, 84.
12 Strauss, *Mark*, 637.
13 Douglas Sean O'Donnell, "'If You, Then, Who Are Evil': Sin in the Synoptic Gospels and Acts," in *Ruined Sinners to Reclaim: Human Corruption in Historical, Biblical, Theological, and Pastoral Perspective*, eds. David Gibson and Jonathan Gibson (Wheaton, IL: Crossway, forthcoming).
14 Graham Greene, *The Heart of the Matter* (New York: Viking, 1948), 211.

Sunday best. I came into a large church building. I needed to get to the nursery. I saw a slide that went from the sanctuary down to the nursery. I thought it would be fun to slide down it. So I jumped through the hole and slid down. About halfway down this abnormally long slide I got stuck. I could not turn to the right or to the left. I could not push myself down any further. And I was too far down and too far up for anyone to hear my shouts for help. Moments later I could not hear the noise of children. Soon thereafter the lights were turned off. I was alone and scared. I could not have envisioned a worse hell than that.

We recite in the Apostles' Creed that Jesus "descended into hell." Christian scholars debate what the term "hell" means and whether that event happened. But surely no Christian should debate the fact that Jesus experienced God's judgment. He was forsaken so we might be forgiven.

I do not know what hell would be like. Jesus speaks of fire, darkness, and destruction of the body and soul.[15] It might be climbing a never-ending stone mountain. It might mean being alone and stuck by yourself in a frightening dark place of torment, both emotionally and physically. But what I do know is that Jesus took into his own body and soul that hell for me. Do you know that? Believe that? Rejoice in that? Stop to give an emotionally charged thanks for that?

Now, as we are first exploring the details of Jesus' death in Mark 15:33–37, we have looked, first, at the timing of Jesus' death and, second and third, at the outer and inner darkness. Fourth, notice that the greatest theological pronouncement in history ("Eloi, Eloi, lema sabachthani?" 15:34) is met with misunderstanding. In verses 35–36 we read: "And some of the bystanders hearing it said, 'Behold, he is calling Elijah.' And someone ran and filled a sponge with sour wine, put it on a reed and gave it to him to drink, saying, 'Wait, let us see whether Elijah will come to take him down.'"

When some of the Jews at the foot of the cross hear what they think is a cry to Elijah, they wonder whether the wonder-working prophet will save the wonder-working Jesus. The Jews at this time view Elijah "as a kind of 'patron saint' of lost causes"[16] and as the one who would return "before the great and awesome day of the LORD" (Mal. 4:5).

As they try to revive Jesus and then wait to see whether a whirlwind from heaven might come down to earth (see 2 Kings 2:11), we know that Elijah has already appeared at the transfiguration (Mark 9:4–5) and that John the Baptist, in this role as the prophet ushering in the last days, has already

15 Matthew 5:22; 10:28; 18:9; Mark 9:43.
16 Donald Senior, *The Passion of Jesus in the Gospel of Matthew* (Collegeville, MN: Liturgical Press, 1985), 137.

accomplished his mission ("Elijah has come," 9:13). We also understand that Jesus does not need anyone to save him (he has the power to save himself) but has freely chosen to stay on the cross and not be rescued from it.

The fifth and final detail from Mark 15:33–37 moves beyond misunderstanding to the fulfillment of Jesus' mission. We read in verse 37, "And Jesus uttered a loud cry and breathed his last." In John 19:30 we read that Jesus' "loud cry" was "It is finished" and in Matthew 27:50 that Jesus "yielded up his spirit." Those Evangelists portray something of Jesus' power (he is sovereign over his sufferings and he shouts a victor's cry). Mark is less dramatic. His version sounds anticlimactic. Jesus' last words are "My God, my God, why have you forsaken me?" (Mark 15:34) and his last breath so human. He loses too much blood, his heart ruptures, or his lungs asphyxiate. Whatever the final cause of death,[17] he stops breathing. Jesus dies like an ordinary man dies.

This final detail separates Christianity from all world religions. It is not just that all religions say "do" (you need to do something to be right with God) while Christianity says "done" (Jesus has done something for you so you might be right with God); it is what Jesus has done that is so remarkable. For example, Islam believes Jesus existed and that he was a great prophet. However, the Qur'an teaches that it is "inappropriate that a major prophet of God should come to such an ignominious end,"[18] and thus, according to Islam, Allah saved Jesus "from the shame of crucifixion."[19] Before Jesus breathed his last breath, "Allah took [Jesus] up to himself."[20] Christianity, however, pictures Jesus' diving headfirst into the cesspool of sin! Jesus is presented as the God-man sent to save godless men.

Before Jesus hung his head and died, he took on all the sins of his people. Perhaps the first wave of sins rolled over him at 9 a.m., the sins of adultery, arrogance, backbiting, bearing false witness, bitterness, blasphemy, boasting, bribery; then the second wave at 10 a.m., the sins of complaining, contention, course joking, coveting, deceit, defrauding, despising the poor, dishonoring the government, disregarding the Lord's people on the Lord's Day, disrespecting one's elders; then the third wave at 11 a.m., the sins of envy, evil thoughts, fornication, fortune-telling, fraud, giving begrudgingly, gluttony, gossip,

---

17 On the possible medical reasons for Jesus' death see Raymond E. Brown, *The Death of the Messiah: From Gethsemane to the Grave; A Commentary on the Passion Narrative in the Four Gospels*, 2 vols. (New York: Doubleday, 1994), 1088–92.

18 As summarized by Stott, *Cross of Christ*, 40.

19 As summarized by Daniel M. Doriani, *Matthew*, REC, 2 vols. (Phillipsburg, NJ: P&R, 2008), 2:495.

20 Qur'an 4:157–158. I used *The Qur'an: The First American Version*, trans. T. B. Irving (Brattleboro, VT: Amana, 1985), 50–51.

greed; then the fourth wave at 12 p.m., the sins of harsh words, hating one's brother, holding a grudge, idleness, idolatry, immodesty, losing one's temper, lust, lying, malice, murder, prayerlessness; then the fifth wave at 1 p.m., the sins of racism, rage, rape, resisting the Holy Spirit, returning insult for insult, rioting; then the sixth wave at 2 p.m., the sins of scoffing, selfish ambition, showing favoritism, slander, sloth, speaking idle words, stealing, violence, witchcraft. Christ bore God's wrath for each and every one of our sins. We stand forgiven! That is the power of the cross!

The Power of the Cross to Do the Impossible

In Mark 15:33–37 a seemingly powerless man dies. But then in **15:38–47** we quickly learn that Jesus' death is not in vain. The power of the cross takes immediate effect. Mark moves from "And Jesus . . . breathed his last" (15:37) directly to "And the curtain of the temple was torn in two, from top to bottom" (15:38). Immediately after Jesus' death God shows a sure sign of his vindication and victory: he rends the temple's veil! The detail about its being "torn in two, from top to bottom" highlights the impossibility of this event. No human, not even Samson in all his strength, could do what Mark records here.

The Evangelist does not tell us whether this curtain is the curtain that separated the Holy Place from the Most Holy Place, the Holy of Holies that housed the ark of the covenant and could be entered only by the high priest on the Day of Atonement, or whether this curtain was the larger outside veil that divided the Court of the Jews from the Court of the Gentiles. Mark is intentionally vague. He wants us to imagine the significance of both. Dale Bruner summarizes the significance in this way: "The split veil of the temple says two truths about the temple: (1) judgment ("It is all over!") and (2) salvation ("It is all open!").[21] Jesus' death ushers in God's judgment against the corruption of the temple in Jesus' day. Jesus is now the great high priest, the ultimate Lamb of God, our atonement. There is no longer a need for an earthly high priest, animal sacrifice, or Day of Atonement. It is all over for the temple.

Yet now it is also all open. Through Jesus' death both Jews and Gentiles gain access, through faith (Rom. 5:2), to God. Those "who once were far off"—as near as the Court of the Gentiles and as far as those pagans who had never heard the name of Yahweh—"have been brought near by the blood of Christ" (Eph. 2:13). Hebrews 10:19–22 teaches this same truth in this way:

---

21 Frederick Dale Bruner, *Matthew: A Commentary, Volume 2: The Churchbook, Matthew 13–28*, rev. ed. (Grand Rapids, MI: Eerdmans, 2007), 757.

Since we have confidence to enter the holy places by the blood of Jesus, by the new and living way that he opened for us through the curtain, that is, through his flesh, and since we have a great priest over the house of God, let us draw near with a true heart in full assurance of faith, with our hearts sprinkled clean from an evil conscience and our bodies washed with pure water.

Through faith in Jesus we walk straight through the first and second temple curtains into the throne room of God (see 4:16; 6:19). The beautiful lesson of the supernaturally split veil is that all who believe in Jesus have access to God—even, as we shall see next, a Roman centurion at the foot of the cross.

The Power of the Cross to Soften the Hardest Hearts

Immediately after Jesus' death the power of the cross is on display. First, we saw how the power of the cross does the impossible—the temple curtain is torn in two. Second, we will see that the cross has the power to soften the hardest hearts.

Notice the correlation between the ways in which the word "and" is used to start Mark 15:37, 38, and 39: "And Jesus . . . breathed his last" (15:37); "And the curtain of the temple was torn in two" (15:38); "And when the centurion" (15:39). One event seemingly triggers the next. It is remarkable here in verse 39 who confesses ("the centurion, who stood facing him"), why he confesses (he "saw that in this way he breathed his last"), and what he confesses ("Truly this man was the Son of God!" 15:39).

How remarkable that the first postcrucifixion confession comes from a high-ranking Roman soldier. The theology of the torn veil is immediately acted out.[22] It is not Peter who walks through the crowd to the foot of the cross and makes this great confession. It is not one of the religious leaders who has a sudden change of mind. Rather it is a centurion, the leader of the men who tortured and killed Jesus. If there ever were a Gentile sinner, he was it.[23] He certainly was part of the crucifixion crew and likely one of the men responsible for mocking and scourging Jesus. To say to Jesus hours ago, in

---

[22] Psalm 22 predicts not only the sufferings of the righteous suffering king but also that the nations would worship him (see Ps. 22:27).

[23] "The theme of salvation of the Gentiles is not as prominent in Mark as it is in Luke (his gospel and Acts). Yet it has been hinted at throughout Mark's gospel. This is true in the healing of the Syrophoenician woman's daughter (7:24–30), other healing in the Decapolis (7:31–37), the feeding of the four thousand (8:1–9), Jesus' predictions that the 'vineyard' will be given to 'others' (12:9), and the declaration that the gospel will be preached to all the nations (13:10). This theme should not have been surprising to the Jewish nation, since the OT repeatedly predicted that God's salvation would one day go forth to all people everywhere" (Strauss, *Mark*, 712–13).

utter scorn, "Hail! King of the Jews!" (15:18), and now to declare Jesus to be more than a king can be attributed only to the power of God.

But how does this radical conversion occur? This enemy has drawn near to God through witnessing the death of Jesus (cf. Rom. 5:10). That is the only reason Mark offers. He does not say that the centurion got word of what happened to the temple's curtain; Mark does not add the possible aid of an earthquake followed by bodies' being raised from their graves ("When the centurion . . . saw the earthquake and what took place, [he was] filled with awe and said. . . ." Matt. 27:54). This centurion's heart, according to Mark's record, is changed by simply looking at the crucified Christ.

Finally, notice what this man says of Jesus: "Truly this man was the Son of God!" (Mark 15:39). It is possible that he is confused and labels Jesus "Son of God" like a pagan would a "Greco-Roman 'divine man' (a great human hero who is deified upon his death)."[24] It is possible that this man simply speaks better than he knows. Or it is possible, and most likely, that the power of the cross has penetrated this man's soul. He knows who Jesus is because God has revealed that identity to him. When Jesus is on trial before the Sanhedrin the high priest asks, "Are you . . . the Son of the Blessed?" (14:61). Jesus answers that he is (14:62). This centurion, then, is the first to agree. He takes Jesus to be the divine Son of God. He agrees with Mark's assessment of Jesus in the opening line of his Gospel. Jesus is the "Christ" and "Son of God" (1:1). The centurion also echoes the Father's voice at Jesus' baptism and transfiguration (1:11; 9:7).[25]

The power of the cross! Do you believe in the power of the cross to change people's lives—that someone can look upon the crucified Jesus and move from being a mocker to being a worshiper? I do. I have witnessed it with my own eyes. Shortly after I finished college I traveled with a group of missionaries to Malawi. We traveled around the country and most nights gave a long Christian concert, followed by a short gospel message. I played bass guitar in the band and then preached. In one of the venues, a packed university auditorium, I preached on the rich young ruler. In the balcony to my right was a group of rowdy students. One student was an absolute annoyance. She sang and danced and clapped. She stood up and yelled. She even directly taunted me.

After a while I drowned out the noise. I got used to her like one would a fussy baby on a plane from Singapore to Newark. That night I walked through

---

24 Craig L. Blomberg, *Matthew*, NAC (Nashville: Broadman, 1992), 422. This is not Blomberg's view.
25 "Shockingly, it is this Gentile centurion who first recognizes that Jesus' divine sonship and messianic identity are confirmed *not through conquest, but through suffering*" (Strauss, *Mark*, 706).

the way Jesus dealt with this self-righteous and sinful person, and I talked about the impossibility of salvation by works and the possibility of salvation through faith in Christ. I preached the cross. At the end of the talk, instead of giving a traditional invitation to come forward, I reversed the call of commitment. I said, "If you are interested in giving your life to Christ, simply stay where you are. Stay in your seats, and someone will come to talk to you."

Only a few students stayed, most notably that girl. In fact, she sat in the balcony all alone. She sat there with tears of sorrow and joy. That night she repented, embraced Jesus, and received forgiveness. That night, I will tell you, I witnessed a camel pushed through the eye of a needle! The possibility of an impossibility. I witnessed the power of the cross. The point here is plain: there is no one you know—no matter how sinful he is, no matter how far removed she might seem from Christian commitment—that is beyond the reach of God's grace, beyond experiencing the heart-softening power of the cross.

The Power of the Cross to Use the "Weak" to Witness to the World!

So then, the power of the cross is manifested not only in the temple curtain's being torn in two and in softening the hardest hearts but also in using the so-called "weak" to witness effectively to the world.

Today, in the day of women's empowerment, many people would never attach the word "weak" to "women." Yet in the time of Jesus women were so marginalized that they could not serve in a court of law as reliable witnesses.[26] So what does God decide to do? He records a number of women as official eyewitnesses. In Mark the centurion witnesses the crucifixion and Joseph of Arimathea the burial. But only the women see and testify to Jesus' death, burial, and resurrection.

First, they witness Jesus' death. "There were also women looking on from a distance, among whom were Mary Magdalene, and Mary the mother of James the younger and of Joses, and Salome" (15:40).[27] Deuteronomy 19:15 requires that at least two witnesses must testify for something to be valid. Mark provides three of the names from the "many . . . women" who have been with Jesus since his early Galilean ministry ("When he was in Galilee, they followed him and ministered to him,[28] and there were also many other women who came up with him to Jerusalem," Mark 15:41).

---

26 See m. Roš Haš. 1:8; Josephus, *Ant.* 4.219.
27 Salome is the mother of the sons of Zebedee (Matt. 27:56).
28 In several ways the women embody qualities of discipleship. First, "they followed" Jesus. Second, they followed him a great distance, some 100 miles from Galilee to Jerusalem, to the cross. Third, on the way, they served him ("ministered to him," Mark 15:41).

Two of those witnesses to the crucifixion also witness the tomb where Jesus' body is placed. "Mary Magdalene and Mary the mother of Joses saw where he was laid" (15:47). These two Marys, along with another one ("Mary the mother of James") and, again, "Salome" (16:1), witness the empty tomb. Four witnesses!

This is one of the most remarkable details about the Christian story. In a world dominated by male leaders (in the Gospels all the Roman leaders, Jewish authorities, and apostles are male), God sends a few select women to the witness stand to testify to the gospel. Christ has died. Christ was buried. Christ is risen. The world would not know this good news if not for these women.

It is true that ever since Eve's catastrophic blunder women have received bad press. Here, however, at the end of Mark's Gospel, the ladies line up for the cover photo for the front-page story of the Jerusalem Times: "Women Witness Three Greatest Events in World History." Read all about it! And realize that there is a pattern, namely, that God often chooses "what is foolish in the world [like the cross] to shame the wise," and "what is weak in the world [like these women who look from a distance upon Christ crucified and then see him alive again] to shame the strong" (1 Cor. 1:27).

The Power of the Cross to Turn Scared, Secret Disciples into Courageous Servants

We come to our final point.

Immediately after Jesus' death the power of the cross is on display. We have seen how the power of the cross (1) does the impossible, (2) changes the hardest of hearts, and (3) employs the so-called "weak" of this world to witness effectively to the world. The final point of this power, as illustrated in verses 42–46, is that the cross can turn cowardly and self-preserving secret disciples into courageous servants of God.

> And when evening had come, since it was the day of Preparation [Thursday sundown to Friday sundown], that is, the day before the Sabbath, Joseph of Arimathea, a respected member of the council, who was also himself looking for the kingdom of God, took courage and went to Pilate and asked for the body of Jesus. Pilate was surprised to hear that he should have already died. And summoning the centurion, he asked him whether he was already dead. And when he learned from the centurion that he was dead, he granted the corpse to Joseph. And Joseph bought a linen shroud, and taking him down, wrapped him in the linen shroud

and laid him in a tomb that had been cut out of the rock. And he rolled a stone against the entrance of the tomb.

Before I focus on Joseph's transformation, notice again that Mark is keen on eyewitness testimony. The women, from a distance, saw Jesus die. But the centurion, up close, saw the same reality. This is why Pilate summoned him to make sure Jesus was actually dead.[29] Likewise, Joseph of Arimathea was not only an eyewitness to Jesus' death but a hand-witness. He touched Jesus' dead body.[30] For, as verse 46 records, Joseph took Jesus down from the cross, "wrapped" the body in a "linen shroud," carried the corpse to the tomb, "laid him" in it, and "rolled a stone against the entrance of the tomb" (15:46). If anyone knew that Jesus had died, it was Joseph. And if anyone was a reliable witness in those days, he was. He was "rich" (Matt. 27:57). A tomb like this was expensive.[31] He was important. He was a "respected member of the council" (Mark 15:43). He was influential. He not only had access to Pontus Pilate; he had Pilate's ear.

But it is not his wealth, reputation, or clout on which we should focus. Rather, it is his courage and service. Mark tells us that Joseph was a "respected member of the council" and that he "was also himself looking for the kingdom of God" (15:43). He was part of the Sanhedrin and he was a devout Jew. Yet Mark gives no record of his attendance or his part in Jesus' trial before the Sanhedrin.[32] John tells us that he identified himself as a "disciple of Jesus," but a secret one (John 19:38). Joseph kept his views about Jesus to himself because he feared his fellow Jews ("a disciple of Jesus, but secretly for fear of the Jews," John 19:38). But now, after Jesus' death, look at him! He moved from fear to faith: "Joseph . . . took courage [or "took a risk," NLT] and went

---

29 Note the language Mark uses to emphasize this point: "the body of Jesus" (15:43); "already died" (15:44); "he was dead" (15:45); "the corpse" (15:45). Also, for Joseph to wrap Jesus in a shroud that would prevent breathing also points to the fact that Jesus was really dead.

30 John makes clear that Joseph, along with Nicodemus, "took the body of Jesus and bound it in linen cloths" (John 19:40). "The burial custom of the Jews" (John 19:40) would include what John records Joseph and Nicodemus doing (perfuming the body with spices and wrapping it in a linen cloth, John 19:39–40; cf. m. Šabb. 23:5). It also would have included washing the body beforehand. This ritual cleansing would have rendered Joseph and Nicodemus unclean for seven days (Num. 19:11). This makes Joseph's personal sacrifice on behalf of Jesus even more noble.

31 "Poor men were buried in mass paupers' graves. Joseph's tomb had no other bodies in it; it was brand-new; it was above, not below, ground; and it had the expensive, state-of-the-art, rolling-stone feature. Most tombs had small square stones just to keep out animals and thieves. This tomb was the deluxe edition." Douglas Sean O'Donnell, *Matthew: All Authority under Heaven*, PTW (Wheaton, IL: Crossway, 2013), 886.

32 Luke mentions that Joseph did not consent with the Sanhedrin's "decision and action" (Luke 23:51), but he does not make clear whether this lack of consent was voiced during the trial or after, and, if after, privately or publicly.

to Pilate and asked for the body of Jesus" (Mark 15:43). After Jesus' death, Joseph went from bashful to brave. He also went from self-preservation to selfless service and self-sacrifice. He *was* a disciple of Jesus. Now he was finally *acting* like one. His hands (what he did) finally caught up with his head (what he believed). He served Jesus in lowly and loving ways.

After Joseph received permission to collect Jesus' corpse, he attended personally to Jesus. He was a rich and powerful man. But he did not send his servants to secure and care for Jesus' body. He did it himself. He risked his reputation. And notice what he did. In public view he stood at the foot of the cross, took down the bloody body, and wrapped it in a linen shroud (15:46). Then he brought Jesus to "his own new tomb" (Matt. 27:60), an expensive one ("a tomb that had been cut out of the rock," Mark 15:46). He laid the body in the tomb and "rolled a stone against the entrance" (15:46). Here Joseph served the suffering servant, and in doing so he embodied Jesus' teaching: "If anyone would be first, he must be last of all and servant of all" (9:35; cf. 10:43).

Oh, the power of the cross. Do you know its power? Have you experienced its power? God, through Christ crucified, can do the impossible, soften the hardest of hearts, use the weak to witness to the world, and turn fear into faith, self-preservation into selfless, courageous service.

Not Ashamed of the Gospel

It is tempting these days, as the theological and ethical foundation of Western civilization has moved from standing on the rock of Jesus' words to standing on the shifting sands of modernism and postmodernism, to be ashamed of the gospel. But this passage reminds us to take courage and speak out. For there is power in the cross; "There is power, power, wonder-working power in the blood of the Lamb."[33] And that power, through the work of the Holy Spirit, is still available today. Let us renew our commitment to stand upon this saving word. Let us not be ashamed of the gospel, for it is indeed the power of God unto salvation (Rom. 1:16).

---

33   Lewis E. Jones, "Power in the Blood" (1899).

Sometimes It (the Resurrection!) Causes Me to Tremble

MARK 16:1-8

And they went out and fled from the tomb, for trembling
and astonishment had seized them, and they said nothing
to anyone, for they were afraid.
Mark 16:8

Right before I preached on Mark 15:33–47, the congregation sang the old spiritual "Were You There?" We sang five questions: Were you there when they crucified my Lord? Were you there when they nailed him to the tree? Were you there when they pierced him in the side? Were you there when the sun refused to shine? Were you there when they laid him in the tomb? And after each question we replied, "Oh! Sometimes it causes me to tremble, tremble, tremble." We ended the service, as we anticipated Easter, singing, after the benediction, the final stanza of that song:

> Were you there when he rose up from the dead?
> Were you there when he rose up from the dead?
> Sometimes I feel like shouting "Glory, glory, glory!"
> Were you there when he rose up from the dead?

What a fitting response to Easter, to shout, "Glory, glory, glory!" The resurrection is a glorious event. We celebrate Jesus' vindication and victory. We celebrate our justification and the gift of eternal life.

Yet, as we witness the first eyewitnesses to the event (the women who "fled from the tomb" because "trembling . . . had seized them," 16:8), perhaps we should return to the refrain, "Oh! Sometimes it causes me to tremble, tremble, tremble," when we think of Jesus' empty tomb. Also, perhaps fear ("And they said nothing to anyone, for they were afraid," 16:8) is just as natural a response to the news of Jesus' resurrection as is a shout of "glory."

Whatever we make of Mark's ending to his Gospel and his brief account of the empty tomb, one thing that he does that the other Gospel writers do not do is to have us linger at the tomb as we ponder the angel's amazing pronouncement, "Do not be alarmed. You seek Jesus of Nazareth, who was crucified. He has risen; he is not here" (16:6). But as we linger (and watch the trembling, fearful women flee the scene), we notice that Mark's ending is unique in at least two ways when compared to the other Evangelists'. First, Mark 16:1–8 is an unexpected ending; second, it is a seemingly incomplete ending. In this final chapter we will try to make sense of why Mark has left us with this unexpected and incomplete ending, and we will discover that there is a plan to his peculiarities.

An Unexpected Ending

Knowing what we know of OT Sabbath law (that God's people should rest from their labors on the Sabbath), the ladies' break-of-dawn movements ("They went to the tomb") on Sunday ("very early on the first day of the week, when the sun had risen," **16:2**, and "when the Sabbath was past," **16:1**) is expected. It is also expected that these women who had repeatedly "ministered to" Jesus from his early ministry in Galilee to his last days in Jerusalem (15:41), would seek to perform the lowly, loving act of caring for his corpse. It is expected that they, as Jesus' close friends, would seek "to show respect and devotion to the departed loved one," and so they brought "spices" to the tomb (16:1). Moreover, it is expected that they would wonder, on the way to the tomb and having seen the size of the stone rolled across the entrance of the tomb (see 15:47), "Who will roll away the stone for us?" (**16:3**).[1] Where are the strong men to move this "very large" (**16:4**) stone (4–6 feet in diameter)? Where are the men, period? Are they still running (14:50), or have they found a hideout (John 20:19)?

What is *unexpected* is that these women, as Jesus' disciples (they were part of a group of "many women" who followed Jesus from Galilee; Matt. 27:55; Mark 15:41), did not expect him to be alive. I say that is unexpected because Jesus had predicted his sufferings, death, and resurrection. For example, in Mark 9:31 we read that Jesus "was teaching his disciples, saying to them, 'The Son of Man is going to be delivered into the hands of men, and they will kill him. And when he is killed, after three days he will rise.'" He made four other

---

1   "There is a tremendous dramatic touch in the [first part of] the women's question." Grant R. Osborne, *Mark*, TTCS (Grand Rapids, MI: Baker, 2012), 317.

similar statements (see 8:31; 9:9; 10:34; 14:28). So after these women witnessed (or heard about) the absolute accuracy of Jesus' predictions—he was rejected by the Jewish religious leaders, delivered over to the Romans, and then mocked, flogged, and killed—we would expect them to anticipate that three days later (Friday, Saturday, and now Sunday) his word about his resurrection would also come true. Or at the very least to come to the tomb with hopeful expectation of something as miraculous as a man walking on water, something beyond their known categories of comprehension. They should have left their spices at home. They should have come with empty hands but open minds, saying, "What might the Son of God do next?"

It is fine that they were "alarmed" when they entered the opened tomb and saw "a young man sitting on the right side, dressed in a white robe" (**16:5**). He was obviously a supernatural being, because the only reason they could see him in a dark tomb was that this messenger's appearance was like that of "lightning, and his clothing as white as snow" (Matt. 28:3; cf. "shining garments," Luke 24:4 KJV). It would be alarming to see a young man sitting in a tomb. It would be doubly alarming to learn that this young man was an angel. Every biblical character who encounters an angel, from Samson's mother to the mother of our Lord (Judg. 13:6, 22; Luke 1:29), is shocked and troubled at the encounter. And no wonder, for angels are mighty creatures. According to 2 Kings 19:35 one angel destroyed 185,000 Assyrians! Fear is the natural response in encountering such an awesome supernatural being in such an odd locale.

But, that said, what is unexpected is that they do not execute (or Mark does not record their executing) their personal great commission—to "go" and "tell" (**16:7**). They are commissioned to announce to the eleven (Jesus' "disciples and Peter," 16:7) the news of his resurrection ("He has risen," **16:6**)[2] and to meet Jesus in Galilee, the very place where he predicted he would meet them after the resurrection ("After I am raised up, I will go before you to Galilee," 14:28). But we read in the final verse of Mark's Gospel that, instead of heeding that command, "They went out and fled from the tomb, for trembling and astonishment had seized them, and they said nothing to anyone, for they were afraid" (**16:8**).

It could be that we should read "And they said nothing to anyone" (16:8) to indicate that "they said nothing as they made their way to Peter and the

---

2   Mark uses the aorist passive, "which can carry either a passive sense, 'he has been raised' (by God), or an active sense, 'he has risen' (by his power)." Mark L. Strauss, *Mark*, ZECNT (Grand Rapids, MI: Zondervan, 2014), 719. Strauss then lists biblical texts that state that God has raised Jesus from the dead (e.g., Acts 2:24) and others that point to Jesus' laying down his life and taking it up again (e.g., John 10:17–18).

others."[3] That is a charitable reading. The natural sense of the verse, especially in the context of chapters 14–15, in which Jesus' disciples did not score high on their Discipleship Aptitude Test, is that they were scared out of their wits. "They were [so] afraid"—both of the angelic encounter and announcement and of what others might think of such an odd announcement—that they decided, for the time being, to keep the good news to themselves. Of course, we know from Matthew's account that their real fear was mixed with "great joy" (Matt. 28:8), and soon after the joy outweighed the fear. They eventually opened their mouths. As they fled, sometime along the way, they decided "to tell [the] disciples" (Matt. 28:8).

Now, related both to the fulfillment of the woman's commission and to the commission itself, it is unexpected, given what we have read about the apostles since that ominous statement at Jesus' arrest ("Then all the disciples left him and fled," Mark 14:50 NET), that Jesus would single out these three to hear the good news first. Jesus could have chosen Joseph of Arimathea instead of the women to take the news of Jesus' resurrection to Pontus Pilate, King Herod, and Joseph's fellow justices on the Jewish Supreme Court. Instead Jesus chose some of his female disciples to tell some of his male disciples that the tomb was empty and that he had been raised (see Luke 24:9–10).

So then, with all that is expected and unexpected in Mark's final eight verses, here the Evangelist gives the church three reasons to rejoice, to go from "tremble, tremble, tremble" to "glory, glory, glory."

First, let us rejoice that through his resurrection Jesus forever changes history. It is no insignificant detail that Jesus chose to die during the Passover, rest on the Sabbath, and rise on the first day of the week.

> How interesting that God didn't select the Sabbath as the resurrection day. Instead, he chose the next day to be the new holy day. He chose Sunday to be the day we worship his Son (the Lord's Day). Perhaps he chose a new day because a new era was breaking into world history; a permanent cavity was torn in the cosmos to create an eternal eighth day of rest and rejoicing for all who rest and rejoice in Christ.[4]

Second, let us rejoice that Jesus is a merciful Savior. With the phrase "And [tell] Peter" (16:7) Jesus announces that he is ready and willing to forgive his

---

3 R. C. Sproul, *Mark*, St. Andrew's Expositional Commentary (Sanford, FL: Reformation Trust, 2015), 415.

4 Douglas Sean O'Donnell, *Matthew: All Authority under Heaven*, PTW (Wheaton, IL: Crossway, 2013), 899.

disciples, even Peter after he has done the unimaginable and seemingly the unforgivable. How kind our Lord is to single out Peter for restoration.

Let me add here, as I speak of Jesus as the merciful Savior, that he is also the *only* Savior. When we finish reading Mark's Gospel, we honestly wonder: What will become of the church? Of course we know that the church will get its act together in the Acts of the Apostles, but only because the Holy Spirit acts upon her. What we do not wonder is to whom we should go for our salvation. Should we ask imperfect Peter to save us, or the fickle women? God forbid! This abrupt ending, you see, centers our attention on the only character on whom Mark centers his attention throughout his Gospel—Jesus. He is the only Savior.

Third, let us rejoice that God has provided the world with authentic evidence of Jesus' resurrection. Mark not only has, throughout his whole Gospel, been "blunt about the failing of the apostles,"[5] but he also provides an utterly authentic account of the resurrection event. If this were fake news there would be no record of Galilean women as the prime (here in Mark the sole!) witnesses. A Jew from Galilee had little social standing in Jerusalem— especially so within the Roman world. Moreover, women had no legal standing. They could not testify in a court of law. Why then would Mark fabricate this story? Whom is he trying to convince? His first-century Palestinian audience? A broader Greco-Roman readership? If so, he has done a terrible job. However, if his purpose was to highlight not the "status of the witnesses, but the truth to which they testified,"[6] then he has accomplished his goal.

Moreover, if Mark were making up a story that would be better received, there would be no record of the women's spices, fear,[7] or astonishment (they obviously did not think Jesus would rise again). The story could have been circulated that Jesus had taught that he would die and rise, and, sure enough, all his disciples—120 men and women—lined up at the empty tomb, waiting for the prediction to come true. They came in the early morning, dressed in light blue suits, pink dresses, and Easter bonnets, ready to toss a thousand lilies in the air. But that is not what Mark records.

A final mark of Mark's authenticity is both Jesus' (earlier) and the angel's (later) command to travel to Galilee. Why would the indisputable evidence

---

5 Donald English, *The Message of Mark: The Mystery of Faith*, BST (Leicester, UK: Inter-Varsity, 1992), 240. "This story [Mark 16:1–8] is wholly in harmony with that."

6 English, *Message of Mark*, 240.

7 "In Mark's Gospel, this fear is always man's [and woman's!] response to the breaking in of the power of God. It is the fear the disciples experienced when Jesus stilled the story; the fear of the Gerasenes when Jesus delivered Legion; the fear of the disciples as they saw Jesus setting his face to Jerusalem to die on the cross." Sinclair B. Ferguson, *Let's Study Mark* (repr., Carlisle, PA: Banner of Truth Trust, 2016), 271.

of the astonishing news of bodily resurrection take place somewhere like Buford, Wyoming, rather than New York, New York? I will tell you why—because the location of the most glorious event in world history will take place in a setting that mirrors the place of Jesus' birth, a setting that is only befitting our Lord's humble incarnation. Also, Galilee is where Jesus called his first disciples (1:16–20) and first commissioned them as apostles (3:13–19; cf. 6:7). It is thus a fitting setting to re-call and recommission them.[8]

There are other evidences of the resurrection, such as Jesus' bodily appearances to more than five hundred witnesses, the radical and abrupt worldview changes (e.g., monotheistic Jews worshiping the man Jesus as God; belief in an individual's bodily resurrection),[9] and the disciples' inexplicable change from cowards huddled in a locked room to fearless evangelists spreading the word without fear of persecution or death.[10] However, I must say, having studied afresh the validity of Jesus' resurrection, that I am drawn to Mark's subtle apologetic. His short but sincere testimony about a few women's running scared and silent from the scene sounds believable. One reason I believe "He has risen" is because Mark's unbelievably abrupt ending is believable. It rings true. It sounds absolutely authentic.

An Incomplete Ending

As we are still lingering at the empty tomb, we have noticed that the ending of Mark's Gospel is unexpected. Next we will notice that his ending seems incomplete. After we read the angel's announcement ("He has risen"), followed by the suggestion to see the evidence ("See the place where they laid him," 16:6) and then his commission to them to inform the apostles ("Go, tell his disciples," 16:7), we do not expect to read, "And they went out and fled from the tomb, for trembling and astonishment had seized them, and they said nothing to anyone, for they were afraid" (16:8). Or, I should say, we do not expect that to be the last line!

For this day we are glad to see that Mark offers a visible sign of Jesus' resurrection—the moved stone. Who moved the "very large" stone (16:3, 4)? Heaven knows. Heaven did! The verb "Had been rolled back" (16:4) is a divine passive, as the subject, which is not provided, is assumed to be God. God

---

8   Moreover, "Galilee of the Gentiles" (Matt. 4:15) is a fitting place from which to take the gospel to "all nations" (Matt. 28:19).

9   "To all the dominant worldviews of the time [in the Greek and Jewish first-century Mediterranean world], an individual bodily resurrection was almost inconceivable." Timothy Keller, *The Reason for God: Belief in an Age of Skepticism* (New York: Dutton, 2008), 206.

10   "Virtually all the apostles and early Christian leaders died for their faith, and it is hard to believe that this kind of powerful self-sacrifice would be done to support a hoax" (Keller, *The Reason for God*, 210).

rolled back the stone. Mark gives us the testimony of the angel ("A young man sitting on the right side, dressed in a white robe" announces, "He has risen," 16:5–6). No one moved or stole the body. And Mark gives us the testimony of the three women: "Mary Magdalene, Mary the mother of James, and Salome . . . see the place where they laid him" (16:1, 6). They went to the right place and observed the inside and outside of Joseph's empty tomb. But with all that said, where is Jesus? Is he really alive? Did anyone see him alive? Why does Mark not record a bodily appearance of Jesus? For someone who gave us precise details throughout the passion narrative, why such a "remarkably short and puzzling account of the resurrection"?[11]

It is no wonder that Matthew, Luke, and John, writing years after Mark's Gospel, made sure the church had a clear and indisputable record of Jesus' bodily appearances, commission to the church, and ascension into heaven. Also it is no wonder that a copyist likely a century or more after the Four Gospels were written thought it necessary to add an ending that features Mary Magdalene's seeing Jesus himself ("He appeared first to Mary Magdalene," 16:9; "He was alive and had been seen by her," 16:11; cf. Luke 24:11; John 20:11–17). Moreover this copyist, using a "few Markan expressions" and a "compendium" of verses from "the other Gospels and Acts,"[12] also adds two stories of further appearances to thirteen other witnesses ("two" disciples who "were walking into the country," Mark 16:12; cf. Luke 24:13–35; "He appeared to the eleven," Mark 16:14; cf. Luke 24:36–43), along with a great commission ("Go into all the world and proclaim the gospel to the whole creation," Mark 16:15; cf. Matt. 28:18–20) and a prediction of "signs" that will accompany their gospel proclamation (e.g., "They will cast out demons" and "speak in new tongues," the sick will "recover," while the "deadly poison" will not hurt them, even serpents' bites; Mark 16:17–18, 20; cf. Acts 2:4; 28:3–6), followed by Jesus' ascension ("The Lord Jesus . . . was taken up into heaven and sat down at the right hand of God," Mark 16:19; Luke 24:50–51).

I can state with confidence that a copyist added that ending because Mark 16:9–20 is not found in our most reliable Greek manuscripts of the NT.[13] It is also

---

11   Strauss, *Mark*, 714.
12   Osborne, *Mark*, 324. In his *Miracle and Mission: The Authentication of Missionaries and Their Message in the Longer Ending of Mark* (Tübingen: Mohr Siebeck, 2005) James A. Kelhoffer argues that a single author composed Mark 16:9–20 in the early to mid-first century AD, that he drew on the Four Gospels and Acts, and that he "did not intend to create a novel account, but wrote in conscious imitation of traditions which he . . . esteemed" (121).
13   See Bruce M. Metzger and Bart D. Ehrman, *The Text of the New Testament: Its Translation, Corruption, and Restoration* (New York: Oxford University Press, 2005), 322–37; cf. Daniel B. Wallace, "Mark 16:8 as the Conclusion to the Second Gospel," in *Perspectives on the Ending of Mark: 4 Views*, ed. David Alan Black (Nashville: B&H Academic, 2008), 1–39.

not mentioned in the writings of early Christians, such as Clement of Alexandria (d. 215), Origen (d. 253), Eusebius (d. 340), and Jerome (d. 420).[14] Since this is the case, how do we make sense of Mark's seemingly incomplete ending now?

I surmise that Mark has three reasons for his curious and cryptic ending.

First, Mark wants us to trust in Jesus' authoritative word. If Jesus repeatedly said that he would rise from the dead, then that authoritative word should suffice.[15] If Jesus promised that he would rise, and if he guarantees resurrection life to all who lose their lives for his sake (see Mark 8:34–9:1), then we can take him at his word. Unlike Thomas, we are not to doubt the testimony of Jesus even if we ourselves have not seen his resurrected body. If we can trust anything, we can trust the sure foundation of Jesus' word (see Matt. 7:24–27). We can trust what he says. We can trust that it is true: "Blessed are those who have not seen and yet have believed" (John 20:29). And we can trust, whether we are facing death now or loved ones in Christ have already faced it, that what Jesus said to Martha he says to us today: "I am the resurrection and the life. Whoever believes in me, though he die, yet shall he live, and everyone who lives and believes in me shall never die" (John 11:25–26).

The Christian message is not that Jesus has come to end world hunger and military conflict. The message is not that Jesus will bring health and wealth, healing and prosperity. The message is the good news about Good Friday and Easter. Jesus' death destroyed death. His resurrection brings new life. The tomb was empty. The stone rolled away. He has conquered the grave. He is alive! Whether we pass from this life today or decades from now, there is hope for forgiven sinners beyond the grave.

Why? Because Jesus said so. Mark wants us to trust Jesus' authoritative word. That is the first goal of Mark's seemingly incomplete ending. The second follows. Even in the resurrection account Mark takes us to the cross. His ending reemphasizes the importance of the cross.

---

14 "In the oldest commentary on Mark's Gospel, by Victor of Antioch, we find a note attached to the longer ending . . . that says, 'In most copies this additional material according to Mark is not found.'" Eckhard J. Schnabel, *Mark: An Introduction and Commentary*, TNTC (Downers Grove, IL: IVP Academic, 2017), 19. Based on external (see above) and internal (e.g., nine new words are introduced) evidence, the scholarly consensus since 1881 (Westcott and Hort, *The New Testament in the Original Greek*) is that the longer ending is not original. For excellent defenses of this view see James A. Kelhoffer, *Miracle and Mission*, WUNT (Tübingen: Mohr Siebeck, 2000); James W. Voelz, *Mark 8:27–16:8*, Concordia Commentary (St. Louis: Concordia Publishing House, 2013); Christopher W. Mitchell, *Mark 8:27–16:20*, Concordia Commentary (St. Louis: Concordia Publishing House, 2019), 1201–4, 1222–37.

15 This is similar to the point that Jesus makes in the parable of the rich man and Lazarus. As Jesus said to the damned rich man about that man's brothers, "If they do not hear Moses and the Prophets, neither will they be convinced if someone should rise from the dead" (Luke 16:31), so we can say the same of Mark's ending.

The angel speaks of Jesus as the risen Savior ("He has risen"), but he ties even the resurrection to Jesus' death ("You seek Jesus of Nazareth, who was crucified," Mark 16:6). While Mark, with the empty tomb, breaks the pattern of Greco-Roman biographies—which end with a person's death and the way that person died—his focus centers on the final hours of Jesus' life. To him the cross is the center! In these final eight verses on the resurrection he points us back to the preceding 119 verses on Jesus' sufferings and death. As Christians, we never move past the cross. Even throughout eternity we will sing, "Worthy is the Lamb who was slain!" (Rev. 5:12).

So in a world that embraces a God without wrath who brings people without sin into a kingdom without judgment through the ministrations of a Christ without a cross,[16] Mark (even at Easter!) makes sure that we do not forget Good Friday: a just and holy God of wrath and love brought sinners into his righteous kingdom through the sacrifice of Christ crucified.

So how do we make sense of Mark's seemingly incomplete ending? We recognize that he has three goals. First, Mark wants us to trust in Jesus' authoritative word. Second, he wants to take us back to the importance of the cross. Third, he wants to call us to discipleship.

Mark intends to use the failure of the male disciples in chapters 14–15 and of the female disciples in chapter 16 to remind us both that Jesus graciously uses even imperfect sinners to build his perfect kingdom and that their failures serve to call us to be faithful with Jesus' mission. These final verses, especially 16:8, offer a "positive challenge" and an "implicit call to discipleship."[17] He is calling us, even those disciples who are "confused and uncertain,"[18] to get over the confusion and uncertainty, along with the doubt and fear, and to join the victory march and raise high the banner of God's victory over death. As Morna Hooker puts it, "This is the end of Mark's story, because it is the beginning of discipleship."[19]

As readers of this Gospel, and hearers of it preached, we have followed Jesus from his baptism to his resurrection, and, even when everyone around him (the religious leaders, the crowd, and even his own family and disciples) has disowned him, we have followed along. We have not put the book down. We keep coming back for more. But now, as we stand at the end of the story and Mark suddenly stops the narrative, he leaves us with a "decision to

---

16 This is a slight rewording of parts of H. Richard Niebuhr's famous saying, found in *The Kingdom of God in America* (Chicago: Willett, Clark, 1937), 193.
17 Strauss, *Mark*, 723.
18 Strauss, *Mark*, 724.
19 Morna D. Hooker, *The Gospel according to St. Mark*, BNTC (London: A&C Black, 1991), 394.

make."[20] But that decision should be obvious enough. We are to follow Christ by sharing the good news with others.

Think of it this way. We should treat the end of Mark's Gospel like we would the lyrics to a familiar hymn. If I sang, "Christ the Lord is risen today," and left the next ten notes and one word for you, you would add, "Alleluia." The early Christians who heard the death and resurrection proclaimed in the marketplaces, synagogues, and house churches for decades before the penning of Mark's Gospel knew that these fearful women did not bite their tongues for long. So, as at the end of the Acts of the Apostles,[21] the church is not to ask What happened to Paul? or Will the gospel spread to both Jews and Gentiles after the death of Paul? Instead the church is to act—to act like that apostle. Put simply, the end of Mark, like the end of Acts, is an invitation to act. We fill in the notes. We continue the everlasting, unstoppable song.

Mark 16:8 is not an incomplete ending but an "open ending" whereby Mark invites us to "finish the story,"[22] to obey the angelic command. If these ladies will not speak out, then we will. And, if we do not, we can be certain that even the stones will cry out.

Even the Stones Will Cry Out

On Monday, April 15, 2019, the day after Palm Sunday, the beautiful roof and famed tower of the gothic architectural masterpiece Notre-Dame de Paris went up in flames and crashed as burning embers to that cathedral's floor. What a devastating sight! A cultural icon in disrepair. Irreplaceable works of art and architecture forever lost.

That building was dedicated in 1345 and took nearly two centuries to build. It is being restored, not just because the president of France has vowed so but because the human spirit will determine so. However, I must say, as I reflected on that tragedy, that I came to this conclusion, or this reminder of reality: if all the houses of Christian worship—the great European cathedrals

---

20 For the thought process behind this paragraph see Eugene Boring, *Mark*, NTL (Louisville: Westminster John Knox, 2006), 449.

21 John Chrysostom viewed the ending of Acts as an invitation to the hearer: "[Luke] brings his narrative to this point, and leaves the hearer thirsty so that he fills up the lack by himself through reflection." "Homily 55 on Acts 28:1 on Acts 28:17–20," in *Homilies in the Acts of the Apostles*, in *the Nicene and Post-Nicene Fathers of the Christian Church*, ed. Philip Schaff, trans. Henry Browne (Oxford: Oxford University Press, 1956), 326. On this method Shively notes: "First, the open ending is a common literary and rhetorical practice of ancient writers. Second, it functions to invite the hearer to respond with reflection and interpretation. Third, the hearer knows how to respond according to intratextual cues." Elizabeth E. Shively, "Recognizing Penguins: Audience Expectation, Cognitive Genre Theory, and the Ending of Mark's Gospel," *CBQ* 80 (2018): 285–86.

22 Shively, "Recognizing Penguins," 276.

and the simple wood-framed churches of small-town America—were suddenly destroyed, this would perhaps suspend the movement of Christianity for a moment, but it would not stop it. God's truth would still march on through God's people moving forward.

When the center of Notre-Dame was burning—a center that is in the shape of the cross (from the aerial views you could see the cross burning in the night sky)—I thought to myself, "Nothing can stop the message of Christ crucified," and I think now, "Nothing can stop the message of Christ raised from the dead."

Mark's Gospel begins, "The beginning of the gospel of Jesus" (1:1), and it ends with a new beginning. A new era dawns on Easter morning. The Christian church is birthed out of the empty tomb. For the good news that "He has risen" (16:6) has spread and continues to spread to the four corners of the world. For

Christ is risen.
He is risen indeed!

So then, "go." "Go [and] tell." Finish the story.

Select Bibliography

Bayer, Hans F. *A Theology of Mark: The Dynamic between Christology and Authentic Discipleship*. EBT. Phillipsburg, NJ: P&R, 2012.

———. *Mark*. Vol. 8 of ESVEC. Wheaton, IL: Crossway, 2021.

Bock, Darrell. *Mark*. NCBC. Cambridge: Cambridge University Press, 2015.

Boring, M. Eugene. *Mark*. NTL. Louisville: Westminster John Knox, 2006.

Brooks, James A. *Mark*. NAC. Nashville: Broadman, 1991.

Brown, Raymond E. *The Death of the Messiah: From Gethsemane to the Grave: A Commentary on the Passion Narratives in the Four Gospels*. ABRL. 2 vols. New York: Doubleday, 1994.

Bruner, Frederick Dale. *Matthew: A Commentary, Volume 1: The Christbook, Matthew 1–12*. Rev. ed. Grand Rapids, MI: Eerdmans, 2007.

———. *Matthew: A Commentary, Volume 2: The Churchbook, Matthew 13–28*. Rev. ed. Grand Rapids, MI: Eerdmans, 2007.

Cahill, Michael, trans. and ed. *The First Commentary on Mark: An Annotated Translation*. Oxford: Oxford University Press, 1998.

Calvin, John. *A Harmony of the Gospels Matthew, Mark and Luke and the Epistles of James and Jude*. Translated by A. W. Morrison. Grand Rapids, MI: Eerdmans, 1975.

Cole, R. Alan. *Mark*. TNTC. Downers Grove, IL: IVP Academic, 1989.

———. "Mark," in *New Bible Commentary*. Edited by Gordon J. Wenham, J. A. Motyer, D. A. Carson, and R. T. France. Downers Grove, IL: InterVarsity, 1994.

Collins, Adela Yarbro. *Mark*. Hermeneia. Minneapolis: Fortress, 2007.

Cranfield, C. E. B. *The Gospel According to St Mark*. CGTC. Repr., Cambridge: Cambridge University Press, 2000.

Culpepper, R. Alan. *Mark*. SHBC. Macon, GA: Smyth & Helwys, 2007.

Davies, W. D., and Dale C. Allison Jr. *A Critical and Exegetical Commentary on the Gospel according to Saint Matthew*. ICC. Edinburgh: T&T Clark, 1991.

Decker, Rodney J. *Mark 1–8: A Handbook on the Greek Text*. Waco, TX: Baylor University Press, 2014.

———. *Mark 9–16: A Handbook on the Greek Text*. Waco, TX: Baylor University Press, 2014.

Doriani, Daniel M. *Matthew*. REC. 2 vols. Phillipsburg, NJ: P&R, 2008.

Edwards, James R. *The Gospel According to Mark*. PNTC. Grand Rapids, MI: Eerdmans, 2002.

English, Donald. *The Message of Mark: The Mystery of Faith*. BST. Leicester, UK: Inter-Varsity, 1992.

Evans, Craig A. *Mark 8:27–16:20*. WBC 34B. Nashville: Nelson, 1988.

Ferguson, Sinclair B. *Let's Study Mark*. Repr., Carlisle, PA: Banner of Truth Trust, 2016.

France, R. T. *The Gospel of Mark*. NIGTC. Grand Rapids, MI: Eerdmans, 2002.

Garland, David E. *Mark*. NIVAC. Grand Rapids, MI: Zondervan, 1996.

———. *A Theology of Mark's Gospel: Good News about Jesus the Messiah, the Son of God*. Biblical Theology of the New Testament. Edited by Andreas J. Köstenberger. Grand Rapids, MI: Zondervan, 2015.

Giertz, Bo. *The New Testament Devotional Commentary: Volume 1: Matthew, Mark, Luke*. Translated by Bror Erickson. Irving, CA: 1517 Publishing, 2021.

Guelich, Robert A. *Mark 1:1–8:27*. WBC 34A. Nashville: Nelson, 1989.

Gundry, Robert H. *Mark: A Commentary on His Apology for the Cross*. Grand Rapids, MI: Eerdmans, 1993.

Hendriksen, William. *Exposition of the Gospel according to Mark*. Grand Rapids, MI: Baker, 1975.

Hooker, Morna D. *The Gospel according to St. Mark*. BNTC. London: A. & C. Black, 1991.

Hughes, R. Kent. *Mark: Jesus, Servant and Savior*. PTW. 2 vols. Wheaton, IL: Crossway, 1989.

Keller, Timothy. *King's Cross: The Story of the World in the Life of Jesus*. New York: Dutton, 2011.

Lane, William L. *The Gospel of Mark*. NICNT. Grand Rapids, MI: Eerdmans, 1974.

Marcus, Joel. *Mark 1–8: A New Translation with Introduction and Commentary*. AB 27. New York: Doubleday, 2000.

———. *Mark 8–16: A New Translation with Introduction and Commentary*. Anchor Yale Bible 27A. New Haven: Yale University Press, 2009.

Moloney, Francis J. *The Gospel of Mark: A Commentary*. Peabody, MA: Hendrickson, 2002.

Nolland, John. *The Gospel of Matthew*. NIGTC. Grand Rapids, MI: Eerdmans, 2005.

———. *Luke*. WBC 35. 3 vols. Dallas: Word, 1989–93.

Oden, Thomas C., and Christopher A. Hall, eds. *Mark*. ACCS NT. Downers Grove, IL: InterVarsity, 1998.

O'Donnell, Douglas Sean. *Matthew: All Authority under Heaven*. PTW. Wheaton, IL: Crossway, 2013.

Osborne, Grant R. *Mark*. TTCS. Grand Rapids, MI: Baker, 2012.

Rhoads, David, Joanna Dewey, and Donald Michie. *Mark as Story: An Introduction to the Narrative of a Gospel*. 3rd ed. Minneapolis: Fortress, 2012.

Ryken, Philip Graham. *Luke: Knowing for Sure*. REC. 2 vols. Phillipsburg, NJ: P&R, 2009.

Ryle, J. C. *Mark: Expository Thoughts on the Gospels*. CCC. Wheaton, IL: Crossway, 1993.

Schnabel, Eckhard J. *Mark: An Introduction and Commentary*. TNTC. Downers Grove, IL: IVP Academic, 2017.

Senior, Donald. *The Passion of Jesus in the Gospel of Mark*. Collegeville, MN: Liturgical Press, 1992.

Shively, Elizabeth Evans. "Mark." In *The Greek New Testament, Produced by Tyndale House, Cambridge, Guided Annotating Edition*, edited by Daniel K. Eng, 127–133. Wheaton, IL: Crossway, 2023.

Snodgrass, Klyne R. *Stories with Intent: A Comprehensive Guide to the Parables of Jesus*. Grand Rapids, MI: Eerdmans, 2008.

Sproul, R. C. *Mark*. St. Andrew's Expositional Commentary. Sanford, FL: Reformation Trust, 2015.

Stein, Robert H. *Mark*. BECNT. Grand Rapids, MI: Baker Academic, 2008.

Strauss, Mark L. *Mark*. ZECNT. Grand Rapids, MI: Zondervan, 2014.

Voelz, James W. *Mark 1:1–8:26*. Concordia Commentary. St. Louis: Concordia Publishing House, 2013.

———. *Mark 8:27–16:8*; Christopher W. Mitchell. *Mark 16:9–20*. Concordia Commentary. St. Louis: Concordia Publishing House, 2019.

Watts, Rikki E. "Mark." In *Commentary on the New Testament Use of the Old Testament*. Edited by G. K. Beale and D. A. Carson, 111–249. Grand Rapids, MI: Baker, 2007.

Wessel, Walter W. "Mark." In *The Expositor's Bible Commentary*. Edited by Frank E. Gaebelein. 12 vols. Grand Rapids, MI: Zondervan, 1984.

Williams, Joel. *Mark*. EGGNT. Nashville. B&H Academic, 2020.

Scripture Index